Pascal's Triangle

Pascal's Triangle

Reading, Writing, and Reasoning

About Programs

Rick Decker & Stuart Hirshfield

HAMILTON COLLEGE

WADSWORTH PUBLISHING COMPANY

Belmont, California

A Division of Wadsworth, Inc.

Computer Science Editor: **Frank Ruggirello**
Developmental Editor: **Alan Venable**
Editorial Assistant: **Rhonda Gray**
Production Editor: **Donna Linden**
Managing Designer: **Andrew Ogus**
Print Buyer: **Barbara Britton**
Art Editors: **Marta Kongsle and Kelly Murphy**
Permissions Editor: **Peggy Meehan**
Cover and Text Designer: **Al Burkhardt**
Copy Editor: **Elaine Brett**
Cover Photographs: **Granite: © Westlight/H. D. Thoreau**
　　　　　　　　　　Clouds: © Tony Stone Worldwide/John Chard
Compositor: **Thompson Type, San Diego, California**
Printer: **Vail-Ballou Press, Kirkwood, New York**

1　2　3　4　5　6　7　8　9　10—96　95　94　93　92

Library of Congress Cataloging-in-Publication Data

Decker, Rick.
　　Pascal's triangle : reading, writing, and reasoning about programs /
Rick Decker, Stuart Hirshfield.
　　　　p.　　cm.
　　Includes index.
　　ISBN 0-534-16176-6
　　1. Pascal (Computer program language)　2. Electronic digital
computers—Programming.　　I. Hirshfield, Stuart.　　II. Title.
QA76.73.P2D42　　1992
005.13′3—dc20　　　　　　　　　　　　　　　　91-28150

C O N T E N T S

P A R T   T W O

Algorithms   125

CHAPTER 6

Text Processing: Characters, Strings, and Keyboard I/O   223

CHAPTER 7

Subprograms Revisited: Parameters, Scope, and Recursion   268

CHAPTER 8

From Algorithms to Data Structures: User-Defined Types   314

PART THREE

Data Structures   347

CHAPTER 9

Homogeneous Data Structures: Arrays   349

CHAPTER 10

Heterogeneous Data Structures: Records   398

On our bookshelves we have over four dozen CS1 texts. We'd be willing to bet that most of these texts were written for the same reason — someone had an idea of the Right Way to present the introductory course in computer science and couldn't find an existing text that did the presentation in the way it should be done. So it was with us. This package of text and labs is the result of our attempts to address the curricular and pedagogical issues we wrestled with — successfully, we think — over the past ten years or so in the various incarnations of our introductory course.

The first course in computer science generally serves two purposes, as do introductory courses in other areas: to lay the foundation for further study in the discipline, thereby providing for the needs of potential majors, and to provide something worthwhile for those students who never intend to go beyond the first course. Done well, an introductory course also provides a bridge between these two audiences, a one-way bridge, it is hoped, that captures the interest and imagination of some of the latter group and encourages them to delve more deeply into the subject matter.

Traditionally, of course, the introductory offering in computer science has been a programming course, and in recent years, that has meant a course in Pascal programming. We realize that our Right Way of presenting the introduction may not be right for all instructors. Other models of the introductory course may, for instance, follow the lines of our text, *The Analytical Engine*, and concentrate more on a liberal arts approach to the major topics of the discipline and less on programming. We also realize that time constraints often do not leave room for such a gentle introduction and that at most schools the first course must necessarily be a serious introduction to programming in Pascal. In this package of text and labs, we attempt to combine the virtues of both approaches.

Our Assumptions

Computer science is a new discipline, but practitioners in the field are beginning to accumulate some hard evidence about what should and should not be done in the first course. The overwhelming majority of our colleagues whom we've surveyed agree that the single biggest problem novices face in learning to program is what might be called the "facing a blank screen problem," that is, how to go from a vague statement of a problem to a working program that solves the problem. Of course, students face many other difficulties, such as mastering the details of the compiler and operating system, understanding parameter passing, using arrays effectively, and so on, but we feel that these are important primarily insofar as they obstruct the problem-solving process. So how do we teach our students to program effectively? The *triangle* part of *Pascal's Triangle* refers to the three main themes of our introductory programming course: reading, writing, and reasoning about programs. Many of us — your authors included — believe that

- While syntactic difficulties can often stand squarely in the way of solving problems, programming is most effectively taught in the context of a programming language.
- Programming primarily involves problem-solving skills but also involves language skills. While some students may have difficulty expressing themselves using a programming language, most of our students have greater difficulty designing programs.
- Students learn programming best when they read programs as well as write them (in fact, reading should come first, in much the same way as hearing a natural language is a prerequisite for speaking it).
- Both language and problem-solving skills are best learned by doing — by active experimentation in meaningful, motivating contexts.
- Students read and understand a specific program best when they have had experience with it — by using it to the extent that they understand the program's purpose and operation.

Finally, there is growing sentiment among computer science educators that our business is not merely to turn out competent programmers but rather to nurture and train computer scientists. Our future is bleak indeed if the next generation of programmers is adept at writing and modifying Pascal programs that already exist but wholly unprepared to apply their knowledge to new technologies and problems. The current trend, then, is toward a breadth-first curriculum, in which programming is taught in the broader context of the principles and subfields of computer science. By placing our introduction in the framework of the topics of our discipline, we contextualize the material for potential majors who will see these topics later in their education and we disabuse both majors and non-majors of the notion that there's nothing to computer science but programming.

hat We Do

As we said before, this text arose from our attempt to solve the problem of teaching problem solving with computers. It takes into account our collective experience teaching Pascal over the past two decades and, in so doing, enhances both the teaching and learning processes. In particular, there are several points of emphasis and text features that, while not individually unique in the world of CS1 texts, together constitute a package that we have found to be highly effective to teach and learn from.

Laboratories This text fully embraces the lab-based approach to teaching programming. Along with the text we provide the students with a lab manual that includes a complete set of directed exercises for each chapter. These exercises are integrated precisely with the textual material and serve to bring the static text material to life. We've used a lab-based approach at our school for ten years for one main reason—it works. To paraphrase a maxim that is several millennia old, "I hear and forget, I see and remember, I do and understand." Each chapter's lab concludes with a collection of Post-Lab Exercises that may be assigned as extended programming assignments, and most of the labs include a Rehash section, where appropriate, wherein we review the compiler-specific material introduced in the labs. In this sense, the lab's Rehash section serves as a parallel to the Reference section at the end of each text chapter.

We have run our course in three different ways, depending on how rigid our lab schedules have been. All of the following arrangements have worked well for us:

- Closed, scheduled lab sessions with the instructor and teaching assistants available for help.
- More flexibly scheduled open lab sessions, with a teaching assistant available in the evenings for consultation.
- No scheduled sessions at all, where we rely on the students to complete the labs on their own. Each lab has been carefully developed so that students can work through it on their own, without instructor intervention.

At present, there are three available lab manuals: for Turbo Pascal 6.0, THINK Pascal 4.0, and Pascal in the BSD UNIX 4.3 environment. While the text is largely compiler-independent and devoted to ISO standard Pascal, the lab manuals differ in compiler-specific details so that the manuals reflect exactly what the students will experience in the labs. In particular, each set of lab exercises contains specific exercises on debugging and program testing that make full use of the support facilities provided by the individual programming environment.

Case studies Each chapter and associated lab is organized around a complete, meaningful and interesting sample program. These "Programs in Progress" (PIPs) were developed expressly to illustrate the programming concepts described in the text and to serve as the basis for the associated lab exercises. With the exception of the Chapter 1 PIP (which the students type in to gain practice in program editing in their environment), all the PIPs are provided on the lab disk that comes with each manual. Students can run the program they are reading about, experiment with it, and extend it using what they learn from the text.

Emphasis on problem solving We treat problem solving as the foundation on which the text and labs are built. Each PIP begins with a discussion of how the program was designed and developed, during which we lead the student through the software life cycle. Although we realize there are several models for the software development process, we use the conventional model throughout the text:

    I. *Design* the program, describing the problem carefully, specifying the input/output and the user interface.
    II. *Develop* the program, successively refining the original outline.
    III. *Analyze and code* the program, using verification techniques where appropriate.
    IV. *Test* the program as thoroughly as feasible.
    V. *Maintain* and modify the program.

These phases of software development are referred to in section heads throughout the text, so don't be surprised when you find a reference to "Problem Solving X" without a prior reference to "Problem Solving $X - 1$." The reference number is to a specific stage of program design and may or may not have anything to do with the sequence of sections. For example, Chapter 8 contains the sections "Problem Solving V: Modifying *Zeller*," followed by "Problem Solving III: Analyzing the PIP," since in this context it makes more sense to first talk about modifying the program from Chapter 1 and then to talk about subrange types, enumerated types, and sets as they are used in the new version of the program.

In addition, problem-solving techniques are included throughout the text as boxed items and are reiterated at the end of each chapter for easy reference.

Disciplinary context Every chapter contains a "Computer Science Interlude" that puts the programming concepts described in the text and illustrated in the lab in the broader context of computer science. Indeed, the Program in Progress for each chapter relates directly to that chapter's CS Interlude (so when we talk about analysis of algorithms, the associated programs do sorting, and when we discuss language translation, the Program in Progress is a simple parser). Students see why the concepts are relevant, how they can be used to solve real problems, and how those problems fit into the computer science landscape.

Code reuse An ongoing theme in the text is to increase programming efficiency by avoiding reinventing the wheel for each new program. Every text chapter concludes with a set of program "Building Blocks" that are developed in the text and the associated lab. These building blocks constitute a vocabulary from which the design constituents or "modules" of subsequent programs can be drawn.

Reference Each text chapter concludes with a Reference section, which provides a convenient summary of the major points of the chapter. We have found that our students often skim the chapter, look at the reference section, and then reread the chapter in depth at their leisure.

Exercises We provide approximately 400 text exercises, half of which are answered in the text. Many of the answers are in the nature of reviews of the text material, others serve as hints to complete solutions. The instructor's manual provides answers to all the exercises that are not answered in the text.

Chapter Coverage

The thirteen chapters cover the standard Pascal topics in a quite standard order.[1] Each is organized around a Program in Progress that provides a meaningful context for learning as well as a starting point for a directed laboratory experience, and each contains a Computer Science Interlude that puts the chapter itself in context. The lab exercises serve as a source for extended programming exercises and homework assignments, while the text provides exercises of the pencil-and-paper variety to test understanding of specific language features. The text is organized in three major parts:

Part I: programs The first three chapters are devoted to the nature and primary features of programs. Chapter 1 is an introduction to hardware and software, explaining what a Pascal program is, the form it must take, and how it is translated into a sequence of instructions that can be run on a computer. The PIP for this chapter is a program that determines the day of the week on which a date falls. We thus begin with an example that our students find is much more interesting than the canonical first program that displays "Hello" on the screen. In Chapter 2, we cover the simple Pascal data types, representation of information in the machine, and the ways that information may be manipulated by a program. Chapter 2's PIP illustrates these topics in the context of a simple tax preparation program. In Chapter 3, we introduce the notion of subprograms and discuss the values of encapsulation, the nature of parameters, and the calling conventions for functions and procedures. We introduce verification techniques here and conclude with an extended case study in program design, in which we extend the PIP (a collection of geometric calculations).

[1]Reading the comments of the reviewers of the manuscript, we seriously considered numbering each chapter as Chapter 1. For almost every chapter, X, there was a reviewer who said "I liked the manuscript, except for the fact that Chapter X should have been presented before Chapter $X - 3$." We knew you can't please all the people all the time, and it appears that you can't please *any* of the people all the time.

Part II: algorithms Chapters 4 through 8 are devoted to filling in the details, by discussing Pascal's control structures and introducing structured data types. Chapter 4 covers conditional statements using an expert system as our PIP. Chapter 5 is devoted to a discussion of loops. In this chapter, we discuss numerical analysis and design a program to perform numerical analysis. We continue the concept of verification here by introducing loop invariants and exit conditions. In Chapter 6, we discuss text processing and introduce strings. We depart from the Pascal standard here because, first, strings are such a common extension to Pascal that they may almost be regarded as standard and, second, we find that it makes the later introduction of arrays far less painful. The two PIPs for this chapter deal with cryptography, which we also discuss in the Computer Science Interlude. In Chapter 7, we return to subprograms, discussing parameter passing and recursion in detail. The context in this chapter is parsing and the PIP is a simple recursive descent parser that recognizes Pascal identifiers. Chapter 8 concludes this part with a transition from an emphasis on algorithms to the next major part, where the emphasis is on data structures. In this chapter, we discuss the **type** declaration in detail, using subrange and enumerated types. The PIP is a more sophisticated and robust version of the weekday program we introduced in the first chapter. We conclude this chapter and bid farewell to control structures by discussing the use and misuse of the **goto** statement.

Part III: data structures Chapters 9 through 13 conclude our tour of Pascal and problem solving by discussing data structures. In Chapter 9, we introduce arrays and use Selection Sort and Quicksort to illustrate timing analysis of algorithms. Chapter 10 includes a discussion of records, and we begin to construct a line-oriented word processor, PasWord. In Chapter 11, we use files to remedy PasWord's inability to save any of its documents. We finish PasWord in Chapter 12, where we change the representation of a document from a static array of lines to a linked list. Finally, in Chapter 13, we take a step away from the detailed investigation of Pascal so that we may see the principles of abstract data types. In a related vein, the PIPs for this chapter are two units with identical interfaces to implement the List ADT, one using arrays and the other using linked lists. The Computer Science Interlude in this chapter is an introduction to Object-Oriented Programming.

Having experienced programming in this way, we've found that students come away with a solid, comprehensive, and positive background in problem solving using the computer, as well as a good sense of what computer science is about. We devoted a great deal of effort toward making the text and labs interesting, accurate, fun to read, and easy to learn (and teach) from. We hope our package conveys to you and to the students our enthusiasm for all of the topics covered.

Heartfelt Thanks

While this project was in many ways our creation, it would not exist in its present form were it not for the contributions of many talented and dedicated people, each of whom influenced the final product in some significant and positive way. Our thanks go out, in parallel, to: our students in MA/CS 241 (particularly Mauritz Heukamp and Frank Iuorno), for being guinea pigs for the draft version of this text for three years, finding errors beyond number and suggesting better ways of doing things; Frank Ruggirello, for introducing us to the concept of Gu and getting us into this in the first place (may all your projects be blockbusters); Donna Linden, our "personal production editor," who had things well enough under control to take her vacation during the early stages of the production of this book (hugs and kisses for being an island of sanity in the sea of chaos); Stan Loll, our reliable computer guru at Wadsworth; Rhonda Gray, for all her help on the details that go into a project like this; Andrew Ogus, managing designer; Al Burkhardt, for producing a design that knocked our socks off; and to our reviewers—Robert B. Anderson, University of Houston; Anthony Q. Baxter, University of Kentucky; John Buck, Indiana University; Robert Christiansen, University of Iowa; Edmund Deaton, San Diego State University; Chris Dovolis, University of Minnesota, Twin Cities; Robert Holloway, University of Wisconsin, Madison; Leon Levine, University of California, Los Angeles; Abe Low, California State University, Sacramento; Linda Northrop, USAF Academy; Pete Petersen, Texas A&M; Theresa Phinney, Texas A&M; Jeffrey Popyack, Drexel University; Eleanor Quinlan, Ohio State University; William Root, San Diego State University, Ali Salehnia, South Dakota State University, and Stephen Weiss, University of North Carolina—for their insightful comments on the manuscript.

We'd like to say that any errors in the text were the fault of the production staff but honesty forbids. We did everything we could to ensure that the final manuscript was error-free, but even if it was, we're aware of Bit Rot, that law of nature that describes the way errors generate spontaneously in texts (and programs). If you find glitches, please feel free to let us know, either through Wadsworth or by contacting us at the Department of Mathematics and Computer Science, Hamilton College, Clinton, NY 13323. Now, let's get to it.

Pascal's Triangle

Programs

Computer Science and Programming: An Introduction to Pascal

1

This book is about programming—particularly, programming in the Pascal language—and problem solving with computers. Before we lead you into the world of programming, though, we will do our best to orient you, taking a quick look at the surrounding landscape. A computer program is nothing more than a list of instructions that a computer can execute. With this in mind, we'll first take a brief look at computers, discussing how a Pascal program is executed on a computer, and then take a first look at what a Pascal program looks like and the problem-solving techniques we use to build one.

O B J E C T I V E S

In this chapter, we will:

- Describe, at a level appropriate for a fledgling Pascal programmer, what a computer is.
- Describe the process whereby a program is "understood" and executed by a computer.
- Enter and run a complete Pascal "Program in Progress" that performs an interesting calculation.
- Describe the problem-solving process, whereby we go from a vague statement of a task to a finished program that accomplishes that task.
- Review the Program in Progress to describe the basic structure and format of Pascal programs.
- Describe some general features of the Pascal language.

1.1 Why Learn Pascal?

Since you are reading this text, you are presumably enrolled in an introductory programming course. Why is that? Or, more to the point, why should one learn programming? Forget practical answers such as "It's a required course," or "Friends and relatives have told me that it's a good idea." The ability to program in Pascal, or any other language for that matter, is not a requisite for success in society, nor will it ever be. Neither is it a ticket to a fulfilling and high-paying career. The overwhelming majority of people live happy and productive lives—and will continue to do so in the foreseeable future—without ever once having to program a computer. Of course, the same could be said for fixing a car, writing music, or understanding history.

Here are some reasons for learning to program: It is a challenging intellectual pursuit. It is (for some of us) a stimulating activity. It is rewarding to solve a problem on a computer. By programming a computer we can get it to do interesting things—indeed, in order to get a computer to do anything interesting, someone must write a program. Programming gives one a feeling of control over the computer. Learning to program helps one understand how a computer works. Learning to program helps one understand the types of problems that can and cannot be solved by a computer, and to distinguish between the two.

Computers can only do things they can be programmed to do. A large part of learning to program is learning to think in a particularly simple and efficient fashion, to be able effectively to break a problem into finer and finer units until the units can be expressed in a form that the computer can execute. As you will see, writing programs to solve problems demands an attention to details and mastery of the language used for communication with the computer, but the main precepts involve no more than the common-sense rules you already use to manage any medium-to-large cognitive task, such as writing an essay or designing a loft for your room.

In addition, there is a less practical side to learning to program, one that makes it so gratifying to teach. Programming is *fun*. Certainly it is exasperating to spend hours trying to fix errors in a program, only to discover that each fix introduces several new ones. At times you will feel as if you were battling the mythical hydra, where cutting off a head causes two to grow in its place. For all the frustration, though, there will come a time when your program works as you intended and that, we guarantee you, is more satisfying than scratching an itch in a place you couldn't reach before. When you program, you are the creator, in complete control of a small universe. Subject only to a minuscule collection of rules, you are free to shape your microworld in any fashion you wish. In that respect, what you get from programming is similar to the creative satisfaction involved in composing music or writing a story, except that the rules for good programming are simple enough to set down in a single volume like the one you are now holding.

There is another, more profound reason for learning to program. We all have a duty to be able to make informed decisions about the world around us. If we fail to do so, we put ourselves in the hands of the first demagogue that comes along and, in so doing, give ignorant assent to policies about which we know nothing. If, for instance, we are presented with a governmental decision to spend billions of dollars on a computer-controlled battle program that is touted as a shield against intercontinental ballistic missiles, or if we hear about plans to develop a national data bank to store information on all of us, we had better be sure we at least understand what computers can and can't do. The best way to learn that is by finding out directly — by learning ourselves how to make computers do what we want.

1.2 Computer Science Interlude: Hardware and Software

A theme that runs throughout computer science, especially in programming, is that of *levels of abstraction*. One feature that characterizes both computers and their programs is that each is made of a very large number of very simple parts — so many that keeping a mental picture of all the tiny details is often impossible. While this state of affairs is particularly notable in computer science, it is certainly not unique to the discipline; we see the same complexity in writing an essay or designing a house. We can approach mastering this complexity in two ways: We can work from the most complex level down, or we can repeatedly group small elements into larger ones.

The process of *top-down design* is what we do when we write an outline. We begin by identifying the largest conceptual units, then break these into smaller subordinate units, and break these subordinates into smaller units, and so on, until we eventually arrive at the basic building blocks — the sentences, if we're writing an essay, or the individual lines of code, if we're writing a program.

We could also attack a problem in the opposite direction, using *bottom-up design*. Think, for instance, of describing a house. A house, like a computer or a program, is constructed of a large number of simple pieces, in this case pieces of wood, brick, metal, and glass. An architect needs to know that a certain window is made up of four pieces of glass of a certain size and thickness, along with perhaps twenty pieces of wood of particular dimensions and fourteen pieces of metal; that's one level of abstraction, probably the smallest that the architect needs to understand. However, it would clearly be impossible to keep track of this level of detail when designing the entire facade of the house. At the design level, the architect need only be concerned about what the window looks like and what its exterior dimensions are, and can trust that the window manufacturer has kept track of the details of window construction. In what follows, we will use both approaches: We will solve programming problems from the top down, and we'll rely on a growing collection of tested building blocks, which, like the windows of a house, come prepackaged for our use.

Throughout this text, new terms are italicized. Detailed definitions of most of these terms are given in the glossary at the end of the text.

In the next two sections (and throughout the rest of the text) we'll see much more about top-down and bottom-up design.

Hardware

At the lowest level of detail, a computer may be regarded as a very large collection of very small switches. A typical modern computer may have several million of these switches, all packed onto a chip of silicon about the size of a postage stamp. These switches are much like ordinary light switches, except that in addition to input and output wires they also have a control wire that sets the switch on or off, so that the output wires from one switch may be used to control the settings of others. This is the level of abstraction that is the purview of the circuit designers.

The next step up in complexity is to connect these switches together into circuits that can store information and manipulate it. To do this, the circuit designer first chooses a way to represent information using only the values 0 (no current flowing in a particular wire, for example) and 1 (current flowing). To represent the numbers 0, 1, 2, and 3, for instance, the designer may decide to use two wires with the interpretation that the values 00 (no current in wire 1 and no current in wire 2) will be interpreted as the number 0, the values 01 (current in wire 2 only) will represent 1, 10 will represent 2, and 11 will represent 3. In a similar way, we could code alphabetic information using more wires in parallel, letting 1000001 denote A, 1000010 denote B, and so on, up to 1011010 to represent Z. Once we have settled on a code for information, we can connect switches together in such a way as to store information, move information from one storage location to another, and perform simple arithmetic and logical operations on the information. At this level, where we have grouped tens or hundreds of switches into storage and manipulation units, we find ourselves in the domain of the computer architect, whose job it is to combine simple circuits into a functioning whole computer.

At this higher level of abstraction, a computer may be described as consisting of just a few main components, such as:

- A *memory*, which retains information that we can think of as numeric, logical, or alphabetic.
- A *central processing unit*, which performs operations such as addition on numbers, comparisons of numbers or characters, and so on.
- An *input/output (I/O) unit*, which allows the computer to communicate with the outside world by writing on a screen, printing on paper, or reading information from a keyboard or disk.

Software

In the Mesozoic era of computers, a mere fifty years ago, the architectural level was the level at which the programmer was forced to live. In order to add two numbers from memory and store their sum in a different location, for example, one might have to provide the following instructions (we have provided italicized descriptions that would not be part of the actual code):

LOD 2400   *Copy the number stored in memory location 2400 into temporary*
           storage
ADD 2420   *Add to that the number stored in memory location 2420*
STO 1204   *Copy the result into location 1204 in memory*[1]

This kind of programming, in what is known as *assembly language*, was a daunting experience. So much code had to be written to perform even the simplest tasks that the details took up almost all of the programmer's attention, and keeping track of the overall logical organization was well-nigh impossible. In addition, very little was available in the way of automated error-checking, so that a single typographical error could spell disaster, not to mention be very difficult to find after the fact. Because of the nature of the languages and the designs of early machines, much of the early code was replete with tricks to save a line or two, or a fraction of a second, resulting in programs that were not only virtually impossible to explain to someone else, but even difficult for the original programmer to understand and modify. Clearly, something had to be done.

To understand how help came in the decades of the 1940s and 1950s for the problems of programmers, you need to know a bit more about how computers work. A natural question to ask at this stage is: "Where do the instructions to the computer come from?" The very earliest computers received their instructions by someone plugging together the units for storage and manipulation of information in appropriate ways — in a sense, rewiring the computer for each new task. A slight improvement came from using ordinary toggle switches to set the instructions. We owe a debt to John von Neumann, who realized that the list of instructions — what we call a program — could be stored in the computer's memory, along with the data that the computer was to manipulate. In such a *stored-program computer*, the basic sequence of operations is the *fetch-execute cycle*: fetch an instruction from memory, execute that instruction (that is, have the computer do what the instruction asks), fetch and execute the next instruction in memory, and continue this cycle until instructed to halt. This is the heart of the operation of any modern computer — a dazzling electronic dance executed in miniature at the rate of several million repetitions each second.

Once programs could be stored in a computer's memory, they could be treated as ordinary data; in particular, a program may itself be regarded as input data, to be manipulated by another program. This insight led to the notion of *high-level languages*. A high-level language is a programming language that is designed specifically to make programming easier for people. We can't change the native language of the machine — that language is completely determined by the way the computer is built. These native languages, or *machine languages*, will always be

---

[1]In fact, things were even worse. Since the switches that manipulate information can have only two settings — on and off — all information had to be expressed using only the values 0 and 1, so the instructions would actually have looked more like:

```
0110 100101100000
1001 100101110100
0101 010010110100
```

hard for us to use, precisely because they are designed to be easy for the computer. What we can do, though, is design a high-level language that is easier for people to use, and then design a program that will translate *source code* — the original program in the high-level language — into *object code* — the translated program in the only language that the machine can execute, its machine language.

For example, we might, as language designers, realize that a programmer has very little interest in knowing precisely where in memory a piece of information is stored as long as she or he can refer to it in a program. We might then decide that our language will allow reference to information by symbolic names like *sum, oldValue,* or *newValue.* We might also realize that a useful operation is to evaluate an expression and name it so that it can be referred to later. So, we might decide that the combination : = (colon followed by an equal sign with no space between them) will represent the operation "evaluate the expression on the right and place the result in the location corresponding to the name on the left." Having made these (and many other similar) decisions, we then write a translating program, which, when it reads the source code expression

sum : = oldValue + newValue

performs whatever steps are necessary to produce the object code:

```
LOD 2400    Location 2400 corresponds to oldValue
ADD 2420    Location 2420 corresponds to newValue
STO 1204    And the translator has assigned sum to location 1204
```

As you might expect, writing a translator program is a difficult task. The benefits, though, are enormous. We are free to invent a high-level language that is as easy to use and as productive as we can make it, as long as the language we invent can be translated by a program. (We don't yet know how to translate English into machine language, for example.) Once we've done that, the translator acts as an intelligent assistant, handling all the details of translating a program in our language into a sequence of instructions in the computer's language.

In Chapter 7 we'll see a program that performs a small part of this translation.

In essence, then, as a Pascal programmer you can behave as if you are dealing with an imaginary *virtual computer*, one that is designed to execute Pascal statements; you need not be concerned with the reality that your source code is being translated to run on a particular machine, as we illustrate in Figure 1.1.

One of the biggest benefits of this approach is that the virtual machine is the same, whether your Pascal program is actually being run on an IBM, Apple, or Digital Equipment Corporation computer. Different machines have different machine languages, but you need never be concerned with that level of detail. The people who write translators *have* to be concerned — since they must write a translator for each variety of machine on which programs in a particular high-level language will be run — but as long as you have the right Pascal translator available, the code you wrote on your IBM PS/2 will work the same way on an Apple Macintosh IIfx or a Digital VAX 11/780.[2]

---

[2]Well, sort of. The people who design translator programs seem to have a hard time resisting the impulse to add extra features above and beyond the agreed-upon standard for a language. These

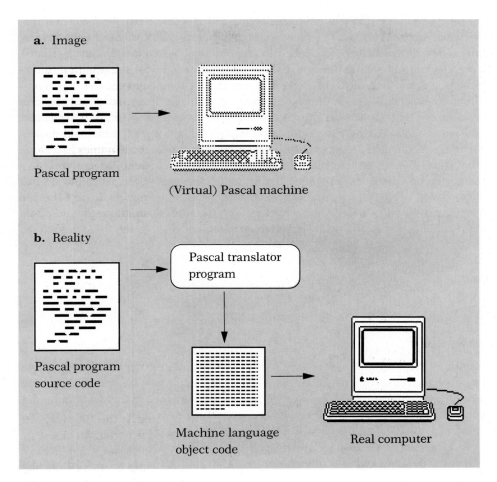

a. Image

Pascal program

(Virtual) Pascal machine

b. Reality

Pascal translator program

Pascal program source code

Machine language object code

Real computer

Figure 1.1. Programming a virtual machine

Writing a translator is a difficult but manageable task, especially with the help of existing utility programs that simplify much of the detail work. As a result, we find ourselves today with a wealth of different high-level languages. There are several hundred of them, designed for different purposes and having different underlying philosophies. Some of the more common ones are: COBOL, designed for business use; FORTRAN, created for scientific applications; LISP and Prolog, used in Artificial Intelligence research; and BASIC and Pascal, developed primarily as teaching languages (although Pascal and its cousin language, C, are frequently used for applications outside of academia).

bells and whistles can be very useful in programming, but using them often means that your program will not be compatible with all translators. In this text, we will stick mainly to the standard set of language features and will clearly indicate any nonstandard ones we use.

As we leave this section, we will bid farewell to the term *translator* in favor of two more precise ones. The process of program translation comes in two flavors: an *interpreter* translates each line of source code just before it is executed, while a *compiler* translates an entire source code program before it is executed. An interpreted program typically takes longer to run than a compiled version of the same program, since translation time is interspersed with run time (not to mention that a statement that is executed a thousand times will necessarily have to be translated a thousand times). One virtue of interpretation, though, is its flexibility. Programs written in some interpreted languages can modify themselves between translations and, thus, alter their behavior on the fly. If a program is compiled, on the other hand, the translation is done once and for all prior to execution. The advantage of compilation is quicker execution time, at the expense of a more static, less flexible program. COBOL, FORTRAN, and Pascal are generally compiled languages, while LISP, Prolog, and BASIC are generally interpreted.

1.3   Problem Solving with Computers

We've said before that a program is a list of instructions for a (virtual) computer. True as that may be, it doesn't afford us much help when we sit down with a blank piece of paper and, more often than not, a blank mind, without any idea of where to begin. The problems of where to begin and where to go from there are not unique to programming—indeed, we face the same difficulties when we attempt any task of similar complexity, such as writing a term paper.

Pick up a typical writing handbook and open it to the chapter on "Writing a Paper." The chapter is usually toward the end and has sections with titles like "Define your topic carefully," "Prepare an outline," "Write a first draft," "Make effective use of the language," and "Revise what you wrote." If you talk to a professional writer, she or he will usually add guidelines like "Consider your audience" and remind you that "Writing is rewriting." The general principles for writing an effective paper have been with us for a long time, which isn't surprising when you consider how long people have been writing. If you stop to think about it, these principles are really little more than codifications of common sense and can be applied to a wide variety of tasks.

The Software Life Cycle

These same principles that work for writing papers hold equally well when it comes to writing programs. In the language of computer science, they are expressed as the *software life cycle*. We can describe the software life cycle as the production of a good program in five major phases:

The software life cycle

I. Design and specify the program.
II. Develop the program.
III. Analyze the program design and write the code.
IV. Test the program and fix any mistakes you find.
V. Maintain, extend, and modify the program.

Let's look at these stages in more detail.

Design. ("Define your topic carefully.") In this phase, you ask yourself questions like these: What, precisely, do I want my program to do? What information will the program require as *input*? What *output* information will the program produce? What will the program look like to the operator while it's running? Unless you can produce answers to these questions, it's pointless to continue, since you'll be working without a clear goal in mind.

Development. ("Prepare an outline," "Produce a first draft.") Once the specifications are clear, you should outline the major tasks that your program needs to perform to accomplish its intended function. You can often go directly from this outline to a program that is a hasty, incomplete, but working first draft, which you can run and test without getting sidetracked by details. The development phase may have to pass through several revisions as you see deficiencies in your first draft program. Just as you fill in the details of a broad outline, you'll probably do several draft programs, each more detailed and closer to the eventual finished product.

Analysis and final coding. ("Make effective use of the language.") Eventually, you'll reach a stage in the development process when you're ready for your final draft. You'll put the finishing touches on your program and take an especially close look at the program statements you've written, with an eye to their correctness and precision. This is when you do whatever you can to make sure that the program will actually do what you intended it to do, tracing its actions by hand if necessary. Don't neglect to look at the parts of the program that are "obviously" correct — a surprisingly large number of errors occur in such places. This is a good time to have someone else go through the code with you, since explaining a program to another person can often force you to make your assumptions explicit.

Testing. ("Writing is rewriting.") By now you have a working program that you've carefully inspected for flaws. The real world, though, is full of surprises, and it's almost impossible to predict all the things that can go wrong with a program. Now's the time to sit down with your program and do as many sample runs as you can, all the time trying to ferret out potential problems. Is the program easy to understand and use? Does it work as it should on "typical" inputs? Does it work correctly on proper but "weird" inputs that might only arise once in a hundred runs? Does it work, or at least fail gracefully, on "pathological" inputs that might arise from misunderstandings or errors on the part of the operator? If you encounter a problem here, you'll have to find it and fix it (*debugging*, as it's called). This usually entails a return to phases II and III.

Maintenance. ("Consider your audience.") For school programs, you'll probably see this phase only rarely. In real-world applications, though, someone will have to see to it that your program is modified to serve new purposes, as your program passes from version 1.0, through 1.1 to 2.0, 3.0, and 4.055b2. It may require adding new features, changing the design to suit new specifications from the boss or the customers, and so on. Here's where there's a big payoff to be gained from writing the program clearly and coherently, with plenty of documentation about what it does and how it does it.

These discrete phases of the software design life cycle are often more of an ideal than they are a reflection of the real programming process. Often, you'll have to backtrack to an earlier phase to correct errors, and we're well aware that you may find it irresistible to rush ahead to the next step before completing an earlier one. Keep in mind, though, that in programming — as in most other tasks — it's almost always better to proceed carefully and systematically. If you don't, you'll discover that it's far more difficult to correct errors than it is to work in such a way that those errors don't appear in the first place.

Things to Come

We'll be the first to admit that these guidelines are little more than empty platitudes unless you have some concrete examples of the problem-solving process in action. With this in mind, we've built this text so that each chapter walks you through this process, applying the guidelines to a realistic problem.

Each chapter is built around a sample program (a "Program in Progress," or "PIP" for short) that illustrates the topics of the chapter. For each PIP, we trace at least the first three stages of the software life cycle: (1) designing and specifying the PIP, (2) showing how we developed the version of the PIP you'll see in the text, and (3) analyzing the PIP's features in terms of the new Pascal constructs we've introduced. In a static text, we can't run and test it, but *you* can in the labs, and we'll direct you in running the PIP, testing it, and modifying it (which is why we call it a "Program in Progress," rather than something like "The Completed Program"[3]). In addition, in all subsequent chapters, we'll use the PIP to illustrate an aspect of the wider world of computer science, because we want to make it

---

[3]There's a maxim among software designers that applies here: "Programs are never finished, only released."

abundantly clear that there's much more to computer science than just programming computers.

1.4   Problem Solving I: Designing the PIP

The Program in Progress for this chapter is one that, when given a day, month, and year, computes and displays the day of the week on which that date falls. That sounds simple enough—the specification is partially written as soon as we finish the first sentence. We could dress it up by stating it formally, and fill in some of the details about the information involved, as follows:

INPUT: Three whole numbers, representing the day, month, and year of a given date.

OUTPUT: The input day, month, and year, along with the day of the week on which that date falls, as, for example, the birthday of one of your authors:

25.12.1945 falls on Tuesday

An explicit description of a program's input and output is a great place to begin designing a program. Obviously, this information must be known before writing the program, and the format of the information will almost certainly dictate decisions later in the problem-solving process.

Problem-solving technique

What information will be provided to the program, and in what form? What information should the program produce as output, and how should it be displayed?

So far, so good. There's a big problem, though, that stands squarely in the way right from the start. How do we figure out the day of the week? You'll have to take our word for it when we tell you that there's no built-in feature in the Pascal language that performs this computation, so we have to look elsewhere. Let's start with the most obvious:

Problem-solving technique

Is it like anything I've done or seen before?

Hmm. We'd guess that the answer to this one is a resounding "No." Don't feel discouraged, though — we'd bet that most professional programmers would give the same answer. What else can we try?

Problem-solving technique

How would I go about solving this problem if I had to do it by hand?

We might get some help here. If we weren't in a computer course and saw this problem, we might first consider counting forward or backward from a known date. Now we take a look at what that approach would involve.

Problem-solving technique

Are there one or more little problems hiding in the big one? Can I break the problem down into smaller parts?

We've exploded the problem into a host of smaller ones, like how to tell whether the input date is before or after our known date, how to count forward and backward, how to keep track of the days in the various months, and how to keep track as we're counting of whether we're in a leap year or not. Ugh. We seem to have gone from one problem we don't know how to solve to a whole collection of problems we don't know how to solve, and that's not progress. We make a mental note to come back to this if we can't do any better, since now it just seems extremely difficult, rather than impossible. Let's try another obvious approach.

Problem-solving technique

Does *anyone* know how to solve this problem? Can I ask someone or do a literature search?

We're in luck here. We ask around, go to the library, and finally ask one of the authors of this text, who vaguely recalls a mention of the problem in a number theory text that went out of print before he was born. With a bit of searching, he even finds it in his files. It's called *Zeller's Congruence*.

Zeller's Congruence takes three whole numbers for the day of the month, the month itself (1 = January, . . . , 12 = December), and the full number for the year (so February 14, 1971, would be represented by the numbers 14, 2, 1971, and *not* 14, 2, 71). It then performs the following steps (which we explain in detail in the exercises):

1. Because February is the only month with a variable number of days, adjust the month and year so that January and February are the last months of the preceding year. For example, February 14, 1971, would have the adjusted day, month, and year numbers 14, 12, 1970, and March 27, 1991, would be adjusted to have the number 27, 1, 1991.

2. Compute the contribution to the day of the week caused by the fact that the months have different numbers of days. To do this, let m be the adjusted month number from step 1 above, compute $26m - 2$ and divide the result by 10, discarding the remainder. For example, if m were 4, then $26m - 2$ would be $26 \times 4 - 2 = 102$, which when divided by 10 yields a month contribution of 10.

3. Compute the contribution to the day of the week caused by the year, using the following steps:

   a. Determine the century and the year within the century of the adjusted year. For 1971, for example, the century would be 19 and the year within the century would be 71.

   b. Add the following four values: (i) the year within the century, (ii) the whole number part of the result of dividing the year within the century by four, (iii) the whole number part of the result of dividing the century by four, and (iv) five times the century. The result is the contribution to the day of the week caused by the year.

4. Add the day number, the contribution from the month, and the contribution from the year. Divide this sum by 7 — the remainder will be the day of the week, where 0 = Sunday, 1 = Monday, . . . , 6 = Saturday.

As an example, let's find the day of the week on which Valentine's Day fell in 1971. We begin with day code = 14, month code = 2, and year code = 1971. In step 1, we adjust the month code to 12 and the year code to 1970. In step 2, we find the month contribution to be the whole number part of $26 \times 12 - 2$ divided by 10, or 31. In step 3, we find the year contribution by adding 70, 17 (the whole number part of 70 / 4), 4 (the whole number part of 19 / 4), and 95 (5×19). The contribution from the year is $70 + 17 + 4 + 95 = 186$. Finally, in step 4, we add 14 (the day), 31 (the month contribution), and 186 (the year contribution) to get $14 + 31 + 186 = 231$. Dividing this by 7 yields a remainder of 0, so we've found that February 14, 1971, fell on a Sunday.

While Zeller's Congruence is a trifle complicated, it's a heck of a lot better than the only other idea we had, so we give it a try. We breathe a sigh of relief, decide to call the program *Zeller*, and go to the next phase of the process.[4]

---

[4] To be candid, we'll admit that Zeller's Congruence is almost completely incomprehensible at first glance. Our choice of this for a first program was guided by two reasons: (1) we wanted to begin

1.5 Problem Solving II: Developing the PIP

At this point, we want to get more precise about the steps involved in solving our problem. In other words, we want to describe the *algorithm*, or sequence of steps to solve a problem, in detail. The top-level algorithm of *Zeller* is quite simple, but it illustrates the structure of a great number of programs.

Problem-solving technique

A great many computer problems take the following form:

I. Get some information.
II. Process the information.
III. Display the results of the processing.

Now the program begins to take shape. We need to describe the information we will get (from the user in this case), the techniques used to process the information, and the form the output will take. Each level of detail, as it is developed, will be listed as subordinate to one of the previous outline items, just as in any other outline. Ultimately, the fully expanded outline will serve as the basis for our program, indicating both the sequence of steps to be performed and the relationships, if any, between these steps.

Problem-solving technique

Use an outline to describe the tasks that need to be performed.

I. Get some information.
   A. Print a message to the user, requesting three whole numbers for the day, month, and year of a date.
   B. Read these three numbers from the keyboard.
II. Process the information.
   Use Zeller's Congruence to produce a number in the range from 0 to 6, where 0 represents Sunday, 1 represents Monday, . . . , 6 represents Saturday.

In this sample, we don't check whether the numbers represent legitimate dates. We'll remedy this deficiency in Chapter 8.

---

with a program that did something interesting, and (2) since we don't expect you to know anything about Pascal at this stage, a complex, incomprehensible example will serve as well as a simple, incomprehensible one.

III. Display the results of the processing.

    A. Repeat the day, month, and year to the user.

    B. Convert the code from Zeller's Congruence to a day name.

    C. Write the day name.

We're almost finished; the input and output sections are broken down far enough that they correspond almost one-for-one with Pascal statements. All that remains is to expand the middle part until we are convinced that it, too, can be expressed readily in Pascal. The final design of our program now looks like this:

I. Get some information.

    A. Print a message to the user, requesting three whole numbers for the *day*, *month*, and *year* of a date.

    B. Read these three numbers from the keyboard.

II. Process the information.

    A. Adjust the month and year.

        1. If *month* is 1 or 2 (January or February), set *adjMonth* to 10 + *month* and set *adjYear* to *year* − 1.

        2. If *month* is not 1 or 2, set *adjMonth* to *month* − 2.

    B. Use Zeller's Congruence to find *weekDay*.

        1. Set *monthCorrection* to the integer part of 26 × *adjMonth* − 2, divided by 10.

        2. Compute *century* and *lastTwo* (year within the century).

        3. Set *yearCorrection* to (*lastTwo*) + (whole part of (*lastTwo* / 4)) + (whole part of (*century* / 4)) + (5 × *century*).

        4. Set *weekDay* to (*day* + *monthCorrection* + *yearCorrection*) / 7.

III. Display the results of the processing.

    A. Display the day, month, and year to the user.

    B. Convert the code from Zeller's Congruence to a day name.

    C. Write the day name.

Problem-solving technique

Expand your outline until each step can be expressed in Pascal.

We're done. Now, and only now, when we have a detailed outline, can we sit down and write Pascal code. It took a few minutes to develop the program, but the time was well spent, since we have a clear outline of what has to be done. The results follow, exactly as we designed and developed our program. As you read it, don't worry too much about what each line means; you'll have plenty of time over the next several weeks to fill in the details. The important thing to notice is not how unfamiliar the details might seem, but rather how easy it is to get a general sense of what's going on, even though you may not know anything about Pascal.

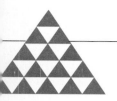

The PIP

```pascal
program Zeller (input, output);
{---------------------------------------------------------------}
{                                                               }
{                  PROGRAM IN PROGRESS                          }
{                                                               }
{                     CHAPTER 1                                 }
{                                                               }
{     This program uses Zeller's Congruence to calculate the day }
{     of the week on which any date falls. For details about     }
{     Zeller's Congruence, see Uspensky and Heaslet, Elementary  }
{     Number Theory, 1939, p. 206.                               }
{     INPUT:    day, month, and year (integer) of a date         }
{     OUTPUT:   day of the week on which the date falls          }
{                                                               }
{---------------------------------------------------------------}

  var
      day, month, year,                  {the date the user provides}
      adjMonth, adjYear,                 {adjusted month and year}
      century, lastTwo,                  {the century and the year within the century}
      monthCorrection, yearCorrection,   {the contribution from the month and the year}
      weekDay: integer;                  {the code for the day of the week on which the date falls}
begin
    {----------------------- GET DAY, MONTH, YEAR -----------------------}
    writeln('At the prompt, ">", enter numbers for day, month, year');
    writeln('Separate the numbers by spaces, and press Return after entering all three. ');
    write('> ');
    readln(day, month, year);

    {--------------------- ADJUST THE MONTH AND YEAR ---------------------}
    {Since February is the only month that has a variable number of days, the program    }
    {temporarily treats January and February as the last two months of the previous year. }

    if month <= 2 then
       begin    {We only do this part if the month entered was Jan. or Feb.}
          adjMonth := 10 + month;
          adjYear := year - 1
       end
    else
       begin    {We do this part if the month entered was not Jan. or Feb.}
          adjMonth := month - 2;
          adjYear := year
       end;
```

```
{————————————— CALCULATE THE DAY CODE ———————————}
{This is where the real work goes on. "weekDay" gets set to a whole number}
{in the range 0 .. 6, which is interpreted as the day Sunday .. Saturday.    }
monthCorrection := (26 * adjMonth — 2) div 10;                {adjustment for
                                                              the month}

century := adjYear div 100;
lastTwo := adjYear mod 100;
yearCorrection := lastTwo + (lastTwo div 4) + (century div 4) + 5 * century;  {adjustment for
                                                                             the year}

weekDay := (day + monthCorrection + yearCorrection) mod 7;
{——————————— CONVERT THE DAY CODE, WRITE THE RESULT ———————————}
writeln;
write(day : 1, '.', month : 1, '.', year : 1, 'falls on ');
case weekDay of
   0:
      writeln('Sunday');
   1:
      writeln('Monday');
   2:
      writeln('Tuesday');
   3:
      writeln('Wednesday');
   4:
      writeln('Thursday');
   5:
      writeln('Friday');
   6:
      writeln('Saturday')
   end
end.
```

1.6   Problem Solving III: Program Analysis

In the analysis section of each chapter, we'll take a close look at the new features of the PIP. This time we'll concentrate on the structure of a Pascal program. Take a close look at the PIP and write down some of the things you notice about its format. Don't concern yourself too much with how the program works — rather, concentrate on the form of the program itself. Take a few minutes to do that before you go on to the rest of the text — we'll wait.

•   •   •

All done? When we ask our students to do this, they usually observe some of the features we've listed on the following pages.

O B S E R V A T I O N 1. *Some of the words are in boldface type.* These are known as *reserved words*. They are words that have special meaning in Pascal and are there to facilitate the translation of your program into a form that the computer can execute. Not all Pascal programming environments use different typefaces for reserved words; you may find other sources that mark reserved words in capital letters, for example. Regardless of how they are indicated, all versions of Pascal treat these words as having predefined meanings. For instance,

> **E**very Pascal program begins with the reserved word **program** and ends with the reserved word **end**, followed by a period.

If you look back at the program, you'll notice also that the reserved words **begin** and **end** almost always come in matching pairs.[5] These two words serve to group statements together—the rules for these grouping words are the same as those for parentheses in algebraic expressions:

> **E**very **begin** must be matched with a subsequent **end**, and groups may be nested within another group, to any depth you wish.

We often indent **begin..end** groups, since it makes programs easier to read.[6] Below, we illustrate two possible program structures: (a) is the simplest possible, and (b) is the structure of our sample program.

a. The simplest possible Pascal program:

```
program Name and other stuff goes here;
begin
    Statements here
end.    Notice the period at the end of the program.
```

b. The structure of the sample program:

```
program Zeller(input, output);
begin
    Statements here;
    if Some condition then
        begin
            Statements
        end
```

---

[5]The **case** statement in the PIP (which we'll explain in Chapter 4) and the **record** declaration (Chapter 10) both contain an **end** that is not matched with a **begin**. However, whenever there's a **begin**, it is *always* matched with an **end**.

[6]Some modern compilers will do this "prettyprinting" for you automatically.

```
    else
        begin
            Statements
        end;
        More statements
    end.
```

You may have also noticed that there are reserved words other than **program**, **begin**, and **end**. The **if..then** pair and the **case** statement, as you may have guessed, are statements that control the execution of other statement groups, depending on certain logical and arithmetic conditions.

We'll have much more to say about these in Chapter 4.

O B S E R V A T I O N 2. *There are semicolons at the ends of some lines, but not others.* The semicolon is the cause of lots of headaches when you are first learning Pascal. Unlike some computer languages, such as COBOL and FORTRAN, which require only one statement per line or require that certain parts of a statement occur in fixed positions on a line, the Pascal standard makes no (or very little) restriction on how your program listing looks. That is to say, Pascal is a *free-format language.* You can format a Pascal program, using tabs, spaces, and returns, in any way that suits you (and those people for whom you're writing programs), just as you can write a paragraph in English with many sentences on a line, spaced as you wish. This implies, though, that the Pascal compiler needs to have some way of telling where one statement stops and the next one starts. That's what the semicolon is for:

> **A** semicolon in Pascal is a *statement separator*, and must always be placed between the end of one statement (or **begin..end** group of statements) and the beginning of the one following.

Take a look at the sample program again. There are 22 semicolons, each of which separates a single statement from the one following. Most of these occur at the ends of lines, but that's only because it makes the program easier to read if we put one statement per line. Had we wished, we could have run the entire listing on one very long line, trusting in the semicolons to provide the compiler with the necessary markers between statements.

You'll notice that there are no semicolons immediately before an **end** word, just as no **begin** is followed by a semicolon. That seems a mite peculiar, until you think of the analogous situation in English. In English, we can group words in parentheses and separate words in a group with commas, as we would if we wrote

The committee (Jones, Mustafa, Chen, O'Leary) convened at 7:00.

We don't need a comma after the left parenthesis or before the right, since the parentheses already serve the purpose of marking word divisions. In the same way, we never need a semicolon after **begin** or before **end**. They themselves serve as statement separators.[7]

Like natural languages such as English, Pascal is governed by its own rules of grammar. Although we may wince when we hear an ungrammatical English sentence, we can usually interpret the speaker's intent. That's because we humans are much better language processors than any program ever written. Fortunately for us, Pascal must be translated by a computer program and run by a computer, so its grammatical rules are much simpler than those of any natural language. This makes learning Pascal much easier than learning a human language, but the price we pay for simple grammar is that the compiler will not try to guess your meaning if you make a grammatical error. A modern compiler is "smart" enough to detect grammatical errors, as you will see, but it will not attempt to figure out what your program means when it does find an error. For our purposes, this means that a program *must* adhere to the rules of the language, with no exceptions whatsoever. If it doesn't, the compiler won't translate it—it's as simple as that.

As we introduce you to Pascal, you will notice that there really are two linguistic points of view at work. The simplest is *syntax*, the rules that dictate the form for programs and statements. This is the grammatical aspect we've mentioned already. More difficult to master is the *semantics* of a language, which is to say what the utterances mean. In English, for example, the sentence "Tom Fido the bone to gave" is syntactically incorrect, but even so we can be pretty sure what it means. On the other hand, the famous sentence by the linguist Noam Chomsky, "Colorless green ideas sleep furiously," gets a perfect score for syntax and zero credit for semantics. In computer languages, we may consider the semantics as concerning what we want to say to the (virtual) computer, and syntax as being the way we must say it.

A simple graphical way of describing what form a statement or group of statements in Pascal must take is a *syntax diagram*. In such a diagram, the components are drawn in boxes, connected with arrows. Any syntactically legal construction—which is to say, any construction that is allowable under the rules for Pascal grammar—is one that can be made by following the arrows and writing down the contents of the boxes as they are encountered. For example, the syntax diagram that describes statements might take the form of Figure 1.2.

You will notice that there are two kinds of boxes in the syntax diagram in Figure 1.2. The rounded boxes contain characters that appear literally in the pro-

---

[7]It doesn't do any harm to include extra semicolons as long as they're in places where a semicolon may legally appear. The rules for Pascal allow *empty statements*, so if you include extra semicolons, the Pascal translator program, which is written with the understanding that semicolons separate statements, will add dummy statements that do nothing at all. For example, the program segment

```
begin
    a := a + 1;;;
end
```

consists of four statements: the one you see and three "no-operation" dummies.

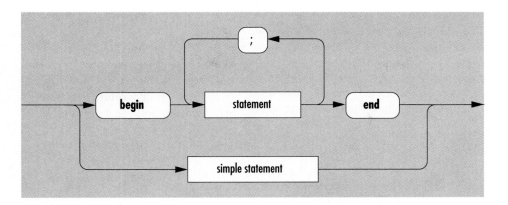

Figure 1.2.   Simplified syntax diagram for Pascal statements

gram statement, exactly as they are written. The rectangular boxes contain the names of constructions that are themselves described by syntax diagrams. In Figure 1.2 we have deliberately left out some of the details, like what a statement really is, but you should get the picture (pun intended): a statement is either (1) a simple statement or (2) a compound statement, consisting of a collection of statements (simple or compound) separated by semicolons and enclosed by a **begin..end** pair. Notice that this definition is not only incomplete (since we haven't yet said what a simple statement can be), but it is also *recursive*, since the definition of a statement includes the term defined ("statement") as part of its definition.

We'll see much more about recursive definitions in Chapter 7.

Consider, for instance, the statement

begin	*Start of outer compound statement*
simple statement1;	
begin	*Start of inner compound statement*
simple statement2;	
simple statement3	
end	*End of inner compound statement*
end	*End of outer compound statement*

The outer compound statement consists of simple statement1 and the inner compound statement. The inner compound statement, in turn, consists of simple statement2 and simple statement3. Notice that each of these compound statements is delineated by a **begin..end** pair, and that the statements within these **begin..end** pairs are separated by semicolons.

O B S E R V A T I O N 3. *There are ordinary English sentences in the program.* These are *comments*, and they consist of any text you wish, enclosed in curly braces (the { and } characters[8]). There are only two rules governing the use of comments in a Pascal program. The first rule is that

> **C**omments may not be nested within each other, and every left brace must be matched with a corresponding right brace.

In simple terms, this means that you may include any text whatsoever within comments, as long as it doesn't include curly braces. (Think about the job of translating a program and see if you can deduce why this restriction holds.) The second rule is almost as simple.

> **C**omments may not break or interfere with Pascal words or numbers.

In the next chapter you will see that

```
runningSum := runningSum + newValue
```

is a syntactically legal Pascal statement, but

```
runningSum := runningSum + new{for this month}Value
```

isn't, because the comment appears inside the identifier *newValue*. The following statements, however, are just fine:

```
runningSum := runningSum + newValue {for this month}
runningSum := runningSum + {for this month} newValue
```

Despite the fact that compilers essentially ignore them (except when they violate one of the simple rules above), we cannot express too strongly the need for comments. We write programs for computers, it is true; but equally important, we write programs for people. Programs have a life cycle: they are born, serve a useful term, and must be adapted to changing circumstances. In the real world of professional programmers, the person who must modify a program is almost never the person who wrote it. Even if the person who must modify a program happens to be the person who wrote it, it is highly likely that the modifier has completely forgotten his or her original intent in writing the program. At the very minimum, a program should include a comment block at the start about the intent of the program, how

---

[8]The Pascal standard allows the character combinations (* for { and *) for }. This alternate form was originally intended for computer keyboards without curly braces; they are syntactically equivalent to braces, so they cannot be nested within braces. A common use nowadays is to use the alternate forms for notes to yourself while developing a program, such as:

```
writeln(iteration, sum, delta);    (*REMOVE THIS LINE IN THE FINISHED PROGRAM*)
```

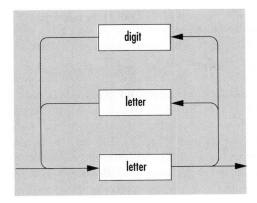

Figure 1.3. Syntax diagram for Pascal identifiers

it works, and what is expected from the operator. The listing should also contain individual comments on any part of the program for which the purpose or details are not completely transparent to a reader.

While it's possible to go overboard and smother the sense of a program with unnecessary comments, a good rule of thumb is: *It is better to err on the side of too many comments, rather than too few.* Comments aren't translated into machine code, so all they do is add to the length of the listing. True, it's easier not to *document* your programs or at best, put the comments in as an afterthought. Don't do it—try to get in the habit of including comments as you write your program. You'll appreciate the value of this Good Habit when you have to go back and modify a program that you wrote a few weeks before and realize how quickly the sense of what a program does evaporates.

O B S E R V A T I O N 4. *There are ordinary words in the program, like* "Zeller," "year," *and* "day." These are *identifiers*: they serve as names for programs, parts of programs called *procedures* and *functions*, and names for numeric, logical, and alphabetic information that is manipulated by a program. It used to be that many computer languages put severe restrictions on the syntax of identifiers, limiting them to single letters or single letters followed by a single digit. Contemporary languages like Pascal typically allow much greater latitude in the form identifiers may take, which makes for much more readable programs. Certainly $area :=$ $length * width$ is a big improvement over the spartan $a := l * w$. In Pascal, an identifier may consist of any combination of letters and digits, as long as the first character is a letter.[9]

Figure 1.3 shows a syntax diagram for identifiers, where the boxes "letter" and "digit" have exactly the meaning you would expect: the letters A through Z

---

[9]Some compilers allow identifiers to be arbitrarily long, but they only pay attention to the first few characters; this means that the compiler wouldn't be able to tell the difference between the identifiers *sumOfTheSquaresOfTheXValues* and *sumOfTheSquaresOfTheYValues*, in spite of the fact that they look different to us.

and the digits 0 through 9, respectively. You can use the diagram to verify that *a*, *area*, *zeta2*, and *dollarsAndCents* are legitimate Pascal identifiers, but that *big sum* (because it includes a space), *2BeOrNot2Be* (because it doesn't begin with a letter), and *$ + ¢* (because these are not letters or digits) are not.

Pascal is *case-insensitive* when it comes to identifiers, which means it makes no difference whether or not a letter is capitalized. The identifiers *INSIDEDIAME-TER*, *insidediameter*, *insideDiameter*, and *InSiDeDiAmEtEr* are all exactly the same as far as Pascal can tell, and you are free to use any capitalization style you wish (preferably one that is consistent and easy to read). Finally, although it is not standard Pascal, many compilers allow the use of the underscore character in identifiers (except as the first character), as in *inside_diameter*. The underscore is useful for making identifiers readable, since a space cannot be used within an identifier. (Can you see why?)

We've actually given you only part of the truth here. Although it is syntactically correct to use any combination of letters as an identifier, it is a semantic error to use any Pascal reserved word as an identifier. That means, for instance, that you could not give a variable the name *begin*, since the compiler is written with the understanding that that particular string of characters has a special meaning and may not be redefined in a program. Subject to that caution, though, you are free to choose any other identifier names you wish in your programs—they're all equally good as far as the compiler is concerned.

OBSERVATION 5. *Some of the other identifiers in our PIP program, like "read" and "writeln," seem to be used in a special way.* Indeed they are. One of the most powerful features of Pascal and many other modern languages is their ability to encapsulate any computational task into a separate routine—named by an identifier—so that the task's statements may be called into execution merely by invoking the routine's name. To use a metaphor from fantasy, one may summon a computational genie by calling its name, and the genie will perform its required task with no further intervention on the part of the summoner. These "genies" come in two basic forms: predefined and programmer-defined.

Pascal comes with a number of predefined commands that are useful for a variety of tasks. The commands *readln* and *writeln*, for example, cause information to be passed from an input device, such as the keyboard, to a program (*readln*), and from a program to an output device, such as the screen (*writeln*). As you might imagine, the details of these routines are very complicated and almost completely incomprehensible except to experts. The best part about using these predefined routines is that we need not be concerned with the details of how they work, only that they do indeed work as they should. Rather than having the same twenty or so lines of opaque code cluttering up your program whenever you want your program to write something on the screen, all you have to do is invoke the previously written code by calling it by name.

The real power of Pascal, though, comes from being able to write routines on your own to insert in your programs as you need them. As you will see in

Chapter 3 and subsequently, this can bring about an enormous saving of effort on the programmer's part, since a commonly used sequence of operations may be written only once and then called into action as needed. Using these *subprograms*, as they are called, has the additional benefit of making a program much easier to understand. In fact, one of the pervasive themes of this text is the building of reliable and verified subprograms that you can reuse across many different programs.

1.7   Reference

- A program is a list of instructions for a computer to perform.
- High-level languages are designed for the programmer's ease of use, while low-level languages reflect the design of the computer. A high-level language like Pascal is one that is translated by another program before being executed by a computer.
- One way of going about program design is to follow the five-step software design life cycle:
  - Design and specify the program, identifying and classifying all program inputs and outputs.
  - Develop the program by identifying its main tasks, then break these down into subtasks when necessary, continuing the process for as many levels as needed.
  - Code and analyze the program, looking for potential errors.
  - Test the program. Test it again. Test it again.
  - Maintain, modify, and extend the program, if necessary.
- When a problem seems to have no obvious solution, consider
  - Whether it is like anything you've done already
  - Whether it would be helpful to decompose the problem into smaller problems
  - Whether someone else has a solution, or whether one can be found in reference materials
  - Relaxing and doing something else for a while
- We write programs for people as well as for computers. Anything we can do to make a program more readable is a Good Thing. Some examples of Good Things are the use of abundant comments and of descriptive identifier names.
- A Pascal program consists of (1) a *header* (the **program** declaration, along with other parts we'll discuss later), followed by (2) a *statement part*, containing zero or more simple or compound statements enclosed in a **begin..end** pair, followed by (3) a period.

- Every Pascal statement has an associated syntax (describing its grammatical form) and semantics (describing how it will be interpreted by a computer).
- The semicolon in a Pascal program is a statement separator, in much the same way that commas are clause separators in English.

1.8 Building Blocks

As we progress through the details of Pascal, we will save any generally useful routines we develop and summarize them at the end of each chapter. As your knowledge of Pascal increases, so too will our stock of modules that we can use to build other programs. This relieves us of the need to reinvent the wheel every time we need some code we've already written and tested. This process of code reuse may seem like self-plagiarism, but far from being morally wrong, it is highly commendable when you are programming. Handel and Beethoven, after all, had no inhibitions about reusing themes that were particularly successful, and we could do much worse than follow their examples.

At this stage, the only building block we have is the shell of a program:

```
program ProgramName(input, output);
{comment block — all about the program}
begin
    Statements here;    {with comments as necessary}
    And here
end.
```

1.9 EXERCISES

Here, and in the exercises at the ends of other chapters, we give you the answers to the odd-numbered exercises so you can check your progress. You'll find the answers immediately after the exercises.

1. Why are you taking this course?

2. Give an example of an impact of technology on society about which it is important for the citizenry to be able to make *informed* policy decisions.

3. Why do we stress the importance of levels of abstraction in computer science and in programming in particular?

4. What is a computer? According to your definition, which of the following are computers?

   a. A dog.
   b. A toaster.
   c. The solar system.
   d. You.
   e. "Malzel's Chessplayer," a nineteenth-century automaton shaped like a man sitting at a chessboard, which was purportedly constructed of clockwork gears, rods, cams, and levers, and was reliably reported to be able to play chess as well as most people. Edgar Allen Poe wrote an essay about The Turk, as it was also known, but it was a real device, not one of Poe's fictions.
   f. A baby.

5. Define the following:

   a. Program
   b. Top-down design
   c. Bottom-up design

6. a. Give an example, other than a computer/program combination, of a situation in which ideas are embodied in a physical object.
   b. The five-step software life cycle is not the only model for managing a large and complex project. Give an example of a design scheme for some task that is different from the one we described.

7. Describe the fundamental entities of a Pascal program.

8. There are 26 shortest legal Pascal programs. Write one of them and tell what it would do when executed.

9. Look at the program *Zeller* and compare it structurally to a recipe in a cookbook.

10. Give an example of a design or description task that would be particularly appropriate for a top-down approach. Find a task for which a bottom-up approach would be more appropriate.

11. What is the rule for determining whether a year is a leap year?

12. The real cleverness behind Zeller's Congruence comes from the term $(26 * adjMonth - 2)$ **div** 10.

   a. Let's return to our original idea for computing the day of the week on which a date falls. We'll begin by computing by hand the contribution to the date caused by the month. Suppose, for instance, that March 1 fell on Tuesday (day code 2). Then, since March has 31 days, April 1 would fall on the day with code $2 + 31 = 33$. Of course, there's no day code 33, but since the days of the week repeat every 7 days, we can ignore any multiples of 7 and consider just the remainder of 33 divided by 7, which is 5. In other words, if March 1 were Tuesday, then April 1 would be Friday (day code 5).

   The Pascal operator **mod**, when applied to positive numbers, yields the remainder of the expression on the left when divided by the expression on the right, so what we've been doing is repeatedly computing the sum of a day code and the number of days in a month and then taking the result **mod** 7.

Write a table with two columns: the first containing the names of the months, starting with March, and the second containing the number of days in each month. Leave some spaces for other columns.

b. In the third column, begin with 2 and fill in the rest of the column by repeatedly adding the number in the column to the number of days in the month for that row, and then taking the sum **mod** 7. For example, the next number in the third column will be found by adding 2 and 31 to get 33, dividing that by 7 to get a remainder of 5, as we've seen. The next entry in that column will be found by adding the 5 we just got to the 30 days in April to get 35, and we then find that 35 **mod** 7 is 0. This column will begin with the numbers 2, 5, 0 (which we've already seen), 3, 5, 1 . . . . The interpretation of this column is that if March 1 were Tuesday, the first days of the following months will be on Friday (code 5), Sunday (code 0), Wednesday, Friday, Monday, ...

c. In the fourth column, write the values of the *adjusted* month codes for each month. This one's easy — the column begins 1, 2, 3, 4, 5, 6, ...

d. Finally, in the fifth column, compute the values of $((26 * m - 2) \textbf{ div } 10) \textbf{ mod } 7$, for the adjusted month codes $m = 1, 2, 3, 4, 5, 6, \ldots$ The Pascal operator **div** is the companion to **mod**, in that it returns the quotient when the expression on the left is divided by the one on the right, so 20 **div** 4 is 5, as is 21 **div** 4. Compare your result with the numbers in column three. They should be the same. In simple terms, what you've just shown is that $(26 * m - 2) \textbf{ div } 10$, when taken **mod** 7, is a compact and elegant way of determining the contribution that each month makes to the day of the week on which a date falls!

e. See if you can use the answer to Exercise 11 to figure out what the rest of Zeller's Congruence does.

f. If each year were exactly 365 days long, what effect would that have on Zeller's Congruence?

13. Even though you know hardly any Pascal, you should be able to design a program, as we did in the section where we traced the top-down design of this chapter's PIP. Design a program that would maintain a checkbook. List the major tasks that such a program would perform, and if any of the tasks need to be separated into subtasks, describe the subtasks as well. In addition, describe the information the program would need to store and manipulate.

14. What is the difference between syntax and semantics? Which has more to do with the machine and which has more to do with the programming language?

15. What is the difference between a compiler and an interpreter?

16. What would be the effect of replacing every semicolon in a program with six adjacent semicolons?

17. If, for the sake of simplicity, we denote **begin** by **b** and **end** with **e**, are the following sequences of **b**'s and **e**'s syntactically legal in a Pascal program?

a. bbebee
b. bbbebe
c. ebbbbeee
d. bbbebebbeeee

18. Give a collection of rules that a compiler might use when translating a program that is designed to determine whether a sequence of **b**'s and **e**'s, as in Exercise 17, is syntactically legal. How does this relate to strings of balanced parentheses, like ((()(())), that could correctly be used in some algebraic expression?

19. Consider the following syntax diagram, which describes some functions in the LISP programming language. Which of the following expressions are allowed by the syntax diagram?

    a. C
    b. AD
    c. CAR
    d. CADDADR
    e. ABRACADABRA

    Describe in words all legal expressions for this diagram.

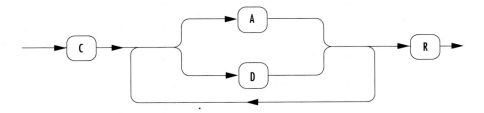

20. Draw the syntax diagram for Pascal comments.

21. Which of the following are illegal Pascal identifiers, and why?

    a. *two*
    b. *2*
    c. *O.K.*
    d. *case*
    e. *the answer*
    f. *supercallifragillisticexpialidocious*
    g. *ReservedWord*

1.10   Answers

1. There is no right answer to this question — sometimes it's just a good thing to reflect on our motivations. Come back to this question after the end of Chapter 13 and see what your answer looks like then.

3. Because the subject matter of computer science — computers and their programs — lends itself naturally to the process of grouping many small details together into larger conceptual units, which can then be grouped into ever larger units. Without this grouping, one quickly becomes swamped by details.

5. **a.** A program is a list of instructions to be executed by a (virtual) computer, written according to the rules of a particular language.

b, c. Top-down design works from the largest, most general, conceptual units and when necessary, repeatedly subdivides design units into smaller ones, continuing the process until the resulting pieces are small enough to manage. Bottom-up design works in the reverse direction, combining small units into successively larger ones.

7. A program header, which begins with the reserved word **program** and includes the name of the program and other declarations, followed by a statement body containing zero or more statements enclosed in a **begin..end** pair, followed by a period.

9. A recipe is a list of instructions to a cook, just as a program is a list of instructions to a computer. They both have a header ("Blackened Liver: An Old Family Favorite"), a list of ingredients that will be used (the **var** part of *Zeller* is equivalent to "18 Tbs butter, ½ pound calf's liver, 3 cups fenugreek"), and a collection of operations that must be performed in sequence ("Heat butter and fenugreek in an iron skillet over high heat until the smoke subsides, then toss in the liver and cook, shaking rapidly, for 25 minutes. Serve with root beer sauce.").

11. A year Y is a leap year if Y is evenly divisible by 4, except that Y is not a leap year if Y is evenly divisible by 100, except that Y is a leap year if Y is evenly divisible by 400. All this because the earth takes slightly more than 365 days to make one complete revolution around the sun.

13. There is no one right way to organize this program. Here's one way.

    I. Initialize and startup.
        A. Write instructions to the operator on how to use the program.
        B. Get the opening balance.
    II. Do a transaction (do this repeatedly, until the user enters Quit command).
        A. Get a command from the operator. (W = write a check, D = deposit money, B = display the current balance, Q = quit the program). Check the command. If it's not valid, tell the user what the commands are, get another, and try again. (Keep doing this until the user gives a valid command.)
        B. Do the command.
            1. If it's a W:
                a. Get the amount to be written.
                b. If the amount is greater than the current balance, inform the user that the check will bounce.
                c. If the amount is less than the current balance, get the name of the payee, print a check, and update the current balance.
            2. If it's a D:
                a. Get the amount to be deposited.
                b. Update the current balance.
            3. If it's a B: Display the current balance.
            4. If it's a Q: Do nothing.
            5. In any case except Q, go back to II and get another command.

15. A compiler translates all the statements of a program and then causes the translated version to be executed (as one would translate a text passage and write the translated version for a homework assignment in a French class). An interpreter translates each statement as it is encountered (as the translators in the U.N. do). Compilers are generally faster, since they don't have to retranslate repeated statements, but interpreters are generally simpler to write.

17. a. Legal
  b. Illegal; there are four **b**'s and only two **e**'s
  c. Illegal; there's no possible match for the first **e**, even though there are an equal number of **b**'s and **e**'s
  d. Legal

19. a. Illegal; to get from start to finish, you must pass through both C and R
  b. Illegal; same reason as answer a
  c. Legal
  d. Legal
  e. Magical, but illegal

All strings must start with C, must be followed by any nonempty sequence of A's and D's, and must be followed by R.

21. a. Legal
  b. Illegal; the first character must be a letter
  c. Illegal; the only characters allowed in identifiers are letters and digits
  d. Illegal; tricky: **case** is a reserved word; look carefully at *Zeller*
  e. Illegal; can't contain spaces
  f. Legal (although some environments wouldn't look at all the letters)
  g. Perfectly acceptable

2

Problem Solving and Programs: Primitive Data Types and Statements

In a sense, the computer is the physical embodiment of a metaphor. While at one level computers deal with the presence or absence of a flow of current, the designers of any computer do not think in terms of "on" or "off"; they think instead of the *interpretation* of current in the language of mathematics. In this chapter, we will concentrate on the interpretation, trusting—like the architect of a house—that the designers have done the job of handling the small details so that the circuits do what they should do. As long as the computer architects have built a machine that can manipulate the familiar forms of information, the compiler designers can write translators to produce machine code that will faithfully perform whatever information manipulation our Pascal programs describe. We programmers can then regard the computer as an information processor without having to be concerned with the low-level details of what goes on in the machine.

In this chapter, we will present the most basic of Pascal's information description and processing capabilities. These include the abilities to represent common *data types* (like integers, real numbers, and characters) and to perform simple operations (like reading, writing, and arithmetic calculations) on them. As your familiarity with Pascal grows, you will see that virtually every Pascal program makes use of these capabilities, and—more important—much of Pascal's power derives from them.

OBJECTIVES

In this chapter, we will:

- Describe the basic information types common to most high-level programming languages.
- Describe techniques for describing such information on modern computers.
- Present the Program in Progress, a tax preparation program that demonstrates Pascal's use of predefined data types.
- Apply our problem-solving techniques to the PIP and describe its development.
- Review the declaration section of a Pascal program.
- Describe Pascal's assignment statement.
- Describe Pascal's simple input-output statements.
- Discuss how to trace the execution of a sequence of assignment statements.

2.1   Computer Science Interlude: Storing Information

Put yourself, for the moment, in the place of Nicklaus Wirth when he invented Pascal in the late 1960s and early 1970s. Of course, we're not being entirely fair here, since Wirth knew a lot more about programming languages when he designed Pascal than you do right now, but our discussion of information should lead you in the right direction. You want to design a language that will be ideally suited for teaching programming. You have an idea of a number of important themes you want to emphasize, some of which are derived from earlier programming languages like Algol, and some of which have not been emphasized enough for your satisfaction. What sort of features would you include?

One of the first things to be considered when designing a high-level language is what kind of basic, primitive information will be available. In order to make this decision, you must ask the right questions. The first question is: "What kind of information should a computer program be able to process?" Some choices are obvious: At the very minimum, a programming language should be able to represent numbers and alphabetic characters and strings of characters like 'A SAMPLE STRING'.[1] If you know a little more about programming, it also becomes clear that it would be very helpful to be able to represent *boolean* information: basically, the two values *true* and *false*.

---

[1]Strictly speaking, strings of characters are not supported as a predefined data type in standard Pascal except in a very limited form, but the majority of Pascal compilers include strings as an extension to the standard. Remember from Chapter 1 our mention of the well-nigh irresistible compulsion that compiler designers seem to have for adding features.

Of course, the information that can be processed in a language like Pascal is directly influenced by the kind of information that can be represented in the computer on which the Pascal program is running. Given the binary nature of computers, we hardly even need to discuss the storage of boolean values: All we have to do is use the two possible states of the hardware—on and off, one and zero—to denote *true* and *false*. How to represent numeric and character information is not so obvious, however; we will provide more explanation about this in the next section. We should mention, though, that numeric, character, and boolean information are not the only forms we could choose in a new computer language. As a simple example, we could design a high-level language that included pictorial information as one of its primitive data types. Pascal does not include this, but it's not hard to imagine a language that would allow us to overlay one picture on another, copy part of a picture and place it in another, or produce a new picture that was the negative of another. So far, we have implicitly couched our discussion in terms of general-purpose computers, since that is the way most modern computers are designed, but it is not difficult to imagine a special-purpose computer embedded in a soft-drink machine that would have as its primitive data types the coin values 5, 10, 25, and the dollar-bill value (if it included hardware for bill changing). The point is that language designers have the flexibility to include any data types they consider appropriate, bearing in mind the constraints imposed by the machines on which they intend to implement their language.

We know that modern computers must represent information using only two possible values: off and on. To save writing, we will represent these states by the digits 0 and 1, respectively. If the computer can only work in terms of two values, 0 and 1, how are we to represent the information we want to store and manipulate?

Integers

We are comfortable with the notion of the computer as a number-cruncher, so we will begin by considering representation of numbers using this limited alphabet {0, 1}. An easy form of representation would be to use *binary-coded decimal* (BCD) notation, in which we invent a "code" for the digits 0, 1, 2, 3, 4, 5, 6, 7, 8, 9, and use this code to represent integers. For example, we might decide to use the code shown in Table 2.1. With this choice of representation, the number 247 would be represented by three groups of four digits: 0010 (for the 2), 0100 (for the 4), 0111 (for the 7), or 001001000111. Of course, we could have chosen any other collection of zeros and ones to represent the numbers, as long as our choice permitted a unique representation for each integer.[2]

BCD representation has the advantage of being relatively easy to read, but it has two serious disadvantages that limit its use. First, it is not efficient in terms of space; and second, arithmetic in BCD notation is more complicated than it is in some other representations. For these reasons, the overwhelming majority of com-

[2]We could not have used, for instance, 1 → 1, 2 → 11, 3 → 111, and so on, since then the code '111' could be interpreted as any of the numbers 111, 12, 21, or 3.

Table 2.1. A Typical Binary Coding of Decimal Digits

Digit	Code	Digit	Code
0	0000	5	0101
1	0001	6	0110
2	0010	7	0111
3	0011	8	1000
4	0100	9	1001

puters today use a different form of representation of numbers, one that is a bit more difficult to learn than BCD, but quite a bit more efficient.

From our earliest years in grade school, we have been taught to represent information in *base-10 positional notation*. Positional notation means that the value represented by a digit in a number depends on where in the number that digit happens to be, and base-10 means that the value of any position is a multiple of a power of ten. The expression 247, for instance, is interpreted as the sum $(2 \times 100) + (4 \times 10) + (7 \times 1)$. Notice, too, that the multipliers 100, 10, and 1 are just powers of 10, arranged in increasing size from right to left, beginning with the 0-th power. Although most people don't give it any thought, the nice thing about positional notation is that it permits unique representation of integers: every possible integer can be represented by this scheme, and every arrangement of strings of digits corresponds to one and only one integer.

There is nothing special about using 10 as our base — we use base 10 and 10 digits only because that's the way things have been done for several thousand years (perhaps having something to do with the fact that most of us have ten fingers). Since the computer could be regarded as having only two fingers, it is appropriate to use *base-2 positional notation*, also known as *binary notation*, instead. Let's see how that would work. The first few powers of 2 are 1, 2, 4 ($= 2 \times 2$, or 2^2), 8 ($= 2 \times 2 \times 2$, or 2^3), 16, 32, 64, 128, 256, 512, 1024, 2048, 4096, and 8192, where we form the sequence by beginning with 1, and multiplying each term by 2 to find the next one. Using only the "digits" 0 and 1 as multipliers of these powers of 2, we find, perhaps by trial and error, that the decimal number 247 would be represented in this scheme as

$$247 = (\mathbf{1} \times 128) + (\mathbf{1} \times 64) + (\mathbf{1} \times 32) + (\mathbf{1} \times 16) + (\mathbf{0} \times 8)$$
$$+ (\mathbf{1} \times 4) + (\mathbf{1} \times 2) + (\mathbf{1} \times 1)$$

or 11110111, as a binary number. Notice that this representation requires only 8 *bits*, (or **b**inary dig**its**) to express 247, whereas the BCD encoding takes 12 bits.

To convert from binary to decimal representation is easy: Below the binary digits we write the powers of 2 in increasing order from right to left; then, for each position, multiply the digit by its corresponding power of 2; and finally, add the terms together.

E X A M P L E 1. To convert the binary number 10111 to decimal notation, we write

Binary string: 1 0 1 1 1
Powers of 2:   16 8 4 2 1 $= 16 + 0 + 4 + 2 + 1 = 23$

Conversion in the opposite direction, from decimal to binary, is a trifle more complicated, but not much more, once we realize that the last digit in the binary representation of n is just the remainder we get when we divide n by 2, and the next digit is obtained by repeating the division on the quotient of the first division. In other words, we can convert a decimal number to binary by repeatedly dividing by 2 and keeping track of the remainders.

E X A M P L E 2. To convert the decimal number 23 to binary, we have the repeated divisions with quotients and remainders:

1. 23 divided by 2 has a quotient of 11 and a remainder of **1**. We remember the remainder and use the quotient in our next step.
2. 11 divided by 2 has a quotient of 5 and a remainder of **1**, which we also save.
3. 5 divided by 2 has a quotient of 2 and a remainder of **1**.
4. 2 divided by 2 has a quotient of 1 and a remainder of **0**.
5. 1 divided by 2 has a quotient of 0 and a remainder of **1**. We have a zero quotient, so we stop the process.
6. The sequence of remainders we obtained, *when presented in this order, from right to left*, is the binary representation of 23, namely 10111.

In more compact notation, our example might take the following form:

```
        0     1
     2 ⌐1     0
     2 ⌐2     1
     2 ⌐5     1
     2 ⌐11    1
     2 ⌐23
```

The binary equivalent of 23 is found by reading the column of remainders from top to bottom, that is, 10111. We stop the process when we have a zero quotient, since any subsequent division by 2 will simply append zeros to the front of our binary answer, and it is clear that 00010111 and 10111 represent the same number.

We implied that binary arithmetic is simpler than decimal. That's because there are only two binary digits. We're used to thinking of $1 + 1$ being equal to 2, but that's just because we customarily use decimal arithmetic. In binary notation, the equivalent expression would be "$1 + 1 = 10$," since 10 is the binary representation of 2. We would say, then, that in binary, "One plus one equals zero; carry one." Binary arithmetic would certainly make a grade-schooler's life easier, since all one needs to know about arithmetic in binary are two simple tables.

All you need to know about binary arithmetic

+	0	1
0	0	1
1	1	10

×	0	1
0	0	0
1	0	1

To perform arithmetic in binary, the algorithms are the same as the ones we all learned in grade school; the only difference is that the digit-wise addition and multiplication are done using the binary tables. To add 12 (= 1100 in binary) to 7 (= 0111), we perform the following steps (note that we carried a 1 in the leftmost sum):

```
    1
  0 1 1 1    binary 7
+ 1 1 0 0    binary 12
1 0 0 1 1    binary 19
```

As another example, we multiply 12 by 7 in the usual way, except that we use base-2 arithmetic:

```
    0 1 1 1    binary 7
  × 1 1 0 0    binary 12
    0 0 0 0
    0 0 0 0
  0 1 1 1
0 1 1 1
1 0 1 0 1 0 0    add four partial products = 84
```

Typically, computers are designed so that a set amount of space is allotted in memory for each integer. If, as is often the case, an integer is represented by 16 bits in memory, then we could represent the values 0 (= 0000000000000000) to 65536 (= 1111111111111111), or we might decide to use the leftmost bit to store the sign (0 for plus and 1 for minus), in which case we'd still have 65536 (= 2^{16}) numbers, but they would range from −32767 (= 1 111111111111111) to 32767 (= 0 111111111111111), along with two expressions for zero. (How would they be represented?)

Characters

Now that we can represent any nonnegative integer[3] as a binary number, we can expand this scheme to represent other information in the computer—we sim-

---

[3]In the exercises, we explore some of the ways we might represent negative integers and real numbers, like 3.1415926535.

Table 2.2.   ASCII Codes

First digits \ Last digit	0	1	2	3	4	5	6	7	8	9
30			space	!	"	#	$	%	&	'
40	(	)	*	+	,	−	.	/	0	1
50	2	3	4	5	6	7	8	9	:	;
60	<	=	>	?	@	A	B	C	D	E
70	F	G	H	I	J	K	L	M	N	O
80	P	Q	R	S	T	U	V	W	X	Y
90	Z	[	\	]	^	_	`	a	b	c
100	d	e	f	g	h	i	j	k	l	m
110	n	o	p	q	r	s	t	u	v	w
120	x	y	z	{	|	}	~			

ply find a suitable coding for the information to be stored in integers and represent the integers as binary numbers. For example, to represent strings of characters, we first decide on a suitable integer code for each character. This coding varies from machine to machine, but many computers represent characters by what is known as *ASCII code*, where ASCII stands for American Standard Code for Information Interchange, and is pronounced "ask'-ee." Table 2.2 lists some characters and their ASCII codes.

    To read the table, note that the code for a character is the sum of the digits in its row and column labels. For instance, the character A is in the row labeled 60 and the column labeled 5, so the ASCII code for A is 65. ASCII codes less than 32 are reserved for nonprinting characters, like the carriage return and tab. Some computers use an extended version of ASCII, in which codes between 128 and 216 are used for special characters like •, ¶, and Δ.

    Now that we have a code for characters, we might decide to represent a string of characters by a number designating the length of the character string, followed by the codes for the characters. For example, the string 'CAB' could be represented by the code for 3 (the number of characters in 'CAB'), followed by the codes 67, 65, 66 for the three letters. In the computer, then, this information would take the form 00000011 01000011 01000001 01000010; note that we've included spaces between groups of eight bits only to make it easier to read. Notice that there is no difference in memory between the representation of the character 'C' and the integer 67—the difference comes from how the program interprets the information.

2.2 Problem Solving I: Designing the PIP

The Program in Progress for this chapter is a simplified tax preparation program. This program differs from commercial tax preparation programs only in its complexity. In this sample, we don't consider itemized deductions, business profits and losses, child-care credits, and all the other items that strike terror into the hearts of taxpayers every April, because these additions would only make our program longer, rather than different in any fundamental respect.

The specification of this Program in Progress is a bit more complicated than it was for *Zeller*. That's to be expected, since there's more information that is used here. The good part is that the algorithm is considerably simpler than Zeller's Congruence. In fact, the algorithm is sufficiently simple that we can describe most of it implicitly within the input/output specification.

INPUT: A character, specifying whether the user is single ('s') or not
The number of dependents (an integer)
A character, specifying whether the user wants a dollar to go to the presidential election campaign fund
The total wages, salaries, and tips (real)
Taxable interest (real)
The tax withheld (real)

OUTPUT: For verification, display marital status, number of dependents, and contribution to campaign fund
The adjusted gross income (wages, salaries, tips + interest)
The standard deduction (real constant)
The taxable income (adjusted gross income − deduction)
Balance owed/overpaid (0.25 * taxable income − tax withheld)

2.3 Problem Solving II: Developing the PIP

The tax preparation PIP, like *Zeller*, is another example of a "Get information/Process information/Display results" program. There is a slight difference between *TaxMan* and *Zeller*, though, in that this program displays its results as it goes, rather than waiting until the end. The top-level outline consists of three main tasks, derived directly from the tax form itself:

- **I.** Certification: Get marital status, dependents, and campaign fund information and display these values.
- **II.** Get income information; compute adjusted gross income and taxable income.
- **III.** Figure tax using taxable income and tax withheld.

Problem-solving technique

If your problem is a model of a process for which there is an established format or established solution, let the initial outline reflect this.

Now that we have the overall organization, all that remains is to describe the three sections in detail. Notice that at this stage we describe the *variables* that will be used in the program, along with the information-processing steps that will be performed. We use variables to store information, and introduce a variable whenever information is solicited from the user or whenever a value must be stored for later use.

Problem-solving technique

Introduce variables into your outline to store inputs and to save the results of calculations.

- **I.** Certification
  - **A.** Display instructions to the user.
  - **B.** Find whether the user is *single* (character), has *numberDependents* (integer) equal to zero, and wants to contribute a dollar to *campaignFund* (character).

    [*Note:* In a more advanced program, we would, for example, check whether the user's responses indicated that he or she could use Form 1040EZ.]
- **II.** Report income
  - **A.** Get total *wagesSalariesTips* (real).
  - **B.** Get taxable *interest* (real).
  - **C.** Compute *adjGrossIncome* (real) = *wagesSalariesTips* + *interest* and display it.
  - **D.** Subtract *STANDARDDEDUCTION* (constant, = 5100.00) from *adjGrossIncome*, to compute and display *taxableIncome* (real).

III. Figure tax

    A. Get *taxWithheld* (real).

    B. Compute and display *taxLiability* (real) = 0.25 * *taxableIncome*.
    [We'll assume a straight 25% tax rate, to make life simple here.]

    C. Compute and display *balance* (real) = *taxWithheld* − *taxLiability*.

That wasn't too bad, was it? We're now ready to write code. Take a close look at the program listing; you'll see that each of the subsections translates almost directly to Pascal statements.

he PIP

```
program TaxMan(input, output);
{——————————————————————————————————————————————}
{                                                              }
{                      PROGRAM IN PROGRESS                     }
{                                                              }
{                          CHAPTER 2                           }
{                                                              }
{       This program is an automated (and simplified) 1040EZ   }
{       Federal tax form.                                      }
{       INPUT:     marital status (char)                       }
{                  number of dependents (integer)              }
{                  campaign fund preference (char)             }
{                  wages, salaries, tips (real)                }
{                  taxable interest (real)                     }
{                  tax withheld (real)                         }
{       OUTPUT:    taxable income (real)                       }
{                  tax liability (real)                        }
{                  balance owed/overpaid (real)                }
{                                                              }
{——————————————————————————————————————————————}

   const
      STANDARDDEDUCTION = 5100.00;    {used in calculating taxable income}
   var
      wagesSalariesTips, interest, adjGrossIncome, taxableIncome,
      taxWithheld, taxLiability, balance: real;
      single, campaignFund: char;
      numberDependents: integer;
```

```
begin
{————————————————— CERTIFICATION —————————————————}
    writeln('This is an automated version of Federal tax form 1040EZ.');
    writeln('To use this form you must be single and have no dependents.');
    writeln;
    write('Certify that you are single by entering s, followed by Return:');
    readln(single);
    writeln;
    write('Certify that you have zero dependents by entering 0, followed by Return:');
    readln(numberDependents);
    writeln;
    writeln('Do you want $1 of your tax to go to the Presidential Election Campaign Fund?');
    write('Enter y (for yes) or n (no), followed by Return:');
    readln(campaignFund);

    writeln;
    writeln('Verification: marital status: ', single, ' dependents: ', numberDependents : 1, ' contribution: ',
            campaignFund);
    writeln;

{————————————————— REPORT INCOME —————————————————}
    write('LINE 1: Enter total wages, salaries, and tips, followed by Return.....$');
    readln(wagesSalariesTips);
    writeln;

    write('LINE 2: Enter taxable interest, followed by Return.....$');
    readln(interest);
    writeln;

    adjGrossIncome := wagesSalariesTips + interest;    {calculate adjusted gross income}
    writeln('LINE 3: This is your adjusted gross income.....$', adjGrossIncome : 10 : 2);
    writeln;

    writeln('LINE 4: Your total standard deduction and personal exemption is.....$',
            STANDARDDEDUCTION : 7 : 2);
    writeln;

    taxableIncome := adjGrossIncome - STANDARDDEDUCTION;    {calculate taxable income}
    writeln('LINE 5: This is your taxable income.....$', taxableIncome : 10 : 2);
    writeln;

{————————————————— FIGURE TAX —————————————————}
    write('LINE 6: Enter Federal tax withheld, followed by Return.....$');
    readln(taxWithheld);
    writeln;
```

{For the sake of simplicity, this program calculates tax liability based on a straight 25% tax rate.}

```
writeln('User is filing as single with no dependents');
writeln;
taxLiability : = 0.25 * taxableIncome;
writeln('LINE 7: Taxes due.....$'; taxLiability: 10 : 2);
writeln;

balance : = taxWithheld — taxLiability;    {Calculate refund or amount you owe.}
writeln('LINES 8–9: YOUR BALANCE IS.....$', balance : 10 : 2);

writeln;
writeln('If balance is > 0, balance represents a refund.');
writeln('If balance is < 0, balance represents amount you owe.');
writeln;
writeln('PROCESSING COMPLETED . . . GOODBYE')
end.
```

2.4 Problem Solving III: Program Analysis

We've said that a program is a list of instructions to a computer to process information in a certain way. To write a program, then, we need to know how to describe information, and we need to know the rules that govern how the information will be interpreted.

Describing Information

When you look over the Program in Progress, notice first that its overall organization is exactly what we have come to expect—it begins with a program declaration, **program** *TaxMan(input, output)*, which names the program with the Pascal identifier *TaxMan* and tells the compiler that the program will expect input (from the keyboard, in this case) and will produce output (to the screen). It continues with a collection of statements enclosed within a **begin..end** pair and ends with a period.

Declarations. The two parts that follow the program declaration are a *constant declaration* and a *variable declaration*. The constant declaration names a value, *STANDARDDEDUCTION*, equal to the real number 5100.00, that is used later in the program in the line *taxableIncome := adjGrossIncome − STANDARD-DEDUCTION* and in the *writeln* above it. Constant declarations all have the form

const
    identifier = some fixed value or previously defined constant name;

and so on, for as many constants as you wish.

In standard Pascal, the constant declaration must come after the program declaration and before the variable declaration.

A typical constant declaration, then, might look like

```
const
    BIGNUM = 10000;
    OKTEMP = 98.6;
    BIGNEGNUM = −BIGNUM;     Notice we can use a previously defined constant.
    ALPHABETSTART = 'A';
```

There are a few minor considerations regarding constants. Two of the three following constant declarations are illegal in Pascal, for the reasons noted.

```
const
    BIGNEGNUM = −BIGNUM;     We can't refer to BIGNUM here, since it
                            hasn't been declared yet.
    BIGNUM = 10000;         This, of course, is acceptable.
    VERYBIGNUM = 2 * BIGNUM − 1;   This is not allowed—the only arithmetic we
                            can do on the right side of a constant
                            declaration is place + or − in front of a
                            constant.
```

You cannot use a constant (or anything else in Pascal) until it has been declared.

With one exception, which we'll see in Chapter 12 when we talk about pointers.

The only arithmetic you can do on the right side of a constant declaration of a real number or an integer is to precede the right side with a + or −.

Constant declarations are most often used in a program that refers several times to a particular fixed value. If, for instance, we had a program that processed a list of one hundred numbers, we might have to use the value 100 several times in the program. If we then wanted to write a program that would perform the same processing steps on a list of 250 numbers, we would have to go through our original program and change every instance of 100 to 250 (except when the 100 referred to a different value—like the number of cents in a dollar—that had nothing to do with the size of the list). The point is that making such a change is fraught with the possibility for error: Have we changed all and only those 100s that refer to the size of the list? It would be much better to design our original program with a constant, *LISTSIZE*, set to 100, and then use that constant whenever the program

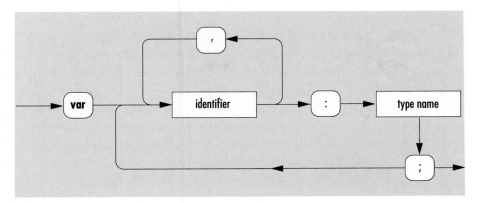

Figure 2.1.   Syntax diagram for variable declarations

refers to the size of the list. Then, changing the program for a different size list would require changing only the constant declaration from *LISTSIZE* = 100 to *LISTSIZE* = 250, making the task of updating much simpler. A cardinal rule is illustrated here:

Use constants for values that don't change while the program is running. In this way, you can write your programs so that they can easily be modified to perform similar, related tasks.

The next part of the Program in Progress is the variable declaration:

```
var
    wagesSalariesTips, interest, adjGrossIncome, taxableIncome,
    taxWithheld, taxLiability, balance: real;
    single, campaignFund: char;
    numberDependents: integer;
```

Variable declarations look very much like constant declarations, except that (1) we use colons rather than equals signs to separate identifiers from what follows, and (2) we can group together several identifiers of the same type, separating them by commas. Figure 2.1 shows the syntax diagram for the variable declaration part of a Pascal program.

Pascal is a *strongly typed language*, in that every variable or constant that is named in a program is associated with a specific data type. In other words, every variable that is used in a program must first be named and described in the variable declaration part of the program, in much the same way that every ingredient in a recipe must be listed at the beginning. In the preceding sample, for instance,

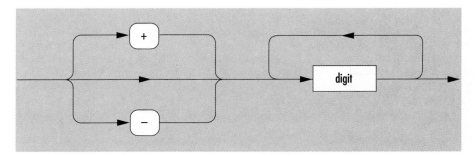

Figure 2.2.   Syntax diagram for integers

numberDependents is a variable that denotes a location in memory where an integer may be stored, and *campaignFund* refers to a (usually smaller) chunk of memory where we may store a single character. In this chapter, we'll discuss four of Pascal's *simple types*: integers, real numbers, characters, and boolean values.

Integers. The variable *numberDependents* is declared to be of type *integer* in our program. As its name implies, it represents the number of qualified dependents that a taxpayer can claim in filing his or her return. An integer-type value represents a whole number, positive, negative, or zero. Of course, not all integers can be represented in a computer, if only because there are numbers that are too large to be stored in any fixed amount of memory. The Pascal language makes no restriction on the size of the integers it uses, leaving that to the compiler writers who must tailor Pascal to a specific machine. There is, though, a predefined constant, *maxint*, that can always be relied on to contain the largest integer available on the machine you're using. This means that if you are writing a program that uses large integers, you can inspect *maxint* to make sure that the numbers will be within the allowable range. Generally, the integers available for use in a program range from $-maxint - 1$ to *maxint*; with compilers that use 16 bits to represent integers, *maxint* is usually 32767 $(= 2^{15} - 1)$, and with 32-bit representation *maxint* is usually 2147483647 $(= 2^{31} - 1)$.

Notice that we didn't use any commas when writing the values of *maxint*. We did that deliberately to prepare you for the syntax of Pascal integers. Figure 2.2 is a syntax diagram for integers; in words, it says that a Pascal integer consists of a string of one or more digits preceded by an optional plus or minus sign. The representation of an explicit value in a program is called a *literal*—thus Figure 2.2 is a syntax diagram for integer literals.

Reals. The other kind of Pascal numbers are, naturally enough, designed to include non-integers (although they may also represent whole numbers, since mathematically the integers are included as a subset of the reals). Elements of the *real* data type come in two forms when written as literals: conventional numbers with fractional parts, like 67.5, 800.0, and -0.82441; and scaled numbers. *Scaled*

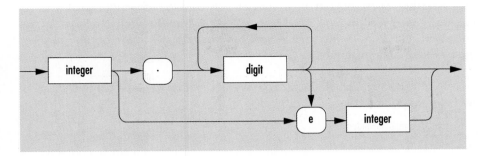

Figure 2.3. Syntax diagram for reals

numbers are closely related to scientific notation, in which reals are represented as a fractional real multiplied by some power of 10, like 45.9×10^{13}. In Pascal, the exponent of the scale is separated from the rest of the number by the character e, so the number 45.9×10^{13} would be written 45.9e13, and we would think of it as 459,000,000,000,000.0 (which should give you an idea of why Pascal has scaled real numbers at all: Which form would you rather type?).

The formal syntax of real numbers (see Figure 2.3), as we would expect, is somewhat more complicated than that of integers. In words, the syntax diagram tells us that a real number is represented in a Pascal program in any of three ways: (1) an integer (positive or negative), followed by a period, followed by a collection of one or more digits, like -983.1001; (2) a number of form (1) followed by an e and an integer, like 18.922e8, with no blanks before or after the e; or (3) an integer followed by an e and an integer, like $82e-9$ (which would represent 82×10^{-9}, or 82 with the decimal point shifted nine places to the left: 0.000000082). If you trace the arrows in Figure 2.3, you will see that .49 is not a syntactically legal real number, because there is no digit in front of the decimal point; nor is 56., because there is no digit after the decimal point. Similarly, $82.e-9$ and $.82e-11$ are not acceptable. The reasons for these restrictions are not too hard to deduce if you think about how the compiler recognizes when a number starts and ends. It's easier to write a compiler if your language says that any number begins and ends with a digit, because then it's easy to tell when a number starts and ends, and hence easy to pick numbers out of the characters that make up the source code program. In addition, it's easier for people to read. The number 0.38 is less likely to be confused with an integer than is .38, for instance.

Notice, by the way, that to complete our description of a Pascal number (or any part of the language), we need to tell you more than just how to write a number; we also have to tell you what these numbers mean. That is, we must define a number's semantics as well as its syntax. Numbers, both integer and real, have semantics that are already familiar to us because what they "mean" in Pascal corresponds closely (although not exactly) with what they mean in mathematics. Note, though, that just because a number conforms to Pascal syntax, it need not conform to Pascal semantics. To make this clear, consider that the integer

123456789123456789123456789 is syntactically correct but would probably be semantically incorrect on most machines, since it is almost surely too large. In another vein, -30.0, $-3.0e1$, and $-30e0$ are syntactically different, but all three represent the same real number.

Characters. The character type is indicated by the type name *char*, as in the Program in Progress:

```
single, campaignFund: char;
```

The variables *single* and *campaignFund* can each represent a single character. In our program, the character values for these variables are provided by the user of the program, who enters them from the keyboard. Character values can be written directly in a program just as integer and real literals can. We do this by enclosing any character in single quotes, as 'A', 'a', or '$'. Although Pascal makes no distinction between upper- and lowercase in identifiers (such as program, constant, and variable names) when implemented on computers that have both uppercase and lowercase letters, Pascal always distinguishes between the two when considering values of character-type expressions. So, while *a* and *A* would be considered by Pascal as naming the same variable, 'a' and 'A' are distinct character values when assigned to a variable of type *char*. The only subtlety about character values lies in using a single quote itself as a character. Since the single quote serves as a *delimiter* for characters, separating them from the other tokens that Pascal recognizes, we must indicate the single quote by a special token, in this case. In other words, the character consisting of a single quote must be represented as ''''; the two outer single quotes serve as delimiters, and the doubled single quotes inside denote a single quote, called an *apostrophe image*, if you want to be precise.[4] The same rule for single quotes holds for strings of characters, as in

```
writeln('Isn''t this grand?')
```

See if you can think like a compiler designer and tell why we don't represent a single quote character by a single quote.

Manipulating Information

Being able to represent information in a program is of little use unless we also have the ability to manipulate it—to read it, to change it from one value to another, and to display it. Pascal is richly endowed with information-manipulating facilities, as you might expect. In this section we will explore the most important ones.

---

[4]The double quote, '', although it resides on most keyboards as the shifted version of the single quote, has no special meaning in Pascal (except, of course, as a character). BASIC users will have to unlearn old habits here.

The assignment statement. One of the fundamental Pascal statements is the *assignment statement*. For example, the Program in Progress contains a number of assignment statements:

```
adjGrossIncome : = wagesSalariesTips + interest;
taxableIncome : = adjGrossIncome − STANDARDDEDUCTION;
taxLiability : = 0.25 * taxableIncome;
balance : = taxWithheld − taxLiability;
```

If you look closely at these statements, you will see that they all take the same form: *variable identifier* : = *expression*. The token : = is the *assignment operator*, and when it appears in a statement (thereby defining the statement as an assignment statement), its semantics are roughly: "Evaluate the expression on the right and, if the evaluation is of the correct type, store the result of the evaluation in the variable on the left." In each of the above examples, the expression on the right is a numeric one involving variables, constants, numeric literals, and arithmetic operators (which we'll discuss shortly). The variables on the left of each statement are declared as either integer or real, depending on the quantity they are intended to represent. After, for example, adding *wagesSalariesTips* to *interest* and arriving at an answer, that value becomes the value of real variable *adjGrossIncome*. Notice very carefully that the left-hand part of an assignment statement is always a variable (or part of a variable, as we'll see later) and never anything else. The line

```
wagesSalariesTips + interest : = adjGrossIncome
```

is not a statement at all, since it has an expression, rather than a single variable, on the left of the assignment operator : = .

Most computer languages include an assignment operator. In APL and Smalltalk, the operator is the left arrow, ←, which perhaps makes the most sense, since it indicates a transfer of information from the right-side expression to the left-side variable. BASIC and FORTRAN, on the other hand, are at the other end of the comprehensibility spectrum, since they use the equals sign, = , as the assignment operator. This leads to assignment statements like $x = x + 1$, which — while it makes perfectly good sense in these languages, serving to increase the value of x by 1 — also looks like the nonsensical statement in algebra that asserts that some number can be equal to one more than itself. In 1971, the year Pascal was introduced, not all keyboards had left arrows (and indeed, the keyboard on which this text was typed still lacks a left arrow character; there's a left arrow, but it moves the blinking cursor on the screen). This may be why Wirth chose an intermediate course and decided to use the character sequence : = for the assignment operator.[5]

[5]Another reason was to distinguish the assignment operator from the boolean comparison operator = , which evaluates the expressions on both sides of the operator and returns *true* if and only if the two expressions have the same value. We will have much more to say about the equality operator soon. The final reason is that Wirth was probably influenced by the language Algol, which also uses : = .

The assignment operator is ubiquitous in Pascal programs, largely because of the central importance of being able to name and move data within a program. The assignment statement can be used in almost any context; while there are some special cases we'll deal with shortly, we can at least assert the fundamental principle of assignments:

> **W**ith the exception of the *file* type, any expression, no matter how complicated, may be assigned to a variable of the same type.

Expressions. We said above that the right-hand side of an assignment statement must consist of an "expression," so it would be appropriate for us to explain what an expression is before we go any further. We'll use a recursive definition here, as we did when we defined "statement." An *expression* may be (1) a constant, (2) a variable, (3) a function designator (which we'll explain shortly), or (4) a collection of expressions combined by operators. The expressions in the preceding assignment statements are all examples of this fourth class of expression. Each involves a pair of variables combined by an arithmetic (in these cases) operator, such as +, −, or *. For example, here are some expressions, where we assume *index* and *sum* are integer-type variables and that *pressure* and *average* are real-type variables.

20	*An integer constant*
index	*A single variable*
sum + 4 * (index − 1)	*An integer arithmetic expression*
(average + sum) / 5.0	*A real arithmetic expression*
sum **div** 6	*An integer arithmetic expression*
index **mod** 3	*An integer arithmetic expression*
sqrt(sqr(pressure) + 1.0)	*A real expression, using two functions,* sqrt *and* sqr

You should be on familiar ground with the integer and real expressions, since Pascal expresses them pretty much as you were taught in school: + adds, − subtracts, * multiplies (that one's a little different[6]), and / divides. There are two operators, though, that were likely not part of your early arithmetic experience. Since division of two integers often yields a result that is not an integer, there is a pair of operators that take the place of integer division. The operator **div**, which we saw in *Zeller*, returns the quotient, ignoring any fractional part, so that 18 **div** 3 is 6, as is 20 **div** 3, since in both instances the quotient is 6. As you would expect, it is an error to have zero for the second operand, since division by zero isn't defined. Whether the two operands are positive, negative, or a mixture of signs, **div** simply throws away the fractional part, rounding toward zero: both 7 **div** (−4) and (−7) **div** 4 represent −1, since −(7 / 4) = −1.75. The operator **mod**, which we also

---

[6]Not only is multiplication indicated by * rather than ×, but it may not be implied: $2y + 1$ is acceptable algebra, but in a program the expression would have to be $2 * y + 1$.

saw in *Zeller*, is complementary to **div**: it returns the remainder of the division, as follows:[7]

$$68 = 1500 \textbf{ div } 22$$

$$
\begin{array}{r}
22\overline{\smash{)}1500} \\
132 \\
\hline
180 \\
176 \\
\hline
4 = 1500 \textbf{ mod } 22
\end{array}
$$

Pascal also has *precedence rules* built in that determine how ambiguous expressions will be interpreted. For instance, we were taught that 2 + 4 * 3 should denote 14 rather than 18, since in the absence of other specifications (like parentheses), multiplication and division are to be completed before addition and subtraction. That's just how Pascal interprets things, too.

We'll come back to precedence rules shortly, in Chapter 4.

For the arithmetic operators we've seen so far, Pascal's rules for evaluating expressions are

1. Expressions in parentheses are evaluated first, from the most deeply nested parentheses outward. Within parentheses, expressions are evaluated according to the rules below.
2. Unary minus is performed first (as in −8.3).
3. Then the operators *, /, **div**, and **mod** are performed, from left to right, if there's more than one.
4. Finally, the operators + and − are performed, again from left to right.

There is a subtle point about numeric expressions, stemming from the fact that Pascal recognizes two different types of numeric information, integers and reals. Just as every quantity (variable, constant, literal) must have an associated type, so too must the value of every expression. What type, though, should a composite expression—one involving quantities of different types, like 2 + 3.9—be? Clearly, the result of any such expression can always be represented as a real (2 + 3.9 is 5.9 and 2 + 3.0 is 5.0) but may or may not be accurately representable as an integer. In general, then, it would make more sense for Pascal to treat this composite expression as real, which is indeed what happens. There is nothing wrong with mixing real and integer types in a single expression, but you should be aware that a mixed expression yields a real-type result.

---

[7]Well, sort of. 7 **mod** 4 is 3, as you would expect, but (−7) **mod** 4 is 1, and not −3. In computing i **mod** j, j may not be negative or zero, and the result is defined to be always (1) between 0 and $j − 1$, and (2) chosen so that it is equal to $i + (k * j)$, for some integer k. If this is confusing, you can always take refuge in the knowledge that for positive integers i and j, i **mod** j is the remainder, as it should be.

The result of an arithmetic expression containing a mixture of real and integer values will be treated as a real-type value. Also, an expression using the real division operator, /, will produce a real result, even if both operands are integers.

A similar form of type mixing is allowed in assignment statements. It is frequently handy to be able to assign one type of expression to a different type of variable. This is known as *type coercion*. Here's another quicky quiz: If *i* is an integer variable and *r* is real, which assignment statement do you think should be allowed: $i := 3 / 4$ (assigning a real value to an integer), or $r := 2 + i$ (assigning an integer value to a real)? Again, because every integer has a possible real interpretation, but only some reals can be thought of as integers, the second is allowed in Pascal, and the first is not.

Any integer-valued expression may be assigned to a real variable. It is illegal to assign a real result to an integer variable (even if the real result is a whole number).

Functions. Pascal provides a wealth of useful built-in functions to manipulate information. Many of the numeric functions will be familiar, but there are others that you may not have seen before. There are eight numeric functions, which take either integer or real arguments:

Function	Description	Argument x	Return Type
$abs(x)$	$\lvert x \rvert$	integer or real	same as x
$sqr(x)$	x^2	integer or real	same as x
$sqrt(x)$	$\sqrt{x}$	integer or real, ≥ 0	real, ≥ 0
$sin(x)$	sine of x	integer or real, interpreted as radians	real
$cos(x)$	cosine of x	integer or real, interpreted as radians	real
$arctan(x)$	inverse tangent of x	integer or real	real, interpreted as radians
$exp(x)$	e^x	integer or real	real
$ln(x)$	natural log of x	integer or real, > 0	real

The argument to a function—the part inside the parentheses—may be any expression of the correct type. We could write, for instance, $sqrt(sqr(a) + sqr(b))$, to compute $\sqrt{a^2 + b^2}$, or even something as intimidating as $arctan(sqr(sin(abs(x))) / cos(abs(x))) + 1.0)$. By the way, Pascal does not have a power operator. To compute a^b, we must, in general, employ the workaround $exp(b * ln(a))$.

Whereas type coercion is implicit in an expression or assignment statement containing mixed types, two *transfer functions* are useful for explicit type coercion. Each forces a real expression to be interpreted as an integer. The function $trunc(x)$ returns the integer part of x, so that $trunc(5.98)$ is 5 and $trunc(-7.2)$ is -7. The function $round(x)$ rounds the real expression x to the nearest integer, so that $round(4.7)$ represents 5, $round(2.5)$ represents 3, and $round(-4.7)$ returns the value -5.

Input and output. So far we haven't provided any way for a program to communicate with the outside world. We can assign values to variables within a program, but that's of limited use unless we can provide the program with data to operate on and then see the results of our computations. Pascal provides four routines that satisfy this basic need for communication, two for getting information into a program while it is running and two for producing output. These are, respectively, the routines *readln, read, writeln,* and *write*.

The Program in Progress makes heavy use of these routines; in fact, if you look closely at the program, you'll notice that almost every statement — 40 out of 44 — uses one of these input/output routines. Let's inspect some of these in detail.

```
writeln('This is an automated version of Federal tax form 1040EZ.');
writeln('To use this form you must be single and have no dependents.');
```

The first two lines show the *writeln* statement in a common use: to display a message on the screen (or paper, or whatever output device happens to be attached to the computer).[8]

Specifically, the action of *writeln* is to write whatever is within the parentheses, then return to the beginning of the line and drop down to the next line (where the writing from the next *writeln* or *write* statement will start). In the preceding examples, the parentheses contain a *string* literal, a collection of characters delimited by single quotes. Anything within the quotes will be written exactly as it appears (except that you cannot include a return character within a literal string), so the two statements above provide an opening message to the user which appears on the screen as

```
This is an automated version of Federal tax form 1040EZ.
To use this form you must be single and have no dependents.
```

The next statement in the program is even simpler. What do you suppose it does?

```
writeln;
```

---

[8]Technically, the standard output is treated as a *textfile*, meaning that it accepts character information, or information in character form that represents integer, real, character, or boolean values. This, by the way, is why we use the word *output* in the **program** declaration: We are informing the compiler that output from the program is to be directed to the standard output file (which is then directed to the screen, for instance). We'll see more about textfiles in Chapter 8.

If you guessed that it produces a blank line on the screen, you're exactly right. A *writeln* with no arguments just sends the carriage return/line feed combination, so that any subsequent writing will occur after a blank line.

The next statement makes use of Pascal's *write* routine. This acts exactly as the *writeln*, except that it doesn't conclude with a carriage return/line feed pair, so that any subsequent writing to the screen will begin on the same line immediately after the last character displayed by the *write* statement.

```
write('Certify that you are single by entering s, followed by Return:');
readln(single);
```

In this case, we used a *write* statement because the next statement requires input from the user, and we wanted that input to be on the same line as the *prompt* (the message that describes what the user is to do). We'll get to the *read* statement shortly; for the time being, all we need to know is that it requires the user to type a character. Using this *write/readln* combination, the screen will look like the following:

```
Certify that you are single by entering s, followed by Return: s
```

Note that the user's response is set in color to distinguish it from what the program produces; we will use this device from now on.

If we had instead used a *writeln*, the screen would have looked like this:

```
Certify that you are single by entering s, followed by Return:
s
```

Certainly the first format is easier on the user: The user is presented with a request for action, and the result of his or her action is visually connected with the request.

The next example occurs later in the program, and it illustrates another feature of the *write* and *writeln* statements: their ability to display the values of variables that are determined as the program is running.

```
writeln('LINE 5: This is your taxable income.....$', taxableIncome : 10 : 2);
```

This *writeln* statement writes two expressions on the same line: the string 'LINE 5: This is your taxable income.....$' and the value of the real variable *taxableIncome*. If, for instance, *taxableIncome* had been 465000.0 (Oh, happy day!), the statement would have displayed the literal string followed by the value of *taxableIncome*, as follows:[9]

```
LINE 5: This is your taxable income.....$ 465000.00
```

---

[9]The *write* statement is also useful in cases where you want output that is described by many strings and variable names in your program to appear on a single line. For example, if it bothers you to have to break a long *writeln* statement, the statement above could have been produced by the statements

```
write('LINE 5: This is your taxable income.....$');
writeln(taxableIncome : 10 : 2);
```

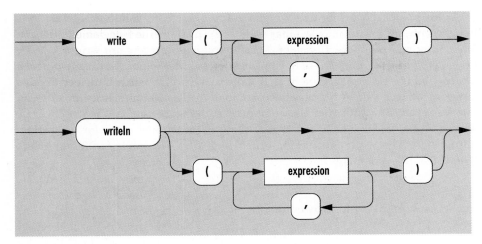

Figure 2.4.   Syntax diagrams for standard output statements

Any expression that has a string, integer, real, character, or boolean value can be part of the arguments to a *write* or *writeln* statement. Figure 2.4 gives the syntax for both statements. In the diagrams, the box "expression" includes any string of characters, delimited by single quotes, and any expression that has a real, integer, character, or boolean value. In words, rather than pictures, the syntax of the *write* statement is identical to that of the *writeln* except for the routine name and the fact that it cannot appear without a parenthesized list of arguments. Each statement type may include within parentheses as many expressions as desired, separated by commas.

Semantically, these statements do an enormous amount of work behind the scenes. First, each of the expressions that does not express a literal value must be evaluated. It is perfectly legitimate, for example, to have a *writeln* statement that includes computations, such as

writeln('The distance between the points is ', sqrt(sqr(v — x) + sqr(w — y)))

Second, the value of any expression that is not of type *char* must be translated into the characters that will eventually appear on the screen. We mentioned earlier that the integer 247 might be represented in memory as the binary number 11110111; in order to write the value of a variable that stored 247, then, the compiler must generate code to instruct the computer to translate the binary 11110111 into the string of characters '247', so that the number appears on the screen in a form we humans can recognize. We are fortunate indeed that these routines are built into Pascal, since it saves us the considerable task of having to invent them ourselves.

We need to say just a little more about the output statements of our Program in Progress, because we have glossed over one final detail. To make the output of a program easier to read, it is often useful to be able to force the values of expressions to appear in a particular format. We may want to line up a list of reals or integers in a column, for instance, or we may want to specify a certain degree of precision for writing real numbers. Consider, for starters, how integers are written. At the time a program is compiled, there is usually no way of knowing how large or small a particular integer variable might be (except that it will fall within the permissible range of integer values for the given computer). The simplest way to write an integer would be to instruct the computer at the start that any integer will be allotted enough space to hold *maxint*, along with another space for a potential minus sign. That's simple enough, except that when *classSize* is 26 and *avg* is 78.038461, the statement

writeln('For your ', classSize, ' students, the average is ', avg)

might result in the rather ugly output

For your   26 students, the average is 7.8038461e + 1

We can coerce information to be written in a tidier, more compact form by using a feature of the output statements known as *format forcing*. If we follow a numeric expression in a *write* or *writeln* statement by a colon and an integer expression, the value of the integer expression dictates the number of characters to be used in displaying the value of the associated numeric expression. That is, the integer is evaluated, and the expression we want to write is placed, right-justified, in that many characters, padding the left end with blanks as necessary. In the example above, we could cause the variable *classSize* to appear immediately after the literal string by rewriting the *writeln* statement as

writeln('For your ', classSize : 2, ' students, the average is ', avg)

The output would then look like

For your 26 students, the average is 7.8038461e + 1

(Notice that in the *writeln* statement, we have put a character space after the word *your* so that the word doesn't run up against the number 26.)

If we wanted the real variable *avg* to be in a more user-friendly form, too, we could perform another sort of format forcing that applies only to real values. If we follow a real expression by $:n:m$, the real number is written in a total of n characters (again, right-justified and padded on the left with blanks, as necessary) and is rounded to m digits following the decimal point (which is counted among the total n characters). If, for instance, *avg* was 78.038461, the statement

writeln('For your ', classSize : 2, ' students, the average is ', avg : 5 : 2)

would produce

For your 26 students, the average is 78.04

In the PIP, each of the output statements that displays a real value uses this formatting ability both to specify a desired precision ($:n:2$ is useful for representing dollars and cents) and to control the spacing of each line. Since *STANDARD-DEDUCTION* is a real constant with value 5100.00, the statement

writeln('LINE 4: Your total standard deduction and personal exemption is.....$',
          STANDARDDEDUCTION : 7 : 2);

would produce

LINE 4: Your total standard deduction and personal exemption is.....$5100.00

Note that seven total spaces are used to represent the value of *STANDARDDE-DUCTION* (including one for the decimal point) and two of the digits are to the right of the decimal. Similarly, if the variable *balance* has the value 6208.879, the statement

writeln('LINES 8–9: YOUR BALANCE IS.....$', balance : 10 : 2);

would display

LINES 8–9: YOUR BALANCE IS.....$ 6208.88

with three blank spaces between the $ and the 6.

Format forcing is designed to lose as little important information as possible. If an integer value doesn't fit in the space allotted, the space is expanded until it is just long enough to hold all the digits of the integer, along with a minus sign if needed (so that :1 will always print an integer in just enough space as it needs). If a real value is forced by :n, and n is small, there will always be enough space provided for a minus sign if needed (or a blank, otherwise), the first nonzero digit, a decimal point, the e, and the exponent with its sign. If a real value is forced into *fixed-point notation* by :n:m and n is small, the sign (if the value is negative), integer part, decimal point, and m fractional digits are written.[10]

Getting information into a program is considerably less complicated than getting it out. In essence, the *read* and *readln* statements contain a list of integer, real, or character variables for which values are to be read. When one of these statements is encountered, the program looks in the standard input file (the keyboard, in our case) for a string of characters that could be interpreted as values for the argument variables, translates them into whatever internal form is necessary, and stores the resulting values in the memory locations corresponding to the variables. If the input file is empty (you haven't typed anything yet, for example) or doesn't have enough characters to fill the pending requests, the program waits until the requests can be filled.

There are five *readln* statements in the Program in Progress. A typical one is

readln(interest);

When this statement is encountered, the computer looks in the input file for any characters that have been typed in. Starting from the beginning, spaces and end-of-line marks (which the user generates by pressing the Return key) are skipped until a character is encountered that could be the start of a real number, since *interest* is a real-type variable. As long as the subsequent characters could be part of a real number, they are consumed and translated into a real number. Finally, a

---

[10]Our experience has been that these standards are honored more in the breach than in the observance. It is a good idea to test your compiler on some sample cases to see what it does.

character is encountered that could not be part of a real number—like a blank, end-of-line, or *, for instance. At this point, everything in the input file, up to and including the next available end-of-line mark, is discarded, and the received characters are translated into a real number. This number is then stored in the variable *interest*.

In the preceding *readln* statement, we could have typed in any of the following four examples, and the result would have been the same:

22.1<RET>	*Fixed-point real*
2.21e1<RET>	*Scientific notation real*
22.1that's all she wrote<RET>	*Real followed by junk*
<RET>	*Real preceded by blanks and returns,*
<RET>	*followed by junk*
22.1*&^%&$*&$<RET>	

In each instance, the real value 22.1 would be stored in *interest*, and the rest of the line, including the return character (which we've indicated by <RET>), would be purged from the input file and ignored by the program.

The only difference between *readln* and *read* is that *read* doesn't discard anything after the characters that represent the required value, so that the remaining contents of the input line are available for subsequent reading.

Each of the input statements in our Program in Progress applies *readln* to a simple variable. When prompted, we enter a value of the appropriate type and press the Return key. As with the *write* and *writeln* statements, it is perfectly legal to include as many variables as we want in a *readln* or *read* statement; the effect is the same as having a sequence of repeated single-argument *read* statements, with the last discarding the end-of-line mark if the statement were a *readln*. For example, suppose that for the statement

readln(aReal, anInteger, aChar, anotherChar, aLastReal)

you gave the input

330.91   −92XY562.9e-2!!!<RET>

Pascal would store 330.91 in *aReal*, skip over the intervening spaces and store −92 in *anInteger*, 'X' in *aChar*, 'Y' in *anotherChar*, and 5.629 in *aLastReal*, and would discard the three exclamation points and the end-of-line character. We need to be careful when reading character values, since the end-of-line character is read as a space.

We'll see why in Chapter 6.

Finally, what happens when a *read* or *readln* tries to read an integer or real and the first nonblank or non−end-of-line character it encounters is something that couldn't be part of a number? That's an error, and most modern programming environments will catch it and inform you that you typed in something wrong. It is not an error, however, to enter 780 in response to

readln(interest)

Even though 780 has the form of an integer, it could also be interpreted correctly as a real, and Pascal allows that, storing 780.0 in *interest*. As you can probably guess, type coercion doesn't work in the opposite direction. (What would happen, do you think? This is actually an interesting question; as a hint, no error would be generated, but some information might be lost.)

2.5 Running a Program Without a Computer

When we write a program, we want it to be correct, which is to say we want to be sure that it does indeed do what we expect it to do. This almost goes without saying—the Program in Progress computes your taxes for you, and you certainly don't want to be wrong there. An error in tax computation can, at best, result in overpaying what you owe, and could lead to penalties and prosecution if it results in underpayment. An anticollision program for aircraft traffic control would have to pass even more stringent tests for correctness, since a small programming error could have consequences far more horrible than underpaying your taxes.

When we described the software life cycle, we mentioned that the third phase was analyzing our program to make sure that it was as error-free as we could make it. Why even bother, since the next step is testing? Testing is a good idea and should always be done, but it suffers from a serious shortcoming. For all but the simplest programs, the number of possible input combinations is so large that we can't be completely sure that a program will work correctly on *all* possible inputs. We are thus forced into a compromise position—we test a program on a "reasonably large" set of normal inputs, and then test the program on a reasonably large set of "pathological," or nonstandard, inputs. We might check to see that the program gracefully handles cases of no input, input that is negative when it should be positive, input that is at or beyond the largest values we ever expect to encounter, and so on. Even if a program works flawlessly on all test inputs, though, we have no guarantee that our test cases cover everything that could happen. There are plenty of documented cases of testing being insufficient, including errors such as the one that occurred on October 5, 1960, when the United States radar defense system triggered an alert of a massive enemy attack because the rising moon was interpreted as a wave of incoming ballistic missiles. During the testing phase everyone was thinking of missiles, and nobody thought to ask, "How would this program react to the moon?" The conclusion is obvious:

Testing can reveal the presence of errors, but never their absence.

— *Edsger Dijkstra*

We can sometimes obtain help if we write our programs *from the start* in a way that allows us to be more confident of their correctness. The analysis stage of the software life cycle is an attempt to increase our confidence in programs while they're being written, in hope that we'll catch some errors before they happen. Now we'll show you how to perform an inspection tour of a section of code, in essence using paper and pencil to step through the code and watch it in action.

Of course, it's not always easy to look at a collection of assignment statements and figure out what they will do. One technique that is often helpful is to use a collection of "memory snapshots," in which we draw boxes representing the contents of variables and update the contents as each statement is executed. Consider the following sequence of three assignment statements, using integer variables a and b:

```
a := a − b;
b := a + b;
a := b − a
```

We've departed from good programming practice here by deliberately making the variable names as unenlightening as possible. We've also chosen a particularly opaque collection of statements, just to make things less obvious.

We might be lucky enough to know what the values of the variables a and b are before executing these three statements, or we might begin by just assigning some values at random. In any case, suppose that before the statements are performed, we know that $a = 9$ and $b = 13$. We draw boxes for each of the variables, representing the memory locations corresponding to the variables, as follows.

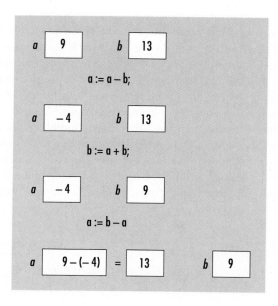

We start with 9 in the a box and 13 in the b box. The first assignment statement, $a := a - b$, means that we evaluate the right-hand expression and store the result in variable a. Using the initial values in the boxes, we see that the expression $a - b$ evaluates to $9 - 13 = -4$, and we store this in the a box below the statement, leaving the current state of the program with -4 in the a box and 13 in the b box. Continuing this process, we perform the next statement, $b := a + b$, using the current values of a and b. This leaves us with $a = -4$, as it was before (since the assignment statement didn't change the value of a), and $b = 9$ (which is what we got when we evaluated $a + b$). Finally, we execute the last statement and find that the variables now have the values $a = 13$ and $b = 9$.

We've demonstrated that if we start with $a = 9$ and $b = 13$ and perform the three statements, we'll end up with $a = 13$ and $b = 9$. We might guess that these three statements interchange the values in a and b, but it's not clear right now that this wasn't just coincidence, and in any case, one example certainly isn't convincing. We can verify that these three statements swap the contents of a and b, though, by a simple modification of the inspection tour we just made. Let's fill the a box with the unknown value A and put another unknown, B, in the b box. By doing this, we're saying, "We don't know what's in the a box, nor do we care. We do know, though, that it is *some* integer, so we may as well represent it by a capital A, to distinguish it from the variable name a." We now mimic the tour we made before:

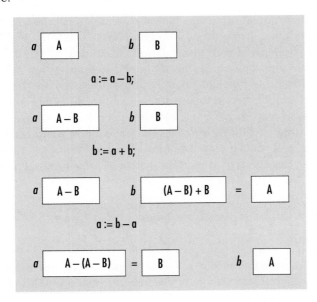

Notice now that if we have $a = A$ and $b = B$ at the start, we'll wind up with $a = B$ and $b = A$ after executing the three statements. In simple terms, we've shown that no matter what values a and b have initially, the end result is that these values will have interchanged after completing the three statements. Thus, the three statements swap the values of a and b for any initial values the variables may have.[11]

To trace one or more assignment statements, perform the following steps:

1. Write the current values of all relevant variables.
2. Use the current values of the variables to evaluate the expression on the right.
3. Store the result in the variable on the left.
4. Repeat the process for any subsequent statements, using the new current values of the variables.

a ⬚ 9 b ⬚ 13

$a := a - b;$

a ⬚ −4 b ⬚ 13

Paper-and-pencil execution of a collection of statements can be helpful in debugging—finding and fixing errors when a program doesn't do what it should. In this case, the memory-snapshot technique allows you to trace by hand and in detail what your code does and sometimes shows where things go wrong. We'd like to avoid debugging as much as possible, though, since tracking down errors is tedious and difficult. It's much better to use these techniques before you start typing code, since you stand a good chance of detecting errors in your design before they ever occur (some authors call this *anti-bugging*). We'll talk about tracing as we learn new statements, and you'll discover that its real power comes in Chapter 5, when we apply it to *loops*, collections of statements that are repeated several times.

2.6
Reference

- Every piece of information used in a Pascal program has a type associated with it. Pascal has four simple data types: integers, real numbers, characters, and boolean values.
- Integers are represented by a string of one or more digits, optionally preceded by + or −. The arithmetic operators on integers are addition (+),

---

[11]Actually, that's not quite correct, since if a and b were very large at the start, the intermediate calculations might produce values that are out of the range of allowable integers. There's a better way to swap, which we'll discover in Chapter 3.

subtraction ($-$), multiplication (*, which cannot be implied) and division (**div**, which yields the quotient, and **mod**, which yields the remainder).

- Reals are represented as unscaled, in which case they consist of one or more digits before the decimal point and one or more digits after the decimal point, optionally preceded by $+$ or $-$; or they may be scaled, in which case they appear as an unscaled real or an integer, followed by an e, followed by an integer exponent. The arithmetic operations on reals are addition, subtraction, multiplication, and division (/).
- Pascal's precedence rules for arithmetic operators are
  - Evaluate parenthesized expressions from the inside out.
  - Perform unary minus first.
  - Then perform *, /, **div**, and **mod**, from left to right.
  - Then perform $+$ and $-$, again from left to right.
- Characters are represented as individual type symbols enclosed by single quotes, except for the single-quote character, which is represented by two single quotes, so a single quote character would be represented by *four* single quotes.
- There are only two boolean values. They are represented in a program by the words *true* and *false*.
- The header of a program may contain a constant declaration part, which begins with the reserved word **const** and is followed by one or more declarations that look like

identifier = some integer, real, character, or boolean constant;

or

identifier = some previously declared constant name;

Constants may not be modified by a program's statements.
- Every variable used in a program must be declared in the variable declaration part of the program header. The variable declaration part begins with the reserved word **var**, followed by a list of variable declarations that look like

list of variable identifiers, separated by commas : type name;

The variable declaration part must follow the constant declaration part.
- An assignment statement looks like

variable identifier : = some expression

and its action is to evaluate the expression and place the value of the expression in the memory location corresponding to the variable. The type of the expression's value must be either the same as that of the variable or compatible with it.
- An expression consists of either a single constant, a single variable, a function call, or a combination of these, connected by arithmetic operators.

- There are eight predefined numeric functions, *abs, sqr, sqrt, sin, cos, arctan, exp,* and *ln*; and two transfer functions, *trunc* and *round.*
- Input to a program from the standard input device (the keyboard, for our purposes) is handled by the predefined *read* and *readln* procedures. Both take a list of variables and assign input from the input device to these variables. In the case of *readln*, after all input has been assigned to its variables, all remaining input, up to and including the next end-of-line character (which you enter by pressing the Return key), is discarded.
- Output from a program to the standard output device (the screen, for us) is handled by *write* and *writeln*. Both take a list of expressions and send them to the output device. In the case of *writeln*, after the expressions have been evaluated and sent to the output device, a return/line feed combination is sent, which moves the position of the next display to the start of the next line.
- We verify the action of an assignment statement by proving that if some condition on the variables is true before the statement is executed, then some other condition must be true after the statement is executed.
- We now know four kinds of statements (out of a total of eleven):
  - *Assignment statements*, of the form *variable := expression.*
  - *Compound statements*, consisting of one or more statements, separated by semicolons and enclosed within a **begin..end** pair.
  - *Empty statements*, like the one Pascal understands as being between two adjacent semicolons.
  - *Procedure calls*, such as Pascal's predefined procedures *readln, read, writeln,* and *write.*
- For all but the simplest sequences of statements, it is often a good idea to use memory snapshots to trace their execution. Doing so can help us verify that the statements do what they should. In the best cases, this can provide us with graphical proof that the statements are error-free.

2.7 Building Blocks

We can now write the basic building block of a program in more detail:

```
program ProgramName(input, output);
{comment block — all about the program}
   const
      CONSTANTNAME = some constant value;
      ANOTHERCONSTANT = some other constant value;
   var
      var1, var2 : some type name;
      var3 : some type name;
```

begin
    Statements here;   {*with comments as necessary*}
    And here
end.

A common way to get information in an interactive environment (such as we are assuming in this course) is to include a prompt before we get information from the operator:

write('Some message goes here ');   *Note that we didn't use* writeln *here.*
readln(*some list of variables*)

2.8   EXERCISES

1. How many different values can we represent with three bits? With sixteen bits? In general terms, how many different sequences of length n can we make, using only zeros and ones?

2. Why did we use 4-bit codes for BCD notation? Could we have shortened the codes to three bits?

3. Find the decimal equivalents of the following binary numbers.
   a. 1101
   b. 10000
   c. 001101
   d. 111111
   e. 1111100111

4. Given a binary number $b_n b_{n-1} \ldots b_1 b_0$, with value b, what is the value of $b_n b_{n-1} \ldots b_1 b_0 000$? In general, how does the value of a binary number change when we append z zeros to its right end?

5. Express the following numbers in binary notation.
   a. 13
   b. 32
   c. 42
   d. 127
   e. 999

6. The first few powers of 8 are 1, 8, 64, 512, 4096. Find a simple rule for the binary expression of 8^n.

7. Add 1101 to 101010, and check your results in decimal form.

8. Invent the binary equivalent of long division, and show what happens when you divide 20 by 3. The fractional part, 2/3, should have the binary equivalent 0.1010101010 . . . . How would you interpret this?

9. Multiply 1101 by 101010, and check your answer in decimal form.

10. One way to represent negative integers is known as *one's complement* form. For example, if we restricted ourselves to 4-bit numbers, the numbers 0 through 7 would be represented as usual:

Number	Binary
0	0000
1	0001
2	0010
3	0011
4	0100
5	0101
6	0110
7	0111

To negate a number, we invert the values of its bits, making every 1 a 0 and every 0 a 1, so that we would represent -2 as 1101 and -6 as 1001.

a. Show that n and $-(-n)$ have the same representation.

b. One number has two representations in this scheme. Which one?

c. Does addition by the usual rules of binary arithmetic work here? Investigate the sums $6 + (-2)$, $5 + (-4)$, $2 + (-6)$, and $4 + (-5)$ and describe what you have to do to add in this representation.

d. In your addition algorithm in part c, what is the sum $5 + 6$? Explain or fix your algorithm. What about $(-5) + (-6)$?

11. Count from 1 to 20 in binary.

12. In constant declarations, the types of the constants are implied, rather than declared explicitly. How do you suppose a Pascal compiler recognizes from the declaration *OKTEMP* = 98.6 that *OKTEMP* should be a real constant and not an integer or character?

13. There are more than a dozen errors in the following horribly flawed program. Find as many as you can and explain why they are errors. Don't try to fix them — the program is such a mess that it can't be retrieved.

```
program Bad Example(input)
[This program has a few {!!} problems, but I was up late last night with a sick friend.};
   var
      temp ; real:
      x, start, end, integer;
   const
      MULTIPLIER = −TEMP + 1;
      TEMP = 160.901;
begin
   writeln(The value of x is, x)
   begin
      readln(start, end, t);
      writeln(start × MULTIPLE : 2 : 6)
end
```

14. Outdo Exercise 13 by producing a 14-line program with as many errors as you can. Only one example of each type of error, please, and make the grader's life easier by including a list of the errors you created.

15. There are no syntax or logic errors in the following program. It runs as it should and correctly computes the area of a rectangle of height a with a half-circle on top of radius b, which (if you remember your high-school math) is $2ab + (\pi b^2) / 2$.

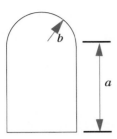

Stylistically, though, the program stinks. Be a grader for this course and correct the style errors.

```
program Problem15(input, output);
    var
        a, b : real;
begin
    readln(a, b);
    writeln(2 * a * b + 1.5708 * b * b)
end.
```

For each of the expressions in Exercises 16 and 17, state whether it is valid or not. For those that are invalid, tell why, and for those that are valid, describe the type of the result. Throughout, assume these variable declarations:

```
var
    x, y : real;
    n, m : integer;
```

16. a. x + y / 2
  b. n **div** (m / 2)
  c. m * x
  d. n − (1 − n **trunc** m)
  e. sqrt(sqr(n))
  f. 3 + sin(3.1416(n / 2))
  g. 4.2122 * sin
  h. −(−x − y)
  i. 1 + n * (1 + n * (1 + n))

17. a. 3 + (x **mod** y)
  b. n + n * n
  c. (m + 4 * n) / 2
  d. 4x − y
  e. 2.0 * n
  f. trunc(abs(x − n))
  g. 3 + sin(n / 2)
  h. sin(abs(round(x)))
  i. 3.1416 + tan(x)

For Exercises 18 and 19, suppose that x, y *are real, and* n, m *are integer variables and that at the time of execution, we had* x = 3.6, y = −0.09, n = 10, *and* m = 8. *What would be the values of the following expressions? Make sure you indicate the type correctly; that is, write the result of a real-value expression as 3.0 rather than 3.*

18. a. n **div** (m − 3)
  b. y / abs(y)
  c. round(x * y) **mod** 4
  d. (n + m) / (n − m)
  e. m + x * n − n
  f. trunc(x) + round(x)
  g. sqr(sqrt(x))
  h. (n + m − abs(n − m)) **div** 2

19. **a.** (4 * n) **div** m
  b. 2 + x * n
  c. 3.3 * abs(m − n)
  d. (x − y) / (x + y)

  e. sqrt(sqr(n))
  f. trunc(abs(x − n))
  g. m * (n **div** m) + n **mod** m
  h. sqrt(sqr(y * n))

20. How could you test whether the integer variable n was evenly divisible by 17?

21. Try some values for x and describe your guess about what the value is of the expression $100 * round(x / 100)$.

22. Write an assignment statement that will set p to the value of q, rounded to the nearest thousand (assume p and q are integer variables). In other words, if q was 27610, p should be set to 28000.

23. The expression $(a + b + abs(a − b)) / 2$ is very interesting. Try some examples, guess what it does, and prove that your guess is correct.

24. Write an expression that finds the minimum of two variables x and y.

25. Write an expression that finds the positive fractional part of a real variable r. In other words, if $r = 78.1099$, the expression will evaluate to 0.1099 and if $r = -45.8121$, the expression will evaluate to 0.8121.

26. Are the two statements below equivalent in the sense that their actions will be the same in all cases?

  c := (sqr(x) − sqr(y)) / (x − y)   and   c := x + y

27. Give the Pascal equivalents of the following expressions, assuming that x and y are real.

  a. $\sqrt{x^2 + y^2}$

  b. $1 + \dfrac{1}{1 + \dfrac{1}{1 + x}}$

  c. $\dfrac{x^4 − x^3 + x^2 − x + 1}{2x^2 + 8x − 17}$

  d. $\dfrac{1}{x + y} + \dfrac{1}{x − y}$

28. What is the output of the following segment, assuming that p, q, and r are real? Be very careful here.

```
p := 2.3;
q := 1 + 2 * p;
r := p − q;
writeln('2 * p + sqr(r)')
```

29. What are the *preconditions* for the following statements — that is, what must be true for the statements to execute without error? Assume all variables are real.

  a. x := y / z
  b. u := 1.0 / sqr(v − 4.0)
  c. t := 2.0 + sqrt(s − 1)

30. This section of code swaps the values of x and y. Or does it? Use memory-snapshot arguments to show what it really does and describe in a concise sentence the action of this code.

```
y := x;
x := y
```

31. a. Use memory snapshots to find the values of a, b, and c after execution of the following three statements. Assume that the initial states of the three variables are $a = 1$, $b = 3$, $c = 5$.

```
a := 2 * b;
b := 2 * c;
c := 2 * a
```

b. Does the order in which we execute these statements have any effect on the final result? Try redoing the problem with the following order:

```
b := 2 * c;
a := 2 * b;
c := 2 * a
```

32. Sometimes we can simplify a collection by eliminating extra variables, so, for instance, the sequence

```
x := 2 * b + 1;
y := a / 2;
a := x - y
```

accomplishes the same thing as the single statement $a := (2 * b + 1) - a / 2$. This process of "folding" statements together doesn't always yield equivalent results, however. Use memory snapshots to show that the following two sequences do not have equivalent results.

```
temp1 := 3 * x - y;          and      x := 3 * x - y;
temp2 := 5 * x - 2 * y;               y := 5 * x - 2 * y
x := temp1;
y := temp2
```

Bonus: We can change $y := 5 * x - 2 * y$ in the second segment so that it is indeed equivalent to the first. What changes would we have to make?

33. Show that $p = 2^n$ is an *invariant* for the following statements, in the sense that if n is some value N, and p is 2^N before the two statements, then after the two statements, we will have $n = M$, for some value M, and $p = 2^M$, so that p and n will still be related by $p = 2^n$.

```
p := 2 * p;
n := n + 1
```

Does the result still hold if we reverse the order of execution of the two statements, doing $n := n + 1$ first?

34. Write a program that will compute property tax. The rules for the tax in this particular town are 1.3% of the assessed value for assessments of $0 to $19,999, 1.325% of the assessed value for assessments of $20,000 to $39,999, 1.350% of the value for values of $40,000 to $59,999, 1.375% of the value for values in the range $60,000 to $79,999, and so on. The operator **div** will be helpful here. You may assume that you are writing for a computer with a very large value of *maxint*, or you may assume that assessments are always in multiples of $1000.

35. Write a complete program that will take as input two integers representing the current cost of a year in college and a future year, and will return the expected cost of a year of college in the given future year. Assuming 12% annual inflation of college cost, you can compute the expected cost by $currentCost \times (1.12)^n$, where n is the number of years from the present to the future year given as input. Remember, Pascal has no exponentiation operator—to compute a^k, you must use $exp(k * ln(a))$. Format your answer so that it looks like a dollars-and-cents amount. Try some examples and get depressed.

36. If a, b, and c are the lengths of the sides of a triangle, *Heron's Formula* tells us that the area of the triangle is given by

$$A = \sqrt{s(s - a)(s - b)(s - c)}$$

where

$$s = \frac{a + b + c}{2}$$

a. Write a top-down design outline for a program that will get three numbers, a, b, and c, and will compute and print the area of a triangle with sides of these lengths.
b. Convert your outline into a program.
c. There are a number of things that can go wrong with this program. Knowing what we do now, it is difficult to guard against such things as operator error. If you were writing a set of instructions to a bright but completely unimaginative person, though, you could say the kind of things you'll eventually be able to say in a program, like "Get a value for a. If a is negative, inform the user that only nonnegative values are allowed and let them enter another value for a." Revise your answer to part a to include error-checking in your design.

37. a. Write a design outline for a program that makes change. The program takes a (real) dollar-and-cents amount, converts it to an equivalent amount of quarters, dimes, nickels, and pennies, and displays the number that is needed of each coin.
b. Convert your outline to a program.
c. Revise your outline from part a to include testing for errors the operator might make.

38. Identification numbers, like those on credit cards, checks, UPC codes on grocery items, driver's licenses, airline tickets, and the like, frequently include a *check digit*, the purpose of which is to guard against input error when the number is read or transcribed. Many countries, for instance, use a check digit as part of a passport number. Write a program for a small country that uses six-digit passport numbers with one check digit, d, so that if n_1, n_2, n_3, n_4, n_5, n_6 are the passport digits, the check digit is defined by

$$d = (7n_1 + 3n_2 + n_3 + 7n_4 + 3n_5 + n_6) \textbf{ mod } 10$$

For example, the passport number 186064 would be assigned a check digit 9, since $(7 \times 1) + (3 \times 8) + (1 \times 6) + (7 \times 0) + (3 \times 6) + (1 \times 4) = 59$, and 59 **mod** $10 = 9$, so the entire passport number would look like 1 8 6 0 6 4 9. Write a program that will take as its input seven digits and tell whether those digits could be a passport number. Use your program to see how useful a check digit is in detecting transposed digits, a common source of input error. Try, for example, the transposed passport numbers 1 6 8 0 6 4 9, 1 8 6 0 6 9 4, and so on.

For more on this subject, you might want to read these two articles: Wagner, N., and Putter, P., "Error Detecting Decimal Digits," *Communications of the ACM 32*, 1 (Jan. 1989), 106–110; and Gallian, J., "Assigning Driver's License Numbers," *Mathematics Magazine 64*, 1 (Feb. 1991), 13–22.

2.9 Answers

1. $2^3 = 8$ values with 3 bits: 000, 001, 010, 011, 100, 101, 110, 111; $2^{16} = 65536$ values with 16 bits. With n bits, there are 2^n values we can represent.

3. a. 13
   b. 16
   c. 13; the leading zeros have no effect
   d. 63
   e. 999

5. a. 1101
   b. 100000
   c. 101010
   d. 1111111
   e. 1111100111

7.
```
        1
   1 0 1 0 1 0    binary 42
 + 1 1 0 1        binary 13
   1 1 0 1 1 1    binary 55
```

9.
```
   1 0 1 0 1 0    binary 42
 × 1 1 0 1        binary 13
   1 0 1 0 1 0
 0 0 0 0 0
 1 0 1 0 1 0
1 0 1 0 1 0
1 0 0 0 1 0 0 0 1 0    binary 546
```

11. 1, 10, 11, 100, 101, 110, 111, 1000, 1001, 1010, 1011, 1100, 1101, 1110, 1111, 10000, 10001, 10010, 10011, 10100.

13. Depending on how you count, there are at least 19 errors.

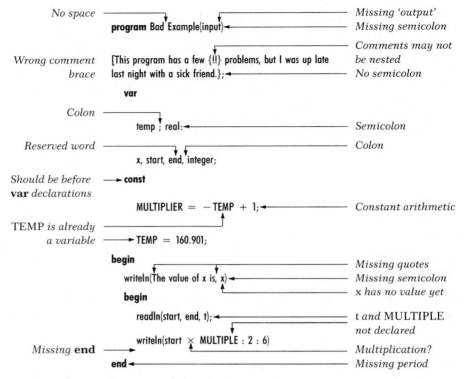

No space ──────── **program** Bad Example(input)◄──────── *Missing 'output'*
── *Missing semicolon*

── *Comments may not be nested*

Wrong comment brace [This program has a few {!!} problems, but I was up late last night with a sick friend.};◄──────── *No semicolon*

var

Colon ──────── temp ; real:◄──────── *Semicolon*

── *Colon*

Reserved word ──────── x, start, end, integer;

Should be before ──► **const**
var *declarations*

MULTIPLIER = − TEMP + 1;◄──────── *Constant arithmetic*

TEMP is already a variable ──► TEMP = 160.901;

begin

writeln(The value of x is, x)◄──────── *Missing quotes*
── *Missing semicolon*
── *x has no value yet*

begin

readln(start, end, t);◄──────── *t and* MULTIPLE *not declared*

writeln(start × MULTIPLE : 2 : 6)

Missing **end** ──────── *Multiplication?*

end ◄──────── *Missing period*

15. **program** Problem15(input, output);   *Use a descriptive name. What is the program supposed to do? How does it do it? Where are your comments?*

var
    a, b : real;   *Use descriptive names.*
begin
    readln(a, b);   *Where is the prompt for the operator? How is the operator supposed to know what to enter?*

    writeln(2 * a * b + 1.5708 * b * b)   *How about using a constant? It's not at all clear that the number 1.5708 is π / 2. Also, the answer should be interpreted for the user; the output should tell what the value means.*

end.

17. **a.** Invalid; can't use **div** or **mod** on real numbers
b. Integer
c. Real
d. Invalid; the multiplication operator may not be implied
e. Real
f. Integer
g. Real
h. Invalid; missing a right parenthesis
i. Real

19. a. 5
 b. 38.0
 c. 6.6
 d. 0.1111111 . . .
 e. 10.0
 f. 6
 g. 10; for positive n and m, this expression is always equal to n
 h. 0.9

21. $100 * round(x / 100)$ rounds x to the nearest multiple of 100

23. If we try a few examples, it seems that $(a + b + abs(a - b)) / 2$ returns the (real) maximum of a and b, that is, the larger of the two values. To prove it, assume first that $a \geq b$. In this case, $a - b \geq 0$, so we can replace $abs(a - b)$ by just $a - b$. The expression then is $(a + b + (a - b)) / 2 = (2a) / 2 = a$, the larger of the two. On the other hand, if b is the larger, we have $a - b < 0$, so $abs(a - b) = -(a - b) = b - a$, so the expression becomes $(a + b + (b - a)) / 2 = (2b) / 2 = b$, which is still the larger of the two.

25. $abs(r - trunc(r))$

27. a. sqrt(sqr(x) + sqr(y))
 b. 1 + 1 / (1 + 1 / (1 + x))
 c. (sqr(sqr(x)) − x * sqr(x) + sqr(x) − x + 1) / (2 * x * sqr(x) + 8 * x − 17)

 By the way, a more efficient way to form this expression is to use the equivalent form:

 (1 + x * (−1 + x * (1 + x * (−1 + x)))) / (−17 + x * (8 + 2 * sqr(x)))

 It's less clear, we admit, but it uses fewer operations and so should run faster.

 d. 1 / (x + y) + 1 / (x − y)

29. a. z cannot be zero.
 b. v cannot be 4 (otherwise we're dividing by zero).
 c. s must be greater than or equal to 1 (otherwise we're attempting to take the square root of a negative number).

31. a.

a	1	b	3	c	5

a := 2 * b;

a	6	b	3	c	5

b := 2 * c;

a	6	b	10	c	5

c := 2 * a

a	6	b	10	c	12

b. The order does indeed make a difference, as it does with most program segments. Starting with $a = 1$, $b = 3$, and $c = 5$, and doing the statements in the order given, we finish with $a = 20$, $b = 10$, $c = 40$.

33. If we have $p = 2^n$ as our initial condition, then there is some number, N, for which $n = N$ and $p = 2^N$. Now, using memory snapshots, we have:

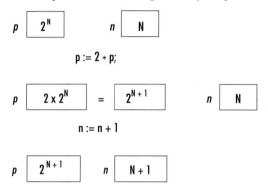

$$p \quad \boxed{2^N} \qquad\qquad n \quad \boxed{N}$$

$$p := 2 * p;$$

$$p \quad \boxed{2 \times 2^N} \;=\; \boxed{2^{N+1}} \qquad\qquad n \quad \boxed{N}$$

$$n := n + 1$$

$$p \quad \boxed{2^{N+1}} \qquad n \quad \boxed{N+1}$$

and we see that after the two statements, we still have $p = 2^n$, in spite of the fact that n has a new value. In this particular case, the order of execution of the statements has no effect on the outcome.

35.

```
program CollegeCost(input, output);
{————————————————————————————————————}
{                                                                    }
{              Computes the cost of college in a given year,         }
{              assuming a 12% annual increase.                       }
{              INPUT:    a future year (integer)                     }
{                        current cost of a year in college (integer) }
{              OUTPUT:   expected cost in the given year (real)       }
{                                                                    }
{————————————————————————————————————}

   const
        INCREASE = 0.12;   {annual rate of increase}
        THISYEAR = 1992;
   var
        futureYear : integer;
        currentCost, futureCost : real;
   begin
        writeln('This program will depress you by');
        writeln('computing the cost of a year of college in the future. ');
        writeln('Enter the current cost of a year and a future year, ');
        writeln('separated by a space, then hit Return');
        writeln;
        write('Future year and current cost? ');
        readln(futureYear, currentCost);

        futureCost := currentCost * exp((futureYear − THISYEAR) * ln(1 + INCREASE));

        writeln('In the year ', futureYear : 1, 'you should expect a cost of $', futureCost : 8 : 2)
   end.
```

37. a.   **I.** Preamble
    A. Display instructions to the user.
    B. Get the *amount* (real) of money to be changed.
   II. Calculations
    A. Convert the amount to *cents* (integer).
    B. Divide cents by 25; the quotient is the number of *quarters* (integer).
    C. Set cents to what's left over after the quarters are taken out; divide by 10 to get number of *dimes* (integer).
    D. Set cents to what's left over; divide by 5 to get *nickels* (integer).
    E. What's left over is *pennies* (integer).
  III. Display results
    A. Repeat amount entered.
    B. Display quarters, dimes, nickels, and pennies.

b.
```
program ChangeMaker(input, output);
{------------------------------------------------------}
{                                                      }
{          This program gets a dollars and cents amount and displays }
{          the number of quarters, dimes, nickels, and pennies needed to }
{          make the amount entered.                    }
{          INPUT:    currency amount (real)            }
{          OUTPUT:   number of quarters, dimes, nickels, }
{                    pennies needed (integer)          }
{                                                      }
{------------------------------------------------------}

var
    amount : real;
    cents, quarters, dimes, nickels, pennies : integer;
begin
    writeln('This program makes change for you. ');
    writeln('Please enter an amount of currency, using only');
    write('two digits after the decimal point: ');
    readln(amount);

    cents := trunc(100 * amount);
    quarters := cents div 25;
    cents := cents - 25 * quarters;
    dimes := cents div 10;
    cents := cents - 10 * dimes;
    nickels := cents div 5;
    pennies := cents - 5 * nickels;

    writeln('The amount $', amount : 10 : 2, ' can be converted to:');
    writeln('      ', quarters : 1, ' quarters');
    writeln('      ', dimes : 1, ' dimes');
    writeln('      ', nickels : 1, ' nickels');
    writeln('      ', pennies : 1, ' pennies')
end.
```

c. In part I of the outline, we might check for errors like this:

   I. Preamble
    A. Display instructions to the user.
    B. Get the *amount* (real) of money to be changed.

1. Read the amount.
2. As long as the amount is negative or contained fractional cents (which we could check by testing whether $trunc(100 * amount)$ is equal to $100 * amount$).
   a. Remind the user (perhaps by example) what the input should look like.
   b. Read the amount again.

Program Design and Subprograms: Procedures and Functions

Building a large program is a complicated task, and anything we can do to help manage this complexity is a Good Thing. We mentioned earlier that many modern languages like Pascal have built-in constructs that allow us to encapsulate in a group a collection of statements so that it can be executed within a program merely by calling the name. This is an excellent idea, but hardly a new one. The designer of a skyscraper doesn't include complete specifications for every I-beam, bolt, and ceiling tile that will be used; if he or she did, the building plans for even a simple building would run to hundreds of thousands of pages. Instead, the specifications might include just the relevant details, like "2 in. #8 machine screw" or "4 in. #10 machine screw." Even though the description of how to make a machine screw would have to include the composition of the steel used, the head and shaft diameters, the screw pitch and shape, the head shape, and the shaft length, all of these are either the same for each machine screw or are determined by the specifications of length and gauge. In other words, the construction of a screw can be specified just once and subsequently referred to by name—"machine screw," and parameters—"3 in. #8."

O B J E C T I V E S

In this chapter, we will:

- Describe Pascal's subprograms: procedures and functions.
- Show how to transfer information to and from subprograms via parameters.
- Demonstrate the usefulness of encapsulating information and program details within subprograms.
- Discuss how the use of procedures and functions can help us in designing programs, through an extended problem-solving example.

3.1 Subprograms

Pascal provides two mechanisms for the kind of encapsulation of details we talked about when we looked at the specification of machine screws earlier. These *subprograms*, as they are called collectively, are known as *procedures* and *functions*. In each, a series of statements are written—like the details of the specifications for a machine screw—and, having been written once, need never be written again. To cause these statements to be executed, one calls the subprogram by name and includes the *parameters*—like length and gauge—that may differ from one invocation of the subprogram to another. You have already seen a number of predefined procedures and functions: *readln* and *writeln* are procedures and *sqr*, *abs*, *trunc*, and *round* are all functions provided as part of the Pascal language. These are very helpful, and you will very quickly become adept in their use, but the best part about using subprograms is that you can also define your own.

There are two distinct advantages to using subprograms. First, subprograms save typing. If you have a program that has the same group of statements repeated several times in different places, you can (and should) write a subprogram containing that code and call it when needed.[1] In these days of program editors with cut-and-paste facilities, saving typing time by replacing lines of code with subprogram calls isn't that much of a big win; after all, one could always select the code to be repeated, copy it, and paste it in the program wherever needed. The true benefit comes from the fact that subprograms reduce the number of statements in the part of the program where they are called, and thus improve the readability of the program for human readers (as opposed to computers, which have yet to express a preference!). In the best of circumstances, program statements are difficult to read,

---

[1]This is why *op. cit.*, *loc. cit.*, and *ibid.* were invented for bibliographic references.

and the more statements there are, the harder it is to keep track of what they're supposed to be doing. Consider, for instance, this very simple example. Which is easier to understand, these three assignment statements:

```
temporary : = a;
a : = b;
b : = temporary
```

or this single procedure call with a descriptive name:

```
Swap(a, b)
```

If you haven't seen these three lines before, it's probably not immediately clear that those statements interchange the values of the variables *a* and *b* in a more efficient way than the swapping algorithm we introduced in Chapter 2. (The complete routine *Swap* is given in the Building Blocks section at the end of this chapter.) True, using a subprogram (a procedure in this case) does force us to look elsewhere for the definition, but having done that, the name serves as a mnemonic; the next time we see a call to *Swap*, we can think, "Right, I looked that up—it swaps two variables. No problem here." Using a procedure or function call chunks many simple ideas (one per statement) into one larger idea that is much easier to handle. Also, like constants, subprograms make it easier to modify a program, because the code in a subprogram is collected in one place rather than spread over several locations in the program.

Finally, subprograms reduce the need for reinventing the wheel. Once we write and test a procedure, we can copy it for use in other programs.[2] From now on, for instance, we never have to bother thinking about how to swap two variables. This code reuse can be a great help in writing programs, and one of our aims in this text is to provide you with a collection of these building blocks in the form of procedures and functions you can hook together to build later programs.

Encapsulation and Compactness

We said that there are two main virtues of using subprograms. Let's consider these two advantages in the context of this chapter's PIP. One of the things the PIP does is the now familiar action of getting some information from the user to be used in later calculations. In particular, the PIP requires the radii of three snowballs, so that it can compute the volume of a snowperson. The input section is a collection of conceptually related tasks, so it would make sense to collect all the prompts and *readln* statements in one clearly defined place. In the PIP, we do this

---

[2]Indeed, in modern implementations of Pascal and other similar languages, we can define "libraries" of subprograms that are generally useful and then reference the subprograms we want from within any program that has access to the library.

by placing the input routines in a single procedure, as follows:

```
procedure GetRadii(var top, middle, bottom : real);
begin
    writeln;
    write('What is the radius of the top snowball? ');
    readln(top);
    write('What is the radius of the middle snowball? ');
    readln(middle);
    write('What is the radius of the bottom snowball? ');
    readln(bottom)
end;
```

Then, when we want these statements to be executed in the main program, all we have to do is invoke the procedure by a statement that gives the procedure name and the name the main program uses for the three variables representing the radii, like this:

```
GetRadii(topRadius, middleRadius, bottomRadius);
```

This makes the main program much easier to read, since the reader needn't be sidetracked by the details of how *GetRadii* does its work and can see immediately that it is the input section of the program. The details are all in the procedure definition at the top of the program, if the reader wants them, and the main program is much more streamlined than it would be if all the code were placed within it.

The other advantage that we gain is that subprograms can encapsulate a group of statements that can be performed several times in the program but only have to be written once. One of the things the PIP does is compute the volume of each snowball. It does this with a function that takes in the radius of a sphere and sends back the volume of a sphere with that radius:

```
function SphereVol(radius : real) : real;
    const
        PI = 3.1415926535;
begin
    SphereVol := (4 / 3) * PI * radius * radius * radius
end;
```

To compute the total volume of our snowperson with snowball radii *top-Radius*, *middleRadius*, and *bottomRadius*, all we have to do is invoke the function *SphereVol* three times in an assignment statement, as follows:

```
totalVolume := SphereVol(topRadius) + SphereVol(middleRadius) + SphereVol(bottomRadius)
```

Of course, we could have simply written the calculations in detail and never used the function at all, but placing the calculations in one place and calling them into action three times certainly makes the assignment statement easier to read (and less likely to be typed erroneously, as well). As we develop the PIP, you'll see how we put these programming principles into practice.

3.2
Problem Solving I: Designing the PIP

We want to write a program that computes the volume of a snowperson, who consists of three snowballs. The specification is simple enough:

INPUT: The radii of the three snowballs (three real values)

OUTPUT: The total volume of the three balls (real)

ALGORITHM: If we call the three radii r_1, r_2, and r_3, we can see (with a little high-school geometry) that the total volume will be
$$(4/3)\pi\,(r_1)^3 + (4/3)\pi\,(r_2)^3 + (4/3)\pi\,(r_3)^3$$

3.3
Problem Solving II: Developing the PIP

It appears that this will be another Get/compute/display program. As usual, in our first outline, we also make note of the variables the program will use.

I. Display an introduction.
II. Get *topRadius*, *middleRadius*, and *bottomRadius* (real).
III. Compute the *totalVolume* (real) by
   totalVolume := $(4/3)$ π * *topRadius* * *topRadius* * *topRadius* + ...
   Use a constant for π.
IV. Display *totalVolume*.

Unlike the PIPs we've seen so far, this time we'll use subprograms to clearly set off the four major tasks. For each subprogram, we also list the variables that must be sent to the routine and the variables that the subprograms will modify and send back, very much as we describe the input and output of the main program. Our first stage outline now looks like this:

I. Call **procedure** *Introduction*. IN: nothing, OUT: nothing. Explain the program and give instructions to the operator.
II. Call **procedure** *GetRadii*. IN: nothing, OUT: *topRadius*, *middleRadius*, *bottomRadius* (real).
III. Call **procedure** *ComputeVolume*. IN: *topRadius*, *middleRadius*, *bottomRadius* (real), OUT: *totalVolume* (real). For each radius, compute the volume of a sphere of that radius, $(4/3)\,\pi\,r^3$, and then set *totalVolume* to the sum of the three volumes.
IV. Call **procedure** *DisplayVolume*. IN: *totalVolume* (real), OUT: nothing. Display the total volume. [We'll do this in the lab.]

Problem-solving technique

Define subprograms for each topic in your design outline.

Note also that we're describing the direction in which information flows between the units: The main program gets information from the procedure *Get-Radii*, sends that information to *ComputeVolume*, and receives in return the volume, which it then sends to *DisplayVolume*, which writes the value it received. This example is typical of many programming problems in that the main program acts as a supervisor, whose job it is to call upon the subordinate routines in the right order and to transfer the necessary information between them so that all the tasks are completed as they should be.

Problem-solving technique

Use the main program to supervise the subprograms, calling them in appropriate order and passing them the information they need.

The first, second, and last procedures are sufficiently straightforward that we could go directly to writing their code. The procedure *ComputeVolume*, though, it still too bulky, since it performs the same computation—for the volume of a sphere—three times. It would be much better to describe outline item III in more detail, explaining how the volume will be calculated. Doing so leads us to the expanded outline below. Following our earlier advice to define subprograms corresponding to outline items, we define a subordinate routine as part of *Compute-Volume*, a subprogram that takes the value of a radius and returns the volume of a sphere with that radius. If we do this, our finished outline now takes this form:

I. Call **procedure** *Introduction*. IN: nothing, OUT: nothing. Explain the program and give instructions to the operator.

II. Call **procedure** *GetRadii*. IN: nothing, OUT: *topRadius*, *middleRadius*, *bottomRadius* (real).

III. Call **procedure** *ComputeVolume*. IN: *topRadius*, *middleRadius*, *bottom-Radius* (real), OUT: *totalVolume* (real).

    A. Use **function** *SphereVol*. IN: *radius* (real), OUT: the volume of a sphere of the given radius. Return $(4 / 3) \pi (radius)^3$. Use a constant for π.

    B. Set *totalVolume* to *SphereVol*(*topRadius*) + *SphereVol*(*middleRadius*) + *SphereVol*(*bottomRadius*).

IV. Call **procedure** *DisplayVolume*. IN: *totalVolume* (real), OUT: nothing. Display the total volume.

Now that we've finished our outline, the program itself is easy to write. It uses four procedures, one of which has a function defined within it. You'll see the reason for our choice of a function for *SphereVol* shortly. When you look over the PIP, *SnowPerson*, notice especially how closely its organization matches that of our outline.

The PIP

```pascal
program SnowPerson(input, output);
{——————————————————————————————————————————————}
{                                                }
{                  PROGRAM IN PROGRESS           }
{                                                }
{                     CHAPTER 3                  }
{                                                }
{    This program computes the total volume of a snowperson }
{    made of three snowballs.                    }
{    INPUT:     topRadius, middleRadius, bottomRadius (real) }
{    OUTPUT:    totalVolume (real)               }
{                                                }
{————————————————————————————————————————————————}
{    SUBPROGRAM LIST                             }
{    Introduction                                }
{    GetRadii(var top, middle, bottom : real)    }
{    ComputeVolume(top, middle, bottom : real ; var }
{                 totalVolume : real)            }
{            SphereVol(radius : real) : real     }
{    DisplayVolume(totalVolume : real)           }
{                                                }
{————————————————————————————————————————————————}

var
    topRadius, middleRadius, bottomRadius, totalVolume: real;

procedure Introduction;
begin
    writeln('This program will compute the volume of snow');
    writeln('required to construct a snowperson. ');
    writeln;
    writeln('You''ll be asked to provide the radius of each of');
    writeln('three snowballs. For each, enter a number (it can');
    writeln('be a decimal number, if you wish), and then press Return. ');
    writeln
end;
```

```pascal
procedure GetRadii (var top, middle, bottom: real);
begin
   writeln;
   write('What is the radius of the top snowball? ');
   readln(top);
   write('What is the radius of the middle snowball? ');
   readln(middle);
   write('What is the radius of the bottom snowball? ');
   readln(bottom)
end;

procedure ComputeVolume(top, middle, bottom : real; var totalVolume : real);
{Sets totalVolume to the sum of the volumes of three spheres }
{of radius topRadius, middleRadius, bottomRadius.            }

   function SphereVol(radius : real) : real;
   {Returns the volume of a sphere of given radius.}
      const
         PI = 3.1415926535;
      begin
         SphereVol : = (4 / 3) * PI * radius * radius * radius
      end;

   begin    {ComputeVolume}
      totalVolume : = SphereVol(top) + SphereVol(middle) + SphereVol(bottom)
   end;

begin    {Main}
   Introduction;
   GetRadii(topRadius, middleRadius, bottomRadius);
   ComputeVolume(topRadius, middleRadius, bottomRadius, totalVolume);
   DisplayVolume(totalVolume)
   writeln;
   writeln('The total volume of the snowperson is ', totalVolume : 7 : 2)
end.
```

3.4 Problem Solving III: Program Analysis Using Procedures

The first thing to notice about the Program in Progress is where the definitions of subprograms—functions and procedures—occur. In the program, they appear immediately before the statement part (which is to say, immediately before the first **begin** of the main program), and that's where the standard says they have to be. This section of a Pascal program is called the *declaration section*. The declaration section describes all of the labels, constants, types, variables, procedures, and functions that are used in the statement part of the program.[3] These declarations serve to alert the compiler so that when it encounters these names later in the program, it will know what those names refer to. In the case of procedures and functions, defining them in the declaration section doesn't cause them to be executed; subprograms are executed only when they are invoked from within the statement part of the program.

If your program has several functions and procedures to declare, they must all appear immediately before the statement part and after any other declarations, like the label, constant, and variable declarations. A general rule of thumb in Pascal is that a name must be defined in the declaration section before it is referenced anywhere else in the program (unless it is a name with predefined meaning to Pascal). So the procedures and functions in a program can be arranged in any order after the variable declarations, unless one subprogram refers to another (which is legal). In that case, a subprogram's definition must precede its use in another subprogram.[4]

Now if you look at the procedure *GetRadii*, you'll notice that it is almost syntactically identical to a small program.

```
procedure GetRadii(var top, middle, bottom : real);
begin
    writeln;
    write('What is the radius of the top snowball? ');
    readln(top);
    write('What is the radius of the middle snowball? ');
    readln(middle);
    write('What is the radius of the bottom snowball? ');
    readln(bottom)
end;
```

In simple terms, the procedure definition above is a chunk of code that is executed whenever it is *called* — referred to by name elsewhere — as in the statement part (the "Main" program) of the Program in Progress:

```
GetRadii(topRadius, middleRadius, bottomRadius);
```

[3]According to the Pascal standard, a program must look like

```
program header;
    constant declarations;
    variable declarations;
    procedure and function declarations;
begin
    statement part
end.
```

Some compilers allow you to modify the order of these declarations, but it's a good idea to stick to the standard order.

[4]This general rule does not apply to the problematic case in which subprogram A references subprogram B, which, in turn, references subprogram A again. Such "mutually recursive" subprograms are legal, and must be defined using a special feature of Pascal that we will see in Chapter 7.

Take another look at the main statement body of the PIP. Notice how easy it is to understand just what it does. The four procedure calls almost read like our outline, especially since we used descriptive names for them. Using procedure calls, we've made a big step toward making the program *self-documenting*. We still need comments to specify and explain the form of the program but the program itself goes a long way toward describing its function.

Now look at the definition of *GetRadii*. The statement part of the procedure definition is clear enough. Whenever the procedure is called, it writes a prompt and gets a value for *topRadius* from the user, writes another prompt, gets a value for *middleRadius*, writes another prompt, and gets a value for *bottomRadius*. In fact, the only part that is different from a complete program is the heading (well . . . that's not exactly true: A program has a period as its last character, while a procedure definition ends with a semicolon). A procedure declaration begins with the reserved word **procedure**, followed by the procedure name (made according to the rules for any other identifier), followed finally by the *formal parameter list*. This last ingredient is the part that needs explaining.

Parameters

Think of the parameter list as the information that can vary every time a procedure or function is invoked. Like a program, a procedure consists of a list of statements that perform the same actions each time the procedure is called. What differs between invocations is the information that the statements use and generate. In our example, we wouldn't want to write a program that computed the volume of the same snowperson every time we used it. We want to be able to vary the radii of the snowballs with each run of the program. Our *GetRadii* procedure, as we said, has the job of soliciting the three values for the radii, to be used in subsequent calculations. Each time we invoke *GetRadii*, we expect it to read three values and make those values available to the rest of the program.

Information that is needed by a procedure or function is passed in to it from the calling routine via the parameters, and information generated within the procedure is passed back to the calling routine via the parameters. This is accomplished by matching the formal parameters in the procedure definition with the *actual parameters* that are used when the procedure is called. Figure 3.1 illustrates this transfer of information.

Notice that the actual parameters in the procedure call and the formal parameters in the procedure heading do not have the same names. This causes some confusion until you realize that the formal parameters are nothing but placeholders for the information that will change every time the subprogram is invoked. If you think about it, it would be impossible to require that the names of the formal parameters and their matching actual parameters always be the same. If at one point in a program it was necessary to swap *a* and *b*, and at another, *newValue* and *oldValue* had to be swapped, there would be no way to write the procedure *Swap* so

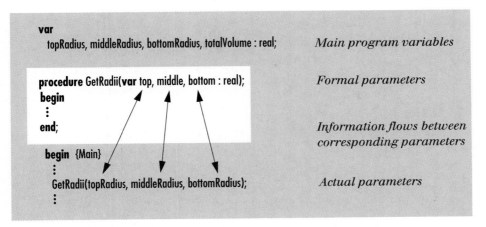

```
var
    topRadius, middleRadius, bottomRadius, totalVolume : real;      Main program variables

procedure GetRadii(var top, middle, bottom : real);               Formal parameters
begin
    ⋮
end;                                                               Information flows between
                                                                   corresponding parameters
    begin  {Main}
        ⋮
        GetRadii(topRadius, middleRadius, bottomRadius);           Actual parameters
        ⋮
```

Figure 3.1. Transfer of information between formal and actual parameters

that its formal parameters had the same names as both sets of actual parameters. Furthermore, if we wanted to use an old procedure in a new program, it would be counter to Pascal's philosophy of ease of use to require that the programmer change the formal names in the procedure to duplicate the actual names in the new program. In our example, the user may enter 55.2 as *top* in *GetRadii*, and this value would be immediately transferred to the matching program variable *topRadius* in the procedure call, exactly as if the user had entered 55.2 as *topRadius*.

Actual parameters must correspond in order and type to their corresponding formal parameters. The names of formal parameters need not be the same as those of the actual parameters.

In the formal parameter list of *GetRadii*, notice the reserved word **var** immediately before the parameters. This is not the same as the **var** in the variable declaration of the program, however much it may look that way. Placing **var** before a formal parameter declaration signifies that these parameters are *variable parameters*, which means that any changes made to the formal parameters are immediately made to the corresponding actual parameters. In fact, Pascal compilers translate variable parameters so that the formal and actual parameters are really just two names for the same location in memory. In other words, variable parameters allow information to pass from a procedure back to the location where the procedure was called. There are times, however, when it is desirable for the flow of information to be one-way in the other direction. When information flows only from the calling routine to the procedure, we may indicate this by leaving out the **var**. Formal parameters without a preceding **var** are known as *value parameters*.

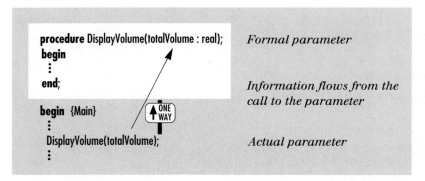

Figure 3.2.   Transfer of information by value parameters is one-way

Information passed to a procedure via a value parameter is copied to the procedure, and thereafter any changes are made only to the procedure's copy, leaving the corresponding actual parameter unchanged (Figure 3.2).[5]

    While in most cases one can safely make all parameters variable parameters, it is good practice to design the formal parameters so that they clearly point out the flow of information.[6] A procedure that has the sole task of writing the values of its parameters, for instance, never changes the parameters, so this could be made obvious by using value parameters, as follows.

```
procedure DisplayVolume(totalVolume : real);    Note: No var here.
begin
    writeln;
    writeln('The total volume of the snowperson is ', totalVolume : 7 : 2)
end;
```

Variable parameters (with a **var** preceding) pass on any of their changes by immediately changing the corresponding actual parameters. Value parameters (without **var**) can be changed within a procedure, but these changes do not affect variables in the calling routine.

[5]In Pascal's big cousin, Ada, the flow of information is made more explicit by specifying *parameter modes* using the reserved words **in**, **out**, and **in out**. This, in our opinion, is one of the few virtues of Ada.

[6]There are times when we might want to violate this guideline. If a parameter occupied a large amount of memory space (if, for example, it were a large array, which we'll see in Chapter 9), it would be better to pass it as a **var** parameter, even if it weren't changed in the subprogram, because it's much more efficient to pass just the address of the parameter than to copy the entire object.

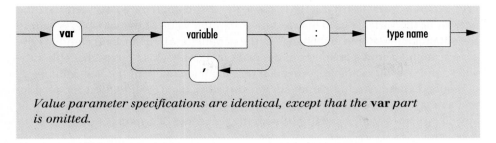

*Value parameter specifications are identical, except that the **var** part is omitted.*

Figure 3.3.   Variable parameter syntax diagram

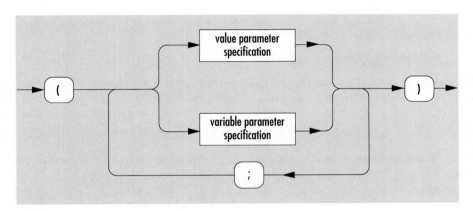

Figure 3.4.   Formal parameter syntax diagram

Figure 3.3 gives a syntax diagram for parameters: a collection of variable names, separated by commas, followed by a colon and the type of the variables. This collection is preceded by **var** if the parameters are to be variable parameters.

The full syntax diagram for formal parameter lists is given in Figure 3.4. Notice that we can mix as many value and variable parameter specifications as we want, as long as the specifications are separated by semicolons. For example, in the procedure heading

    procedure LotsaParams(**var** a, b : integer; c, d: integer; x: real ; **var** y: real);

a and b are integer variable parameters, c and d are integer value parameters, x is a real value parameter, and y is a real variable parameter. Notice that the first **var** part stops at the semicolon; the next parameters (c and d) don't inherit the **var**.

There is one more difference between variable and value parameters— namely, the way they may appear as actual parameters in a procedure or function call. When a variable parameter is passed to a subprogram, we've seen that the *address* of the variable in memory, rather than the value of the variable, is sent to the subprogram (so that any change to the parameter can be made instantly to the corresponding actual parameter in the main program). This implies that only variables (and not, for example, a constant) can be matched with the **var** parameters of a subprogram. A value parameter, on the other hand, is a request for a value, and so may have a corresponding actual parameter that is a variable, constant, or any other expression. For example, with the procedure declaration

      procedure TwoKindsOfParams(**var** a : real ; b, c : integer);   a *is a variable parameter,* b *and*
                                                                c *are value parameters*

we can have calls that look like

      TwoKindsOfParams(mainVariable, 3, (u + v) * 5)

but we cannot make a call like

      TwoKindsOfParams(4.78, u, v)   *Illegal*

Since a literal constant is stored in a different way than a variable is, there would be no way to interpret the meaning of a constant in a call to a variable parameter.

> **V**alue parameters can be called with any expression as the corresponding actual parameter. Variable parameters must have single variables as actual parameters.

Finally, sometimes you may design a procedure that neither generates information nor requires any information from the calling routine. In such instances, it is perfectly legal to write the procedure declaration and its calls without a parameter list. Such routines are often used to encapsulate commonly used output sections; for example:

```
procedure WriteSeparation;
{Writes a blank line, a line of dashes, and another blank line.}
begin
   writeln;
   writeln(' ------------------------------------------------------------------------------------- ');
   writeln
end;
```

which would be called into action simply by invoking the procedure's name:

      WriteSeparation

Local Information

When we said earlier that procedures are almost syntactic twins of the routines in programs, we meant it. That's why they're called "subprograms." A procedure or a function may be quite complicated, though — so complicated that it might need its own *local* constants, variables, and even procedures and functions. If these are defined within a procedure, the standard stipulates that their order of declaration must be the same as that of programs — that is, constants, then variables, then procedures and functions. In Chapter 7 we'll discuss the intricacies of subprograms defined within subprograms, but for the time being, it's enough to tell you that anything declared within a procedure or function is completely inaccessible to the main program, since it is intended for the sole use of the subprogram itself.

> **A**ny constant or variable declared in the main program can be used within a subprogram, but the entities declared within a subprogram — including its parameters and local constants, variables, and subprograms — can only be referred to within the subprogram itself.

In the first section of this chapter, we mentioned the procedure *Swap*. Here's its statement part, with a trace to demonstrate that it does indeed interchange the values in its variables.

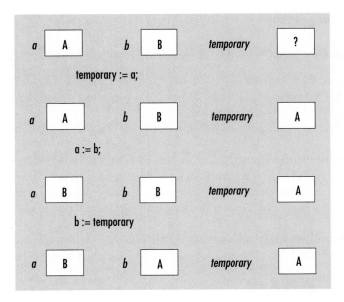

Okay, now we know it works, and we can see that *temporary* is just temporary storage for the value of *a* while we're resetting *a* to *b*'s value in the second statement. We need *temporary*, but we only need it while we're swapping. This means that the main program doesn't need *temporary* at all, once we make *Swap* into a procedure. In this case, we declare *temporary* within *Swap*, making it a *local variable*, and thus "hiding" it from the calling program as follows.

```
procedure Swap(var a, b : real);      Note: We need var here, right?
   var                                Declaration is just as in a program
      temporary : real;               Local variable, hidden from the calling routine
begin
   temporary : = a;
   a : = b;
   b : = temporary
end;
```

This feature of *information hiding* is another of Pascal's efforts to make programs more comprehensible. We could have included *temporary* among the parameters, not using local variables, but then the requirement that formal and actual parameters must match would have forced us to declare a variable in the main program to match *temporary*. In this case, that variable would be completely useless anywhere else in the main program, so it would represent a waste of typing, not to mention that it would add unnecessary clutter to the main program. As another example, notice that the function *SphereVol* is declared within *ComputeVolume*. Here, too, the main program never directly uses *SphereVol*, but *ComputeVolume* does, so we embed *SphereVol* where it will be needed. Then, if we need to copy *ComputeVolume* to another program, its subordinate function will come along with it. In fact, the main program couldn't even call *SphereVol*, since its name isn't even known at the main level.

> **H**ide information. Anything needed within a function or procedure but not used outside is none of the calling routine's business and should be declared locally within the function or procedure.

Anyone familiar with espionage fiction has seen this principle in action. A cell of spies is told just enough to accomplish its mission and no more. In addition, the spymaster — the main program, in our case — doesn't want to be concerned with the details of how the local cell accomplishes its mission and only requires that it gets the job done.[7]

There's a complementary question about the validity of variables and constants that's appropriate here. The main program cannot refer to local variables

[7]In the world of political corruption, this principle avoids having to answer messy questions, like "What did he know, and when did he know it?"

defined within a subprogram. What about, though, a subprogram referring to variables and constants that are declared outside itself—that is, entities that are *global* with respect to the subprogram and therefore defined at the main program level? The rule is simple enough: Identifiers that are declared at the main program level can legitimately be referred to within a subprogram. We will have much more to say later about the *scope* of names within a program—that is, where they are valid and where they are not. At this stage, we'll just caution you about modifying global variables within any subprogram. Suppose, for example, that we modified *Swap* slightly, so that it counts the number of times it is used. We might do this in a sorting program, for instance, so that we could generate data about how efficient it was. One way to do that would be to use a global variable *swapCount* that was initialized to zero and increased by one whenever *Swap* was called, as follows:

```
program SortTest(input, output);
   var
      swapCount : integer;              {a global variable}
         ⋮
   procedure Swap(var a, b : real);
      var
         temp : real;
   begin
      swapCount : = swapCount + 1;   {the global is referenced}
      temp : = a;
      a : = b;
      b : = temp
   end;
      ⋮
begin                                  {Main}
   swapCount : = 0;                    {assigns a value to the global}
      ⋮
   Swap(oldValue, newValue);          {changes the value of the global}
      ⋮
   Swap(start, finish);               {changes the value of the global}
      ⋮
   writeln('The routine Swap was called ', swapCount : 1, ' times.')
end.
```

There are two problems with this program. First, someone trying to read it is faced with a statement in *Swap* that seems to have nothing to do with the procedure itself. To figure what *swapCount* does, it is necessary to leave the procedure declaration and return to the variable list in the main program. That's not such a burden in this example, but for a procedure that is defined within a procedure that is defined within another procedure, the variable might be declared at any of four possible levels, making for a rather irritating side trip to find what and where the mysterious variable is. Another problem of these *side effects* (as modifications of global variables within subprograms are called) is that they destroy the easy portability of subprograms from one program to the next. If a subprogram modifies a global variable, we must be careful when including it in another program to make sure that the new program has a matching global that is defined as it should be.

There are two ways we could fix our example program so that it handled *swapCount* in a nicer manner. The first would be not to increment *swapCount* within *Swap* at all, and instead do the incrementing at the main program level, just before *Swap* was called, as follows:

```
begin   {Main}
   swapCount := 0;
     ⋮
   swapCount := swapCount + 1;
   Swap(oldValue, newValue);
     ⋮
   swapCount := swapCount + 1;
   Swap(start, finish);
     ⋮
   writeln('The routine Swap was called ', swapCount : 1, ' times.')
end.
```

The other fix would be to increment *swapCount* within *Swap* but pass *swapCount* as a **var** parameter, as follows:

```
program SortTest(input, output);
    var
        swapCount : integer;              {a global variable}
          ⋮
    procedure Swap(var a, b : real ; var count : integer);
        var
            temp : real;
        begin
        count := count + 1;
        temp := a;
        a := b;
        b := temp
        end;
          ⋮
    begin                                 {Main}
       swapCount := 0;
         ⋮
       Swap(oldValue, newValue, swapCount);   {Use global as a parameter.}
         ⋮
       Swap(start, finish, swapCount);        {Use global as a parameter.}
         ⋮
       writeln('The routine Swap was called ', swapCount : 1, ' times.')
    end.
```

A third **var** *parameter is included to make explicit to the reader that the procedure does more than just swap — it counts, too!*

Unless there are compelling reasons to do so, avoid modifying a global variable within a procedure or function.

3.5 Problem Solving III: Program Analysis Using Functions

A function, like a procedure, is a separate piece of code that is called into action by specifying its name. A function differs from a procedure in two important respects. First, it is declared and called in a slightly different way than a procedure. Second, and more important, a function is intended to calculate and return a single value to the calling routine, just like the predefined functions *trunc* and *round*, for instance. That's why it is called a "function"—like a mathematical function, it is applied to a set of arguments and produces a single value as its result. *GetRadii*, from our PIP, is a procedure and should be, since it modifies the values of three variables. *SphereVol*, on the other hand, is a function, since it computes a single value—the volume of a sphere—and returns only that to the main program. Notice that we declared the constant *PI* locally, within *SphereVol*. The main program never uses the value for π, so to make it a global constant would only confuse the reader. In addition, having π defined locally means that we can copy *SphereVol* into another program without having to remember to include a constant declaration in the main program.

```
function SphereVol(radius : real) : real;
{Returns the volume of a sphere of given radius.}
   const
      PI = 3.1415926535;
begin
      SphereVol : = (4 / 3) * PI * radius * radius * radius
end;
```

As you can see, when *SphereVol* is called, it is called in a different way than a procedure is.

```
totalVolume : = SphereVol(top) + SphereVol(middle) + SphereVol(bottom)
```

ComputeArea is called within the context, in this case, of an assignment statement. It appears that a function call is syntactically closer to an expression than it is to an entire statement, such as a procedure call, and indeed that's exactly the case.

> **A** function call may be used anywhere an expression of the same type as the function may be used.

It would be perfectly acceptable, for example, to call *SphereVol* within a complicated expression or within a *writeln* procedure call, as follows:

bubbleVolume : = bubbleVolume + 0.5 * (SphereVol(3.9 + r) − 7.89)

or

writeln('The middle volume is ', SphereVol(middleRadius) : 10 : 2)

Notice the syntactic differences between procedure and function declarations. A function declaration begins with the reserved word **function**. Also, we must indicate explicitly that we are returning a value of a particular type. This is indicated in two ways. The function heading has a type specification after the parameter list indicating, in this case, that *SphereVol* returns a value of type *real*. Which real value is returned is indicated in the body of the function in an ordinary assignment statement, except that the function name appears on the left, as

SphereVol : = (4 / 3) * PI * radius * radius * radius

When a function name is used as the left part of an assignment statement, it is being used as a *function assignment*, to set the value the function will return. The use of a function name anywhere else (such as in the right part of an assignment statement or within something like a *writeln* call) causes the function to be called into action. We may include as many of these function assignments as we want to within a function declaration, as long as we make sure that at least one function assignment is performed before we leave the function.

> **A** function must return *something*. This means that no matter what happens within a function, a function assignment must be performed.

We will discuss the **if** statement in the next chapter, but here is an example that should be clear enough of a function definition that contains an **if** statement and three function assignments.[8]

[8]A shorter, but more opaque, version of this function is

```
function Sign(n : integer) : integer;
begin
    if n <> 0 then
        Sign : = n div abs(n)
    else
        Sign : = 0
end;
```

```
function Sign(n : integer) : integer;
{Returns +1 if n is positive, −1 if n is negative, and 0 if n is zero.}
begin
   if n > 0 then
      Sign := 1
   else if n < 0 then
      Sign := −1
   else
      Sign := 0
end;
```

There's nothing syntactically or semantically incorrect about using **var** parameters in a function declaration, but there are good stylistic reasons for not doing so. The intent of a function is to compute and return a single value. We circumvent that intent if we use **var** parameters that are changed by the function.

> **A** function should compute and return a single value. If you need a **var** parameter in a function definition, consider using a procedure instead.

3.6 Computer Science Interlude: A Case Study in Problem Solving

Subprograms offer us a means of chunking sequences of code into distinct units. This might at first seem to be a frivolous addition—"So what?" is an entirely appropriate response upon first learning about Pascal's procedures and functions. To be sure, subprograms do allow us to eliminate repeated instances of the same code, and they do make programs more readable by collecting sections of code into conceptual units. But, frankly, there's nothing we can do with procedures and functions that we can't do without them. The real benefit of using subprograms is that they help us right from the beginning to design programs efficiently. In this section, we will see how subprograms can be used to facilitate the program design process.

It took quite a while for the programming world to realize that there are good and decidedly less good ways to write programs. Many beginning programmers start writing a program by writing code. "Start with **program** and write statements until you come to the **end**," is their methodology. It's a time-honored notion, true—in a kid's world it leads to the design philosophy that builds tree houses by nailing boards together as they become available—but it's almost always a bad idea. If you want to be a hacker and construct programs by throwing statements together, we probably won't be able to dissuade you, even by telling you that the results will be no more stable than a child's tree house. In both cases, you'll spend all your time patching and fixing design errors that you should never have made in the first place. If you want to get good results, however, and a final product that you can rely on, it's better to take the time to be organized, clear, and concise.

> **I**t's better to work smart than to work hard.

As an extended example of the problem-solving process we're advocating, we'll design a program that is somewhat more complicated than the *Snowperson* PIP. The requirements for our new program will be to compute the volume of snow required to construct a snowfamily, consisting of a snowmomma, a snowpappa, and snowbaby. Each snowperson will be constructed of three snowballs. The user will enter nine radii, and the program will calculate and display the volume of each family member as well as the total volume of the family.

This case study is a typical example of phase five of the software life cycle, the maintenance and modification phase. You'll see that this phase can involve all four of the previous phases, and that as problems become more complex, the number of revisions of the design outline increase, as does the depth of the subordinate tasks. You'll also see how we can use one of the most helpful problem-solving techniques — that of reusing what you've already done.

Stage 1

The top level is easy enough to design, because it's just a variant of our input/processing/output theme. The three major tasks are:

   I. Display instructions to the user.
   II. Compute the volumes of the family members and the total volume.
   III. Display the volumes of the family members and the total volume.

At this level, we encapsulate the major tasks into three subprogram calls. Doing so not only isolates the details of each processing step into an appropriate subprogram, but also means we are nearly ready to write our main program. All that remains is to decide what variables we will need to pass between the three subprograms. Part I neither requires nor generates information; part II will get the nine radii and compute the volumes of the three family members and the total volume, which we will pass to part III, wherein their values will be displayed. Here's our first outline:

   I. Call **procedure** *DisplayInstructions*. IN: nothing, OUT: nothing. Tell the user what the program will do and what is required of the user.

II. Call **procedure** *ComputeFamilyVolume*. IN: nothing, OUT: *mommaVol*, *pappaVol*, *babyVol*, *familyVol* (real). We'll get all the radii and compute the total family volume here.

III. Call **procedure** *DisplayResults*. IN: *mommaVol*, *pappaVol*, *babyVol*, *familyVol* (real), OUT: nothing. Display all volumes.

Our pass at the program is listed below. Notice that we've included a header comment block. It's a good idea to put comments in as you're writing, if only because it eliminates the tendency to leave them off until the end, when things may have become so complicated that you have forgotten your original intent. There are fairly few comments, because the program is clearly enough organized that it essentially documents itself, just by its form.

Note, too, that we've defined subprograms to correspond to each of our outline points. The fact that we don't yet know the details of these parts of our design needn't stop us from writing subprogram *stubs* — subprograms that conform to our design outline but temporarily lack processing substance. Using stubs for subprograms early in the problem-solving process allows us to work on a functioning program throughout the development phase.

Think first, outline second, code later. The longer you delay entering code, the less trouble you'll have in the long run.

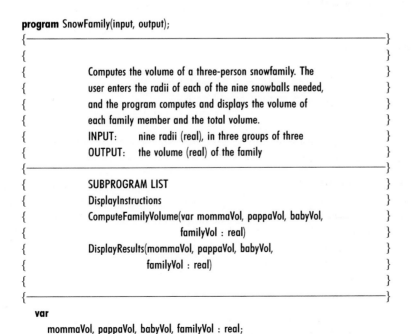

```
program SnowFamily(input, output);
{————————————————————————————————————}
{                                                             }
{            Computes the volume of a three-person snowfamily. The    }
{            user enters the radii of each of the nine snowballs needed, }
{            and the program computes and displays the volume of      }
{            each family member and the total volume.              }
{            INPUT:    nine radii (real), in three groups of three       }
{            OUTPUT:   the volume (real) of the family             }
{————————————————————————————————————}
{            SUBPROGRAM LIST                                   }
{            DisplayInstructions                                }
{            ComputeFamilyVolume(var mommaVol, pappaVol, babyVol,  }
{                          familyVol : real)                     }
{            DisplayResults(mommaVol, pappaVol, babyVol,          }
{                          familyVol : real)                     }
{                                                             }
{————————————————————————————————————}
   var
      mommaVol, pappaVol, babyVol, familyVol : real;
```

```
procedure DisplayInstructions;
begin
    writeln('Instructions go here')
end;

procedure ComputeFamilyVolume(var mommaVol, pappaVol, babyVol, familyVol : real);
{Compute the volume of a family of three snowpeople. }
{For each of the three snowpeople,              }
{    Get the radii of the three snowballs        }
{    Find the total volume of the three spheres  }
begin
    writeln('Now we compute the four volumes. ');          (*REMOVE LATER*)
    writeln('For now, we'll set the family to 100.1, 200.2, 50.5');  (*REMOVE LATER*)
    mommaVol : = 100.1;   (*REMOVE LATER*)
    pappaVol : = 200.2;    (*REMOVE LATER*)
    babyVol : = 50.5;       (*REMOVE LATER*)
    familyVol : = mommaVol + pappaVol + babyVol
end;

procedure DisplayResults(mommaVol, pappaVol, babyVol, familyVol : real);
begin
    writeln('The volume of momma snowperson is ', mommaVol : 10 : 4);
    writeln('The volume of pappa snowperson is ', pappaVol : 10 : 4);
    writeln('The volume of baby snowperson is ', babyVol : 10 : 4);
    writeln;
    writeln('The total family volume is ', familyVol : 10 : 4)
end;

begin    {Main}
    DisplayInstructions;
    ComputeFamilyVolume(mommaVol, pappaVol, babyVol, familyVol);
    DisplayResults(mommaVol, pappaVol, babyVol, familyVol)
end.
```

We run the program to make sure that the procedure stubs act as they should and that information is being passed between the procedures correctly. Now we can use *stepwise refinement*, breaking down the subprograms into smaller pieces where necessary. In this case, the first and last subprograms, *Display-Instructions* and *DisplayResults*, are sufficiently small that we can code them directly, but *ComputeFamilyVolume* must be subjected to this same kind of top-down decomposition.

Problem-solving technique

Use stepwise refinement to describe complex outline points in greater detail, and continue your refinement until you can use your outline to write the program.

Stage 2

Let's concentrate now on refining routine II of our outline. We could get all nine radii at once, but that seems to be an unpleasant task for the user, so instead we'll do three similar tasks in sequence, along with a final display of the total volume.

   I. Call **procedure** *DisplayInstructions*. IN: nothing, OUT: nothing.

   II. Call **procedure** *ComputeFamilyVolume*. IN: nothing, OUT: *mommaVol*, *pappaVol*, *babyVol*, *familyVol* (real). We'll get all the radii and compute the total family volume here. We'll use a subordinate routine to get and compute the volume of one snowperson, and then we'll call it three times, once for each snowfamily member.

     A. Use **procedure** *ComputePersonVolume*. IN: nothing, OUT: *personVolume* (real). Get three radii and compute the volume of a snowperson.

     B. Do the computations three times and keep track of the running sum of all three volumes in *familyVol*.

       1. Mamma

         a. Display a prompt.

         b. Call *ComputePersonVolume(mommaVol)*.

       2. Pappa

         a. Display a prompt.

         b. Call *ComputePersonVolume(pappaVol)*.

       3. Baby

         a. Display a prompt.

         b. Call *ComputePersonVolume(babyVol)*.

       4. *familyVol := mommaVol + pappaVol + babyVol*.

   III. Call **procedure** *DisplayResults*. IN: *mommaVol*, *pappaVol*, *babyVol*, *familyVol* (real), OUT: nothing.

Our expanded outline helps us fill in the stub of procedure *ComputeFamilyVolume*. Notice that nothing else in the program has changed, and that we can (and should) run and test it again.

program SnowFamily(input, output);

```
{————————————————————————————————————————}
{                                                          }
{              Computes the volume of a three-person snowfamily. The      }
{              user enters the radii of each of the nine snowballs needed,  }
{              and the program computes and displays the volume of        }
{              each family member and the total volume.                    }
{              INPUT:     nine radii (real), in three groups of three        }
{              OUTPUT:   the volume (real) of the family                    }
{————————————————————————————————————————}
{              SUBPROGRAM LIST                                              }
{              DisplayInstructions                                          }
{              ComputeFamilyVolume(var mommaVol, pappaVol, babyVol,        }
{                                  familyVol : real)                        }
{                  ComputePersonVolume(var personVolume : real)            }
{              DisplayResults(mommaVol, pappaVol, babyVol,                  }
{                                  familyVol : real)                        }
{                                                          }
{————————————————————————————————————————}
```

var
    mommaVol, pappaVol, babyVol, familyVol : real;

procedure DisplayInstructions;
begin
    writeln('This program will compute the volume of a snowfamily.');
    writeln('You''ll be asked for the radii of three snowballs for each family member.');
    writeln('When asked, enter the required value,');
    writeln('and then press the Return key.');
    writeln
end;

procedure ComputeFamilyVolume(**var** mommaVol, pappaVol, babyVol, familyVol : real);
{Compute the volume of a family of three snowpeople.}
{For each of the three snowpeople,   }
{   Get the radii of the three snowballs   }
{   Find the total volume of the three spheres   }
    procedure ComputePersonVolume(**var** personVolume : real);
    begin
        writeln('Compute a person''s volume.');   (*REMOVE LATER*)
        writeln('For now, we''ll set everyone''s to 33.3.'); (*REMOVE LATER*)
        personVolume : = 33.3   (*REMOVE LATER*)
    end;
```
```

```
begin    {ComputeFamilyVolume}
    writeln('Computing momma snowperson.');
    ComputePersonVolume(mommaVol);

    writeln('Computing pappa snowperson.');
    ComputePersonVolume(pappaVol);

    writeln('Computing baby snowperson.');
    ComputePersonVolume(babyVol);

    familyVol := mommaVol + pappaVol + babyVol
end;

procedure DisplayResults(mommaVol, pappaVol, babyVol, familyVol : real);
begin
    writeln('The volume of momma snowperson is ', mommaVol : 10 : 4);
    writeln('The volume of pappa snowperson is ', pappaVol : 10 : 4);
    writeln('The volume of baby snowperson is ', babyVol : 10 : 4);
    writeln;
    writeln('The total family volume is ', familyVol : 10 : 4)
end;

begin    {Main}
    DisplayInstructions;
    ComputeFamilyVolume(mommaVol, pappaVol, babyVol, familyVol);
    DisplayResults(mommaVol, pappaVol, babyVol, familyVol)
end.
```

The advantage of this methodology is that at every step we have a working program that we can test. If, after dividing a task, we test our program and find that it doesn't act as we expect it to, we have good reason to suspect that the error must be in the new code we just wrote. Compare this with the hacker's typical problem[9]: The hacker wrote several pages of code all at once and then tried to run the program. It failed, as all new programs do, and the poor hacker had to locate the error in hundreds of lines of code, rather than being fairly sure that the error resided in the twenty or so lines of code that were added between the time when the partially completed program ran just fine and the time it blew up.

Try to design a program so that you never have to write more than a page of code (hand-traced, where appropriate) before testing what you wrote. Preparation now may avert disaster later.

---

[9]To lessen the pain of stepping on sensitive toes, we should mention that we're using "hacker" in its pejorative sense here, meaning an undisciplined (however clever) programmer. Some people use the term in the sense of a witty and innovative initiate to the minutiae of programming. The use of the term tends to be generational—positive by younger programmers, negative by their elders.

Stage 3

All that remains is to expand *ComputePersonVolume*, which we do now. We recognize that we've already written and tested a routine that does exactly what is required, namely the *SnowPerson* PIP. All we have to do is copy the code from *SnowPerson* and change the former PIP from a program to a procedure.

I. Call **procedure** *DisplayInstructions*. IN: nothing, OUT: nothing.

II. Call **procedure** *ComputeFamilyVolume*. IN: nothing, OUT: *mommaVol*, *pappaVol*, *babyVol*, *familyVol* (real).

    A. Use **procedure** *ComputePersonVolume*. IN: nothing, OUT: *personVolume* (real). We'll need three local variables here, too, for the three radii. Call them *topRadius*, *middleRadius*, *bottomRadius* (real).

        1. Call **procedure** *GetRadii*. IN: nothing, OUT: *top*, *middle*, *bottom* (real).

        2. Use **function** *SphereVol*. IN: *radius* (real), OUT: volume of a sphere of given radius.

        3. *personVolume* := *SphereVol(top)* + *SphereVol(middle)* + *SphereVol(bottom)*

    B. Do the computations three times and keep track of the running sum of all three volumes in *familyVol*.

III. Call **procedure** *DisplayResults*. IN: *mommaVol*, *pappaVol*, *babyVol*, *familyVol* (real), OUT: nothing.

We're done. The finished program looks like this.

```
program SnowFamily(input, output);
{----------------------------------------------------------------}
{                                                                }
{          Computes the volume of a three-person snowfamily. The }
{          user enters the radii of each of the nine snowballs needed, }
{          and the program computes and displays the volume of   }
{          each family member and the total volume.              }
{          INPUT:    nine radii (real), in three groups of three }
{          OUTPUT:   the volume (real) of the family             }
{----------------------------------------------------------------}
{          SUBPROGRAM LIST                                        }
{          DisplayInstructions                                   }
{          ComputeFamilyVolume(var mommaVol, pappaVol, babyVol,   }
{                      familyVol : real)                         }
{              ComputePersonVolume(var personVolume : real)      }
{                  GetRadii(var top, middle, bottom : real)      }
{                  SphereVol(radius : real) : real               }
{          DisplayResults(mommaVol, pappaVol, babyVol,           }
{                      familyVol : real)                         }
{                                                                }
{----------------------------------------------------------------}
```

```
var
    mommaVol, pappaVol, babyVol, familyVol : real;

procedure DisplayInstructions;
begin
    writeln('This program will compute the volume of a snowfamily.');
    writeln('You''ll be asked for the radii of three snowballs for each family member.');
    writeln('When asked, enter the required value,');
    writeln('and then press the Return key.');
    writeln
end;

procedure ComputeFamilyVolume(var mommaVol, pappaVol, babyVol, familyVol : real);
{Compute the volume of a family of three snowpeople. }
{For each of the three snowpeople,                    }
{    Get the radii of the three snowballs             }
{    Find the total volume of the three spheres       }

    procedure ComputePersonVolume(var personVolume : real);
    {Computes the volume of a snowperson comprised of three snowballs.}
        var
            top, middle, bottom : real;
        procedure GetRadii(var top, middle, bottom : real);
        begin
            writeln;
            write('What is the radius of the top snowball? ');
            readln(top);
            write('What is the radius of the middle snowball? ');
            readln(middle);
            write('What is the radius of the bottom snowball? ');
            readln(bottom)
        end;

        function SphereVol(radius : real) : real;
        {Returns the volume of a sphere of given radius.}
            const
                PI = 3.1415926535;
            begin
                SphereVol := (4 / 3) * PI * radius * radius * radius
            end;
    begin   {ComputePersonVolume}
        GetRadii(radius1, radius2, radius3);
        personVolume := SphereVol(radius1) + SphereVol(radius2) + SphereVol(radius3)
    end;
```

```
begin    {ComputeFamilyVolume}
    writeln('Computing momma snowperson.');
    ComputePersonVolume(mommaVol);

    writeln('Computing pappa snowperson.');
    ComputePersonVolume(pappaVol);

    writeln('Computing baby snowperson.');
    ComputePersonVolume(babyVol);

    familyVol : = mommaVol + pappaVol + babyVol
end;

procedure DisplayResults(mommaVol, pappaVol, babyVol, familyVol : real);
begin
    writeln('The volume of momma snowperson is ', mommaVol : 10 : 4);
    writeln('The volume of pappa snowperson is ', pappaVol : 10 : 4);
    writeln('The volume of baby snowperson is ', babyVol : 10 : 4);
    writeln;
    writeln('The total family volume is ', familyVol : 10 : 4)
end;

begin    {Main}
    DisplayInstructions;
    ComputeFamilyVolume(mommaVol, pappaVol, babyVol, familyVol);
    DisplayResults(mommaVol, pappaVol, babyVol, familyVol)
end.
```

3.7

Reference

- Subprograms are sections of code that are performed when called by a currently executing statement. The two types of Pascal subprograms are functions, which return single values and are invoked as parts of expressions; and procedures, which are invoked as separate statements.
- Subprograms called by the main program are defined in the declaration section of the main program, immediately before the statement part, and must conform to Pascal's declare-before-use restriction.
- Functions and procedures are syntactically similar to programs, in that they may have local constants, variables, and subprogram declarations before the subprogram's statement part.
- Locally declared entities (such as constants, variables, functions, and procedures) are valid only within that part of the subprogram where they are defined, that is, from the location in the subprogram where they are first defined to the last **end** in that subprogram, and may not be referenced outside of the subprogram.
- A subprogram may refer to global entities that are declared at the level of the main program, but it is usually a bad idea to modify the value of a

global variable within a subprogram unless the global variable has arrived via a **var** parameter.

- Information is passed between subprograms and the statements that call them by parameters. The header of a subprogram has a formal parameter list with identifiers that must match the actual parameter list of the sub-program call in number, type, and order, but do not have to match in name.
- Variable parameters appear in formal parameter lists with a preceding **var** and permit information to pass in both directions between the subprogram and its call.
- A variable parameter must have a variable, rather than a constant or other expression, as its actual parameter.
- Value parameters pass information into, but not out of, subprograms. The actual parameter of a value parameter can be any expression.
- A subprogram may have any number of parameters, including none at all. (Actually, there is a compiler- and machine-specific upper limit to the number of parameters a subprogram may have but it's unlikely you'll ever reach it—you'll get tired of typing long before you reach the limit.)
- A function is designed to return a single value to its calling statement. The header of a function must include a reference to the type of the returned value, and the value must be explicitly returned by one or more function assignment statements.
- Functions are invoked in a different way than are procedures. While a procedure call is a statement, function calls are made within expressions, where they may be made anywhere a reference to a variable may be.
- Subprograms are useful because they encapsulate sections of code into single conceptual units. Thus, they simplify the task of designing pro-grams, and they may be reused in other programs.
- Top-down design is a process in which the major tasks are first identified and then divided as needed into subtasks, which are themselves decom-posed if necessary. This process continues until the tasks are small enough to be translated directly into Pascal statements.
- Coupled with top-down design is the process of stepwise refinement, in which each task is identified as a subprogram, usually as a stub that will be filled in later.

3.8 Building Blocks

From now on, most of the building blocks we will present will be pro-cedures or functions, since they can easily be copied from one program and used in another.

A pair of very common building blocks is concerned with getting information to and from a program. As we learn more about Pascal, we will improve these two to be truly error-resistant and general-purpose.

```
procedure GetData(var variable1, variable2 : some type);
begin
   write('Some prompt goes here');
   readln(variable1, variable2)
end;

procedure WriteData(variable1, variable2 : some type);
begin
   writeln('Some information about what we"re writing goes here');
   writeln(variable1, variable2)
end;
```

While it may not seem so right now, you'll discover that there are lots of times when you'll use *Swap*, so we'll include it in your toolkit.

```
procedure Swap(var variable1, variable2 : some type);
{Interchanges the values in variable1 and variable2.}
   var
      temp : same type as parameters;
begin
   temp := variable1;
   variable1 := variable2;
   variable2 := temp
end;
```

The function that computes the volume of a sphere is typical of a number of simple functions that perform some geometric calculation. It's not hard to come up with a host of others that you can use as needed.

```
function SphereVol(radius : real) : real;
{Computes the volume of a sphere of radius r, using the fact that volume = (4 / 3) π r³.}
   const
      PI = 3.1415926535;
begin
   SphereVol := (4 / 3) * PI * r * r * r
end;
```

Finally, here are some functions that Pascal should have but doesn't. They're not used all that often, but they're handy when you need them. Don't be intimidated by the **if** statements—we'll see them in the next chapter, and you'll see that they act pretty much as they appear to act.

```
function Sign(v : integer or real) : same type as v;
{Returns +1 if v > 0, 0 if v = 0, and −1 if v < 0.}
```

```
begin
   if n > 0 then
      Sign : = 1
   else if n < 0 then
      Sign : = −1
   else
      Sign : = 0
end;
```

function Max(v, w : *integer, real, or char*) : *same type as v and w;*
{Returns the larger of v and w.}
```
begin
   if v > w then
      Max : = v
   else
      Max : = w
end;
```

3.9   E X E R C I S E S

1. Why is it generally not a good idea to refer to a global variable in a subprogram?

2. Why is it generally not a good idea to have **var** parameters in a function?

3. In what ways is *Swap* better than the swapping routine we introduced in Chapter 2?

Identify which of the subprogram headers in Exercises 4 and 5 are incorrect. For those that are incorrect, identify the error or errors in each.

4. a. function ReadyToQuit : boolean;
   b. SphereVolume(radius : real) : real;
   c. procedure Solve(a, b ; **var** x, y : real);
   d. function FirstLetter(name) : char;
   e. procedure Permute(**var** p1, p2, p3 : char);

5. a. procedure SetUp;
   b. function Wages(regular, overtime : integer);
   c. procedure Determinant(a, b, c, d : integer; **var** det : integer);
   d. procedure Swap(a, b : integer);
   e. procedure Permute(**var** p1 : char; **var** p2 : char; **var** p3 : char);

6. Here's another flawed program that may look somewhat familiar. Identify as many errors as you can. You don't have to fix the program—just be a grader and tell where it's wrong.

```
program SnowPerson(input, output);

   procedure GetBallSizes(radius1, radius2, radius3 : real);
```

```
begin
    writeln('We"re going to build a snowperson.');
    write('Enter the radii for the three snowballs');
    readln(radius1, radius2, radius3)
end;
function TotalVolume(r1, r2, r3 : real) : real;
    var
        vol : integer;
    begin
        vol : = SphereVol(r1) + SphereVol(r2) + SphereVol(r3)
    end;
function SphereVol(var radius);
    const
        PI = 3.1415926535;
    var
        radius : real;
    begin
        SphereVol : = (4 / 3) * PI * radius * radius * radius
    end;
    var
        bottom, middle, top : integer;
begin
    GetBallSizes(bottom, middle, top);
    writeln('The amount of snow needed is ', TotalVolume(bottom, middle, top) : 10 : 4)
end.
```

Write procedure or function headers for each of the tasks in Exercises 7 and 8. We're particularly interested in your choice of parameters and whether they are variable or value parameters.

7. a. Convert Fahrenheit to Celsius. If F is the Fahrenheit temperature, its Celsius equivalent is $(5 / 9)(F - 32)$.

   b. Convert miles, feet, and inches to meters, given that 1 inch is approximately 2.54 centimeters.

   c. Make change by taking an amount in cents and returning the number of quarters, dimes, nickels, and pennies required to make the given amount.

   d. Convert polar coordinates in the plane to Cartesian coordinates. If a point in the plane has polar coordinates (r, θ), then its Cartesian coordinates are given by $x = r\cos(\theta)$ and $y = r\sin(\theta)$.

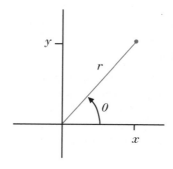

8. a. Convert Celsius to Fahrenheit.
   b. Tell whether one integer is evenly divisible by another.
   c. Convert degrees to degrees, minutes, seconds of arc. A degree is made up of 60 minutes and a minute is divided into 60 seconds. For example, 45.8326 degrees is 45 degrees, 49 minutes, 57.36 seconds.
   d. Compute the distance between two points in the plane, given their coordinates (x_1, y_1) and (x_2, y_2).

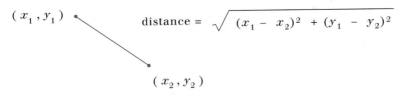

$$\text{distance} = \sqrt{(x_1 - x_2)^2 + (y_1 - y_2)^2}$$

9. Given the following declarations, which of these procedure calls is allowable? For those that are wrong, tell why.

```
program Test(input, output);
   const
      TEMP = 98.6;
   var
      p, q, r : real;
      n, m : integer;
   procedure DoSomething(var x, y : real ; z : real ; var i : integer);
```

   a. DoSomething(p, p, q, m)
   b. DoSomething(p, q, n)
   c. DoSomething(p, r, q, p − q)
   d. DoSomething(2.45e2, p, q, m)
   e. DoSomething(r, p, − 0.0934, n)
   f. DoSomething(r, p, n / m, m)
   g. DoSomething(m, TEMP, n / m, m)

10. Fix the program in Exercise 6.

11. Write the procedures or functions described in Exercise 7.

12. Write the procedures or functions described in Exercise 8.

13. Use calls to *Swap* to write **procedure** *CyclicShift*(**var** a, b, c : integer). In a cyclic shift, the values of the first two variables are shifted to the right, for instance, and the value of the rightmost variable gets shifted into the leftmost variable. For example, if we had $a = A$, $b = B$, and $c = C$ prior to the call, we would have $a = C$, $b = A$, and $c = B$ upon completion of the procedure.

14. Extend Exercise 13 by finding a pattern of swaps that performs a cyclic shift on more than three variables. What is the smallest number of swaps required to perform a cyclic shift on n variables?

15. Using the function $Max(a, b : \text{integer}) : \text{integer}$, which returns the larger of a and b, write **procedure** *Order*(**var** a, b : integer), which arranges a and b in order, so that after a call to *Order* we'll always have $a \leq b$. You may assume that *Max* has already been written and declared before *Order*.

16. Two functions, $f(x)$ and $g(x)$ are said to be *inverses* of each other if $f(g(x)) = x$ and $g(f(x)) = x$, for all values of x for which the functions are defined. For example, $f(x) = 2x$ and $g(x) = x / 2$ are inverses, since doubling a number and halving the result yields the original number. Write a program to support the assertion that $f(x) = (3x + 4) / (2x - 1)$ and $g(x) = (x + 4) / (2y - 3)$ are inverses. Does your program *prove* that f and g are inverses?

17. Rewrite *Zeller* as a function, and write a program that uses it.

18. The *mean* of two numbers is another number, suitably chosen to be between the two original numbers. If a and b are two numbers, the *arithmetic mean* (a.k.a. the average) is $(a + b) / 2$; the *geometric mean* is $\sqrt{ab}$; and the *harmonic mean* is $2ab / (a + b)$.

  a. Write functions for each of the three means.
  b. As long as both a and b are positive, these three means will always have the same numeric order (for instance, the harmonic mean is always less than or equal to the arithmetic mean). Write a program using these three means and test enough values to suggest which mean is smallest, which is largest, and which is in the middle. Include a top-down design outline for your program.
  c. Using a little elementary algebra, prove your conjectures from part b.
  d. If we call these three functions $Arith(a, b)$, $Geom(a, b)$, and $Harm(a, b)$, what is $Geom(Arith(a, b), Harm(a, b))$—namely, the geometric mean of the arithmetic and harmonic means of two numbers?

19. One of the nice features of user-defined subprograms is that you can define your own extensions to Pascal. For example, Pascal doesn't have an exponential operator to compute a^b. We've said that we can compute exponentials (if $a > 0$) by using the fact that $a^b = exp(b * ln(a))$. Use this to write a function, *Power*, that takes in real values a and b and returns the value of a^b. Add this function to your collection of building blocks.

20. For a number $a > 0$, with $a \neq 1$, we can define the *logarithm* function to the *base a*, written $\log_a x$, in such a way that $\log_a x = n$ if and only if $a^n = x$. For example, $\log_2 8 = 3$, since $2^3 = 8$.

  a. What is $\log_2 64$, $\log_2 (1/16)$ (*Hint*: $1/16 = 2^{-4}$), $\log_2 1$, $\log_2 2$?
  b. The *natural logarithm* that Pascal uses (which we write as *ln*) takes for its base the value 2.718281828459045 . . . , which mathematicians and computer scientists call e, just as they use π to represent 3.1415926535 . . . . To find $\log_2 n$, we can use the formula

$$\log_2 n = \frac{\ln(n)}{\ln(2)}$$

Write a function, $Log2(x : real) : real$, that returns the logarithm to the base 2 of x. Test your function by embedding it in a small *driver program*, whose only job is to get some input value(s), call the function suitably on the input, and display the results. Be sure to test *Log2* on the values of part a.

   Exercises 21–24 require you to design programs in a good top-down fashion. Show the final stage in your program design in an outline that specifies the subprograms your program will require, the variables and constants they will use, and the variables the main program will use to facilitate communication between the subprograms.

21. Write a program that will compute the weighted average of three exams and a final. The four weights (for example, 0.10, 0.25, 0.25, and 0.40) will be built into the program, and the program will get four exam scores (integers, in the range 0–100) from the user and then display the weights, the four scores, and the weighted average. For example, if the scores were 82, 88, 79, and 90, the weighted average would be $(0.10 \times 82) + (0.25 \times 88) + (0.25 \times 79) + (0.40 \times 90) = 85.95$.

22. Write a program that tells how much paint will be needed to paint the four walls of a room. The input will be the length, width, and height of the room, in feet and inches, along with the number of windows and the number of doors. The program will compute the total area of the walls and subtract 16.5 square feet for each door and 10 square feet for each window. The output will consist of the paintable surface area and the number of gallons of paint required, assuming a gallon of paint will cover 200 square feet. Round the result up to the next gallon, so if the paintable area was 500 square feet, the program would inform the user that 3 gallons were required.

23. Write a program that will calculate an employee's pay. The program will get from the operator the base hourly rate and the number of hours worked. Any hours over 40 will be compensated at 1.5 times the base rate; so, for example, an employee with a base rate of $7.75 who worked 49 hours would be paid $(7.75 \times 40) + 1.5 \times (7.75 \times 9)$, or 414.625 dollars, which we would round to $414.63. From the wages, subtract 35% for withholding taxes and $5.00 for union dues, so in our example the take-home pay would be 414.63 minus 0.35×414.63, which rounds to $145.12, minus $5.00, for a take-home total of $264.51. Make the output look like a wage statement, displaying the base rate, regular hours, overtime hours, withholding taxes, dues, and take-home pay.

24. In many states, the law requires that a lender must disclose the total interest cost before a borrower takes out a loan. If an amount A is borrowed, the monthly payment is given by

$$A\frac{i\,(1 + i)^N}{(1 + i)^N - 1}$$

where i is the annual rate of interest divided by 12, and N is twelve times the length of the loan in years. For example, a 25-year mortgage at 9.75% would have $i = (0.0975\,/\,12) = 0.008125$ and $N = 25 \times 12 = 300$. If the amount loaned was $75,000, the monthly payment would then be

$$75000\frac{(0.008125)(1.008125)^{300}}{(1.008125)^{300} - 1}$$

or $668.35, rounded to the nearest cent. The total payment, then, would be 300 times this amount, or the staggering sum of $200,505. In this case, the interest paid over the life of the loan would be $200,505 − $75,000, or $125,505. Write a program that will get the annual interest rate as a percentage (which would be 9.75 in our example), the length of the loan in years (25 in our example), and the amount of the loan, and then compute and display the monthly payment and the total interest paid. For the figures we've given, see how much change a 1% change up or down in the interest rate makes on the total interest paid. Be impressed.

24 + _n._ Write the program you designed in Exercise 20 + _n_, for $n = 1 \ldots 4$.

3.10 Answers

1. It hinders portability, since when copying the subprogram to another program, we would have to take the time to make sure that the new program had a global variable of the right name, type, and interpretation. It also makes the routine harder to read, since the global variable might be defined at a far-distant remove from the subprogram.

3. *Swap* avoids the problem of overflow that could cause difficulties in the Chapter 2 version. It is also applicable to types other than *integer* and *real*, which is not the case with the other version, since it performs arithmetic (and so couldn't swap *char* or *boolean* variables, for example).

5. **a.** There's nothing wrong here — a procedure need not have parameters.
   b. The return type isn't specified.
   c. There's a comma separating the two groups of parameters. It should be a semicolon.
   d. There's nothing syntactically wrong, though it seems likely from the procedure name that the parameters should be **var** parameters.
   e. Nothing wrong here, though we could have written all three parameters in a single **var** list.

7. **a.** **function** Celsius(fahrenheit : real) : real;

   This could equally well be a procedure; it depends on your sense of style, and how the subprogram will eventually be used:

   procedure ConvertToCelsius(fahrenheit : real ; **var** celsius : real);
   b. **function** Meters(miles, feet : integer; inches : real) : real;
   c. **procedure** MakeChange(amount : integer ; **var** quarters, dimes, nickels, pennies : integer);
   d. **procedure** PolarToCartesian(r, theta : real ; **var** x, y : real);

9. **a.** DoSomething(p, p, q, m)   *Nothing wrong here.*
   b. DoSomething(p, q, n)   *Too few parameters.*
   c. DoSomething(p, r, q, p − q)   *Can't use the expression* p − q *as an actual parameter to a* **var**.
   d. DoSomething(2.45e2, p, q, m)   *Can't use a constant as an actual parameter to a* **var** *parameter.*
   e. DoSomething(r, p, −0.0934, n) *This is just fine.*
   f. DoSomething(r, p, n / m, m)   *So's this.* n / m *gives a real result, so it is appropriate for a real value parameter.*
   g. DoSomething(m, TEMP, n / m, m) *Type of first actual parameter* (m) *doesn't match the formal parameter. Also, we can't use a constant as an actual parameter to a* **var** *parameter.*

11. **a.** **function** Celsius(fahrenheit : real) : real;
    begin
       Celsius : = (5 / 9) * (fahrenheit − 32.0)
    end;

b. **function** Meters(miles, feet : integer; inches : real) : real;
    var
        totalInches : real;
    begin
      totalInches : = 5280 * 12 * miles + 12 * feet + inches;
      Meters : = (2.54 * totalInches) / 100
    end;

c. **procedure** MakeChange(amount : integer ; **var** quarters, dimes, nickels, pennies : integer);
    {NOTE: Since amount is a value parameter, we don't change }
    {its value in the main program, even when we modify it here.}
    begin
      quarters : = amount **div** 25;
      amount : = amount − 25 * quarters;   {how much is left over}
      dimes : = amount **div** 10;
      amount : = amount − 10 * dimes;
      nickels : = amount **div** 5;
      pennies : = amount − 5 * nickels
    end;

d. **procedure** PolarToCartesian(r, theta : real ; **var** x, y : real);
    begin
      x : = r * cos(theta);
      y : = r * sin(theta)
    end;

13. **procedure** CyclicShift(**var** a, b, c : integer);
  begin
    Swap(a, c);
    Swap(b, c)
  end;

This is a good example of how verification comes in handy in designing a routine. Here's the verification of *CyclicShift*:

Swap(a, c);

Swap(b, c)

Your answer may not have looked like this. It could be different and still be correct—the two calls to *Swap* given here are by no means the only way to perform a cyclic shift to the right. There are two other combinations of two calls to *Swap* that work—what are they? Do you see the pattern common to all three combinations?

15. **procedure** Order(**var** a, b : integer);

```
    var
        sum : integer;
  begin
    sum : = a + b;
    b : = Max(a, b);
    a : = sum - b
  end;
```

17. **program** Zeller (input, output);

```
    var
        day, month, year, weekDay: integer;

    function ZellerDay(day, month, year : integer) : integer;
        var
            adjMonth, adjYear : integer;
            century, lastTwo : integer;
            monthCorrection, yearCorrection : integer;
    begin
      if month < = 2 then
        begin
            adjMonth : = 10 + month;
            adjYear : = year - 1
        end
      else
        begin
            adjMonth : = month - 2;
            adjYear : = year
        end;
      monthCorrection : = (26 * adjMonth - 2) div 10;

      century : = adjYear div 100;
      lastTwo : = adjYear mod 100;
      yearCorrection : = lastTwo + (lastTwo div 4) + (century div 4) + 5 * century;

      ZellerDay : = (day + monthCorrection + yearCorrection) mod 7
    end;

begin    {Main}
    writeln('At the prompt, ">", enter numbers for day, month, year');
    readln(day, month, year);
    weekDay : = ZellerDay(day, month, year);
```

```
write(day : 1, '/', month : 1, '/', year : 1, ' falls on ');
case weekDay of
    0:
        writeln('Sunday');
    1:
        writeln('Monday');
    2:
        writeln('Tuesday');
    3:
        writeln('Wednesday');
    4:
        writeln('Thursday');
    5:
        writeln('Friday');
    6:
        writeln('Saturday')
end
end.
```

Even better would be to put the input and output parts into procedures. You should try that, too, so that the program's statement part would then look like this:

```
begin
    GetData(day, month, year);
    weekDay : = ZellerDay(day, month, year);
    DisplayResults(weekDay)
end.
```

19. ```
    function Power(base, exponent : real) : real;
    {Computes base raised to the exponent power.}
    {NOTE: This function requires that base > 0.}
    begin
        Power : = exp(exponent * ln(base))
    end;
    ```

21. Keep *WEIGHT1*, *WEIGHT2*, *WEIGHT3*, *WEIGHT4* (real) as global constants.

    I. Call **procedure** *ShowInstructions*. IN: nothing, OUT: nothing. Tell the user what the program does and what's expected.

    II. Call **procedure** *GetScores*. IN: nothing, OUT *score1*, *score2*, *score3*, *score4* (integer). Read the four scores.

    III. Use **function** *WeightedAverage*. IN: *score1*, *score2*, *score3*, *score4*, (integer), *WEIGHT1*, *WEIGHT2*, *WEIGHT3*, *WEIGHT4* (real), OUT: weighted average.

    IV. Set *average* (real) equal to *WeightedAverage(score1, score2, score3, score4, WEIGHT1, WEIGHT2, WEIGHT3, WEIGHT4)*.

    V. Call **procedure** *DisplayResults*. IN: *score1*, *score2*, *score3*, *score4*, (integer), *WEIGHT1*, *WEIGHT2*, *WEIGHT3*, *WEIGHT4*, *average* (real), OUT: nothing. Display the results.
    ```

23.
    I. Call **procedure** *ShowInstructions*. IN: nothing, OUT: nothing. Tell the user what the program does and what's expected.

    II. Call **procedure** *GetHours*. IN: nothing, OUT: *hours, rate* (real). Get the number of hours worked and the base rate.

    III. Call **procedure** *CalculatePay*. IN: *hours, rate,* (real), OUT: *regHours, otHours, wages, withheld, paycheck* (real). Define OTMULTIPLE = 1.5, WITHHOLDINGRATE = 0.35, DUES = 5.00 as local constants.

        A. Use **function** *RoundToCents*. IN: *amount* (real), OUT: amount, rounded to two decimal places. Use $round(amount * 100) / 100$ from Chapter 2.

        B. Use **function** *Max*. IN: x, y (real), OUT: the larger of x and y. Use $(x + y + abs(x - y)) / 2$ from Chapter 2.

        C. Calculate all variables.

            1. $otHours := Max(0, 40 - hours)$. Find overtime hours.

            2. $regHours := hours - otHours$

            3. $wages := RoundToCents(rate * regHours) + OTMULTIPLE * rate * otHours$

            4. $withheld := RoundToCents(WITHHOLDINGRATE * wages)$

            5. $paycheck := wages - withheld - DUES$

    IV. Call **procedure** *MakePayStub*. IN: *regHours, otHours, wages, withheld, paycheck* (real), OUT: nothing. Display the variables suitably.

25.
```
program Grader(input, output);

{------------------------------------------------------------------}
{                                                                  }
{          Computes and displays the weighted average of four exam }
{          scores.                                                 }
{          INPUT:    4 integers, for exam scores                   }
{          OUTPUT:   echo the scores, show the weights, and show the}
{                    weighted average.                             }
{                                                                  }
{------------------------------------------------------------------}

const
    WEIGHT1 = 0.10;                    {the weights of the four exams}
    WEIGHT2 = 0.25;
    WEIGHT3 = 0.25;
    WEIGHT4 = 0.40;
var
    score1, score2, score3, score4 : integer;   {the four exam scores}
    average : real;                              {the weighted average}

procedure ShowInstructions;
begin
    writeln('This program will compute a weighted average of four exam scores. ');
    writeln('You will be asked for four exam scores. For each score, enter');
    writeln('a whole number and press the Return key. ');
    writeln('When all four scores have been entered, the program will');
    writeln('display the scores you entered, the weights of each score, and the average. ');
    writeln
end;
```

```
procedure GetScores(var s1, s2, s3, s4 : integer);
begin
   write('First exam score? ');
   readln(s1);
   write('Second exam score? ');
   readln(s2);
   write('Third exam score? ');
   readln(s3);
   write('Final exam score? ');
   readln(s4)
end;

function WeightedAverage(s1, s2, s3, s4 : integer ; w1, w2, w3, w4 : real) : real;
begin
   WeightedAverage := s1 * w1 + s2 * w2 + s3 * w3 + s4 * w4
end;

procedure DisplayResults(s1, s2, s3, s4 : integer ; w1, w2, w3, w4, avg : real);
begin
   writeln;
   writeln(' ---------------------------------------------------------------------------- ');
   writeln('   Exam Score   Weight');
   writeln(   s1 : 3,'   ', w1 : 4 : 2);
   writeln(   s2 : 3,'   ', w2 : 4 : 2);
   writeln(   s3 : 3,'   ', w3 : 4 : 2);
   writeln(   s4 : 3,'   ', w4 : 4 : 2);
   writeln;
   writeln('Weighted average of all scores:', avg : 6 : 2)
end;

begin   {Main}
   ShowInstructions;
   GetScores(score1, score2, score3, score4);
   average := WeightedAverage(score1, score2, score3, score4, WEIGHT1, WEIGHT2, WEIGHT3, WEIGHT4);
   DisplayResults(score1, score2, score3, score4, WEIGHT1, WEIGHT2, WEIGHT3, WEIGHT4, average)
end.
```

27.
```
program Payroll(input, output);
{----------------------------------------------------------------------}
{                                                                      }
{              Generates an employee pay stub.                         }
{              INPUT:    number of hours worked, base pay rate         }
{              OUTPUT:   regular hours (smaller of hours or 40)        }
{                        overtime hours (larger of (hours — 40) or 0)  }
{                        wages (before withholding)                    }
{                        amount withheld (fixed percentage of wages)   }
{                        union dues                                    }
{                        net pay (wages — withheld — dues)             }
```

```
{-----------------------------------------------------------------}
{                SUBPROGRAM LIST                                  }
{         ShowInstructions;                                       }
{         GetHours(var hours, rate : real);                       }
{         CalculatePay(hours, rate : real ; var : regHours, otHours, }
{                      wages, withheld, paycheck : real);         }
{            RoundToCents(amount : real) : real;                  }
{            Max(x, y : real) : real;                             }
{         MakePayStub(regHours, otHours, wages, withheld,         }
{                      paycheck : real);                          }
{-----------------------------------------------------------------}
```

```
const
    DUES = 5.00;       {union dues — used in CalculatePay and MakePayStub}
var
    hours, rate : real;   {hours worked and base pay rate}
    regHours,             {hours or 40, whichever is smaller}
    otHours,              {hours over 40}
    wages,                {gross wages before withholding}
    withheld,             {amount withheld}
    paycheck : real;      {amount left from gross wages after subtractions}

procedure ShowInstructions;
begin
    writeln('This program will compute the paycheck for a week''s work. ');
    writeln('You will be asked for the number of hours worked and the hourly rate. ');
    writeln('For the hours, type a number (it may be a decimal, like 42.5) and press Return. ');
    writeln('For the rate, enter the hourly amount without a dollar sign');
    writeln('(for example, 8.75), and then press the Return key. ');
    writeln('Once these amounts have been entered, the program will');
    writeln('generate a pay stub for this employee. ');
    writeln
end;
procedure GetHours(var hours, rate : real);
begin
    write('Enter number of hours worked: ');
    readln(hours);
    write('Enter base pay hourly rate: ');
    readln(rate)
end;

procedure CalculatePay(hours, rate : real ; var : regHours, otHours, wages, withheld, paycheck : real);
{NOTE: This routine requires a global constant DUES.}
    const
        OTMULTIPLE = 1.5;          {time-and-a-half for overtime over 40 hours}
        WITHHOLDINGRATE = 0.35;    {35% withholding rate}
    function RoundToCents(amount : real) : real;
    {Rounds amount to two decimal places.}
    begin
        RoundToCents := round(amount * 100) / 100
    end;
```

```
    function Max(x, y : real) : real;
    {Returns the larger of x and y.}
    begin
      if x > y then
        Max : = x
      else
        Max : = y
    end;

  begin   {CalculatePay}
    otHours : = Max(0, 40 − hours);
    regHours : = hours − otHours;
    wages : = RoundToCents(rate * regHours + OTMULTIPLE * rate * otHours) ;
    withheld : = RoundToCents(WITHHOLDINGRATE * wages);
    paycheck : = wages − withheld − DUES
  end;

  procedure MakePayStub(regHours, otHours, wages, withheld, paycheck : real);
  {NOTE: This routine requires a global constant DUES.}
  begin
    writeln;
    writeln(' ---------------------------------------------------------------------------------------- ');
    writeln;
    writeln(' CATEGORY                AMOUNT');
    writeln('Regular hours:          ', regHours : 5 : 2);
    writeln('Overtime hours:         ', otHours : 5 : 2);
    writeln('Gross wages:          $', wages : 6 : 2);
    writeln;
    writeln('Gross wages:          $', wages : 6 : 2);
    writeln('Withholding:          $', withheld : 6 : 2);
    writeln('Union dues:          $', DUES : 6 : 2);
    writeln;
    writeln('Net wages:          $', paycheck : 6 :2);
    writeln;
    writeln(' ---------------------------------------------------------------------------------------- ')
  end;

begin   {Main}
  ShowInstructions;
  GetHours(hours, rate);
  CalculatePay(hours, rate, regHours, otHours, wages, withheld, paycheck);
  MakePayStub(regHours, otHours, wages, withheld, paycheck)
end.
```

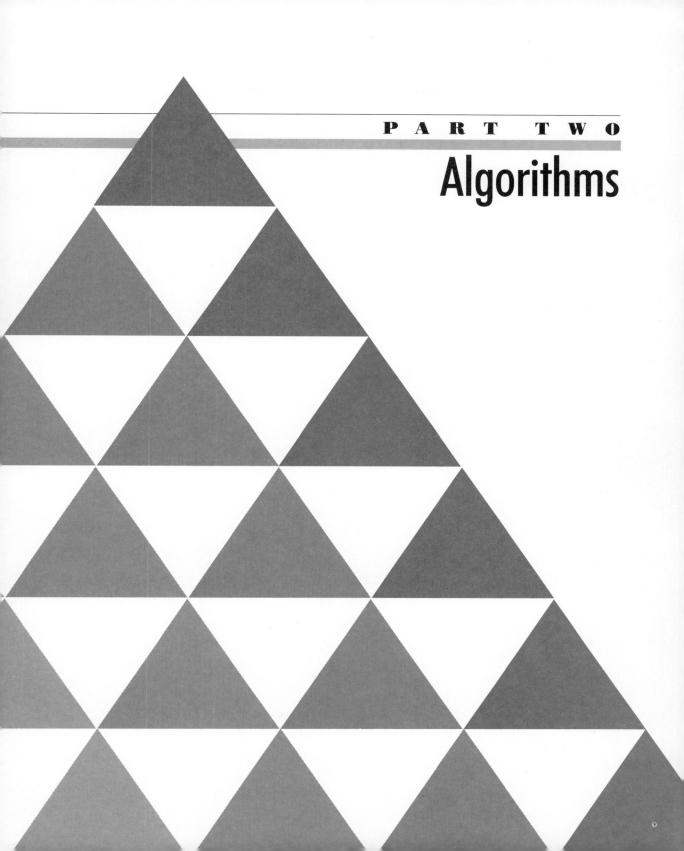

Algorithms

To Do, or Not to Do

So far, the only programs we can write are straight-line collections of statements to be executed one after the other:

```
do this;
next do this;
    ⋮
then do this;
finally, do this
```

In a sense, the programs we've written up to now are all examples of a computer equivalent of predestination—the order of execution is strictly set when we write the program, and that order can never be altered while the program is running. In this chapter and the next, we will explore statements that give our programs the computer version of free will. With such statements, the order of execution may depend on information that exists at run-time—information that may not be known at the time we write the program and that may change each time we run it. All of these statements *transfer control* to another statement, based on the state of the program's information at the time, breaking us out of the straight-line lockstep of execution we've seen so far (Figure 4.1).

Many algorithms exploit the machine's ability to base the flow of control on conditions that we describe so that, for example, a group of statements can be performed only if a condition is met. In this chapter and the next, we will see how

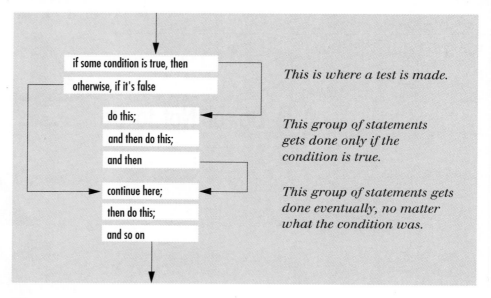

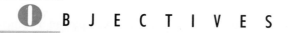

Figure 4.1.   Conditional order of execution

a Pascal program can be written that takes one of several courses of action, depending on information that is available only at run-time. You'll also see how extraordinarily powerful this ability is—there are things we'll be able to do that we simply couldn't do otherwise.

O B J E C T I V E S

In this chapter, we will:

- Describe the primitive data type *boolean*.
- Describe various kinds of expressions that yield boolean values.
- Conduct another problem-solving session with our Program in Progress, a simple expert system for weather forecasting.
- Define the syntax and semantics of Pascal's **if** statement.
- Define the syntax and semantics of Pascal's **if..else** statement.
- Describe structured and nested statements.
- Define the syntax and semantics of Pascal's **case** statement.

4.1 Boolean Values and Expressions

If we're going to break out of the straight-line mode of "First do this statement, next do this, next do this, . . . ," we need to have a feature in our language that permits us to test the *state* of a program's variables, that is, their values at a given instant, and use the result of the test to say something like, "If this condition is true, then do this, otherwise do this other thing."

We've mentioned this *conditional execution* of statements before. In the Chapter 3 building blocks, for instance, there is a passing mention of a function *Max* that returns the larger of its two parameters.

```
function Max(v, w : real) : real;
begin
    if v > w then
        Max := v
    else
        Max := w
end;
```

This **if** statement does exactly what it appears to do. It first tests the boolean expression $v > w$, which evaluates to *true* if v is greater than w, and *false* otherwise. If the expression evaluates to *true*, then v is greater than w, so the **if** statement causes the function assignment $Max := v$ to be executed, thus returning the larger value. On the other hand, if v is not greater than w, control passes to the statement $Max := w$, again returning the larger value. Notice how easily this reads: in simple terms, we could describe the action of the function by saying "If v is greater than w, then return v, and otherwise return w."

Although it would be possible to write *Max* without using an **if** statement (see the answer to Exercise 23 in Chapter 2 for a much less obvious alternative), there are some problems that would be almost completely impossible without the help of the **if** statement (and its relative, the **case** statement), as you'll see in this chapter's PIP.

If we're going to control the execution of one or more statements by an **if** statement that tests whether a condition is satisfied or not, we'll need a different kind of expression than the arithmetic expressions we've seen already. What we need are *boolean expressions*, whose values are *true* or *false*.

We know that we can, for example, declare simple variables to be of type *boolean*, thereby restricting them to take on the values of *true* or *false*. As you'll see, our Program in Progress defines a number of variables to be of boolean type (like *barFalling*, *barRising*, and *barSteady*) and directly assigns them boolean values (using Pascal's standard assignment statement), such as *barRising := false* and *barFalling := true*. We use boolean variables just as we use variables of any other type—to store information so that it can be saved at one time to be referred to later.

The real utility of boolean data, though, stems from our ability to apply a variety of boolean operators to data and produce more sophisticated boolean expressions, just as we use the arithmetic operators $+$, $*$, and **mod** to build complicated numeric expressions from simpler ones. There are several boolean-valued operators. These fall into two classes: the *relational operators* are used to compare expressions for inequality, equality, and relative order; whereas the *boolean operators* act like arithmetic operators to combine boolean expressions and produce boolean results.

Relational Operators

There are six relational operators: $<$, $>$, $<=$, $>=$, $=$, and $<>$. Each takes an expression on the left and an expression on the right, compares them, and returns a boolean value describing the results of the comparison.

Operator	True If and Only If
exp1 $<$ *exp2*	*exp1* is less than *exp2*
exp1 $>$ *exp2*	*exp1* is greater than *exp2*
exp1 $<=$ *exp2*	*exp1* is less than or equal to *exp2*
exp1 $>=$ *exp2*	*exp1* is greater than or equal to *exp2*
exp1 $=$ *exp2*	*exp1* is equal to *exp2*
exp1 $<>$ *exp2*	*exp1* is not equal to *exp2*

We can use these relational operators whenever the relations they describe are defined for a given data type. Since integers, reals, and characters all have an intrinsic ordering, for example, all six relational operators may be used to compare expressions of these types. Of course, it goes without saying that the expressions on the left and right may be arbitrarily complicated. Here are some examples of boolean-valued expressions using relational operators:

3 < 8	*is* true
(5.6 − 0.009) <= 0.0	*is* false
'B' > 'F'	*is* false
sqrt(abs(t)) >= 0	*is* true (*as long as* t *is integer or real*)
3.56 + 2 <> 4.0 * (sqr(7))	*is* true
x = x + 1	*is* false (*for any number* x)
(x = x + 1) = false	*is* true (*for any number* x. *Do you see why?*)
false < true	*is* true (*Pascal just happens to order the boolean values that way. There's a reason for it, but it's not important here.*)

There are three cautions that you need to bear in mind when using relational operators, and the reasons for all of them are easy to deduce.

1. The expressions on the left and right of a relational operator must be the same type or compatible types (like integer and real).
2. The two-character relational operators, $>=$, $<=$, and $<>$, must appear exactly as written here, with the two characters in the proper order and without intervening spaces.
3. Don't confuse the assignment operator $:=$ with the relational operator $=$. The operator $:=$ has no place in a boolean expression.

The first restriction is for semantic reasons. There doesn't seem to be any sensible interpretation for the boolean expression $3 < \,'G'$, so Pascal disallows it, but it makes perfect sense to test whether $3 < 3.74883$, so the compiler coerces the integer expression on the left to be real, then compares the two real values 3.0 and 3.74883, and answers *true*. The second caution is clearly for syntactic reasons, since it's much easier to write a compiler that doesn't have to deal with alternative constructions for an operator. A common typographic error is to type $=>$ instead of $>=$, or to accidentally put a space in $<\,>$. The third caution is both syntactic and semantic. Since assignment statements generally outnumber relational expressions, it's easy to inadvertently use $:=$ in a comparison, but there is never a case when that is meaningful. Don't worry — the compiler will usually be quite adept at telling you you've typed something it doesn't recognize.

We first saw type coercion in Chapter 2.

Boolean Operators

The operators **and**, **or**, and **not** operate on boolean expressions in much the same way that $*$, $+$, and $-$ operate on arithmetic expressions.

Suppose p and q are boolean expressions, then

1. The expression p **and** q is true only when p and q are both true, and false otherwise.
2. The expression p **or** q is true when either p or q (or both) are true, and false otherwise.
3. Finally, **not** q "negates" the value of q so that **not** q is true when q is false, and false when q is true.

There are two ways to remember how **and**, **or**, and **not** work. The first is to think of their English interpretations: "It's raining and my umbrella is broken" is true if and only if both the statements "It's raining" and "My umbrella is broken" are true. "Do you walk to school or carry your lunch?" has a "yes" answer if and only if the answer to "Do you walk to school?" or "Do you carry your lunch?" is affirmative.[1] The other way to remember the action of these connectives is to think of the way they are represented in some computers: *false* is coded internally as 0, and *true* is coded as 1. Then **and** acts internally just as multiplication (you get a 1 as the answer if and only if both factors are 1), **or** acts somewhat like addition (the only way to get a 0 answer is to have both terms equal to 0), and **not** inverts the values, changing 0 to 1 and vice versa.[2]

To test your understanding of boolean connectives and expressions, you should take the time to verify the following assertions. In these examples, suppose that *ans* = 'Y', *sum* = 45, *index* = 31, *r* = 2.5, and *done* = *false*.

(ans = 'Y') **and** (index <> 0)	*is* true
not (ans < 'Z')	*is* false (*equivalent to* ans >= 'Z')
(sum = 45) **or** (index < r)	*is* true (*since one of the terms is* true)
(**not** done) **and** (index < 30)	*is* false (*since one of the terms is* false)
done **and** (**not** done)	*is* false (*always*)
(1 = 1) **or** done	*is* true (*no matter what value* done *has*)

It is interesting to note that the relational operators may be used on character-valued expressions, too. The Pascal standard, recognizing that the numeric codes associated with individual characters may differ between machines, stipulates that: (1) the codes for '0' through '9' be ordered numerically (so that '1' < '8' is true), (2) the characters 'A' through 'Z' be ordered alphabetically (so that 'H' < 'T' is true, but there is no guarantee that '9' < 'A' is true), and (3) the lowercase alphabetic characters 'a' through 'z'—if they are available at all—are also ordered alphabetically (though this order need not have any specific relation to the uppercase alphabetics or the digit characters). In general, the order of characters is derived from the underlying numeric code used to represent characters, so in a system that uses ASCII order we would have '+' < '@', since the ASCII code for '+' (43) is less than the code for '@' (64). Placing an order on characters may seem of limited use, until you consider how useful a program to sort a list of names might be, for example.

Refer to Table 2.2.

We'll end this subsection with a small note, a very small one. We've talked about boolean operators and compared them to numeric operators. The astute reader may have noticed that there are several predefined numeric functions, like *sqrt*, and that we have not mentioned any boolean-valued functions. Are there any? Yes—in fact there are three, only one of which we'll discuss here. The function

*T*he other two are eoln *and* eof, which we'll see in Chapters 6 and 11, respectively.

---

[1]We have to be a little careful with the interpretation of **or**, since we commonly use "or" in its *exclusive* sense of "one or the other (but not both)," which is why the example above probably struck you as a trifle peculiar. The Pascal expression *p* **or** *q* is still true even when both *p* and *q* are true.

[2]This explains why the expression *false* < *true* has the value *true* in Pascal.

odd(n) takes an integer parameter n and returns *true* if and only if n is an odd number, so *odd*(0), *odd*(20), and *odd*(-8192) are *false*, whereas *odd*(1), *odd*(-455), and *odd*(7887) are *true*.[3]

Precedence

Things have suddenly become much more complicated. When we introduced arithmetic expressions in Chapter 2, we mentioned that each of the numeric operators +, −, *, /, **div**, and **mod** had a *precedence* associated with it, and that this precedence was used to determine the order in which these operators would be performed in the absence of parentheses to serve as a guide. For example, the expression 3 + 4 * 5 would be evaluated in the order 3 + (4 * 5), rather than as (3 + 4) * 5, since multiplication has a higher precedence than addition. Now, though, along with the seven numeric operators, we have six new relational operators and three boolean operators, and one more, **in**, that we'll see in Chapter 8, for a total of seventeen operators.

While the precedence of the numeric operators is more or less familiar to us from our elementary algebra days, it's perhaps not at all clear whether < should have higher precedence than + or **not**. Pascal groups the seventeen operators into four levels of precedence, as described below. In evaluating an expression, operations are performed in order of their precedence, from highest to lowest. Operations of equal precedence are performed from left to right.

Precedence	Operator(s)
1 (highest)	**not** − (unary minus)
2	**and div mod** * /
3	**or** + − (binary minus)
4 (lowest)	**in** = <> < <= > >=

Parentheses and function calls, while technically not operators, have "precedence" higher than any of these, since they force evaluation as soon as possible.

This is a big chunk of information to digest at once, so let's start with a few nibbles. We'll give some expression and show with parentheses how they would be evaluated. In these examples, assume that a, b, c, d are integer variables and that p, q, r are boolean.

---

[3]It has always struck us as odd that Pascal has *odd*, which could easily be implemented using **mod**, and doesn't have an exponentiation operator.

This Expression	Would Be Evaluated as	
a + b **mod** c	a + (b **mod** c)	
a * b + c * d	(a * b) + (c * d)	
a − b − c	(a − b) − c	*Equal precedence, so left-right*
a − b * sqr(b)	a − (b * (sqr(b)))	
not p **and** q	(**not** p) **and** q	
p **and** q **or** r	(p **and** q) **or** r	
p **or** **not** q **and** r	p **or** ((**not** q) **and** r)	
a < b **or** c < d	(a < (b **or** c)) < d	*ERROR!*
0 < a **and** < 101	?	*ERROR!*

Notice particularly the last two expressions, since they embody two common errors in the use of the more complicated boolean expressions. In the example $a < b$ **or** $c < d$, the intent was probably to test whether either a was less than b or c was less than d. However, since the relational operator $<$ has lowest precedence, the **or** operator would be performed first, resulting in an attempt to perform **or** on the two integer expressions b and c. Since **or** is a boolean operator, it makes no sense in Pascal to "**or**" two integers, so we would have a type incompatibility, and things would grind to a halt. The correct way to write this expression would be to use parentheses to override the normal order of evaluation, since expressions are always evaluated from the most deeply nested parentheses outward. In this case, we should write $(a < b)$ **or** $(c < d)$, forcing evaluation to be performed in the way we intended.

The second error is also not syntactically legal. Evidently, the intent in writing $0 < a$ **and** < 101 was to check that a was within the range 1 to 100. This is a common syntax error and typically stems from thinking that the logic expression "$0 < a < 101$" — which makes perfectly good mathematical sense — should make Pascal sense. It doesn't. There's a missing variable here — do you see why? In an attempt to evaluate this expression, the compiler would try to perform the highest-precedence operator, **and**, first, leading to an attempt to evaluate "a **and** $<$". This clearly makes no sense; we don't even have to do type checking to discover that. To fix this error, we must explicitly test a twice, and — as in the first error — use parentheses to force the correct evaluation: $(0 < a)$ **and** $(a < 101)$.

Finally a note on style. While the first seven of the example expressions are syntactically correct, and might even do what the author intended, they are certainly not as easy to read as the parenthesized versions on their right. We've said this before, but it bears repeating here.

When in doubt, parenthesize. Even if you don't need them, use parentheses to improve readability.

Complicated Boolean Expressions

We don't have too much trouble analyzing complicated arithmetic expressions, but a boolean expression like

$(a < 100)$ **or not** $((t = MAX)$ **and** $((a - MAX) > 0))$

gives one pause. Because few of us have the depth of experience with boolean expressions that we have with numeric expressions, it'll be helpful for you to know some of the tricks for analyzing them and generating them when you need to.

Analyzing boolean expressions is relatively simple in principle. Since any boolean expression can only be true or false, all we have to do to analyze a complicated expression is to test all possible cases (something that would clearly be impossible with integer or real expressions). One of the simplest ways to do this is to use a *truth table*. In a truth table, you begin by making rows for all possible values of the variables involved, and then in subsequent columns, use the known values to find the values of increasingly complicated expressions, until you find the value of the expression you want. There are three basic truth tables, and all the rest are made by suitable combinations of these. You already know these tables—they merely represent what you know in a tabular form:

a	*b*	*a* **and** *b*	*a*	*b*	*a* **or** *b*	*a*	**not** *a*
T	T	T	T	T	T	T	F
T	F	F	T	F	T	F	T
F	T	F	F	T	T		
F	F	F	F	F	F		

To find the value of an expression for a particular combination of variable values, simply find the values of the variables in the left columns (we've used T to represent *true* and F to represent *false* to make the tables easier to write), and read the value of the expression in its column. For example, (T **and** F) is F, (F **or** T) is T, and **not** F is T. Notice, by the way, that for n variables, there will be 2^n rows to represent all possible combinations of values for those variables: $2^2 = 4$ for the *dyadic* (two-operand) **and** and **or**, and $2^1 = 2$ for the *monadic* (one-operand) **not**.

It's important to realize how simple life is for us when we're dealing with boolean expressions. To prove the algebraic identity $(x + y)^2 = x^2 + 2xy + y^2$, we have to resort to a moderately complex proof using algebra, since there's no possible way to test whether this equation is true for all of the infinitely many possible values of x and y. On the other hand, to show that the expression a **and** $(a$ **or** $b)$ always has the same boolean value as a, all we do is write a truth table for the expression and then compare its values with those of a, like this:

a	*b*	*a* **or** *b*	*a* **and** $(a$ **or** $b)$
T	T	T	T
T	F	T	T
F	T	T	F
F	F	F	F

Notice that the first and last columns are identical. In other words, we've shown that (a **and** (a **or** b)) = a, for any possible values of a and b. Things are simple in the world of logic precisely because there are only two possible values for any boolean variable. A truth table is nothing more than a mechanical way of evaluating all possible cases.

To build a truth table for a more complicated expression, all you have to do is write the expression as it would be evaluated, and evaluate each row by using the values of the variables. For example, the expression

$$(a < 100)\ \textbf{or}\ \textbf{not}\ ((t = \text{MAX})\ \textbf{and}\ ((a - \text{MAX}) > 0))$$

has the form p **or** **not** (q **and** r), where, for ease of writing, p represents ($a < 100$), q represents ($t = MAX$), and r represents (($a - MAX$) > 0). Building this up in the truth table, we see

p	q	r	(q **and** r)	**not**(q **and** r)	p **or** (**not**(q **and** r))
T	T	T	T	F	T
T	T	F	F	T	T
T	F	T	F	T	T
T	F	F	F	T	T
F	T	T	T	F	F
F	T	F	F	T	T
F	F	T	F	T	T
F	F	F	F	T	T

It's easy to see from the last column of the truth table that this expression is false only when $p = false$, $q = true$, and $r = true$, so we can say

$$(a < 100)\ \textbf{or}\ \textbf{not}\ ((t = \text{MAX})\ \textbf{and}\ ((a - \text{MAX}) > 0))$$

is false only when $a \geq 100$, $t = MAX$, and $a - MAX > 0$.

Truth tables are very helpful when you're trying to analyze someone else's boolean expression, but what do you do when you want to build a boolean expression that corresponds to conditions of your own? There are lots of logical identities, like **not** (**not** a) = a, that any good logic text can give you (and that we'll explore in the exercises). Two classes of identities are particularly helpful to programmers.

The Distributive Laws

(p **and** q) **or** (p **and** r) is equivalent to p **and** (q **or** r)
(p **or** q) **and** (p **or** r) is equivalent to p **or** (q **and** r)

DeMorgan's Laws

not (p **and** q) is equivalent to (**not** p) **or** (**not** q)
not (p **or** q) is equivalent to (**not** p) **and** (**not** q)

You've seen numeric versions of some of these. The distributive laws allow you to "factor out" a common expression,[4] as we might do in algebra when we replaced $xy + xz$ by $x(y + z)$. In other words, you can replace the expression

((t > 0) **and** (s <= g)) **or** ((t > 0) **and** (r <> MAX + 1))

by a simpler one, obtained by factoring out the common expression "$t > 0$."

(t > 0) **and** ((s <= g) **or** (r <> MAX + 1))

The distributive laws allow you to simplify a complicated expression, but we could always leave the expression alone if we couldn't remember the distributive laws. DeMorgan's laws, on the other hand, often tell us how to do things that we might not think of doing otherwise. Consider the following problem: We want to tell whether a character variable, *thisChar*, is a capital letter. We could rely on the order of characters and say that *thisChar* is a capital letter if it is alphabetically greater than or equal to 'A' and less than or equal to 'Z'.[5] Thus we could test *thisChar* by

(thisChar >= 'A') **and** (thisChar <= 'Z')

Now suppose we wanted to test whether *thisChar* was *not* among the uppercase letters? We could write

not ((thisChar >= 'A') **and** (thisChar <= 'Z'))

but this isn't particularly transparent, nor is it as simple as it could be. Realizing that DeMorgan's laws say "The negation of an **and** expression is the **or** of the negation of its components," we could write

(**not** (thisChar >= 'A')) **or** (**not** (thisChar <= 'Z'))

which is equivalent to the much simpler

(thisChar < 'A') **or** (thisChar > 'Z')

Notice, by the way, how we negated the pair of relational operators. We can summarize this by saying

not $(a < b)$ is equivalent to $a >= b$.
not $(a > b)$ is equivalent to $a <= b$.
not $(a = b)$ is equivalent to $a <> b$.

[4]We couldn't interchange the operators though: $(x + y) \times (x + z)$ is most emphatically not the same as $x + (y \times z)$. In algebra, multiplication distributes over addition, but addition doesn't distribute over multiplication. In logic, both **and** and **or** distribute over the other.

[5]This cannot be relied on to work all the time. The standard doesn't stipulate that there are no extra characters interposed among the uppercase letters. On all the computers that this text is written for, this is a moot point, since the uppercase letter characters have no strangers among them.

Although the distributive laws and DeMorgan's laws can help to simplify complicated boolean expressions, the biggest help is to avoid complicated expressions of any kind, numeric or boolean. To use our complicated expression as an example, it would be much better to replace the expression

$$(a < 100) \text{ or not } ((t = MAX) \text{ and } ((a - MAX) > 0))$$

entirely, by first using auxiliary assignment statements to three boolean variables, *aIsInRange*, *tIsAtLimit*, and *aIsOverLimit*:

```
aIsInRange : = (a < 100);
tIsAtLimit : = (t = MAX);
aIsOverLimit : = ((a - MAX) > 0)
```

and then representing the expression by the much clearer version

aIsInRange **or not** (tIsAtLimit **and** aIsOverLimit)

We did the same thing with *Zeller* in Chapter 1. If you look at the way we computed *weekDay*, you'll see that we used five assignment statements and four auxiliary variables — *monthCorrection*, *century*, *lastTwo*, and *yearCorrection* — to find a value that could have been computed in one hideously complicated assignment statement. To see just how hideous, try writing the code that computes *weekDay* using a single assignment statement.

4.2
Computer Science Interlude: Artificial Intelligence

The sample program for this chapter is a simple expert system. Such a program falls under the heading of *Artificial Intelligence* — that branch of computer science that attempts to build programs that embody an expertise that we could call intelligent if it were performed by a person.

Alan Turing's 1950 paper, entitled "Computing Machinery and Intelligence," is generally regarded as the first to propose that the computer be brought to bear on the problem of simulating human behavior. It was certainly the first to juxtapose the words *computing* and *intelligence*, and, in so doing, propose the computer as a metaphor for human intelligence — a metaphor that permeates our culture today. Like the forms of automation that preceded them chronologically, the first computers were powerful enough to inspire their programmers to attempt to develop programs that played checkers and chess, translated natural language, proved theorems, and learned from their experience. By 1956, the phrase "Artificial Intelligence" had been coined to describe the use of computers for studying and modeling certain problem-solving tasks that were, prior to the invention of the computer, thought to be uniquely human.

After some thirty years, Artificial Intelligence (AI) is a central and exciting part of the computer science landscape. All of its successes and failures have contributed to our understanding both of the practical powers of digital computers and of how we as humans perform a variety of intellectual tasks. Indeed, many of the tasks that had been historically equated with superior human "intelligence" (such as chess playing and theorem proving) were among the first to be simulated successfully by a computer. Others that at casual glance seemed readily amenable to automation (natural language translation, common-sense reasoning) have to this day proven elusive.

Language, for example, is regarded by many as a skill that distinguishes humans from other species and, as such, is considered a potentially fruitful source of insight into our intellectual behavior. Similarly, there is great practical motivation for developing computers that understand language. Not surprisingly, researchers have been writing programs to process and respond to natural language input, in both typed and spoken form, since the early days of computing. In such programs, "understanding" is demonstrated when they accept natural language text from the keyboard as input and either produce comprehensible text on the screen or carry out some motor command as output. An entirely separate branch of AI is devoted to the problems of getting computers to "hear" natural language. Because these problems deal with physical phenomena (sound waves) and require special equipment to record and produce the data upon which they operate, this subfield takes on an engineering, as opposed to a psychological, flavor.

Knowledge representation is an implicit concern of all computer programs. For AI programs, representation schemes merit additional attention for two reasons. First, the adequacy of the chosen method for representing knowledge often dictates more than the storage or processing efficiency of the program. The method may determine what kinds of behavior can be achieved by a program, and ultimately whether or not the program is judged a success. Second, given that the domain of AI is human intellectual tasks, programs that experiment with knowledge representation schemes are a means of evaluating and refining theories of human memory.

As our understanding of particular domains increased, and as programs were pushed to higher levels of sophistication, the need for domain-specific information became evident. Many of today's *expert systems*, programs that perform humanlike diagnostic and analysis functions in a specific field or task, are based on general problem-solving and knowledge representation techniques that have been customized to incorporate and take advantage of domain-specific information.

Partly because of this practical need for imparting knowledge to computers, and partly because of the theoretical fascination it holds for researchers, the topic of learning is one of the most provocative for AI. Programs that learn on their own are representative of the state of the art in AI for at least three reasons. First, they simulate a fundamental human intellectual skill—one that may be the basis for all other skill development. Second, they accomplish their behavior by surprisingly mechanical means. Finally, the possibility that we can program learning skills opens the door to an uncertain future.

Indeed, our notion of a computer continues to expand, as does our understanding of human development and behavior. In recognition of this (and only somewhat facetiously), AI has been defined as "whatever hasn't been done yet." This description emphasizes at once the elusive natures of intelligence and computation. If history is an accurate predictor, there is every reason to believe AI will continue to present a moving target toward which our scientific energies will be directed.

4.3 Problem Solving I: Designing the PIP

In this *very* simple example of an expert system, the program asks the user for answers to questions about the weather and "predicts" the likelihood of rain, based on the user's responses. We'd be the first to admit that this is a pretty simplistic program, but we'd also point out that we could improve it considerably by including other rules that would lead to more accurate predictions—at least as good as those of the old farmer leaning on the fence, feeling his bunions and looking at the sky.

We'll first ask a number of questions that seem to us to be predictors of rain, such as "Does it feel like rain?" Depending on the responses, we'll compute a numeric score of the likelihood of rain and use that score to determine the message that the program displays.

INPUT: Character responses to
"Does it feel like rain?" (char, 'y' or 'n')
"Is it raining now?" ('y' or 'n')
"Was rain predicted for today?" ('y' or 'n')
"Are your bunions aching?" ('y' or 'n')
"What is the state of the barometer?" ('r'(ising), 's'(teady), or 'f'(alling))

OUTPUT: A statement, depending on the computed likelihood of rain

ALGORITHM: Pick one of four responses, depending on the score, where the score is given by the sum of the following:
+1, if it feels like rain,
+2, if the bunions ache,
+1, if it is raining and the barometer is steady,
+2, if rain was predicted and the barometer is falling,
-2, if the barometer is rising and it is not the case that it is raining or it feels like rain.
If the score is -2, -1, or 0, write a message that rain is unlikely,
if the score is 1 or 2, write a message that rain is slightly likely,
if the score is 3 or 4, write a message that rain is likely,
if the score is 5, write a message that rain is highly likely.

4.4 Problem Solving II: Developing the PIP

We start, as usual, with our basic outline of three steps: solicit the inputs, process the data, display the results. Given the number of inputs to this program, we are justified in breaking the input phase into two steps — one of which displays instructions for the program's use, and the other of which asks weather-related questions. Processing in this case consists primarily of calculating a score, based on our algorithm. The displayed result depends on the calculated score and will indicate the program's weather prediction. Our initial outline, then, looks like this:

I. Introduce program and display instructions.
II. Ask questions and record answers.
III. Calculate the score based on the answers.
IV. Make a prediction based on the score.

Describing each of these steps as a subprogram yields the following description and allows us to write our program. You will see as you read further that these subprograms are readily describable in Pascal.

I. Call **procedure** *Introduction*. IN: nothing, OUT: nothing. As usual, describe the program and display instructions to the user.

II. Call **procedure** *AskQuestions*. IN: nothing, OUT: *feelsLikeRain*, *isRaining*, *rainPredicted*, *bunionsAche*, *barFalling*, *barRising*, *barSteady* (boolean). These will be *true* if the user answered "yes" to the corresponding question. In each case, we'll read the character, *response* (local variable), and set the corresponding boolean value by, for example, *feelsLikeRain* := (*response* = 'y').

III. Call **function** *DetermineScore*. IN: *feelsLikeRain*, *isRaining*, *rainPredicted*, *bunionsAche*, *barFalling*, *barRising*, *barSteady* (boolean), OUT: a *score* (integer) based on the truth or falsehood of these variables.

IV. Call **procedure** *MakePrediction*. IN: *score* (integer), OUT: nothing. Display the message corresponding to the score.

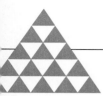

The PIP

program Weather(input, output);

```
{--------------------------------------------------------------}
{                                                              }
{                  PROGRAM IN PROGRESS                         }
{                                                              }
{                     CHAPTER 4                                }
{                                                              }
{   This program predicts the likelihood of rain based on      }
{   the user's responses to questions about the weather. The   }
{   prediction reflects a numeric scoring system that weights  }
{   and combines the weather factors.                          }
{   INPUT:     Character responses to                          }
{                   "Does it feel like rain?" ('y' or 'n')     }
{                   "Is it raining now?" ('y' or 'n')          }
{                   "Was rain predicted for today?" ('y' or 'n') }
{                   "Are your bunions aching?" ('y' or 'n')    }
{                   "What is the state of the barometer?"      }
{                        ('r'(ising), 's'(teady), or 'f'(alling)) }
{   OUTPUT:    A message, depending on the computed            }
{                   likelihood of rain.                        }
{                                                              }
{--------------------------------------------------------------}
{   SUBPROGRAM LIST                                            }
{   Introduction                                               }
{   AskQuestions (var feelsLikeRain, isRaining, barFalling,    }
{                   barRising, barSteady, rainPredicted,       }
{                   bunionsAche: boolean)                      }
{   DetermineScore (feelsLikeRain, isRaining, barFalling,      }
{                   barRising, barSteady, rainPredicted,       }
{                   bunionsAche: boolean) :integer             }
{   MakePrediction (score: integer)                            }
{                                                              }
{--------------------------------------------------------------}

var
{The following are boolean flags, which will be set based on user's responses.}
    feelsLikeRain, isRaining, barFalling,
    barRising, barSteady, rainPredicted, bunionsAche: boolean;

    score: integer;    {score is the numeric rating of the likelihood of rain}
```

```
procedure Introduction;
{Display brief introduction to the program.}
begin
    writeln;
    writeln('This program will predict the likelihood of rain based upon your');
    writeln('responses to questions about the weather. Answer each question');
    writeln('with a single key response, followed by a Return. ');
    writeln
end;

procedure AskQuestions (var feelsLikeRain, isRaining, barFalling, barRising, barSteady,
                            rainPredicted, bunionsAche: boolean);
{Ask questions and solicit responses from the user that}
{allow all of the boolean parameters to be set.        }
    var
        response: char;    {user's response from the keyboard}
begin
    write('Does it feel like rain? (enter y for yes; n for no): ');
    readln(response);
    writeln;
    feelsLikeRain : = (response = 'y');

    write('Is it raining now? (enter y for yes; n for no): ');
    readln(response);
    writeln;
    isRaining : = (response = 'y');

    write('Was rain predicted for today? (enter y for yes; n for no): ');
    readln(response);
    writeln;
    rainPredicted : = (response = 'y');

    write('Are your bunions aching? (enter y for yes; n for no): ');
    readln(response);
    writeln;
    bunionsAche : = (response = 'y');

    writeln('What is the status of the barometer?');
    write('(enter r for rising; s for steady; f for falling): ');
    readln(response);
    writeln;
    barRising : = false;
    barSteady : = false;
    barFalling : = false;
```

```
        {Set one of the barometer flags to true.}
        if response = 'r' then
            barRising : = true
        else if response = 's' then
            barSteady : = true
        else
            barFalling : = true    {Assume barometer is falling if bad response was chosen.}
    end;

    function DetermineScore (feelsLikeRain, isRaining, barFalling, barRising, barSteady, rainPredicted,
                             bunionsAche: boolean): integer;
    {Calculates numeric score based on values of boolean parameters.}
    var
        score : integer;
    begin
        score : = 0;
        if feelsLikeRain then
            score : = score + 1;
        if bunionsAche then
            score : = score + 2;
        if isRaining and barSteady then
            score : = score + 1;
        if rainPredicted and barFalling then
            score : = score + 2;
        if not (isRaining or feelsLikeRain) and barRising then
            score : = score − 2;
        DetermineScore : = score
    end;

    procedure MakePrediction (score: integer);
    {Use the value of score to make a guess about the weather.}
    {The higher the value, the more likely rain is.              }
    begin
        case score of
            −2, −1, 0:
                writeln('No chance of rain . . . put the top down!');
            1, 2:
                writeln('Slight chance of rain . . . save your rain check. ');
            3, 4:
                writeln('Good chance of rain . . . bring your umbrella. ');
            5:
                writeln('Major storm coming . . . build an ark!')
        end
    end;
```

```
begin    {Main}
    Introduction;
    AskQuestions(feelsLikeRain, isRaining, barFalling, barRising, barSteady, rainPredicted, bunionsAche);
    score := DetermineScore(feelsLikeRain, isRaining, barFalling, barRising, barSteady, rainPredicted,
                                bunionsAche);
    MakePrediction(score)
end.
```

4.5 Problem Solving III: Analyzing the **if** Statement

We've referred to the **if** statement several times already, so it should come as no surprise that it is used to control whether or not a group of statements will be executed, depending on the value of a boolean expression. Syntactically, the **if** statement comes in two forms: the simple **if** and the **if..else**. Figure 4.2 shows the syntax of these two variants.

You can probably figure out what these statements do just by looking at their syntax. In each, the boolean expression is evaluated; if the expression evaluates to *true*, the statement after the **then** is executed, and control then passes to the statement after the **if** statement. If the boolean expression of a simple **if** evaluates to *false*, the **if** statement passes control to whatever follows it. If the boolean expression of an **if..else** statement is false, whatever follows the **else** is executed, and then control is passed to the next statement.

These **if** statements are the first examples you've seen of *structured statements*, which is to say, statements that monitor the action of other statements. The action controlled by an **if** statement, for example, may very well consist of several statements, such as

```
if numberOfSides = 2 then
    begin
        writeln('You haven''t entered enough data yet');
        writeln('to determine a triangle.');
        write('Please enter another side length : ');
        readln(sideLength);
        numberOfSides := numberOfSides + 1
    end;
```

Way back in Figure 1.2, we indicated that a statement in Pascal can be either a simple statement or a collection of statements grouped within a **begin..end** pair. Now at long last we see why Pascal permits this grouping. In the preceding example, there is a single statement that is executed if the boolean expression *numberOfSides* = 2 is true. That the statement to be executed also consists of four

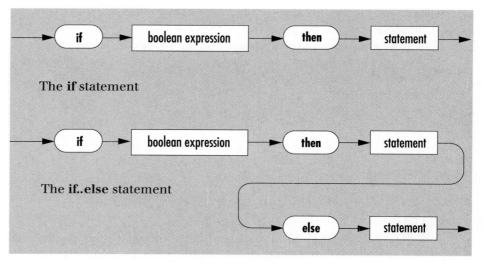

The **if** statement

The **if..else** statement

Figure 4.2.   Syntax diagrams for the **if** and **if..else** statements

procedure calls and an assignment statement is immaterial here. Pascal expects an **if** statement to contain a single statement after the reserved word **then**, and that's exactly what the **begin..end** pair indicates. This is an important feature of modern languages. In many languages of the old days, statements couldn't be grouped, so the clauses of an **if** or **if..else** statement could be only one simple statement. It doesn't take much imagination to see how limiting that would be.

If you are in the habit of automatically including a semicolon after every statement, you'll have to unlearn that habit when using the **if** statements. You'll notice that the syntax diagrams in Figure 4.2 don't have any semicolons, and if you put them in where they don't belong, you'll be asking for confusion at best, and disaster in some cases. Here are two common errors. Before you continue past them, see if you can figure out what would happen in each case. Remember, a semicolon is a statement separator; it signals the end of one statement and the beginning of another.

```
if number > 1e + 34 then ;     probable error: a semicolon after then
    writeln('That''s a big number!');
```

```
if sample > 0 then
    writeln('Positive number');     certain error: a semicolon before else
else
    writeln('Negative or zero')
```

•   •   •

Got it? In the first example, the *writeln* would be executed no matter what the value of *number* was, since the semicolon signals the end of the **if** statement.

If *number* was large, the **then** clause would be executed, but in this case that's just the empty statement, and control would pass to the *writeln*. On the other hand, if *number* was not large, the empty **then** clause would be skipped over, and control would still pass to the *writeln* statement.[6]

While there's nothing syntactically wrong with the first example, the next one has a problem so severe that it would make compilation impossible. In the second example, the semicolon is interpreted, as usual, as separating two statements, but the result is the two "statements"

   if sample $>$ 0 **then** writeln('Positive number')

and

   else writeln('Negative or zero')

While the first statement is perfectly acceptable (it conforms to the format of a simple **if** statement), there is no Pascal statement that may legally begin with the word **else**. The only things we know so far that can begin a statement are variables (in an assignment statement), procedure names (in a procedure call), and the word **if**. Since **else** is a reserved word, it couldn't be used as the name of anything we can define in a program, like variable or procedure names.

It is legal to place a semicolon after **then** (but there's almost never a good reason to do so). It is a syntax error to put a semicolon before **else**.[7]

4.6 Using Conditionals

The Program in Progress uses a sequence of **if** statements in the section that computes the value of *score* — the likelihood that it will rain.

---

[6]Some Pascal environments automatically format source code for you. In some such environments, the peculiar but not illegal construction of the first example would be made more obvious by being written

   if number $>$ 1e $+$ 34 **then**
      ;
   writeln('That''s a big number!')

[7]Or after **if** or before **then**, for the same reasons.

```
score := 0;
if feelsLikeRain then
    score := score + 1;
if bunionsAche then
    score := score + 2;
if isRaining and barSteady then
    score := score + 1;
if rainPredicted and barFalling then
    score := score + 2;
if not (isRaining or feelsLikeRain) and barRising then
    score := score − 2;
```

Look at the first **if** statement. If the boolean variable *feelsLikeRain* is *true*, the clause *score* := *score* + 1 will be executed, increasing *score* by 1. Notice that *feelsLikeRain* is set earlier in the program by the assignment statement

```
feelsLikeRain := (response = 'y');
```

This probably looks a bit peculiar at first, but if you understand what is going on, you can take comfort in having mastered the difference between the assignment operator := and the boolean comparison operator =. The variable *response* is a character variable, so we can compare it with the character constant 'y'. If *response* is 'y', the test for equality is *true*, and if *response* is any other character, the comparison is *false*. In other words, the right-hand part of the assignment statement (*response* = 'y') is a boolean expression that is evaluated and used to set the value of the boolean variable *feelsLikeRain*. We could have used another **if** statement to set the value of *feelsLikeRain*:

```
if response = 'y' then
    feelsLikeRain := true
else
    feelsLikeRain := false;
```

This has exactly the same effect as *feelsLikeRain* := (*response* = 'y'), but the assignment statement version saves keystrokes and is common enough that we didn't feel like hackers by using a somewhat less transparent method. We should mention here that the assignment *feelsLikeRain* := (*response* = 'y') leaves room for a potential logic error. Remember that the character 'y' and the character 'Y' are different, so if *response* was 'Y', *feelsLikeRain* would be set to *false*, which is certainly not what was intended. A much better assignment would be

```
feelsLikeRain := (response = 'y') or (response = 'Y')
```

The other four simple **if** statements are then executed in turn, increasing or decreasing the value of *score* as determined by the boolean expressions. Each of the five **if** statements is executed in this case, which is not the case with the more complex statement that appears earlier.

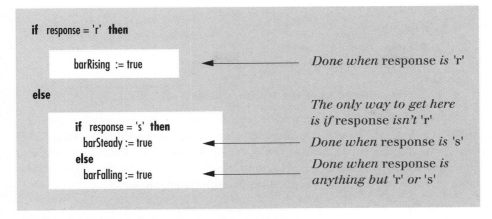

```
if  response = 'r'  then
        barRising := true                    ← Done when response is 'r'

else
                                             The only way to get here
                                             is if response isn't 'r'
        if  response = 's'  then
            barSteady := true                ← Done when response is 's'
        else
            barFalling := true               ← Done when response is
                                               anything but 'r' or 's'
```

Figure 4.3.   Nested **if..else** statements

```
if response  =  'r' then
    barRising : = true
else if response  =  's' then
    barSteady : = true
else
    barFalling : = true
```

This is syntactically a single **if..else** statement, one that contains an **if..else** statement as its **else** clause. Pictorially, we would view it as in Figure 4.3. The indentations of Figure 4.3 make the structure of the statement clear, but not all Pascal environments handle these indentations automatically for you. This means that you'll have to be careful when an **if** statement contains another **if** statement as one of its clauses.

There are, in fact, times when a complex **if** statement even seems as if it may be open to two interpretations. Consider for a moment a syntactically simpler statement, written without indentations.

if *B1* **then if** *B2* **then** *S1* **else** *S2*

This "dangling **else**" could be interpreted in two ways:

```
if B1 then
    if B2 then      {Done if B1 is true}
        S1          {So this is done only when B1 and B2 are true}
    else
        S2          {And this is done only when B1 is true and B2 is false}
```

or

```
if B1 then
    if B2 then    {Done if B1 is true}
        S1        {So this is done only when B1 and B2 are true}
else
    S2            {But this is done when B1 is false, regardless of B2}
```

There's no obvious reason for Pascal to prefer one interpretation over the other, even though the two interpretations have different semantic readings and, thus, present different problems to compiler designers. This is similar to the ambiguity in the expression $2 + 3 * 4$ and is handled by Pascal in the same way: by more or less arbitrarily choosing what the interpretation will be.

> **P**ascal interprets **if..else** statements so that every **else** clause is matched to the nearest **if** clause preceding it that has not already been matched with an **else**.

With this convention, it is clear that the first of the two preceding interpretations is the one that Pascal would use—the **else** S2 clause would be considered to be paired as part of the nearest unmatched **if** statement, namely, the **if** B2 **then** S1 part. If we wanted to force the second interpretation, we could indicate to the compiler that the inner **if** statement had no **else** part by bracketing the inner statement within a **begin..end** pair, such as in the example below (just as we would force a different evaluation in an arithmetic expression by using parentheses).

```
if B1 then
    begin
        if B2 then
            S1
    end    {This concludes the inner if statement,        }
else        {so this else can be matched only with the outer if.}
    S2
```

Practicing Safe Computing

The fact that we can use any statement as a clause of an **if** statement is very handy, particularly in cases when we need to *guard* another statement. Suppose that we needed to make the assignment statement *avg* := *sum* / *num*. This statement looks simple enough, and it will work just fine as long as *num* isn't zero, but it contains a hidden trap. If *num* happens to be zero at the time of execution, division by zero isn't defined, and the program will halt in error at that stage, perhaps reporting "Attempted division by zero." A good program is *robust*, which is to say that it handles errors in such a way as to avoid crashing. In this situation, we could modify the program by guarding the assignment statement with an **if** statement:

```
if num <> 0 then      Here's where we guard the assignment.
   avg := sum / num
else
   begin
      writeln('No values entered, so average is undefined');
      avg := 0   {a dummy value}
   end
```

Now, even if *num* is zero, the program will continue without crashing.

We often use a guard to protect against operator error, too. If a grade-keeping program is supposed to get test scores in the range 0–100, we want to make sure that the operator enters numbers that are in the expected range. A possible guarded input statement might look like this:

```
readln(score);
if (score < 0) or (score > 100) then
   begin
      writeln(score : 1, ' Is not in the right range.');
      write('Please enter a number in the range 0 .. 100 : ');
      readln(score)
   end
```

While this doesn't completely protect against operator error,[8] it is certainly better than blindly accepting any input that is offered.

It's not paranoid to think the world's out to get you if it truly is. Assume that the worst will happen, and guard against all the errors you can think of.

---

[8]What happens, for example, if the operator makes two consecutive input errors? We need to check repeatedly for numbers in the right range, and we'll see how to do that in the next chapter and in the exercises for this chapter.

Let's look more closely at guards. We've been talking about a hypothetical grade-keeping program in which the user enters several scores, and the program computes the average of all the scores entered. Part of the program might include a section that reports the average and writes a message if the average is below a particular range. Our first thought might be to use a statement like

```
if sum / num < 60 then
    writeln('This student is in trouble.')
```

We've seen enough by now to know that we should guard against the possibility of division by zero, so we might think of including the guard in the boolean expression, like this:

```
if (num <> 0) and (sum / num < 60) then
    writeln('This student is in trouble.')
```

The only problem with this is that we can't be sure that it will work. The boolean expression p **and** q is *true* only when both p and q are true. If p is *false*, we really don't even need to look at q—we know the expression will be *false*, regardless of the value of q. We might, then, expect that as soon as *num* is found to be zero, the whole expression will be known to be *false*, and the part that checks *sum / num* < 60 will be passed over as redundant in this case. That's what some languages do, using what are known as "conditional **and**" and "conditional **or**," and it's also a feature of some Pascal compilers, but the standard stipulates that you can't count on it.

> **T**he Pascal standard makes no stipulation about the order in which the clauses of an **and** or **or** connective are evaluated. Don't assume that your compiler is smart enough to quit evaluating an expression when enough information is known. Assume that your compiler evaluates all logical clauses completely.

In the preceding example, for instance, it might happen that even though *num* is determined to be zero, the computer will still try to evaluate *sum / num*, which in this case would lead to a division-by-zero error. A better way to guard the original **if** statement would be with a separate nested statement, such as

```
if (num <> 0) then
    if (sum / num < 60) then
        writeln('This student is in trouble.')
```

More on Nested **if** Statements

We could expand the grade-reporting part of our example to print letter grade equivalents by using a "waterfall" of nested **if..else** statements.

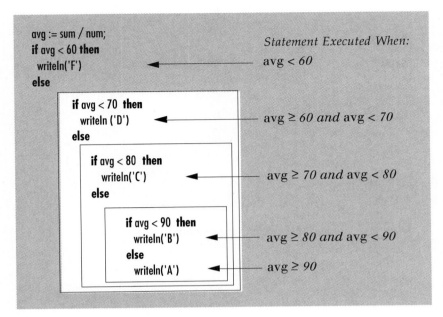

Figure 4.4.   A waterfall of nested **if..else** statements

```
avg : = sum / num;      We do this first to avoid recomputing sum / num every time.
if avg < 60 then
    writeln('F')
else if avg < 70 then
    writeln('D')
else if avg < 80 then
    writeln('C')
else if avg < 90 then
    writeln('B')
else              Do you see why we don't need an if here?
    writeln('A')
```

In such an arrangement, each **if** statement is executed only if none of the previous boolean conditions are true. If *avg* = 75, for instance, the first boolean expression is false, so control passes to the **else** part, which checks whether *avg* < 70. This is also false, so control passes to the next **else** part, which checks whether *avg* < 80. This is true, so 'C' is written, and control passes completely over any subsequent **else** clauses. To make this clear, Figure 4.4 shows the same statement with inclusion of substatements indicated by indentation.

When using nested **if..else** statements, we have to be careful of the order in which we use the boolean expressions. Each successive boolean condition must be true for at least all the cases that were true in the preceding condition. If that's

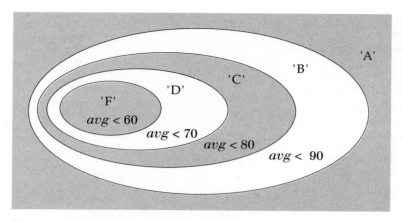

Figure 4.5.   Truth sets for successive boolean expressions in nested
if..else statements should also be nested

too much of a mouthful, look at the following example. First, consider the nested
if..else statements in Figure 4.4. Now consider what would happen if we mixed
up the order of the **if** statements in our grade-writing example. Trace through the
following rearranged code, and see how it responds to various values of *avg*.

```
if avg < 60 then
    writeln('F')
else if avg < 90 then
    writeln('B')
else if avg < 70 then
    writeln('D')
else if avg < 80 then
    writeln('C')
else
    writeln('A')
```

If *avg* is 63, for instance, the segment would write B, because the second **if**
statement's boolean condition is satisfied by 63. The student with a 63 would
undoubtedly be very pleased with this logic error, since he or she deserved only a
D, but it's probably not what the program design called for. The reason this error
happened, of course, is that not enough filtering took place. Before we ever got to
the weak comparison *avg* < 90 to find the B grades, we should have taken care of
all the cases that resulted in grades lower than B.

We could explain this in terms of Figure 4.5 by saying that the cases we are
interested in are in the rings formed by the regions. If we are working our way out

from the interior, we must arrange the statements in the order we encounter them on our journey to eliminate each region in turn.

In a related vein, what would happen to our example if we removed the nesting and wrote the following?

```
if avg < 60 then
    writeln('F');
if avg < 70 then
    writeln('D');
if avg < 80 then
    writeln('C');
if avg < 90 then
    writeln('B')
else
    writeln('A')
```

Now things are even worse. A person with an average of 63 gets a grade of 'DCB', on three lines since each **if** statement is executed in turn. This is also a common error, but now at least you should be able to recognize its cause when such multiple selections happen to you.

4.7 The **case** Statement

Another method for handling mutually exclusive conditions that makes use of another Pascal statement is illustrated in the Program in Progress. The procedure *MakePrediction* writes one of four different messages, depending on whether the value of *score* is in the sets $\{-2, -1, 0\}$, $\{1, 2\}$, $\{3, 4\}$, or $\{5\}$. We could use nested **if..else** statements to do this, as follows:

```
if (score = -2) or (score = -1) or (score = 0) then
    writeln('No chance of rain . . . put the top down!')
else if (score = 2) or (score = 1) then
    writeln('Slight chance of rain . . . save your rain check.')
else if (score = 3) or (score = 4) then
    writeln('Good chance of rain . . . bring your umbrella.')
else
    writeln('Major storm coming . . . build an ark!')
```

Pascal provides a more compact way to write such multiple selections: the **case** statement. The **case** statement evaluates an expression of an *ordinal* type, such as integer, character, or boolean, and uses that value to determine which of several statements is to be executed. Compare the preceding **if..else** statement with its analogous **case** version.

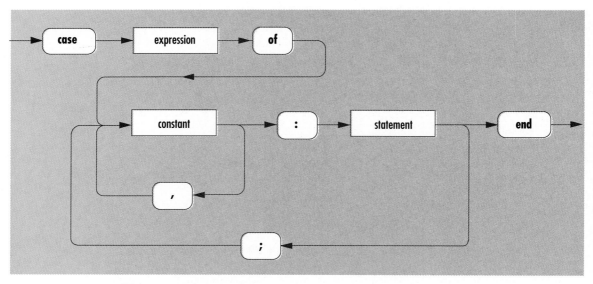

Figure 4.6.   Syntax diagram of the **case** statement

```
case score of
    −2, −1, 0:
        writeln('No chance of rain . . . put the top down!');
    1, 2:
        writeln('Slight chance of rain . . . save your rain check. ');
    3, 4:
        writeln('Good chance of rain . . . bring your umbrella. ');
    5:
        writeln('Major storm coming . . . build an ark!')
end
```

This **case** version is certainly easier to read than the analogous **if..else** version (and when compiled it may run faster, too), and that's why **case** statements are included in Pascal. We can do without the **case** statement, since its action can always be duplicated by a waterfall of nested **if..else** statements, and there are things we can do with the waterfall that we can't do in a **case** statement. One of the design goals of Pascal, though, was to make programs easier to read, and **case** statements certainly do that.

Figure 4.6 illustrates the syntax of the **case** statement. It's certainly one of the most intimidating syntax diagrams you've seen so far, but it's not too bad if you break it into its components: (1) the *header*, consisting of the reserved word **case**, followed by an expression (which, given what we know now, can be of integer, character, or boolean type, but *not* real, (2) a collection of *case lists*, each of which consists of a list of constants separated by commas, followed by a colon and a statement, ending with (3) the reserved word **end**, serving an extra duty here as the terminator of the statement. The case lists are separated from each other by semicolons, just as ordinary statements are.

There are a few cautions to be noted about the **case** statement. First, the constant lists may not have any overlaps, since it is the intention of the **case** statement to perform exactly one of its case list statements, no matter what the value of the expression that appears in the header. The second point is closely related to the first. Every possible value of the header expression must appear in one and only one constant list. The **case** statement is not equipped to handle the situation when the value of the expression doesn't match any of the constant values.[9] In cases where you're pretty sure (but not certain) that the expression will never evaluate to anything but one of the case constants, it's a good idea to guard the **case** statement with an **if**, as in

```
if (c = 'A') or (c = 'E') or (c = 'I') or (c = 'O') or (c = 'U') then
   case c of
      'A', 'E', 'I' :
         earlyVowels : = earlyVowels + 1;
      'O' :
         middleVowels : = middleVowels + 1;
      'U' :
         lateVowels : = lateVowels + 1
   end
```

Now, even if the character variable c somehow gets set to a non-vowel, the **case** statement is protected from trying unsuccessfully to match c with one of the constants.

This is particularly helpful in **case** statements that use an integer expression. If we had to have a constant for every possible integer, we would spend all our time typing the thousands of integers that can be represented, especially since we are not allowed to write constant lists in any shortcut form like -32768 .. 0 : *writeln*('Negative').[10] A constant list must be just that: a list of constants, either literals like 3, *true*, or 'B', or user-defined constants that appeared in a **const** declaration, or Pascal constants like *maxint*. This is a good time, too, to restate

---

[9]This is a common area for Pascal extensions. Many compilers allow an **otherwise** clause to be added that takes action if none of the constants are matched, as, for example,

```
case value of
   0 :
      writeln('Divisible by 3');
   1 :
      writeln('Remainder of 1');
   2 :
      writeln('Remainder of 2')
otherwise
   writeln('Something weird happened with value')
end
```

[10]Some compilers allow this.

what we said before: The expressions and constant lists in **case** statements cannot be of *real* type.

Before we leave the **case** statement, there are a few observations and pitfalls to mention. First, the header expression can be any expression at all, as long as it is of the proper type. We could use single variables,[11] complicated integer arithmetic expressions, or function calls. Second, the statement parts of a **case** statement can be as complex as you want them to be, as long as you observe the rules about grouping compound statements with **begin..end** pairs. Third, it should go without saying that the statement parts can consist of any statements: assignment statements, procedure calls, **if** statements, and even other **case** statements. Finally, the **case** statement is the only Pascal statement that has the reserved word **end** as part of its definition. It is a common error to forget the **end**, thereby sending the compiler—and you—into fits of confusion.

*The only other time an **end** may appear without a matching **begin** is in a record declaration, which we'll see in Chapter 10.*

4.8 Reference

- Along with real and integer types, Pascal includes a *boolean* type. Boolean variables, constants, and expressions take the values *true* or *false*.
- There are six *relational operators*: <, >, <=, >=, =, <>, which take two expressions, compare them, and return a boolean value.
- Boolean expressions may be combined by the *boolean operators* **not**, **and**, and **or**.
- The seventeen Pascal operators are grouped into four levels of precedence that control the order in which expressions are evaluated. From highest precedence to lowest, these groups are:

  1. **not**, − (unary minus: negation).
  2. **and**, **div**, **mod**, *, /.
  3. **or**, +, − (binary minus: subtraction).
  4. **in**, =, <>, <, <=, >, >=.

- The **if** statement looks like

  if *boolean expression* **then**
     statement part   {can be any simple or compound statement}

  The action of the **if** statement is as follows:

  1. The boolean expression is evaluated.
  2. If the expression evaluates to *true*, the statement part is executed.
  3. Otherwise, the statement part is not executed.
  4. And in any case, execution then proceeds to the next statement following the **if** statement, if any.

- The **if** statement may have an **else** clause, like this

---

[11]Or even constants, although that would be very peculiar: **case** 3 **of** . . . ?

```
if boolean expression then
    statement1   {done only when expression is true}
else
    statement2   {done only when expression is false}
```

- The **if** statement is a structured statement, which expects a simple or a compound statement (that is, a group enclosed within a **begin..end** pair) immediately after the reserved word **then**.
- It is almost never a good idea to place a semicolon separator after the word **then**.
- It is an error to place a semicolon separator before **else**.
- Along with their other uses to control the execution of statements in a program, **if** statements are commonly used to guard against errors that might crash a program.
- A **case** statement is related logically to an **if..else** statement. It specifies a series of mutually exclusive statements, one of which is chosen for execution based on the value of a single expression. **Case** statements have the form

```
case expression of
    value1: statement1;   {done only when expression = value1}
    value2: statement2;   {done only when expression = value2}
    ⋮
    valuen: statementn    {done only when expression = valuen}
end;
```

When the case selector expression has value i, statement i is the one and only statement executed. In standard Pascal, if the value of the expression matches none of the specified values, a run-time error results.

4.9 Building Blocks

We promised that we'd improve *GetData*. Here it is with a guard against bad input. It gives the user one chance to correct his or her error.

```
procedure GetData(var variable : some type);
begin
    write(Some prompt goes here);
    readln(variable);
    if variable is out of range then
        begin
            writeln(Error message, describing the proper range);
            writeln(Some prompt goes here);
            readln(variable)
        end
end;
```

Of course, *GetData* might get several pieces of information. If, however, it is supposed to get a single datum, it might profitably be written as a function, like this:

```
function NewData : some type;
    var
        variable : same type as return value;
begin
    write(Some prompt goes here);
    readln(variable);
    if variable is out of range then
        begin
            writeln(Error message, describing the proper range);
            writeln(Some prompt goes here);
            readln(variable)
        end;
    NewData : = variable
end;
```

There's a more sophisticated version of this function in the exercises.

When we need to check that a variable v is in the right range, between or equal to the endpoints to the range *low .. high*, we can use a simple boolean function

```
function IsBetween(low, high : some type; v : same type) : boolean;
begin
    IsBetween : = ((low < = v) and (v < = high))
end;
```

For example, we might use this with *NewData*, as

```
function NewData(lowRange, highRange : some type) : same type;
    var
        variable : same type;
begin
    write('Enter a value between ', lowRange : 1, ' and ', highRange : 1, ':');
    readln(variable);
    if not IsBetween(lowRange, highRange, variable) then
        begin
            writeln('Please reenter your value.');
            writeln('Make sure it''s between ', lowRange : 1, ' and ', highRange : 1);
            write('Enter your value now: ');
            readln(variable)
        end;
    NewData : = variable
end;
```

A similar function is designed to ask for a positive or negative response from the user and to return *true* if and only if the user answers 'y' or 'Y'.

```
function PositiveResponse : boolean;
   var
      ans : char;
begin
   write(Put the question here);
   readln(ans);
   if (ans <> 'y') and (ans <> 'Y') and (ans <> 'n') and (ans <> 'N') then
      begin
         writeln('Please limit your response to "y" or "n" (without quotes)');
         write(Put the question here);
         readln(ans)
      end
   PositiveResponse : = (ans = 'y') or (ans = 'Y')
end;
```

A very common use of the **if** statement is as a guard. Suppose that the boolean expression *B* is a necessary precondition for statement *s* to execute without error. In that case, our program should handle the possibility that *B* may be false — and therefore that *S* should not be executed — by doing something like this:

```
if B then
   S
else
   begin
      writeln(Some error message);
      and do whatever is necessary to recover from the error
   end
```

4.10   EXERCISES

Assume n = 3, x = 6.7, c = 'K', *and* p = false. *Evaluate the boolean expressions in Exercises 1 and 2.*

1. a. p and (n <= x)
   b. (c <= 'A') or (2 * n − x < 0)
   c. (c <= 'A') and (2 * n − x < 0)
   d. abs(x) <> n − 8
   e. odd(n) and (not p or (x < 5))
   f. (n < 0) or ((c < 'M') and p)

2. a. p and not (x / 2 < round(x))
   b. not (2 * n − x <= 3)
   c. (trunc(x) = 6) or ('T' <> c)
   d. (x = n) = p
   e. (4 − n >= x) and not (n < n)
   f. (odd(trunc(x))) or ((n = 0) and p)

In Exercises 3 and 4, use parentheses to show how the expressions that are valid would be evaluated. For those that are invalid, explain why. Assume that n *and* m *are integer variables,* c *is a character, and* p *and* q *are boolean.*

3. a. (n = > 0) or p
   b. not 2 * n < m
   c. (n = m) < p
   d. not not not (c = 'G')
   e. (n not > 0) or p
   f. (n < 0) and (c < '0') and p

4. a. p and not q or not p
   b. n > 0 and m
   c. (n := m) or (c >= '0')
   d. not n > 0
   e. odd(n) and odd(m) or p
   f. (n = m) = (c = 'A')

5. Express each of the following sentences as boolean expressions.

   a. *x* is greater than 10.
   b. *temp* is strictly between 3.7 and 3.8.
   c. At least one of *j*, *k*, or *l* is odd.
   d. *j*, *k*, and *l* are all odd.
   e. Exactly one of *index* and *count* is positive.
   f. *theChar* is an uppercase vowel.
   g. *newCharacter* is not a digit character.
   h. $- limit \leq sum < limit$.
   i. *shot* is no farther than 1.5 away from *target*.
   j. *sign* is positive or *x* and *y* are both negative.

6. Verify the distributive laws using truth tables.

7. Verify DeMorgan's laws using truth tables.

8. In the statement $x := (x = x)$, what type must x be? Tell why this is an inefficient statement and provide a simpler, more comprehensible equivalent.

9. In the following statements, there are a number of boxes. Into which boxes could we put a semicolon without causing a syntax error? Of the "legal" boxes, which are most likely to receive semicolons in normal programs?

   a. if ☐ x >= 0 ☐ then ☐
            x := sqrt(x) ☐

   b. if ☐ odd(x) ☐ then ☐
            x := 3 * x + 1 ☐
           else ☐
            x := x div 2 ☐

10. In the statement of Exercise 9b, if you ignore the boxes and perform the statement repeatedly on various values of x, what happens? Try it repeatedly for starting values $x = 32, 7,$ and 25. This is known as *Ulam's function*, and nobody has yet been able to prove that it always reaches 1 for any starting value of x. If you'd like to become famous, you're welcome to try to show that it always does or to find an x for which it never reaches 1.

11. Define a *robust program*, and give an example of how you would improve the robustness of a program.

12. Define the following terms:

   a. Artificial Intelligence
   b. Expert system

13. Using DeMorgan's laws, show that you don't need **and** if you have **not** and **or** available.

14. a. We need to remember that Pascal evaluates expressions in a left-associative way. Demonstrate this by showing that the left-associative evaluation of the expression $5 - 4 - 3, (5 - 4) - 3$, is different from the right-associative way, which would yield $5 - (4 - 3)$.

b. Show by example that it doesn't matter whether + is evaluated left-associative or right-associative.

c. Explain the difference between parts a and b.

15. When we filled in the rows of a three-variable truth table, we used TTT, TTF, TFT, TFF, FTT, FTF, FFT, FFF. Explain the pattern we used, ideally relating it to something we discussed in Chapter 2.

16. Using the result that **and**, **or**, and **not** are sufficient to produce any boolean operator, show that either of the two following boolean operators alone suffice to produce any boolean operator by suitable combinations.

a. The *Sheffer stroke* (also called *nand*, for **n**ot **and**), |, defined by

a	*b*	*a* | *b*
T	T	F
T	F	T
F	T	T
F	F	T

b. The *Pierce arrow*, ↓ (honest, that's what it's called, at least when it's not being called *nor*, for **n**ot **or**), defined by

a	*b*	*a* ↓ *b*
T	T	F
T	F	F
F	T	F
F	F	T

17. This is a somewhat peculiar but perfectly legal statement

```
case height > 75 of
    false : ;
    true : writeln('This is a tall person')
end
```

What is the simplest equivalent that doesn't use a **case** statement?

18. Is the following a legal statement? Whether it's legal or not, what does the compiler do with it?

```
if sqr(b) < 4 * a * c then
    ;
else
    writeln('Negative discriminant. Can"t compute roots')
```

19. Fill in the blanks. We haven't indented the statements so as not to give you extra clues.

```
if n > 1 then
if m < = 0 then
S1    Executed when _____
else
S2    Executed when _____
else
S3    Executed when _____
```

20. Suppose that *B1* and *B2* are boolean expressions and that *S* is a statement. What is the difference between these two statements, if any?

if B1 and B2 then	if B1 then
S	if B2 then
	S

21. Write a **function** *Ordered*(*a*, *b*, *c* : integer) : boolean that returns *true* if *a*, *b*, and *c* are in order, that is, if $a < b < c$, and that returns *false* otherwise.

22. Write a **function** *IsSum*(*a*, *b*, *c* : integer) : boolean that returns *true* if any of the values is equal to the sum of the other two (if, for example, we had $a + b = c$) and that returns *false* otherwise.

23. Write a procedure that determines eligibility for student financial aid. The rules for eligibility are

   1. Count the number of children under age 21 in the family.
   2. If the family income minus $2,500 times the number of children is less than $20,000, then the family is eligible for aid.

The procedure should check for potential errors in its parameters by returning a boolean flag *error*. In particular, *error* should be set to *true* if the income is negative or larger than $10 million, or the number of children is negative or larger than twenty. The procedure header should look like

procedure TestEligibility(income : real ; children : integer ; **var** error, isEligible : boolean);

24. One problem with the grade-keeping segment we showed on page 151 is that the guard for the *readln* statement is performed only once. Ideally, we'd like to guard against repeated operator errors and to keep asking for data in the right range until the operator finally catches on and enters a number in the right range. We can do that right now, using recursion. Recall that a recursive procedure or function is one that can call a copy of itself, and consider the function *GetGrade*:

```
function GetGrade : integer;
    var n : integer;
begin
    write('Enter a number in the range 0 .. 100 :');
    readln(n);
    if (n < 0) or (n > 100) then    {negation of (n > = 0) and (n < = 100)}
        begin
            writeln('OOPS! You goofed.');
            n : = GetGrade        {Call a copy of GetGrade.}
        end;
    GetGrade : = n
end;
```

Trace what happens when *GetGrade* is called and the operator enters −1, then −1 again, then finally 89.

25. The tax rate schedules for the 1990 U.S. federal taxes contain, in part, the following directions for a person filing with single status.

If your taxable income is Over–	But not over–	Enter on form 1040, line 38	of the amount over–
$0	$19,450	.....................15%	$0
19,450	47,050	**$2,917.50 + 28%**	19,450
47,050	97,620	**10,645.50 + 33%**	47,050

a. Write a function that will take as its parameter an amount of taxable income (real) between 0.0 and 97620.0 and will return the tax payment to be entered on line 38 of Form 1040. If the amount is not in the range 0.0 to 97620.0, the function should write an appropriate error message and return -1.0.

b. Is the tax rate schedule *continuous*, that is, does the tax that must be paid make a smooth transition between 19,450.0 and 19,450.01 and between 47,050.0 and 47,050.01?

26. Rewrite the PIP for this chapter using the building block function *PositiveResponse* where appropriate.

27. In a quadratic equation, such as $ax^2 + bx + c = 0$, we are given three real coefficients, a, b, and c, and are to find the values of x that make the equation true. The nature of the solution depends on the coefficients as follows:

If $a = 0$ and $b \neq 0$, there is one solution.

If $a = 0$ and $b = 0$, then there are no solutions if $c \neq 0$, and all x values are solutions if $c = 0$.

If $a \neq 0$, let d denote $(b^2 - 4ac)$. If $d < 0$, then there are two complex solutions. If $d = 0$, then there are two equal real solutions. If $d > 0$, then there are two unequal real solutions.

a. Write a program that will read three coefficients, and describe the type of solutions that the corresponding quadratic equation will have.

b. Extend part a so that the program displays the solution(s), where appropriate.

28. Rewrite the *SnowPerson* PIP from Chapter 3 to make it more robust.

4.11
Answers

1. a. False
   b. True
   c. False
   d. True
   e. True
   f. False

3. a. (n => 0) or p   *Invalid; the token should be $<=$ or $>=$*
   b. ((**not** 2) * n) < m   *Invalid; can't perform* **not** *2*
   c. (n = m) < p   *Valid, but strange. True only when* n $\neq$ m *and* p *is* true.
   d. **not** (**not** (**not** (c = 'G')))   *Valid*
   e. (n **not** > 0) or p   *Invalid; compiler would attempt to evaluate "**not** $>$"*
   f. ((n < 0) **and** (c < '0')) **and** p   *Valid*

5. a. x > 10
   b. (temp > 3.7) **and** (temp < 3.8)
   c. odd(j) **or** odd(k) **or** odd(l)
   d. odd(j) **and** odd(k) **and** odd(l)
   e. ((index > 0) **and** (count <= 0)) **or** ((index <= 0) **and** (count > 0))

   A shorter, but less obvious, way is (index > 0) <> (count > 0)

   f. (theChar = 'A') **or** (theChar = 'E') **or** (theChar = 'I') **or** (theChar = 'O') **or** (theChar = 'U')
   g. (newChar < '0') **or** (newChar > '9')
   h. (−limit <= sum) **and** (sum < limit)
   i. abs(shot − target) <= 1.5
   j. (sign > 0) **or** ((x < 0) **and** (y < 0))

7. We'll do just one here; the other is similar:

a	b	a **and** b	**not** (a **and** b)	**not** a	**not** b	(**not** a) **or** (**not** b)
T	T	T	F	F	F	F
T	F	F	T	F	T	T
F	T	F	T	T	F	T
F	F	F	T	T	T	T

In both parts, the result column on the right is the same (F, T, T, T), so we've proved that **not**(a **and** b) is equivalent to (**not** a) **or** (**not** b).

9. We've darkened the boxes where we could legally place a semicolon. In each statement, the last box is the one most likely to receive a semicolon in practice.

   a. **if** ☐ x >= 0 ☐ **then** ■
        x := sqrt(x) ■
   b. **if** ☐ odd(x) ☐ **then** ☐
        x := 3 * x + 1 ☐
      else ■
        x := x **div** 2 ■

11. A robust program is tolerant of errors of input or calculation. To make a program more robust, guard (using **if** statements, for example) against every potential error you can think of.

13. Whenever we need p **and** q, just use **not**((**not** p) **or** (**not** q))

15. The leftmost column goes T, F, T, . . . , the next goes T, T, F, F, . . . , and so on, with each column taking twice as long to change values as the one on its right. If we represent T as 1 and F as 0, we are counting down in binary.

17. **if** height > 75 **then**
        writeln('This is a tall person')

19. We've indented these as they should be:

   if n > 1 **then**
      if m <= 0 **then**
         S1   *Executed when*   (n > 1) **and** (m ≤ 0)
      else
         S2   *Executed when*   (n > 1) **and** (m > 0)
   else
      S3   *Executed when*   (n ≤ 1)

21. function Ordered(a, b, c : integer) : boolean;
    begin
        if (a < b) **and** (b < c) **then**
            Ordered : = true
        else
            Ordered : = false
    end;

There's a shorter way to write this:

function Ordered(a, b, c : integer) : boolean;
begin
   Ordered : = (a < b) **and** (b < c)
end;

23. procedure TestEligibility(income : real ; children : integer ;
                         var error, isEligible : boolean);
    begin
        error : = false;
        if (income < 0) **or** (income > 1e7) **then**
            error : = true
        else if (children < 0) **or** (children > 20) **then**
            error : = true
        else
            isEligible : = ((income − 2500.0 * children) < 20000.0)
    end;

25. a. function TaxAmount(income : real) : real;
        const
            BREAK1 = 19450.00;
            BREAK2 = 47050.00;
            UPPERLIMIT = 97620.00;
            RATE1 = 0.15;
            RATE2 = 0.28;
            RATE3 = 0.33;
            BASE2 = 2917.50;
            BASE3 = 10645.50;
        begin
            if (income < 0) **or** (income > UPPERLIMIT) **then**
                begin
                    writeln('Error in function TaxAmount.');
                    writeln('Income must be between 0 and ', UPPERLIMIT : 7 : 1);
                    TaxAmount : = −1.0
                end
            else if income < = BREAK1 **then**
                TaxAmount : = RATE1 * income
            else if income < = BREAK2 **then**
                TaxAmount : = BASE2 + (income − BREAK1) * RATE2
            else
                TaxAmount : = BASE3 + (income − BREAK2) * RATE3
        end;

    b. Yes. We don't have to run the function to observe that $2,917.50 = 0.15 * $19,450, and $10,645.50 = $2,917.50 + 0.28 * ($47,050 − $19,450).

27. In the outline for this program, we separated the solution into two parts: the part that computes the solutions to the linear equation $bx + c = 0$ (when $a = 0$) and the part that computes the solution to the quadratic equation (when $a \neq 0$). The outline looks like this:

> **I.** Call **procedure** *GetData*. IN: nothing, OUT: the coefficients a, b, c (real). Explain the program, and get the coefficients.
>
> **II.** If $a = 0$, then call **procedure** *SolveLinear*. IN: b, c coefficients (real), OUT: nothing. If $b \neq 0$, then there's a single solution, else if ($b = 0$ and $c = 0$), then any number is a solution, else ($b = 0$ and $c = 0$), there is no solution.
>
> **III.** If $a \neq 0$, then call **procedure** *SolveQuadratic*. IN: a, b, c coefficients (real), OUT: nothing.
>
> > **A.** Compute *discriminant* $= b^2 - 4ac$ (real).
> >
> > **B.** If *discriminant* $= 0$, then there are two equal real solutions.
> >
> > **C.** Else if *discriminant* > 0, then there are two unequal real solutions.
> >
> > **D.** Else (*discriminate* < 0), there are two complex solutions.

We've folded the answers to parts a and b of this problem together — the only differences between the two parts are labeled by the comment (****(b)****).

program Quad(input, output);

```
{————————————————————————————————————————————————}
{                                                                          }
{              Solves a quadratic equation.                                }
{              INPUT:    coefficients (three reals)                        }
{              OUTPUT:   messages about the nature of the solutions.       }
{                                                                          }
{              NOTE:   Because of internal roundoff, this will not always  }
{              produce the correct solutions. This is particularly apparent}
{              when the two solutions are very close in value (try it for  }
{              a = 1, b = −6.001, and c = 9.003, which should have         }
{              solutions x = 3.001 and 3).                                 }
{————————————————————————————————————————————————}
```

var
    a, b, c: real;   {coefficients of x^2, x, 1, respectively}

procedure GetData (**var** a, b, c: real);
{Get the coefficients of the quadratic equation.}
begin
    writeln('This program solves the quadratic equation');
    writeln;
    writeln('   a * x^2 + b * x + c = 0');
    writeln;
    writeln('Enter the values of the coefficients a, b, and c. ');
    writeln;
    write('Coefficients? ');
    readln(a, b, c);
    writeln
end;

```
    procedure SolveLinear (b, c: real);
    {Solves the linear equation b * x + c = 0.}
    begin
        writeln('For the equation ', b : 9 : 4, '* x + ', c : 9 : 4, ' = 0,');

        if b <> 0 then
            writeln('there is a single solution: x = ', −c / b : 9 : 4)    (****(b)****)
        else if c = 0 then
            writeln('Any real number is a solution.')
        else
            writeln('There is no solution.')
    end;

    procedure SolveQuadratic (a, b, c: real);
    {Solves the quadratic equation a * x^2 + b * x + c = 0.}
    {Assumes a ≠ 0.                                        }
        var
            discriminant: real;
    begin
        discriminant := sqr(b) − 4 * a * c;
        writeln('For the equation ', a : 9 : 4, 'x^2 + ', b : 9 : 4, '* x + ', c : 9 : 4, ' = 0,');

        if discriminant = 0 then
            begin
                writeln('there are two identical real solutions:')
                writeln(' x = ', −b / (2 * a) : 9 : 4)    (****(b)****)
            end
        else if discriminant > 0 then
            begin
                writeln('there are two real solutions:');
                writeln('   x = ', (−b + sqrt(discriminant)) / (2 * a) : 9 : 4);    (****(b)****)
                writeln('   x = ', (−b − sqrt(discriminant)) / (2 * a) : 9 : 4)    (****(b)****)
            end
        else
            begin
                writeln('there are two complex solutions:');
                (****(b)****)
                writeln('   x = ', −b / (2 * a) : 9 : 4, '+', sqrt(abs(discriminant)) / (2 * a) : 9 : 4, 'i');
                writeln('   x = ', −b / (2 * a) : 9 : 4, '−', sqrt(abs(discriminant)) / (2 * a) : 9 : 4, 'i')
            end
    end;
begin
    GetData(a, b, c);
    if a = 0 then
        SolveLinear(b, c)
    else
        SolveQuadratic(a, b, c)
end.
```

5

Do It Again, and Again: for, **while**, and **repeat** Loops

In Chapter 4, we saw that we can use **if** and **case** statements to vary the order of execution of a program, based on information about the state of a program's variables at run-time. When you are writing many programs, though, it quickly becomes obvious that it would be very helpful to be able to repeat a sequence of statements several times, something that we can't do (at least not easily) with what we've seen so far. Fortunately, Pascal provides us with three different ways to perform such *loops*, and each method will be investigated in this chapter. Once you know how to use loops, you will know essentially all you need to describe any kind of algorithm. In Chapter 7, we'll return to a more detailed discussion of functions and procedures, and your collection of algorithm building blocks will be complete. After that, we'll devote the rest of the text to managing the data that algorithms act on. Then you'll know all there is to know about Pascal.

O B J E C T I V E S

In this chapter, we will:

- Demonstrate the need for iteration in programming.
- Review the PIP for this chapter, a program that approximates the value of pi using numerical analysis techniques.
- Define the syntax and semantics of Pascal's **for**, **while**, and **repeat** statements.

- Provide a variety of examples of Pascal loops.
- Describe common programming errors when using loops and ways to avoid them.
- Add to our problem-solving techniques some valuable tools to help design loops correctly, and test that they work as they should.

5.1 Why Do We Need Loops?

Suppose we wished to write a routine that would compute the average of three integers entered by the user. One way to do it would be as follows:

```
sum : = 0;
writeln('When asked for a value, enter an integer and then press Return.');

write('Value 1?');
readln(n);   {Get the first integer.}
sum : = sum + n;
write('Value 2?');
readln(n);   {Get the second integer.}
sum : = sum + n;
write('Value 3?');
readln(n);   {Get the third integer.}
sum : = sum + n;

writeln('The average is ', sum / 3)
```

That's not too bad, but suppose we had to compute the average of one hundred integers—the modified code would require 303 statements! What we need is a way to do something like this

```
sum : = 0;
writeln('When asked for a value, enter an integer and then press Return.');
```
Execute one hundred times everything from here ...
```
    write('Value ', i : 1);
    read(n);
    sum : = sum + n
```
down to here, using i = 1, 2, 3, . . . 100.
```
writeln('The average is ', sum / 100)
```

Fortunately, Pascal provides us with just the mechanism we need to do this repetition: the **for** statement. The **for** statement causes a statement or group of statements to be executed a specified number of times, determined by a variable like *i* above:

```
sum : = 0
writeln('When asked for a value, enter an integer and then press Return.');
```

```
for i : = 1 to 100 do
   begin
      write('Value ', i : 1);
      read(n);
      sum : = sum + n
   end;
writeln('The average is ', sum / 100)
```

As powerful as the **for** statement is, there are situations when we simply don't know in advance how many times we want to execute a statement or group of statements. Suppose, for example, we wanted to find the first positive value x for which a function $f(x)$ was negative. We decide that we'll test f for values $x = 0.01$, 0.02, 0.03, and so on. We know that we want to repeatedly increase x and stop increasing x as soon as $f(x) < 0.0$, but we have no idea how many increments it will take, so we can't use a **for** statement. Pascal's **while** statement is just what we need—it keeps executing its statements until some boolean condition is *false*, as follows:

```
x : = 0.01;
while f(x) > = 0.0 do
   x : = x + 0.01;
{We leave the loop and get here when f(x) < 0.0.}
write('The first negative value of f occurs at x = ', x : 10 : 3)
```

Closely related to the **while** statement is the **repeat** statement. A **repeat** statement executes other statements until a boolean condition is *true*. In the following example, the **repeat** loop continues to read temperature values (from some sensor, for example) until it receives three consecutive values that are over 200. Once this has happened, the program leaves the loop and invokes a user-defined procedure that sounds an alarm.

```
consecutiveHighs : = 0;
repeat
   read(temperature);
   if temperature > 200.0 then
      consecutiveHighs : = consecutiveHighs + 1   {Increment the counter.}
   else
      consecutiveHighs : = 0                      {Reset the counter.}
until consecutiveHighs = 3;
{We leave the loop and get here when we've seen three consecutive high temperatures.}
SoundAlarm
```

In each of our three examples, we've used loops to repeat execution of a collection of statements. Each example could be done without Pascal's loop statements, but the results would be far more difficult to write and very hard to understand. In what's to come, we'll look at **for, while,** and **repeat** loops in detail and see how powerful and useful they are.

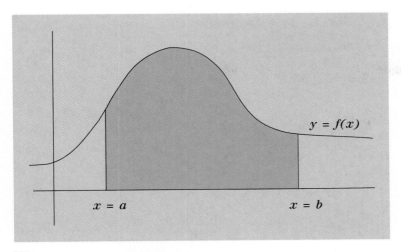

Figure 5.1.   Finding the area under a curve

5.2

Computer Science Interlude: Numerical Analysis

The Program in Progress for this chapter needs a bit of explanation. It falls in the area of *numerical analysis*, the machine implementation of numerical calculations. The PIP finds the area of a quarter circle of radius 1 and in so doing, makes approximations of π. Recall that the area of a circle of radius r is given by the formula πr^2, so that finding the area of a quarter circle of radius 1 will give a value for $\pi / 4$. You might argue that we already know the value of π, so writing a program to find the value is pointless.[1] How do we know the value, though? Somebody had to find approximations to π in the first place, and it is valuable to see how such approximations are discovered. In addition, knowing approximations to π ahead of time allows us to investigate the behavior of our program and to verify that it works as it should.

The essential idea of the Program in Progress is to find an approximation to the area under a curve $y = f(x)$, between the limits $x = a$ and $x = b$, as in Figure 5.1. Those of you with some calculus experience might recognize this as *numerical integration*. In the old precomputer days, this problem could have been solved by a

[1]In fact, we *don't* know the value of π and never will. The constant π is an irrational number, which means that its decimal expansion is of unlimited length and nonrepeating. In a sense, we "know" the values of rational numbers like 1/3, since their decimal values repeat and so can be described in finitely many terms: "1/3 = 0.333 . . . and all subsequent digits are 3," but such a simple description doesn't exist for π. We know that π begins 3.14159265358979323846264633 . . . and we know the next two hundred million or so digits, but we'll never know more than a negligibly small fraction of all its digits.

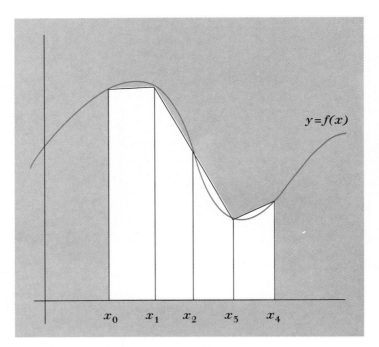

Figure 5.2.   Trapezoidal approximation of area

wonderfully clever device called a *planimeter*: After making a careful picture of the region whose area we wished to find, we would trace the border with a pointer attached to the planimeter, and gears would spin, wheels would turn, and finally we could read the area of the figure from a dial. Nowadays, though, we can rely on a much more accurate machine and use the computer to produce a "virtual" planimeter that we can use to find areas.

We may approximate the area under a curve by calculating the area of a collection of *trapezoids*, that is, four-sided figures with two parallel sides. As you can see in Figure 5.2, it seems reasonable that using trapezoids of successively smaller width should provide successively closer approximations to the true area, and indeed that's the case for a large variety of curves. In fact, as long as the boundary curve is fairly well behaved (without too many discontinuities and with no regions where the curve increases or decreases without limit), the trapezoidal approximation does indeed get closer to the actual area as the width of the trapezoids decreases.[2]

[2]In theory, that is. In practice, the closeness of the approximation depends on many factors such as machine accuracy and accumulated error due to rounding off values to fit the number of bits allowed for representation of real numbers. A large body of scholarship in numerical analysis is devoted to what can go on at the slippery edge between theory and practice. We'll explore the topics of accuracy and round-off error in the lab.

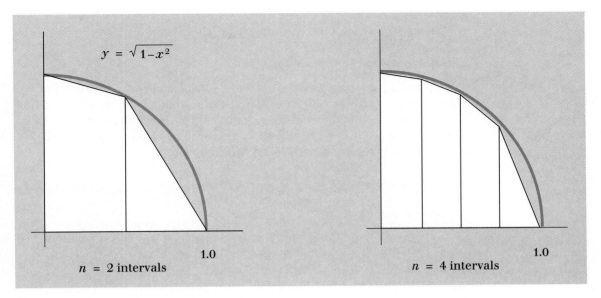

$y = \sqrt{1-x^2}$

$n = 2$ intervals   1.0

$n = 4$ intervals   1.0

Figure 5.3. Approximating the area under a circle

5.3
Problem Solving I: Designing the PIP

Now that we understand one form of numeric integration, we can begin to design our program. We want to use trapezoids to approximate the area under a quarter circle, bounded above by the curve $y = \sqrt{1 - x^2}$, on the left by the y-axis, and below by the x-axis, as illustrated in Figure 5.3.

INPUT: n (integer), the number of trapezoids we'll use for the approximation.

OUTPUT: The total area of the n trapezoids under the curve $y = \sqrt{1 - x^2}$.

ALGORITHM: Compute the area of each trapezoid in turn, adding them all as we go.

5.4
Problem Solving II: Developing the PIP

The first pass at the program is, as usual, a very rough approximation to the finished solution and reflects the three basic steps of input, processing, and output.

I. Get the value of n (integer), the number of trapezoids we'll use.
II. Add the areas of n consecutive trapezoids under the curve
$y = \sqrt{1 - x^2}$.
III. Display the sum of the areas (real).

This is a good example of our problem-solving strategy of breaking down a big problem into smaller ones. Parts I and III of the outline are simple enough to code right away—after all, we've done similar things several times already. There are several tasks within part II, though. Let's look more closely at what's involved. We'll adopt another of our problem-solving techniques.

Problem-solving technique

When breaking a problem down into subproblems, insights can often come from asking yourself, "How would I solve this problem if I had to do it by hand?"

Our guess is that your answer might be something like, "I'd find the area of the leftmost trapezoid, then find the area of the one after that, then the one after that, and so on, until I'd found the area of all of them. Then I'd add up all the answers to get the total approximation." Thinking of similar problems, we recognize that we've seen such summation tasks before. What we can do is keep a running *sum*, and, for each trapezoid, we add its area to *sum* by the statement *sum := sum + (the new area)*.

Notice that our description consists essentially of a list of similar tasks to be repeated one after the other. The fundamental task seems to be "find the area of the i-th trapezoid, and add it to the running sum." What we need (and what Pascal provides for us) is a way to make part II look like this:

II. Add the areas of n consecutive trapezoids under the curve.

A. Initialize *sum* (real) to 0.0.
B. Repeat the following steps, with i (integer) varying from 0 to $n - 1$.[3]

1. Find the area of the i-th trapezoid from the left.
2. Add that area to *sum*.

Problem-solving technique

If a problem has steps that are performed repeatedly, use a loop to control execution of those steps. In the loop, place the part of the task that is common among all repetitions.

[3]Computer scientists often begin counting from zero rather than one. There's a good reason for this, which you'll see shortly.

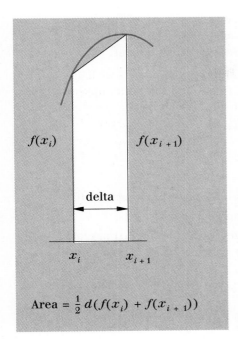

$$f(x_i)$$

$$f(x_{i+1})$$

delta

$$x_i$$

$$x_{i+1}$$

Area $= \frac{1}{2} d(f(x_i) + f(x_{i+1}))$

Figure 5.4.   The area of a trapezoid

We're getting there, but there's still a small problem hiding in the big one —
how do we find the area of the i-th trapezoid in part II.B.1 of our outline? Here we
are likely to rely on the technique of looking up the answer. If we do, we find that
the area of a trapezoid is the width times the average of the heights of the parallel
sides. Now we have two further problems: What is the width of each trapezoid, and
what are the heights of its parallel sides? If we're dividing the region between the
bounds *lower* and *upper* into n equal parts, the width of each trapezoid will clearly
be $((upper - lower) / n)$. Of course, we know that in this problem, we'll always
have *upper* = 1.0 and *lower* = 0.0, but we want to make the trapezoid-finding
routine as general-purpose as possible. Let's call this width *delta*.

Now we can find the area of the i-th trapezoid, as soon as we figure out what
the lengths of its parallel sides are. Look at Figure 5.4 — if the left and right bound-
aries are given by x_i and x_{i+1}, then the heights of the parallel sides under the
curve $y = f(x)$ will just be $f(x_i)$ and $f(x_{i+1})$. The x's will be evenly spaced *delta*
apart, so we'll have $x_0 = lower$, $x_1 = lower + delta$, $x_2 = lower + 2 * delta$, and,
in general, we'll have $x_i = lower + i * delta$.

Our expanded outline for item II.B.1 now looks like this:

1. Find the area of the i-th trapezoid from the left.

    a. Compute the left and right boundaries using i and *delta*.

    b. Compute the area of the trapezoid using the formula for area and the
        values of the circle function.

We're finally done. How do we know? Because we can see clearly how to
code each step in our outline. Of course, we've been writing our program as we go,

using a stub for part II. We elected not to make separate subprograms for parts I and III in this case, since each was only a single line long and easy to understand without a descriptive name. Our final outline now looks like this:

I. Get the value of n (integer), the number of trapezoids we'll use.

II. Call **function** *Trapezoid*. IN: n (real), and the limits *upper* and *lower* (reals), OUT: the total area of the n trapezoids (real).

    A. Use **function** f. IN: x (real), OUT: $sqrt(1.0 - sqr(x))$.

    B. Initialize variables.

        1. Set *sum* (real) to 0.0.

        2. Set *delta* (real) to $((upper - lower) / n)$.

    C. Repeat the following steps, with i (integer) varying from 0 to $n - 1$:

        1. Find the area of the i-th trapezoid from the left.

            a. Compute the left and right boundaries of the trapezoid:

                i. Set $lowx = lower + i * delta$.

                ii. Set $highx = lower + (i + 1) * delta$.

            b. Compute the area $0.5 * delta * (f(lowx) + f(highx))$.

        2. Add that area to *sum*.

    D. Have the function return *sum*.

III. Display the sum of the areas (real).

Brief Digression into Problem Solving V: Modifying the PIP

Flushed with the success of being able to repeat a collection of statements in the function *Trapezoid*, we notice during testing that it's a pain to have to rerun our program anew every time we want to try a different value of n. "Why not," we ask ourselves, "enclose the entire program within a big loop, one that keeps running the program over and over, until we tell it we've seen enough?" That's just what we do, using a modification of our building block function that prompts the user for a yes or no answer to a question. The result follows.

The PIP

```
program TrapezoidTest(input, output);
{——————————————————————————}
{                                                            }
{                    PROGRAM IN PROGRESS                      }
{                                                            }
{                         CHAPTER 5                          }
{                                                            }
{      This program uses trapezoidal approximations to the area }
{      under a quarter of a circle to find approximations to pi. }
{      INPUT:      the number of trapezoids to use           }
{      OUTPUT:   the trapezoidal area approximation          }
{                                                            }
{——————————————————————————}
{           SUBPROGRAM LIST                                   }
{           Trapezoid(lower, upper: real; n: integer): real   }
{               f(x : real) : real                           }
{           ReadyToQuit : boolean                            }
{                                                            }
{——————————————————————————}

  var
     n: integer;
     area : real;

  function Trapezoid (lower, upper: real; n: integer): real;
  {Approximates the area under y = f(x) between     }
  {x = lower and x = upper by using n trapezoids. }
     var
        sum,                    {the running sum of the trapezoid areas}
        delta,                  {the width of each trapezoid}
        lowx, highx: real;      {the left and right endpoints of each trapezoid}
        i: integer;

     function f (x : real): real;
     {The graph of this function is the upper half of a circle with given radius.}
        const
           RADIUS = 1;
        begin
          if x > RADIUS then
             f := 0
          else
             f := sqrt(sqr(RADIUS) − sqr(x))
        end;
```

```pascal
begin   {Trapezoid}
    delta := (upper — lower) / n;    {Compute the width of each trapezoid.}
    sum := 0.0;                      {Initialize the running sum of the areas.}
    for i := 0 to n — 1 do           {Do the following for each trapezoid . . . .}
      begin
      {Compute the area of each trapezoid and add it to the running sum.}
          lowx := lower + i * delta;        {Find the left endpoint of the trapezoid.}
          highx := lower + (i + 1) * delta;   {Find the right endpoint.}
          sum := sum + 0.5 * delta * (f(lowx) + f(highx))   {Compute the area of a trapezoid.}
      end;
    Trapezoid := sum                        {Return the sum of the trapezoid areas.}
end;

function ReadyToQuit : boolean;
{Ask if the user wants to run the program again and return true}
{if and only if the user fails to answer 'Y' or 'y'. In other words,}
{a yes answer means that the user is not ready to quit.          }
{This routine keeps asking for another response as long as the   }
{user enters a wrong answer: one that isn't 'Y', 'y', 'N', 'n'.   }
    var
        ans : char;
begin
    write('Do you wish to run the program again (type Y for yes, N for no)? ');
    readln(ans);
    while (ans <> 'Y') and (ans <> 'y') and (ans <> 'N') and (ans <> 'n') do
    {Prompt and get another answer as long as a bad answer character is entered.}
        begin
            writeln('Please answer with either Y or N');
            write('Run the program again? ');
            readln(ans)
        end;
    ReadyToQuit := (ans = 'N') or (ans = 'n')   {Return true if the answer is a big or little 'n'.)
end;

begin   {Main}
  repeat
      write('Please enter the number of intervals to use in the approximation: ');
      readln(n);
      area := Trapezoid(0.0, 1.0, n);
      writeln(n : 2, ' intervals. Pi approximation = ', 4.0 * area : 9 : 7)
  until ReadyToQuit
end.
```

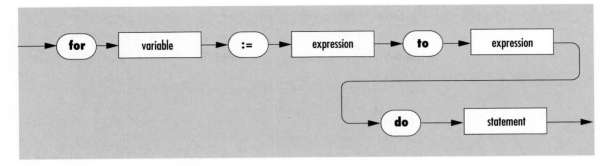

5.5 Problem Solving III: Analyzing the **for** Statement

In the PIP, the function *Trapezoid* adds the areas of *n* trapezoids. This is accomplished with a **for** statement, as follows:

```
for i := 0 to n − 1 do
    begin
        lowx := lower + i * delta;
        highx := lower + (i + 1) * delta;
        sum := sum + 0.5 * delta * (f(lowx) + f(highx))
    end;
```

The action of the **for** statement in this case is to execute repeatedly the three statements grouped by **begin..end**, first with $i = 0$, then with $i = 1$, then with $i = 2$, and so on, until the last repetition with $i = n - 1$. The syntax of the **for** statement is given in Figure 5.5. As with the **if** statement, the statement part can be a simple statement (we now know five kinds of statements: assignment statements, procedure calls, **if** and **case** statements, and the **for** statement) or any collection of statements grouped within a **begin..end** pair. The two expressions that control the lower and upper limits of the variable *i* (the *index* or *control variable*) can be any Pascal expressions that match the type of *i*: in this case, integer constants, variables, function calls, or integer expressions such as $n - 1$.

Semantically, the **for** statement is more complicated than most of the statements we've seen so far.

When a **for** statement is executed, the following steps are performed:

1. The lower and upper limit expressions are evaluated, and their values are saved.
2. The control variable is set equal to the lower limit value (that is, that of the first expression).
3. If the control variable is greater than the upper limit value, execution passes to whatever statement follows the **for** statement.
4. If the control variable is less than or equal to the upper limit value, the statement part of the **for** statement is executed.
5. After performing the statement part, the control variable is increased to its next possible value, and control is passed to step 3.

Avoiding **for** Statement Errors

There are a number of cautions that must be observed when using a **for** statement, some of which are consequences of the semantics, and some of which follow from Pascal's design philosophy. First, if the lower limit expression is greater than the upper limit expression, the **for** loop will not be executed. This is a consequence of step 3 in the description of the **for** statement. It implies, for instance, that the following loop will do nothing:

> **for** index : = **7 to 2 do**
>> writeln('something happens')   *This will never be executed.*

Another caution is similar to the implied use of the semicolon we saw with the **if** statement. If the reserved word **do** is immediately followed by a semicolon separator, the statement part of the **for** loop is empty. For example, the following statement will not act as we might expect it to, in spite of the fact that the lower and upper limits are in the proper order.

> **for** index : = **2 to 7 do**;   *Notice the semicolon.*
>> writeln('something happens')   *This gets done just once.*

This may appear to be a single **for** statement until we notice the semicolon. It is actually two statements: a **for** loop with an empty statement part, followed by a *writeln* procedure call. The **for** statement will do nothing (in fact, it will do nothing six times[4]), and the *writeln* call will be executed once, after the loop is finished.

---

[4]This is a cheap but not very reliable way of making your program pause briefly; since a computer takes a small amount of time to do nothing, a loop like this

> **for** i : = **1 to 10000 do**;

will effectively stall the computer for a time. The problem is that you have no easy way to tell how long the delay will be, not to mention that the delay will depend on the machine.

Another caution is exemplified by the following segment:

```
for i := 1 to 8 do
    begin
        Some statements;
        i := i - 1    Illegal. Why?
    end
```

Trace the possible action of this statement according to the five semantic rules we outlined above—something is decidedly peculiar here, since the loop will never terminate. The **for** loop is intended to describe very clearly how many iterations will be performed simply by reading the conditions of the **for** part. That intent is clearly violated when we modify the control variable inside the loop part, and so the standard disallows it.

It is an error to *threaten* the control variable of a **for** loop by including in the loop part any statement that could modify the control variable, such as a *read* or *readln* of the control variable, using it as the left side of an assignment statement, or by using the control variable in a procedure as a **var** parameter.

For example, all of these statements would result in an error.

```
for i := 1 to 8 do
    begin
        ⋮
        i := i - 1;      Error: using i on the left of an assignment
        ⋮
    end
for i := 1 to 8 do
    begin
        ⋮
        readln(i);       Error: reading the control variable
        ⋮
    end
for i := 1 to 8 do
    begin
        ⋮
        Modify(i, j, k); Error: if i matches a var parameter in Modify
        ⋮
    end
```

If we can't modify the control variable, or put it in danger of being modified, what about the lower and upper limit expressions? Could we do the following, and if we could, what would be the result? Before you read the explanation that follows, see how well you can second-guess the Pascal standard.

```
for i : = firstValue to lastValue do
   begin
      ⋮
      firstValue : = firstValue − 1;
      lastValue : = 2 * lastValue;
      ⋮
   end
```

The answer follows almost directly from semantic condition 1. The limit expressions are evaluated and saved *before* the loop is executed, and so any modification to the limit expressions will not affect the number of iterations. The standard allows a bit more latitude with the limit expressions than it does with the control variable, however.

It is not an error to modify the limit expressions of a **for** statement within the loop part. However, any modifications to the limit expressions will not alter the original number of loop iterations. In addition, it's usually a stylistically bad idea to do *anything* in a program that's not obvious.

As an example, the segment

```
firstValue : = 3;
lastValue : = 5;
for i : = firstValue to lastValue do
   begin
      writeln('i = ', i : 1, '   first = ', firstValue : 1, '   last = ', lastValue : 1);
      firstValue : = firstValue − 1;
      lastValue : = 2 * lastValue
   end;
writeln('Done!   first = ', firstValue : 1, '   last = ', lastValue : 1)
```

will have output

```
i = 3    first = 3    last = 5
i = 4    first = 2    last = 10
i = 5    first = 1    last = 20
Done!    first = 0    last = 40
```

Notice that *i* takes the values 3, 4, 5, and the loop then stops, in spite of the fact that we have modified *firstValue* and *lastValue* within the loop. Notice also that we didn't try to write *i* after the loop ended. There's a good reason for that, a reason that is the cause of headaches for beginning programmers.

After the completion of a **for** loop, the value of the control variable is undefined.

In this context, *undefined* means that you cannot rely on the value of the control variable to be anything predictable. It may be the upper limit, it may be the value after the upper limit, it may be zero, or it may not be any legal value at all. This is different from the situation in some other languages and is a consequence of Pascal's design philosophy. The control value is regarded as "local" to the loop, in that its sole purpose is to control the loop. To underscore its special nature, the standard stipulates that the control variable only has a reliable value within the loop.

We'll have much more to say about this principle of locality in Chapter 7.

The final caution is a consequence of semantic condition 5. After each iteration of the **for** loop, condition 5 says that the control variable is increased to the *next possible* value. If you think about it for a moment, you'll see that this could cause real problems if the control variable were a real-type variable (pun intended). Put simply, what's the next real number after, say, 3? It's not 4, obviously, but is it 3.1, 3.01, 3.001, 3.0001, or some other number?

What mathematicians mean by real numbers and what computer scientists mean are most emphatically not the same thing, since computers must represent each piece of information in a finite (usually fixed) number of binary digits. That means that the overwhelming majority of real numbers can't be represented exactly in the computer, but rather must be approximated to a degree of accuracy that depends on the way the circuits are designed. In decimal terms rather than binary, the real number immediately after 3 might be 3.00001 on a small microcomputer but might be 3.00000000000000000001 on a powerful supercomputer. A mathematician knows that there is *no* immediate successor to any real number — computer scientists know this, too, but realize that real numbers in a computer aren't the same thing as the Platonic ideal of real numbers we learn in school. The point is that a computer language should be, as much as possible, machine independent, and for that reason, Pascal restricts the type of the index variable in a **for** loop.

The index variable of a **for** loop must be of *ordinal* type — that is, a type in which each value has a well-defined successor, if it has a successor at all. For now, that means that the type of an index variable must be integer, character, or boolean.

There are other ordinal types. We discuss them in Chapter 8.

The order of character values varies from machine to machine, but 'A' always comes before 'B', and so on (though we can't be sure in general that 'A' comes before 'a'). We'll have more to say about the order of character values shortly. For no reason other than having to settle on one way to order values, the Pascal standard stipulates that *false* comes before *true*. In other words, both of these loops would iterate twice.

```
for c : = 'E' to 'F' do      {c is a character type variable}
   Some statement

for b : = false to true do   {b is a boolean type variable}
   Some statement
```

*S*ee Chapters 9 and 10.
*S*ee Chapter 7.

There are two final cautions about the control variable, which won't really concern us until later: (1) It must be an *entire* variable, not part of a record or an array, and (2) it must be declared as a variable in the same block as the **for** statement and cannot be a subprogram parameter.

Iterating with Other Increments

There are many times when we might want to count down in a **for** loop rather than up. Pascal is very accommodating in this respect, recognizing that there's no particular reason to prefer one direction over the other. Remember the semantics of the **for** loop. A variant of the **for** loop changes semantic condition 5 (and 3 and 4, too) to change the control variable to be the *previous*, rather than the subsequent, value by using the reserved word **downto** in place of **to**, as in

```
for i : = 10 downto 1 do
   writeln(i);
writeln('Blast off!')
```

Of course, when using the **downto** version of the **for** loop, we would normally have the first limit expression evaluate to a value *greater* than or equal to the second limit expression.

Although Pascal provides us with loops that iterate both up and down, in both cases we are restricted to increasing the index variable to the next value (or previous, as the case might be). Suppose, though, we wanted to have a loop in which the index took on the seven equally spaced values 3, 9, 15, 21, 27, 33, and 39? Some languages, like BASIC and C, allow you to specify the step size in the heading of the **for** loop, but in Pascal one must resort to a workaround. Here are two simple ways to step by different values, both of which use an auxiliary variable, *stepIndex*, which acts in place of the index.

```
stepIndex : = −3;
for index : = 1 to 7 do              for index : = 1 to 7 do
   begin                                begin
      stepIndex : = stepIndex + 6;        stepIndex : = 6 * index − 3;
      {Process, using stepIndex}          {Process, using stepIndex}
   end                                  end
```

The left-hand example begins with the element -3, which would come before the first value in the sequence to be processed, and since each element in the sequence is 6 more than the previous one, it adds 6 to *stepIndex* at each pass through the loop. In the right-hand example, we find a formula for each element in the list and use that formula to recalculate *stepIndex* at each iteration. Notice that in the left example, the index variable controls only the number of iterations; we could have equally well used any other limits that differ by the same amount, such as **for** *index* := 3 **to** 9 or even **for** *index* := 7 **downto** 1. In the example on the right, on the other hand, the assignment *stepIndex* := $6 * index - 3$ requires that the limits be 1 and 7. Using different limits would be acceptable, but we'd have to change the expression in the assignment.

Given that the Computer Science Interlude for this chapter is numerical analysis, it is appropriate to consider which of these schemes is better. You probably know enough by now to guess the answer: "This is one of those engineering-type tradeoffs; each has its advantages and disadvantages." The left loop will usually run faster than the right, since addition on most computers typically runs three to ten times faster than multiplication. Of course, for a small loop like this with only seven iterations, that's not important—most people couldn't tell the difference between 0.12 milliseconds and 1.2 milliseconds anyway. The left example is perhaps slightly more comprehensible, since it's immediately obvious that *stepIndex* is being increased by 6 at each iteration. At this stage, the odds seem to be tilted slightly in favor of the additive loop rather than the multiplicative one.

However, there's a subtle difference between the two that tips the balance in favor of the formula version on the right for some uses. Indeed, that's why we adopted the formula version for use in our Program in Progress. The function *Trapezoid* performs some computations using a real variable that takes on a sequence of values like 0.1, 0.2, 0.3, . . . 12.0. If we used the left-hand, additive loop, it seems at first that we'd generate the real numbers 0.1, 0.2, . . . and so on. But in fact, 1/10 in binary—the way numbers are stored in a computer—is an infinite, repeating binary fraction, namely, 0.00011001100110011. . . . If, for the purposes of argument,[5] we had to store real numbers with eight bits of precision, the computer might represent 1/10 as the truncated binary fraction .00011001. This is not 1/10, but is $25/256 = 0.09765625$, and is as close as we can come with eight bits. We are too low by 0.00234375, and because we are basing the new value of *sum* on the old value of *sum*, that error is compounded each time we add 0.1 to our auxiliary index. That means we'll be off by at least 0.00468750 at the next iteration, by at least 0.00703125 at the third, and so on.[6] Of course, we face a similar problem with multiplication, but in this case the value of *sum* is found by a single multiplication rather than by 120 additions. In effect, the additive version has 120 operations to introduce accumulating roundoff errors in the final value rather than just one in

---

[5]This argument is a considerable simplification of the way real numbers are represented on most computers, but the conclusion is the same no matter how the actual representation works.
[6]We said that the error was *at least* 0.00234375 times the number of iterations. In fact, it can be even worse than that, since every sum is truncated to eight bits.

the multiplicative loop. Try it yourself: Run the following program, and look at the results.

```
program IterationTest(output);
    var
        index : integer;
        stepIndex : real;
begin
    {Find 1000 by 10000 additions of 1/10.}
    stepIndex : = 0.0;
    for index : = 1 to 10000 do
        stepIndex : = stepIndex + 0.1;
    writeln(stepIndex : 19 : 13);
    {Now find 1000 by a single multiplication.}
    writeln(10000 * 0.1 : 19 : 13)
end.
```

When we tested this program, the additive answer was too low by almost 0.1, whereas the multiplication was correct to thirteen decimal places.

Loops Within Loops

As we said earlier, the statement part of a **for** loop can contain any Pascal statement, including another **for** statement. We could, for instance, use *nested loops* to print a very simple addition table.

```
for n : = 1 to 3 do
    begin
        for m : = 1 to 3 do
            write(n + m);
        writeln
    end
```

The output would look like this:

```
2    3    4
3    4    5
4    5    6
```

What happens here? For each iteration of the outer loop, the inner loop will be executed three times, writing numbers in a row, and then pass control to the *writeln* statement, which drops the writing down to the next line. The successive values of the (n, m) pair will then be $(1, 1)$, $(1, 2)$, $(1, 3)$ [finished with the first circuit of the inner loop here], $(2, 1)$, $(2, 2)$, $(3, 3)$ [and now the inner loop has rolled over again], $(3, 1)$, $(3, 2)$, and $(3, 3)$. There will be nine numbers written: three sums from the inner loop for each of the three iterations of the outer loop. If you want a mental hook for the behavior of nested loops, think of a car's odometer: The inner loop represents tenths of miles, and the outer loop represents miles.

With nested loops, the inner loop cycles through all of its index values for each value of the outer loop.

A consequence of the syntax of **for** loops is that we can nest loops as deeply as we wish. For example, the following segment with three nested loops writes 60 (= 3 × 4 × 5) three-letter "words."

```
for c := 'A' to 'C' do        {three character values used}
    for d := 'P' to 'S' do        {four values here}
        for e := 'B' to 'F' do    {and five values here}
            writeln(c, d, e)
```

Realizing that the inner loops iterate more rapidly than the outer ones, you should be able to see that the first few words printed will be APB, APC, APD, APE, APF, AQB, AQC, AQD, AQE, and AQF.

Of course, **for** loops do not have to execute a fixed number of times. Even though it is fixed at the time of execution, the number of iterations may be dependent on the value of another variable. Suppose, for example, that we wished to investigate the series $1 + 2 + \cdots + n$. We might design a routine to write the partial sums $1, 1 + 2, 1 + 2 + 3$, and so on. Each partial sum could be controlled by a **for** loop, and we could include the summation loop in a larger loop that controls the upper limit of the partial sums, as below:

```
for limit := 1 to 100 do        {Find the first 100 partial sums.}
    begin
        partialSum := 0;            {Initialize the partial sum.}
        for i := 1 to limit do      {Find the partial sum 1 + 2 + ⋯ + limit.}
            partialSum := partialSum + i;
        writeln('The sum of the integers from 1 to ', limit : 1, ' is ', partialSum)
    end
```

Take careful notice of where we initialized *partialSum*. It must be inside the outer loop, since it must be reset to zero each time we find a new partial sum. Placing an initialization outside of the loop where it should be is a very common error. What would happen if we placed the initialization before the header of the outer loop? What would happen if we placed the initialization inside the inner loop?

If a loop or a nested collection of loops appears to give the wrong values, make sure that any initializations are placed where they should be.

This example of nested loops, by the way, can be made slightly easier to read if we hide the inner loop in a function, as follows.

```
function SumUpTo(limit : integer) : integer;
   var
       i, partialSum : integer;
begin
   partialSum := 0;
   for i := 1 to limit do
       partialSum := partialSum + i;
   SumUpTo := partialSum
end;
   ⋮
begin    {Main}
   ⋮
   for limit := 1 to 100 do
       writeln('The sum of the integers from 1 to ', limit : 1, ' is ', SumUpTo(limit))
```

5.6 Problem Solving III: Analyzing the **while** Statement

The **for** statement repeats a loop a specified number of times, which is known prior to the execution of the loop. What happens, though, when we need to repeat a collection of statements, and the number of iterations we'll need is not known ahead of time, but rather is dependent upon something that can change while the loop's statement is executed? Pascal provides two kinds of loops that are *conditionally executed*, which means that the loop part will be executed as long as a certain condition is satisfied.

The **while** statement is the first of the two conditional loops we'll investigate. Consider the following section from the PIP. This section is part of the function *ReadyToQuit* and is used to read a single character from the keyboard. The character is expected to be 'Y' or 'N'—as long as the character read is not one of these, the loop will remind the user what the correct input should be and read another character.

```
write('Do you wish to run the program again (type Y for yes, N for no)?');
readln(ans);
while (ans <> 'Y') and (ans <> 'y') and (ans <> 'N') and (ans <> 'n') do
   begin
       writeln('Please answer with either Y or N');
       write('Run the program again? ');
       readln(ans)
   end
```

The syntax of the **while** statement is simple enough (Figure 5.6): It begins with the reserved word **while**, followed by a boolean expression and the reserved word **do**, followed by the statement or statements to be repeated.

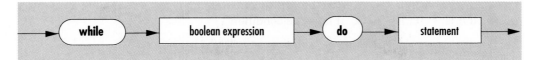

Figure 5.6.   Syntax of the **while** statement

The semantics of the **while** statement are relatively simple, as well.

The **while** statement acts as follows:

1. The boolean expression is evaluated.
2. If the expression is *true*, the loop statement is executed, and control passes to step 1.
3. If the expression is *false*, control passes to the statement following the loop part of the **while** statement.

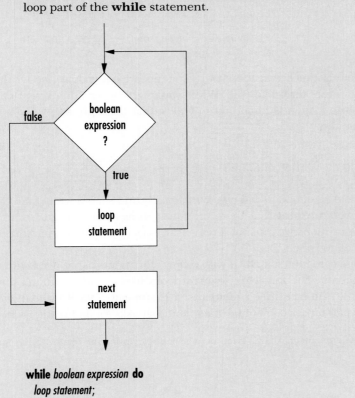

In the segment from the PIP, the answer character is read and tested to see if it is 'Y', 'y', 'N', or 'n'. If it is, the condition

(ans <> 'Y') **and** (ans <> 'y') **and** (ans <> 'N') **and** (ans <> 'n')

is *false*, and the loop is skipped. If the character entered is not one of these letters, the loop statements are executed, and a new value for *ans* is read. As a result of the *readln* statement, the value of *ans* — and thus the values of the boolean expression — may change. The new value is then tested, and the loop either terminates or is repeated until *ans* is one of the acceptable inputs.

Notice now that, strictly speaking, we no longer need the **for** statement. The following two statements are equivalent (although we'd be the first to admit that the **for** version is considerably easier to read).

```
                                        lower : = exp1; upper : = exp2;
                                        index : = lower;
      for index : = exp1 to exp2 do     while index < = upper do
            Statement                       begin
                                                Statement;
                                                index : = next value of index
                                            end;
                                        if index = upper then
                                            Statement
```

If you can satisfy yourself that these two segments are equivalent, the **while** loop should hold no future terrors for you. While you might never want to replace a **for** loop with a **while** loop, it is important to realize that there are many roads to the top of the mountain.

Avoiding **while** Statement Errors

The **while** statement is simpler syntactically and semantically than the **for** statement, so you'd expect that there are fewer things that can go wrong. Still, there are some cautions we must observe — warnings of potential errors that creep into programs all too often.

The same care must be taken with empty statements as we used with the **if** and **for** statements. The following segment looks like a *readln* call and a **while** statement, but it is in fact three statements: a *readln* call, a **while** statement with an empty loop part, and a compound statement that asks for and reads a value.[7]

---

[7]Some Pascal environments make this error more obvious by writing the code with the "proper" indentations:

```
readln(n);
while n < = 0 do
    ;
begin
    writeln('That''s negative. Please enter a positive integer : ');
    readln(n)
end
```

```
readln(n);
while n <= 0 do;     Notice the semicolon
   begin
      writeln('That''s negative. Please enter a positive integer : ');
      readln(n)
   end
```

Pretty clearly, the intent of this segment is to keep trying until a positive number is entered. In fact, what happens is that if a positive number is entered first, the (empty) loop will be skipped and the segment will ask for another number, even though the original input was correct. Even worse, if the original number is negative or zero, the condition $n <= 0$ will be *true* and will remain so forever. In this case, the empty loop will execute forever, never reaching the compound statement, since n is never changed by the "no-operation" loop statement.

This segment not only indicates that we have to be careful about following **do** immediately by a semicolon but also points out a caution about the boolean expression of the **while** loop.

If the boolean expression that controls a **while** loop stays *true* forever, the loop will execute forever. That's almost always wrong, so be sure to include some statement(s) in the statement part of a **while** loop that have the potential to change the loop's boolean expression.

The previous example is a typical use of conditional loops. Consider a slight variant, where we want to accept a collection of numbers in the range from 0 to 100, and average them, as might be the case in a grade-keeping program. We won't know ahead of time how many numbers will be entered, so we allow the operator to signal the end of input by using a *sentinel*—that is, a value that couldn't possibly be one of the acceptable inputs. For this example we'll choose −1 as the sentinel. We first design our routine in *pseudocode*.

```
numInputs := 0;
total := 0;
Get a grade from the user that is −1 or in the range 0 .. 100;
while grade <> −1 do
   begin
      numInputs := numInputs + 1;
      total := total + grade;
      Get a grade from the user that is −1 or in the range 0 .. 100
   end;
average := total / numInputs[8]
```

---

[8]There's a potential error lurking in this segment. We'll find it in the lab.

Now all we have to do is expand the routine that gets the "legal" inputs. Since this is done twice and is a complete logical unit, it makes sense to encapsulate it in a procedure. We've almost done this already, in the example segment that gets positive numbers. All we have to do is change the condition of the **while** loop. A legal input is a number, n, for which ($n = -1$) **or** (($n >= 0$) **and** ($n <= 100$)). We want to execute the body of the loop when the input is *not* legal. So the negation of this boolean expression is ($n <> -1$) **and not** (($n >= 0$) **and** ($n <= 100$)), which is the same as ($n <> -1$) **and** (($n < 0$) **or** ($n > 100$)), either of which could serve as our loop condition. The routine is to return a single value—the grade—so it would be a good choice for a function, except that *GetGrade(grade)* seems to be a better way to invoke the routine than *grade := GetGrade*. Okay, we'll write it as a procedure. Notice that the procedure comment block includes a *postcondition*, which is a description of the condition that will be true when the procedure terminates. It is a good idea to include postconditions as part of the description of subprograms. It is also a good idea to include *preconditions*, which tell what is assumed to be true before the subprogram begins execution. Preconditions and postconditions provide a compact description of what the subprogram does.

```
procedure GetGrade(var n : integer);
    {Returns an integer that the user entered.    }
    {Postcondition: n = -1 or 0 ≤ n < 100.}
begin
    write('Grade: ');
    readln(n);
    while (n <> -1) and ((n < 0) or (n > 100)) do
        begin
            writeln('Wrong input. Enter an integer between 0 and 100,');
            writeln('or enter -1 to signal that there is no more input.');
            write('Your number : ');
            readln(n)
        end
end;
```

All we have to do now is replace each pseudocode line *Get a grade from the user that is* -1 *or in the range* 0 .. 100 with a call *GetGrade(grade)*, and our job is done.

We'll conclude this section with a brief mention of a topic we'll return to later. The condition of the loop in *GetGrade* is somewhat complicated. It might be better to split the two conditions—that the number is the sentinel and that the number is in the right range—into two distinct conditions. We can do this efficiently with a *flagged loop*, that is, one in which a separate boolean variable controls the loop. Below we've rewritten *GetGrade* with a boolean flag *done* that becomes *true* when something happens that would cause an exit from the loop. That something is, of course, $(n = -1)$ **or** $((n >= 0)$ **and** $(n <= 100))$.

We'll use flagged loops again. They're particularly useful with arrays (Chapter 9) and pointers (Chapter 12).

```
procedure GetGrade(var n : integer);
{Returns an integer that the user entered.    }
{Postcondition: n = −1 or 0 ≤ n < 100.}
    var
        done : boolean;         {flag to control the loop}
begin
    done : = false;             {We're not done yet—we haven't tested anything.}
    while not done do
        begin
            write('Grade: ');
            readln(n);          {Get a number to test.}
            if n = −1 then
                done : = true    {We can leave the loop now.}
            else if (n >= 0) and (n <= 100) then
                done : = true    {We can leave the loop here, too,}
            else
                begin            {but here we have to get another value to test.}
                    writeln('Wrong input. Enter an integer between 0 and 100,');
                    writeln('or enter  −1 to signal that there is no more input.');
                    write('Please enter your number again: ')
                end
        end
end;
```

5.7   Problem Solving III: Analyzing the **repeat** Statement

The grade-keeping segment and the procedure *GetGrade* are both slightly awkward, since in both we have to "prime the pump" of the **while** loops by reading a value or setting the flag first, before we enter the loop. We have to do this because the semantics of the **while** statement dictate that the test for loop termination be done before we enter the loop, so we have to give the boolean expression something to test before we do the loop statements. Pascal provides another conditional loop that avoids this awkwardness. The other statement is in a sense the mirror image of the **while** loop—the **repeat** loop.

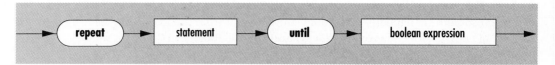

Figure 5.7.   Syntax diagram for the **repeat** statement

A **repeat** loop is used in the Program in Progress, enclosing the entire main program statement body.

```
repeat
    write('Please enter the number of intervals to use in the approximation: ');
    readln(n);
    writeln(n : 2, ' intervals. Pi approximation  =  ', 4.0 * Trapezoid(0.0, 1.0, n) : 9 : 7)
until ReadyToQuit
```

This statement reads as if it does one pass through the loop and tests for the exit condition (returned by the boolean function *ReadyToQuit*) at the *end* of the loop, rather than at the beginning, and that's exactly what it does. The syntax of the **repeat** statement is given in Figure 5.7.

The semantics of the **repeat** statement are very similar to those of the **while** statement.

The **repeat** statement acts as follows:

1. The loop body (which could be several statements) is executed.
2. The boolean expression is evaluated.
3. If the expression is *false*, control passes to step 1.
4. If the expression is *true*, control passes to the statement following the loop part of the **repeat** statement.

Notice the differences between the **while** and **repeat** loops:

The test for loop exit is done *before* the loop statement in the **while** loop, whereas in the **repeat** statement the test is done *after* the loop statement. That means that the statement part of a **repeat** loop is always done at least once (the statement part of a **while** loop, as we've seen, might never be executed). Furthermore, in a **while** statement, the loop is performed when the boolean condition is *true*; whereas in a **repeat** statement, the loop is performed as long as the boolean expression is *false*.

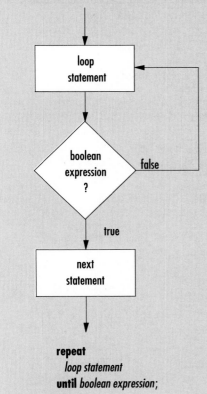

```
repeat
    loop statement
until boolean expression;
```

If you have trouble remembering something like "The **while** loop iterates when the boolean expression is *true*," just read the Pascal loops in English: "**while** boolean expression [is true] **do** statement" does the loop as long as the expression is true; "**repeat** statement **until** boolean expression [is true]" does the loop as long as the expression is *not* true.

Notice, by the way, that we didn't enclose the statement part of the **repeat** statement above in a **begin..end** pair. That's because the statements are already bracketed between the reserved words **repeat** and **until**, and Pascal doesn't require any further grouping. This, of course, is not the case with **while** and **if** statements: **begin** and **end** are the only ways we can tell where the statement parts of these statements end. You can use **begin** and **end** to bracket the loop part of a **repeat** statement if you wish—it's just not required.

We could recast our grade-keeping segment with **repeat** loops. It would make good sense to do this since, as we mentioned, each loop must iterate once anyway to get at least one value. The segment would look like this.

```
procedure GetGrade(var n : integer);
begin
   repeat
      write('Grade: ');
      readln(n);
      if (n <> −1) and ((n < 0) or (n > 100)) then
         begin
            writeln('Wrong input. Enter an integer between 0 and 100,');
            writeln('or enter −1 to signal that there is no more input.')
         end
   until (n = −1) or ((n >= 0) and (n <= 100))
end;
   ⋮
begin    {Main}
   ⋮
numInputs := 0;
total := 0;
repeat
   GetGrade(grade);
   if grade <> −1 then
      begin
         numInputs := numInputs + 1;
         total := total + grade
      end
until grade = −1;
average := total / numInputs
```

Although using **repeat** loops means we don't have to feed the loops with initial *readln* or *GetGrade* calls, notice the price we have to pay. In both cases, we need **if** statements to make sure that we don't perform the loop statements if the eventual exit condition is satisfied. In this case, it's a judgment call as to which version is easier to read (or easier to invent in the first place). Our feeling is to give the nod to the **while** version, in spite of the fact that we have to do a little work to get the loop going in the first place. Just as the **for** statement is semantically superfluous in the sense that any **for** statement can be replaced by a **while** state-ment, we can write either of the **while** or **repeat** statements using the other (along with some others). We'll explore this interchangeability further in the lab and the exercises.

5.8
Program Analysis in Practice: Tracing Loops

We've seen how to trace programs that are more or less static, but how do we guarantee that a loop does what we expect it to do? Showing the correctness of loops is, as you'd expect, somewhat more complicated than the examples we've seen so far, but it is vitally important. Based on what you've seen so far, you could argue that all this tracing is simply more trouble than it's worth. In the case of a collection of assignment statements and **if** statements, you can generally tell whether they do what they should without going through the hassle of a trace. We'd agree with you there, but with the proviso that things change radically when we introduce loops into a program. In fact, it's precisely because loops are compli-cated to understand at first glance that we need to be able to demonstrate their correctness. Even in the simplest cases, it's generally not at all obvious what a loop does.

Question 1: When Do We Get Out?

We'll start with an example that shows just how hard it is to tell at a glance what a loop does. Consider the following three segments. They're all intended to compute the sum $1 + 2 + 3 + 4 + 5$. Do they all accomplish the same thing, though?

Sample 1
```
sum : = 0;
for k : = 1 to 5 do
    sum : = sum + k;
```

Sample 2
```
sum : = 0;
k : = 1;
while k < 5 do
    begin
        sum : = sum + k;
        k : = k + 1
    end;
```

Sample 3
```
sum : = 0;
k : = 1;
repeat
    sum : = sum + k;
    k : = k + 1
until k > 5;
```

We can get some help here by considering the *exit condition* of each loop.

Sample 1. This loop terminates after k has taken the value 5, so the last value added to *sum* is 5, and hence we have $sum = 1 + 2 + 3 + 4 + 5 = 15$.

Sample 2. In this sample, the loop iterates as long as $k < 5$, so the loop will terminate as soon as $k \geq 5$. Because the increment statement $k := k + 1$ occurs after the statement $sum := sum + k$, the last value that will be added to *sum* will be 4, so in the second sample after termination of the loop we will have $sum = 1 + 2 + 3 + 4 = 10$, rather than 15, as we had in the first sample.

Sample 3. This loop will terminate as soon as $k > 5$, so when $k = 6$ the loop will terminate. As in the second sample, the loop will terminate before the last value of k (6, in this case) is added to *sum*. In other words, the third sample will leave the loop with $sum = 1 + 2 + 3 + 4 + 5$.

The moral here is that however much these three segments might appear to be similar, only the first and the third accomplish the same thing. We can summarize these arguments in a precise way as follows:

The exit conditions for **while** and **repeat** loops are as follows:

while *expression* **do**
    statement
{At this point in the program, (**not** expression) is known to be true.}

repeat
    statement
until *expression*
{At this point in the program, (expression) is known to be true.}

For example, in the loop controlled by **while** $k < 5$ **do**, we know that after the loop finishes we must have **not** ($k < 5$), which is the same as saying $k \geq 5$. In a loop that looks like **repeat..until** $k > 5$, we know $k > 5$ must be true after the loop finishes. Generally, of course, we can't say anything at all about the value of k after a loop like **for** $k := 1$ **to** 5, since we know that the value of the control variable is undefined after completion of a **for** loop. We can, though, make use of the limit expressions to tell what the index will be *during* the last iteration of the loop.

The difference between these three samples points out something we should always be careful about when we use loops.

Problem-solving technique

A common problem with loops is to be off by one iteration. Always look closely at the exit condition to make sure that the loop does no more and no fewer iterations than expected.

One of the more distressing errors that can happen when you use a loop is that the loop never terminates. This problem is generally easy to recognize—you run your program and eventually it seems to lock up, apparently doing nothing at all—or, worse still, a kind of computerized psychosis seems to take hold wherein the program either produces the same output over and over or refuses to halt when you expect it to.

Problem-solving technique

When a program refuses to halt as expected, or produces an endless stream of the same output, there's an excellent chance that it's locked in a loop where the exit condition is never reached.

When you write a loop, always check to make sure that there is an exit condition and, especially, that the program will eventually reach that exit condition. Suppose, for example, that we had designed the function *Trapezoid* like the following code using a **while** loop in an attempt to eliminate reference to the integer variable k of the **for** loop.

```
delta : = (upper − lower) / n;
sum : = 0.0;
lowx : = lower;          {left boundary of the first trapezoid}
highx : = lower + delta;   {right boundary of the first trapezoid}
while highx <> upper do
   begin
      {Find the area of a trapezoid, and add it to the running sum.}
      sum : = sum + 0.5 * delta * (f(lowx) + f(highx));

      {Advance boundaries to the next trapezoid.}
      lowx : = lowx + delta;
      highx : = highx + delta
   end;
```

This seems to be an improvement over the original version, since it's simpler and easier to read. It appears that it should work, and nothing seems to be improper when we trace it by hand in a simple case. If we try it, though, we find that the program hangs up and never prints the approximation. What went wrong?

The problem here is caused by the necessarily inexact representation of real numbers that we mentioned earlier. Even though *delta* is defined to be one *n*-th of the distance between *lower* and *upper*, it will generally not be exactly that value. Thus, adding *n* copies of *delta* to *lower* will usually produce a value close to *upper* but not precisely the same. In this case, *highx* will eventually skip right past *upper*, the exit condition *highx* = *upper* will never be met, and the loop will never terminate. Even changing the boolean expression to *highx* < *upper* won't make the loop correct. It will halt, but it may be off by one and halt before evaluating the last trapezoid. As one of our colleagues says (the pun is important here), "You can't count on real numbers."

Question 2: What Happens Inside?

If a loop performs a collection of statements repeatedly, modifying its variables as it goes, how can we know what will be true when repetition halts? We need to turn a dynamic situation, in which some action is performed an arbitrary number of times, into a static one in which some assertion is true and remains so throughout. What we need is a boolean expression that remains true at the end of each iteration through a loop. Then, you see, we'll have a single statement that, since it's true after each iteration, will also be true when the loop terminates, and that's exactly what we're looking for.

To show this principle in action, consider the following code, intended to produce the values of the sums of the first *n* odd numbers, $1 + 3 + \cdots + (2n - 1)$.

```
sum := 0;
k := 1;
while k <= n do
    begin
        sum := sum + (2 * k - 1);
        k := k + 1
    end
```

Let's do a trace of the first few iterations of the loop, doing a snapshot at each iteration:

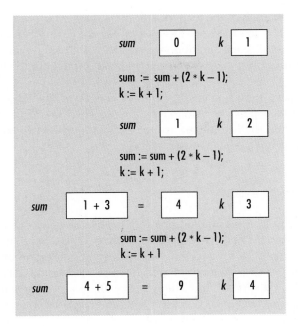

If we didn't know what the loop was supposed to do, we might have a little difficulty guessing the pattern: What sequence goes 0, 1, 4, 9, . . . ? It looks like the sequence of squares, so we'd guess that at the start of each iteration, we'd have $sum = (k - 1)^2$. That's clearly true before we enter the loop. Let's prove that it's always true, again using a hand trace. This time, we don't know the values of k and sum, so we just fill in the boxes in accord with the supposed condition: k is some value K, and sum is then $(K - 1)^2$.

Note that after one iteration of the loop we still have $sum = (k - 1)^2$, since after the loop we have $sum = K^2 = ((K + 1) - 1)^2 = (k - 1)^2$. In other words, after the loop body, we have the same condition we started with, using a different value for k. Thus, the identity $sum = (k - 1)^2$ is unchanged throughout the life of the loop.

Now we can state what the loop does. If $sum = (k - 1)^2$ is true after each iteration of the loop, and the loop exit condition is $k > n$ (so, since the loop counts up, we have $k = n + 1$ when the loop quits), we may combine these two facts to show that after the loop is completed, we must have

$$sum = (k - 1)^2 = ((n + 1) - 1)^2 = n^2.$$

Our loop calculates squares, as we guessed.

The process we followed is a common one for tracing the action of loops. We'd be the first to admit that it's not a trivial process, but we'd also add that it's a process that can be very helpful in some cases. As you become more comfortable with loops, you'll find that you can often take a quick look at a loop and verify that it does what you expect it to do. You'll find, though, that there are times when a loop is not completely transparent. In these cases, the time taken to prove that a loop works correctly pays off as an investment in not having to find and fix errors after they occur.

To demonstrate that a loop works correctly, follow these five steps:

1. Verify that the loop will reach its exit condition eventually.
2. Perhaps using examples as guides, try to find a condition that holds throughout the life of the loop. Look particularly for one that, when combined with the exit condition, will produce a statement that implies the intended goal of the loop.
3. Show that the condition is true before entering the loop.
4. Trace the loop body to show that if the condition is assumed to be true at the start of the loop body, then it will be true after the body.
5. Combine the loop condition with the exit condition to produce a statement that is true upon completion of the loop.

These five steps can, and should, be used when you design a loop as well. While you're writing a loop, you should make sure that it will terminate. You should have a goal in mind for the loop, and you should write the loop body so that each iteration makes progress toward that goal. Finally, you should convince yourself that the goal will indeed be met when the loop terminates.

5.9   Reference

- The **for** statement looks like

  for *control variable* : = *lower limit* **to** *upper limit* **do**
  statement part;

  The action of the **for** statement is as follows:

  1. Evaluate the lower and upper limits (since they may be arithmetic expressions).
  2. Set the control variable equal to the lower limit.
  3. If the control variable is less than or equal to the upper limit, do the statement part; otherwise, go to step 5.
  4. Increase the control value by 1, and go back to step 3.
  5. Continue on to whatever follows.
- The **for** statement is a structured statement, which expects a simple or a compound statement (that is, a group enclosed within a **begin..end** pair) immediately after the reserved word **do**.
- After executing a **for** loop, the value of the control variable is undefined.
- It is an error to modify the value of the control variable within the loop.
- It is not an error to modify the limit values within the loop, but it is usually not done, since such modification has no effect on the number of times the loop iterates.
- Since **for** loops are statements, they may appear anywhere a statement may appear, including within another loop.
- The **while** statement looks like

  while *boolean expression* **do**
  statement part   {Can be any simple or compound statement.}

- The **repeat** statement looks like

  repeat
  statement part   {Can be any simple or compound statement.}
  until *boolean expression*

- Their actions are shown in Figure 5.8.
- The **while** statement performs its test *before* the loop statement is executed and executes the loop statement if the boolean expression is *true*.
- The **repeat** statement performs its test *after* the loop statement is performed (thus, it always does the loop statement at least once) and repeats the loop statement if the boolean expression is *false*.
- The loop statements of both loops can be compound statements—the **while** statement requires that the compound statement be grouped within a **begin..end** pair, whereas the **repeat** statement does not.
- When you design loops, make sure that the exit condition will be met eventually, and that upon termination, the desired result holds. If necessary, trace the loop to verify its action.

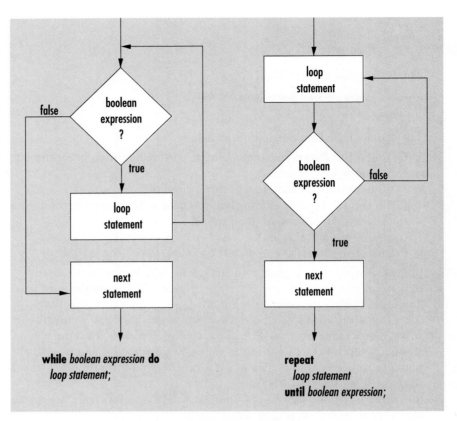

Figure 5.8.   The actions of **while** and **repeat** statements

5.10
Building Blocks

In this chapter, you have seen many forms and uses of Pascal loops. The building blocks that follow are the general forms as well as a few of the more common and generally useful applications.

The **for** loop that follows illustrates two very important concepts: the use of an auxiliary variable for indices other than 1 and the use of an *accumulator* variable to keep a running sum.

```
sum : = 0.0;
for i : = 0 to 99 do
    begin
        newIndex : = i * 0.031416;      {newIndex steps in multiples of π / 100}
        sum : = sum + cos(newIndex)   {Compute a value, and add it to the accumulator.}
    end
```

A common use of loops is to provide a more complicated guard than is available from the **if** statement. The general form is to place the guard loop before the guarded statement so that the loop will not permit access to the statement until the proper conditions have been met. Here's an example, used in a boolean function:

```
function ReadyToQuit : boolean;
    var
        ans : char;
begin
    write('Do you wish to run the program again (type Y for yes, N for no)?');
    readln(ans);
    while (ans <> 'Y') and (ans <> 'y') and (ans <> 'N') and (ans <> 'n') do
        begin
            writeln('Please answer with either Y or N');
            write('Run the program again? ');
            readln(ans)
        end;
    {Execution can't get here until the exit condition of the loop is met.}
    ReadyToQuit : = (ans = 'N') or (ans = 'n')
end;
```

Often, a list of data to be processed may have a length that's not known until run-time. One way to process the list is to terminate it with a sentinel value that is clearly distinguishable from the "actual" data. Then, to process the list, you can use a loop that terminates as soon as the sentinel is seen, as follows.

```
readln(n);
while n <> −1 do
    begin
        {Do processing, using n.}
        readln(n)   {Get another value to process.}
    end
```

Another way to process a list of information is to use a *counted loop*. In such a loop, the first entry is the length of the list, and that is followed by the list elements. Such a loop might take the following form:

```
readln(count);
for i : = 1 to count do
   begin
      readln(n);
      {Do processing, using n.}
   end
```

Finally, a flagged loop can be useful in cases where the loop has a complicated terminating condition, like C_1 **or** C_2 **or** C_3, especially if C_1 must be false for us to evaluate C_2 without error.

```
done : = false;        We're not done yet — we haven't tested anything.
while not done do
   if C1 then
      done : = true     We can leave the loop now.
   else if C2 then
      done : = true     We can leave the loop here, too,
   else if C3 then
      done : = true     and here.
   else
      begin
         ⋮            This is where the processing goes on.
      end
```

5.11   EXERCISES

1. Give a geometric proof that the area of a trapezoid is the width times the average of the lengths of the parallel sides. It's not hard to find a proof that doesn't require any words.

2. In the three samples we compared in the text to compute $1 + 2 + 3 + 4 + 5$, show that order matters in the **while** and **repeat** versions by interchanging the order of the two statements within the loops. What do the new versions of the loops compute now?

For Exercises 3 and 4, identify and correct the syntax errors, if any, in the following segments. Don't worry about whether these loops do anything useful — you're interested here only in whether they'll compile.

3. a.
```
readln(n);
while n = −1 do
   sum : = sum + n;
   readln(n)
```

b.
```
repeat until n = −1
   begin
      readln(n);
      sum : = sum + n
   end
```

   c. **for** x + 1 := 2 **upto** 78 **do**
        t := t + sqr(x + 1)

4. a. repeat
       g := g + 1;
   until g > g

   b. read(n);
    t := 0;
    for k = 1 **to** n **do**
      begin
        k := 2 * k − 1;
        t := t + sqr(k)
      end

   c. n := 0;
    while n > 0 **do**;
      begin
        readln(n);
        sum := sum + n
      end

    Exercises 5 and 6 refer to Exercises 3 and 4, respectively.

5. For the corrected segments in Exercise 3, try to guess the programmer's intention and then point out the likely semantic problems that would keep the routines from working as you think they should or that would lead to a run-time error.

6. For the corrected segments in Exercise 4, do the same thing.

7. In the following segments, how many times is the statement S executed?

   a. **for** n := 1 **to** 5 **do**
      for m := 1 **to** 5 **do**
        S

   b. **for** n := 1 **to** 5 **do**
      for m := n **to** 5 **do**
        S

   c. **for** n := 1 **to** 5 **do**
      for m := n **to** 5 − n **do**
        S

8. Assume that S is a statement or group of statements and that B is a boolean expression.

   a. Using the **while** statement, write the equivalent of

      repeat
        S
      until B

   b. Using the **repeat** statement, write the equivalent of

      while B **do**
        S

9. The following segment is supposed to produce a list of integers from 2 to 1000. For each number, the sum of its proper divisors is computed and displayed. For example, 8 has proper divisors 1, 2, and 4 (we don't count 8 itself here), so the sum of the divisors is $1 + 2 + 4 = 7$. The number 28 is an example of a rare *perfect number*, that is, one that is equal to the sum of its proper divisors, since $1 + 2 + 4 + 7 + 14 = 28$. The organization is simple enough:

> For all numbers, n, from 2 to 1000,
>> Test all trial divisors from 2 to $n - 1$ to see if they divide n evenly.
>>> If a divisor is found, add it to a running sum of divisors.

The segment fails to work as we intended, though. Describe the first three lines of its output, and fix the segment so it works properly.

```
trialDivisor := 1;
for n := 2 to 1000 do
   begin
      while trialDivisor < n do
         begin
            sumOfDivisors := 0;
            if n mod trialDivisor = 0 then
               sumOfDivisors := sumOfDivisors + trialDivisor;
            trialDivisor := trialDivisor + 1
         end;
      writeln(n, sumOfDivisors)
   end
```

10. The *harmonic series*,

$$1 + \frac{1}{2} + \frac{1}{3} + \frac{1}{4} + \cdots + \frac{1}{n}$$

increases without limit, as n increases. We could, for instance, ask how big n has to be before the harmonic series has a value greater than 20. That seems simple enough—all we'd have to do is write a routine like this:

```
sum := 0.0;
denominator := 0;
repeat
   denominator := denominator + 1;
   sum := sum + (1 / denominator)
until sum > 20.0;
writeln('It took ', denominator, ' terms to get above 20')
```

That may not work, though. Why?

11. Write a routine that will read a collection of positive integers, separated by spaces, with sentinel value -1 at the end, and that will stop reading at the sentinel or at the first instance of a repeated pair of numbers. In other words, the routine, when given $8, 90, 12, 12, 41, 86, -1$, would stop reading as soon as it saw the second 12.

a. Write this routine using a flagged loop, as we did at the end of Section 5.6.
b. Write this routine using a **repeat** loop without a boolean flag.
c. Compare the two routines. Which was easier to write? To understand?

12. There are two fundamental ways to read a list. In a sentinel-controlled loop, the loop is controlled by searching for a sentinel at the end of the input, signaling that there is no more data to be processed. The grade-keeping routine in the text is an example of a sentinel-controlled loop. In a counted loop, the first value to be read is not part of the data but rather represents the number of data elements that follow. Write a routine to read positive integers and compute their sum, first using a sentinel and then using a count, so that typical inputs would be

> 45 81 12 −1

for the sentinel-controlled loop, and

> 3 45 81 12

for the counted loop. Discuss the advantages and disadvantages of each, from the point of view of the programmer and the user.

13. A *prime number* is an integer (generally assumed to be greater than 1) that has no proper divisors except for itself and 1. We see that 7 is prime, but 6 is not, since 6 can be divided evenly by 2 and 3, as well as 1 and 6. The first few primes are 2, 3, 5, 7, 11, 13, 17, 19, 23, 29, 31, 37, 41, and 43.

   a. Write **function** *IsPrime*(n : *integer*) : *boolean*, that returns *true* if and only if n is prime. Remember that you can test whether b divides a by the condition (a **mod** b) = 0. It's also helpful to know that when testing whether n is prime, one needs to test only divisors that are less than or equal to $sqrt(n)$.

   b. *Wilson's theorem* states that p is a prime if and only if the expression ((p − 1)! + 1) **mod** p is equal to zero. (See Exercise 26 for a definition of !.) Use this to produce a new prime-testing function. *Hint*: Since factorials grow so quickly, you should do all arithmetic **mod** p to avoid integer overflow.

14. Investigate the following conjecture: The value of the expression $n^2 + n + 41$ is prime for any integer n. *Bonus*: Draw a valuable conclusion from this exercise.

15. We can find the square root of a nonnegative number N without using Pascal's built-in *sqrt* function by performing the following segment:

```
a := N;   {a is a real variable}
repeat
    a := a − (sqr(a) − N) / (2 * a)
until abs(sqr(a) − N) < 1e − 8
```

In this segment, we do the loop until the answer a has a square that is within 0.00000001 of N. This technique is known as *Newton's method*, and the nice part about it is how fast it works. Try it, writing the current value of a within the loop, and see how many iterations it takes to find the square root of 100 to within 8 places. Try it again, this time to find the square root of 10,000.

16. A growing use of the computer in mathematics is to use it as an assistant, having it do the dirty work of calculation so that the mathematician can use the results to conjecture results that can then be proved. Here's an example. The *triangular numbers*, 1, 3, 6, 10, 15, . . . , are formed by the partial sums of the sequence of positive integers, so 3 = 1 + 2 and 6 = 1 + 2 + 3, for example. Write a function *Triangle*(n), which returns the n-th triangular number, and use that function to investigate the sum of the n-th and (n + 1)-th triangular numbers. Notice anything interesting?

17. Design and write a program to write sums of the form

$$\frac{1}{1 \times 2} + \frac{1}{2 \times 3} + \frac{1}{3 \times 4} + \cdots + \frac{1}{n \times (n + 1)}$$

and see if you can guess a simple expression for such sums in terms of n.

18. Write a program that prints the values of the following sequence:

$$1, 1 + \sqrt{1}, 1 + \sqrt{1 + \sqrt{1}}, 1 + \sqrt{1 + \sqrt{1 + \sqrt{1}}}, \ldots$$

You might want to make use of the fact that if x is the n-th term in the sequence, then the next term is $1 + \sqrt{x}$. By the way, if the sequence *converges* (that is, eventually gets arbitrarily close) to a single value, we can say — very loosely — that successive terms are equal, so we can sometimes find the value to which a sequence converges by setting adjacent terms equal to each other. In this case, if we set the successive terms equal to each other, we have $x = 1 + \sqrt{x}$. Try solving this equation for x, and see if one of the values you get is what the program suggests.

19. The following loop takes a number, n, assumed to be composed only of the digits 0 and 1, and sets *num* equal to the decimal equivalent of n, so if n were 1101, the loop would set *num* to 13. Fill in the boolean expression to control the loop. You might want to look back at Chapter 2, where we discussed binary-to-decimal conversion.

```
num : = 0;
power : = 1;
while _____ do
    begin
        digit : = n mod 10;    {Get the rightmost digit of n.}
        num : = num + power * digit;
        power : = 2 * power;
        n : = n div 10        {Remove the rightmost digit from n.}
    end
```

20. Write **function** *Digits*(n : *integer*) : *integer*, which counts the number of digits in n. *Hint*: Look at Exercise 19.

21. a. Write **function** *Reverse*(n : *integer*) : *integer*, which reverses n, so that *Reverse*(4723) = 3247. This is a tricky problem. It involves extracting the digits from the right of n and building the reverse using these digits as they come in. *Hint*: Look at Exercise 19.

b. Use *Reverse* to write function *Palindrome*(n : *integer*) : *boolean*, which returns *true* if and only if n is a *palindrome*, that is, reads the same left to right as right to left, as do 454 and 3333.

c. An interesting problem that appeared on *Square One* (a Public Broadcasting System kids' show about mathematics) is the following: Take a starting number, n, add it to its reverse, and continue this process until the result is a palindrome. For example, starting with 95, we add it to its reverse to get 95 + 59 = 154. Add this to its reverse, and we get 154 + 451 = 605. Add this to its reverse, and we have 605 + 506 = 1111, which is a palindrome after three iterations. Write a program to count the number of iterations this process takes to produce a palindrome, and try it for some starting values. Since the numbers can get pretty big, you might want to use the nonstandard *longint* type (available in THINK Pascal and Turbo Pascal, among others), which allows you to represent integers up to 2,147,483,647. Even that won't help for the starting value 98—that takes 24 iterations and results in the palindrome 8,813,200,023,188. Don't even think about trying it on 295—if that ever results in a palindrome, the result is at least 3200 digits long. Does the process always result in a palindrome for any starting value? *Note*: In Chapter 9, you'll see a way to do this problem that doesn't limit you to 13 digits.

22. Discover the next term in the sequence 24, 20, 4, 16, 37, . . . , and write a program to generate such a sequence from any starting value (which in itself is a hint). We were humbled to discover that a ten-year-old in our local school system got the answer before we did, so congratulate yourself if you get it quickly, and don't feel bad if you didn't.

23. Design a program that prints a tree like the one shown here.

```
      *
     ***
    *****
   *******
  *********
 ***********
*************
     ***
     ***
     ***
```

Write your program so that it is general enough to be able to draw other figures with fairly little modification. You might, for instance, design a procedure that prints a centered line consisting of an odd number of stars.

24. It's not always easy to show that a loop will terminate. Consider the following loop, whose body was introduced in Chapter 4, Exercise 9b.

```
while n > 1 do
   if odd(n) then
      n := 3 * n + 1
   else
      n := n div 2
```

a. It's not known whether this loop terminates for all values of n. Try it for $n = 160$, $n = 15$, and $n = 1920$. *Hint*: $1920 = 128 \times 15$.

b. Write a program that counts how long the loop takes to terminate for starting values $n = 1, 2, 3, . . . , 100$.

c. Prove that the loop terminates for all positive starting values. Write to us and let us see your proof. We promise to share the credit with you for your discovery.

25. If a and b are integers, the *greatest common divisor* (*gcd*) of a and b is the largest number that divides both a and b evenly. For example, the *gcd* of 15 and 24—which we would write *gcd*(15, 24)—is 3, whereas *gcd*(15, 16) = 1, since 1 is the largest number that divides both 15 and 16. The following function computes the *gcd* of two nonnegative integers.

```
function GCD(a, b : integer) : integer;
begin
   repeat
      a := a mod b;
      Swap(a, b)    {This is our building block that swaps values.}
   until b = 0;
   GCD := a
end;
```

It's tricky to prove that the function is correct. In fact, it's not even trivial to show that the loop terminates. The nice part, though, is that the function is *fast*. Try it with $a = 1377$ and $b = 1088$, listing the values at the start of each iteration of the loop.

26. As we've mentioned, a recursive subprogram is one that includes a call to itself in its definition. We could, for instance, define the *factorial* function of n, written $n!$, by the recursive definition

$$1! = 1$$

$$n! = n \times (n - 1)!, \text{ for } n > 1$$

or by the nonrecursive definition

$$n! = n \times (n - 1) \times (n - 2) \times \cdots \times 2 \times 1$$

For example, we can verify that $3! = 6$, $5! = 120$, and $7! = 5040$ (that's why the factorial function is written as an exclamation mark—it grows surprisingly! fast). Any recursive routine may be written without recursion. Using informal arguments, show that the following two functions both compute $n!$

```
function RecursiveFactorial(n : integer) : integer;
begin
   if n <= 1 then
      RecursiveFactorial := 1
   else
      RecursiveFactorial := n * RecursiveFactorial(n - 1)
end;

function IterativeFactorial(n : integer) : integer;
   var
      i, product : integer;
begin
   product := 1;
   i := n;
   while i >= 1 do
      begin
         product := i * product;
         i := i - 1
      end;
   IterativeFactorial := product
end;
```

27. Now you can write the checkbook management program we outlined in Chapter 1, Exercise 13. Do so.

28. In the function f in the PIP, there is an **if** statement that begins "**if** $x > RADIUS$ **then** $f := 0 \ldots$." The trapezoids are all bounded above by $x = 1$ (which is *RA-DIUS*), so the first clause of the **if** statement seems to be superfluous, since it'll never be executed. Why did we include it?

29. Modify the PIP so that it automatically sets the number of intervals to 2, 4, 8, 16, 32, and 64 and runs the approximation for the specified number of intervals.

30. Modify the PIP so that it keeps track of the last approximation, and does repeated approximations, doubling the number of intervals until the last approximation and the newest differ only in the eighth or higher decimal place. This technique of terminating a series of repetitive calculations when successive calculations differ only by a small amount is called the *method of relaxation*.

31. In the PIP, if we replace the function f by one that returns the values of the straight line $1 - x$, we should get 0.5 as the area of the resulting triangular region, so the program should return 2.0 as the approximation, since it multiplies the area by 4. Try it, and check that the number of intervals has almost no effect on the program's results. Why is that?

32. Modify the PIP for this chapter so that instead of approximating the area under a curve by trapezoids, it uses rectangles of height equal to the function value at the right side, as shown here. Compare your results with the original PIP for various numbers of intervals. Which method seems better?

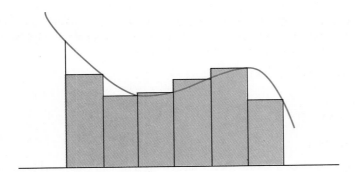

33. An even better way to approximate the area under a curve is to use *Simpson's rule*, which says that if the number, n, of intervals is even, the area can be approximated by

$$\frac{1}{3} \Delta \left[f(x_0) + 4 f(x_1) + 2 f(x_2) + 4 f(x_3) + \cdots + 2 f(x_{n-2}) + 4 f(x_{n-1}) + f(x_n) \right]$$

where Δ is the width of each interval. Modify the PIP to use Simpson's rule, and try it to see whether the results are closer to the actual value of π than those obtained by using trapezoids.

5.12
Answers

1.

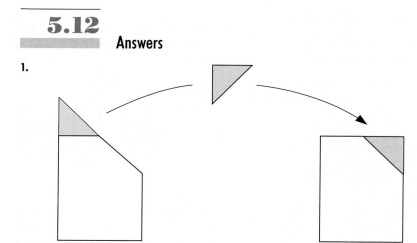

3. a. Nothing's wrong here.
   b. Move the **until** $n = -1$ part to the bottom, and eliminate the **begin** and **end**.
   c. The statement should be something like **for** $x := 2$ **to** 78 **do**. You can't have anything but a variable as an index, and **upto** sounds good but has no Pascal meaning.

5. a. This appears to be a sentinel-controlled loop that sums the values entered. The exit condition, then, is wrong, and both statements after **while** should be in the loop:

```
readln(n);
while n <> -1 do
    begin
        sum := sum + n;
        readln(n)
    end
```

   b. This also appears to be a sentinel-controlled loop. The exit condition is okay, but the sentinel is included in the running sum, so we have to adjust the sum upon completion:

```
repeat until n = -1
begin
    readln(n);
    sum := sum + n
end;
sum := sum + 1
```

   c. It's not easy to figure out *what* this is supposed to do, but it appears to add the squares from 2 to 78. The variable t hasn't been initialized, and that might be a mistake, too.

```
t := 0;
for x := 2 to 78 do
    t := t + sqr(x)
```

7. a. 25; five times in the inner loop for every iteration of the outer loop
   b. As the outer loop changes m from 1 to 5, the inner loop iterates 5, 4, 3, 2, and 1 times, so S is executed $5 + 4 + 3 + 2 + 1 = 15$ times.
   c. As above, the inner loop executes 4, 2, 0, 0, 0 times (when n is 3 or more, the upper limit $5 - n$ is less than the lower limit n, so the inner loop doesn't execute at all). S is executed 6 times.

9. The first three lines written have the values 2 1 (which is correct), 3 0 (which isn't), and 4 0 (which is also wrong). The problem is that the variables *trialDivisor* and *sumOfDivisors* aren't initialized where they ought to be. Since both of these need to be reset for every iteration of the outer loop, they should be initialized inside the outer loop, but outside the inner one, as follows.

```
for n := 2 to 1000 do
    begin
        sumOfDivisors := 0;
        trialDivisor := 1;
        while trialDivisor < n do
            begin
                if n mod trialDivisor = 0 then
                    sumOfDivisors := sumOfDivisors + trialDivisor;
                trialDivisor := trialDivisor + 1
            end;
        writeln(n, sumOfDivisors)
    end
```

11. a.
```
oldValue := -999;    {a dummy old value, just to get things started}
done := false;
while not done do
    begin
        read(n);
        if n = oldValue then
            begin
                writeln('Found an adjacent pair.');
                done := true
            end
        else if n = -1 then
            done := true
        else
            oldValue := n
    end;
readln                     {Discard the rest of the line.}
```

   b.
```
oldValue := -999;
n := -998;
repeat
    oldValue := n;
    read(n);
    newValue := n;
    if n = oldValue then
        writeln('Found an adjacent pair.');
until (oldValue = n) or (n = -1);
readln;
```

    c. While we wouldn't want to put words in your mouth, we found the flagged loop easier to write and, because of its directness, easier to understand.

13. a. **function** IsPrime(n : integer) : boolean;

There's a fairly simple way to speed this up by a factor of 2. Hint: If 2 doesn't divide n, *we don't need to check any other even divisors.*

```
    var
        divisor : integer;
    begin
        divisor : = 2;
        while (n mod divisor <> 0) and (divisor < trunc(sqrt(n))) do
            divisor : = divisor + 1;
        IsPrime : = (n mod divisor <> 0)
    end;
```

    b. **function** IsPrime(n : integer) : boolean;

```
    var
        i, prod : integer;
    begin
        prod : = 1;
        for i : = 1 to n − 1 do
            prod : = (prod * i) mod n;
        IsPrime : = (prod + 1) mod n = 0
    end;
```

15. Here are the sequences of *a* values we got.

100.00000000	10000.00000000
50.50000000	5000.50000000
26.24009859	2501.25000000
15.02552986	630.30364990
10.84043503	323.08450317
10.03257847	177.01808167
10.00005245	101.20218658
10.00000000	100.00714111
	100.00000000

Notice particularly that it took only one more iteration to go from 10,000 to 100 than it did to go from 100 to its square root, 10.

17. **program** SequenceTest(output);

```
    var
        sum: real;
        i, n: integer;
    begin
        for n : = 2 to 10 do
            begin
                sum : = 0.0;
                for i : = 1 to n do
                    sum : = sum + 1 / (i * (i + 1));
                writeln(n : 3, ' ', sum : 10 : 8)
            end
    end.
```

Well, well. It appears that the sum is $1 - 1/(n + 1)$. The trick here is to recognize that $1/(n(n + 1)) = (1/n) - (1/(n + 1))$, so the sum looks like this:

$$\left(\frac{1}{1} - \frac{1}{2}\right) + \left(\frac{1}{2} - \frac{1}{3}\right) + \cdots + \left(\frac{1}{n} - \frac{1}{n+1}\right) = 1 - \frac{1}{n+1}$$

There's a moral lurking here. While we might not have immediately seen the *partial fraction* decomposition of $1/(n(n + 1))$, we should not jump in and write code immediately. Sometimes, thinking can substitute for programming altogether.

19. **while** n $<>$ 0 **do**. We stop when we've used all the digits of n.

21. a. **function** Reverse(n : integer) : integer;
```
        var
            digit, r, powerOf10 : integer;
        begin
          r := 0;
          powerOf10 := 1;
          while n <> 0 do
            begin
              digit := n mod 10;        {Get the rightmost digit still in n,}
              n := n div 10;            {. . . strip it away from n,}
              r := powerOf10 * digit + r;   {. . . and place it on the left of r.}
              powerOf10 := 10 * powerOf10
            end;
          Reverse := r
        end;
```

b. **function** Palindrome(n : integer) : boolean;
```
        begin
            Palindrome := (n = Reverse(n))
        end;
```

c. The solution is left to the reader.

23. **program** DrawTree (output);
```
        const
            WIDTH = 41;   {the width of the print area; should be odd}
        var
            i: integer;

        procedure PrintStars (n: integer);
        {Print an odd number of stars, centered in the print area.          }
        {If we're printing n centered stars, there must be (WIDTH − n) / 2}
        {blanks on each side, particularly on the left.                     }
            var
                i: integer;
        begin
            for i := 1 to (WIDTH − n) div 2 do
                write(' ');
            for i := 1 to n do
                write('*');
            writeln
        end;
```

```
begin
  {Print the foliage.}
  for i : = 1 to 7 do
    PrintStars(2 * i − 1);
  {Print the trunk.}
  for i : = 1 to 3 do
    PrintStars(3)
end.
```

25.

a	b
1377	1088
1088	289
289	221
221	68
68	17
17	0

Done. $17 = gcd(1377, 1088)$

You can check that $1377 = 3^4 \times 17$ and $1088 = 2^6 \times 17$, so 17 is indeed the largest number that divides both.

27. We'll use the outline we generated in Chapter 1. We won't fill in all the details, but rather we'll show the state of the program midway through the development stage, concentrating on the parts that are particularly relevant for this chapter.

```
program CheckbookManager(input, output);
  var
    done : boolean;
    balance : real;

  procedure Startup(var openingBalance : real);
  begin
    writeln('We''ll give instructions here. ');
    write('What is the current balance? ');
    readln(openingBalance)
  end;

  function GetCommand : char;
    var
      c : char;
  begin
    write('Command? ');
    readln(c);
    while (c <> 'W') and (c <> 'w') and (c <> 'D') and (c <> 'd') and (c <> 'B') and
          (c <> 'b') and (c <> 'Q') and (c <> 'q') do
```

```
      begin
         writeln('Please enter a single letter, then press Return.');
         writeln('The command codes are:');
         writeln('   W: to write a check');
         writeln('   D: to deposit funds');
         writeln('   B: to see the current balance');
         writeln('   Q: to quit this program.');
         writeln;
         write('Command? ');
         readln(c)
      end;
   GetCommand : = c
end;

procedure WriteCheck(var balance : real);
begin
   writeln('This will have error-checking features like MakeDeposit.')
end;

procedure MakeDeposit(var balance : real);
   var
      deposit : real;
begin
   write('Amount to be deposited? ');
   readln(deposit);
   while deposit < 0 do
      begin
         writeln('You can''t deposit a negative amount.');
         writeln('Please enter a new deposit amount.');
         writeln('Just enter 0 if you want to get back to other transactions.');
         write('Amount to be deposited? ');
         readln(deposit)
      end;
   balance : = balance + deposit;
   writeln('The current balance is $', balance : 7 : 2)
end;

procedure DisplayBalance(balance : real);
begin
   writeln('The current balance is $', balance : 7 : 2)
end;

begin
   Startup(balance);
   done : = false;
   repeat
      case GetCommand of
         'w' : WriteCheck(balance);
         'd' : MakeDeposit(balance);
         'b' : DisplayBalance(balance);
         'q' : done : = true
      end
   until done
end.
```

29. This isn't too hard. All we do is replace the main **repeat** loop by a loop that doubles *n* each time, as shown here. We can eliminate *ReadyToQuit* from the program as a result.

```
begin   {Main}
   n := 2;
   while n <= 64 do
      begin
         writeln(n : 2, ' intervals. Pi approximation = ', 4.0 * Trapezoid(0.0, 1.0, n) : 9 : 7);
         n := 2 * n
      end
end.
```

31. If the upper boundary is a straight line, the trapezoidal regions, having straight tops, will give the area exactly. The only thing that can give us trouble, then, is round-off error, and that's not significant here, as you can see by running the modified PIP.

33. Replace *Trapezoid* by the following function, where we've omitted the function *f* for brevity.

```
function Simpson (lower, upper: real; n: integer): real;
{Approximates the area under y = f(x) between x = lower }
{and x = upper by using Simpson's method.                }
{NOTE: This requires that n be even, so if it's not, the  }
{function uses n + 1.                                     }
   var
      sum: real;    {the running sum of the terms in the series}
      delta: real;  {the width of each subinterval}
      i: integer;
begin
   if odd(n) then
      n := n + 1;
   delta := (upper - lower) / n;   {Compute the width of each subinterval.}
   sum := f(lower) + f(upper);      {Take care of the end cases.}
   for i := 1 to n - 1 do
      if odd(n) then
         sum := sum + 4.0 * f(lower * i)
      else
         sum := sum + 2.0 * f(lower * i);
   Simpson := (1 / 3) * delta * sum
end;
```

Text Processing: Characters, Strings, and Keyboard I/O

Almost by definition, computers have always had a facility with numbers, but people do not communicate solely in numbers. Textual information, like the paragraph you're reading right now, is perhaps even more common than numeric information. We read and generate written passages, our names and addresses are naturally expressed in textual form, the items in a store's inventory have descriptions as well as numeric inventory codes—all of these pieces of information, and many more, are examples of textual information that could profitably be manipulated by a computer.

In this chapter, we will discuss some of the ways that we can program a computer to process text. We will begin with the basic units of text, describe how they are manipulated, and then do something we have yet to do in this text: spend a considerable amount of time discussing a nonstandard—but quite common—extension to standard Pascal.

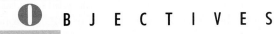

OBJECTIVES

In this chapter, we will:

- Describe in detail the primitive data type *char* and the internal codes by which characters are represented.
- Review the relational operators and functions applicable to *char* data.
- Discuss standard input and output statements as they relate to character data.

- Introduce the nonstandard data type **string**, and describe the common procedures and functions that operate on strings.
- Present our PIP for this chapter, which applies Pascal's text manipulation facilities to the problem of decoding encrypted messages.

6.1 Characters: Starting from the Bottom

Since all text is made by stringing characters together, the natural starting point for our discussion of text processing techniques is the *char* type. We've already seen that the type *char* represents single characters and that character literals in a program are represented by a character (only one!) enclosed in single quotes, like 'A', 'a' (which is not the same as the capital version, recall), '%', or '0'. It is important *not* to give any interpretation to the characters themselves; in particular, the character '0' has nothing whatsoever to do with the integer 0. This is a frequent source of confusion for beginning programmers. We have also seen that characters are stored in the memory of a computer as numbers represented by a preset code, like the ASCII code that assigns the number 65 to 'A', 66 to 'B', 97 to 'a', 48 to '0', 32 to ' ' (the space character), and so forth.

These codes were explained at the end of Section 2.1.

Character Operations

Characters have a natural linear order in some cases: 'A' comes before 'P' in alphabetic order, and it seems reasonable that '0' should come before '7'. The Pascal standard stipulates that this must be true: If the system supports alphabetic characters, the codes for uppercase letters must be strictly increasing in alphabetic order, and the same must be true for lowercase letters if they are available (as they are in most modern implementations). The standard for representing the digit characters '0', '1', . . . , '9' is even stricter: They must not only occur in numeric order but must also be *contiguous*, so the code for '2' must be one more than the code for '1'. Except for these requirements, the codes are left to the Pascal implementers. In the two most common code schemes, for example, these collections of characters occur in very different orders. In ASCII, the digit characters are before the capital letters, which are before the lowercase letters; in EBCDIC (Extended Binary Coded Decimal Interchange Code), the groups are arranged lowercase, then uppercase, then digits, which is about as different from ASCII as can be. In short, if you are writing a program that should run on all machines, you can assume 'G' < 'T', 'g' < 't', and '1' < '8', but you can make no assumption that 'G' < 'g' or '5' < 'R'—which leads us to the subject of this subsection.

Notice that we used the relational operator <. This makes sense according to the way we think of characters, and the requirements just mentioned guarantee that Pascal reflects our expectations. Since characters are represented internally as integers, it is a small step to extend the natural order of integers to an order on characters.

> The relational operators $=$, $<>$, $<$, $>$, $<=$, and $>=$ may be applied to characters. For characters $c1$ and $c2$ and relational operator OP, the expression $c1$ OP $c2$ is *true* if and only if (the code for $c1$) OP (the code for $c2$) is *true*, so $c1 < c2$ is true if and only if the code for $c1$ is less than the code for $c2$.

This *lexicographic order* is very useful. Suppose, for instance, we wanted to test whether a character variable ch represented a digit. In the standard, the digit character '0' . . . '9' are contiguous, so all we need to do is test whether ch occurs at or after '0' and also at or before '9', as in the following example:

```
if ('0' <= ch) and (ch <= '9') then
    writeln('This is a digit')
```

In a similar way, we could test whether a character, ch, was a vowel by

```
if (ch = 'A') or (ch = 'a') or (ch = 'E') or (ch = 'e') or (ch = 'I') or (ch = 'i') or (ch = 'O')
        or (ch = 'o') or (ch = 'U') or (ch = 'u') then
    writeln('This is a vowel')
```

Since we may generally assume that the letter characters are consecutive within each case, we can use them as we do integers to control a loop, as we might do to print the alphabet:

```
for ch := 'A' to 'Z' do
    writeln(ch);
```

Character Functions

Along with the relational operators, Pascal provides us with four predefined functions that act on characters or produce character values as their results. All of these depend on the internal code, though in most cases, you will never need to know codes of individual characters (thank goodness!). Three of these functions can also be applied to other types of data in Pascal.

The functions ord, pred, *and* succ *may be applied to values of any ordinal* type. *See Chapter 8.*

The *chr(integer)* function. The first function we'll discuss applies only to character-type information. The function *chr(integer)* returns the character with code equal to the integer argument. For example, on systems that use ASCII coding for characters, *chr*(65) is 'A', and *chr*(36) is '$'. You could discover the internal code your system uses for characters by running the following program:

```
program MakeCharTable(output);
   var
      i : integer;
begin
   for i := 0 to 127 do     The upper limit is 255 on some systems.
      writeln(i : 3, '*', chr(i), '*')
end;
```

We enclosed the character corresponding to the code *i* between stars ('*') in the *writeln* statement, since the first 32 characters in ASCII order (with codes 0 through 31) are nonprinting characters like the Tab and Return characters, which don't leave an image on the screen. Using the stars at least gives us a clue about their effects, if any, when they are sent to the screen. Except as a means of writing characters that happen not to be on the keyboard, like '¶', the function *chr* is rarely used by itself. You'll see it most often used with the *ord* function.

The *ord*(*character*) function. The inverse function to *chr* is *ord*(*character*). Given a character as argument, *ord* returns the integer code for that character so that in ASCII systems, *ord*('A') is 65, and *ord*('$') is 36. This function and *chr* are frequently used together. Since we can do arithmetic on integers, we can find the *ord* of a character, do something to the value, and send the result to *chr* to get a different character, depending on the original character. That probably seems somewhat cryptic, so we'll give you a useful example. In both ASCII and EBCDIC, the codes for 'A' through 'Z' and the codes for 'a' through 'z' all differ by a common amount for corresponding letters. As we've seen, the ASCII code for 'A' is 65, and the code for 'a' is 97, a difference of 32. Not surprisingly, the ASCII codes for 'B' and 'b' are 66 and 98, also differing by 32. What happens, then, when we perform the following operation on a lowercase alphabetic character *ch*?

```
chr(ord('A') + (ord(ch) − ord('a')))
```

Hmm . . . that's not at all obvious, so let's pick it apart from inside out, as we do with any complicated expression. First, if *ch* is a lowercase letter, the difference between its *ord* and the *ord* of 'a' tells us how far away *ch* is from 'a', as, for example, in ASCII *ord*('d') = 100, so *ord*('d') − *ord*('a') = 3 tells us that 'd' is three characters beyond 'a'. Now what happens when we add that number to *ord*('A')? The result will be the code of the character that is that many positions beyond 'A' — which is 'D', in this case. We then convert the result back to a character by applying *chr* to this result. Okay, we put in 'd' and got out 'D' — so what? You've probably guessed the answer: We've come up with an expression that changes lowercase letters to their uppercase equivalents. We'll talk about this particular expression in the lab for this chapter, and we'll use a similar expression in the Program in Progress.

$chr(n)$, for integer n, returns the character with internal code n.
$ord(ch)$, for character ch, returns the integer code of ch.

The *pred(ch)* and *succ(ch)* functions. The next two functions apply to characters and other types, as you will see. If ch is a character, $pred(ch)$ is the character whose code is one less than that of ch, if such a character exists at all. For instance, $pred('D')$ is 'C' in virtually all representation schemes. It happens that $pred('A')$ is '@' in ASCII (though not in other representations), as you can see by looking back to Table 2.2 (page 40) — $ord('A')$ is 65, and $ord('@')$ is 64. Although it's not likely to happen, it is possible that a call to $pred('A')$ might be an error, if you happen to be on a system in which there was no character before 'A'. Since the standard stipulates that alphabetic characters occur in order (though not necessarily consecutively), it will never be an error to call $pred('B')$ — it might not be 'A', but it will certainly be *some* character.[1]

The inverse to *pred* is *succ*; if ch is a character variable, $succ(ch)$ is the character whose code is one more than that of ch, so in ASCII $succ('A')$ is 'B', and $succ('Z')$ may be undefined (again, see footnote 1). Just as *chr* and *ord* undo each other, *succ* and *pred* are inverses, so $succ(pred(ch))$ and $pred(succ(ch))$ are both equal to the character ch (with two exceptions, right?). If we needed to test whether the uppercase characters were contiguous in our system, for instance, we could use the following program.

```
program TestUpperCase(output);
    var
        ch : char;
begin
    ch := 'A';
    writeln(ch);
    repeat
        ch := succ(ch);    Very much like i := i + 1, for integers.
        writeln(ch)
    until ch = 'Z'
end;
```

[1]This is really a nonproblem, since the two most important internal representations for letters have no nonletters lurking within them. They are also not at the ends of the character set, so there's a character before 'A' and after 'Z'. The standard notwithstanding, unless you are programming in some alternative universe, you can count on 'B' immediately following 'A', and you can be sure that $succ('Z')$ and $pred('A')$ are defined.

For a character, *ch*, *pred*(*ch*) returns the character immediately before *ch* (if any — it's an error if there isn't one), and *succ*(*ch*) returns the character immediately after *ch* (if any — it's an error if there isn't one).

Character Input and Output

If we think of it at all, most of us probably think of the keyboard and the screen as integral parts of a computer system, since that's generally the way the hardware is arranged. The screen and the keyboard sit on the same table, are physically attached to, and often even contained in, the same box that holds the computer's central processing unit and memory. In a sense, though, the screen and the keyboard are different from the computer proper. These *I/O devices* (for *input/ output*) are the windows to the human world that we use to get information into the computer and to display information that the computer processes.

At the conceptual level just below the one we see when we sit down to the computer, there are two storage areas that sit between the I/O devices and the computer. These are known as *buffers,* and they provide temporary storage for the characters that the computer has generated that are waiting to be sent to the screen or that have been typed and are waiting for the computer to read them. These buffers are collectively known also as the *standard textfiles* and are individually called *input* and *output*. That's what we mean when we write a program heading **program** *Sample*(*input*, *output*) — we are instructing the system that the program *Sample* will use both of the standard textfiles for communicating with its user. Figure 6.1 portrays the system at this conceptual level.

When you enter information from the standard input device, usually the keyboard, the typed characters go into the input buffer in the order in which you type them. A call to *readln* or *read* causes information to be removed from the input buffer and transferred to the variables in the *read* or *readln* calls. If there is not enough data in the input buffer to satisfy the call, the system suspends operation of the program until sufficient information is received. The Return key also sends a character to the input buffer, and this character is special. When the Return key is pressed, it sends a character that is referred to as the *end-of-line mark*. When the program sends a *readln* call to get some information, that information is transferred from the input buffer to the program, and all remaining characters up to and including the next end-of-line mark are discarded from the input buffer. A *read* call, on the other hand, transfers the requested information without discarding anything else, as indicated in Figure 6.2.

It is possible to read the end-of-line mark, but when you do, it is translated to a blank. Generally, you will not read the end-of-line mark but will rather use it as a sentinel and discard it by using a *readln* call. We'll soon see why you won't want to read the end-of-line mark and how to discard it.

T extfiles are Pascal entities themselves and are not limited to the two standard ones. We'll discuss this at length in Chapter 11.

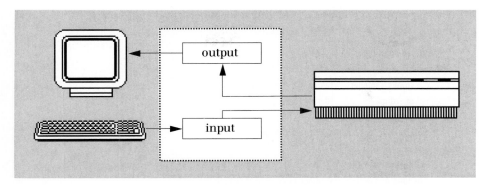

Figure 6.1. Communicating between I/O devices and a program using input and output buffers

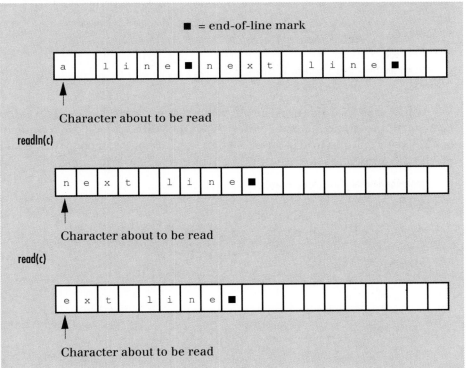

Figure 6.2. The different actions of *read* and *readln* on the input buffer

We mentioned that the end-of-line mark was special. That's because we don't need to read the input buffer to test for the mark. The predefined boolean function *eoln* (which stands for *end of line*) returns *true* if and only if the character about to be read is the end-of-line mark. This is often used as a sentinel to indicate to the program that nothing more is to be read. For example, the following program reads a line of characters and counts the number of vowels entered. For the sake of simplicity, we'll just count the lowercase vowels.

```
program VowelCount(input, output);
    var
        vowels : integer;     {number of vowels seen so far}
        ch : char;            {the character just read}
begin
    writeln('Type anything, ending with Return.');
    vowels : = 0;
    while not eoln do
    {As long as the character about to be read isn't the}
    {end mark, get the character from input and test it.}
        begin
            read(ch);
            if (ch = 'a') or (ch = 'e') or (ch = 'i') or (ch = 'o') or (ch = 'u') then
                vowels : = vowels + 1
        end;
    writeln('There were ', vowels : 1, ' vowels in that line.')
end.
```

This seems clear enough: The program reads and tests characters up to the first end-of-line mark in the input buffer. When the **while** loop is complete, then, the next character to be read is the end-of-line mark. Suppose, though, that we do some further reading, as in the following extension of the example program.

```
program NewVowelCount(input, output);
    var
        vowels : integer;     {number of vowels seen so far}
        ch : char;            {the character just read}
begin
    repeat
        writeln('Type anything, ending with Return.');
        vowels : = 0;
        while not eoln do
            begin
                read(ch);
                if (ch = 'a') or (ch = 'e') or (ch = 'i') or (ch = 'o') or (ch = 'u') then
                    vowels : = vowels + 1
            end;
        writeln('There were ', vowels : 1, ' vowels in that line');
        write('Do you want to try again? Answer N for no, Y for yes: ');
        readln(ch)
    until (ch = 'n') or (ch = 'N')
end.
```

This seems reasonable at first glance, but it has a serious flaw—it won't allow the user to quit. See if you can tell why before you read further.

Aha! The *readln(ch)* call at the end of the **repeat** loop will do just as requested — it will read the next character in the input buffer, which in this case, happens to be the leftover end-of-line sentinel that we used to control the **while** loop. The user might enter 'n' as an answer to "Do you want to try again?" but the *readln* that gets the user's response will never see it. We need to throw away the end-of-line mark before we call *readln* to get the user's response. How do we do that? With another *readln*!

```
program NewVowelCount(input, output);
    var
        vowels : integer;    {number of vowels seen so far}
        ch : char;           {the character just read}
begin
    repeat
        writeln('Type anything, ending with Return.');
        vowels : = 0;
        while not eoln do
            begin
                read(ch);
                if (ch = 'a') or (ch = 'e') or (ch = 'i') or (ch = 'o') or (ch = 'u') then
                    vowels : = vowels + 1
            end;
        readln;            {THROW AWAY THE END MARK!}
        writeln('There were ', vowels : 1, ' vowels in that line');
        write('Do you want to try again? Answer N for no, Y for yes: ');
        readln(ch)
    until (ch = 'n') or (ch = 'N')
end.
```

A call to *readln* with no parameters discards everything from the front of the input buffer through the first end-of-line mark. If you use the end-of-line mark as a sentinel to signal no further input, you must discard it by a *readln* call before you do any further reading.

There is no easy way to test for the end-of-line mark besides using *eoln*. Remember, though, that *eoln* is a boolean function, not a character. This confusion of names often leads people to try something like this:

```
read(ch);
if ch = eoln then        NO, NO, NO!
    writeln('This is the end of the line')
```

or the very natural-sounding

```
for i : = 1 to eoln do    NO, NO, NO!
    read(ch)
```

Don't do it. Actually, you don't have to worry. The Pascal compiler won't let you do it. The expression $ch = eoln$ mixes incompatible types: *char* on the left and *boolean* on the right, which is the same problem with **for** $i := 1$ **to** *eoln* **do**.

Notice, too, that you can't test for the end-of-line mark after you've read it. Since the mark reads as a blank, you can't tell whether the character you just read was an ordinary blank or the end-of-line mark, and the value of boolean function *eoln* will have changed back to *false*.

6.2 Strings: Extending the Standard

One of the most obvious deficiencies of the *char* type is that its elements are just too small. While we can do anything we need with text at the character level, most of the time we're working on larger objects—*strings* of characters, consisting of zero or more characters arranged in linear order. Pascal provides a limited string capability that you've already seen, namely, the literal strings that can appear in the parameters to *write* and *writeln* calls. Strings in the standard are written by enclosing zero or more characters within single quotes, as we're accustomed to doing: 'This is a string', for example, is a string of 16 characters (blanks count, remember), whereas '', written with two adjacent single quotes, is the *null string* consisting of no characters at all.

Because strings are so useful, many compilers include them as extensions to Pascal, enough so that it is worthwhile discussing them in a text that is otherwise implementation independent. In this section, we'll discuss the **string** type as it is implemented in Symantec's THINK Pascal and Borland's Turbo Pascal. The two environments include different string-handling routines, but to avoid complicating things too much, we'll discuss only the features that are common to both. Just remember that throughout this section we will be talking about nonstandard extensions, so be careful when transporting your string-using routines to other environments.

Syntax

A string-type object consists of an ordered collection of characters, along with two attributes: a maximum *size* that is set when the object is first declared and a *length* that may vary during the life of the object from zero to the maximum size declared. In no case can the size of a string be larger than 255 characters.

A variable of type **string** is declared just as other variables are, by following its name by a type name in a **var** declaration. There are two forms of **string** type specifications: **string** and **string** [n], where n is a constant between 0 and 255.

We'll see the reason why the size limit is 255 when we talk about arrays in Chapter 9.

The following are all legal string-type declarations:

```
const
   STRSIZE = 6;
var
   address : string;        Can be as long as 255 characters.
   name : string [32];      Can never have more than 32 characters.
   ID : string [STRSIZE];   We can use previously defined constants.
```

String variables can be used as entire objects, or we can refer to their *components* — namely, the characters of which they are composed. To refer to the *i*-th character in a string-type variable *str*, we use the *selector* for string variables. For strings, we enclose the position in square brackets so that *name*[3] is the third character in the string *name*. Positions can be any integer from 1 to the length of the string. Given the declaration above, *ID*[−2] and *ID*[99] would always be incorrect since they refer to locations out of the size range 1 . . . 6, and *ID*[4] may be invalid, depending on the current length of *ID*. Since strings are composed of characters, we can do anything with their components that we can do with characters. For example, the following statements are all legal.

We'll see selectors used again in Chapters 9 and 10.

```
name := 'Jones, K., M.';
if name[6] = ',' then
   writeln('Found a comma');
name[1] := 'B';
name[1] := chr(ord(name[1]) − ord('A') + ord('a'))
```

String Operations

In the preceding example, you've already seen the first string operation we will discuss: the assignment statement. As with other Pascal types, you can assign to a string variable any string expression whose result is compatible with the variable. *Assignment compatibility* for strings is simple — if *s* is a string and *v* is a string-type variable, the assignment statement *v* := *s* is legal as long as the maximum allowed size of *v* is greater than or equal to the current length of *s*, as we demonstrate below:

```
var
   word : string [7];
   bigWord : string;          Could be up to 255 characters long.
begin
   ⋮
   word := 'A';               OK. There's room for one character in word.
   bigWord := word;           OK. Plenty of room in bigWord.
   bigWord := '123456789';    OK. Note that this is not an integer.
   word := bigWord            NO. bigWord has length 9 now, but word has size 7, so
                              there's not enough room.
```

Notice in this example that there is no contextual clue that tells us that 'A' should be a character constant or a string of length one. Since there's no way of telling, Pascal allows characters to be considered as strings of length one when appropriate. In the example, we could equally well have used a character variable *ch* and made the assignment *word := ch*, for instance.

The relational operators $=$, $<>$, $<$, $>$, $<=$, and $>=$ can be applied to strings. Although the rule for string comparisons sounds complex, it is really nothing more than the computer version of the *lexicographic order* that we use to locate items in a dictionary:

Suppose *s* and *t* are strings, then $s < t$ if any of the conditions below hold.

1. The length of *s* is zero, and the length of *t* is positive.
2. The first *n* characters of *s* and *t* match and either
   a. *s* has length *n* and *t* has length greater than *n*, or
   b. *s* and *t* are longer than *n* characters, and $s[n + 1] < t[n + 1]$ in the underlying order on characters.

Condition 1 asserts that the null string is less than any other; condition 2a implies that 'HOT' < 'HOTTENTOT'; and condition 2b implies that 'BRAINS' < 'BRAWN'. Hidden in this definition is the consequence that strings of different length can never be equal.

One of the nicest features of strings for text-processing purposes is that they can be read and written as entire units. This relieves us not only of having to read or write textual information character by character but also frees us from having to worry about reading end-of-line markers. Using strings, we can read or write a whole chunk of text at once. This should come as no surprise, since we're used to statements like *writeln*('This whole string'). The good news is that we can read that way, too.

Recall from Chapter 2 that a string can never contain a Return character. This determines in part how strings are read.

- *read*, applied to strings, gets characters from the input buffer up to but not including the first end-of-line mark. It's an error if the number of characters available in the buffer is larger than the length of the string(s) being read. Note that *read*ing strings always leaves the end-of-line mark in the input buffer, so subsequent reads will read nothing unless you discard the end-of-line mark.
- *readln*, applied to strings, acts like *read*, except that it discards the end-of-line mark. Generally, you will use *readln* to read strings.

String Procedures and Functions

There are six subprograms that are common to the compilers we're discussing—four functions and two procedures. In this section, we'll describe each of the routines briefly. We'll show how they are used when we discuss the Program in Progress. In the descriptions below, the name *string-type* refers to either **string** or the size-limited **string** [*K*], for some constant *K*.

String functions

- *Length*(*str* : *string-type*) : *integer*, returns the current length of *str*. If *str* = 'Moo', *Length*(*str*) is 3, regardless of the size limit on *str*.
- *Pos*(*substr*, *str* : *string-type*) : *integer*, returns the location of the start of the first instance of *substr* in the string *str*, if any, and returns 0 if *substr* is not found in *str*. For example, *Pos*('is', 'Mississippi') is 2, since the first 'is' in 'Mississippi' begins in position 2. *Pos*('os', 'Mississippi') is 0, since 'os' does not occur in the target string.
- *Concat*(*s1*, *s2*, . . . , *sn*: *string-type*) : *string-type*, returns the string that results from combining the arguments in order into one large string, so *Concat*('Wom', 'bat') is the string 'Wombat'. It is an error if the result is longer than the allowed size of the string.
- *Copy*(*str* : *string-type* ; *index*, *count* : *integer*) : *string-type*, returns a string of length *count* copied from the locations beginning at *index* in *str*. For example, *Copy*('quiddity', 5, 3) returns 'dit'. *Copy* does the best it can if given bad parameters. If *count* is ≤ 0, it returns the null string. If *index* is negative or *index* + *count* is larger than the length of *str*, only the characters in range are copied, so *Copy*('quiddity', 5, 9999) returns 'dity'. This relieves us of the need to keep track of the length of *str*.

String procedures

- *Delete*(**var** *str* : *string-type* ; *index*, *count* : *integer*), changes *str* by deleting *count* characters, starting from position *index*. If *str* is 'mustard', *Delete* (*str*, 3, 4) results in *str* = 'mud'. Like *Copy*, *Delete* does the best it can with faulty inputs. If *index* or the combination of *index* and *count* are out of the range of positions in *str*, only those characters in range will be deleted.
- *Insert*(*source* : *string-type* ; **var** *dest* : *string-type* ; *index* : *integer*), alters *dest* by inserting the string *source* into *dest*, starting at position *index*. After insertion, the substring *source* is found in *dest* beginning at position *index*. In a sense, *Insert* is the inverse of *Delete*, so that if *str* = 'mud', *Insert*('star', *str*, 3) results in *str* = 'mustard'. If *index* ≤ 0, *source* is inserted at the beginning of *dest*, and if *index* > *Length*(*dest*), *source* is inserted after the end of *dest*.

6.3
Computer Science Interlude: Cryptography

The development of the computer owes much to code-breaking, and indeed one of the first major applications of computers was to aid the Allies in the decoding of German messages during World War II. At that time, the German military used a code machine called ENIGMA, which looked something like a typewriter with a collection of rotating disks attached. The action of such a disk machine is simple in principle: Each disk had a collection of metal contacts around its circumference, and these buttons were connected in pairs by wires. When the operator typed 'a', for instance, the key sent a current to one of the contacts on the disk, the current traveled to another contact, perhaps the one for 'h'. By itself, this is a simple *substitution cypher* that might be represented

```
input:   a b c d e f g h i j k l m n o p q r s t u v w x y z
output:  h p w j r o t a n d z q v i f b l e x g y m c s u k
```

Notice that the letters are grouped in pairs so that input 'b' gives output 'p' and *vice versa*. This of course is a consequence of the way the wires are connected. The message 'happy birthday', then, would be encoded 'ahbbu pnegajhu'. Such ciphers are too simple to provide any real security. Since each letter is always represented by the same coded letter, one can rely on the frequency of letters to guess that in a message with many 'r's, the frequent 'r's represented 'e' ('e' being the most common English letter).[2]

A rotor machine extends this substitution notion as follows. After each letter is entered, the wheel rotates a specified number of positions. In Figure 6.3, we show what happens after a clockwise rotation by one position. Notice that 'a' translates as 'h' in the first position, but after a rotation, 'a' translates to 'l'. The old 'a'–'h' wire is set in color to make the rotation clearer: After rotation, that wire is now the 'b'–'i' wire, and after another rotation, it would become the 'c'–'j' wire. You can show (with some mental rotation of your own) that the word 'aaa' would be encoded as 'hlw', giving little clue to the coding scheme that could be deduced by letter frequencies in the original text.

Complex rotor machines make the cryptologist's job even more difficult by using several rotors, arranged so that the output of one rotor becomes the input of the next and designed so that they rotate at different rates. If that weren't enough, the ENIGMA machines sent each letter through the rotors twice: once through the rotors in one direction, then reflected back through the rotors in the opposite direction.[3]

---

[2]Of course, the frequencies are different if the source language is German, but the same principle applies. Although 'e' is the most common letter in English and German, 't' is the second most common letter in English, whereas 'n' is the second most common in German, for example.

[3]This had the advantage that the same machine with the same settings could be used both to encode and decode messages.

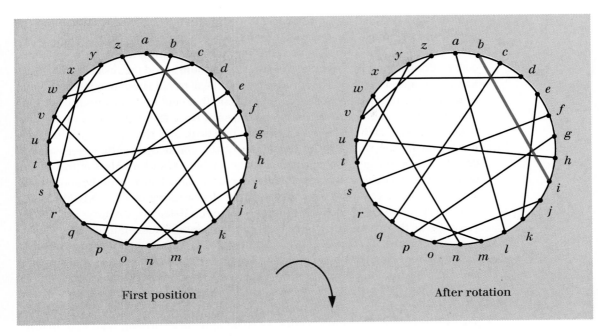

First position   After rotation

Figure 6.3. The action of a rotor encryption machine

Rotor machines had been commercially available since 1921, and British intelligence knew that ENIGMA was such a device, but most of the details of ENIGMA remained a mystery until Polish agents managed to smuggle an ENIGMA machine to the British. Even with the machine in their possession, decoding messages was hellishly difficult, since, for example, the starting position for the rotors was changed on a regular basis, and each time the settings were changed the code had to be broken anew.

Put yourself in the position of the cryptanalysis group at Bletchley Park in England in 1940. You had the exact machine that the enemy was using but had no clue to the settings used to generate a message. One way to decode a message, of course, would simply be to run the message through the machine for all settings, and wait until you found text that made sense. With five rotors, there would be $26 \times 26 \times 26 \times 26 \times 26 = 11,881,376$ possible settings. If you were very dextrous, you could change the rotor settings and run the message through at the rate of about one trial per minute, which means that it would take until 1962 to decode a single message. With one additional rotor, the time goes up to over 387 years, which you'll admit is a completely useless time frame.

We're vastly oversimplifying the procedures the code-breakers had at their command, but even with sophisticated group-theoretic and statistical techniques available, the problem was the same. There was simply too much computational work for any unaided group of people to complete in a useful time frame. Fortunately, the group had the services of Alan Turing, the brilliant British mathematician and one of the founders of computer science. Turing and others set about constructing a computer, named Colossus, that would speed the task of calculation. Keeping in mind the fact that our example is a near-trivial simplification of the real task, suppose that we had a computer available that could test a thousand settings per second. Suddenly, the decoding task shrinks from 22 years to just under four hours! Breaking new codes now becomes practical, and that's exactly what happened during the war. For the remainder of the conflict, the Allies were able to decode Axis messages, giving them an incalculable advantage. Most of the details of what went on during that period have been declassified only recently, and several authorities have gone so far as to claim that the breaking of the ENIGMA codes could very well have spelled the difference between defeat and victory.

Since then, computers have been an indispensable tool for intelligence agencies such as the National Security Agency (NSA) and its counterparts in other nations. These agencies have at their disposal the state of the art in computation, and common rumor has it that they often have equipment that is more sophisticated than anything that is commercially available. Whether that is true or not, the computer remains of primary importance since encryption algorithms have kept pace with the ability to break codes. Cryptography is a thriving branch of mathematics and computer science today, investigating problems such as that of factoring a large number efficiently, which lies at the heart of a sophisticated modern encryption scheme. It may sound strange that an efficient algorithm for factoring a 300-digit number would be a matter of national security, but it's true.

Encryption

The *Caesar cypher* is the first documented use of what we would call true cryptology, although contemporary accounts imply that it was not new at the time. Julius Caesar is reported to have communicated to some of his acquaintances through a substitution cypher in which every letter was replaced by one three places further in the alphabet, wrapping the letters around to fill the last three places. In modern terms, and using the English alphabet, we have the following correspondence between the *plaintext* input and the *cyphertext* output.

```
input:    a b c d e f g h i j k l m n o p q r s t u v w x y z
output:   d e f g h i j k l m n o p q r s t u v w x y z a b c
```

According to this scheme, the first sentence of Caesar's *Gallic Wars*, 'OMNES GALLIA EST DIVISA IN PARTES TRES' would become 'RPQHV JDOOL DHVWG LYLVD QSDUW HVWUH V', separating the cyphertext into groups of five letters, according to time-honored tradition.

We'd bet most of you have seen a Caesar cypher encryption/decryption device, though you probably didn't know the name at the time. You can make your own by making two copies of Figure 6.4 (don't try to snip it from the text!), cutting

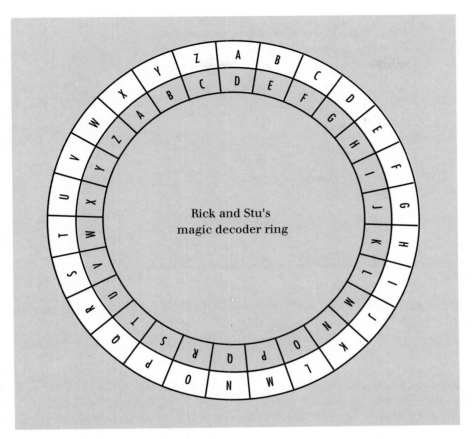

Rick and Stu's
magic decoder ring

Figure 6.4.   Collect 'em, trade 'em with your friends!

the inner disk of one copy free from the outer ring, pasting them on cardboard, and fastening the centers together. You can see, for instance, that by rotating the ring, you are not limited to Caesar's offset of three but could choose any offset that suited you — and there's where the fun comes in, as we'll see.

Decryption

Suppose you intercepted an encyphered message that read NMDLJ CRXWR BFQJC BDAER ENBFG NWCQJ CFQRL QQJBK NNWUN JAWNM QJBKN NWOXA PXCCN W. How would you begin to decipher it?

The first thing you might notice is that the *frequency* of letters is different from that of English: There are too few 'E's and too many 'Q's for the message to be the result of a *transposition cypher*, in which letters of the input text are merely rearranged to form the cyphertext. An example of a transposition cypher is the

---

Table 6.1.   Frequencies of Letters in a Representative Sample Text (this text, Chapters 1–5, in fact)

Letter	Frequency (%)	Letter	Frequency (%)
E	13.04	M	2.69
T	9.76	P	2.57
A	8.61	F	2.18
O	7.31	G	2.01
N	7.07	W	1.89
I	6.88	B	1.64
R	6.73	Y	1.39
S	6.41	V	0.97
L	4.22	X	0.55
H	4.21	K	0.41
D	3.25	Q	0.14
C	3.10	Z	0.09
U	2.80	J	0.07

railfence cypher that would take 'FOOLED YOU DIDNT I', write its letters alternately on two rows:

```
F   O   E   Y   U   I   N   I
  O   L   D   O   D   D   T
```

and then string the rows together: 'FOEYUINIOLDODDT'. Since the frequency gives us a clue that we might be dealing with a substitution cypher, we look further at the frequency of letters. Of the 66 letters in the cyphertext, 'N' occurs most often, followed by a tie between 'Q' and 'R', closely followed by a tie between 'C' and 'J'. These might represent the commonest English letters, which we can find by looking them up in a table like Table 6.1, prepared from the 162,353 letter characters in Chapters 1–5.

It took us about twenty minutes to write the program and a minute for it to compute the frequency of all 162,353 characters. You'll know how to do what we did when you finish Chapter 11.

Our first attempt is to guess that this is a Caesar cypher and that plaintext 'E' corresponds to cyphertext 'N'—the two commonest letters in English and the cyphertext, respectively. We test our guess by setting our decoder ring to an offset of 9 (the difference between 'N' and 'E' in alphabetic order) and—lo and behold!—the answer pops right out the first time. Try it and see for yourself. If we had gotten junk, the next step would be to guess that 'E' cyphers as either 'Q' or 'W' and to try those. There are more sophisticated techniques, of course, some of which we'll explore later.

6.4 Problem Solving I: Designing the PIP

The Program in Progress for this chapter is actually two programs, designed to give you a taste of computational cryptography. Since this text is not primarily devoted to making and breaking codes, we'll have to settle for the bare minimum, enciphering and deciphering according to an old and—by today's standards—simple coding scheme. Much of what we'll say about our PIP, though, applies equally well to far more sophisticated enciphering and deciphering programs, like the ones the NSA uses.

The first of the two Programs in Progress is the encryption program *EncryptCaesar*. We'll work through the design and development process for this one, trusting that you'll be able to see how the other was made. This program asks the user to enter a plaintext string to be encrypted, along with the offset to be used, and produces the cyphertext output, collected in groups of five. Here's the specification:

INPUT: The offset to be used in the Caesar cypher (integer).
A collection of characters to be decoded (string).

OUTPUT: The encrypted version of the input message (string).

ALGORITHM: Produce the output by taking each letter in the input message in turn and shifting it in the alphabet by the offset.

6.5 Problem Solving II: Developing the PIP

The first outline is the usual input/process/output format. By now, we're familiar enough with this form that we can actually flesh it out somewhat right at the start.

I. Get information.
   A. Read the *offset* (integer) to be used in the Caesar cypher.
   B. Read the *plaintext* message (string).
II. Encode the plaintext to produce the *cyphertext* (string).
III. Display the cyphertext in groups of five.

Outline item I needs no further expansion, so we move on to item II. We do this just as we would do it by hand. In other words, we consider each character in turn, from left to right, determine the letter that is *offset* away from the one we're considering, and place the encrypted character in its proper place in the cyphertext message. When defined as a subprogram, outline item II will look like this:

II. Call **procedure** *CaesarCypher*. IN: *offset* (integer), *inStr* (string), OUT: *outStr* (string).

    A. Initialize *outStr*.

    B. Repeat processing for characters 1 to the length of *inStr*.

        1. Find the character shifted *offset* beyond the i-th *inStr* character.

        2. Place that character in the i-th position in *outStr*.

We can find the i-th character of *inStr* easily enough — we just use the string selector square brackets. In other words, *inStr*[i] will be the i-th character in *inStr*. The coding will be done by the machine version of Rick and Stu's Magic Decoder Ring. We'll discuss the shifting process to produce the cypher in the analysis section that follows, but clearly the result will be assigned to *outStr*[i]. We want *outStr* to be the same length as *inStr*, so how do we initialize *outStr*? Well, since we're going to replace each of its letters, we could start with any string of the same length as *inStr*. Why not simply use a copy of *inStr* itself? Now we have expanded outline item II to look like Pascal, since we're just about ready to finish the procedure.

II. Call **procedure** *CaesarCypher*. IN: *offset* (integer), *inStr* (string), OUT: *outStr* (string).

    A. *outStr* := *inStr*

    B. **for** i := 1 **to** *Length*(*inStr*) **do**

        outStr[i] := the shifted result of *inStr*[i]

Oops! We forgot something. We flashed past the input part, thinking that we could just use *readln*(*plaintext*), but any old text at all won't serve as input to *CaesarCypher* — the decoder ring that we're modeling expects only uppercase letters.

Problem-solving technique

Look at each new routine carefully. Are you making any implicit assumptions that need to be guarded?

In this case, we'd better make sure that the plaintext string that *CaesarCypher* gets consists only of uppercase letters. What we could do is read the plaintext and convert it by discarding all non-alphabetic characters and changing any lowercase letters to their uppercase equivalents. The input part IB is complicated enough to deserve its own procedure, which will have its own subordinate procedure for converting to uppercase.

I. Get information.

    A. Read the *offset* (integer) to be used in the Caesar cypher.

    B. Call **procedure** *GetAString*. IN: nothing, OUT: *enteredStr* (string).

        1. Read *enteredStr*.

        2. Call **procedure** *ConvertToCapAlpha*. IN, OUT: *s* (string).

            a. Set *t* (string) to the empty string.

            b. For every character in *s*,

                i. If the *i*-th character in *s* is a lowercase letter, use **function** *Cap* to convert it to uppercase, and insert it at the right end of *t*.

                ii. If the *i*-th character of *s* is an uppercase letter, insert it at the right end of *t*.

                iii. Otherwise, do nothing.

We'll look more closely at *ConvertToCapAlpha* and *Cap* in the analysis section.

Finally, we can expand the item III output part. To print *cyphertext* in groups of five, we'll write the string character by character, keeping a count of the position of the character we're writing. When the count gets to 1, 6, 11, 16, and so on, we write an extra blank. The final outline now looks like this:

I. Get information.

    A. Read the *offset* (integer) to be used in the Caesar cypher.

    B. Call **procedure** *GetAString*. IN: nothing, OUT: *enteredStr* (string).

        1. Read *enteredStr*.

        2. Call **procedure** *ConvertToCapAlpha*. IN, OUT: *s* (string).

            a. Set *t* (string) to the empty string.

            b. For every character in *s*,

                i. If the *i*-th character in *s* is a lowercase letter, use **function** *Cap* to convert it to uppercase, and insert it at the right end of *t*.

                ii. If the *i*-th character of *s* is an uppercase letter, insert it at the right end of *t*.

                iii. Otherwise, do nothing.

II. Call **procedure** *CaesarCypher*. IN: *offset* (integer), *inStr* (string), OUT: *outStr* (string).

    A. *outStr* := *inStr*

    B. **for** *i* := 1 **to** *Length*(*inStr*) **do**
        outStr[*i*] := the shifted result of *inStr*[*i*]

III. Call **procedure** *PrintInGroups*. IN: *s* (string), OUT: nothing.

    A. **for** *i* := 1 **to** *Length*(*s*) **do**

        1. **if** (*i* **mod** 5) = 1 **then** write a space.

        2. In any case, write *s*[*i*].

    B. Call *writeln* to move the cursor to the start of a new line.

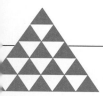

This is certainly the most complex program we've designed so far. In light of this, you'll notice that we've included in each subprogram's comment header a list of the places where it's called and what subprograms, if any, it calls.

The PIP: Coding

```
program EncryptCaesar (input, output);
{——————————————————————————————————————————————————}
{                                                                          }
{                        PROGRAM IN PROGRESS—1                             }
{                                                                          }
{                              CHAPTER 6                                   }
{                                                                          }
{         This program encodes a plaintext message using a Caesar          }
{         cypher.                                                          }
{         INPUT:     offset used in decryption (integer)                   }
{                    plaintext message (string)                           }
{         OUTPUT:    cyphertext (string)                                  }
{                                                                          }
{         NOTE: This uses strings, so is nonstandard.                      }
{                                                                          }
{——————————————————————————————————————————————————}
{         SUBPROGRAM LIST                                                   }
{         ConvertToCapAlpha (var s: string)                                }
{              Cap (ch: char): char                                       }
{         GetAString (promptStr: string; var enteredStr: string)          }
{         PrintInGroups (s: string)                                       }
{         CaesarCypher (offset: integer; inStr: string;                   }
{                       var outStr: string)                               }
{                                                                          }
{——————————————————————————————————————————————————}

var
    plaintext, cyphertext: **string**;
    offset: integer;
{——————————————————— TEXT-HANDLING ROUTINES ———————————————————}
procedure ConvertToCapAlpha (**var** s: **string**);
{Strips all non-alphabetic characters from the input string }
{and converts what remains to uppercase letters.            }
{Called by : Main    Calls : Cap (internal)                 }
    var
        i,          {the current position in the input string}
        j: integer;  {the position just after the end of the output string}
```

```
function Cap (ch: char): char;
{If ch is a lowercase letter, return its uppercase equivalent,}
{otherwise return the character itself.                    }
begin
    if ('a' < = ch) and (ch < = 'z') then
        Cap : = chr(ord(ch) − ord('a') + ord('A'))
    else
        Cap : = ch
end;

begin   {ConvertToCapAlpha}
    t : = ";   {Start with an empty output string.}
    i : = 0;
    for i : = 1 to Length(s) do
    {for every character in the input string . . .}

    s : = t    {Send the output string out of the procedure.}
end;

procedure GetAString (promptStr: string; var enteredStr: string);
{Prompts the user with 'promptStr' to enter   }
{a line of text and converts the entered string }
{to uppercase letters. Called by : Main        }
begin
    writeln;
    writeln(promptStr);
    writeln;
    write('> ');
    readln(enteredStr);
    ConvertToCapAlpha(enteredStr)
end;

procedure PrintlnGroups (s: string);
{Prints string s in groups of size GROUPSIZE.}
{Called by : Main                           }
    const
        GROUPSIZE = 5;
    var
        i: integer;
```

```
    begin
      for i := 1 to Length(s) do
        begin
          if (i mod GROUPSIZE) = 1 then
            write(' ');
          write(s[i])
        end;
      writeln
    end;
```

{────────────────────────── CYPHER ROUTINE ──────────────────────────}

```
  procedure CaesarCypher (offset: integer; inStr: string; var outStr: string);
  {Convert each character in the input to one that is  }
  {further in the alphabet by a given offset. The only}
  {tricky part is the use of modular arithmetic to     }
  {wrap around the end of the alphabet.                }
  {Called by : Main                                    }
    var
      i: integer;
  begin
    outStr := inStr;
    for i := 1 to Length(outStr) do
      outStr[i] := chr(ord('A') + (ord(outStr[i]) − ord('A') + offset) mod 26)
  end;
```

{────────────────────────── MAIN PROGRAM ──────────────────────────}

```
begin   {Main}
  write('Offset to be used in encryption? ');
  readln(offset);

  GetAString('At the ">" prompt, enter a line of text to be encrypted.', plaintext);

  CaesarCypher(offset, plainText, cypherText);

  writeln;
  writeln('The encrypted text is:');
  writeln;
  PrintInGroups(cypherText)
end.
```

The second of the Programs in Progress takes a cyphertext message and attempts to decrypt it by finding the most frequently occurring character in the cyphertext and decoding the message on the assumption that the most frequent character corresponds to one that the user enters. For the sake of brevity, we haven't included the complete code for the routines that have already been defined in *EncryptCaesar*.

We haven't provided a development outline here. Instead, we'll leave it up to you to figure out how this program works. This is a common problem that

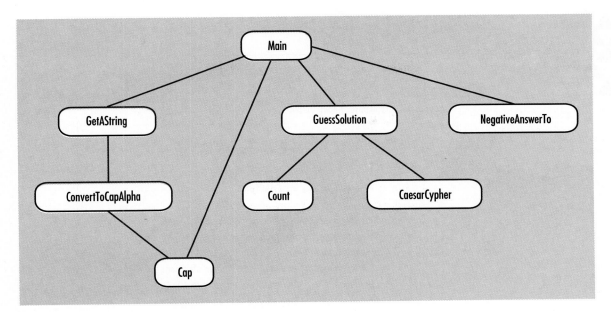

Figure 6.5. Subprogram calling diagram of *DecryptCaesar*

programmers face: You're given a moderately large program that someone else has written, and you have to read and understand it. There are two general schemes for reading programs, known as front-to-back and back-to-front.

In a *front-to-back reading*, you begin with the program header and read through until you come to the last statement in the main program. As you go, take note of what the subprograms do (with luck, you'll have comments to guide you), and make note of their dependencies. In other words, keep track of which routines are called by each new subprogram and how the subprograms are nested within each other. You'll produce an outline very much like the subprogram list, which, fortunately, has been provided in the comment header block. While doing this, you should also note the information that is passed to and from the subprograms.

In a *back-to-front reading*, you begin with the main program and list the subprograms it calls. For each of these subprograms, you note the subprograms that they call, and so on, until you've produced a hierarchical diagram like the one in Figure 6.5.

In practice, one generally reads a program in both directions, often several times. Ultimately, your goal should be to produce something very much like the outline that would have been used to develop the program in the first place. Try it.

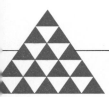

The PIP: Decoding

program DecryptCaesar (input, output);

```
{————————————————————————————————————————————————}
{                                                  }
{              PROGRAM IN PROGRESS—2               }
{                                                  }
{                    CHAPTER 6                     }
{                                                  }
{    This program takes a cyphertext and decodes it, based on   }
{    the assumption that the cyphertext was constructed by using }
{    a Caesar cypher.                              }
{            It uses a procedure, GuessSolution, that finds the  }
{    commonest letter in the cyphertext and uses that to find    }
{    the Caesar cypher offset, which it then uses to produce a   }
{    trial decryption.                             }
{    INPUT:      a cyphertext (string)             }
{                guesses about the most common character }
{                in the cyphertext (char)          }
{    OUTPUT:     the trial decryptions (string)    }
{                                                  }
{    NOTE: This uses strings, so is nonstandard.   }
{                                                  }
{————————————————————————————————————————————————}
{    SUBPROGRAM LIST                               }
{    Cap (ch: char): char                          }
{    ConvertToCapAlpha (var s: string)             }
{    GetAString (promptStr: string; var enteredStr: string) }
{    Count (theChar: char; s: string): integer     }
{    GuessSolution (cypherText: string; targetChar: char) }
{            CaesarCypher (offset: integer; inStr: string; }
{                            var outStr: string)   }
{    NegativeAnswerTo(prompt: string): boolean     }
{                                                  }
{————————————————————————————————————————————————}
```

    var
       cypherText: **string**;   {the text to be decoded}
       likelyChar: char;   {our guess of the likeliest character in the plaintext}

{────────────────── TEXT-HANDLING ROUTINES ──────────────────}

```
function Cap (ch: char): char;
begin
   {See EncryptCaesar.}
end;

procedure ConvertToCapAlpha (var s: string);
   var
      i, j: integer;
      t: string;
begin
   {See EncryptCaesar.}
end;

procedure GetAString (promptStr: string; var enteredStr: string);
begin
   {See EncryptCaesar.}
end;

function Count (theChar: char; s: string): integer;
{Returns the number of occurrences of theChar in s.}
{Called by : GuessSolution                           }
   var
      n, i: integer;
begin
   n := 0;
   for i := 1 to Length(s) do
      if s[i] = theChar then
         n := n + 1;
   Count := n
end;
```

{────────────────────── CYPHER ROUTINES──────────────────────}

```
procedure GuessSolution (cypherText: string; targetChar: char);
{Produce a trial decryption of the cyphertext by finding   }
{the most common letter and assuming that it is the        }
{encrypted form of targetChar in a Caesar cypher.          }
{Called by : Main       Calls : Count, CaesarCypher (internal) }
   var
      maxCount, thisCount, offset: integer;
      ch, thisChar: char;
      plainText: string;

   procedure CaesarCypher (offset: integer; inStr: string; var outStr: string);
   begin
      {See EncryptCaesar.}
   end;
```

```
begin    {GuessSolution}
   maxCount : = 0;
   for ch : = 'A' to 'Z' do
      begin
         thisCount : = Count(ch, cypherText);
         {Find the number of occurrences of the character ch.}
         if thisCount > maxCount then
         {If there are more than the old maximum . . .}
            begin
               maxCount : = thisCount;    {Record the new maximum.}
               thisChar : = ch            {Record which character it was.}
            end
      end;
   offset : = ord(thisChar) − ord(targetChar);
   writeln;
   writeln('The most likely offset is ', offset : 1, ' and the decrypted message is:');
   writeln;
   CaesarCypher(26 − offset, cypherText, plainText);
   writeln(plainText)
end;
```

```
{──────────────────────── NEW QUIT UTILITY ────────────────────────}
function NegativeAnswerTo(prompt: string): boolean;
{Returns true if and only if user enters}
{'n' or 'N' to the prompt string.        }
{Called by : Main                        }
   var
      ans: char;
begin
   writeln;
   writeln(prompt);
   write('Type "y" for yes or "n" for no and then press Return: ');
   readln(ans);
   while (ans <> 'y') and (ans <> 'Y') and (ans <> 'n') and (ans <> 'N') do
      begin
         writeln;
         writeln('*** Please limit your response to "y" or "n" (without quotes). ');
         write('Try again: "n" for no, "y" for yes: ');
         readln(ans)
      end;
   writeln;
   NegativeAnswerTo : = (ans = 'n') or (ans = 'N')
end;
```

```
{———————————————— MAIN PROGRAM ————————————————}
begin   {Main}
    GetAString('Please enter a line of text to be decrypted.', cyphertext);

    repeat
        writeln('The commonest letters in English are');
        writeln(' "E", "T", "A", "O", "N", and "I" ');
        write(' What''s your guess for the most likely character? ');
        readln(likelyChar);

        likelyChar := Cap(likelyChar);
        GuessSolution(cypherText, likelyChar)
    until NegativeAnswerTo('Do you want to try again?')
end.
```

6.6 Problem Solving III: Analyzing the PIPs

The heart of both programs is the procedure *CaesarCypher*, and the heart of *CaesarCypher* is the statement that converts characters and places them in the output string:

```
outStr[i] := chr(ord('A') + (ord(outStr[i]) — ord('A') + offset) mod 26);
```

If you look closely, you'll see that in essence this statement is no different from the one we used to convert lowercase letters to uppercase. In both cases, the statement is nothing but

```
aCharacter := chr(ord('A') + something involving ord(aChar))
```

In the lower- to uppercase conversion, the *something* was the offset between the lowercase *aChar* and the start of the lowercase alphabet, 'a', namely, $ord(aChar) - ord('a')$. In *CaesarCypher*, the *something* is again an offset, only this time it is the number *offset* added to the location of the uppercase *aChar*. For example, with Caesar's offset of 3, the character 'G' is first compared to 'A' to discover that 'G' is six characters beyond 'A' in the alphabet, so after an offset of 3, we will have $6 + 3 = 9$, and the ninth letter after 'A' is 'J'—the encrypted form of 'G'. (See Figure 6.6.)

The algebraically astute have probably noticed that the expression in Figure 6.6 can be simplified to $chr(ord(ch) + offset)$. That would work correctly for some letters but not for all. If, for instance, the character to be encrypted was 'Y', then adding 3 would give us a character three beyond 'Y', the 28th "letter" in the alphabet, which in ASCII is '\', not the 'B' we want on the code wheel. Since **mod** 26 gives the remainder upon division by 26, the value 28 becomes 2, and the second letter in the alphabet is indeed the 'B' we need. In effect, taking the result $(ord(ch) - ord('A') + offset)$ **mod** 26 "wraps" the numbers around the wheel.

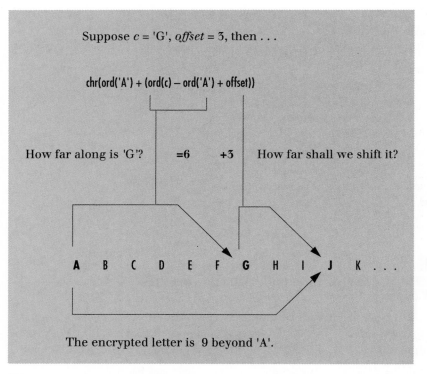

Figure 6.6.   Coding the Caesar cypher in Pascal

We used **mod** again in the procedure *PrintInGroups*:

```
procedure PrintInGroups (s: string);
    const
        GROUPSIZE = 5;
    var
        i: integer;
begin
    for i := 1 to Length(s) do
        begin
            if (i mod GROUPSIZE) = 1 then
                write(' ');
            write(s[i])
        end;
    writeln
end;
```

In this routine, we loop i from 1 to the length of the string s (given by the predefined string function *Length*) and when i is 1, 6, 11, 16, . . . , we write a blank before writing the i-th character, $s[i]$, of the string s, thus writing the string in groups of five.

Although we can read or write strings character by character as we did in *PrintInGroups*, we don't have to. We mentioned earlier that one of the nicest features of strings was that they could be read as a chunk, as we do in *GetAString*:

```
procedure GetAString (promptStr: string; var enteredStr: string);
begin
    writeln;
    writeln(promptStr);
    writeln;
    write('> ');
    readln(enteredStr);
    ConvertToCapAlpha(enteredStr)
end;
```

Without strings, we would have to replace the procedure call *readln(enteredString)* by a more complicated version that looked something like this:

```
i := 0;
while not eoln do
    begin
        i := i + 1;
        read(s[i])
    end;
readln;   {to discard the end-of-line mark}
```

Notice another nice feature of *GetAString*: One of the parameters is *promptStr*, a string. The value of *promptStr* is written when the procedure executes, and it can be changed by changing the actual parameter in the procedure call. In *EncryptCaesar*, for example, we call it by

```
GetAString('At the ">" prompt, enter a line of text to be encrypted.', plaintext);
```

In *DecryptCaesar*, when we want a different prompt, the call looks like

```
GetAString('Please enter a line of text to be decrypted.', cyphertext);
```

We use the same trick in the latest modification of our old friend *ReadyToQuit*, which we introduced in Chapter 3 and modified in Chapters 4 and 5. Now it appears with a string prompt as its sole parameter and has the more descriptive name *NegativeAnswerTo*. We call it in *DecryptCaesar* when we want to control a **repeat** loop:

```
repeat
    ⋮
until NegativeAnswerTo('Do you want to try again?')
```

The other predefined string routine that is used in the Programs in Progress is *Insert*, which is used to construct the output in *ConvertToCapAlpha*. The goal of the procedure is to revise its input string so that it contains only alphabetic characters. We start with an empty string, *t*, and successively fill it by inserting characters from the original string, *s*, at its end:

```
procedure ConvertToCapAlpha (var s: string);
    var
        i,              {the current position in the input string}
        j: integer;     {the position just after the end of the output string}
        t: string;      {the converted string}
begin
    t := ";
    j := 0;
    for i := 1 to Length(s) do
        if ((s[i] >= 'a') and (s[i] <= 'z')) or ((s[i] >= 'A') and (s[i] <= 'Z')) then
        {If the character is a letter, convert to uppercase, if}
        {necessary, and insert it at the end of the output.  }
            begin
                j := j + 1;
                Insert(Cap(s[i]), t, j)
            end;
        s := t
end;
```

The important part here is the section

```
j := j + 1;
Insert(Cap(s[i]), t, j)
```

In *ConvertToCapAlpha*, the integer *j* marks the position of the end of the string *t*. When we have a character to append to *t*, we increase *j* by one, making it refer to the position just beyond the end of *t*, and call *Insert*(*s*[*i*], *t*, *j*) to place the *i*-th element of string *s* (also a character—remember that characters and individual elements of strings may be used interchangeably!) at position *j* in the string *t*. Notice, by the way, that we could have dispensed with *j* entirely if we had wished to use an extra function call:

```
Insert(Cap(s[i]), t, 1 + Length(t))
```

Since all the insertions were at the end of *t*, we could have further simplified the insertion routine by concatenating instead with:

```
t := Concat(t, Cap(s[i]))
```

6.7
Reference

- Elements of the *char* type consist of single characters. Character constants are written by enclosing a printable character within single quotes, as 'A' or '%'. Although Pascal is case-insensitive when it interprets identifiers, the character 'g' is different from the character 'G'.
- The set of characters has a linear order, given by the numeric codes used to represent characters internally. The relational operators $=$, $<>$, $<$, $>$, $<=$, and $>=$ may be applied to characters. The standard stipulates that the alphabetic characters be ordered in alphabetic order, but they need not be contiguous. The digit characters '0' through '9' must not only be in order but must also be consecutive with no intervening characters. There is no set relation among the subsets of uppercase letters, lowercase letters, and digit characters.
- The *char* type has four predefined functions available:
  - *chr(n)*, which returns the character with a given numeric code *n*.
  - *ord(ch)*, which returns the numeric code corresponding to a character *ch*.
  - *pred(ch)*, which returns the character (if any) immediately before the character *ch*.
  - *succ(ch)*, which returns the character (if any) immediately after the character *ch*.
- Character I/O is accomplished by the predefined procedures *read*, *readln*, *write*, and *writeln*. The procedure *read* reads the first character from the standard textfile *input*. The procedure *readln* acts like *read*, except that it also discards everything from the front of the input buffer to the first end-of-line mark.
- The predefined boolean function *eoln* is *true* if and only if the character about to be read (the one at the front of the input buffer) is the end-of-line mark.
- If you *read* the end-of-line mark, it is translated as a blank. It is better to test for the end-of-line mark using *eoln* and then discard it using *readln*.
- Strings are a common but nonstandard extension to Pascal. The only required strings in the standard are string constants, consisting of any collection of 0 to 255 printable characters (so you can't use the Return character), enclosed within single quotes. Within a string, a single quote must be represented as two single quotes.
- The **string** type (in the compilers we discussed) may be declared using the reserved word **string**, or it may have a size limit of less than 255 characters by using a declaration like **string** [16]. Within a string variable *s*, the *i*-th character (starting from 1) may be referred to by using $s[i]$.
- The lexicographic order on strings is an extension of the order on the underlying character set. All of the relational operators may be applied to strings.

- Strings may be read or written character by character, but they may also be read or written as entire units, using *read, readln, write,* or *writeln.*
- There are six operators that may be applied to strings:
  - *Length(s)* returns the current length of the string *s.*
  - *Pos(substr, str)* returns the location of the start of the first instance of *substr* in the string *str,* if any, and returns 0 if *substr* is not found in *str.*
  - *Concat(s1, s2, . . . , sn)* returns the string that results from combining the arguments in order into one large string.
  - *Copy(str, index, count)* returns a string of length *count* copied from the locations beginning at position *index* in the string *str.*
  - *Delete(str, index, count)* changes the string *str* by deleting *count* characters, starting from position *index.*
  - *Insert(source, dest, index)* changes the string *dest* by inserting the string *source* into *dest,* starting at position *index.*

6.8 Building Blocks

There are many building blocks that can be gleaned from this chapter; this is a consequence of how useful text-processing routines are. Most of these routines are purely for text manipulation, but the last two show how we might use a variable prompt string in a routine so that we can use the same subprogram call in several different contexts without any rewriting.

To test whether a character, *ch,* lies within a given range, we compare the character to the endpoints of the range, so for most compilers in common use, we could test *ch* to determine whether it was an uppercase letter by

('A' <= ch) **and** (ch <= 'Z')

Using the functions *ord* and *chr,* we can change a character to one of a given offset by using *ch := chr(ord(ch) + offset),* as in the function that follows, which changes lowercase letters to uppercase:

```
function Cap(ch : char) : char;
{If ch is a lowercase letter, return its uppercase  }
{equivalent, otherwise return the character itself.}
begin
   if ('a' <= ch) and (ch <= 'z') then
      Cap := chr(ord(ch) − ord('a') + ord('A'))
   else
      Cap := ch
end;
```

The standard loop to read a line of characters uses the *eoln* function to test for the end-of-line sentinel:

```
while not eoln do
    begin
        read(ch);
        Process ch
    end;
readln;
```

The next procedure reads a string and uses a string parameter to write a prompt to the operator, indicating what is expected:

```
procedure GetAString (promptStr: string; var enteredStr: string);
{Prompts the user with 'promptStr' to enter a line of text.}
begin
    writeln;
    writeln(promptStr);
    writeln;
    write('> ');
    readln(enteredStr);
    ConvertToCapAlpha(enteredStr)    {optional, depending on use}
end;
```

Finally, we've improved the quit response boolean function so that it can be used in a variety of contexts, requiring only a prompt string from the calling routine:

```
function NegativeAnswerTo(prompt: string): boolean;
{Returns true if and only if user enters}
{'n' or 'N' to the prompt string.        }
    var
        ans: char;
begin
    writeln;
    writeln(prompt);
    write('Type "y" for yes or "n" for no, followed by Return: ');
    readln(ans);
    while (ans <> 'y') and (ans <> 'Y') and (ans <> 'n') and (ans <> 'N') do
        begin
            writeln;
            writeln('*** Please limit your response to "y" or "n" (without quotes).');
            write('Try again: "n" for no, "y" for yes: ');
            readln(ans)
        end;
    writeln;
    NegativeAnswerTo : = (ans = 'n') or (ans = 'N')
end;
```

1. Write the boolean expressions to test whether the character c is

   a. Something other than a digit.
   b. A punctuation mark that could end a sentence.
   c. An uppercase consonant.
   d. A nonprinting character (assuming that the system uses ASCII code).

2. Write a line of code that would set the integer variable *digit* to the value represented by the digit character c. In other words, if $c = \text{'3'}$, the line would set *digit* to 3.

3. The assignment statement $c := chr(ord(\text{'a'}) + ord(c) - 65)$ is intended to convert uppercase letters to lowercase. What's wrong with it?

4. Which of the following are true inverses, in the sense that $ord(chr(x))$ is x for all integers x, or $chr(ord(c))$ is c for all characters c?

5. What's a simpler way to write the boolean expression $(ord(c) >= ord(\text{'A'}))$ **and** $(ord(c) <= ord(\text{'Z'}))$? Assume c is a character variable.

6. For what—if any—characters c is $pred(succ(c)) \neq c$? What about $succ(pred(c))$?

7. This looks like a reasonable routine to read and process a line of characters. What's wrong with it? How would you fix it?

```
repeat
    read(c);    {c is a character}
    {Process c}
until eoln
```

8. When reading integers, Pascal finds the integer to be read by skipping blanks until it comes to the first character that could be part of an integer. Write **procedure** *SkipBlanks*(**var** $c : char$), which reads characters until it comes to the first character, c, that isn't a blank or until it comes to the end of the current line. If there are no nonblank characters to be found, the procedure should signal that by returning a blank in c.

In Exercises 9–11, we will explore different representations of numbers.

9. a. *Hexadecimal* notation expresses a number in base 16, using the "digits" 0 . . . 9, A (= 10), B, (= 11), . . . , F (= 15). The hexadecimal number 5E, then, represents 94, since $94 = 5 \times 16 + 14$, and 1A0 represents 416, since $416 = 1 \times 256 + 10 \times 16 + 0 = 1 \times (16^2) + 10 \times (16^1) + 0 \times (16^0)$. Write a routine that reads a hexadecimal number and displays its decimal equivalent.
   b. Write a routine that reads an integer and writes its hexadecimal representation.

10. a. In the Roman numeral representation of numbers, I = 1, V = 5, X = 10, L = 50, C = 100, D = 500, and M = 1000. Other numbers are made by repeating these symbols, so 32 would be represented XXXII. To save writing, there is a convention that IV = 4, XL = 40, CX = 90, CD = 400, and CM = 900 so that the number 2947 would be represented MMCMXLVII. Write a routine that reads a Roman numeral and writes its decimal equivalent.
   b. Write a routine that reads an integer and writes it in Roman numerals.

11. a. Write **procedure** *NumWord*(*num* : **string** ; **var** *word* : **string**), which takes as a parameter a string representing an integer between 0 and 9999 and returns the word equivalent. For example, if *num* = '423', we'll have *word* = 'four hundred twenty-three'.

   b. Use *NumWord* in a program that reads a sentence like "John had 130 hogs that he traded for 4091 guinea pigs" and translates all numbers to words, displaying, in this case, "John had one hundred thirty hogs that he traded for four thousand ninety-one guinea pigs."

12. *Planit reduction* transforms English words into a coded form using the following rules, in order:

   a. Replace each character in the word using the following rules:

   A, E, I, O, U, Y → A
   B, F, P, V → B
   C, G, J, K, Q, S, X, Z → C
   D, T → D
   H, W → H
   L → L
   M, N → M
   R → R

   b. For any consonant that's followed by H, eliminate the H so that DH would be replaced by D, for instance.
   c. For any repeated sequences of consonants, replace the repeats by a single instance. For example, MM would be replaced by M.
   d. Finally, eliminate all A's.
   For example, the Planit reduction of THINNING is

   THINNING → DHAMMAMC, after step a
            → DAMMAMC, after step b
            → DAMAMC, after step c
            → DMMC, after step d

   Planit reduction is useful in automated dictionaries, since variant spellings often have the same Planit reduction. Write a program to perform Planit reduction, and test it on THEIR, THERE, THEYRE, and EITHER.

13. Write a program that will read text and produce a classified ad by deleting all lower-case vowels. For example, given the input

   1989 Ferrari Testarossa. Auto, air, awesome stereo.
   Some minor body damage, mostly small holes.
   Contact Sonny, this paper, box MH1765.

the program will produce

   1989 Frr Tstrss, At, r, wsm str.
   Sm mnr bdy dmg, mstly smll hls.
   Cntct Snny, ths ppr, bx MH1765.

(Clearly, this algorithm needs some fixing. We particularly like what happens to "Ferrari" and "air.") You may use '*' to signal that there is no further input.

14. Write a routine that will read a name of the form "Smith, Sally S." and write the name in the form "Sally S. Smith." You may assume that the input ends with a return.

15. Most Pascal environments will generate a run-time error when reading integer values if they encounter input like 'g45' or 'two'. Rather than having the system take over when such an error occurs, we might want a robust integer-reading routine of our own, which, when it encounters an error, will retain control within the program. Write **procedure** *GetInteger*(**var** n : integer) that will act like *readln(n)*. The procedure should read and skip blanks until it comes to a $+$, $-$, or digit and then keep reading and converting characters to build an integer until it comes to the end of the line. During this process, if the procedure encounters a character that can't be part of an integer, it should handle the error gracefully by ignoring the bad character. You could improve this routine by including another parameter **var** *ok* : boolean that is set to *false* if the line is empty, consists of a bad character, or consists of all blanks.

16. Why can strings of different length never be equal? If $Length(s) = 1$ and $Length(t) = 3$, is it always true that $s < t$ in lexicographic order?

17. If $Length(dest) = n$, how many different strings are possible by changing *index* in $Insert(source, dest, index)$?

For Exercises 18 and 19, suppose s and t are strings, with s = 'flabbergasted' and t = 'berg'. What would be the result of the following string operations?

18. **a.** Pos(Copy(s, 2, 3), s)
    b. Length(Concat(t, t))
    c. Concat(Copy(s, 1, 1), Copy(s, 2, Length(s) − 1))
    d. Delete(s, Length(s) − 3, 2)
    e. Insert(Copy(t, 2, 2), s, 5)
    f. Insert(s, Copy(t, 2, 2), 5)
    g. Copy(Delete(s, 1, 1), 3, 3)

19. **a.** t <= s
    b. Pos(t, s)
    c. Pos(s, t)
    d. Concat(t, s, t)
    e. Copy(s, 6, 3)
    f. Delete(s, 6, 10)
    g. Insert(t, s, 8)

20. **a.** Write an improved version of *Pos*. The new version, **function** *NewPos(subStr, str* : **string** ; *from* : *integer*) : *integer*, will find the starting position of the first instance of *subStr* in *str*, starting from position *from*. If *subStr* isn't found or the value of *from* makes such finding impossible, the function should return zero.
    b. Write your own version of *Insert*.

21. Write **function** *Reverse(s* : **string**) : **string**, which returns the reverse of s, so if s = 'alligator', then $Reverse(s)$ = 'rotagilla'.

22. **a.** Write **function** *Palindrome(s* : **string**) : *boolean*, which returns *true* if and only if s is a palindrome—that is, it is the same as its reverse.
    b. Extend *Palindrome* so that it ignores all nonletters, so, for example, it would recognize 'Madam, I"m Adam.' as a palindrome. Don't reinvent the wheel— you've seen almost everything you need to solve this problem.

23. **a.** Write **function** *NumToStr(n* : integer) : **string**, which returns the string that represents n. For instance, if $n = -267$, we'd have $NumToStr(n)$ = '−267'.
    b. Write *StrToNum*, that is, the inverse of *NumToStr*. You may assume that the input string is the correct representation of an integer.

24. a. Write a procedure that will sort the characters in a string of four digits in increasing order so that the string '6174' would become '1467'.

   b. Use your procedure to investigate what happens when you perform the following sequence of operations repeatedly on different four-digit numbers:

   1. Take the digit string, and sort it.
   2. Reverse the result.
   3. Convert the sorted and reversed strings to numbers, and subtract the smaller from the larger.
   4. Convert the difference to a string, and go back to step 1.

25. The following function is supposed to find the position of the first instance of repeated characters in a string. For example, given the string 'I and thee see the fool', the function would return 9, the position of the start of the leftmost 'ee'. If there are no adjacent repeated characters, the routine should return zero. It's not correct. Why?

```
function FindRepeats(s : string) : integer;
    var
        index : integer;
begin
    index : = 1;
    while (s[index] <> s[index + 1]) and (index < Length(s)) do
        index : = index + 1;
    if s[index] <> s[index + 1] then
        index : = 0;
    FindRepeats : = index
end;
```

26. a. In a string that represents a sentence, how would you recognize a word? Look at this (or any other) sentence, for instance: You can see that it's not enough — not nearly enough! — to say that a "word" is characterized by a collection of letters with a blank at either end.

   b. Use your criteria for words to write a routine that will count the number of words in a string.

27. a. Write a procedure to take a string *s* and return the string that results after applying the railfence cypher to *s*. To make life easier, assume that *s* has an even length.

   b. The railfence cypher has the interesting property that if it is applied repeatedly to a string, eventually the original string is produced. The number of repetitions needed to get back to the original is a function of the length of the string. For instance, for strings of length 2, one iteration of the cypher obviously leaves the string unchanged; for strings of length 32, five iterations suffice, whereas for strings of length 30, it takes 28 iterations. Write a program to investigate the number of iterations of the railfence cypher it takes to bring a string to its original form. What conclusions can you draw?

28. Modify *EncryptCaesar* to accept multiple lines. The only difficult part of this modification is producing the output in groups of five.

29. A *columnar cypher* places the plaintext in columns and then produces the cyphertext by extracting characters by rows. For example, with five rows, the message I CANT MEET YOU ON TUESDAY would be arranged as follows:

```
I   M   O   U   Y
C   E   U   E
A   E   O   S
N   T   N   D
T   Y   T   A
```

Then, generating the message by rows would produce IMOUYCEUEAEOSNTND-TYTA, which we would group as usual to give the cyphertext IMOUY CEUEA EOSNT NDTYT A. Notice that the railfence cypher is just a two-row columnar cypher.

a. Rewrite *CaesarCypher* to generate a columnar cypher, given the number of rows and the plaintext message. Incorporate this in a driver program like *EncryptCaesar*.

b. (This is harder.) Write the program that the recipient of the cyphertext would use to decode your message, assuming that he or she knows the number of rows you used.

30. (Hard.) Given a restricted alphabet of characters from 'A' to some character LAST, we want to find a string of length n, constructed only of characters in our limited alphabet, that has no adjacent equal substrings. For example, the string 'CBACABA' satisfies our requirements, whereas 'ABCABCAAC' doesn't, since the underlined portion consists of adjacent copies of 'BCA'.

We can try to construct such a sequence by inserting characters at the front of a trial string. Every time we attach a new character to the front, we test whether the new character produces a repeat. If it does, we replace it with its successor and test again for repeats. If we run out of successors without producing a good string, we delete the first character and try the same process of testing and replacing the first character with its successor until we either find a good string or run out of characters to change. For the alphabet 'A', 'B', 'C' and length $n = 5$ as our goal, we would start with the good string 'A' and produce the following strings:

'AA'	*Bad string, replace first character.*
'BA'	*Good, so make the next one.*
'ABA'	*Good, keep going.*
'AABA'	*Bad, so replace first character.*
'BABA'	*Oops! Still bad, replace again.*
'CABA'	*Finally, a good one. Make the next one.*
'ACABA'	*Good, and the length we want. We're done.*

Write a program that reads values for n and produces a "good" string of length n or reports that no such string can be made. Try it several times with an alphabet of three characters and then for a two-character alphabet. Does the alphabet size have an effect on the strings that can be made?

6.10 Answers

1. **a.** $(c < '0')$ **or** $(c > '9')$

b. $(c = '.')$ **or** $(c = '!')$ **or** $(c = '?')$ **or** $(c = '"')$

The last character is a double quote enclosed within two single quotes.

c. $((c >= 'A')$ **and** $(c <= 'Z'))$ **and not** $((c = 'A')$ **or** $(c = 'E')$ **or** $(c = 'I')$ **or** $(c = 'O')$ **or** $(c = 'U'))$

d. $\text{ord}(c) < 32$

3. It only works for ASCII encodings. A system-independent way would be to use $c := chr(\text{ord}('a') + \text{ord}(c) - \text{ord}('A'))$.

5. $(c >= 'A')$ **and** $(c <= 'Z')$

7. There are two problems here. First, if the input is empty, consisting just of a return, it will read the end-of-line mark (as a blank) and try to process it. If the processing did any character counting, for instance, the result would be off by one. Second, the routine leaves the end-of-line mark in the buffer, which could interfere with any subsequent *read*s that expect something other than an empty line. We could fix these problems by testing for the end-of-line sentinel before doing any reading and then, when processing is complete, discarding the end-of-line mark.

```
while not eoln do
    begin
        read(c);
        {Process c}
    end;
readln
```

9. **a.** We'll use a flagged loop here and stop reading when we reach the end of the line or when we first see a character that couldn't be part of a hexadecimal number.

```
done := false;
number := 0;
while not done do
    if eoln then
        begin
            done := true;
            readln    {Discard end-of-line mark.}
        end
    else
        begin
            read(c);    {c is a character}
            if (c >= '0') and (c <= '9') then
                number := 16 * number + (ord(c) - ord('0'))
            else if (c >= 'A') and (c <= 'F') then
                number := 16 * number + (10 + ord(c) - ord('A'))
            else
                done := true
        end;
writeln('The hex number represents ', number : 1)
```

b. The solution is left to the reader.

11. a. There are two essential parts to this procedure. First, we can use a **case** statement to determine the word equivalent of a digit, as in

```
case ord(s[i]) − ord('0') of
    0:  {we'll have to take care of this separately};
    1: word : = 'one';
    2 : word : = 'two';
    ⋮
    9 : word : = 'nine'
end
```

The other part is to use the length of *num* to determine what follows each word. For example, if *Length(num)* = 4, the first word would be followed by 'thousand', but if the length were 3, the first word would be followed by 'hundred'. We'll have to take care of the last two digits, if any, by other **case** statements that would either write 'twenty', and so on, or would write, for instance, 'thirteen'.

b. The solution is left to the reader.

13. The essential part of the program is:

```
c = '\';           {a dummy character to feed the loop}
while c <> '*' do
    begin
        while (not eoln) and (c <> '*') do
            begin    {read and process one line}
                read(c);
                if (c <> 'a') and (c <> 'e') and (c <> 'i') and
                        (c <> 'o') and (c <> 'u') and (c <> '*') then
                    write(c)
            end;
        readln       {Discard end-of-line mark, or anything}
    end          {beyond the first '*' seen.}
```

A flagged loop makes this easier to read. Try it.

15. The important part of this routine is the following procedure:

```
procedure ReadPastJunk(var c : char ; var lineEnd : boolean);
    var
        done : boolean;
begin
    lineEnd : = false;
    done : = false;
```

```
        while not done do
            if eoln then
                begin
                    c := ' ';              {can't read any more, so return a dummy char}
                    lineEnd := true;
                    done := true
                end
            else
                begin
                    read(c);
                    if ((c >= '0') and (c <= '9')) or ((c = '+') or (c = '−')) then
                        done := true    {found a good char—quit reading}
                end
        end;
```

(Notice how similar this is to the solution of Exercise 9.) The routine will repeatedly call *ReadPastJunk*, until it returns a *true* value for *lineEnd*. While the reading is going on, we will look at the character returned via *c*, and if it is a digit, we'll update the parameter *n* by $n := 10 * n + (ord(c) − ord('0'))$. We have to be careful to treat '+' and '−' differently, depending on whether we're within the number or at its start. We also have to be careful to handle the case where the input represents an integer larger than *maxint*.

17. $n + 1$.

19. a. *true*
  b. 5
  c. 0
  d. 'bergflabbergastedberg'
  e. 'erg'
  f. s = 'flabb'. There are only eight characters after 'flabb', but *Delete* will handle that gracefully, even if asked to delete ten characters.
  g. s = 'flabberberggasted'. Notice here, as in part f, that the operator is a procedure rather than a function.

21. Normally, a Pascal function can return only a *simple* type, such as an integer, real, char, or boolean (or a *pointer*, as we'll see in Chapter 12). For the string extensions in the compilers we've discussed, this restriction is relaxed. We use a character version of our *Swap* building block here.

```
        function Reverse(s : string) : string;
            var
                r : string;
                i, len : integer;
        begin
            r := s;
            len := Length(s);    {so we don't have to recompute it each time}
            for i := 1 to len div 2 do
                Swap(r[i], r[len − i + 1]);
            Reverse := r
        end;
```

23. a. **function** NumToStr(n : integer) : **string**;
{We build the answer string by getting successive digits from the right of n}
{and inserting their character equivalents at the front of the answer string.}

```
    var
        negative : boolean;
        digit : integer;
        num : string;
begin
    negative : = (n < 0);
    if n = 0 then
        NumToStr : = '0'
    else
        begin
            num : = '';
            while n <> 0 do
                begin
                    digit : = n mod 10;    {Get the rightmost digit of n}
                    n : = n div 10;         {and then remove it from n.}
                    Insert(chr(ord('0') + digit), num, 1)
                end;
            if negative then
                Insert(' − ', num, 1);
            NumToStr : = num
        end
end;
```

b. We've done almost the same thing in Exercises 9 and 15.

25. Look at the exit condition for the loop. If there are no repeated characters, the loop will increment *index* until $index = Length(s)$, at which time the clause ($index < Length(s)$) will become false, so the loop will terminate. Unfortunately, the compiler might try to evaluate the other clause, ($s[index] <> s[index + 1]$), and that will require a reference to a location that's beyond the current size of s, an error. In many cases, this problem is tricky to fix, but here the fix is to change the second clause of the **while** statement to ($index < Length(s) - 1$). Then, the final comparison will be between the last two elements of s, so we're okay.

27. a. **procedure** Railfence(plain : **string** ; **var** cypher : **string**);
{This produces the cyphertext by using the railfence cypher.}
{NOTE: Requires the length of the plaintext to be even.   }

```
    var
        i, half : integer;
begin
    {This is to make sure that the two strings are the same length.}
    cypher : = plain;
    half : = Length(plain) div 2;
    for i : = 1 to half do
        begin
            cypher[i] : = plain[2 * i − 1];
            cypher[i + half] : = plain[2 * i]
        end
end;
```

b. The number of iterations it takes to get the original string has something to do with the powers of 2 in the length of the input. Try it for strings of length 2, 4, 8, and 16. Then try it for strings of length 2×3, 2×7, and 2×15. The general rule is not obvious.

29. a. The principle here is very much as we used with the railfence cypher, except that in place of *half* we use *Length(plain)* **div** *rows*, and we have *rows* assignment statements in the body of the loop. It's much easier to write the routine when the length of the plaintext is a multiple of *rows*, so first pad the end of the plaintext with as many dummy '%' characters as are needed to make the length divisible by *rows*, and then strip them from the cyphertext.

b. The solution is left to the reader.

7 Subprograms Revisited: Parameters, Scope, and Recursion

We have seen that procedures and functions are of fundamental importance in a programming language. First, subprograms allow us to collect related sections of code into manageable conceptual units, thereby making it easier for us to keep a grasp on the logical structure of an entire program. It is easier to write any nontrivial program in top-down fashion: We first decide on the major tasks to be performed and represent each task as a subprogram. If any of those tasks is too large or complex to handle as a single conceptual chunk, it can be further divided into physically and conceptually smaller subprograms. Eventually, the separate pieces will be simple enough to visualize, and then *and only then* should we start to write code.

Another big advantage of subprograms is that they can be reused. A single procedure or function may be called several times in a single program, eliminating duplicate or near-duplicate sections of code. Subprograms of general utility can even be copied from one program for use in another. It saves a considerable amount of time and effort when you build parts of a program from a library of useful subprograms.

Once you accept the idea that procedures and functions are useful in the design and development of a program, a host of questions arise—questions that until now we've glossed over or simply ignored. Most of these questions stem from the same main concern: If we are going to allow "plug-in" subprograms in a language, how can we design our language so that the pieces fit together smoothly and with a minimum of modification? In essence, the semantic features of Pascal procedures and functions are all related to the goal of ensuring that a program built of subprograms will not have any conflicts caused by unintended interaction between its subprograms. At first glance, some of the details of subprograms may seem capricious or arbitrary and certainly confusing. Because of this, we'll start by explaining a variety of simple examples. Ultimately, we will build up to our PIP, which illustrates that there are almost always good reasons for the way subprograms work.

 B J E C T I V E S

In this chapter, we will:

- Define Pascal's concept of *scope*.
- Discuss local and global variables and Pascal's mechanism for resolving name conflicts.
- Review and describe in detail Pascal's methods for defining and manipulating subprogram parameters.
- Introduce the topic of language parsing, and review all of the above topics in the context of this chapter's PIP, a simple parser.
- Illustrate how collections of subprograms (and other declarations) can be grouped together into units in many Pascal environments and how they can be reused by any program.

7.1 Scope

Every identifier in a Pascal program has a domain — a part of the program — in which it is defined. This domain is called the *scope* of the identifier. Every object — a constant, type, variable, procedure, or function identifier — may be referred to only within its scope. Basically, there are two different scopes, *global* and *local*. Objects with global scope may be used anywhere in a program. Locally defined objects are valid only within the particular procedure or function in which they are defined. Consider the following example.

```
program VerySimple(input, output);
   var
      x, y: real;
   procedure Double(var a, b : real);
      var
         total: real;
```

```
    begin
        a := 2.0 * a;
        b := 2.0 * b;
        total := a + b;
        writeln('First value = ', a, 'second value = ', b, 'their sum = ', total)
    end;
begin    {Main}
    readln(x, y);
    writeln('You entered ', x, y);
    Double(x, y)
end.
```

This program doesn't do very much, but it does illustrate some of Pascal's basic scope rules. The variables *x* and *y* are global, since they are declared in the main program's variable declaration part. They may be used anywhere, not only in the statement part of the program, as above, but also in the procedure *Double* had we decided to do so (we didn't, for reasons that will be clear shortly). The variable *total*, on the other hand, is a local variable. It was defined within *Double* and has meaning only within *Double*. It would be an error for us to refer to *total* anywhere except within *Double*, so we could not have legally made any reference to it in the main statement part. The same is true for the formal parameters *a* and *b*. They may be used only within *Double*, since that's where they are declared. On the other hand, the procedure identifier *Double* is defined at the global level as part of the main program's procedure declarations. This means that *Double* could be called anywhere within the program, even within the definition of *Double* itself.

That's called re-cursion, *and we'll talk about such self-referential pro-cedures shortly.*

We can look at scope pictorially, as in Figure 7.1. Each procedure (and the main program itself) defines a *block* in which its identifiers have their scope. Notice that the procedure name itself has its scope *outside* of the procedure's block. The reason for this is clear: Otherwise we'd never be able to call any procedure from the main program! With this in mind, we can see that the block structure of the sample program *VerySimple* is that of Figure 7.2.

If you think about it for a while, you'll see that Pascal's scope rules are a natural consequence of the goal of reusability. If there were no limits to the scope of either parameters or local variables, whenever we plugged a previously written procedure or function into a new program, we'd have to check the program carefully to ensure that none of the parameter or variable names matched those already in the program. Otherwise we would be leaving ourselves open to the possibility that our new subprogram could introduce entirely unexpected changes in the existing program variables. Indeed, some early implementations of high-level languages (BASIC, for one) lacked Pascal's notion of scope and left it up to the programmer to ensure that there were no conflicts between names in subprograms. Pascal's scope rules explicitly limit the influence of identifiers in a subprogram. It's much easier to understand what is going on in a program if you can be sure that

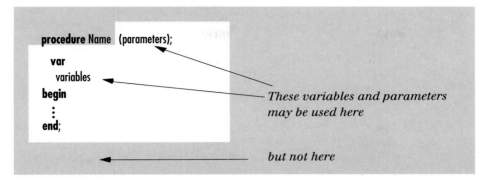

Figure 7.1. Scope of local variables and parameters

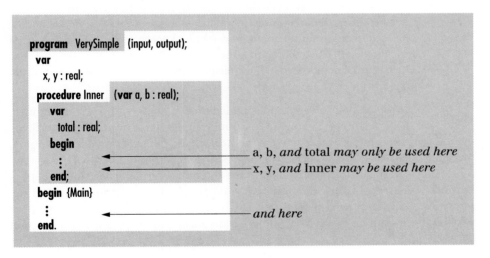

Figure 7.2. The block structure of the program *VerySimple*

identifiers defined within a subprogram don't have far-reaching consequences outside the subprogram's scope.

Resolving Name Confusion

Suppose we had a program with a variable x and we plugged in a procedure with a local variable that was also named x, as follows.

```
program Main(input, output);
    var
        x : integer;
```

```
procedure Conflict(t : integer);
    var
        x : integer;
    begin
        ⋮
        x := x + 1;     Which x is being modified here?
        ⋮
    end;
begin    {Main}
    ⋮
end.
```

It's not hard to imagine at least three different ways Pascal could deal with such name confusion.

1. The global interpretation could take precedence so that the line $x := x + 1$ in procedure *Conflict* would modify the global variable named x.
2. The local interpretation could be the one in force so that the instance of x local to *Conflict* would be modified.
3. The compiler could flag such duplicate names as an error and not run the program.

The third option is clearly undesirable for reasons we've already mentioned. When we insert a subprogram into a new program, we don't want to have to check all the program's identifiers to make sure there are no duplicate names. Assuming, correctly, that Pascal allows duplicate names, it seems that the first option is inappropriate as well, since it clearly violates the intent of Pascal's scope rules. Scope is a means of encapsulating details that should be of no concern to the rest of the program. We want to, and indeed are able to, make changes to the local x without having those changes in any way influence any instances of x in the main program or elsewhere.

> **I**t is an error to declare an identifier twice at the same level. If an identifier is declared at two different levels and is then used, the most local definition is the one that is in force.

The first part of this principle implies, for instance, that a program cannot have a variable and a procedure declared at the same level with the same name (or two variables, or a variable and a constant, and so on). Similarly, a procedure cannot have a parameter and a local variable (or constant, and so on) with the same name. The second part implies that you may feel free to use any names you like for the parameters and locally defined objects (variables, constants, other subprograms) within a function and procedure, confident that they will never conflict with other identically named objects outside the subprogram's block.

To illustrate the principles of scope and name resolution, consider the following program.

```
program Example(output);
  var
      x : integer;
  procedure A;
      var
          x : integer;
      begin
          x := 1      This value for x holds only within A.
      end;

  procedure B;
      begin
          writeln(x)   There's no local x here, so this statement can only refer to the
      end;             global x.

  procedure C;
      var
          x : integer;
      begin
          x := 2;      This value for x holds only within C.
          B
      end;
  begin   {Main}
      x := 3;
      C
  end.
```

What gets written in procedure B: 1, 2, or 3? Let's trace the action of the program and find out. The first statement to be executed in the main program is $x := 3$. The program then calls procedure C and control passes into that procedure. Within C, the local identifier is the one in force, and that x gets set to the value 2. As long as we're in C, the local x overrides the global one (although the global x still has the value 3). Once procedure C calls B, however, we're out of the scope of C's local variable, so which x do we refer to while in B? The global one! The main program's x is the only one available within B, so the value 3 is written. Don't be confused by the x in procedure A: it may be typographically near procedure B, but that x is defined only within the scope of A and hence is in force only when we're within A.

Parameters and Aliasing

Since the scope of a global variable is the entire program, it is perfectly possible for a procedure to modify a global variable (assuming that there is no name confusion between the global variable and any locally defined identifiers). We mentioned in Chapter 3 that this was not a good idea, and now we can see why: It violates the design goal of locality that tries to ensure that the data items and values a subprogram deals with are all defined within the subprogram. Locality makes a program much easier to read and maintain. It would, for example, be a real bother to read a procedure like this:

```
procedure ProcessData(var a, max : real; count : integer);
    var
        index, temp : integer;
    begin
        ⋮
        squareSum : = squareSum + sqr(a);    ???
        ⋮
    end;
```

We would look at the line $squareSum := squareSum + sqr(a)$ and probably say something like, "Now where in the world is $squareSum$ defined and what is it supposed to represent?" (Long pause with grumbling while we look back through the program listing to find out.) Even worse, though, is that such a *side effect* effectively destroys the portability of this procedure. Before plugging this procedure into another program, we would have to make sure that the new program had a global variable $squareSum$ and that the program handled the variable appropriately.

To be fair, we should admit that there are times when side effects make it easier to write a program. If we have a program that keeps some statistics on its own behavior, for example, and the statistics use fifteen variables in each of ten separate procedures, passing all of them as parameters in each subprogram might make the parameter list uncomfortably bulky.[1] In this case, it might be barely acceptable to ignore the stricture against side effects. Such a decision, though, should be weighed carefully, with thought toward the mental health of any future reader of the program. Although the rule against side effects is not graven in stone, it was, like all rules of style, born of extensive experience and should not be violated lightly.

Another very serious problem with side effects occurs when the global variable being changed is one that happens to be used as the actual parameter corresponding to a formal **var** parameter. Consider the following example.

```
program VeryBadPractice(input, output);
    var
        clarkKent, bruceWayne : integer;
```

There are ways to collect several variables into one, though, as you'll see when we cover records in Chapter 11.

---

[1] We might, for instance, want to record how many times a procedure is called. This is really only the procedure's business, so this number should be a local variable. Unfortunately, in Pascal (though not in some other languages), the values of all local variables are lost when the procedure returns, thus forcing us to use a parameter or side effect.

```
procedure WhatGoesOnHere(var superman, batman : integer);
begin
    superman : = 2 * superman;        This is just fine,
    batman : = 2 * batman;            and so is this,
    bruceWayne : = bruceWayne + 1;    but this is a side effect.
    writeln(superman, batman)         What gets written is not 2, 4.
end;

begin
    clarkKent : = 1 ; bruceWayne : = 2 ;
    WhatGoesOnHere(clarkKent, bruceWayne)
    ⋮
end.
```

When called with *clarkKent* = 1 and *bruceWayne* = 2, *WhatGoesOnHere* immediately doubles *clarkKent*, since the actual parameter *clarkKent* is matched to the formal **var** parameter *superman*. Similarly, *bruceWayne* is doubled. That's all reasonably clear. What is not obvious when reading *WhatGoesOnHere* is that the line *bruceWayne* := *bruceWayne* + 1 not only adds 1 to the global variable *bruceWayne* but also adds 1 to the parameter *batman*! Because *bruceWayne* is the actual parameter matched to the formal **var** parameter *batman*, they both refer to the same object. Any change made to one is immediately made to the other. In technical (and nontechnical) terms, *batman* and *bruceWayne* are *aliases*, with the customary meaning that they are different names for the same entity. Remember, in the real world, aliases are designed for confusion, and they can also cause confusion in the world of programming. It is virtually impossible to read and understand a procedure that modifies aliases—unless you are in on the secret. It appears to the casual observer that the line *bruceWayne* := *bruceWayne* + 1 changes *bruceWayne* only, not *batman* as well. Needless to say, this could cause all sorts of confusion, especially if *batman* were used later in the procedure.

Avoid aliasing. In fact, it's a good idea to avoid any modification of global variables within a subprogram.

Nested Blocks

As we have seen, procedures and functions are syntactically and semantically similar to "mini-programs," in that they may have locally declared labels, constants, types, variables, and subprograms. In particular, you've also seen that it is quite possible (and often desirable) to declare a procedure or function within another subprogram. The scope rules for such nesting are the same as we have discussed, but it is confusing enough at first glance that we'll take some time here to provide a bit of clarification.

We might, for example, want to declare a function inside a procedure if the function provides some help to the procedure and that help is of such a specialized nature that it is of no use outside the procedure's block. The following procedure, for instance, takes a real number, *money*, writes it as a dollar amount rounded to two places, and returns the difference between the actual and the rounded amount.[2]

```
procedure WriteDollars(money : real ; var difference : real);

   function RoundToTwoPlaces(amount : real) : real;
   begin
      RoundToTwoPlaces : = Round(amount * 100.0) / 100.0
   end;
begin
   write('$', money : 8 : 2);
   difference : = amount − RoundToTwoPlaces(amount)
end;
```

It's unlikely that the special-purpose function *RoundToTwoPlaces* would be used elsewhere in any program that used *WriteDollars*, so a good place to put the function is within the procedure. Doing that rather than making *RoundToTwo-Places* external to *WriteDollars* has two advantages. First, placing *RoundToTwo-Places* within the procedure makes it obvious to the reader that the function is used only within the procedure. The reader doesn't have to remember the function outside of the block of *WriteDollars*. Second, if we ever needed to include *Write-Dollars* in another program, we could simply copy it whole, carrying its helper function along and not having to bother with remembering that in order to transport *WriteDollars* to a new program, we have to copy its helper, too.

We could include *WriteDollars* in a program with, perhaps another global-level procedure *SomethingElse*. If we did this, the block structure would be that of Figure 7.3.

The program *Finance* has four blocks defined by the program itself, the two procedures, and the internal function. Any parameters or local variables, constants, types, or labels of *RoundToTwoPlaces* would be valid only within Block R and could not be used elsewhere. The function identifier (that is, the name "RoundToTwo-Places"), however, exists within Block W, defined by *WriteDollars*. We could thus call *RoundToTwoPlaces* anywhere within Block W—in *WriteDollars* or in *Round-ToTwoPlaces* itself. We could not, however, call *RoundToTwoPlaces* from the main program or from *SomethingElse*. *WriteDollars* (the procedure identifier), however,

---

[2]This difference of fractional cents is the basis of an interesting piece of computer fraud known as a *salami scam*. In such a scheme, a programmer for a bank inserts a routine to *truncate*, rather than round, all transactions (such as calculations of loan payments) to the nearest cent and to keep track of the total of the differences. Every so often, the total of differences will be credited to the programmer's account. Done correctly, the bank's books always balance, and the programmer reaps a nice steady income. In the folklore of one such instance, the programmer was caught only when he began living conspicuously beyond his apparent means.

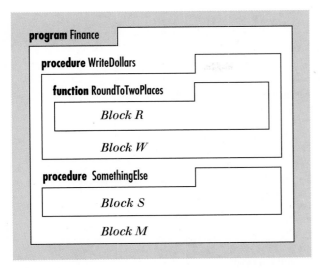

Figure 7.3.   A somewhat complicated block structure

is declared within the main block, M, and so could be called anywhere in the main block: from within *RoundToTwoPlaces*, from itself, from *SomethingElse*, or in the statement part of the main program.

Pascal, you'll recall, has a fairly strict "declare before use" rule, so although the identifier *SomethingElse* is declared in the main block, M, we could not ordinarily call it in either *WriteDollars* or *RoundToTwoPlaces*. There are times when we'd like to be able to do so, however, and Pascal provides us with a means for circumventing the rule about declaring a procedure or function before we use it, as you'll see shortly.[3]

One can nest subprograms as deeply as needed. Whether to include a subprogram within another is often a judgment call, as in the following example.

```
procedure WriteDollars(money : real ; var difference);

    function RoundOff(places : integer ; amount : real) : real;
        var
            multiplier : real;

        function Exponent(a, b : real) : real;
        {This returns a raised to the power b and is the way}
        {we must do exponentiation in Pascal.              }
```

---

[3]There are also times when it is unavoidable, as we will see when we discuss recursion.

```
begin
   if a > 0 then
      Exponent : = exp(b * ln(a))
   else
      begin
         writeln('The base in exponentiation must be > 0');
         Exponent : = 0
      end
end;
begin   {Roundoff}
   multiplier : = Exponent(10.0, places);                = 10^places
   RoundOff : = Round(amount * multiplier) / multiplier
end;
begin   {Main}
   write('$', money : 8 : 2);
   difference : = amount − RoundOff(2, amount)
end;
```

For ease of future use, it is a good idea to write a subprogram in as general a fashion as possible. For example, it is a simple modification to write a rounding routine that rounds to a number of decimal places specified by a parameter rather than just to two places. To round a number x to n places, all one has to do is compute $Round(x * 10^n) / 10^n$ (try a few examples to see how this works). We've done that in the function *RoundOff*, defined within *WriteDollars*. To compute 10^n, we could have used a loop, multiplying 10 as often as needed; instead, we used the unfortunate but necessary workaround that Pascal requires, namely, $a^b = e^{b\ln a}$. (Using the rules for exponents and the fact that $e^{\ln a} = a$, we see that $e^{b\ln a} = (e^{\ln a})^b = a^b$.)

The point here is that both *RoundOff* and *Exponent* are sufficiently useful that they might be used elsewhere in this program or in others. In that case, we wouldn't want to embed them within the somewhat special-purpose routine *WriteDollars* but might instead have them as part of our collection of useful building blocks. Whether or not they were used elsewhere in the program, it might well turn out that we would be willing to pay the price of having to copy them individually rather than placing them inside a routine that we might never plug into another program. For routines of general utility such as these, it is often a good idea to collect them in a section in the program with a comment header like

{———————————————— NUMERIC UTILITIES ————————————————}

where they can be found easily and reused later.

It is often easier to read a program if logically related routines are grouped together, even though these routines might be used only within a single special-purpose procedure or function.

7.2 Recursion

A *recursive definition* is one that uses the term being defined as part of its own definition. Recursion is one of the most powerful tools in the programmer's kit. The basic principle behind recursion is very simple.

Lurking inside many problems is a smaller problem. Often we can solve the big problem by using the solution to the smaller one. The key is to ask, "How could I solve this problem if I already had a solution to a smaller instance of the same problem?"

We'll start with the canonical recursion problem—the one almost everyone uses as the first example. If n is a positive integer, $n!$ (which we call "n factorial") is defined to be the product of all integers from 1 to n, so $4! = 4 \times 3 \times 2 \times 1 = 24$. The factorial operator is the basis for a lot of other mathematical functions. In particular, $n!$ is the number of ways of arranging n different objects in a row. Let's design a function to compute factorials. The key here comes from looking at, say, $4!$ in a slightly different way. Notice that we can write $4! = 4 \times (3 \times 2 \times 1)$, and the parenthesized expression is just $3!$. In other words, we can define the factorial of n in terms of a smaller factorial, as follows.

$1! = 1,$
$n! = n \times (n - 1)!,$ if $n > 1$

This is classic recursion: We have an *exit case* (or *terminating condition*) that says there's no more work to be done if $n = 1$, and we have a *recursive case* that finds $n!$ in terms of the smaller problem $(n - 1)!$. The function definition follows directly.

function Factorial(n : integer) : integer;
{Returns n!, for n ≥ 1.}

```
begin
  if n = 1 then      EXIT CASE: We're done immediately if n = 1.
    Factorial := 1
  else                 RECURSIVE CASE: We find n! by computing n * (n − 1)!.
    Factorial := n * Factorial(n − 1)
end;
```

With a little thought, you can see that we don't really need recursion to define *Factorial*. It would be easy enough to design an iterative version.

```
function IterativeFactorial(n : integer) : integer;
  var
      i, product : integer;
begin
  product := 1;
  for i := 1 to n do
      product := product * i;
  IterativeFactorial := product
end;
```

The recursive version is certainly more elegant and—once you understand recursion—simpler to understand at a glance. There's a hidden disadvantage to the recursive version, though. Recursive routines typically take longer to run than the equivalent iterative versions. The reason is that whenever a procedure or function call is made, recursive or not, the system must store a moderately large amount of information so that it can invoke the subprogram correctly and return from the call. Typically, each time a subprogram is invoked, the system must store the location to which execution will pass when the subprogram is finished, as well as any parameters, local entities like constants and variables, links to nonlocal entities used in the subprogram, temporary values for pending calculations, and the like. Moving this information (called an *activation record*) takes time (and space) for each subprogram call. A recursive routine, which may make a large number of calls to itself, will cause the system to eat up time and memory reserving one activation record for each call. To be honest, though, that's no problem for our factorial routine, since n (and hence the number of function calls that have to be made) will have to be small for the function to work at all. Even with $n = 13$, $13! = 6,277,020,800$, will probably be larger than *maxint* on most computers.[4]

So, *Factorial* could be done without recursion. In fact, it can be shown that with a little work any recursive routine whatsoever can be written without recursion. Given this, and the fact that recursion seems to be difficult to get used to at first, why bother with it at all? Believe us, we don't do it solely to bedevil our students. The simple answer is that there are some problems that are easy to solve recursively and very difficult indeed to solve without recursion. Here's an example.

---

[4]Which is usually the reason given for the choice of the exclamation mark for the factorial operator—factorial grows surprisingly! quickly.

We've already seen how to represent a nonnegative integer in binary form, that is, as a sum of the powers of 2. The number 13, for example, has binary representation 1101, reflecting the fact that $13 = 1 \times 2^3 + 1 \times 2^2 + 0 \times 2^1 + 1 \times 2^0 = 8 + 4 + 1$. We've also seen a simple algorithm to convert a nonnegative integer to its binary form: Repeatedly divide the number by two, keeping track of the remainders of each division. In the example of 13, the first division has remainder 1 and quotient 6; the second division, of 6, has remainder 0 and quotient 3; division of 3 has remainder 1 and quotient 1; and the final division, of 1, has remainder 1. The remainders, in order, are 1, 0, 1, 1, which is the binary representation of 13, albeit in reverse order.

It is the problem of reverse order that we can address most easily with a recursive routine, and only with difficulty (knowing what we do now at least) without recursion. Look, though, at the recursive form:

To write the binary representation of $n \geq 0$:

1. If n is 0 or 1, we're done: n is its own binary form.
2. If $n > 1$, write the binary representation of n **div** 2, and follow that by the remainder we get when we divide n by 2.

We have solved the problem of binary representation by *assuming* that we are able to solve the same problem for smaller values. The algorithm looks like this:

```
procedure WriteBinary(n : integer);
{We assume here that n is not negative.}
begin
   if n <= 1 then
      write(n : 1)
   else
      begin
         WriteBinary(n div 2);
         write(n mod 2 : 1)
      end
end;
```

In Figure 7.4, we trace the execution of this procedure and its recursive calls when *WriteBinary* is originally called with parameter n equal to 13. The procedure is cloned three times, each time with a smaller parameter. Finally, the parameter becomes 1, and the routine can backtrack out of the stack of pending procedure calls, writing as it goes.

Another, even more practical (and certainly more relevant) problem is that of defining the components of a programming language. Consider, for instance, an unsigned Pascal integer. We could define it *iteratively*:

Iterative Definition

An unsigned integer consists of a string of one or more digits.

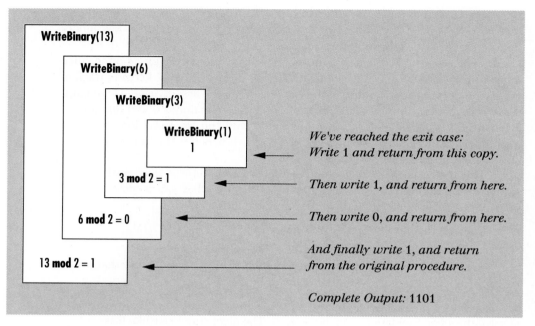

Figure 7.4.   Tracing the action of *WriteBinary*(13)

Or we could define unsigned integers recursively:

Recursive Definition

An unsigned integer consists of either (1) a single digit or (2) a digit followed by an unsigned integer.

The string of characters 458 is an unsigned integer, since it consists of the digit 4 followed by 58, and 58 is an unsigned integer, since it consists of the digit 5 followed by 8, which is an unsigned integer since it is a single digit. This seems much more cumbersome than the iterative definition and indeed it is — for people, that is. Computers, however, are very good at handling such sequences of pending questions. We might, for example, have a function that takes a string of characters as input and returns *true* if the string of characters represents an unsigned integer.

```
function UnsignedInteger(s : string of characters): boolean;
begin
    if s is a single digit, then return true
    else
        Remove the first character from s;
        Return true if and only if (the first character is a digit)
            and (UnsignedInteger returns true when called on what remains)
end;
```

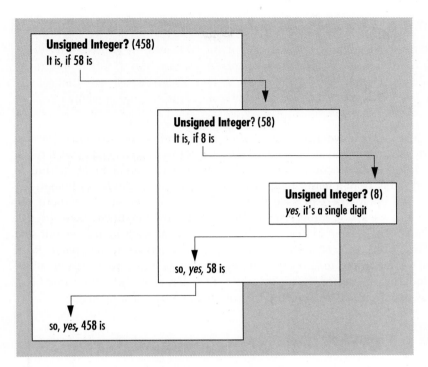

Figure 7.5. A sequence of recursive function calls

Each time *UnsignedInteger* is called, it inspects the first character and calls a clone of itself on what remains of the string. This is important — control does not pass to the start of the block. Rather, a new copy of *UnsignedInteger* is invoked, and control passes to the start of the new copy, as pictured in Figure 7.5.

Even in this skeletal form, *UnsignedInteger* illustrates the two-part form of any recursive definition: There is a recursive part that calls a copy of the routine, almost always on a smaller instance of the problem (in this case, a number with fewer digits), and there is an exit, a condition that will sooner or later become true and cancel any further recursive calls. A common error in designing a recursive algorithm is to neglect to include an exit or to write the exit condition so that it will never be satisfied. If that happens, the algorithm continues to make recursive calls forever, getting more and more deeply buried, usually until the copies of the subprogram that have been invoked, but not completed, overflow the amount of available space in memory. Boom! The program crashes.

> **A** recursive subprogram always contains two parts: (1) an *exit* or *terminating condition* that will eventually cause the procedure or function to return without making any subsequent calls and (2) a *recursive part* that calls a copy of the subprogram on a smaller version of the original problem.

Writing a recursive algorithm is similar in its effect to skydiving: We can confidently jump out of an airplane if we are sure of two things: (1) that we'll reach a lower altitude (the recursive case: solve the smaller problem of getting to the ground safely from a lesser height) and (2) that at a certain lower height, the parachute will open (the exit case that gets us out of recursion). Without the recursive case, we spend forever suspended at the same height; without the exit case, we fall until disaster strikes. Together, the two conditions guarantee our safe arrival. This is the leap of faith we have to make when using recursion. With recursion, we don't need to know how to solve the big problem from scratch; all we have to do is solve it assuming we can solve a smaller problem of the same kind. The messy details are all hidden, and the solution appears, as if by magic.

The **forward** Directive

There are some cases in which we must override Pascal's "declare before use" rule, not just for convenience but because it is absolutely necessary. Consider, for example, two *mutually recursive* subprograms, ones that call each other:

```
procedure A(var x, y : integer);
  var
      n, m : integer;
begin
  ⋮
  m := B(n);     OOPS! We don't know what B is here.
  ⋮
end;
function B(var t : integer) : integer;
  var
      u : integer;
begin
  ⋮
  A(u, t);
  ⋮
end;
```

If we had to declare a procedure before we called it, there would be no way to write these declarations, since procedure *A* calls *B*, so *B* would have to be declared before *A*, but *B* calls *A*, so *A* would have to be declared before *B*. We can't possibly declare *A* before *B* and also declare *B* before *A*, so there would be no way to write these two routines without violating the "declare before use" principle. Although it may seem that this is a problem that is too weird to be worth worrying about, there are times when the only easy way to solve a programming problem is to use mutually recursive routines. This chapter's PIP is an instance of a class of programs, called *recursive descent parsers*, that often make use of mutual recursion.

For a similar dilemma that is solved in a different way, see Chapter 12.

The primary reason for the "declare before use" principle is to make the job of the compiler designer easier. While translating a source code program, the compiler must keep track of details like the types of variables, the definition of named types, and — of particular importance here — the parameters and names of procedures and functions. Requiring that an entity be defined before it is referred to means that the compiler doesn't have to backtrack to fill in definitions, which speeds up compilation considerably. In the case of procedures and functions, though, the most important information that the compiler needs is the name of the subprogram and its parameters. The code of the subprogram isn't needed if all we're interested in is whether the subprogram is being called correctly.

Pascal allows the headers of procedures and functions to be defined without their code, thereby providing a way out of the bind we saw when we tried to define two routines that called each other. The **forward** compiler directive is not a statement; rather, it tells the compiler, in effect, "Here is the header for a subprogram that we'll define later, so you can use it to check any subsequent references for consistency." When we follow the header of a procedure or function with the reserved word **forward**, we are directing the compiler to record the name and parameter list and to defer translation of the body of the subprogram until later. In our example, we can use the **forward** directive to make the function B known to the compiler early enough so that it can translate the code for the procedure A, as follows:

```
function B(var t : integer) : integer;
    forward;        The rest of the definition will come later.
procedure A(var x, y : integer);
    var
        n, m : integer;
begin
    ⋮
    m : = B(n);     Now the compiler can check that B is called correctly.
    ⋮
end;
function B;         Finally, here's the rest of the declaration for this function. We just
    var            use the name, since the compiler has seen the rest of the header.
        u : integer;
begin
    ⋮
    A(u, t);        A has been declared, so we can refer to it here.
    ⋮
end;
```

Note that we didn't include the rest of the header of the function B, since it had been declared in the **forward** directive. In fact, for some compilers, it would be an error to declare the header redundantly. To make it easier on the ultimate reader, though, it is very common to include the header specifications of a subprogram that has been declared **forward** by using comment braces to show what belongs there, as in

```
function B    {(var t : integer) : integer};
    var
        u : integer;
begin
    ⋮
    A(u, t);
    ⋮
end;
```
The comment braces enclose what would be the header if it hadn't been declared previously.

Some authors, particularly when they are writing very complex programs, declare all subprograms using **forward** directives at the start, whether they are needed or not. The intent is to provide a procedure list at the start and to eliminate having to worry about which subprogram depends on which. Others say that this practice obscures the logical hierarchy of the subprograms and they use **forward** directives only when absolutely necessary. We say that this isn't a big enough problem to waste much page space on and leave the decision up to you.

7.3 Computer Science Interlude: Translating a High-Level Language

We've discussed the fact that almost without exception computers are not built expressly to run Pascal programs — and with good reason. A computer that was designed specifically to recognize Pascal would likely be very efficient at Pascal, but would be hideously complicated to construct, not to mention that it would be completely useless for FORTRAN, C, LISP, Ada, Modula-2, and any other language. Modern computers can run programs in any language, as long as they are equipped with a program that translates programs in a given language into the language of the machine. We've talked about the compilers and interpreters that perform this translation, but we haven't said much about how this translation takes place.

The first task of a program translator is called *scanning* or *lexical analysis*. This task is devoted to breaking up the original source code (which is really nothing but a long string of characters) into *tokens* — that is, the smallest units of meaning in the language. Scanning is the machine equivalent of what we do when we read a sentence and take note of the words and punctuation marks it contains. Scanning a Pascal program involves recognizing and separating its identifiers, numbers, operators, and the like. The scanning program must have a knowledge of Pascal's rules for constructing entities like identifiers. Such rules are not arbitrary but rather exist to make scanning easy.

A simplified scanning algorithm can be described as follows:

repeat
    skip over blanks in the source string;
    if *a letter is seen* **then**
        save it and all following characters, up to a blank or end of line
    else if *a digit or minus sign or plus sign is seen* **then**
        save it and all following characters, up to a blank or end of line
    else if *a special symbol (like =) is seen* **then**
        save that symbol
    else
        something wrong happened — send an error message;

    send what has been saved to token storage
until *the end of the line has been reached*

Tokens are stored in a coded form that frees the rest of the parser from having to deal with strings of characters. Included in each token is a description of its meaning in the language. For example, if a token represents an operator in the language, the code for the token might tell us which operator it is. A token describing a variable or constant would contain information about the allocated storage in memory. Scanning lies at the heart of every high-level programming environment, as well as this chapter's Program in Progress.

7.4 Problem Solving I: Designing the PIP

This chapter's PIP is an example of a very small part of the translating task — the part that accepts a string of characters and decides whether or not that string represents a legal Pascal identifier. The rough specification of the design is simple:

Repeat the following steps:

INPUT: A string, *testString*

OUTPUT: A message describing whether or not *testString* is a legal
           Pascal identifier
           Prompt the user whether to test another string.

until the user indicates with an 'n' or 'N' that there are no more strings to test.

Now we must specify the algorithm we'll use to test a string. Recall that a legal Pascal identifier (used to name programs, constants, variables, and subprograms) must begin with a letter and can then be followed by a string composed

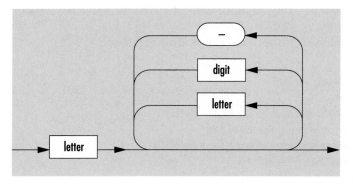

Figure 7.6.   Syntax diagram for extended Pascal identifiers

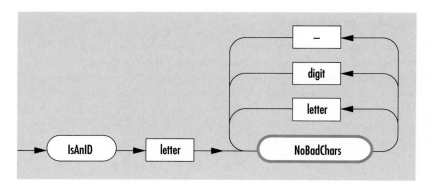

Figure 7.7.   Implementing a syntax diagram using subprograms

solely of letters and digits. In the Program in Progress, we also allow the nonstandard, but commonly used, underscore character to follow the initial letter, as we indicate in the syntax diagram of Figure 7.6.

Until now, we have interpreted such diagrams as describing the syntactic structure of Pascal. In this case, the diagram tells us that a Pascal identifier consists of a letter (an upper- or lowercase alphabetic character), followed immediately by zero or more letters, digits, and underscore characters. The same diagram, though, can be interpreted in procedural terms — that is, as prescribing an algorithm for recognizing Pascal identifiers — and herein lies its relevance to scanning.

One can think, for example, of each box on the diagram as a distinct subprogram and of the arcs between boxes as subprogram calls that process successive characters of an input string, as in Figure 7.7.

In Figure 7.7, each box now refers to a subprogram that tests whether a certain condition has been met. We've added two subprograms, *IsAnID* and *NoBadChars*, whose job it is to manage communication as the string is being processed. You can read Figure 7.7 as stating the definition of a legal identifier: "The string is an ID if it begins with a letter and is followed by a string with no bad characters. A string with no bad characters is either empty or consists of a letter, digit, or underscore, followed by a string with no bad characters." The *NoBadChars* box is highlighted to indicate that if processing stops there (that is, *NoBadChars* finds itself looking at an empty string), then the original string was indeed a legal identifier. If any character of the original string is not a letter, digit, or underscore, the entire string is rejected, and processing stops. This process should sound familiar—it's almost exactly what we did to scan and recognize an unsigned integer in Figure 7.5.

7.5   Problem Solving II: Developing the PIP

Our PIP, *IDTester*, will have the usual input/process/output form, but this time we'll enclose the three-step process in a loop so that we can test as many strings as we wish without having to exit and restart the program. By now, you've had enough experience with development outlines to be ready to try a somewhat more sophisticated approach. We'll replace the outline with a program that we'll fill in as we go. The first stage of development results in a program that looks like this:

```
program IDTester(input, output);

{———————————————}
{To save space, we've omitted the comment }
{block that would normally appear here.   }
{———————————————}
uses
   Quitter;

var
    testString: string;

procedure SolicitInput (var s: string);
{This reads and returns a value for string variable s, from the keyboard.}
{Called by : Main                                                        }
begin
   writeln;
   writeln('Enter string to be tested, ending with Return.');
   readln(s);
   writeln;
end;
```

```
procedure TestAString (s: string);
{This function will test whether s is a legal Pascal}
{identifier and will print an appropriate message.}
{Called by : Main      Calls : IsAnID (internal)   }

    function IsAnID (s: string): boolean;
    {Returns true if and only if s is a legal Pascal identifier.}
    {Called by : TestAString                              }
    begin
       writeln('**In IsAnID. Just return true, for now.');
       IsAnID : = true
    end;

begin    {TestAString}
   write('The string ', s, ' is ');
   if IsAnID(s) then
       writeln('an identifier')
   else
       writeln('NOT an identifier')
end;

begin    {Main}
   repeat
       SolicitInput(testString);
       TestAString(testString)
   until NegativeAnswerTo('Do you want to test another string? ')
end.
```

We test the program and see that information is being passed as it should be. Notice that there's something new here. The program begins with the lines **uses** *Quitter*. We'll explain this in Section 7.7, but for now, all you need to know is that the file *Quitter* is where the Chapter 6 building block function *Negative-AnswerTo* resides.

In the next step in our process of stepwise refinement, we need to expand *IsAnID*. Here's where the organization of Figure 7.7 comes in. We want *IsAnID* to return *true* if the first character of *s* is a letter and the rest of *s* has no bad characters. It appears that we'll need

1. A boolean function *IsALetter* that will return *true* if and only if the character $s[1]$ is a letter. That's no problem; we did that in Chapter 6.
2. A function *Tail* that will return the tail of *s*, that is, *s* without its first character. That's also no problem, since we can use the string function *Copy* to return all but the first character of *s*.
3. A function *NoBadChars* that returns *true* if its argument has no bad characters, which we'll invoke as *NoBadChars(Tail(s))*.

Time for an assumption check: Is there any condition on *s* that needs to be guarded? Indeed there is. If *s* is the empty string, we can't inspect its first character (not to mention that it won't be a legal identifier), so we have to check that in

IsAnID before we call *IsALetter* or *NoBadChars*. We can expand *IsAnID* with its helper functions as follows:

```
procedure TestAString (s: string);
{This function will test whether s is a legal Pascal}
{identifier and will print an appropriate message.}
{Called by : Main      Calls : IsAnID (internal)   }

   function IsALetter (c: char): boolean;
   {Determines if a single character is an alphabetic character.}
   begin
      IsALetter := ((c >= 'A') and (c <= 'Z')) or ((c >= 'a') and (c <= 'z'))
   end;

   function Tail(s: string): string;
   {Returns the string that results if we strip the first character from s.}
   {Called by : IsAnID                                         }
   begin
      Tail := Copy(s, 2, Length(s) − 1);
      writeln('**In Tail. The parameter is ', s);               (***REMOVE LATER***)
      writeln('and string returned is ', Copy(s, 2, Length(s) − 1))   (***REMOVE LATER***)
   end;

   function NoBadChars (s: string): boolean;
   {Determines if a string is composed solely}
   {of letters, underscores, and digits.      }
   {Called by : IsAnID                        }
   begin
      writeln('**In NoBadChars. The parameter is ', s);   (***REMOVE LATER***)
      writeln('For now, we''ll just return true.');         (***REMOVE LATER***)
      NoBadChars := true
   end;

   function IsAnID (s: string): boolean;
   {Returns true if and only if s is a legal Pascal identifier.   }
   {Called by : TestAString    Calls : IsALetter, NoBadChars}
   begin
      if Length(s) = 0 then
         IsAnID := false   {The empty string can't be an identifier.}
      else
         IsAnID := IsALetter(s[1]) and NoBadChars(Tail(s))
   end;

begin   {TestAString}
   write('The string ', s, ' is ');
   if IsAnID(s) then
      writeln('an identifier')
   else
      writeln('NOT an identifier')
end;
```

Again, we test our program on strings like 'ABC', '5BCDE', 'A', '7', and the empty string, ''. Everything seems to be working so far, so we can think about how to expand *NoBadChars*. Looking at Figure 7.7 again, we see that *NoBadChars(s)* should return *true* if and only if *s*[1] is a letter, digit, or underscore and if the tail of *s* has no bad characters. Aha! *NoBadChars* is a natural candidate for recursion. That means that there are two questions we must ask: (1) What's the exit condition? and (2) What's the recursive part?

Problem-solving technique

1. To find the exit condition for a recursive routine, look for the most trivial case the routine could deal with — a case that requires no recursive calls to answer.
2. To design the recursive case, look for a way to perform the routine, assuming that you can solve a smaller version of the problem.

In the case of *NoBadChars*, the most trivial case is when *s* is the empty string. The empty string certainly doesn't have any bad characters, so we leave the function, returning *true*. We've already described the recursive case: *s* has no bad characters if *s*[1] is a letter, digit, or underscore and if the tail of *s* has no bad characters. It appears that we'll need two more helper routines, *IsADigit* and *IsAnUnderscore*, but, again, they can be pulled almost whole from Chapter 6. Here's *NoBadChars*:

```
function NoBadChars (s: string): boolean;
{Recursively determines if a string is composed}
{solely of letters, underscores, and digits.      }
{Called by : IsAnID                                }
{Calls : IsALetter, IsADigit, IsAnUnderscore       }
begin
   if Length(s) = 0 then
      NoBadChars := true              {EXIT CASE: The empty string never has bad characters.}

   else if IsALetter(s[1]) or IsADigit(s[1]) or IsAnUnderscore(s[1]) then
      NoBadChars := NoBadChars(Tail(s))   {s now has no bad chars if its tail doesn't.}

   else
      NoBadChars := false             {The first character of s is bad, so s is.}
end;
```

We're done. We test everything we can think of, like the empty string, legal and illegal strings of length one, legal and illegal strings of length two, including those where the bad character is in the first or second position, and so on. Once we're as sure as we can be that things work as they should, we remove the diagnostic *writeln*s, tidy up the output by having the program write blank lines and spaces as appropriate, and sit back to appreciate our handiwork, which follows.

Programs like *IDTester* that are organized along these lines are known as *recursive descent parsers*. *IDTester* is probably the most conceptually complex program you've seen so far, but you saw that the development wasn't too difficult, as long as we resisted the urge to code everything at once and thought carefully about the algorithms at each stage.

The PIP

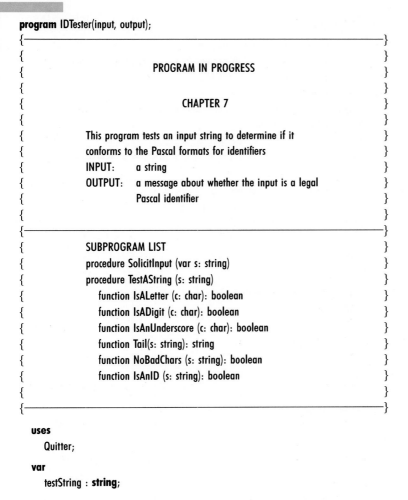

```
program IDTester(input, output);
{─────────────────────────────────────────────────────────}
{                                                           }
{                   PROGRAM IN PROGRESS                     }
{                                                           }
{                        CHAPTER 7                          }
{                                                           }
{       This program tests an input string to determine if it }
{       conforms to the Pascal formats for identifiers      }
{       INPUT:      a string                                }
{       OUTPUT:     a message about whether the input is a legal }
{                   Pascal identifier                       }
{                                                           }
{─────────────────────────────────────────────────────────}
{           SUBPROGRAM LIST                                 }
{           procedure SolicitInput (var s: string)         }
{           procedure TestAString (s: string)              }
{               function IsALetter (c: char): boolean      }
{               function IsADigit (c: char): boolean       }
{               function IsAnUnderscore (c: char): boolean }
{               function Tail(s: string): string           }
{               function NoBadChars (s: string): boolean   }
{               function IsAnID (s: string): boolean       }
{                                                           }
{─────────────────────────────────────────────────────────}

uses
    Quitter;

var
    testString : string;
```

```
procedure SolicitInput (var s: string);
{This reads and returns a value for string variable s from the keyboard.}
{Called by : Main                                                      }
begin
   writeln;
   writeln('Enter string to be tested, ending with Return.');
   write('> ');
   readln(s);
   writeln
end;

procedure TestAString (s: string);
{This function will test whether s is a legal Pascal}
{identifier and will print an appropriate message. }
{Called by : Main      Calls : IsAnID (internal)   }
   function IsALetter (c: char): boolean;
   {Determines if a single character is an alphabetic character.}
   {Called by : IsAnID, NoBadChars                           }
   begin
      IsALetter : = ((c > = 'A') and (c < = 'Z')) or ((c > = 'a') and (c < = 'z'))
   end;

   function IsADigit (c: char): boolean;
   {Determines if a single character is a Pascal digit.}
   {Called by : NoBadChars                   }
   begin
      IsADigit : = ((c > = '0') and (c < = '9'))
   end;

   function IsAnUnderscore (c: char): boolean;
   {Determines if a single character is an underscore character.}
   begin
      IsAnUnderscore : = (c = '_')
   end;

   function Tail(s: string): string;
   {Returns the string that results if we strip the first character from s.}
   {Called by : IsAnID, NoBadChars                             }
   begin
      Tail : = Copy(s, 2, Length(s) − 1)
   end;

   function NoBadChars (s: string): boolean;
   {Recursively determines if a string is composed solely}
   {of letters, underscores, and digits.               }
   {Called by : IsAnID                      }
   {Calls : IsALetter, IsADigit, IsAnUnderscore        }
```

```
  begin
    if Length(s) = 0 then
      NoBadChars := true                      {EXIT CASE: The empty string never has bad
                                               characters.}

    else if IsALetter(s[1]) or IsADigit(s[1]) or IsAnUnderscore(s[1]) then
      NoBadChars := NoBadChars(Tail(s))    {s now has no bad chars if its tail doesn't}

    else
      NoBadChars := false                     {The first character of s is bad, so s is.}
  end;

  function IsAnID (s: string): boolean;
  {Returns true if and only if s is a legal Pascal identifier.    }
  {Called by : TestAString        Calls : IsALetter, NoBadChars}
  begin
    if Length(s) = 0 then
      IsAnID := false                         {The empty string can't be an identifier.}
    else
      IsAnID := IsALetter(s[1]) and NoBadChars(Tail(s))
  end;

begin    {TestAString}
  writeln;
  write('The string ', s, ' is ');
  if IsAnID(s) then
    writeln('an identifier')
  else
    writeln('NOT an identifier ');
  writeln;
  writeln('        *********          ');
  writeln
end;

begin    {Main}
  repeat
    SolicitInput(testString);
    TestAString(testString)
  until NegativeAnswerTo('Do you want to test another string? ')
end.
```

7.6

Problem Solving III: Analyzing the Structure of the PIP

The operation of *IDTester* is remarkably straightforward once the organization of the program becomes clear. Notice, for example, that there are only four names that have global scope. One is the function *NegativeAnswerTo*, which is global by virtue of being included in unit *Quitter*, as we'll see. The others are the variable *testString* and the procedures *SolicitInput* and *TestAString*, which are used only in the main program.

Now look at the body of procedure *TestAString*. It directly references two other subprograms, *IsALetter* and *IsAnID*, which we have chosen to define within the block of *TestAString*. We did so because the main program, as written, does not need to know about or directly invoke either of these routines. Their implementation is the sole concern of *TestAString*, which relies on them to do its job. Indeed, all of the remaining subprograms (functions *IsADigit*, *IsALetter*, *IsAnUnderscore*, and *NoBadChars*) are nested within and defined locally to *TestAString* for the same basic reason — *TestAString*'s block is the only location where these functions are used.

> **I**n general, subprograms should be defined as locally as possible to allow for the required communication between parts of the program, and as globally as possible to ensure that they are available to any other parts of the program that could use them.

The first part of this tenet explains why we have nested subprograms. The second part — the one espousing the need for global availability of useful subprograms — explains why we have left all of the *IsWhatever* functions at the same level within procedure *TestAString*. In this way, we not only ensure that each of these routines can call the others (as *NoBadChars* and *IsAnID* do), but we also acknowledge that these subprograms are general enough that they could (and will!) serve us if we were to extend the scanner to recognize other syntactic structures. Figure 7.8 shows the block structure of program *IDTester*.

7.7 Units: Larger Organizations

We mentioned that our PIP's declaration section begins with a statement that we have not seen before. The line **uses** *Quitter*, like **forward**, is a compiler directive — an instruction to the Pascal compiler that helps it to accomplish the task of translating the PIP. In this case, the directive informs the compiler that in order to fully translate this program, it will have to refer to some additional Pascal code stored elsewhere. Most current implementations of Pascal allow collections of related declarations to be grouped together, compiled, and stored as separate "units," which can then be referenced by other programs.[5]

---

[5]The use of units here is the second and last significant departure from the Pascal standard in this text. Units are not defined in the standard, but all the compilers for which our labs were written allow units as extensions to the standard. There are some minor differences between the way these compilers treat units, but we will concentrate here only on the areas in which they are identical.

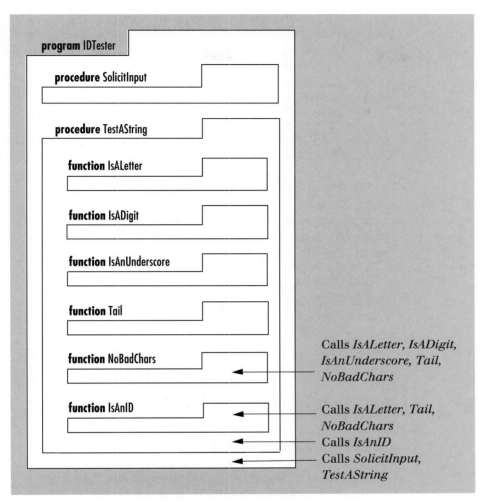

Figure 7.8. Block structure of program *IDTester*

A unit is a separately compileable file, like a program. Like a program, a unit may contain its own constant, type, variable, and subprogram declarations. Unlike a program, a unit has no statement part, that is, no "main" program. The only statements in a unit occur in its procedure and function declarations. The purpose of units is to enhance the encapsulation of code. In a sense, units act like "meta-subprograms" in that they collect together commonly used declarations and code and make them available to any program (or other unit) that calls them. In this example, we have extracted a procedure from the building blocks of Chapter 6 (the one that asks the user whether the program should be run again) and placed it in a unit named *Quitter*, which follows. *Quitter* contains the function *Negative-*

AnswerTo so that it can be invoked from any program that needs to do so. The programmer indicates his or her intention to make use of a *NegativeAnswerTo* (and any of the declarations in the top, interface part of unit *Quitter*) by including a **uses** *Quitter* directive at the start of the program.

```
unit Quitter;
   interface
      {————————————————————}
      {This is the "public" part of the unit. Any identifiers declared here }
      {may be referred to in the program or unit that uses this one.      }
      {————————————————————}
         function NegativeAnswerTo(prompt: string): boolean;

   implementation
      {————————————————————}
      {This is the "private" part of the unit. Any identifiers declared here }
      {are local to this unit and may not be used outside.               }
      {————————————————————}
         function NegativeAnswerTo; {(prompt: string): boolean}
         {Returns true if and only if user enters}
         {'n' or 'N' to the prompt string.        }
            var
               ans: char;
         begin
            writeln;
            writeln(prompt);
            write('Type "y" for yes or "n" for no: ');
            readln(ans);
            while (ans <> 'y') and (ans <> 'Y') and (ans <> 'n') and (ans <> 'N') do
               begin
                  writeln;
                  writeln('*** Please limit your response to "y" or "n" (without quotes). ');
                  write('Try again: "n" for no, "y" for yes: ');
                  readln(ans)
               end;
            writeln;
            NegativeAnswerTo : = (ans = 'n') or (ans = 'N')
         end;
   end.    {NOTE: A unit ends with an end and a period, just like a program.}
```

The obvious advantage of using units, in this case, is that we no longer have to duplicate the *NegativeAnswerTo* function in each of our programs. We can encapsulate it in a unit, compile the unit, and **use** the unit in any program.

In general, a program can refer directly to all declarations — constants, variables, types, and subprograms — that appear in the **interface** section of any units that it uses. Of course, we could, as we have in the past, accomplish the same thing by writing all of these declarations directly into each program that references them. With a unit, though, we write it once and then never have to touch it again — all we need to do to include it in a program is to make a single **uses** directive. It's then exactly as if we had defined the parts of the unit within the program itself.

Way back in Chapter 3, we mentioned that one of the ways subprograms make programs easier to understand is that they hide information. It's much easier to understand a main program listing that contains just the procedure and function calls without all the details of each subprogram's code standing in the way of comprehension. Units carry this information-hiding a step further. Each unit has two parts: an **interface** and an **implementation**.

The **interface** part of a unit is the public part, visible to the program that uses the unit. It can contain constant, type, and variable declarations, and the headings of subprograms (without their code). A program that uses the unit may refer to anything that appears in the **interface** part, just as if it were written into the program itself. The **implementation** part is private to the unit and invisible to the program. This is where information is hidden, in much the same way that local variables in a procedure are hidden from the main program. In simple terms, anything that the program is not going to use itself belongs in the implementation part of a unit, including: the statement parts of the unit's subprograms; any constants, types, and variables that the program has no need to use; and subprograms that are helpful to the unit but of no use to the program. Notice, too, that we didn't duplicate the parameter list of *NegativeAnswerTo* in the **implementation** part. We saw this same behavior when we discussed the **forward** declaration, and the reason is the same — we don't need the parameter list in the **implementation** part because the compiler has already seen it.

In general, a unit takes the following form:

unit *Identifier,*

   interface
      Constant, type, and variable declarations;
      Procedure and function headings only;

   implementation
      Constant, type, and variable declarations;
      Complete procedure and function declarations;
  end.   *Note the period.*

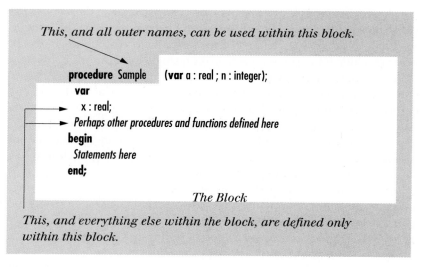

This, and all outer names, can be used within this block.

```
procedure Sample    (var a : real ; n : integer);
   var
      x : real;
      Perhaps other procedures and functions defined here
   begin
      Statements here
   end;
```

The Block

This, and everything else within the block, are defined only within this block.

Figure 7.9.   Elements of a block

7.8
Reference

- Every identifier in Pascal has a *scope*, or collection of lines within which the identifier is defined.
- For scope purposes, a Pascal program is considered to be divided into (perhaps nested) *blocks*. A block consists of all lines between a program, procedure, or function header, and the last **end** statement of the program, procedure, or function (Figure 7.9).
- Global declarations are made at the top, program, level (between the program header and the program statement body) and are defined anywhere within a program, including within any procedures or functions in the program. These include variables, constants, and procedure and function names.
- Local declarations are any made between a procedure or function header and the corresponding statement body. These names are defined throughout the block and throughout any interior block.
- Although it is good programming practice to use parameters to communicate information to and from procedures and functions, it is also possible to use global variables for this purpose.
- Pascal's "declare before use" convention implies that a procedure or function name must have been declared earlier in a program before it can be referred to in the program. There are times when we need to use a **for-**

ward directive to make the name and parameter list of a subroutine known before we declare the routine itself.

- It is legal to define a recursive procedure or function that includes calls to itself. A recursive subprogram must include an exit case that—like the exit condition of a loop—is always satisfied eventually. It must always include a recursive case that calls the subprogram on a (generally) smaller instance of the parameter—one that makes progress toward the exit.
- A common, but nonstandard, extension of Pascal is the unit. Units contribute to the ease of understanding a large project by encapsulating related data and operations and by hiding information that is not needed to understand the main program. A unit is made available to a program by including a **uses** clause in the program heading.
- A unit consists of a public interface part and a private implementation part. The identifiers in the interface part are available to the using program; the details hidden in the implementation part may not be referred to by the using program.

7.9 Building Blocks

A common use of recursion is to process a string, character by character. Generally, we do this by processing the first character of the string, and then call the subprogram on the tail of the string. To get the tail of a string, we can define the function as:

```
function Tail(s : string) : string;
begin
    Tail := Copy(s, 2, Length(s) − 1)
end;
```

and then use *Tail* in the recursive subprogram, like this:

```
procedure ProcessString(s : string);
begin
    if length(s) > 0 then
        begin
            Process s[1] as needed;
            ProcessString(Tail(s))
        end
end;
```

If we need to process the string back-to-front, we can reverse the order of processing within the recursive routine, processing the tail before we do anything with the first character:

```
procedure ProcessString(s : string);
begin
   if length(s) > 0 then
      begin
         ProcessString(Tail(s));
         Process s[1] as needed
      end
end;
```

The basic format of a **unit** looks like this:

```
unit Name;
interface
   {A unit can use other units, too. If it does, the uses directive goes here.}

   const
      {any public constant declarations}
   var
      {any public variable declarations}
   function Sample(parameter list) : boolean;
   {any other subprogram headers}
implementation
   const
      {any private constant declarations, used only within the unit}
   var
      {any private variable declarations}

   procedure Hidden(parameter list);
   {This can be called within the unit, but anything that}
   {uses the unit cannot access this procedure.          }
   begin
      ⋮
   end;

   function Sample;     Don't need the rest of the header here.
   begin
      ⋮
   end;
   {any other subprogram declarations}
end.
```

To access a unit from a program, we include a **uses** compiler directive.

```
program UseAUnit;
   uses Name;
   var
      ⋮
   begin
      ⋮
   end.
```

7.10 EXERCISES

For the following program skeleton, fill in the tables in Exercises 1 and 2 by checking the appropriate boxes.

```
program Scoper;
  procedure A;
    function B;
    begin   {B}
      {1}
    end;   {B}
    procedure C;
      function D;
      begin   {D}
        {2}
      end;   {D}
    begin   {C}
      {3}
    end;   {C}
  begin   {A}
    {4}
  end;   {A}
  function E;
  begin   {E}
    {5}
  end;   {E}
begin   {Main}
  {6}
end.
```

1.

May be called in locations

Subprograms	1	2	3	4	5	6
A						
B						
C						
D						
E						

2.

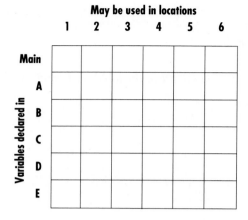

3. Not only is the following program skeleton very confusing, but there are also quite a few name conflicts. After each *x*, we've placed a label within comment braces.

```
program X {1};
   const
      X {2} = 100;
   var
      x {3}: integer;
   procedure X {4}(var x {5}: integer ; x {6} : char);
      var
         x {7} : integer;
   begin
   end;
begin    {Main}
end.
```

Fill in the following table by placing a check in each box corresponding to pairs of labeled identifiers that *cannot* have the same name.

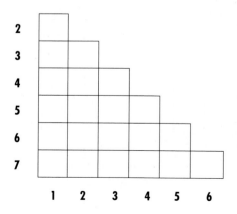

4. Look at the block structure of *IDTester* in Figure 7.8. In the following, we've suggested placing subprograms in different locations. For each placement, either tell why we couldn't do it or discuss whether it would be a good idea or not in terms of readability and reusability.

  a. *IsADigit* within *NoBadChars*.
  b. *IsALetter* within *NoBadChars*.
  c. *IsAnID* immediately before *NoBadChars*.
  d. *IsALetter* immediately before *TestAString*.
  e. *IsALetter* immediately after *TestAString*.
  f. *Tail* outside of *TestAString*.
  g. *Tail* within *IsAnID*.

5. Fill in the blanks, indicating the values of the variables at the given time of execution. We've used comments to label the lines.

```
program Recondite(output);
   var
      x, y, z : integer;
   procedure VeryConfusing(var v, w, x : integer);
      var
         z : integer;
      begin
      {1} v = _____   w = _____   x = _____   y = _____   z = _____
         z := 2;
         v := 4;
         x := 6;
         y := 8
      {2} v = _____   w = _____   x = _____   y = _____   z = _____
      end;
   begin
      x := 1;
      y := 3;
      z := 5;
   {3} v = _____   w = _____   x = _____   y = _____   z = _____
      VeryConfusing(x, y, z)
   {4} v = _____   w = _____   x = _____   y = _____   z = _____
   end.
```

6. Some teachers of programming insist that the statement part of a program should consist only of a single procedure call, like this:

```
begin   {Main}
   GlobalFilter
end.
```

where the procedure *GlobalFilter* contains all necessary constants, variables, and subprograms. Discuss whether this is a good idea or not.

7. Explain why we need the **forward** declaration by going to Exercise 8.

8. Explain mutual recursion and the need for an exit case by going to Exercise 7.

9. What does this procedure do? What does it do if you reverse the order of the *ProcessText* and *write* statements in the body of the **if** statement? What would happen if you moved the call to *ProcessText* before the *read* statement?

```
procedure ProcessText;
    var
        c : char;
    begin
        if not eoln then
            begin
                read(c);
                write(c);
                ProcessText
            end
    end;
```

10. a. A *palindrome* is a string, like 'DEED' or 'STATS', that is the same as its reverse. Write a recursive definition of palindromes by filling in the blanks below.

Any string of length _____ is automatically a palindrome. For longer strings s, we can say s is a palindrome if _____ and also _____ .

b. Use your definition to write a recursive **function** *Palindrome*(s : **string**) : *boolean* that returns *true* if and only if s is a palindrome.

11. The following functions both raise x to the n-th power, for $n \geqslant 0$. Trace the action of each with $x = 2$ and $n = 13$. Which is more efficient, in the sense of using fewer recursive calls to reach the exit case?

```
function Power1(x, n : integer) : integer;
begin
    if n = 0 then
        Power1 := 1
    else
        Power1 := x * Power1(x, n − 1)
end;

function Power2(x, n : integer) : integer;
begin
    if n = 0 then
        Power2 := 1
    else if odd(n) then
        Power2 := x * Power2(sqr(x), n div 2)
    else
        Power2 := Power2(sqr(x), n div 2)
end;
```

12. Modify the functions in Exercise 9 so that they compute x^n for any integer n, positive, negative, or zero.

13. What does *What* do?

```
function What(a, b : integer) : integer;
    var
        r : integer;
    begin
        r : = a mod b;
        if r = 0 then
            What : = b
        else
            What : = What(b, r)
    end;
```

14. Since $n! = (n + 1)! / (n + 1)$, why couldn't we compute factorials this way?

```
function Upfact(n : integer) : integer;
    begin
        if n = 1 then
            Upfact : = 1
        else
            Upfact : = Upfact(n + 1) div (n + 1)
    end;
```

15. Sometimes we can trace the action of a recursive routine by making a *tree diagram* of its calls. For instance, we can define the *Fibonacci numbers* by $Fib(0) = Fib(1) = 1$, and for $n > 1$, $Fib(n) = Fib(n - 1) + Fib(n - 1)$. In other words, the sequence of Fibonacci numbers begins with 1, 1, and continues with each term being the sum of the two preceding values, so the sequence starts 1, 1, 2, 3, 5, 8, 13, 21, 34, 55, ...
    The definition of *Fib* is naturally recursive, so we could write a functional definition, as

```
function Fib(n : integer) : integer;
    begin
        if (n = 0) or (n = 1) then
            Fib : = 1
        else
            Fib : = Fib(n − 1) + Fib(n − 2)
    end;
```

If we trace this algorithm for $n = 3$, we have the following sequence of calls:

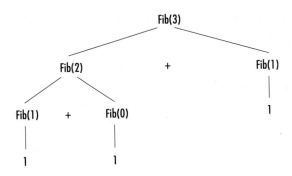

We can use such a diagram to show that the implementation above is terribly inefficient.

a. Do a trace for $n = 6$, and use your findings to support this claim.

b. Find a nonrecursive routine that takes less computer time to compute $Fib(n)$.

c. The Fibonacci numbers have many interesting properties. For example, what can you say about $Fib(n - 1) * Fib(n + 1) - sqr(Fib(n))$? What can you say about the sum $Fib(0) + Fib(1) + \cdots + Fib(n)$? Find an interesting property of your own.

16. Part of the power of recursion is that even simple recursive routines can act in strange and wonderful ways. Trace the action of the following two functions on some sample input values. Try a tree diagram as in Exercise 15 to trace their action on some sample inputs. It would be instructive to code and run these routines.

a. function Ackermann(n, m : integer) : integer;
   {This gets big *very* rapidly, as n and m increase.}
   begin
      if n = 0 **then**
         Ackermann : = m + 1
      else if m = 0 **then**
         Ackermann : = Ackermann(n − 1, 1)
      else
         Ackermann : = Ackermann(n − 1, Ackermann(n, m − 1))
   end;

b. function Takeuchi(p, q, r : integer) : integer;
   {This takes a *lot* of calls to produce a result.}
   begin
      if p < q **then**
         Takeuchi : = r
      else
         Takeuchi : = Takeuchi(Takeuchi(p − 1, q, r),
                              Takeuchi(q − 1, r, p),
                              Takeuchi(r − 1, p, q))
   end;

17. a. Modify the PIP so that it recognizes Pascal integers.

b. (Harder.) Modify the PIP so that it recognizes Pascal numbers, both real and integer.

18. Does Pascal need loops? Explain.

19. The numbers $C(n, k)$ are defined for all $n, k \geqslant 0$ by the following three rules:

$$C(n, 0) = 1$$
$$C(n, k) = 0, \text{ if } k > n$$
$$C(n, k) = C(n - 1, k) + C(n - 1, k - 1), \text{ for } n \geqslant k > 0.$$

a. Write a recursive function that computes $C(n, k)$, given n and k.

b. These numbers are called the *binomial coefficients* and appear in a number of areas. They count the number of arrangements in a row that one can make from n balls, k of which are white and $n - k$ of which are black. They also are the coefficients of $x^n y^{n-k}$ in the expansion of $(x + y)^n$. For instance, $(x + y)^3$ may be written $x^3 + 3x^2y + 3xy^2 + y^3$, and 1, 3, 3, 1 are $C(3, 0)$, $C(3, 1)$, $C(3, 2)$, and $C(3, 3)$. If we write the binomial coefficients in a table, with k increasing to the left and n increasing as we go down the table, we produce what is known as *Pascal's triangle* (the original one, from which we took the name for this book). We've drawn the first four rows below. Notice that it mirrors the definition, since each term is the sum of the one above it and the one above and to the left:

```
1
1  1
1  2  1
1  3  3  1
```

Write a program to print the first n rows of Pascal's triangle.

20. In an attempt to discover a new encryption algorithm, a programmer thought of the following scheme, "I could divide a string into halves and interchange them. In fact, I could do this recursively, dividing each half in half and interchanging the pieces. That ought to mix things up pretty well." If you think about it for a while, you'll discover another nice feature of this scheme: The same algorithm can be used for coding and decoding. This was the algorithm that resulted:

```
procedure Shuffle(var s : string);
    var
        half : integer;                                    {half the length of s}
    begin
        if Length(s) > 1 then                              {no need to shuffle a string of length 1}
            begin
                half := (Length(s) + 1) div 2;
                leftHalf := Copy(s, 1, half);              {Get the left half of s.}
                rightHalf := Copy(s, half + 1, Length(s) − half);   {Get the right half of s.}
                Shuffle(leftHalf);                         {Recursively shuffle the left half.}
                Shuffle(rightHalf);                        {Recursively shuffle the right half.}
                s := Concat(rightHalf, leftHalf)           {Put the halves together in new order.}
            end
    end;
```

   a. Unfortunately, this algorithm doesn't mix up the characters of a string very well at all. What does *Shuffle* do? What would be the result of applying the encryption scheme to the string 'ABLE WAS I ERE I SAW ELBA'?
   b. Write a simpler recursive routine that does what *Shuffle* does.

21. Write a recursive function that counts the number of vowels in a string. Think before you write: What is the exit case (think of the most trivial case you can), and how should we cut the problem down to size? *Hint*: Use *Tail*.

22. Write a recursive **function** $Find(s : \textbf{string} ; c : char) : integer$ that returns the position of the first instance of c in s, if any, and returns zero if there is no instance of c in s. *Hint*: This is hard to do as stated if you use one function. Try to transform the problem by returning a negative number if c is not found, and then have *Find* call this routine and transform negative results to zero. This technique—using a small driver subprogram that calls a recursive one to do all the real work—is fairly common in practice.

7.11 Answers

1.

May be called in locations

Subprograms	1	2	3	4	5	6
A	✔	✔	✔	✔	✔	✔
B	✔	✔	✔	✔		
C		✔	✔	✔		
D		✔	✔			
E					✔	✔

3. Variables labeled 2, 3, and 4 are all declared at the same level, so they must have distinct names. Similarly, variables labeled 5, 6, and 7 are all declared at the same level, so must also have distinct names. There are no other name conflicts.

	1	2	3	4	5	6
2						
3		✔				
4		✔	✔			
5						
6					✔	
7					✔	✔

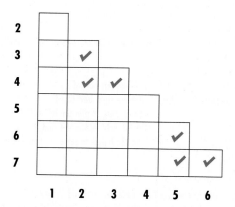

5. Formal parameter v and global variable x are aliases, as are parameter w and global y and parameter x and global z. Within *VeryConfusing*, the identifiers x and z have their local interpretations. Here's a full trace, where we use ! to indicate terms that have no meaning at that location (since they're out of their scope) and use ? to indicate values that are undefined (because of not having been initialized). We've highlighted the values that are changed at each step.

```
procedure VeryConfusing(var v, w, x : integer);
  var
    z : integer;
begin
Globals: x = 1     y = 3     z = 5
Locals:  v = 1     w = 3     x = 5               z = ?
{1}      v = 1     w = 3     x = 5     y = 3     z = ?
  z := 2;
```

```
Globals: x = ___1___   y = ___3___   z = ___5___                        z = ___2___
Locals:  v = ___1___   w = ___3___   x = ___5___
    v := 4;
Globals: x = ___4___   y = ___3___   z = ___5___                        z = ___2___
Locals:  v = ___4___   w = ___3___   x = ___5___
    x := 6;
Globals: x = ___4___   y = ___3___   z = ___6___                        z = ___2___
Locals:  v = ___4___   w = ___3___   x = ___6___
    y := 8
Globals: x = ___4___   y = ___8___   z = ___6___                        z = ___2___
Locals:  v = ___4___   w = ___8___   x = ___6___                        z = ___2___
{2}      v = ___4___   w = ___8___   x = ___6___   y = ___8___          z = ___2___
end;
begin
    x := 1;
    y := 3;
    z := 5;
{3}      v = ___!___   w = ___!___   x = ___1___   y = ___3___   z = ___5___
    VeryConfusing(x, y, z)
{4}      v = ___!___   w = ___!___   x = ___4___   y = ___8___   z = ___6___
end.
```

7. What are you doing here? You should still be locked in Exercises 7 and 8.

9. The procedure, as written, does nothing more than echo the input. The algorithm says, in effect, "Read a character, write it, and then do the same for the tail of the list." If you process the text after reading but before writing it, you read and call, then read and call, and so on, until there's nothing more to read. Finally, then, you write the last character, back out of the procedure call, write the next-to-last character, back out again, and so on. In simple terms, if you process before writing, you'll write the input string in reverse order. If you process before reading, you'll keep stacking pending procedure calls forever, never reaching the exit — the procedure will eventually use up all available memory and fail, never having reached the exit condition.

11. The second function is much more efficient than the first. *Power1* will take $n + 1$ function calls to find x^n, whereas *Power2* will take about $1 + \log_2(n)$ calls. For instance, to find x^{1024} using *Power1* will take 1025 function calls, whereas *Power2* will take just 11.

13. It returns the greatest common divisor of a and b, as does the nonrecursive version of Exercise 25, Chapter 5.

15. a. It takes 25 function calls to find $Fib(6)$. You can show that the number of function calls this algorithm takes to compute $Fib(n)$ is $2Fib(n) - 1$, so to compute $Fib(10)$ takes 177 calls.

b. function Fib(n : integer) : integer;
   {Iterative Fibonacci calculation. This uses the two most}
   {recent values of the sequence to compute the next.   }
       var
           old, recent, current, i: integer;

```
begin
   if n = 0 then
      Fib : = 1
   else
      begin
         old : = 0;
         recent : = 1;
         for i : = 1 to n do
            begin
               current : = old + recent;
               old : = recent;
               recent : = current
            end;
         Fib : = current
      end
end;
```

c. The solution is left to the reader.

17. a. If we translate the syntax diagram for integers into a functional description, we get a diagram much like Figure 7.7. From this, it's not hard to write the routines we need.

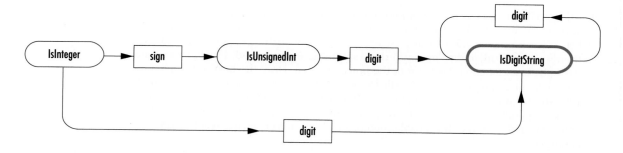

b. The solution is left to the reader.

19. a.
```
function C(n, k : integer) : integer;
   begin
      if k = 0 then
         C : = 1
      else if k > n then
         C : = 0
      else
         C : = C(n − 1, k) + C(n − 1, k − 1)
   end;
```

b. The solution is left to the reader.

21. **function** VowelCount(s : **string**) : integer;
{This routine uses a boolean function, Vowel(c),   }
{that returns true if and only if c is a vowel. It also }
{uses the Tail function from the building blocks.   }
begin
    if Length(s) = 0 **then**   {EXIT}
       Count : = 0
    else if Vowel(s[1]) **then**   {RECURSION}
       Count : = 1 + Count(Tail(s))
end;

8

From Algorithms to Data Structures: User-Defined Types

Pascal provides a wealth of predefined features for you to use in the course of writing programs. As generous and insightful as they were, though, the designers of Pascal recognized from the start that they couldn't possibly anticipate all of the language features you might want for every program you might write. One of the most powerful aspects of modern programming languages is their ability to allow the programmer to add features to the language, in effect tailoring the language to meet the needs of a programming task. Though you might not have thought about it in quite this way, you've already seen this facet of Pascal in the ability of a programmer to define his or her own procedures and functions. Every time you write a procedure or function declaration in a program, it is as if those subprograms have been temporarily added to Pascal for you to call upon, and you can use them as you would any of the features that the standard program provides.[1]

It is also possible for users to define data structures and types that extend beyond the four basic types: *integer*, *real*, *char*, and *boolean*. In one sense, what we will do in this chapter will set the tone for the next four chapters. In the first part of this text, we concentrated on discussing the action part of Pascal. In this chapter and the next four, we will introduce a number of *user-defined data types* that may be customized to suit the processing needs of your program.

---

[1]The user-defined features of Pascal exist only for the duration of the active life of the program in which they are defined. Some languages, like Smalltalk, take this even further and allow user-defined extensions to persist forever.

OBJECTIVES

In this chapter, we will:

- Introduce you to Pascal's facilities for defining your own data types.
- Define and illustrate user-defined **subrange** types.
- Define and illustrate user-defined **ordinal** types.
- Define and illustrate user-defined **sets** of values and the specific operations that apply to sets.
- Discuss this chapter's PIP, a version of program *Zeller* (from Chapter 1) revised to make use of user-defined types.
- Describe Pascal's facilities for labeling statements and for executing **goto** commands.

8.1 The **type** Declaration

We have seen that you can add subprograms to a program by defining them in **procedure** or **function** declarations. To add types of your own, use a **type** declaration, which looks like this:

```
type
    TypeName = some type specification;
    AnotherTypeName = some other type specification;
```

and so on. Syntactically, this looks like a **const** declaration, except that there is a type description on the right of the equals sign. Don't confuse the syntax of **type** and **var** declarations; in a **type** declaration, you use an =, not a :, and only one identifier may appear on the left side of a **type** declaration. This is a very common source of error; experience reduces—but never entirely eliminates—the tendency to use colons in **type** declarations.

Although some compilers allow you some latitude about where the **type** declaration goes, the standard is very clear on the subject:

Type declarations must come after **const** declarations, if any, and before any **var** declarations.

Thus, a standard program must look like this:

program *Name and other specifications*;
    const
        Constant declarations;
    type
        Type declarations;
    var
        Variable declarations;
        Procedure and function declarations;
begin
    Statements
end.

As with other declarations, **type** declarations may be defined within a subprogram and have meaning only within the scope of the subprogram in which they are defined.

Once you have declared a type, you may then use it, within its scope, anywhere you may use a predefined type name. That is to say, you may use a user-defined type name as the type specification of a variable or a formal parameter in a procedure or a function (which — given Pascal's "declare before use" principle — is why the standard requires that **type** declarations occur before variable and subprogram declarations).

Beware of another common misconception about **type** declarations. Declaring a type does not create data objects (constants or variables) for your program to operate on. **Type** declarations merely name and describe a kind of data that can be referred to in your program if you choose to declare any objects to be of that type. The **type** declaration alone does not do this; it is up to you to use the types you define in other declarations so that their potential can be realized in your program.

8.2   Subrange Types

Suppose that you had to design a grade-keeping program and that the test scores your program had to manipulate were all to be integers in the range 0 .. 100. Certainly you would write in guards to ensure that when the user entered a test score, it was in the correct range. However, behind the scenes, the program might do a considerable amount of work that had nothing to do with the actions of the user. It might, for example, adjust the scores to correct for a question that nobody was able to answer, or it might add appropriate scale factors to compress or expand the range of scores to fit some predetermined distribution. During all this, you might assume that, at any time, the test scores—no matter how they were adjusted—were all properly within the 0 .. 100 range. If, as a result of a logic error in your program, a test score strayed outside its allowed range, you would certainly prefer being informed of this fact to having your program produce results that were not obviously incorrect.

The first user-defined type we will discuss allows the programmer to specify that a type will represent a contiguous subset of an *ordinal* type. "Ordinal," in this context, means a class of objects for which there is a first object, which is followed by a second, which is followed by a third, and so on, up to a last object, which is not followed by any other. Integers, for example, are ordinal, in that 45 is immediately followed by 46, and so on. Reals are not, since there is no immediate successor to 3 (what should it be, 3.1, 3.01, 3.001?). Of the four simple types, integers, characters, and boolean types are ordinal types, whereas reals are not.

To declare a subrange type, one specifies the first and last values in the range, using two adjacent periods to separate the endpoints of the range, as in

Recall that false *comes before* true *in the ordering of boolean values.*

    first value .. last value

Any variable or parameter of this type, then, must lie within the specified range. It is an error if the value is not in the range, and the system will generally inform you of that fact while the program is running. The endpoints must be constants, either previously defined constants or literal values, as in the examples that follow.

```
const
    LIMIT = 100;
type
    Score = 0 .. LIMIT;         Can use previously declared constants,
    PositiveNums = 1 .. maxint;  or Pascal constants
    Letters = 'A' .. 'Z';        or literals.
    TruthValues = false .. true; Weird, since it's equivalent to boolean.
    TinyRange = 1 .. 1;
```

Two cautions are in order: (1) The lower limit of the subrange must be less than or equal to the upper limit, and (2) the two periods must not be separated by a space. The first caution is nothing but a codification of common sense. The second is for technical reasons, since it simplifies the job of the compiler writer.

We've been discussing type specifications in the **type** part of a program or within other type specifications, but that's only part of the story. There are two other places you have used type specifications—in a variable declaration and in the formal parameter list of a procedure or a function. Type specifications in these two locations are called *anonymous* in the standard, since they do not have explicit

You'll see a very common use of subrange type specifications in the next chapter, when we talk about arrays.

names associated with them. You can use a type specification anonymously in a variable declaration, as in

```
var
    grade1, grade2 : 0 .. 100;
    inputChar : 'A' .. 'Z';
```

but you cannot use an anonymous **type** declaration in a formal parameter list:

```
procedure IllegalParameters(g : 0 .. 100 ; var letterGrade : 'A' .. 'E');
```

Since Pascal isn't "smart" enough to decode a type specification within a formal parameter list, the standard insists that actual parameters match the type of their corresponding formal parameters exactly — that is, they must have the same name. If you need to pass a parameter of some user-defined type, you must have declared the type in a named **type** declaration at some time previously, as in

```
type
    ExamScore = 0 .. 100;
    GradeType = 'A' .. 'E';
⋮
procedure LegalParameters(g : ExamScore ; var letterGrade : GradeType);
```

You can use anonymous type specifications in variable declarations and in other **type** declarations; you can't use them in formal parameter declarations.

Using Subrange Types for Program Correctness

In our grade-keeping example, by declaring any test score variable, such as *score*, to be of the subrange type 0 .. 100, you are in effect instructing the compiler to test the precondition

```
{(0 ≤ score) and (score ≤ 100)}
```

before every instance of *score* in your program. You could, of course, do the same thing, by inserting this type of a code throughout your program:

```
if (0 <= score) and (score <= 100) then
    writeln('score variable out of range')
```

This would be extremely tedious if your program had twenty variables of this type used in four hundred statements. Why not let the compiler do it for you and alert you with an error message if a variable strays out of its type range? We'll see shortly that it's not a good idea to turn over *all* range checking to the compiler but that there are times when it will be very useful to have the compiler do some of the work for you.

8.3   User-Defined Ordinals

Elements of all ordinal types have literal names that are used to specify single fixed values, like the integer -56, the character '%', and the boolean value *true*. In Pascal, you may construct your own *enumerated* type of ordinals merely by listing the literal values in a type specification. For example, if you wrote a program that deals with days of the week, you could code them as we did in the original version of *Zeller*, using the integers 0 through 6, and assigning 0 to be Sunday, 1 to be Monday, and so on. The problem, of course, is that in the middle of reading such a program, it's a bother to have to remember what the interpretation of **for** *day* := 1 **to** 5 **do** should be. In a situation like this, the readability of the program is certainly enhanced if we define our own enumerated type for days of the week:

```
type
    WeekDays = (Sun, Mon, Tue, Wed, Thu, Fri, Sat);
```

Then, with *day* defined to be of type *WeekDays*, we can make the much more understandable statement

```
for day := Mon to Fri do
```

This not only enhances the readability of the **for** statement, but it works! Enumerated types are ordinal types, with their order being exactly as described in the type specification. In other words, the literal values defined above have the properties *Sun < Mon < Tue < Wed < Thu < Fri < Sat*, and we can iterate over these values in a **for** statement just as we can with any other ordinal type. Since user-defined ordinals behave like any other ordinal types, we may use them to define subrange types as well:

```
type
    WeekDays = (Sun, Mon, Tue, Wed, Thu, Fri, Sat);
    WorkDays = Mon .. Fri;
```

In general, the constraints on user-defined ordinals are fairly easy to anticipate if you remember that including a name (like *Sun*) in a description of an ordinal type (*WeekDays*) amounts to declaring the name to be of that type. That's really what we're doing when we define an enumerated type. We are creating new names, identifying them as being of a new type, and ordering the type. Thus, we can't expect to use a literal name in a type specification if that name has already been defined elsewhere in the same scope — there's no reasonable way we can expect the compiler to understand the ambiguous name in the body of the program. For that reason, the last three of the following four declarations are wrong.

type
    WeekDays = (Sun, Mon, Tue, Wed, Thu, Fri, Sat);
    WorkDays = (Mon, Tue, Wed, Thu, Fri);
        NO. These have already been defined as literals of type WeekDays.
    SmallNums = (1, 2, 3);
        NO. The integer names have already been defined as part of Pascal.
    Location = (beginning, middle, end);
        NO. **end** *is a reserved word and can't be redefined.*

Similarly, once we have defined *Sun* to be a value of type *WeekDays*, we cannot use *Sun* as the name of a variable, since there might be absolutely no way to determine the correct interpretation of the use of *Sun* in the statement **while** *day* <> *Sun* **do**. The rule for resolving name conflicts in these cases is quite complicated, but you can avoid these problems altogether if you adopt the general principle of never allowing this type of conflict to occur.

> **A**ny legal identifier may be used as the name of an enumerated type value. The safest rule to follow is never to have the name of the value of an enumerated type match any other identifer or word in your program.

Remember, we first saw ord, pred, *and* succ *in connection with the* char *type in Chapter 6.*

There are some things that you can do with user-defined ordinals and some things that you can't. Since they are ordinals, the predefined functions *ord*, *pred*, and *succ* work as they should (the *ord* values of enumerated types always start at 0, so in our example *ord(Sun)* = 0, *ord(Sat)* = 6, *pred(Mon)* = *Sun*, *succ(Sun)* = *Mon*, and *succ(Sat)* is undefined). One of the things you can't do becomes a frequent source of minor errors:

> **A**lthough some compilers are smart enough to allow you to do so, the standard stipulates that user-defined ordinals can be neither read nor written.

Because you cannot read or write enumerated types, they are most commonly used for communication within the program and to help improve the readability of a program. Some frequent uses are as status conditions (*incoming*, *running*, *waiting*, *completed*), which describe the state of an object, or as error flags (*badInput*, *noInput*, *needsMore*), which might be used to control a routine that received input from the user. We might see these values used in a statement like this:

```
case jobStatus of
   incoming :
      HandleNewJob;
   running, waiting :
      KeepProcessingJob;
   completed :
      begin
         writeln('Job is completed');
         DeleteFinishedJob
      end
end;
```

8.4   Sets

A *set* in Pascal, like its counterpart in mathematics, is an unordered collection of zero or more objects. This is an instance of one of Pascal's *structured types* like **strings**, in which each instance may consist of a collection of several simpler elements. For example, in a Pascal program we could denote a set of even single-digit integers by [0, 2, 4, 6, 8] and use the operator **in** to test whether an integer was a member of that set. Doing this, we could rewrite the complicated boolean expression in the following **if** statement

The other structured types you'll see are arrays, records, *and* files.

```
if (n = 0) or (n = 2) or (n = 4) or (n = 6) or (n = 8) then
   numCount := numCount + 1
```

by the much simpler (and more readable) version using sets:

```
if n in [0, 2, 4, 6, 8] then
   numCount := numCount + 1
```

In Pascal, all of the elements of a set must be the same type, and the type of the members of a set must be ordinal. In general, a set's type specification looks like

set of *ordinal type specification*

as in the following examples:

```
type
    CharSet = set of char;        Can use predefined ordinal types.²
    SmallNums = 0 .. 20;
    NumSet = set of SmallNums;    Can use subrange types.
    WeekDays = (Sun, Mon, Tue, Wed, Thu, Fri, Sat);
    Absent = set of WeekDays;     Can use user-defined ordinals.
    CapSet = set of 'A' .. 'Z';   Can use anonymous ordinal type.
var
    letters, punctuation : CharSet;
    vowels : CapSet;
    noPay : Absent;
    divisors, evens : NumSet;
    units : set of −2 .. 2;       Anonymous type here, too.
```

Notice that Pascal's "declare before use" principle holds *within* **type** declarations, as well. It's perfectly acceptable, for example, to use a user-defined type name as part of another **type** declaration, as long as the type name being used has appeared prior to the line in which it is used to define another type. This implies that in the example above we could not have written the declaration *NumSet =* **set of** *SmallNums* before we had declared the type *SmallNums*.

Set literals are specified by enclosing elements from the member type in square brackets, using either single elements or ranges, as in the following assignment statements:

```
letters := ['A' .. 'Z', 'a' .. 'z'];
punctuation := ['.', ',', '?', '!', ':', ';'];   Yes, this is hard to read.
vowels := ['A', 'E', 'I', 'O', 'U'];
noPay := [Sun .. Tue, Sat];          Missed work Monday and Tuesday.
divisors := [1 .. 4, 6, 12];         The divisors of 12.
units := [−1, 1];
```

As with other Pascal types you've seen so far, you can assign set-type variables to each other as long as they are compatible. For our purposes, this means that the base types are both subtypes of the same general type and that all members of one set are members of the other. For example, the assignment *letters := vowels* would be allowable. The base types of the two are compatible, and every possible element of *letters* is also in the member set of *vowels*. (The member type of *letters* is all letters, which contains the member type of *vowels*, which is just the capital letters, so nothing could possibly go wrong with the assignment.) On the other hand, the assignment *vowels := letters* is an error, since *letters* might be equal to ['d', 'z'], and so couldn't be assigned to something of type *CapSet*, like *vowels*.

---

²The size of allowable member types depends upon the implementation. Some compilers do not allow large member types. For example, **set of** *integer* is syntactically correct but may not be allowed in some Pascal implementations.

Similarly, although the base types of *divisors* and *units* are compatible (they are both subranges of integers), neither assignment *units* := *divisors* nor *divisors* := *units* would be acceptable, since neither of the base types contains the other.

One set constant is compatible with all others, though, no matter what their base type is: The *empty set*, which contains no elements, is represented by [ ] and is considered a permissible value for a variable of any set type.

Set Operations

There are eight operations that can be performed on sets. All but one use the operator tokens you've seen before, although their meanings are very different for sets.

The first three set operators take two sets and produce a third.

* * Denotes set *intersection*. The result of $S1$ * $S2$ is the set consisting of all the elements common to $S1$ and $S2$, so [1, 2, 5, 6] * [2, 3, 4, 5] is [2, 5].
* \+ Denotes set *union*. The result of $S1$ + $S2$ is the set consisting of all the elements in $S1$ or $S2$, or both, so [1, 2, 5, 6] + [2, 3, 4, 5] is [1 .. 6].
* − Denotes set *difference*. The result of $S1$ − $S2$ is the set consisting of all the elements in $S1$ that are not in $S2$, so [1, 2, 5, 6] − [2, 3, 4, 5] is [1, 6].

The set operator * has the same precedence as the multiplication operator *, and the + and − operators have the same precedence as the arithmetic operators + and − (specifically, they have lower precedence than *). The sets operated on by these operators must have member sets that are subranges of the same ordinal type. Note that * and + (like the arithmetic operators of the same name) are *commutative* so that $S * T = T * S$ and $S + T = T + S$, but in general $S - T$ is not equal to $T - S$.

The remaining five set operators are relational operators; they take two sets (or a member and a set, in one instance) and produce a boolean value.

* = Denotes set *equality*. The result of $S1 = S2$ is *true* if and only if $S1$ and $S2$ have exactly the same members, so [1, 2, 5, 6] = [2, 3] is *false*.
* <> Denotes set *inequality*. The result of $S1 <> S2$ is *true* if and only if $S1$ and $S2$ are not equal, so [1, 2, 5, 6] <> [2, 3] is *true*.
* <= Denotes set *containment*. The result of $S1 <= S2$ is *true* if and only if every member of $S1$ is a member of $S2$, so [2, 5] <= [1, 2, 5, 6] is *true*.
* >= Denotes set *containment*, in the reverse direction as <=. The result of $S1 >= S2$ is *true* if and only if every member of $S2$ is a member of $S1$, so [2, 5] >= [1, 2, 5, 6] is *false*. In other words, $S1 >= S2$ is the same as $S2 <= S1$.

> **in**   Denotes *membership*. If m is of the base type of S, m **in** S is *true* if and only if m is a member of the set S. For example, 2 **in** [1, 2, 3] is *true*, and 4 **in** [1, 2, 3] is *false*.

All five relational operators have the same precedence as the relational operators for other types. Notice, though, that $<$ and $>$ are undefined for sets.[3]

By the way, a common error with **in** comes from reading more into its syntax than is really there. It is tempting to write x **not in** S, but because of precedence rules, the order of evaluation would be x **not** (**in**) S, and this clearly makes no sense. To write the expression that is true when x is not a member of the set S, we must write **not** $(x$ **in** $S)$, which doesn't sound right in English but makes perfect sense in Pascal. Notice that since **not** has a higher precedence than **in**, it would also be incorrect to omit the parentheses and write **not** x **in** S (unless S were a **set of** boolean, in which case the expression would be syntactically correct but would have a different meaning).

$\mathbf{U}$sing Sets

As we've seen, sets provide a convenient way to simplify many complicated boolean expressions. For example, suppose we wrote a program that counted the number of vowels in a text input. To test whether a character was a vowel, we could use a complicated boolean expression in an **if** statement:

```
if (c = 'A') or (c = 'a') or (c = 'E') or (c = 'e') or (c = 'I') or (c = 'i') or (c = 'O') or (c = 'o')
    or (c = 'U') or (c = 'u') then
  vowelCount : = vowelCount + 1
```

Look how much simpler and easier to read the boolean expression becomes when we use sets:

```
if c in ['A', 'a', 'E', 'e', 'I', 'i', 'O', 'o' 'U', 'u'] then
  vowelCount : = vowelCount + 1
```

We could even expand this to count vowels and consonants by writing

```
if c in ['A', 'a', 'E', 'e', 'I', 'i', 'O', 'o', 'U', 'u'] then
  vowelCount : = vowelCount + 1;
if c in (['A' .. 'Z', 'a' .. 'z'] − ['A', 'a', 'E', 'e', 'I', 'i', 'O', 'o', 'U', 'u']) then
  consonantCount : = consonantCount + 1
```

Notice that because of precedence rules we need the parentheses here. You should be able to tell why the example above would be wrong if we left out the parentheses.

---

[3]Although if we wanted to interpret analogous relations for sets, we could indicate that $S1$ was *properly* contained in $S2$ by writing $(S1 <= S2)$ **and** $(S1 <> S2)$.

Sets also provide a convenient way to guard **case** statements. Recall that it is an error if a case index has no match among the case constants; we can protect against this kind of error by doing something like the following:

```
if ch in ['A' .. 'Z', '.', ',', '?', '!', ':', ';'] then
   case ch of
      'A', 'E', 'I', 'O', 'U':
         vowels := vowels + 1;
      'B', 'C', 'D', 'F', 'G', 'H', 'J', 'K', 'L', 'M':
         earlyConsonants := earlyConsonants + 1;
      'N', 'P', 'Q', 'R', 'S', 'T', 'V', 'W', 'X', 'Y', 'Z':
         lateConsonants := lateConsonants + 1;
      '.', ',', '?', '!', ':', ';':
         punctuations := punctuations + 1
   end
```

Although the most common use of sets is probably for comparisons, as we've done here, we can also make use of sets as variables that change during the execution of a program. Suppose that we wanted to keep track of all the letters that appeared in a text sample. One way to do it would be to use a set consisting of all the letters we had read so far, as follows.

```
program TrackLetters(input, output);
   var
      c : char;
      letters, caps, lettersSoFar : set of char;
begin
   letters := ['A' .. 'Z', 'a' .. 'z'];
   caps := ['A' .. 'Z'];
   letterSoFar := [ ];
   writeln('Type in anything, ending with the Return key');
   while not eoln do
      begin
         read(c);
         if c in letters then                      {If c is a letter...}
            begin
               if not (c in caps) then             {if letter isn't a cap,}
                  c := chr(ord(c) − ord('a'));      {convert lowercase to caps,}
               lettersSoFar := lettersSoFar + [c]   {and add to set of letters.}
            end
      end;
   writeln('The letters used in this passage were:');
   for c := 'A' to 'Z' do
      if c in lettersSoFar then
         write(c : 2);
   writeln
end.
```

8.5 Problem Solving V: Modifying *Zeller*

The Program in Progress for this chapter is our old friend *Zeller* from Chapter 1. When we first introduced *Zeller*, we didn't worry about its details or robustness. At that point, we simply wanted to show you an interesting example that illustrated the basic form of a Pascal program. We know a lot more now than we did before, so we can modify *Zeller* to make it clearer and more robust. Go back to Chapter 1 and look over the original before returning to see the new, improved version.

The first major improvement was achieved by encapsulating some of the processing into two functions and a procedure. In addition, we've made the program more robust by using subrange types and improved its readability by using sets.

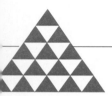

The PIP

```
program ImprovedZeller(input, output);
{—————————————————————————————————————}
{                                                           }
{                    PROGRAM IN PROGRESS                     }
{                                                           }
{                         CHAPTER 8                          }
{                                                           }
{   This program uses Zeller's Congruence to calculate the day }
{   of the week on which any date falls.                     }
{             This is an improved version of the Program in  }
{   Progress of Chapter 1, using ordinal types and sets.     }
{   INPUT:    day, month, and year (integer)                 }
{   OUTPUT:   the day of the week on which the input date     }
{                  falls                                      }
{                                                           }
{—————————————————————————————————————}

type
    DayRange = 1 .. 31;
    MonthRange = 1 .. 12;
    WDNumber = 0 .. 6;

var
    day: DayRange;           {the day provided by the user}
    month: MonthRange;       {the month provided by the user}
    year, adjYear: integer;  {the year provided by the user}
    weekDay: WDNumber;       {the code for the day of the week on which the date falls}
```

```
function FindDay (d : DayRange; m : MonthRange; y : integer) : WDNumber;
    {Returns a whole number in the range 0 .. 6, which is }
    {interpreted as the day Sunday .. Saturday, respectively}
    {on which the given date falls.                        }
    var
        adjMonth: MonthRange;    {adjusted month}
        adjYear: integer;        {adjusted year}
        century, lastTwo,        {the century and the year within the century}
        monthCorrection,         {the contribution from the month}
        yearCorrection: integer; {the contribution from the year}
begin
    if m <= 2 then
        begin    {We only do this part if the month entered was Jan. or Feb.}
            adjMonth := 10 + m;
            adjYear := y - 1
        end
    else
        begin    {We do this part if the month entered was not Jan. or Feb.}
            adjMonth := m - 2;
            adjYear := y
        end;

    monthCorrection := (26 * adjMonth - 2) div 10;

    century := adjYear div 100;
    lastTwo := adjYear mod 100;
    yearCorrection := lastTwo + (lastTwo div 4) + (century div 4) + 5 * century;

    FindDay := (d + monthCorrection + yearCorrection) mod 7
end;

procedure WriteDay(weekDay : WDNumber);
begin
    case weekDay of
        0:
            writeln('Sunday');
        1:
            writeln('Monday');
        2:
            writeln('Tuesday');
        3:
            writeln('Wednesday');
        4:
            writeln('Thursday');
        5:
            writeln('Friday');
```

```
                6:
                    writeln('Saturday')
            end
        end;
    function NegativeAnswerTo(prompt : string) : boolean;
        var
            resp : char;
            goodResponses : set of char;
    begin
        goodResponses : = ['n', 'N', 'y', 'Y'];
        write(prompt);
        readln(resp);
        while not (resp in goodResponses) do
            begin
                writeln('Please respond "y" for yes and "n" for no (without the quotes)');
                write(prompt);
                readln(resp)
            end;
        NegativeAnswerTo : = (resp = 'N') or (resp = 'n')
    end;

begin
    repeat
        writeln('At the prompt, ">", enter numbers for day, month, year.');
        writeln('Separate the numbers by spaces, and press Return after entering all three.');
        write('> ');
        readln(day, month, year);
        weekDay : = FindDay(day, adjMonth, adjYear);
        writeln;
        write(day : 1, '.', month : 1, '.', year : 1, ' falls on ');
        WriteDay(weekDay)
    until NegativeAnswerTo('Do you want to try another date? ')
end.
```

8.6

Problem Solving III: Analyzing the PIP

The first thing to notice in this program is the **type** declarations:

```
type
    DayRange  = 1 .. 31;
    MonthRange = 1 .. 12;
    WDNumber  = 0 .. 6;
```

The only allowable dates in a month lie in the range 1 .. 31, and there are twelve months in a year. Since these are assumptions under which we wrote the program, we include them explicitly by stipulating subrange types. In fancy words, using subrange types in this way has made at least that part of the program *self-documenting*. That is, the interpretations of the variables are given in their definitions rather than just mentioned in comments.

The use of subrange types here is good, but there's a serious style deficiency, nonetheless. Because of the way the program is written, we halt the program with an error if the user enters a month or day that is out of range, since most compilers will catch the range error and terminate the program with an error message. A good program should be friendlier than that: It should catch the range error before the compiler does and give the user a chance to try again. A better (but still not failsafe) way would be to replace the call *readln(day, month, year)* with a procedure that would handle the input:

```
procedure GetDate(var day : DayRange ; var month : MonthRange ; var year : integer);
   var
      d, m, y : integer;     Note here we allow any integers for input, then we check
                             them.
begin
   writeln('At the prompt, ">", enter numbers for day, month, year.');
   write('> ');
   readln(d, m, y);
   while (m < 1) and (m > 12) do
      begin
         writeln('Your month number, ', m : 1, ', is out of range.');
         writeln('Please try again, with a number in the range 1 .. 12.');
         write('New month number: ');
         readln(m)
      end;
   month := m;            Now we know the month is in the right range.
   ⋮                      Similar code for day and year.
end;
```

Even though a compiler will normally catch subrange errors, it is always the responsibility of the program to make sure that these errors are handled gracefully.

We don't have to put in the same kind of code to test *weekDay* or the result of *FindDay*, since the variable and the function values are set within the program and not subject to user error. In this case, the assumption is that the values of these variables will never stray out of the range 0 .. 6. If they do, we *want* something serious to happen, since that would indicate a major error in either our thinking or our algorithms that should immediately be brought to our attention.

The other improvement in *ImprovedZeller* is the use of a set of characters to clarify the building block function *NegativeAnswerTo*.

```
function NegativeAnswerTo(prompt : string) : boolean;
   var
      resp : char;
      goodResponses : set of char;
begin
   goodResponses : = ['n', 'N', 'y', 'Y'];
   write(prompt);
   readln(resp);
   while not (resp in goodResponses) do
      begin
         writeln('Please respond "y" for yes and "n" for no (without the quotes). ');
         write(prompt);
         readln(resp)
      end;
   NegativeAnswerTo : =  (resp  =  'N') or (resp  =  'n')
end;
```

The heart of this function is the **while** loop, which keeps requesting a response from the user until the input character is 'Y', 'y', 'N', or 'n'. As we mentioned in the preceding section, we could have dispensed with the set of characters and used a compound boolean expression in the **while** statement. We think you'll agree that this version is easier to understand, in spite of the overhead necessary to declare and initialize the variable *goodResponses*.

8.7 Labels and **goto**

This section does not discuss user-defined types. It belongs here, though, because this chapter lies at the boundary between the first part of the text, in which we discussed the flow of control in a program, and the latter part, in which we will concentrate on representation of data. We will bid farewell to control here by introducing the last of Pascal's control structures, the controversial **goto** statement.

Part of the modular structure of Pascal, and one of its overriding design goals, is that every statement, no matter how complex, has a single entrance and a single exit. Although a compound statement like a **repeat** loop may contain several other statements, it is still true that each of these statements has only a single entry point and a single exit, as does the **repeat** itself. Figure 8.1 illustrates a moderately complicated section of code with this nested, single-in, single-out structure. Experience has shown that this structure tends to make programs easier to understand and, for the most part, easier to write. We'll explore this idea further in

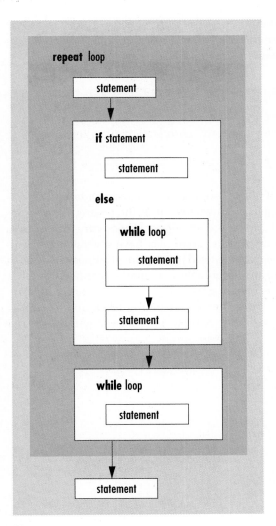

Figure 8.1. The one-entrance, one-exit structure of a typical Pascal program

the Computer Science Interlude in the next section. In this section, we'll show you how, with proper motivation, you can override the linear flow of execution in a Pascal program.

Before we begin, we'll warn you that this is an issue about which some people feel very strongly. The debate over whether to use (or to teach others how to use) the **goto** statement has all the fervor of a religious or political argument. Over the years, it has generated as much heat as it has light. For what it's worth, we take a moderate position: Unrestricted use of the **goto** statement causes more harm than good, but there are a few situations where the **goto** statement can be very helpful if used with care. Given the fact that the **goto** statement is so often the subject of strongly held opinions, we thought it would be appropriate for you to take note of the prevailing political climate in your local environment:

Before continuing, write your instructor's answer to this question in the space provided: "Am I allowed to use the **goto** statement in this class?" Answer: _____

A *label* in Pascal is a string of one to four digits, declared in a **label** declaration. The **label** declaration must appear immediately after the program or subprogram header in which it is defined and before any **const**, **type**, **var**, **procedure**, or **function** declarations. A single **label** declaration may have several labels, separated by commas. The labels themselves are used to mark the destinations of **goto** statements. They may appear before any executable statement, separated from that statement by a colon. When it is executed, a **goto** statement causes an immediate transfer of control to the statement with the corresponding label, and execution proceeds from that location. Here's a simple example of a program with labels and **goto**s:

```
program LabelExample(input, output);
  label
    1, 2;
  var
    n : integer;
begin
  readln(n);
  if odd(n) then
    goto 1;
  writeln('Message A');
  goto 2;
1: writeln('Message B');
2: writeln('Message C')
end.
```

What on earth does this program do? That's a good question, one which points out why many computer scientists are opposed to the unrestricted use of **goto** statements. If you trace the execution of the program for various values of n, you might eventually figure out that it writes 'Message A' if n is even, 'Message B' if n is odd, and then 'Message C' in either case. You'd probably agree that there is a much more comprehensible way to write the program, though. In fact, Pascal's control structures were designed precisely to facilitate and clarify this type of control.

```
program NoLabelExample(input, output);
    var
        n : integer;
begin
    readln(n);
    if odd(n) then
        writeln('Message B')
    else
        writeln('Message A');
    writeln('Message C')
end.
```

Label Restrictions

A label, like all other Pascal objects, has a scope in which it is defined. The scope of a label is limited to the block in which it is declared, so a label declared in a subprogram overrides any exterior labels of the same value, and a label declared within a subprogram cannot be used as a destination outside of the subprogram. Once a label has been declared within a block, a **goto** statement may be used anywhere within that block. A **goto** statement may pass control to any statement within the scope of its label, with two exceptions:

See Chapter 7 for a discussion of Pascal's scope rules.

1. A **goto** statement cannot refer to a destination label inside a block within its own scope.
2. A **goto** statement cannot refer to a destination label inside a compound statement at a level deeper than itself.

If that seems confusing, consider the following pairs of examples. Our first pair illustrates restriction 1. In the program on the left, the **goto** is not allowed because its destination is inside an enclosed block within the scope of the label. The **goto** in the program on the right is legal since its destination is not interior to the scope of the label:

```
program NoGood;                          program OK;
    label                                    label
        1;                                       1;
    procedure Inside;                        procedure AlsoInside;
    begin                                    begin
    1: writeln('Can"t jump here')               goto 1
    end;                                     end;
begin {Main}                             begin    {Main}
    ⋮                                        ⋮
    goto 1;                              1: writeln('Can jump here');
    ⋮                                        ⋮
end.                                     end.
```

The next two segments illustrate restriction 2. The **goto** on the left is in error, since it would cause a jump into a compound statement at a level of nesting below itself, whereas the **goto** on the right is acceptable. It does not cause a jump to a deeper level (in fact, its destination is on a shallower, less deeply nested level).

```
goto 1;                              1: writeln('Can jump here');
while x < 0 do                          while x < 0 do
  begin                                   begin
    ⋮                                       ⋮
  1: writeln('Can''t jump here');         goto 1;
    ⋮                                       ⋮
  end                                     end
```

A little thought will make the reasons for these restrictions clear. In both cases, a jump into a structure (subprogram or compound statement) carries with it too much chance for confusion, since such jumps ignore the orderly sequence of events that are supposed to take place in these structures. Think of the analogue in school: It's much simpler to drop out of a course in the middle of the term than it is to enter a course in the middle and expect to complete it successfully with no idea of what went on during the first six weeks.

Using **goto** Statements Wisely

For all the controversy about whether the **goto** statement is even worth teaching, let alone using, there is one case in which most computer scientists would agree that **goto** is appropriate: beating a hasty retreat from a situation in which recovery is impossible (as in the aforementioned case of deciding to drop a course). Such situations often occur when a fatal error is encountered while a program is deeply buried in nested compound statements or in nested procedure calls. Rather than having to complete all the pending loops, or exit from all the uncompleted procedure calls one by one, the program can use a **goto** to exit immediately. Here's a skeleton of such an immediate abort:

```
program BigAndComplex(input, output);
  label
    99;
  ⋮
  procedure GetData;
  begin
    ⋮
```

```
        if some error condition then
            begin
                writeln('***Can''t continue to read data***');
                goto 99
            end
        else
            Continue normally
    end;   {GetData}
    procedure ProcessData;
    begin
        ⋮
        GetData;
        ⋮
    end;   {ProcessData}
begin   {Main}
    ⋮
    ProcessData;
    ⋮
99 : end.
```

Upon encountering an error in *GetData*, the **goto** immediately transfers control to the end of the program. The bad news is that *GetData* now violates the single-entry, single-exit principle (it has two exit points). The good news is that this use of the **goto** eliminates the code we would otherwise need to write in order to (1) back out of *GetData*, (2) signal to the calling routine *ProcessData* that there was no sense in going on, (3) back out of *ProcessData*, and (4) signal to the main program that it, too, should not attempt to continue processing.

8.8 Computer Science Interlude: **goto**s and Structured Programming

Few topics, if any, in the history of computer science have generated the intensity of debate that has the use of the goto statement in high-level programming languages. Goto statements — unconditional transfers of control from one point in a program to another — were central to the earliest high-level languages. Although available in many modern languages (including, as we have seen, Pascal), they have steadily fallen into disfavor over the past 25 years on the grounds that to use them violates many of what are currently regarded as good programming practices. The debate, which began in the mid-sixties and continues to rage today, is over whether such a control structure is valuable or a hindrance to the production of programs of quality.

On at least one level, the question seems frivolous. After all, who cares today whether languages allow, or programmers use, goto statements. The relative wealth of control structures available in Pascal and other similar languages at the very least minimizes the need to use gotos; some would say they render gotos unnecessary. In either case, it wasn't always this way. The fact that this is still a topic of considerable interest to the programming community after 25 years of debate indicates that there may be more here than meets the eye.

Few would argue with the comment that the goto statement is a vestige of the early days of computers. In the old days, if one wanted to express logical constructs like loops and conditionals in an assembly language program, there was no choice except to use unconditional jumps. In addition, at the time Pascal was invented, very little was known about program methodology or what made a program easy to understand and modify. In short, many assembly- and machine-language programmers were trained in writing code that jumped around from one place in a program to another, and few questioned whether that was the right way to write programs. For many years, it was the only way.

Even though the first high-level languages did have simple versions of conditional (**if..then**) and iterative (**for..do**) statements, they also included labels and gotos among their control structures. As our understanding of programming languages evolved, so did our ability to develop compilers for new, useful constructs. Most notable among these were more sophisticated conditional and iterative forms (**if..else**, **case**, **while**, **repeat**), as well as subprograms and recursion.

Our practical experience with writing programs, though, lagged behind these theoretical developments. By the late 1960s, there were books and papers published that recounted horror stories of failed software projects; missed deadlines; and incorrect, unfixable, and unmaintainable programs. Software was under fire, and Edsger Dijkstra was convinced that he knew where to lay the blame.

In what was to become an influential series of papers, Dijkstra argued persuasively that programming should be recognized as a "human activity." His premise was that when writing programs, we should take into account our conceptual and memory limitations, not ignore them, and that we should organize programs in ways that help us manage and understand them better. This holistic approach to programming was motivated by his practical experience, which indicated that uncontrolled use of the goto statement inherently hindered our ability to write and understand programs because it served to obscure the organization of the program. He went so far as to say that "the quality of . . . programmers was inversely proportional to the density of goto statements in their programs."

His position was supported by the theoretical work of two mathematicians, Bohm and Jacopini, who demonstrated the sufficiency of iteration, conditional, and sequential control for expressing any algorithm. In essence, their work proved that any algorithm of the type represented by programs could be represented by a program that did not use gotos.

That the controversy these articles evoked is still with us today is interesting.[4] That the point of view espoused by Dijkstra and his followers (among them,

Nicklaus Wirth, the developer of Pascal) has had such a profound effect on computer science ranks it as one of the most influential in the history of the discipline. In hindsight, Dijkstra was among the first to recognize what we've been saying throughout this text: Programs are written for people as well as for computers. He effectively shifted our collective focus from merely getting programs to run, to writing programs so that they could be understood, managed, and as a result, made to run. In so doing, he invented the notion of program style.

In many ways, Pascal and other modern programming languages are direct byproducts of the structured programming movement that grew out of Dijkstra's early works. The idea of single-entry, single-exit pieces of programs, or modules, led to increased reliance on subprograms, parameters, and local variables. These same concepts have been extrapolated even further in languages today that support units, libraries, and more formal notions of program interfaces.

It is probably only a modest overstatement to say that what started as a debate about the value of a single statement has led to the development of a thriving subfield of computer science, software engineering (SE). The roots of this subfield are found scattered throughout the early work in structured programming. In fact, the goals of Dijkstra's earliest inquiries and of modern SE are virtually the same. Both are primarily concerned with describing program quality and with developing methods and tools that facilitate and support the development of programs that exhibit quality. Modern SE has, to be sure, taken the notion of program quality far beyond the question of whether a program contains goto statements.

Today, all activities related to producing programs have been subject to the same type of formalization and analysis that the goto was in the 1960s. Software engineers have defined a variety of "life cycle" models for the programming process. Such models typically describe, among other things, how program requirements get defined and expressed, how programs are designed, how designs are represented, how designs are evaluated, how designs are manipulated to reflect changes in requirements, effective design techniques, modern programming practices, testing and review techniques, and testing criteria. A great deal of work has gone into developing, experimenting with, and refining tools to support these pursuits. Modern programming environments (like the one you have been working with) reflect the state of the art in SE research. Automated tools for recording and tracking requirements and for performing systems analysis are commonplace. Formal measures of quality, "software metrics," have been proposed and evaluated. A variety of management and cost estimation techniques have been either borrowed from other disciplines (including psychology, engineering, and economics) or developed originally to help in the process of coordinating the activities of increasingly large teams of programmers.

---

[4]During the period from May to December, 1987, nearly 60% of all letters published in *Communications of the Association for Computing Machinery* (one of the profession's most prestigious technical journals) were devoted to the goto statement.

As computing hardware evolves, providing programmers with more powerful machines to work on, and as programming languages are refined and developed to support newfound capabilities, our software ambitions continue to grow. The limits of what software can accomplish expand almost daily as we tackle larger, more complex problems. Software engineering attempts to provide us with a deep human understanding of programs and the programming process and with tools that reflect this understanding so that the software we develop can keep pace with our ambitions.

8.9 Reference

- In addition to the predefined simple types, Pascal permits user-defined types. A **type** declaration has the form

type
    Identifier = *type name*;
    Identifier = *another type name*;

- The standard order for declarations is **label**, **const**, **type**, **var**, followed by **procedure** and **function** declarations.
- A type name may be used as part of the definition of another type, providing that the type name is defined before it is used.
- A subrange specification has the form

constant1 .. constant2

where *constant1* and *constant2* are of the same ordinal type. As with all other user-defined types, subrange types do not need to be named, but type specifications in formal parameter lists must be named by type name and cannot be anonymous.

- User-defined ordinals, also called enumerated types, take the form of a list of identifiers, separated by commas and enclosed within parentheses, as

(identifier1, identifier2, identifier3)

- Although there are exceptions, it is good practice to avoid duplicating the names of any identifier in a program within the enumerated type list. Under no circumstances can the names of constants of a user-defined ordinal be the same as any reserved word.
- User-defined ordinals are like other ordinals, in that the functions *ord*, *pred*, and *succ* may be applied to them. The order of user-defined ordinals is that given in their type specification, beginning with the *ord* value 0. As with other ordinal types, you may apply any relational operator to user-defined ordinal operands.
- User-defined ordinals may not be read or written.

- A set consists of an unordered collection of members of a given ordinal type. The type specification for sets looks like

  set of *ordinal type specification or name*

  A set constant is written as a list of constants and subrange specifications, separated by commas and enclosed in square brackets, as

  [*constant1 .. constant2, constant3, constant4*]

  The *set descriptor*, as the list of members of a set constant is called, may be empty. The empty set is a constant of all set types and is written [ ].
- The three set operators are * for intersection, + for union, and − for set difference. These have the same precedence as their counterparts for integers.
- There are five boolean operators that apply to sets: = for equality, <> for inequality, <= and >= for subset containment, and **in** for membership testing. These have the same precedence as any other relational operator.
- A label is a string of one to four digits. A statement is labeled by placing a label and a colon before the statement. A labeled statement may be the destination of a **goto** statement. A **label** declaration takes the form

  label
  > *label1, label2, label3;*

  Labels obey the same scope rules as all Pascal objects.
- A **goto** *label* statement, when executed, causes control to pass immediately to the statement with the given label. A **goto** statement cannot cause a jump within the block of a subprogram that is internal to the block of the **goto**, nor can it cause a jump within a compound statement that is at a deeper level than the **goto**.
- Some people think **goto** statements should not be used in high-level languages.

8.10   Building Blocks

Using sets, we can sometimes replace a complicated boolean expression by a test for set membership, as we do in the improved version of the quit function.

```
function NegativeAnswerTo(prompt : string) : boolean;
   var
      resp : char;
      goodResponses : set of char;
```

```
begin
   goodResponses : = ['n', 'N', 'y', 'Y'];
   write(prompt);
   readln(resp);
   while not (resp in goodResponses) do
      begin
         writeln('Please respond "y" for yes and "n" for no (without the quotes)');
         write(prompt);
         readln(resp);
      end;
   NegativeAnswerTo : = (resp = 'N') or (resp = 'n')
end;
```

8.11 EXERCISES

1. Given the **type** declaration

```
type
   Days = (Sun, Mon, Tue, Wed, Thu, Fri, Sat);
```

What are the values of the following expressions?

a. ord(Sun)
b. pred(Tue)
c. Mon < Wed
d. succ(Sat)

2. Define, and give an example of, the following terms:

a. Anonymous type declaration
b. Subrange type
c. Enumerated type
d. Set, in Pascal
e. Label

3. Suppose that we have $O = [1, 3, 5, 7, 9, 11, 13, 15]$, $P = [2, 3, 5, 7, 11, 13]$, and $E = [2, 4, 6, 8, 10, 12, 14, 16]$. What are the values of the following expressions?

a. O − P
b. O + E
c. O − P − E
d. O − (P − E)
e. P − E < O
f. 16 in (O * E)

4. What's wrong with the following statements?

   a. if c in ['A' .. 'Z'] — ['A', 'E', 'I', 'O', 'U'] **then**
   writeln(c)
   b. if c in (('A' .. 'Z') — ('A', 'E', 'I', 'O', 'U')) **then**
   writeln(c)
   c. if c in [('A' .. 'Z') — ('A', 'E', 'I', 'O', 'U')] **then**
   writeln(c)
   d. if c in [['A' .. 'Z'] — ['A', 'E', 'I', 'O', 'U']] **then**
   writeln(c)

5. The Pascal standard doesn't allow you to write or read enumerated types.

   a. Fix part of this shortcoming by defining **procedure** *WriteDay*(*d* : *Days*), which writes the value of the literal *d*, of type *Days* defined in Exercise 1.
   b. (Harder.) Fix the other part of the shortcoming by defining **procedure** *ReadDay*(**var** *d* : *Days*), which acts like *readln* for this enumerated type.

6. We've seen that the function *ord* takes an ordinal argument and returns the integer code of the ordinal. How would we go in the reverse direction? In other words, could we write a **function** *dro*(*n* : *integer*) : *some ordinal type* that takes an integer *n* and returns the ordinal with code *n*? You might want to look at this problem in the context of the ordinal type *Days* = (*Sun, Mon, Tue, Wed, Thu, Fri, Sat*) of Exercise 1.

7. a. Given the design goal of Pascal to make it as simple as possible to plug in subprograms from other programs, do you think that you could have an integer variable *mon* in a procedure, even though *Mon* was the name of an enumerated type constant in the main program?
   b. Can you have a procedure named *True*?
   c. Could you have an enumerated type of the form (*true, almost, never*)? Could you have an enumerated type of the form (*start, middle, end*)?

8. How many elements are there in each of the following types? Where feasible, list all the values in the given type.

   a. boolean
   b. char
   c. (yes, no, maybe)
   d. **set of** (yes, no, maybe)
   e. 3 .. 8
   f. **set of** 3 .. 8
   g. **set of** boolean
   h. **set of** char

9. Strings, as we've seen, have a natural linear order, <. Does this make **string** an ordinal type that we could use in a type specification such as 'aa' .. 'zz' or in **set of string**?

10. All of the following statements or specifications are incorrect. For each, tell what's wrong.

   a. **type** Grades = ('A', 'B', 'C', 'D', 'F');
   b. if x **in** ['a' .. 'z', 0 .. 9] **then** count := count + 1
   c. **type** SmallNums = −1.0 .. 1.0;
   d. workDay := today **in** (Mon, Tue, Wed, Thu, Fri)

11. Write **function** *EveryVowel*(*s* : **string**) : *boolean* that returns *true* if *s* contains all five vowels, as it would if *s* were 'sequoia' or 'miaoued'. To simplify things, you may assume that the string contains only lowercase letters.

12. Make the necessary modifications to make the new version of *Zeller* more robust. In particular, the program should test input values to ensure that they will be within the correct ranges.

13. Suppose we were given the **type** declaration:

    ```
    type
        ChrSet = set of char;
    ```

    Write **procedure** *WriteChrSet*(*s* : *ChrSet*) that would display all elements in the character set *s*.

14. The rules for determining the day on which Easter falls are somewhat complex: (1) Easter must be celebrated on a Sunday. (2) This Sunday must follow the 14th day of the paschal moon so that if the 14th day of the paschal moon falls on a Sunday, then Easter must be celebrated on the following Sunday. (3) The paschal moon is that full moon that the 14th day falls on or that next follows the vernal equinox, which is set to be March 21.

    An algorithm to find the date of Easter for any year after 1582 has been set in modern notation by Donald Knuth in *The Art of Computer Programming*, vol. 1 (Reading, MA: Addison-Wesley, 1973, 1968), pp. 155–156, and takes the following form in Pascal:

    ```
    procedure Easter(year : integer ; var day, month : integer);
        var
            g, c, x, z, d, e, n : integer;
    begin
        g := 1 + year mod 19;
        c := 1 + year div 100;
        x := (3 * c div 4) - 12;
        z := (8 * c + 5) div 25 - 5;
        d := (5 * year) div 4 - x - 10;
        e := (11 * g + 20 + z - x) mod 30;
        if ((e = 25) and (g > 11)) or (e = 24) then
            e := e + 1;
        n := 44 - e;
        if n < 21 then
            n := n + 30;
        n := n + 7 - (n + d) mod 7;
        if n > 31 then
            begin
                day := n - 31;
                month := 4;
                writeln('April', day : 1, ',', year : 1)
            end
    ```

```
    else
        begin
            day : = n;
            month : = 4;
            writeln('March', day : 1, ',', year : 1)
        end
    end;
```

a. Write a program that reads an integer representing the year and prints the date on which Easter falls for that year. To aid in checking your program, Easter occurs on the following dates:

April 1, 1956
March 29, 1959
April 7, 1985
March 31, 1991
April 3, 1994
April 16, 1995
March 27, 2005

b. Use the routines from *Zeller* to check that this algorithm generates dates that fall on Sundays for all years from 1583 to the present.

15. Write the following segment without using **goto**s. Comment on whether your version is more comprehensible than this one.

```
sum : = 0.0;
n : = 1;
1 : if n = 10 then
        goto 9;
    readln(x);
    sum : = sum + x;
    n : = n + 1;
    goto 1
9 : writeln(sum)
```

8.12
Answers

1. a. 0
   b. *Wed*
   c. *true*
   d. Undefined; there is no successor for *Sat* in this type

3. a. [1, 9, 15]
   b. [1 .. 16]
   c. [ ], the empty set
   d. [2, 3, 5, 7, 11, 13] = P, since $O - E$ is empty
   e. *true*
   f. *false*, for any integer, since $O * E$ is empty

5. a. procedure WriteDay(d : Days);
      begin
         case d **of**
            Sun : write('Sun');
            Mon : write('Mon');
            Tue : write('Tue');
            Wed : write('Wed');
            Thu : write('Thu');
            Fri : write('Fri');
            Sat : write('Sat')
         end
    end;

b. The solution is left to the reader.

7. a. Yes. Within the scope of the procedure, *mon* would refer to an integer; outside the procedure, *Mon* would be an enumerated type constant.

b. This one's not as obvious, but the answer is yes. In spite of the fact that *true* has a predefined meaning in Pascal, it doesn't have the status of a reserved word, such as **begin**, which can never be redefined. There are forty such *standard identifiers*, like *eoln*, *maxint*, *read*, and *real*, that can be altered as you wish. Of course, if you declare a procedure named *True*, that identifier no longer has its standard meaning in the block within which it has been redefined. See the Appendix for a complete list of the standard identifiers.

c. For the reasons given earlier, (*true, almost, never*) is perfectly acceptable. However, (*start, middle, end*) is illegal, since it uses the reserved word **end**.

9. No; no more than reals are an ordinal type. Which string comes immediately after 'aa', for example?

11. function EveryVowel(s : **string**) : boolean;
    var
        vowels, test : **set of** char;
        i : integer;
    begin
      for i := 1 **to** Length(s) **do**
        if s[i] **in** vowels **then**
           test := test + [s[i]];
      EveryVowel := (test = vowels)
    end;

13. procedure WriteChrSet(s : ChrSet);
    var
        i : integer;
    begin
      for i := 0 **to** 255 **do**
      {Here, we're assuming that the characters have codes 0 .. 255.}
        if chr(i) **in** s **then**
           writeln(chr(i), ' ')
    end;

15.
```
sum : = 0.0;
for n : = 1 to 9 do
   begin
      readln(x);
      sum : = sum + x
   end;
writeln(sum)
```

Data Structures

Homogeneous Data Structures: Arrays

So far, we have discussed eight Pascal data types—integers, real numbers, characters, boolean values, user-defined ordinals, subranges of ordinal types, sets, and strings. Each of the first six types consists of single values, in the sense that a variable of type *integer*, for example, may contain only a single integer value at one time. There are many instances, however, in which we group together logically related collections of values. The *set* and *string* types are designed so that we can collect several data values in one named object. We can talk about a set, *digits*, consisting of the integers 0, 1, 2, 3, 4, 5, 6, 7, 8, 9, and 0, and a string like 'faz-baz', for example.

Pascal offers three additional structured types that, like sets and strings, allow us to group collections of data together under a single name. These three types are *arrays*, *records*, and *files*. We'll discuss arrays in this chapter, and we'll see records and files in Chapters 10 and 11. All of these types also permit us to refer directly to individual elements of the collections. This is accomplished by using the name of the collection, followed by some sort of *selector* that refers to a particular element within the collection, in much the same way that we use the selector [*i*] to select the *i*-th character from a string.

O B J E C T I V E S

In this chapter, we will:

- Define Pascal arrays, and describe the basic means of declaring and accessing them.
- Review our Program in Progress, a program that sorts lists of numbers, as a common application of arrays.
- Describe how arrays can be used to define more complex data structures such as multidimensional arrays.
- Discuss a variety of searching algorithms as another common application of arrays, and evaluate them using standard timing techniques.

9.1

The **array** Type

An array is an ordered collection of elements of a single type. That's why it is referred to as a "homogeneous structured type." Every array has (1) a name—which identifies the entire structure, (2) a range of indices used for accessing individual elements of the array, (3) an associated type for the elements of the array, and (4) values of the prescribed type for the array's individual elements. In the example in Figure 9.1, we see an array named *storage* of type integer, which uses the subrange 3 .. 7 as indices to its elements, and which contains five different integer values. Notice, by the way, that if an array is indexed by an integer subrange *lower .. upper* it will contain *upper − lower* + 1 elements.

To see why we would want arrays in a programming language, consider the problem we might encounter in writing a grade-keeping program. We might, for instance, want to have the user enter five scores, compute the average of the five values, and then report the number of scores that were below the average. Of course, computing the average is no problem, but once we've done that we can see that we have to have some way to save the five scores so that we can compare them to the average. Simply put, there's no obvious way to count the below-average scores until we've seen all of them. We could, of course, do something like this:

```
readln(score1);
⋮
readln(score5);
average : = (score1 + score2 + score3 + score4 + score5) / 5;
lowCount : = 0;
```

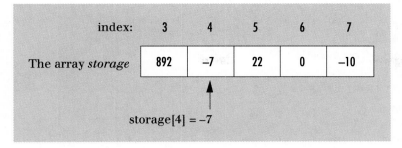

Figure 9.1.   An array of integers

```
if score1 < average then
    lowCount : = lowCount + 1;
    ⋮
if score5 < average then
    lowCount : = lowCount + 1;
writeln('The average was ', average : 6 : 2);
writeln(' and ', lowCount : 1, ' scores were below the average.')
```

If you fill in the details, this simple problem requires nineteen lines of code. You can see how impractical this would be if we had a hundred scores rather than just five — a quick count shows that we'd need 304 lines.

   Using arrays, though, we can collect all the scores in a single variable and refer to individual scores by using the array name and the index in the array where the score was located. The array version of our problem has the same logic as the version above but look how much simpler it is:

```
const
    NUMSCORES = 5;
type
    GradeArray = array [1 .. NUMSCORES] of integer;
var
    score : GradeArray;
    sum, lowCount, i : integer;
    average : real;
    ⋮
    sum : = 0;
```

```
for i : = 1 to NUMSCORES do
   begin
      readln(score[i]);
      sum : = sum + score[i]
   end;
average : = sum / NUMSCORES;

lowCount : = 0;
for i : = 1 to NUMSCORES do
   if score[i] < average then
      lowCount : = lowCount + 1;

writeln('The average was ', average : 6 : 2);
writeln(' and ', lowCount : 1, ' scores were below the average.')
```

This solution requires thirteen rather than nineteen lines, which isn't a great improvement, but notice that simply by replacing each constant 5 by the value 100 the *same thirteen lines* will solve the problem for a hundred scores! Keep this example in mind as you read this chapter—there are many problems that would be completely infeasible without a way to group values of the same type into arrays.

The syntax of arrays is simple. To specify an array type, one uses the reserved word **array**, followed by a collection of ordinal type descriptions enclosed in square brackets and separated by commas, followed by the reserved word **of** and ending with the name of the element type. Figure 9.2 gives the syntax diagram for array type specifications.

All of the following are legal array type declarations:

array [1 .. 100] **of** real;	*One hundred real numbers in a row.*
array [0 .. 10, 1 .. 100] **of** real;	*Eleven hundred reals, in a table of 11 rows of 100 elements.*
array ['A' .. 'Z'] **of** integer;	*26 integers.*
array [char] **of** integer;	*The array size depends on how big the computer's character set is.*

The last example points out that we can use any ordinal type specification in the index description. In theory, then, we could have an array declaration **array** [*integer*] **of** *real*, since *integer* is an ordinal type. That's perfectly correct from a syntactic point of view but may cause problems on some machines. Do you see why? It is common on many computers for integers to range from -32768 to 32767, which means that **array** [*integer*] **of** *real* would contain 65,536 real numbers. That's a big structure—bigger, in fact, than many computers can handle for reasons that have to do with the way they are constructed. So though some **type** declarations are syntactically legal, we must exercise some care to remember that individual compilers may or may not accept them, depending on whether they can be implemented on their machines.

It is worth noting that the index specification can be any ordinal that the compiler recognizes at the time of declaration, including those that have been

We saw the same conflict between Pascal standard syntax and machine-specific semantics when we talked about sets of integers in Chapter 8.

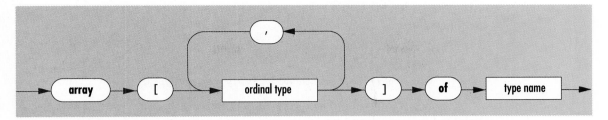

Figure 9.2. Syntax diagram for array type declarations

previously defined in the program and those that rely on user-defined constants, as in the declarations that follow.

```
const
    MAX = 100;
    MIN = 0;
type
    ScoreArray = array [MIN .. MAX] of integer;
    DayType = (Sun, Mon, Tues, Wed, Thur, Fri, Sat);
    ReportType = array [DayType] of real;
    UpperCase = 'A' .. 'Z';
    CountArray = array [UpperCase] of integer;
```

DayType is a user-defined ordinal that is used as the index of arrays of type *ReportType*. That means that if *currentWeek* were a variable of type *ReportType*, it would be correct to refer to the real number *currentWeek*[*Mon*]. Similarly, since *UpperCase* had been defined prior to *CountArray*, it can be used as *CountArray*'s index, so if *theCount* was a variable of type *CountArray*, we could refer to *the-Count*['D']—this would be the integer that was stored in the fourth location in the array *theCount*.

A frequent source of confusion with arrays is that an array declaration uses *two* types: the ordinal, or *index type*, which defines how individual array elements are referenced, and the *element type*, which defines the uniform type of the elements.

Much of what we described above as applicable to index types also applies to element types. In particular, the elements of an array can be of *any* previously defined type: those that are built into Pascal as well as those that have been defined earlier in the program. We could define a type and then use elements of that type as components in an array, as follows.

```
type
    ScoreType = 0 .. 100;
    Class = array [1 .. 30] of ScoreType;    Thirty scores of type 0 .. 100.
```

When we first introduced **type** declarations in Chapter 8, we were careful to point out that declaring a type does not declare a variable. **Type** declarations merely describe and name a form that can later be used to declare and reference specific data objects. Now that we've seen how to declare arrays, how do we use them?

The rules for accessing and using individual elements in an array are simple: To access an element of an array, you select the element by writing the array name followed by the index of the desired element in square brackets. The index may be specified directly, as a literal from the ordinal set of array indices, or as a variable or expression of type that matches the ordinal. Once an individual array element has been selected, it can be used anywhere it makes sense to use a variable of the array's designated type (except that an individual array element cannot be used as the control variable in a **for** loop).

For example, if we have the following declarations

```
type
    TemperatureArray = array [1 .. 31] of real;
var
    thisMonth, lastMonth : TemperatureArray;
    i, j : 1 .. 31;
    avgTemp : real;
```

then all of the following statements are legal:

thisMonth[1] : = 0.0	*thisMonth[1] refers to the first element of the array and is of type real.*
readln(thisMonth[15])	*Read a real value into the fifteenth element.*
thisMonth[32 − j] : = lastMonth[j]	*Variables and expressions allowed as indices; assign one element to another.*
for j : = 1 to 31 do thisMonth[j] : = 0.0	*Initialize — set every element to zero.*

The last example illustrates one of the powers of arrays. Since the elements of an array are indexed by a contiguous sequence of ordinals (which, you recall, is exactly the way we control a **for** loop), and array indices can be expressed as variables, we can use a loop to perform some action on every element in an array. The preceding example sets the value of every element of array *thisMonth* to 0.0. We could similarly set every element of *thisMonth* to its corresponding value in *lastMonth* by saying

```
for i : = 1 to 31 do
    thisMonth[i] : = lastMonth[i];
```

Notice how in such loops, the control variable, i, of the **for** loop is the same variable used as the array index within the loop.

Although it may seem surprising, we could accomplish the same effect as that of the preceding loop with a single assignment statement *thisMonth* := *lastMonth*. When we perform an assignment between two arrays of the same type, Pascal graciously handles all the details for us, in effect performing this **for** loop behind the scenes. This doesn't necessarily save time but it does save writing. With one exception, we can assign variables of any type to others of the same type, whether they are simple or compound. The ability to operate on an array as a whole provides the other level of abstraction we mentioned earlier. An array can be conceived of as a single entity and so can be assigned according to Pascal's assignment rules. It is also composed of several smaller pieces, each of which can be selected and used individually.

File *types cannot be assigned to each other. See Chapter 11.*

The last example, *thisMonth*[32 − *j*] := *lastMonth*[*j*], illustrates two other features of arrays. First, the selector index can be any expression of the proper value, as is 32 − *j*. For example, it is perfectly allowable to use a complicated expression like 1 + (*abs*(15 − *j*) **div** 2) as a selector, as long as the result is within the correct ordinal range. This brings us to the second point: It would not be a violation of Pascal syntax to refer to *thisMonth*[*sqr*(*j*)]. If, though, *j* had the value of 15 when the reference was made, we would be in the position of trying to refer to element 225 in an array indexed by 1 .. 31. Clearly, something would be wrong with this. Unfortunately, the compiler has no way of knowing the value of *j* without actually running the program. The standard allows the possibility of such *out-of-range errors* to pass unchallenged in compilation. Most modern systems optionally can monitor index values while the program is running to make sure that they stay within the range of the ordinal specification, just as range checking is performed on any other ordinal types.[1]

Be sure that index values keep within their prescribed ranges. Failure to do so is usually a logic error and may lead to run-time errors, as well.

One of the biggest problems beginning programmers face is getting used to the fact that programming languages have constructs that do exactly what they are supposed to do—no more and no less. Errors often crop up because we learn something of what statements can do and then incorrectly infer that they can do related operations. The following examples are things we might like to do, but simply cannot (at least in standard Pascal), because they are not part of Pascal's definition.

---

[1] Usually by inserting checks into the compiled code, as we saw for subrange types in Chapter 8.

The array *class*	'A'	'B'	'C'	'D'	'E'
false	0	4	18	9	2
true	1	6	11	5	0

class[true, 'D'] = 5

Figure 9.3.   A two-dimensional array

```
const
    FixedArray  =  [1, 2, 3, 4];
```
We can't have array constants, only simple types and strings.

```
type
    VowelArray  =  array ['A', 'E', 'I', 'O', 'U'] of integer;
```
These indices aren't contiguous — gaps aren't allowed.

```
thisMonth : = 2 * lastMonth;
```
We can't perform wholesale arithmetic on arrays — only assignments to individual elements.

```
readln(thisMonth);
```
We have to read and write arrays element by element.

Finally, notice that according to the syntax diagram, it is quite possible to arrange the elements in an array with more than one ordinal, so we could have a *two-dimensional array* or *matrix* (one-dimensional arrays are often called *vectors*). The array in Figure 9.3 is indexed by the character subrange 'A' .. 'E' in one dimension and by the boolean subrange *false .. true* in the other dimension. Such an arrangement would be appropriate, for example, for storing the number of students in a class whose letter grades fell in the range 'A' to 'E', and who either did or did not do the optional final project. If the array was named *class*, the entry *class*[*true*, 'D'] would, under this interpretation, contain the number of students who received a letter grade of D and completed the final project (five students, in this case).

Pascal permits an arbitrarily large number of array dimensions, although the pictures get a little tricky to draw if an array has more than two dimensions.

A Brief Digression: Strings, Again

By now, you should have experienced a sense of *déjà vu*. Arrays look suspiciously like the **string** type that we saw in Chapter 6, and with good reason. A string is conceptually nothing more than an **array** [1 .. 255] **of** *char*, along with a number of built-in routines that aren't applicable to arrays in general. We can't read entire arrays with a single statement as we can with strings. We can, though, refer either to the entire array in an assignment statement or procedure parameter list or to the individual elements by using the square bracket selector. In reality, a string is often represented as an **array** [0 .. 255] **of** *byte*, where a byte, as we've seen, is eight binary digits. With eight zeros or ones, we have two choices for the first digit, two for the second, and so on, so a single byte can represent $2 \times 2 \times 2 \times 2 \times 2 \times 2 \times 2 \times 2 = 256$ values. These values can be the binary numbers corresponding to the numbers 0 .. 255, which happens to be sufficient for the numeric code for characters. The clever part of this is that we can keep the length of the string in the zero-th byte, so the string 'CAB' could be represented internally by the array whose first four elements are 3, 67, 65, 66—the first byte tells us that the string has length 3, and the next three bytes are the ASCII codes for the letters 'C', 'A', and 'B', respectively. This explains why strings can have a length of no more than 255, since 255 is the largest number that can be represented by eight bits. It also demonstrates how easy it is to write a *Length* function for strings according to this implementation. For string s, the *Length* function simply returns the value of $s[0]$.

We'll see in the next chapter how we can do the same thing ourselves, by attaching a length variable to an array.

9.2 Problem Solving I: Designing the PIP

A very common task for computers is sorting a list of objects. If the objects in the list have a natural linear order, as in the case for numbers, characters, and strings, we can talk about the smallest element in the list, the next smallest, and so on. To sort a list is to rearrange the list so the elements are in increasing or decreasing order. We explore one sorting technique in the PIP, and in the later part of the text, in the lab, and in the exercises we explore others.

We want the PIP to sort a list of numbers, displaying first the unsorted list and then the sorted version. The data structure is clear enough—we'll use an array of integers to represent the list. That leaves us with two major problems: (1) How shall we produce the unsorted list, and (2) how shall we do the sorting?

To answer the first part, we decide to let the computer generate its own list of numbers by filling each entry of the array with a randomly chosen integer. That's not hard to do, as you'll see. The tricky part is doing the sorting, and we'll talk about that in the next section. With these provisos, we can specify the program.

INPUT: None. The program will generate a list of randomly chosen integers, which we'll store in an array.

OUTPUT: The original list, in sorted order. In other words, we'll rearrange the list so that it consists of numbers $a_1, a_2, \ldots, a_n$, with $a_1 \leq a_2 \leq \ldots \leq a_n$.[2]

[2]Which we can write in more compact form by asserting $a_k \leq a_{k+1}$, for $k = 1, \ldots, n-1$.

9.3
Problem Solving II: Developing the PIP

The first stage in our development process is almost our standard input/processing/output format, except that the input portion has been replaced by a routine to generate an array of random integers. As we did before, we'll suppress most of the comments to save space here. Of course, we'd actually generate the comments as we went, but you'll see that the sense of the program will be easy enough to understand even without them.

```
program Sorter(output);
  const
    ARRAYSIZE = 100;     {the size of the array}
  type
    NumArray = array [1 .. ARRAYSIZE] of integer;
    We use a named type, since we intend to send an array as parameter to
    subprograms.
    Recall from the last chapter that we can't use anonymous types as
    descriptors of parameters.
  var
    theArray: NumArray;    {the array to be sorted}
  procedure BuildArray (var a : NumArray);
    var
      i : integer;
  begin
    {For now, we'll just put 1, 2, . . . , n in the array.}
    for i : = 1 to ARRAYSIZE do
      a[i] : = i
  end;

  procedure DisplayArray (a : NumArray);
    var
      i : integer;
  begin
    for i : = 1 to ARRAYSIZE do
      begin
        write(a[i] : 5);
        if (i mod 10) = 0 then
          writeln
      end;
    writeln
  end;
```

```
procedure Sort (var inArray : NumArray);
begin
    writeln('Here''s where we'll sort the array.')
end;

begin   {Main}
    BuildArray(theArray);       {Generate a random array,}
    DisplayArray(theArray);     {show the original,}
    writeln;

    Sort(theArray);             {sort it,}
    DisplayArray(theArray)      {and print sorted version.}
end.
```

Now we need to fill in the details. We'll defer discussion of the details of how to build the array until we get to the labs. Suffice it to say that we'll use a function *Random*, which returns a randomly chosen number. Though such a function is a common extension to Pascal, its action is different among compilers.

How shall we sort the list? Here's a good place to ask whether we can find a solution by looking at what other people have done. There are *many* different ways to sort a list—the standard reference, *Sorting and Searching* (*The Art of Computer Programming*, vol. 3) by Donald Knuth, is 723 pages long! We'll use a simple (but not particularly efficient) sorting algorithm, called *Selection Sort*. This technique is the one that people often use to sort a hand of cards in bridge, for example. To use Selection Sort, one finds the smallest element in the list, marks where in the list it was found, and then swaps the smallest element with the first element in the list, thus putting the smallest element at the front of the list. The algorithm then finds the smallest remaining element and swaps that into the second position in the list, then continues this process with the third smallest, the fourth smallest, and so on, until the entire list has been sorted from smallest to largest. The outline of **procedure** *SelectionSort* looks like this:

```
procedure SelectionSort (var inArray : NumArray);
{Precondition: inArray is an array of integers, indexed from 1 to ARRAYSIZE.}
{Postcondition: inArray is sorted from smallest to largest.              }
    var
        current,        {This is where we'll place the current smallest element}
        where: integer;  {and this is where the current smallest element resides.}
begin
    for current := 1 to ARRAYSIZE − 1 do
        begin
            Starting at index current, find the location, where, of the smallest element to the right of
            location current;
            Swap the elements in locations current and where
        end
end;
```

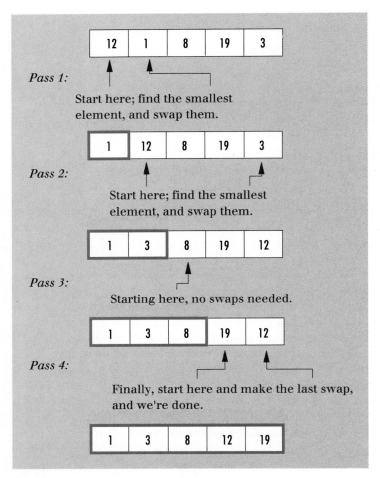

Figure 9.4. An example of Selection Sort

Notice that the input parameter, *inArray*, is used to hold the sorted array when the procedure is completed, which is why we made *inArray* a **var** parameter. Also, note that *current* and *where* are declared locally to *SelectionSort* since they are used only in this procedure and are of no interest to the main program.

Figure 9.4 traces the action of Selection Sort on a list of five integers. At each stage, the figure indicates where we begin looking for the smallest element, the location of the smallest element, and that portion of the array that is already sorted.

The next step is to fill in the details of the routines that find the minimum element and swap two elements, and here's where reusable code comes in handy. We've already written and verified a swapping routine in Chapter 3, so all we have to do is copy it into our program. Since *Swap* will be called only within *Selection-Sort*, it makes sense to define it locally, within the definition of *SelectionSort*.

The only task that remains now is to write the routine that finds the minimum element in an array, starting at a given location. The basic idea isn't too hard.

Loops and arrays are natural companions. A common array operation is: *Step through every element in turn, doing the same processing on each element encountered.*

In our case, the operation is probably described pretty much as you would describe your personal algorithm for finding the smallest number in a list. You might say, "I'll step through the array, looking at each element in turn. If the element I am looking at is smaller than the smallest I've seen so far, remember the new minimum and remember where in the list the new minimum is located." Well, heck, that's almost Pascal as it stands, so let's write the function that returns the location of the minimum value. We'll need two parameters: where to start searching and the array itself. The calling routine doesn't need to know the minimum value. It needs to know only where it is, so we'll keep the minimum value as a local variable. Our procedure heading and local variable list now look like this:

```
function FindMin(a : NumArray ; start : integer) : integer;
    var
        min : integer;
```

The only question that remains is: What will we use for the initial value of the minimum element? Hmm. Before we've looked at any element in the array, we have no idea what the minimum should be, so let's peek ahead and begin by setting the minimum element to the value of the first element in the array. Finally, we can write our procedure:

```
function FindMin(a : NumArray ; start : integer) : integer;
{Finds the location of the smallest element in the array a, at or      }
{after the index start.                                                 }
{Precondition:    a is an array of integers, indexed from 1 to ARRAYSIZE.}
{                 1 ≤ start ≤ ARRAYSIZE                                  }
{Postcondition:   The returned index value, r, satisfies                }
{                 start ≤ r ≤ ARRAYSIZE                                  }
{                 a[r] ≤ a[i], for all i = start, . . . , ARRAYSIZE     }
    var
        min, i : integer;
begin
    min := a[start];                    {Begin with the min at the first element}
    FindMin := start;
```

```
for i := start + 1 to ARRAYSIZE do      {inspect the other elements in turn,}
    if a[i] < min then                  {if we found a new minimum,}
        begin
            min := a[i];                {update the minimum value,}
            FindMin := i                {and record where we found it.}
        end
end;
```

As with *Swap*, we'll use only *FindMin* within *SelectionSort*, so we'll also define it locally within *SelectionSort*. Our sorting algorithm now takes the following form:

```
procedure SelectionSort(var inArray : NumArray);
{Sorts the elements of an array in ascending order.                          }
{Precondition: inArray is an array of integers, indexed from 1 to ARRAYSIZE.}
{Postcondition: inArray is sorted from smallest to largest.                  }
    var
        current,            {The location of the element to be added to the sorted part of the array.}
        where : integer;    {The location of the smallest element at or after position current.}

    function FindMin(a : NumArray; start : integer) : integer;
    {This function returns the location of the smallest element in array a,    }
    {beginning at location start.                                             }
    {Precondition:   a is an array of integers, indexed from 1 to ARRAYSIZE.}
    {               1 ≤ start ≤ ARRAYSIZE                                     }
    {Postcondition:  The returned index value, r, satisfies                   }
    {               start ≤ r ≤ ARRAYSIZE                                     }
    {               a[r] ≤ a[i], for all i = start, . . . , ARRAYSIZE         }
        var
            i, min : integer;
    begin
        min := a[start];
        FindMin := start;
        for i := start + 1 to ARRAYSIZE do
            if a[i] < min then
                begin
                    min := a[i];
                    FindMin := i
                end
    end;
```

```
procedure Swap(var thingOne, thingTwo : integer);
{This procedure exchanges the values of two integer variables.}
    var
        temp : integer;
    begin
        temp : = thingOne;
        thingOne : = thingTwo;
        thingTwo : = temp
    end;
begin    {SelectionSort}
    for current : = 1 to ARRAYSIZE − 1 do
        begin
            where : = FindMin(inArray, current);
            Swap(inArray[current], inArray[where])
        end
end;
```

Modularity: The Unit *Arrays*

We're ready now to write the finished version of the PIP. As we designed the program, we tested it as much as we could, and it appeared that everything worked as expected. Now's a good time to step back and take a good long look at what we have. The program sorts an array of integers, and we can now see that it actually uses two kinds of routines and declarations. The **type** declarations for the array of integers and the subprograms *BuildArray*, *DisplayArray*, and *Swap* have rather little to do with sorting. The main program uses the declarations and subprograms, along with some extra code, to do its job of sorting. We can easily imagine that the array-handling part could be used for other programs that manipulate arrays, so why not include it in a unit of its own? That way, if we need to use the array part in another program, all we'd have to do is include a **uses** directive that refers to the array unit. This would save us the bother of deciding which declarations and subprograms to cut from the PIP and paste into the new program.

Putting the general array-related code in a unit yields this:

```
unit Arrays;

interface
    const
        ARRAYSIZE = 100;

    type
        NumArray = array [1 .. ARRAYSIZE] of integer;

    procedure BuildArray (var a : NumArray);
    procedure DisplayArray (var a : NumArray);
    procedure Swap (var thingOne, thingTwo : integer);
```

implementation

```
procedure BuildArray    {var a : NumArray};
{This procedure fills an array a with random values.    }
{It uses a nonstandard, built-in function, Random, that}
{is a common, but not universal, Pascal extension. See }
{the lab manual for compiler-specific details.          }
    var
        i : integer;
begin
    for i : = 1 to ARRAYSIZE do
        a[i] : = 1 + (abs(Random) mod 1000)
            {This is the THINK version. The Turbo and UNIX versions appear in the labs.}
end;

procedure DisplayArray    {var a : NumArray};
{This procedure displays array a on the screen.}
    var
        element : integer;
begin
    for element : = 1 to ARRAYSIZE do
        begin
            write(a[element] : 5);
            if (element mod 10) = 0 then
                writeln    {Do a carriage return for every tenth element.}
        end;
    writeln
end;

procedure Swap    {var thingOne, thingTwo : integer};
{This procedure exchanges the values of two integer variables.}
    var
        temp : integer;
begin
    temp : = thingOne;
    thingOne : = thingTwo;
    thingTwo : = temp
end;
end.
```

With most of the detail work hidden, the program becomes very easy to read.

The PIP

program Sorter(output);

```
{--------------------------------------------------------------}
{                                                              }
{                    PROGRAM IN PROGRESS                       }
{                                                              }
{                         CHAPTER 9                            }
{                                                              }
{        This program produces five arrays of random integers and }
{        sorts them using the selection sort algorithm.        }
{        INPUT:      Nothing. The program produces the random  }
{                    arrays.                                   }
{        OUTPUT:     The original, unsorted array, followed by the }
{                    sorted version                           }
{                                                              }
{--------------------------------------------------------------}
```

uses Arrays;

```
  var
     runs: integer;
     theArray: NumArray;   {the array to be sorted}

procedure SelectionSort(var inArray : NumArray);
{Sorts an array in ascending order of its elements.            }
{Precondition: inArray is an array of integers, indexed from 1 to ARRAYSIZE.}
{Postcondition: inArray is sorted from smallest to largest.    }
{Called by : Main       Calls : FindMin (internal), Swap       }
     var
        current,           {the location of the element to be added to the sorted part of the array}
        where : integer;   {the location of the smallest element at or after position current}

     function FindMin(a : NumArray; start : integer) : integer;
     {This function returns the location of the smallest element in array a,  }
     {beginning at location start.                                          }
     {Precondition:     a is an array of integers, indexed from 1 to ARRAYSIZE}
     {                  1 ⩽ start ⩽ ARRAYSIZE                                }
     {Postcondition:    The returned index value, r, satisfies               }
     {                  start ⩽ r ⩽ ARRAYSIZE                                }
     {                  a[r] ⩽ a[i], for all i = start, . . . , ARRAYSIZE    }
     {Called by : SelectionSort                                             }
        var
           i, min : integer;
```

```
        begin
            min : =  a[start];
            FindMin : =  start;
            for i : =  start + 1 to ARRAYSIZE do
                if a[i] < min then
                    begin
                        min : =  a[i];
                        FindMin : =  i
                    end
        end;

    begin    {SelectionSort}
        for current : =  1 to ARRAYSIZE − 1 do
            begin
                where : =  FindMin(inArray, current);
                Swap(inArray[current], inArray[where])
            end
    end;      {procedure SelectionSort}

    procedure Header(message : string);
    begin
        writeln;
        writeln(message);
        writeln
    end;

begin    {Main}
    for runs : =  1 to 5 do              {We will repeat the sorting process for 5 arrays.}
        begin
            BuildArray(theArray);        {Generate a random array.}

            Header('The original array is: ');
            DisplayArray(theArray);      {Print the original array,}
            writeln;

            SelectionSort(theArray);     {sort it,}

            Header('The sorted array is: ');
            DisplayArray(theArray);      {and print the sorted version.}

            writeln;
            writeln(' Hit Return to continue . . .');
            readln
        end;    {for runs . . .}
    writeln('Processing completed . . . goodbye.')
end.    {Main}
```

9.4   More About Arrays

There are many things that arrays allow us to do that would be difficult or impossible to do without them. Because of the power of the **array** type, there are a number of features that deserve an extended discussion.

Arrays of Arrays

We have already seen that the elements of an array can be of *any* previously defined type. We can define a type and then use elements of that type as components in an array, as follows.

```
type
    Line = array [1 .. 80] of char;      {eighty letters in a row}
    Page = array [1 .. 100] of Line;     {one hundred lines in a page}
var
    document : Page;
    currentLine : Line;
```

Given these declarations, we could refer to $currentLine[20]$, which would represent the twentieth character in the line. We could also refer to $document[3]$, which would represent the third line on the page. Since *document* is made up of an array of lines, at one conceptual level we could think of *document* as consisting of one hundred elements. Since each of these elements is itself an array of characters, it would also be correct to think of it at a finer level of detail and refer to $document[3][20]$, which would be the twentieth character in the third line of *document*. To make sense of this, think in terms of levels: $document[3]$ is the name of an array of characters; since $document[3]$ is an array, we can refer to its elements by using its name, $document[3]$, followed by the element selector, $[20]$, that singles out the twentieth element in the array $document[3]$.

Since *document* is a one-dimensional array of one-dimensional arrays, we could also look at it as if it were a two-dimensional array, in spite of the fact that it was not declared that way. Pascal supports these two views by allowing individual elements at the lowest level to be accessed as if the array of arrays were a two-dimensional entity. This means that we could refer to the twentieth character in the third line of *document* as either $document[3][20]$ (thinking of it as the left-hand view in Figure 9.5) or as $document[3, 20]$ (thinking of it as the right-hand view).

Linear Search and Flagged Loops

One-dimensional arrays allow us to store information in a list format, so they are particularly handy in situations where we want to inspect all or part of the list in turn. In the procedure *FindMin*, for instance, we began at a start index and

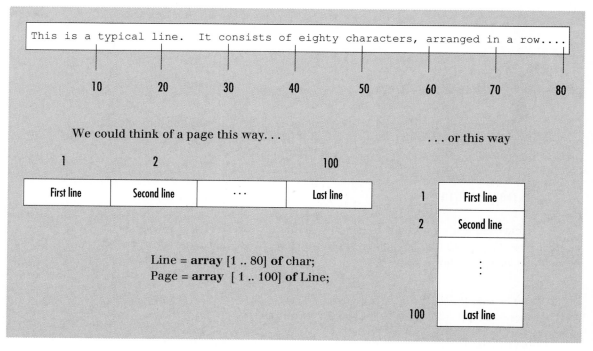

This is a typical line. It consists of eighty characters, arranged in a row....

10   20   30   40   50   60   70   80

We could think of a page this way. . .   . . . or this way

1	2		100
First line	Second line	. . .	Last line

Line = **array** [1 .. 80] **of** char;
Page = **array** [1 .. 100] **of** Line;

1	First line
2	Second line
	⋮
100	Last line

Figure 9.5.   Arrays of arrays

performed a *linear search*, looking at each subsequent element for the minimum. Consider now the problem of finding the location, if any, of the first non-zero element in *a*, an **array** [1 .. *MAX*] **of** *integer*. We could use a **for** loop to step through the indices, but that would be inefficient in many cases, since if we found a non-zero element in the first position, there would be no nice way out of the loop. We would have to continue to inspect all the rest of the elements, even though we would have already found the answer. It seems more appropriate to use a conditional loop, incrementing the array index by 1 until we either inspect the entire array or find a non-zero element. If we find a non-zero element, we signal that by setting the boolean variable *success* to *true*; otherwise, we set *success* to *false*.

Incorrect array search
```
index := 1;
while (index <= MAX) and (a[index] = 0) do
    index := index + 1;
success := (index > MAX)    Did we run out of array elements before finding a non-
                            zero one?
```

This program segment is labeled "incorrect" and indeed it is, in spite of the fact that it seems perfectly okay at first glance and is what many people would try first. Before you look at the next page, take a minute to see whether you can spot the error.

Got it? The problem is that the algorithm will fail when the array has no non-zero elements. In that case, the **while** loop will inspect the array at *index* = 1, . . . , *MAX* just as it should, but at the last iteration, the index will have as its value *MAX* + 1. That will cause the condition *index* <= *MAX* to be *false*, but in evaluating the other part of the test, *a[index]* = 0, a reference is made to a location that is out of the array range. Remember, in Chapter 4, we said that we couldn't rely on the order of evaluation of subexpressions of a boolean expression. In this case, that means that we can't use *index* <= *MAX* as a guard for *a[index]* = 0, since we can't be sure in what order they will be evaluated.

Where we had the incorrect **if** (num <> 0) **and** (sum / num < 60) **then** . . .

A good way around this problem, where there is more than one exit condition for a loop and the exit conditions are logically related, is to separate the exit conditions and use them to control a *flag*. The flag is a variable whose job it is to pass information about the state of a program. Here's our linear search written — correctly, this time — with a flagged loop.

```
Correct array search
index : = 1;
done : = false;              This is the flag that controls the loop.
while not done do
    if index > MAX then      This is one way out of the loop. It also guards the
                             reference to a[index] below.

        done : = true
    else if a[index] <> 0 then
        done : = true        This is another way out of the loop.
    else
        index : = index + 1;  If we're still in the loop, do this.
success : = (a[index] <> 0)   Did we find a non-zero element at index?
```

The flag *done* serves to communicate to the **while** loop whether we should stay in the loop or exit. The nice part of such a flagged loop is that it separates the exit condition into its component parts for ease of comprehension, and — once the **if** tests are placed in the correct order — we can use one exit condition to guard against an incorrect reference in subsequent conditions. In this case, we check *index* > *MAX* first. Then, and only if that isn't true, we evaluate the next expression of the exit condition, *a[index]* <> 0. Doing the tests in this order, we've thereby eliminated the possibility that we'll ever check array *a* at an out-of-range location.

We'll see a very similar use of flagged loops in Chapter 12 when we talk about linear search in linked lists.

Yet another way to solve this problem is to modify the structure of the array. We could, for instance, declare the array as follows:

```
const
    MAX = 100;        Or any other positive integer
    ONEMORE = 101;    One more than MAX
var
    a : array [1 .. ONEMORE] of integer;
```

We would then write our array routines so that they only stored elements in locations 1 .. *MAX*, but we would have the dummy element at location *MAX* + 1 so that our original, "incorrect" routine would never refer to an illegal location in the array. With this change, the original routine now will be correct. We've complicated the concept of the array by having two upper bounds—a "real" one at *ONEMORE* and the "effective" one at *MAX*—but we've gained a simpler algorithm by so doing.

Sometimes we can solve a problem more efficiently by modifying its data structures than by changing its algorithms.

Faster Searching

Here are two similar-sounding problems. Which one could you perform faster using a conventional phone directory?

1. Find someone's phone number, given his or her name
2. Find the name of a subscriber, given his or her phone number

Clearly, you could perform the first task far more quickly than the second. In fact, the second task would be almost completely impractical except for extremely small telephone books. The reason is obvious—the entries in phone books are sorted by name, not by number. That means that to find a name, given a number, one couldn't do much better than to perform a linear search. That is, you'd have to start with the first number, go on to the second, the third, and so on, until either the number was located or the end of the book was reached. In the first problem, though, we gain a considerable advantage from the fact that the entries are in the form of a *sorted list*, with the first name in alphabetic order first, followed by the second, and so on. In a sorted list, we could look at the middle element of the list, compare that element with our target element, and then use that information to decide where to search next, as follows.

This algorithm is called *binary search*, and, appearances aside, the idea behind it is very simple. To find an element, x, in a sorted list that is stored in array locations *start* to *finish*, we look at the element in the middle of the list (or as close to the middle as possible). If the list has only one element or if x is the middle element, we're done, and we return the position of x or the position where x would belong. On the other hand, if x is less than the middle element, we know that we must search for it in the first half of the list. We do this by calling *Find* recursively to continue its search in the sublist from *start* to *middle*. Similarly, if x is greater than the middle element, we know that we must search for it in the second part of the list, from *middle* + 1 to *finish*. We know the recursive algorithm will terminate eventually, since at each stage we divide the sublist in which we search for x in half.[3]

```
function Find(x : DataType ; start, finish : integer ; a : SortedArray) : integer;
{Returns the index of x in the segment of the array a from       }
{start .. finish, or zero if x is not in the array.              }
{Preconditions:    a is a sorted array, in increasing order,     }
{                  indexed from 1, . . . , MAX                   }
{                  When first called, 1 ≤ start ≤ finish ≤ MAX.  }
{Postconditions:   returns a value r, where                      }
{                  a[r] = x, or r = 0 and x is not in a          }
    var
        middle : integer;
begin
    if start > = finish then                  {No need to search one-element lists.}
        if x <> a[start] then
            Find : = 0
        else
            Find : = start
    else
        begin
            middle : = (start + finish) div 2;      {Find the middle index.}

            if x < a[middle] then               {x can only be in the left half,}
                Find : = Find(x, start, middle − 1, a)   {so look there.}
            else if x > a[middle] then          {x can only be in the right half,}
                Find : = Find(x, middle + 1, finish, a)  {so look there.}
            else
                Find : = middle                 {Quit! We found x.}
        end
end;
```

Figure 9.6 illustrates the action of this binary search when we look for the element 12 in the array containing 3, 8, 12, 17, 24, 30, 39, 44, 54.

---

[3]We can get more information from this function with very little work. If we replace the lines

```
if x <> a[start] then
    Find : = 0
```

by

```
if x < a[start] then
    Find : = − start
else if x > a[start] then
    Find: = − (start + 1)
```

the function will return the location of x if it is in the array, and the negative of the location where x would belong, if it is not in the array.

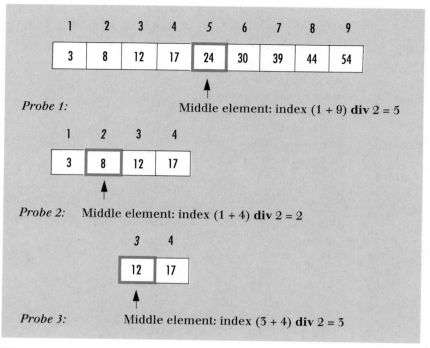

Figure 9.6.   Searching for 12 in a sorted list

Binary search is *much* faster than a linear search. To find an element in a list of 1000 numbers, for example, at the very worst we'd only need to look in sublists of size 1000, 500, 250, 125, 63, 32, 16, 8, 4, 2, and 1, for a total of 10 *probes*, or inspections of array elements. Even in a list of a million elements, we'd require at most 20 probes to find any element — an enormous improvement over the million probes it might take with a linear search.[4]

9.5
Computer Science Interlude: Analysis of Algorithms

We have seen Selection Sort in action; it's simple enough to understand, but it isn't frightfully efficient. The drawback to Selection Sort is that it repeatedly uses a linear search on the unsorted part of the array to find the next element to be

---

[4]For the mathematically inclined, it's not hard to see that it takes at most $1 + \log_2 n$ probes to find whether or not an element is in an array of n elements. This, by the way, is why the game Twenty Questions works so well — if the questions are chosen well, 20 questions will serve to identify any element out of a collection of a million items. We'll see more about this shortly.

inserted. It's not that the repeated calls to *FindMin* are redundant—the inefficiency stems from the basic idea behind Selection Sort: It forces us to inspect the
tail of the list over and over again.

Saying that Selection Sort is inefficient is somewhat imprecise. What exactly
do we mean by the efficiency or inefficiency of an algorithm? One way to measure
this is to count the number of statements that are executed when the algorithm
runs and to express this number as a function of the size of the input. This has
the advantage that it ignores the running speed of different computers. An algorithm that takes n^2 steps to run on an input of size n may run in $0.087n^2$ seconds
on a desktop computer and $0.000026n^2$ seconds on a fast supercomputer, but the
essential behavior is the same on both machines: double n and the algorithm will
take four times longer; triple n and the algorithm will take nine times longer.

For example, the number of statements Selection Sort takes to sort an array
of n elements depends on how many comparisons it takes to find the minimum
element in the range i to n. We clearly have to inspect each of the $n - i + 1$
elements to find the minimum. So the number of comparisons it takes to perform
Selection Sort will be n, to find the first element, plus $(n - 1)$ to find the second,
and so on, for a timing of $n + (n - 1) + (n - 2) + \cdots + 2 + 1$. What is that
sum? Well, if we group the first and last terms, we get $(n + 1)$. If we group the
second and the next-to-last, we get $(n - 1 + 2)$, which is also $(n + 1)$. In fact,
there are $n / 2$ such pairs, each equal to $n + 1$, so the running time of Selection
Sort on an array of size n is just

$$n + (n - 1) + (n - 2) + \cdots + 2 + 1 = ((n + 1)n) / 2$$

or approximately $(n^2) / 2$. This kind of analysis can get quite tricky, but the essential
idea is simple enough: To estimate the time an algorithm takes to run, we can
count the number of steps it takes on input of size n, expressing our answer as a
timing function for the algorithm.

Big-O

When we estimate the timing function of an algorithm on inputs of size n,
we can for the most part ignore any constant multiples and concentrate only on the
terms that involve n. For purposes of estimation, two algorithms that run in time
$2n^2$ and $10n^2$ may both be lumped together in the class of n^2 algorithms and
considered as substantively different from those in the class of, say, 2^n algorithms.
Let's see why we can get away with this simplification. Suppose that we have two
algorithms, A and B, that do the same thing but in different ways and that by
counting statements performed on inputs of size n we find that A runs in time $10n^2$
and B runs in time 2^n. Which one is faster? If we look at the first few values of n,
we can compare the two algorithms as shown in Table 9.1.

For n up to 9, the 2^n algorithm has smaller timing function values, so B runs
faster, but once $n \geq 10$, the $10n^2$ algorithm takes over and thereafter is much faster
than the 2^n one. The multiplicative constant in front of n^2 makes the n^2 algorithm

Table 9.1.   Comparison of two algorithms

n	$10n^2$ (A)	2^n (B)	Faster Algorithm
5	250	32	B
6	360	64	B
7	490	128	B
8	640	256	B
9	810	512	B
10	1000	1024	A
11	1210	2048	A
12	1440	4096	A

slower for a while, but eventually the 2^n algorithm dominates and stays slower for all other values. If we had increased the multiplicative constant to 200 and compared $200n^2$ against 2^n, we would have observed the same behavior, except that the crossover point would be later — 16 rather than 10.

In the long run, a constant multiple will have no effect in the relative behavior of the timing function of an algorithm. An n^2 algorithm will eventually beat an n^3 algorithm, no matter what multiplicative constants are in front of the terms, and any *polynomial-time algorithm* with timing function n^k for some fixed k will eventually beat an *exponential algorithm* with a timing function like 2^n or 3^n. Similarly, a *logarithmic algorithm* with timing function no larger than a multiple of $\log n$ will eventually beat any polynomial algorithm.

Logarithmic algorithms are very efficient; polynomial algorithms are at least worth the effort of programming; but exponential algorithms are so inefficient that they aren't practical, no matter how fast the computer is that executes them. Consider Table 9.2, in which we compare some timing functions. The logarithmic algorithm is clearly the winner — notice that doubling the size of the input increases the timing by a single statement. Also look at the columns for $n\log_2 n$ and n^2. Notice how much more slowly the $n\log_2 n$ column increases. Finally, look at the exponential column for 2^n. An algorithm with this timing function might be practical for inputs of size 16 or (on a fast computer) 32, but even on a computer that can execute a trillion operations per second (far faster than anything you can buy today), it would take 213 days to execute on an input of size 64. For inputs of size 128, it wouldn't finish for ten billion billion years!

Table 9.2. Relative growths of some functions

n	$\log_2 n$	$n\log_2 n$	n^2	2^n
8	3	24	64	256
16	4	64	256	65,536
32	5	160	1024	4.3×10^9
64	6	384	4096	1.8×10^{19}
128	7	896	16384	3.4×10^{38}
256	8	2048	65536	1.2×10^{77}

Exponential-time algorithms are infeasible except for the smallest problems, no matter how much computational power is available.

There is a convenient shorthand that computer scientists use to express timing functions. We say that a timing function, $T(n)$, is "big-O" of another function, $f(n)$, if there are two constants, $k > 0$ and $N \geq 0$ such that $T(n) \leq | kf(n) |$, for all $n \geq N$. In other words, T is big-O of f (which we write as $T(n) = O(f(n))$) if T is eventually always smaller than some multiple of f, as illustrated in Figure 9.7. By this definition, the quadratic functions $4n^2$ and $89n^2 + 233n + 101$ are both $O(n^2)$. A function that is constant, or never rises above a fixed value, is said to be $O(1)$; an algorithm with an $O(1)$ timing function is about as good as we can hope for, since it takes no more than a constant amount of time to execute, no matter what the size of the input is.

Don't worry if big-O and timing seem confusing now: There'll be plenty of time to cover these topics in subsequent courses. For now, keep in mind that how an algorithm is expressed may have significant implications for its feasibility. Computer scientists know that there is a practical side to program style.

Faster Sorting

Selection Sort is what we called an $O(n^2)$ algorithm, since its running time is no worse than a multiple of n^2. That's not terrible, but we can do better if we scrap the whole idea and start fresh, using the idea of binary search as a basis for sorting. The power of binary search comes in part from the fact that it solves the problem of finding an element by dividing the problem in half. This *divide and conquer* scheme appears in many programming applications, and it often leads to a better (faster) solution than would be obtained by an attack on the entire problem at once. In this section, we'll talk about a divide and conquer algorithm for sorting.

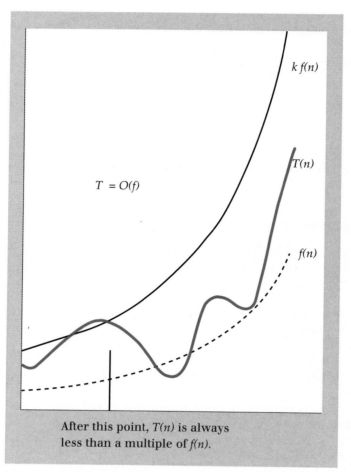

After this point, $T(n)$ is always less than a multiple of $f(n)$.

Figure 9.7.   Graphical representation of big-O

Suppose that we have a list of numbers that we want to sort, and suppose that we were willing to settle for a partial sorting with the following property: After the partial sorting, the list will be divided into a left and a right sublist in such a way that every element in the left sublist is less than or equal to every element in the right sublist. For example, starting with the list 4, 5, 2, 1, 3, we might be content to wind up with the arrangement 3, 1, 2; 5, 4. In this arrangement, every element in the left sublist 3, 1, 2 is less than or equal to every element in the right sublist 5, 4. Does this lead to anything useful? It sure does.

Notice that the left sublist is in its correct position. The *elements* of the sublist aren't where they should be, but the sublist itself is. The same, of course, holds for the right sublist. Here's the clever part—what happens if we apply the same partial sort, *recursively*, to the left and right sublists? Nothing we do to either

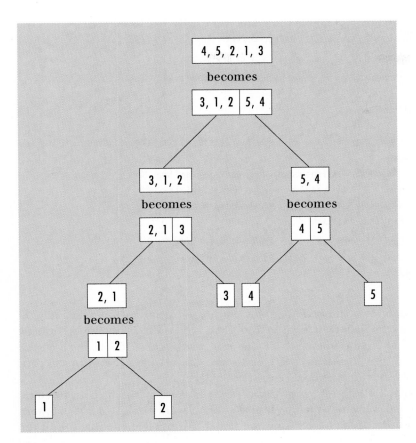

Figure 9.8.   Quicksort in action

sublist alters the fact that the lists are where they should be, and every time we apply the partial sort to a sublist, we'll wind up with two smaller sublists, each of which is now in its correct position. For example, the sublist 3, 1, 2 might wind up as 2, 1; 3, and the right sublist must necessarily become the two smaller lists 4; 5. Now our entire list looks like 2, 1; 3; 4; 5. That's almost perfectly sorted and indeed becomes perfectly sorted as soon as we do a partial sort on the sublist 2, 1. This algorithm is called *Quicksort* and was invented by C. A. R. Hoare in 1962. We illustrate Quicksort in Figure 9.8.

Quicksort is almost too good to be true. Since the elements in every sublist are no farther from their correct sorted positions than the size of the sublist, then as long as we can guarantee that at every stage a sublist list will be split into nonempty sub-sublists, we will eventually wind up with a collection of lists of size one, each of which consists of a single element in its correct position. *Quicksort* is basically a procedure that makes three procedure calls: one to split the list and two recursive calls to sort the sublists. It looks like this:

```
procedure Quicksort(var a : NumArray ; start, finish : integer);
{Sorts part of an array in place, from position start to position finish.}
   var
      split : integer;
begin
   if start < finish then                {We don't need to sort a one-element list.}
      begin
         {Rearrange a into two subarrays, from start .. split, and from    }
         {split + 1 .. finish, in such a way that every element of the left}
         {part is less than or equal to every element in the right part.    }
         Partition(a, start, finish, split);

         Quicksort(a, start, split);        {Now sort the left sublist,}
         Quicksort(a, split + 1, finish)    {and the right sublist.}
      end
end;
```

This seems too simple to be right, but, based upon our understanding of recursion, it seems as though it has to work. This procedure clearly works correctly on lists with a single element (that's our exit case), and if it sorts lists of size smaller than n, it will certainly work on lists of size n (that's the recursive part, after we invoke *Partition* to produce the two sublists).

Of course, all the real work of *Quicksort* is done by the helper procedure *Partition*. The idea behind *Partition* is also rather clever: We work our way inward from *start* and *finish*, and every time we find a pair of elements that are in the wrong sublists, we just swap them.

I. Pick an array value, *pivot*. We'll rearrange the list by putting on the left all values $\le pivot$ and on the right all values $\ge pivot$.

II. Use two indices, *left* and *right*. We'll walk these indices toward each other, using them to swap array elements as we go.

    A. Begin with $left = start - 1$ and $right = finish + 1$.

    B. As long as *left* is less than *right*, do the following:

        1. Keep increasing *left* until we come to an element $a[left] \ge pivot$.

        2. Keep decreasing *right* until we come to an element $a[right] \le pivot$.

        3. Swap $a[left]$ and $a[right]$.

    C. Do one last swap of $a[left]$ and $a[right]$.

III. Return *split* equal to *right*.

Figure 9.9 shows how *Partition* works on the list 4, 5, 2, 1, 3. After two swaps we're done, having produced the sublists 3, 1, 2 and 5, 4.

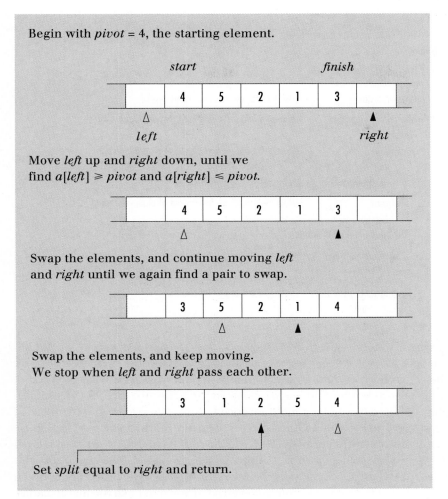

Begin with *pivot* = 4, the starting element.

Move *left* up and *right* down, until we
find $a[left] \geq pivot$ and $a[right] \leq pivot$.

Swap the elements, and continue moving *left*
and *right* until we again find a pair to swap.

Swap the elements, and keep moving.
We stop when *left* and *right* pass each other.

Set *split* equal to *right* and return.

Figure 9.9.   Tracing the action of *Partition*

The code for *Partition* follows. To get a better picture of how *Quicksort*
works, refer to Figure 9.10, where we show the contents of the sublists that are
used in each of the nine recursive calls that the algorithm makes when given the
initial list 4, 5, 2, 1, 3.

```
procedure Partition(var a : NumArray; start, finish : integer; var split : integer);
{Precondition:     a is an array of integers, indexed from 1 to ARRAYSIZE.          }
{                  1 ≤ start, finish ≤ ARRAYSIZE                                     }
{Postcondition:    split satisfies start ≤ split ≤ finish                           }
{                  a is rearranged so that                                           }
{                      a[i] ≤ a[j], for all i = start, . . . , split and j = split, . . . finish}
```

```
var
    left, right, pivot : integer;
begin
  left : = start − 1;
  right: = finish + 1;
  pivot : = a[start];              {Use the starting element as the pivot.}

  while left < right do            {Walk the indices inward until they pass each other.}
    begin
      repeat                       {Move left until we find an out-of-place element.}
        left : = left + 1
      until a[leftIndex] > = pivot;

      repeat                       {Move right until we find an out-of-place element.}
        right: = right − 1
      until a[right] < = pivot;

      Swap(a[right], a[left])
    end;

    Swap(a[right], a[left]);       {Swap the out-of-place elements.}
    split : = right
end;
```

As if it weren't enough for Quicksort to be elegant and simple, we get another benefit as well: Except for very small lists, Quicksort is considerably faster than Selection Sort. If that's still not enough for you, the advantage in speed of Quicksort over Selection Sort increases as you increase the size of the lists. Although you'll have to wait for a more advanced course to see a proof of the speed of Quicksort, we'll tell you that Quicksort, on the average, runs in time $O(n \log_2 n)$. This is a significant difference — for $n = 512$, $\log_2 n$ is 9 (since $2^9 = 512$), so $n \log_2 n$ is $512 \times 9 = 4608$, whereas n^2 is 262,144. Of course we're ignoring any constant multiples that might appear in the real timing function, but the difference between the two sorting algorithms is significant even so. If you don't like the mathematics, you can run the two on the same list and time the results. We did, and found that for lists of 500 random numbers, Quicksort was 7.77 times faster than Selection Sort, and for lists of size 1000, Quicksort beat Selection Sort by a factor of better than 14.36. For lists of size 2000, Quicksort was nearly thirty times faster than Selection Sort! Think of it this way: For really large lists, you might have time to go out for coffee while Quicksort was running, but for Selection Sort, you would have time to go to Colombia and pick the beans.

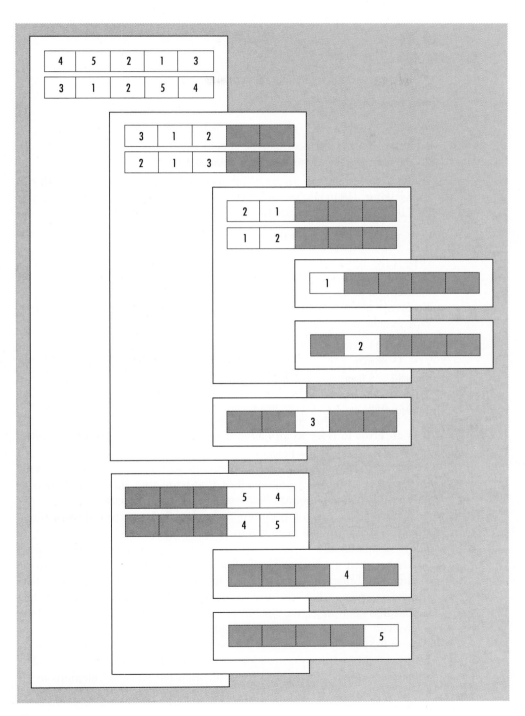

Figure 9.10.   Procedure calls in *Quicksort*

9.6
Reference

- Array-type variables are specified as follows:

array [index range] **of** element type;

where

1. *index range* is any ordinal type specification.
2. *element type* is any previously declared type.

- Individual elements in an array are accessed by the array name, with the index value following in square brackets. For example, if we have the declaration

count : **array** [3 .. 100] **of** integer

then if the integer variable x was equal to 15, it would be legal to refer to $count[4 * x - 1]$, since at the time of reference, we would be using element 59 of the array *count*.

- Elements of arrays may be used anywhere simple variables of the same type may be used, such as

count[x + 1] : = 1;
x : = 3 * count[7];
if count[i] > 0 **then**
    t : = t + 1;
writeln(count[i])

- It is an error to refer to an element of an array that is out of the index range.
- Arrays may be assigned as entire elements, so the assignment statement *thisArray* : = *thatArray* copies all of *thatArray* into *thisArray*, which is permissible if *thisArray* and *thatArray* are of the same type.
- An array may have as many dimensions as needed. An array of two dimensions, for instance, will need two indices in its selector.
- There are generally several ways to solve any problem. Selection Sort builds a sorted list by repeatedly finding the smallest element yet to be included and places that element in its proper position in the sorted list. Quicksort splits a list into two sublists, with each element in the left sublist less than or equal to each element in the right sublist, and then recursively sorts the left and right sublists.
- We can find an element in a sorted list much more rapidly than we can in an unsorted list. Binary search looks at the middle element in a sorted list and uses the comparison of the middle element with the element to be found to recursively look for the target in the left and right halves of the list.
- We can get an estimate of the running time of an algorithm by looking at a big-O upper bound for the timing function. Big-O ignores constant multiples and looks at long-range effects.

- Selection Sort runs in time $O(n^2)$ on lists of size n, whereas Quicksort, on the average, runs in time $O(n\log_2 n)$. Linear search in unsorted lists of size n runs in time $O(n)$, whereas binary search in sorted lists runs in time $O(\log_2 n)$.

9.7   Building Blocks

To read elements into an array, we must read each element in turn.

```
procedure ReadArray(var a : NumArray);
    var
        i : integer;
begin
    for i := 1 to ARRAYSIZE do
        read(a[i])
end;
```

We write the contents of an array in the same way as we read them: element by element.

```
procedure WriteArray(a : NumArray);
    var
        i : integer;
begin
    for i := 1 to ARRAYSIZE do
        write(a[i])
end;
```

Here's a simplified version of the function that finds the smallest element in an array, at or after location *start*.

```
function FindMin(a : NumArray; start : integer) : integer;
{This procedure returns the location of the largest }
{element in array a beginning at location start.   }
    var
        i : integer;
begin
    where := start;
    for i := start + 1 to ARRAYSIZE do
        if a[i] < a[where] then
            where := i;
    FindMin := where
end;
```

If we need to find an element, x, in an array n of type *NumArray* = **array** [1 .. *MAX*] **of** *integer*, we can use a linear search. In the algorithm that follows, we return the dummy index value zero if the search fails to find an instance of the target x. This is another example of a flagged loop.

```
function LinearSearch(x : integer ; a : NumArray) : integer;
{Finds the first location, if any, of x in array a.   }
{Returns zero if x is not an element of the array. }
    var
        index : integer;
        done : boolean;
begin
    index : = 1;
    done : = false;
    while not done do
        if index > MAX then
            begin
                done : = true;
                LinearSearch : = 0
            end
        else if a[index] = x then
            begin
                done : = true;
                LinearSearch : = index
            end
        else
            index : = index + 1
end;
```

If the array is known to be sorted, we can find an element much more quickly by using a binary search algorithm.

```
function BinarySearch(x : integer ; start, finish : integer ; a : SortedArray) : integer;
{Returns the index of x in the segment of the array a from         }
{start .. finish, or zero if x is not in the array.                }
{Preconditions:    a is a sorted array, in increasing order,       }
{                  indexed from 1, . . . , MAX                     }
{                  When first called, 1 ≤ start ≤ finish ≤ MAX.}
{Postconditions:   returns a value r, where                        }
{                  a[r] = x, or r = 0 and x is not in a            }
    var
        middle : integer;
begin
    if start > = finish then
        if x <> a[start] then
            Find : = 0
        else
            Find : = start
```

```
    else
      begin
        middle : = (start + finish) div 2;

        if x < a[middle] then
            BinarySearch : = BinarySearch (x, start, middle — 1, a)
        else if x > a[middle] then
            BinarySearch : = BinarySearch (x, middle + 1, finish, a)
        else
            BinarySearch : = middle
      end
end;
```

The first — and less efficient — of our two sorting algorithms is Selection Sort, using the building block procedure *Swap*, along with *FindMin*, defined earlier.

```
procedure SelectionSort(var a : NumArray);
{This procedure sorts list a using the Selection Sort algorithm.}
    var
        current, where : integer;
begin    {SelectionSort}
  for current : = 1 to ARRAYSIZE — 1 do
    begin
        where : = FindMin(a, current);
        Swap(a[current], a[where])
    end
end;
```

Quicksort is a very efficient sorting technique. It uses a helper procedure, *Partition*, which in turn uses *Swap*.

```
procedure Quicksort(var a : NumArray ; start, finish : integer);
{Sorts part of an array in place, from position start to position finish.}
    var
        split : integer;

    procedure Partition (var a : NumArray; start, finish : integer; var split : integer);
        var
            left, right, pivot : integer;
    begin
        left : = start — 1;
        right : = finish + 1;
        pivot : = a[start];
        while left < right do
          begin
            repeat
                left : = left + 1
            until a[leftIndex] > = pivot;
```

```
        repeat
            right : = right − 1
        until a[right] < = pivot;
        Swap(a[right], a[left])
    end;
    Swap(a[right], a[left]);
    split : = right
  end;

begin   {Quicksort}
  if start < finish then
    begin
      Partition(a, start, finish, split);
      Quicksort(a, start, split);
      Quicksort(a, split + 1, finish)
    end
end;
```

9.8 EXERCISES

1. Given the following declarations, which of the statements are incorrect, and why?

```
const
    CLASSIZE = 50;
    NUMTESTS = 3;
type
    CharArray = array [1 .. 64] of char;
    LineNums = 1 .. 50;
    PageArray = array [LineNums] of CharArray;
    Caps = 'A' .. 'Z';
    Grades = (A, B, C, D, F);
    Distribution = array [Grades] of integer;
    ClassList = array [1 .. CLASSIZE, 1 .. NUMTESTS] of Grades;
var
    thisLine : CharArray;
    page : PageArray;
    g : Grades;
    csDept : Distribution;
    cs241 : ClassList;
    i, j, sum : integer;
```

a. `for j : = 1 to 64 do`
       `read(page[i][j])`

b. j := 1;
   while not eoln **do**
      begin
         read(page[i, j]);
         j := j + 1
      end

c. page[3] := thisLine

d. page[3] := thisLine[4]

e. writeln(thisLine)

f. **for** g := 'A' **to** 'F' **do**
      writeln(csDept[g])

g. sum := 0;
   for g := A **to** F **do**
      sum := sum + csDept[Grades]
      writeln(csDept[g])

h. **for** i := 1 **to** CLASSIZE **do**
      writeln(cs241[i])

i. **for** i := 1 **to** CLASSIZE **do**
      begin
         for j := 1 **to** NUMTESTS **do**
            write(cs241[j, i] : 7);
         writeln
      end

2. Why does Pascal include the **array** type? "It makes programming easier" is not an acceptable answer.

3. Given the declarations of Exercise 1, how many elements are contained in variables that are of these types?

   a. *CharArray*
   b. *PageArray*
   c. *Distribution*
   d. *ClassList*

4. Write array-type declarations that would be appropriate to store the following information:

   a. An inventory of 300 part names
   b. An inventory of the number of pants a store has in stock, where the pants are designated by waist size (24–54 inches) and inseam length (28–39 inches)
   c. The scores (0–20) of five quizzes for 22 students
   d. For 3500 students, whether each student has completed requirements in science, history, foreign language, physical education, and humanities
   e. The high temperature at a given location for each day in a year
   f. The position in a string of the first instance of a capital letter

5. Which of the following declarations would be most appropriate to store a line of text, as we might use in a word processor, for example?

    array [char] **of** char;
    array ['A' .. 'Z', 'a' .. 'z'] **of** integer;
    array [1 .. 80] **of** char;
    array ['A' .. 'Z'] **of** integer;
    array [1 .. 80] **of** integer;

6. Write a procedure that reads 25 real numbers and computes and displays any value that appears more than once. What would you have to do if you weren't allowed to use arrays?

7. Design a function that takes an array of type *NumArray*, as defined in the text, and returns the *median* value of the array. The median of an array is a number, m, for which half of the elements in the array are above that value and half are below. Just do the design — you needn't write code.

8. Assuming we're using the declarations of the *Arrays* unit, why is the following function not correct?

```
function Find(value : integer ; a : NumArray) : boolean;
{Returns true if and only if value is in array a.}
    var
        i : integer;
begin
    i := 1;
    Find := false;
    while i <= ARRAYSIZE do
        if a[i] = value then
            Find := true
        else
            i := i + 1
end;
```

9. Consider the following program:

```
program Puzzle(input, output);
    var
        list : array [1 .. 5] of integer;
        p, q, n : integer;
begin
    for p := 1 to 5 do
        read(list[p]);

    for p := 1 to 5 do
        begin
            n := 0;
            for q := p + 1 to 5 do
                if list[q] > p then
                    n := n + 1;
            write(n : 1, ' ')
        end
end;
```

a. What would be the output of the program on the following three sets of input?

```
4 5 6 7 8
5 4 3 2 1
4 5 2 1 3
```

b. In a sentence, describe what this procedure does.

10. Suppose that p is an array of n integers, consisting of the numbers $1 .. n$ arranged in an arbitrary order, like 4, 5, 2, 1, 3. Such an array is called a *permutation* of the numbers 1 through n. For any permutation, we can generate the *inversion table*, an array t, indexed by $1 .. n$, so that $t[i]$ is the number of elements of p that are to the left of i and greater than i. For instance, the permutation

```
4 5 2 1 3
```

has inversion table

```
3 2 2 0 0
```

The first element of the table is 3, since in the p array the elements 2, 4, and 5 are to the left of 1 and greater than 1.

a. Write **procedure** *InversionTable*(p : *NumArray* ; **var** t : *NumArray*) that produces the inversion table for a permutation p.

b. The inversion table, interestingly enough, determines a permutation uniquely. Write a procedure that takes an inversion table for a permutation and produces the original permutation.

11. Write a procedure that will delete the n-th character from an array of type *CharArray* = **array** [1 .. 80] **of** *char*, moving the elements to the right down to fill the "hole."

12. Write a procedure that will insert a new character, c, in position n in an array *CharArray* as defined in Exercise 11. The routine should move the rest of the characters to make room for the newly inserted one. *Hint*: Be careful about boundary cases.

13. Write a recursive **function** *Member*(n, *start*, *finish* : *integer* ; a : *NumArray*) : *boolean* that returns *true* if and only if n is contained in that part of the array a between positions *start* to *finish*. You can do this by testing whether n is the first element of a or whether n is in the tail of a (the part of the array after the first position).

14. Write a **procedure** *Move*(*fromStart*, *toStart*, n : *integer* ; **var** a : *ArrayType*) that copies n elements of array a, starting at location *fromStart*, to the locations starting at *toStart*.

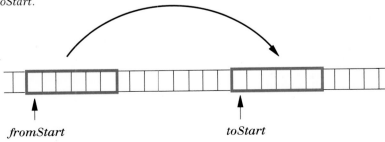

fromStart   *toStart*

a. Do this problem assuming that the region from which the elements are to be copied and the region into which the elements are copied do not overlap.

b. Do this problem without the no-overlap assumption.

15. Many times, we don't need all of the space in an array. If, for example, we have an array that stores quiz scores for a student, we might have no scores at the start of the term and ten scores at the end of the term. Although we can't shorten or lengthen an array at run-time, we can mimic strings and use the zero-th element for a length field, storing the number of valid array entries there. For example, if we had the **type** declaration *ScoreArray* = **array** [0 .. 10] **of** *integer*, the array with three scores 89, 72, 91 would begin 3, 89, 72, 91. . . . Write routines that:

a. Delete the k-th element from such an array.

b. Insert a new k-th element in the array.

c. Write the contents of the array.

d. Compute the average of the elements in the array.

16. One very old way of producing a list of prime numbers is called the *Sieve of Eratosthenes*. To use this algorithm, we begin with a list of integers from 2 to N, for some upper-limit N. The first number in the list is 2, so we cross off every second number in the list (replacing it by zero, for instance). This leaves us with a list 2, 3, 0, 5, 0, 7, 0, 9, 0, 11, ... The next number in the list is 3, so we cross off every third number in the list, leaving us with 2, 3, 0, 5, 0, 7, 0, 0, 0, 11, ... We continue this process, stopping when the number we're about to use for crossing off is bigger than $sqrt(N)$. The numbers that have not been crossed off are the primes less than or equal to N.

a. Use this method to generate the primes less than 300.

b. *Goldbach's Conjecture*, as yet unproved, states that every even integer greater than 2 can be expressed as the sum of two primes. Use your list of primes to verify Goldbach's conjecture for all even numbers from 4 to 300.

c. To generate the *lucky numbers*, we use a technique very much like the Sieve of Eratosthenes, but instead of crossing off every k-th element in the list, we cross off every k-th number *that hasn't already been crossed off*. The first few lucky numbers are 2, 3, 5, 7, 11, 13, 17, 23, 25, 29. Generate the lucky numbers less than 300.

d. Can every even number from 4 to 300 be expressed as the sum of two lucky numbers?

17. Pascal compilers frequently represent a **set of** *OrdinalType* as the internal equivalent of an **array** [*OrdinalType*] **of** *boolean*. For example, if v was of type **set of** 1 .. 3, and v was equal to [1, 2], the compiler would place *true* in positions 1 and 2 in the array and *false* in position 3. Using *OrdinalType* = 'A' .. 'Z', write the array equivalents of the following:

a. *Union*

b. *Intersection*

c. *Difference*

d. **in**

18. This is an interesting routine:

```
var
    s : array [1 .. 100] of boolean;
    i, j : integer;
```

```
begin
    for i : = 1 to 100 do
        a[i] : = true;
    for i : = 2 to 100 do
        for j : = 1 to (100 div i) do
            a[i * j] : = not a[i * j];
    for i : = 1 to 100 do
        if a[i] then
            writeln(i)
end
```

a. What is its output?
b. (Harder.) Why?
c. (Even harder.) Generalize it.

19. In *InsertionSort*, we sort an array by inspecting elements from left to right, building a sorted list as we go. For each element, we place it in its correct position among the values to its left. For instance, we could sort the list 4, 5, 2, 1, 3 by the following steps, where we've set in color the element we're about to place among its neighbors to its left.

4 5 2 1 3	*The first element never needs to be moved.*
4 5 2 1 3	*5 is larger than 4, so it doesn't have to be moved.*
4 5 2 1 3	*2 will have to be inserted in its place at the start.*
2 4 5 1 3	*1 will have to be moved.*
1 2 4 5 3	*3 will have to be moved down.*
1 2 3 4 5	*We're done, and the list is sorted.*

a. Write **procedure** *InsertionSort*(**var** a : *NumArray*).
b. How many times will elements have to be moved when we apply the procedure *InsertionSort* to the following two lists?

```
6 7 8 3 4 5
3 8 4 7 5 6
```

c. For which orderings of the input does *InsertionSort* have to make the fewest data moves? The most data moves?

20. There are many situations in which we want to perform the "opposite" of sorting, by shuffling the elements of an array into a random order. One way to do this is motivated by the way we shuffle a deck of cards. In a *riffle shuffle*, the deck is divided into two equal parts and recombined alternately. For example, if the deck originally contained the "cards" 1, 2, 3, 4, 5, 6, 7, 8, we would cut the deck into the piles 1, 2, 3, 4 and 5, 6, 7, 8, and combine the cards alternately, yielding 1, 5, 2, 6, 3, 7, 4, 8.

a. Write a routine that would initialize a deck of N cards so that $deck[i] = i$.
b. Write a procedure that performs a riffle shuffle on a deck of N cards. (You may assume N is even.)
c. A practiced card player can perform a perfect riffle shuffle. Show that this would be a useful skill to cultivate by writing a program to repeatedly do a riffle shuffle on an array. What interesting thing happens, and when does it happen, as a function of N?
d. How does your answer to part c change if the riffle shuffle starts with the first card in the other pile, yielding 5, 1, 6, 2, 7, 3, 8, 4 for eight cards?

21. a. What condition is true if and only if a list is in sorted order, from smallest to largest?

    b. Write a function, *IsSorted*, that returns *true* if and only if an array is already in sorted order, from smallest to largest.

22. a. Change procedure *SelectionSort* so that it sorts from largest to smallest.

    b. Change procedure *Quicksort* so that it sorts from largest to smallest.

23. a. Is Selection Sort sensitive to the order of the original array, in the sense that there is an arrangement of the input that requires particularly many operations to sort?

    b. In the sense of part a, is Quicksort sensitive to the arrangement of the original array?

24. In *Quicksort*, why do we need the last call to *Swap*?

25. We could represent the action of a sorting routine graphically, by letting the horizontal coordinate represent the array indices and the vertical coordinate the value of the element in that position. Initially, the array would be a cloud of points, since the element in a given position might have any value. For a completely sorted array, the picture would look like a diagonal line, since as we increase the array indices from left to right, the elements in those positions would have increasing heights. The two pictures below represent the behaviors of Selection Sort and Quicksort at some time during their executions. Which is which?

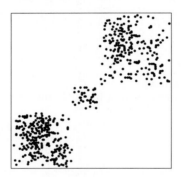 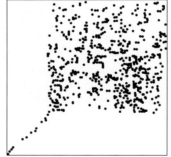

26. a. What would the output displayed by *Quicksort* be if we inserted a *writeln* statement in the function so that the statement body looked like this?

```
if start < finish then
    begin
        Partition(a, start, finish, split);
        Quicksort(a, start, split);
        Quicksort(a, split + 1, finish)
    end
else
    writeln(a[start])
```

    b. What would be the output from the modified algorithm if we also reversed the order of execution of the two recursive calls?

27. Trace the action of the binary search function *Find*:

    a. By searching for 212 in the list 7, 10, 39, 52, 77, 91, 178, 209, 212, 304, 456, 518, 590, 889.

    b. By searching for 212 in the list 1, 2, . . . , 100,000.

    c. By searching for 212 in the list 1, 2, 3, 4, 5, 6, 7, 8, 9, 10, 11, 12, 13, 212.

28. Another way to implement *Find* is to use *Interpolation Search*. Interpolation Search is very much like the algorithm most of us use to search for a word in a dictionary. If we're looking for a data value, *d*, in the part of the array from *start* to *finish*, we first calculate how far proportionally *d* is from *a*[*start*], and then probe to that location. For example, to find "gauge," we wouldn't look at "nab" (the middle of the dictionary). Instead, we'd compute that "gauge" was about 7/26 of the way along, so we'd look at the entry in the (7 / 26) * (size of dictionary) location. Show how Interpolation Search would work:

    a. By searching for 212 in the list 7, 10, 39, 52, 77, 91, 178, 209, 212, 304, 456, 518, 590, 889.

    b. By searching for 212 in the list 1, 2, . . . , 100,000.

    c. By searching for 212 in the list 1, 2, 3, 4, 5, 6, 7, 8, 9, 10, 11, 12, 13, 212.

    d. Implement this version of *Find*. If you run it, you should be able to conclude that in most cases Interpolation Search is *very, very* fast (in fact, it can run as fast as $\log(\log(n))$, on lists of size n).

29. Do Selection Sort and Quicksort still work correctly if we allow duplicate elements in the original array?

30. In *Partition*, the selection of the pivot can have a profound effect on the running time of *Quicksort*. The way *Partition* presently chooses a pivot is to pick the first element of the list. If the pivot happens to be the smallest element of the list, the left sublist will consist of a single element.

    a. Show how choice of the pivot effects *Quicksort* by tracing the action of *Quicksort* on the list 1, 2, 3, 4, 5, where the original arrangement guarantees that the pivot will always be the smallest element of the list. Compare your trace with Figure 9.10.

    b. One way to improve the selection of the pivot is to select three elements from the list at random, find the median value of the three selected list elements (see Exercise 7), swap that value with *a*[*start*], and then run *Partition* as usual. Rewrite *Partition* to use this median-of-three selection, and run the original and new versions of *Quicksort* on the same arrays. Is there a significant difference between the two?

31. We've seen that recursive calls take time, especially if an algorithm has to make a lot of them. We can speed Quicksort up if we eliminate the calls on small sublists by using Insertion Sort (see Exercise 19) if the sublist has length, say, five or less. Modify procedure *Quicksort* this way, and try it out.

32. (Big problem.) Pascal suffers from the deficiency that integers cannot be larger than *maxint*. This causes problems when we want to do arithmetic on 200-digit numbers, for instance. We can get around this problem if we define our own *multiprecision* integer routines. We could, for instance, represent integers as arrays of digits. If we declare *Number* = **array** [1 .. 500] **of** *integer*, we could represent big integers of up to 500 digits.

   a. Write procedures that read and write arrays of type *Number*. *Hint*: For this and
   the parts that follow, its easiest to represent numbers in reverse of their normal
   order, padded with zeros on the right, so the number 4782 would be represented
   as 2, 8, 7, 4, 0, 0, 0, ...

   b. Write **procedure** *Add*(*a*, *b* : *Number* ; **var** *sum* : *Number*) that returns the array
   that represents the sum of the digit arrays *a* and *b*.

   c. Write **procedure** *Multiply*(*a*, *b* : *Number* ; **var** *prod* : *Number*) that returns the
   array that represents the product of the digit arrays *a* and *b*.

   d. Use your routines to find 100! and 2^{512}. Both of these numbers have more than
   150 and less than 200 digits.

9.9   Answers

1. a. This is legal. *page*[*i*] is of type *LineNums*. Since *LineNums* is an array of characters, it makes sense to talk about the *j*-th character in the *i*-th line of the page.

   b. This is legal, as long as we don't try to read more than 64 characters. Pascal allows
   us to refer to an array or arrays as if they were two-dimensional.

   c. This is legal. *page*[3] is an array of characters of the same type as *thisLine*, so we
   can assign the two.

   d. This is not legal, since the types don't match. On the left we have an array, and
   on the right we have a character.

   e. We can't do this. *thisLine* is an array, and we have to write arrays element by
   element.

   f. This is not legal. Since *csDept* is a variable of type *Distribution*, the index type
   must be *Grades*. We're using characters here rather than the enumerated type (A,
   B, C, D, F). Take the quotes from around 'A' and 'F' and the segment is correct.

   g. This is not legal. The index type is correct, but we have a type name inside the
   selector for *csDept* rather than an expression of type *Grades*.

   h. This is not legal. We have too few indices in the selector, since an array of type
   ClassList is two-dimensional.

   i. This would be legal if we reversed *i* and *j* in the selector for *cs241*. As it is now,
   the segment would refer to an out-of-range index as soon as *i* got to 4.

3. a. 64 characters
   b. 50 lines of 64 characters, that is, $50 \times 64 = 3200$ characters
   c. 5 integers
   d. $50 \times 3 = 150$ grades

5. **array** [1 .. 80] **of** *char* is the only declaration that's appropriate here.

7. If *a* was the array, we could sort it first, and then return the middle element if there
   were an odd number of elements. If there were an even number, we could return
   the average of the two middle elements. There are more efficient ways to do this, but
   they're not obvious.

9. a. 4 3 2 1 0
0 0 0 0 0
1 0 1 1 0

b. It reads five integers into an array *list*. The *i*-th value displayed counts the number of elements in the array that are greater than *list*[*i*] and to the right of the *i*-th position.

11. **procedure** Delete(n : integer ; **var** a : CharArray);
    var
        i : integer;
    begin
        if (n < 1) **or** (n > 80) **then**
            writeln('There is no ', n : 1, '-th element to delete. ')
        else
            for i : = n **to** 79 **do**
                a[i] : = a[i + 1]
    end;

13. **function** Member(n, start, finish : integer ; a : NumArray) : boolean;
    begin
        if start > finish **then**
            Member : = false
        else if a[start] = n **then**
            Member : = true
        else
            Member : = Member(n, start + 1, finish, a)
    end;

15. a. **procedure** Delete(n : integer ; **var** a : ScoreArray);
        var
            i : integer;
        begin
            if (n < 1) **or** (n > a[0]) **then**
                writeln('There is no ', n : 1, '-th element to delete. ')
            else
                begin
                    for i : = n **to** a[0] − 1 **do**   {Shift the array to fill the hole.}
                        a[i] : = a[i + 1];
                    a[0] : = a[0] − 1   {Reset the length field.}
                end
        end;

b. **procedure** Insert(x, n : integer ; **var** a : ScoreArray);
        var
            i : integer;
        begin
            if (n < 1) **or** (n > a[0] + 1) **then**
                writeln('There is no ', n : 1, '-th position in the array. ')
            else if a[0] = 10 **then**
                writeln('The array is full. There''s no room to insert. ')

```
      else
         begin
            for i : = a[0] downto n do
               a[i + 1] : = a[i];
            a[n] : = x;
            a[0] : = a[0] + 1
         end
   end;
```

c., d. The solutions are left to the reader.

17.   We'll use the following declarations

```
   type
      MySet = array ['A' .. 'Z'] of boolean;
```

Now notice that an element is in the union of two sets if it is in one or the other, so we can write:

```
   procedure Union(a, b : MySet ; var result : MySet);
      var
         ch : char;
   begin
      for ch : = 'A' to 'Z' do
         result : = a[ch] or b[ch]
   end;
```

The rest of the routines are similar.

19. **a.**
```
   procedure InsertionSort(var a : NumArray);
      var
         i, j, currentElement : integer;
   begin
      for i : = 2 to ARRAYSIZE do
         begin
            currentElement : = a[i];
            j : = i;
            while a[j − 1] > currentElement do
            {As long as currentElement doesn't belong in position (j − 1),}
            {shift the element at position (j − 1) one place to the right  }
            {and look at the next element to the left.                    }
               begin
                  a[j] : = a[j − 1];
                  j : = j − 1
               end;
            a[j] : = currentElement    {Put currentElement where it belongs.}
         end
   end;
```

b. 9 and 6, respectively.

c. On lists that are already sorted, no data moves are required. On lists of size n that are sorted in reverse order, $n (n − 1) / 2$ moves will be required.

21. a. $a[k] \leq a[k+1]$, for $k = 1, \ldots, N - 1$, where N is the size of the array.

b.
```
function IsSorted(a : NumArray) : boolean;
    var
        i : integer;
        done : integer;
    begin
        done := false;
        i := 1;
        while not done do
            if i >= ARRAYSIZE then        {We reached the end. It's sorted.}
                begin
                    done := true;
                    IsSorted := true
                end
            else if a[i] > a[i + 1] then   {We found two elements out of order.}
                begin
                    done := true;
                    IsSorted := false
                end
            else
                i := i + 1                 {We're not done yet. Look at the next pair.}
    end;
```

23. a. No. Selection Sort performs the same operations, no matter how the array is arranged.

b. Yes. If the array is already sorted in either order, *Partition* quickly splits the list into sublists of size 1 and $n - 1$. However, this makes Quicksort use many more recursive calls than would be the case if the list were split nearly in two. Try a trace on 1, 2, 3, 4, 5 to see what happens. In essence, for sorted lists, Quicksort acts almost exactly like Selection Sort, so it runs in $O(n^2)$ time rather than in $O(n \log n)$ time. Fortunately, these "bad" inputs occur rarely enough that on average Quicksort is still a $O(n \log n)$ algorithm.

25. The left picture shows Quicksort; the right shows Selection Sort.

27. a. It takes three probes, to elements 178 (position 7), 456 (position 11), and 212 (position 9).

b. It requires 14 probes, to elements (and hence positions) 50,000, 24,000, 12,500, 6250, 3125, 1562, 781, 390, 195, 292, 243, 218, 206, and 212.

c. It requires four probes, to positions 7, 11, 13, and 14.

29. Yes.

31. On lists of size 500, 1000, and 2000, the modified version of Quicksort runs 150% faster than the original. If we use Insertion Sort when the sublist is of size 10 or less, the new version is roughly 165% faster than the original. It's interesting to explore the best cutoff for Insertion Sort, as a function of the size of the list.

CHAPTER

10 Heterogeneous Data Structures: Records

The elements of both sets and arrays must all be of the same type. That's just fine for many applications. There are many times when we want to group together a related collection of similar information, such as numbers in a sorted list, grades in a class, or characters in a line or page. Often, though, a single logical entity may be characterized by a collection of information of different types. For example, a person has a name (an array of characters), more often than not has an address (several arrays of characters, one for each line in the address), may have a Social Security number (nine digits — too large to be an integer on many computers, so make it an array of 0 .. 9), and certainly has a sex (a boolean or user-defined ordinal), an age (an integer between 0 and 150, perhaps), a height and weight (two real numbers), and so on. In traditional data processing parlance, a chunk of related information is called a *record*, and Pascal borrowed the term to refer to its own collections of heterogeneous information. In this chapter, we will discuss the definition and use of the Pascal **record** type.

OBJECTIVES

In this chapter, we will:

- Define Pascal **records**.
- Illustrate how records can be used to build complex data structures.
- Describe and illustrate Pascal's naming conventions for composite data structures.

398

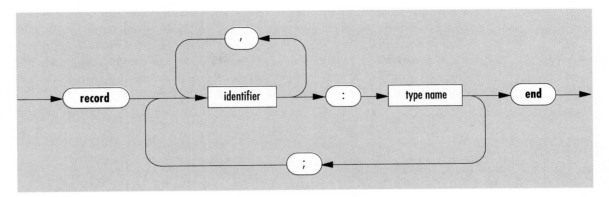

Figure 10.1. Syntax diagram for the (fixed) **record** type

- Review the PIP for this chapter, a simple word processor that will serve as the basis for our lab work in this and the next two chapters.
- Describe additional Pascal features that relate to records, including variant records and the **with** statement.

10.1 The **record** Type

The syntax of a record-type declaration is decidedly more complicated than for most Pascal features. That is because a record may have a *fixed part* that is the same for all instances of that type and a *variant part* that differs among variables of the same type. For the time being, we will concentrate exclusively on records that have only a fixed part and delay discussion of variant records until you have had a chance to become comfortable with fixed ones. Just keep in mind that what we'll be talking about for now is most—but not all of—the whole story.

A Pascal record is divided into *fields*, again mirroring the terminology of the data processing world. To define a record type, one uses the reserved word **record**, followed by specifications of the fields in the record, followed by the word **end** (so that the compiler can tell where the record definition ends and the next type declaration begins). The field declarations look very much like variable declarations: They consist of a list of identifiers separated by commas, followed by a type specification. A record may have as many fields as you need, as long as each field definition is separated from the others by a semicolon. Figure 10.1 gives the syntax diagram for the fixed part of the **record** type.

We use record type specifications as we do any type specifications. They can appear as named types in a **type** declaration, or they can appear anonymously as

*We'll complete the definition of the **record** type in Section 10.5.*

*Record specifications and the **case** statement are the only two instances where an **end** is not matched with a **begin**.*

the type specification of a variable declaration. As with other user-defined types, record type declarations may not be made anonymously in procedure or function formal parameter lists — if they are to be used there, they must have been previously defined elsewhere. Remember, too, that declaring a record type does not define any variables. It prescribes a name and a format for subsequently defined variables. All of the following are valid record type declarations:

```
type
   StudentRec = record
                   average : real;
                   didProject : boolean;
                   letterGrade, modifier : char
                end;
   Fraction = record
                 numerator, denominator : integer
              end;
   MachineState = record
                     on : boolean;
                     pressure, temperature : real;
                     delaySetting : integer
                  end;
```

As we would expect, the fields in a record can be of any type whatsoever, including those that have been previously declared in the program. We could expand the definition of *StudentRec* above, for instance, by including the three exam scores that contributed to the average.

```
type
   GradeRange = 0 .. 100;
   GradeArray = array [1 .. 3] of GradeRange;
   BigStudentRec = record
                      tests : GradeArray;
                      average : real;
                      didProject : boolean;
                      letterGrade, modifier : char
                   end;
```

In addition, we can use the **record** type as a part of other compound types, such as arrays and records.[1] We could further expand our grade-keeping declarations to include a description of an entire class by making the following declaration:

```
type
    GradeRange = 0 .. 100;
    GradeArray = array [1 .. 3] of GradeRange;
    BigStudentRec = record
                        tests : GradeArray;
                        average : real;
                        didProject : boolean;
                        letterGrade, modifier : char
                    end;
    Class = array [1 .. 30] of BigStudentRec;
```

Now that you've seen the way record types are declared, it's not a big step to discuss how they are used in a program. The most important thing to remember is that record-type variables, like array-type variables, consist of a name for the entire object, optionally followed by a selector for the component. In an array, the selector is an ordinal expression enclosed in square brackets. In a record, the selector is the field name, which is separated from the variable name by a period.

> **T**o select an element in a record, follow the name of the record variable by a period and the field name of the element. As with array elements, record fields may be selected and used anywhere variables of that type may be used, with the single exception that a record field cannot be used as the control variable in a **for** statement.

In the example

```
type
    StudentRec = record
                    average : real;
                    didProject : boolean;
                    letterGrade, modifier : char
                 end;
var
    currentStudent : StudentRec;
```

we could refer to *currentStudent.average* or *currentStudent.didProject*, as in Figure 10.2.

[1]We can't use records (or arrays, for that matter) as elements in a **set** type, since neither arrays nor records are ordinal types.

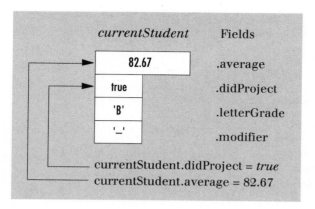

Figure 10.2.   Selecting an element in a record

We refer to elements within records in the way we have come to expect of Pascal, working from the outside in, starting with the variable name, followed by a selector for the element. If the element is itself structured, we continue with the selectors for the structured subtype until the desired piece of the record is described, as in the example below.

```
type
    GradeRange = 0 .. 100;
    GradeArray = array [1 .. 3] of GradeRange;
    BigStudentRec = record
                        tests : GradeArray;
                        average : real;
                        didProject : boolean;
                        letterGrade, modifier : char
                    end;
var
    currentStudent : BigStudentRec;
```

In this example, it would be perfectly legitimate to refer to *current-Student.tests*[2]. The record variable name is *currentStudent*; the field selector is *.tests*. The field *tests* is a structured type (an array), so we may refer to its components by using the array selector [2], as in Figure 10.3.

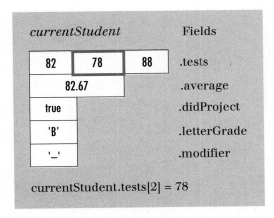

currentStudent   Fields

| 82 | 78 | 88 | .tests
|----|----|----|

| 82.67 | .average

| true | .didProject

| 'B' | .letterGrade

| '_' | .modifier

currentStudent.tests[2] = 78

Figure 10.3.   Selecting elements from a complicated
record structure

Finally, we mentioned that we could use records as part of other types. We could, for example, have an array of records:

```
type
    GradeRange = 0 .. 100;
    GradeArray = array [1 .. 3] of GradeRange;
    BigStudentRec = record
                        tests : GradeArray;
                        average : real;
                        didProject : boolean;
                        letterGrade, modifier : char
                    end;
    Class = array [1 .. 30] of BigStudentRec;
var
    thisClass : Class;
```

We have talked about levels of abstraction throughout this text, and in this example we have several levels available. We can use these declarations to describe:

1. The entire variable, *thisClass*, an array of 30 records
2. A component of the (array-type) variable, *thisClass*[2], one particular record
3. A field of this component, such as *thisClass*[2].*tests*, itself an array of integers
4. An element of this field, which we would access by *thisClass*[2].*tests*[1], which happens to be 79, as illustrated in Figure 10.4

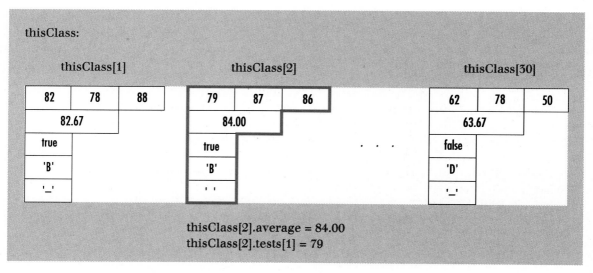

thisClass:

Figure 10.4. An array of records

This probably seems complicated now, but you'll be both pleased with the expressive power such declarations afford you as a programmer and surprised at how fast you catch on to the notation. Just remember:

To access elements in a structured variable, always work from the top level down, following each component by its selector.

The only other caution about using records is not to confuse field types with the names of field selectors. In the following example, for instance, it would be a violation to refer to *currentStudent.GradeArray*, since *GradeArray* is a type name and not a field selector. This is a common mistake — fortunately, most modern compilers will catch it for you.

```
type
    GradeRange = 0 .. 100;
    GradeArray = array [1 .. 3] of GradeRange;
    BigStudentRec = record
                    tests : GradeArray;
                    average : real;
                    didProject : boolean;
                    letterGrade, modifier : char
                end;
```

```
var
    currentStudent : BigStudentRec;
    scores : GradeArray;
⋮
begin
   ⋮
    currentStudent.GradeArray := scores;        Error—confusing type descriptor GradeArray
                                                with field selector.
    currentStudent.tests := scores;             OK—using field selector tests.
```

Type names are *never* used as parts of variables. To refer to elements in a compound type variable, never use a type name—always use the selector name.

10.2 Problem Solving I: Designing the PIP

The Program in Progress for this chapter, named *PasWord*, illustrates a common application of computers, a word processor. Your PasWord will allow insertions, deletions, and changes in a document, and it will grow in later chapters to save documents as files, allow old documents to be retrieved and modified, and eventually permit the user to copy and paste from one document to another. This particular word processor may seem primitive by today's standards, and indeed it is, but its lack of sophistication should not obscure two very important points. First, *you* will write it and its subsequent releases. We will use PasWord as our sample program in this and the next two chapters, and by the end, you will have custom designed—more or less on your own (with a little help from us)—a fully functional word processor, with all of the important features of commercial-quality products.

The second point relates to the progress that the world of programming has made in the last three decades. Your version of PasWord will be equivalent to the state of the art in word processing applications only 15 years ago. If you ask a faculty member about text editing back in the early 1970s, you'll very likely get a description of a system that might not even have been as sophisticated as your PasWord. Think about that. Thanks to modern programming environments, an improved understanding of what introductory computer science courses should be, and a lot of hindsight, you, as a novice programmer, will build an application that a short time ago would have made you famous (not to mention rich).

In fact, the main things missing from PasWord when compared to modern programs like Microsoft Word, WordPerfect, and WriteNow fall into two categories, both of which can be excused for being absent in PasWord. The most obvious, if you have any experience with modern word processing, is a sophisticated user interface. PasWord doesn't have pull-down menus, command-key equivalents of operations, the ability to wrap long lines onto several lines, or the ability to display or print your document in different type faces, sizes, or styles. The excuse here is that capturing total control of a computer to do these things, rather than doing them within your particular programming environment, requires highly specialized knowledge about a specific machine and isn't really our purview here. Given a few months after you finish this text, you could learn the intricacies of the Macintosh, PS/2, NeXT, or VAX machine you wanted to use PasWord on and go from there to make your program as friendly and useful as anything that's around today.

The other omission stems from the fact that PasWord is *line-oriented*. Since the basic unit of operation is the line rather than the word, such features as global search and replacement and spell-checking are not readily available to us. The excuse in this case is a common one in the world of professional programming: "That feature was not available at time of release, due to the need to have a functioning product ready by the scheduled date." This is usually closely followed by the promise that the missing feature will surely be included in version 2.0 (or 7.2.2a, or whatever). The simple fact is that our journey through the land of Pascal programming and problem solving is almost at an end. You *could* include all these missing features in PasWord 4.0. Indeed, by the time you finish this course, you will know very nearly all you need to have mastered in order to write any feature you can dream up into PasWord.[2] We decided on a simple version so as not to obscure the important details and to give you a project you could complete in the few remaining weeks.

Specifying PasWord

In a complicated program such as PasWord, it is often the case that the customer will not specify in complete detail what the program will do. Instead, you, the system designer, would be given a sample of what a session with the program should look like. From there, you would work with the customer to make the specifications more precise by asking questions like "Exactly what do you want to happen here? How should the program handle bad input from the user? What, exactly, would constitute bad input in this context?" We'll take this prototype approach here by providing you with a sample PasWord session.

PasWord is *menu-based*, meaning that the user selects commands to be executed from a menu of choices. Since we don't have pull-down menus available to us, commands to PasWord consist of characters entered from the keyboard, followed by optional parameters that describe what lines the commands are to act on. Each line in a PasWord document has a line number associated with it, so, for

[2]In the interest of getting you excited about the extent of your own knowledge, we're actually fudging a bit here. *Advertisement*: Some things like spell-checking can be performed much more efficiently if you have the background in data structures and algorithms that comes with completion of the two or three courses that follow this one.

example, to insert a new line in position 8 in our document we would type i8, followed by the line that we wanted to go in that position. What follows is an example of what PasWord should look like in action.

Transcript of a PasWord Session

Note that the lines the user typed are highlighted in color. Comments inserted after the session are in italics and would not be part of what the user saw.

```
At the prompt ' > ' enter an operation code        Show the menu.
(with integers n and m where indicated ) :
        I n - Insert a new line at position n
        D n - Delete the line at position n
        C n - Change the line at position n
        P n m - Print lines n through m on the screen
        ? - Display this menu
        Q - Quit PasWord
> i1                                               Insert a first line.
...This is the first line
> i2                                               Insert a second line.
...this is the second line
> i3                                               And a third.
...and this is the third (and last) line
> g9                                               Try an invalid
                                                   command.

***OOPS!***
Invalid command character. Please try again.      We get a warning
                                                   and the menu
At the prompt ' > ' enter an operation code        again.
(with integers n and m where indicated ) :
        I n - Insert a new line at position n
        D n - Delete the line at position n
        C n - Change the line at position n
        P n m - Print lines n through m on the screen
        ? - Display this menu
        Q - Quit PasWord
> p1 3                                             Print lines 1
                                                   through 3.

1  This is the first line
2  this is the second line
3  and this is the third (and last) line
> i3                                               Insert a line at
...THIS IS A NEW THIRD LINE                        position 3.
```

```
> pl 200

1  This is the first line
2  this is the second line
3  THIS IS A NEW THIRD LINE
4  and this is the third (and last) line
> c4

...and this is the third (and last) line


...and this is the fourth line

> pl 100

1  This is the first line
2  this is the second line
3  THIS IS A NEW THIRD LINE
4  and this is the fourth line
> d2

> pl 10

1  This is the first line
2  THIS IS A NEW THIRD LINE
3  and this is the fourth line
> i2

...)*&*&%^%$^#**^##@$#*&^%∆·©∆¨¥†¨¥†√¢¥†®¨¥†
> pl 2

1  This is the first line
2  )*&*&%^%$^#**^##@$#*&^%∆·©∆¨¥†¨¥†√¢¥†®¨¥†
> ?
```

Now look at the change we just made. Notice 200 for upper limit just gives all lines.

To change the fourth line, we get the original one and enter the new one. See what we've done.

Delete the second line.

Yup, that works as it should.

Add a new second line.

And print lines 1 through 2.

Let's see the menu again.

```
At the prompt ' > ' enter an operation code
(with integers n and m where indicated ) :
     I n - Insert a new line at position n
     D n - Delete the line at position n
     C n - Change the line at position n
     P n m - Print lines n through m on the screen
     ? - Display this menu
     Q - Quit PasWord

> q
```

And quit.

10.3 Problem Solving II: Developing the Main Program

We want PasWord to be able to insert a new line of text at a given location, delete a line of text, moving subsequent lines down to fill the hole, change a line, and print all lines within a given range. We'll need menu entries for those four options, and we decide to include entries for displaying the menu instructions and quitting the program. The basic operation of the program is quite simple:

I. Initialize a PasWord document, and display the menu.

II. Repeat the following steps until the user chooses the quit command:

A. Read a character command, along with any necessary line numbers (like the line number of the line to be deleted).

B. Do the operation indicated by the command.

In fact, you've learned enough by now that the program shell that follows should be just about what you'd invent after a little thought.

```pascal
program PasWord(input, output);
   var
      choice: char;                    {command character}
      doc: Document;                   {current working document}
      param1, param2: integer;         {line numbers for insert, delete, change, print commands}

   procedure ShowMenu;
   begin
      writeln;
      writeln('Here''s where we''ll show the menu of commands. ');
      writeln
   end;

   procedure GetCommand (var c: char; var param1, param2: integer);
   begin
      writeln('We''ll read a character for a command, and as many parameters');
      writeln('as we need to execute the command. ');
      write('For now, just enter "I", "D", "C", "P", "?", or "Q"');
      readln(c)
   end;

begin   {Main}
   Initialize(doc);
   ShowMenu;

   repeat
      GetCommand(choice, param1, param2);
      case choice of
         'i', 'I':
            DoInsertion(doc, param1);
```

```
            'd', 'D':
                DoDeletion(doc, param1);
            'c', 'C':
                DoChange(doc, param1);
            'p', 'P':
                ShowDoc(doc, param1, param2);
            '?':
                ShowMenu;
            'q', 'Q':
         end    {case}
    until (choice = 'Q') or (choice = 'q')
end.
```

The job of our main program, as is often the case, is to manage the calls to the routines that do all the real work. This real work will be done by the document-handling routines *Initialize*, *DoInsertion*, *DoDeletion*, *DoChange*, and *ShowDoc*. In essence, all the main program has to do is handle the command structure and call the appropriate document routines. As a matter of fact, we won't even put any of the document routines or declarations in the main program. Instead, we'll put them in the unit *DocHandler*, which will hide all the messy details from the command-handling *front end* (the part that the user sees). Here's the main program in its finished form. Notice that the procedure that gets a command is just a slight modification of the input building block that we saw, in various incarnations, in Chapters 4, 5, 6, and 8. Notice, too, how closely the main program reflects our high-level outline.

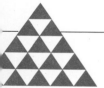

The PIP

```
program PasWord (input, output);
{------------------------------------------------------------------}
{                                                                  }
{                      PROGRAM IN PROGRESS                         }
{                                                                  }
{                          CHAPTER 10                              }
{                                                                  }
{      Simple line-oriented word processor. Allows users to insert,}
{      delete, change, display lines in a document.                }
{                                                                  }
{------------------------------------------------------------------}
{                                                                  }
{      SUBPROGRAM LIST:                                            }
{      ShowMenu                                                    }
{      GetCommand(var c : char; var param1, param2 : integer)      }
{                                                                  }
{------------------------------------------------------------------}
```

```
uses
    DocHandler;
var
    choice: char;                 {command character}
    doc: Document;                {current working document}
    param1, param2: integer;      {line numbers for insert, delete, change, print commands}
procedure ShowMenu;
{Displays the menu.        }
{Called by : Initialize, Main}

begin
    writeln;
    writeln('At the prompt " > " enter an operation code ');
    writeln('(with integers n and m where indicated) :');
    writeln('        I n — Insert a new line at position n');
    writeln('        D n — Delete the line at position n');
    writeln('        C n — Change the line at position n');
    writeln('        P n m — Print lines n through m on the screen');
    writeln('        ? — Display this menu');
    writeln('        Q — Quit PasWord');
    writeln
end;

procedure GetCommand(var c: char; var param1, param2: integer);
{Gets a command character from operator. If command  }
{is not a legal command, shows menu and keeps trying  }
{until legal command is entered. If command is for an  }
{operation that requires a line number (insert, delete, or}
{change), it gets that parameter as 'param1', and if the }
{command is to print, it gets start and finish line nums  }
{as 'param1' and 'param2'.                            }
{Called by : Main                                     }

    var
        needsParams, oneParam, legal: set of char;
begin
    legal := ['I', 'i', 'D', 'd', 'C', 'c', 'P', 'p', '?', 'Q', 'q'];
    needsParams := ['I', 'i', 'D', 'd', 'C', 'c', 'P', 'p'];
    oneParam := ['I', 'i', 'D', 'd', 'C', 'c'];

    writeln;
    write('> ');
    read(c);
```

```
          while not (c in legal) do
             begin
                writeln('***OOPS!***');
                writeln('Invalid command character. Please try again. ');
                readln;                    {Discard anything else on the line and try again.}
                ShowMenu;
                write('Command: ');
                read(c)
             end;

          if not (c in needsParams) then   {Discard the rest of the line, if no numbers needed.}
             readln
          else if c in oneParam then        {If we need one line number, read it now.}
             readln(param1)
          else                              {If we need two line numbers, get them.}
             readln(param1, param2)
       end;

begin    {Main}
   Initialize(doc);
   ShowMenu;

   repeat
      GetCommand(choice, param1, param2);
      case choice of
         'i', 'I':
            DoInsertion(doc, param1);
         'd', 'D':
            DoDeletion(doc, param1);
         'c', 'C':
            DoChange(doc, param1);
         'p', 'P':
            ShowDoc(doc, param1, param2);
         '?':
            ShowMenu;
         'q', 'Q':

      end    {case}
   until (choice = 'Q') or (choice = 'q')
end.
```

10.4 Problem Solving II, Continued: Developing the *DocHandler* Unit

Although it is virtually impossible to write some kinds of programs without arrays, we can generally get along without records. They only serve to make our programs easier to understand (which is, of course, no small benefit). However, the ability of records to clump logically related data of different types together is used to good advantage in PasWord, as we'll see.

*O*ne situation in which records are well-nigh indispensable is in data structures linked with pointers. See Chapters 12 and 13.

Dynamic Lists

The basic data structure of our program is the *Document* type, a record containing an array of lines that comprise the document, along with a field, *.totalLines*, that stores the number of lines currently in the document. The structure of a *Document*-type variable is illustrated in Figure 10.5.

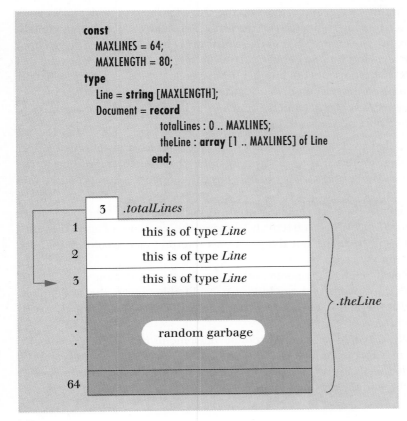

```
const
    MAXLINES = 64;
    MAXLENGTH = 80;
type
    Line = string [MAXLENGTH];
    Document = record
                    totalLines : 0 .. MAXLINES;
                    theLine : array [1 .. MAXLINES] of Line
               end;
```

Figure 10.5. A document made up of lines

Notice that this arrangement of a document—a record containing an array and a field that contains the conceptual length of the array—allows us to simulate at the level of a document precisely what strings do for us at the level of an individual line. That is, it allows us to simulate a dynamic structure—one that seemingly shrinks and grows according to its use in the program. Arrays in Pascal are *static*. That is, once an array type is declared, we cannot change the size of a variable of that type while the program is running. An array with 64 elements will take up the same amount of space in memory, whether or not all 64 elements are being used. If only two entries have been filled, the remaining 62 will contain whatever random garbage was left over in memory when the array was allocated. In the case of a document, the number of valid entries in the array might change during execution (due to changes specified by the user, for instance), so we need to keep track of how many entries in the array of lines are actually valid at any time. We do that by enclosing the array in a record, along with a field that indicates the last valid entry in the array.

Now, although the document array is still static in memory, we may think of it as a *dynamic* entity. The size of a document may now shrink and grow as we dictate, subject only to the condition that its conceptual size may never exceed its real size (64, in this case). Notice, too, that the range for the size field *.totalLines* is not the same as the range of indices for the array. The field *.totalLines* may contain the value zero, in spite of the fact that there is no array index 0. We are *overloading* the size field, allowing it to do double duty as both a pointer to the last valid cell and as a value that represents the number of valid cells (which, of course, will take the value zero when the document is initialized in the procedure *Initialize*).

This description of a document affords us at least four levels of abstraction, depending upon how we view our document.

- We could look at a document as a single monolithic variable so that if *doc1* and *doc2* were variables of type *Document*, we could assign one to the other by *doc1* := *doc2*. This would copy the complete contents of *doc2* into *doc1*.
- We could refer to fields within a document, so we could write *doc.totalLines* := 0, effectively clearing the contents of *doc* (the lines would still be there, but the program's interpretation would be that *doc* was empty).
- We could refer to elements within the fields of a document so that if *currentLine* were of type *Line*, we could then make the assignment *doc.theLine*[2] := *currentLine*, replacing the second line of *doc* with *currentLine*.
- Finally, we could refer to components of elements of fields of a document, writing, for example, *doc.theLine*[3][14] := '$' (or, equivalently, *doc.theLine*[3,14] := '$'), placing a dollar sign in the fourteenth place in line three in the document named *doc*.

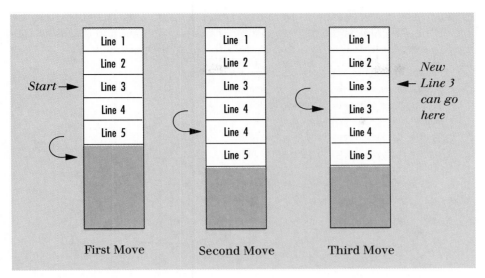

Figure 10.6.   Shifting an array down one place

The Heart of PasWord

We can appreciate this two-field description of dynamic arrays if we consider the process whereby lines get inserted into a PasWord document. We've seen how to insert an element into an array. To put the new element into position k, we first move the elements from the (conceptual) end of the array to k down one position, and then put the new element into the hole we made by shifting, as illustrated in Figure 10.6. Deleting an element is very similar, except that to delete the element in position k, we shift the elements from $k + 1$ to the conceptual end up one place. PasWord combines these two operations into one procedure, *ShiftArray*. This routine takes three parameters. Parameter *start* indicates the starting line number of the segment to be shifted. Parameter d represents the document itself (which is a **var** parameter, since we're changing the array when we shift part of its contents). The only new part of the formal parameter list is *direction*, which tells which direction (up or down) to shift. If *direction* is positive, the routine will shift down (or up, if your conceptual direction is in order of increasing array indices), making room for a line; if it is negative, the shift will be up, decreasing the length of the document by one. If it is zero, no shifting at all will take place.

Notice that we use the document's *.totalLines* field to determine the conceptual end of the list. We don't need to refer to a separate variable, since the length field is now part of the record, as is the list of lines itself. This is a good time to test your understanding of how to access components of a complicated data structure: The lines are the elements of the array, and to shift the element in position $i - 1$ up one place, we make the assignment $d.theLine[i] := d.theLine[i - 1]$.

Remember, we select elements from the biggest conceptual chunk down: d is the document, $d.theLine$ is the field consisting of an array of lines, and $d.theLine[i]$ is the i-th element in that array—that is, the i-th line of the document.

```
procedure ShiftArray (direction, start: integer; var d: Document);
{Shifts the contents of the line array 'doc' from position }
{'start' to end of array one position to the left (if       }
{direction is < 0) or to the right (if direction is > 0).   }
{NOTE: It is the responsibility of the calling routine      }
{(1) To make sure that a shift will not cause the array     }
{to fall out of its bounds.                                 }
{(2) To make sure that 'start' is within the array bounds.  }
{(3) To update the size of the array.                       }
{Called by : DoInsertion                                    }
   var
      i: integer;
begin
   if direction > 0 then
   {Shift elements from the end to 'start' up 1 position.}
      for i := d.totalLines + 1 downto start + 1 do
         d.theLine[i] := d.theLine[i − 1]

   else if direction < 0 then
   {Shift elements from 'start' to end down 1 position.}
      for i := start to d.totalLines − 1 do
         d.theLine[i] := d.theLine[i + 1]
end;
```

Finally, notice that *ShiftArray* does no error checking. In particular, it delegates to the calling routine the responsibility of assuring that an insertion will not cause the array to overflow its range. Deletion, of course, doesn't have that problem. The worst that could happen is that the array would be completely emptied. Notice, too, that there is no internal checking to make sure that *start* is in the right range, namely, $1 \le start \le d.totalLines$. We could have included these checks in *Shift-Array* but elected to get by with a comment of caution in the procedure's heading. We have weakened *ShiftArray* by doing so, but since this routine is almost always done in the context of insertion or deletion, we decided to put the precondition checking in these routines instead.

Notice also that it is the responsibility of the calling routine to update the *.totalLines* field by adding or subtracting 1 after calling *ShiftArray*. Where this responsibility lies is one of the judgment calls that is common in computer science. We could have modified the *.totalLines* field within *ShiftArray* but (1) the subprogram seems to have more to do with the array of lines than with the entire document, and (2) it would have slightly complicated the calling routine *DoInsertion* (do you see why?). This is an example of a *de gustibus non est disputandem* situation—"there's no arguing with taste." Take a look at the insertion routine to see how it does error checking and uses *ShiftArray*:

```
procedure DoInsertion (var d: Document; lineNum: integer);
    var
        newLine: Line;
begin
    write('...');
    GetALine(newLine);                              {Get line to be inserted.}
    writeln;

    if d.totalLines = MAXLINES then
        writeln('***Sorry, no more room in this document.***')

    else
        begin
            if lineNum < 1 then                      {Fix lineNum if too low.}
                lineNum := 1;

            if lineNum > d.totalLines then           {Fix lineNum if too high}
                d.theLine[d.totalLines + 1] := newLine   {and insert.}

            else
                begin                                {Inserting into interior,}
                    ShiftArray( + 1, lineNum, d);    {shift right to make room,}
                    d.theLine[lineNum] := newLine    {and put the new line in.}
                end;
            d.totalLines := d.totalLines + 1         {Update document line count.}
        end
end;
```

We begin by calling *GetALine*, which reads and returns *newLine*, the line to be inserted. Then we check to make sure that the document isn't full. If it is (as indicated by the line counter being equal to the maximum size of the array), there's nothing that can be done except to print an error message. If the position of the new line, *lineNum*, is less than 1, the routine defaults to 1 as the insertion point. Similarly, if the value of *lineNum* is larger than *d.totalLines*, the routine defaults to insertion immediately after the conceptual end. Since, in this latter case we don't need to shift to make room for the new line, we do the insertion immediately by performing the assignment *d.theLine*[*d.totalLines* + 1] := *newLine*. Finally, if we are inserting into the interior of the list, we invoke *ShiftArray* to make room for the new line and then put the new line in its proper place. The last thing we do is to update the length field to reflect the fact that the list is one element longer than it was before by using *d.totalLines* := *d.totalLines* + 1.

When using dynamic arrays, a frequent source of error is forgetting to update the length field.

The remaining subprograms of *DocHandler*, though not specifically related to records, do serve to illustrate a number of interesting Pascal features that have been mentioned in previous chapters and are applied here to the task of word processing. Notice, for example, how simple the *GetALine* and *PrintALine* procedures are, thanks to our use of strings for storing the lines of a document. By using strings, we are saved from two cumbersome (although manageable) tasks. First, we need not resort to performing input and output on a character-by-character basis. Simple *readln* and *writeln* statements work fine. Second, we are freed from having to track the length of each individual line of a document in the same way that we do for the document as a whole.

Now you've seen the essentials of the *DocHandler* unit, which follows. Look back over what we've said, and you'll find that you can use the code provided to write your own deletion and modification routines.

```
unit DocHandler;
{——————————————————————————————————————————————}
{                                                                              }
{              Support routines for managing a PasWord document.               }
{                                                                              }
{              This unit contains subprograms that handle insertion,           }
{              deletion, modification, and printing of lines in a document.    }
{                                                                              }
{——————————————————————————————————————————————}
{              SUBPROGRAM LIST:                                                }
{              Initialize (var d: Document)                                    }
{              DoInsertion (var d: Document; lineNum: integer)                 }
{              DoDeletion (var d: Document; lineNum: integer)                  }
{              DoChange (var d: Document; lineNum: integer)                    }
{              ShowDoc (d: Document; start, finish: integer)                   }
{——————————                                                                   }
{              ShiftArray (direction, start: integer; var d: Document)         }
{              GetALine (var newLine: Line)                                    }
{              PrintALine (d: Document; lineNum: integer)                      }
{              Swap (var thingOne, thingTwo: integer)                          }
{                                                                              }
{——————————————————————————————————————————————}
interface
  const
     MAXLINES  = 64;      {max lines per document}
     MAXLENGTH = 80;      {max characters per line}
  type
     Line = string[MAXLENGTH];
     Document = record
                   totalLines: integer;
                   theLine: array [1 .. MAXLINES] of Line
                end;
```

procedure Initialize (**var** d: Document);
procedure DoInsertion (**var** d: Document; lineNum: integer);
procedure DoDeletion (**var** d: Document; lineNum: integer);
procedure DoChange (**var** d: Document; lineNum: integer);
procedure ShowDoc (d: Document; start, finish: integer);

implementation

{————————————— PRIVATE ROUTINES ————————————}

These are support routines for the other subprograms in the unit. Because they are never intended to be called by the using program, their headers never appear in the **interface** *part of the unit.*

   procedure ShiftArray (direction, start: integer; **var** d: Document);
   {Shifts the contents of the line array 'doc' from position }
   {'start' to end of array one position to the left (if   }
   {direction is < 0) or to the right (if direction is > 0). }
   {NOTE: It is the responsibility of the calling routine   }
   {(1) To make sure that a shift will not cause the array }
   {to fall out of its bounds.   }
   {(2) To make sure that 'start' is within the array bounds.}
   {(3) To update the size of the array.   }
   {Called by : DoInsertion   }
     var
       i: integer;
   begin
     if direction > 0 **then**   {Shift elements from end to 'start' right 1 position.}
       for i := d.totalLines + 1 **downto** start + 1 **do**
         d.theLine[i] := d.theLine[i − 1]
     else if direction < 0 **then**   {Shift elements from 'start' to end left 1 position.}
       for i := start **to** d.totalLines − 1 **do**
         d.theLine[i] := d.theLine[i + 1]
  end;

   procedure GetALine (**var** newLine: Line);
   {Reads one line into a string.}
   {Called by : DoInsertion   }
   begin
     readln(newLine)
  end;

   procedure PrintALine (d: Document; lineNum: integer);
   {Prints a single line from document.}
   {Called by : ShowDoc   }
   begin
     writeln(d.theLine[lineNum])
  end;

```
procedure Swap (var thingOne, thingTwo: integer);
{This procedure exchanges the values of two integers.}
{Called by : ShowDoc                                }
   var
      temp: integer;
begin
   temp : =  thingOne;
   thingOne : =  thingTwo;
   thingTwo : =  temp
end;
```

{─────────────────────────── PUBLIC ROUTINES ───────────────────────────}

*These are the routines that are called by the using program, so their headers
appear in the* **interface** *part of the unit.*

```
procedure Initialize;    {(var d: Document)}
{Initializes document to zero lines.}
begin
   d.totalLines : =  0
end;

procedure DoInsertion;    {(var d: Document; lineNum: integer)}
{Given a line number in the document, gets a new line and}
{inserts that line into the document, shifting other lines up }
{to make room for new line. If line number was out of     }
{range, automatically defaults to insertion at beginning   }
{or end of document.                                       }
{Calls : GetALine, ShiftArray                              }
   var
      newLine: Line;
begin
   if d.totalLines = MAXLINES then
      writeln('***Sorry, no more room in this document.***')
   else
      begin
         write('. . .');
         GetALine(newLine);                        {Get the line to be inserted.}
         writeln;

         if lineNum < 1 then                        {Fix lineNum if it's too low.}
            lineNum : = 1;

         if lineNum > d.totalLines then             {Fix lineNum if it's too high, and insert.}
            d.theLine[d.totalLines + 1] : = newLine
```

```
        else
          begin                              {Inserting into interior—shift to make room.}
            ShiftArray(+1, lineNum, d);      {Shift up, from insertion point,}
            d.theLine[lineNum] := newLine    {and put the new line into 'hole'.}
          end;
        d.totalLines := d.totalLines + 1     {Update document line count.}
    end
end;

procedure DoDeletion; {(var d: Document; lineNum: integer)}
{Deletes a line from the document by shifting part}
{of the line array one position down. Error if line }
{number if out of range of lines in document.      }
begin
    {You'll fill this in. For the time being, it's just a stub.}
    writeln('Here''s where we''ll delete line ', lineNum : 1, '   NOT IMPLEMENTED')
end;

procedure DoChange;    {(var d: Document; lineNum: integer)}
{Change a specified line. Prints the original line, allows   }
{user to type in new line to replace one to be changed.      }
{Error if line number is out of range of lines in document. }
begin
    {You'll fill this in later.}
    writeln('Changing line ', lineNum : 1, '   NOT IMPLEMENTED')
end;

procedure ShowDoc; {(d: Document; start, finish: integer)}
{Prints lines of document from position 'start' }
{to position 'finish'. If these limits are invalid, }
{defaults to printing entire document.           }
{Calls : PrintALine                              }
    var
        lineNum: integer;
begin
    if start > finish then                 {limits out of order—swap them}
      Swap(start, finish);

    if start < 1 then                      {lower limit too small—set to array start}
      start := 1;

    if (finish > d.totalLines) or (finish < 1) then  {upper limit wrong—set to array end}
      finish := d.totalLines;
```

```
        for lineNum := start to finish do        {for each line specified . . .}
            begin
                write(lineNum : 3, ' ');          {Write line number,}
                PrintALine(d, lineNum)            {and print the line.}
            end
        end;
    end.
```

10.5   Miscellaneous **record** Topics

Before we leave our discussion of records, there are two topics—variant records and the **with** statement—that we should discuss for the sake of completeness. Although both are standard Pascal features, they are seldom used in practice. There are times, though, when they can come in handy.

Variant Records

We began this chapter by defining the **record** type; we mentioned then that our definition was deliberately incomplete. The **record** type is indeed more complicated than we let on at the time, and this is a good place to fill in the holes in the definition. We'll begin with an example.

Suppose we were designing a program for the payroll department of a company. The data on each employee is described to us as follows:

1. Every employee has a name.
2. Every employee has a Social Security number.
3. Some employees are paid an hourly wage. For those employees, we need to know their pay rate per hour.
4. Some employees are paid a straight salary, independent of the number of hours they work. For those employees, we need to know their weekly pay.
5. Some employees are temporary consultants who are paid a flat rate that extends over a certain number of weeks. For those employees, we need to know the start and finish dates of their contract in weeks from the start of a year and the total amount they are to be paid.

We could make a record to store the payroll information on each employee (and then collect all the records in an array, perhaps). The record might have a field for each piece of information in the specification and might be specified as:

```
type
    EmpType = (hourly, salaried, consultant);
    EmployeeRec = record
                name : string [30];            {applies to everyone}
                ssnum : array [1 .. 9] of 0 .. 9;   {applies to everyone}
                paySchedule : EmpType;         {applies to everyone}
                hourlyRate : real;             {only for hourly employees}
                weeklyRate : integer;          {only for salaried employees}
                startWeek, endWeek : 1 .. 52;  {the rest is only for consultants}
                fee : integer
        end;
```

There are two problems here: (1) Since not all fields of the record apply to all employees, each record has a lot of wasted space, and (2) there is an implicit dependence between these fields, in the sense that if *.paySchedule* has the value *hourly*, only the field *.hourlyRate* among the last four fields has any meaning. There's just too much chance of error here. It would be very easy to write a program that accidentally used the *.fee* field of an hourly employee, which would make no sense. Even worse, the *.fee* field would probably have only junk values in this case. We could build in checks against this sort of thing, but it would be tedious in the extreme.

Pascal has a way to avoid some of these problems by allowing part of a record to be defined conditionally depending on the value of one of its fields, called the *tag field*. In the example above, we really want three similar, but slightly different, record definitions of the type *EmployeeRec* — one each for hourly workers, salaried workers, and consultants. Figure 10.7 illustrates what we'd like the record to be in these cases.

In Pascal, we can construct these three different but related records by using *record variants*. A record variant is a collection of fields that is controlled by a tag field, which in our example, is the field *.paySchedule*. Depending on the ordinal value of the tag field, one field list of the variant part is the one assumed to be in force. For example, if the tag field *.paySchedule* has the value *hourly*, it is legal to refer to the field *.hourlyRate*, but it would be an error to refer to *.startWeek*, since that field identifier is not part of the variant field list that is associated with the tag field value *hourly*.

The record variant version of *EmployeeRec* would be defined this way:

```
type
    EmpType = (hourly, salaried, consultant);
    EmployeeRec = record
                name : array [1 .. 30] of char;
                ssnum : array [1 .. 9] of 0 .. 9;
```

Figure 10.7.   The three conceptual forms of *EmployeeRec*

```
          case paySchedule : EmpType of
             hourly : (hourlyRate : real);
             salaried : (weeklyRate : integer);
             consultant : (startWeek, endWeek : 1 .. 52; fee : integer)
          end;
```

The fields *.name* and *.ssnum* are called *fixed fields* — they remain the same for any variant of the record. Pascal overloads the **case** construct to refer to the variant fields. The tag field must be an ordinal type, since *paySchedule* is of type *EmpType*. The tag field is followed by a list of variants, consisting of *all* possible values that the tag field can assume.[3] Each tag field is followed by a list of fields that apply when the tag field has a specific value or values.

---

[3]Which, for obvious reasons, effectively excludes tag fields of large ordinal types like *integer* or *char*: Nobody in their right minds would want to specify all possible values of these types in the variant parts.

There is no requirement that the variant field lists have any fields at all. We could expand the above **type** declaration to include employees who are on unpaid leaves. In this case, the payroll office might need no further information other than the leave status of the employee, so we could write

```
type
    EmpType = (hourly, salaried, consultant, unpaidLeave);
    EmployeeRec = record
                    name : array [1 .. 30] of char;
                    ssnum : array [1 .. 9] of 0 .. 9;
                    case paySchedule : EmpType of
                        hourly : (hourlyRate : real);
                        salaried : (weeklyRate : integer);
                        consultant : (startWeek, endWeek : 1 .. 52 ; fee : integer);
                        unpaidLeave : ( )
                end;
```

We leave as an exercise the task of writing the syntax diagram for the complete **record** type declaration. Some things you need to know: (1) The variant part must come after all the fixed parts, if any, (2) the **case** reserved word doesn't need its own **end**, unlike the statement version of **case**, and (3) the tag field must have a type but doesn't need a name.

We use a record variant by first checking or setting its tag field and then referring to the associated variant fields. With our example, for instance, we could use the following statements, assuming that *currentEmp* was a variable of type *EmployeeRec*:

```
if currentEmp.paySchedule = hourly then
{This guards against setting time-and-a-half for any but hourly employees.}
    overtimeRate : = 1.5 * currentEmp.hourlyRate;

currentEmp.paySchedule : = salaried;
currentEmp.weeklyRate : = 1500;
{A working stiff just got promoted to management at a nice salary.}
currentEmp.fee : = 12000
{ERROR! Salaried workers can't get fees for consulting. }
{In Pascal terms, the .fee field name has no meaning   }
{when the tag field has the value salaried.             }
```

The **with** Statement

If we have to do a lot of work on a particular record, it can be tedious to type the record name over and over again when referring to its individual fields. In line with its philosophy of making life easier for the programmer, Pascal provides a way to circumvent the need to repeat a record name. If *longRecordIdentifier* is a record-type variable with fields *.this*, *.that*, and *.whatsis*, we can simplify the statements

```
readln(longRecordIdentifier.this, longRecordIdentifier.that);
if longRecordIdentifier.this > 0 then
    longRecordIdentifier.whatsis : = longRecordIdentifier.whatsis + 1
```

by using the **with** statement

```
with longRecordIdentifier do
    begin
        readln(this, that);
        if this > 0 then
            whatsis : = whatsis + 1
    end
```

You can probably figure out what the **with** statement does just from the example. It tells the compiler, in effect, "As long as you're within the scope of this statement, any identifier that is a field name of the record *longRecordIdentifier* should be treated as if it had the record name appended to the front." In simple terms, the **with** statement is a shorthand that allows you to dispense with the name of a record variable and refer to its fields by their field names alone, without the period or variable name. We could modify PasWord's *DoInsertion* procedure, for instance, by writing it as

```
procedure DoInsertion (var d: Document; lineNum: integer);
    var
        newLine: Line;
    begin
        with d do                                    Within this statement, we don't
            begin                                    need the variable name
                write('. . .');
                GetALine(newLine);
                writeln;
                if totalLines = MAXLINES then                 here,
                    writeln('***Sorry, no more room in this document.***')
                else
                    begin
                        if lineNum < 1 then
                            lineNum : = 1;
                        if lineNum > totalLines then            here,
                            theLine[totalLines + 1] : = newLine    here,
                        else
                            begin
                                ShiftArray( +1, lineNum, d);
                                theLine[lineNum] : = newLine        here,
                            end;
```

```
            totalLines := totalLines + 1          or here (twice).
        end
    end
end;
```

A **with** statement may contain several record identifiers; these are separated by commas in the heading of the statement. Also, **with** statements, like any other compound statements in Pascal, may be nested within one another, so long as the two records involved have no field names in common. Consider this example.

```
var
    machine : record
                isOn : boolean;
                rpm : real
              end;
    system : record
                isOn : boolean;
                inputs : integer
              end;
    ⋮
with system do
    with machine do
        begin
            readln(rpm);            This refers to machine.
            inputs := inputs + 1;   This refers to system.
            isOn := false           But which does this refer to?
        end
```

The statement *isOn* := *false* could refer either to the *.isOn* field of *machine* or the field of the same name of the variable *system*. Which should it be, if any? Well, we gave you a hint at the start of this discussion when we used the phrase "the *scope* of the **with** statement." Scope rules for nested **with** statements (including those that are implied by using several record names separated by commas) are like those for nested subprograms:

Recall the scope rules for subprograms in Chapter 7.

The scope of a field identifier in a **with** statement is defined to be within the smallest statement block that pertains to that field identifier.

This means that in the preceding example the statement *isOn* := *false* would refer to the *.isOn* field of *machine*, since the **with** *machine* **do** statement is contained within the **with** *system* **do** statement. If we had wanted *isOn* to refer to the record *system*, we would have had to make that explicit by writing the record name:

```
with system do
   with machine do
      begin
         readln(rpm);              This refers to machine.
         inputs : = inputs + 1;    This refers to system.
         system.isOn : = false     And now this also refers to system.
      end
```

We'll be honest with you; we — and many other computer scientists — are underwhelmed by the **with** statement. Like the **goto** statement, it has good, legitimate uses in making a program easier to write, but it can be abused too easily. In most cases, the programmer receives a benefit (easier typing) that the subsequent reader has to pay for (in trying to figure out whether the identifiers are field names or variable names). Unless the record variable has a *very* long name, we normally avoid the **with** statement.

10.6 Computer Science Interlude: Standard Applications

Revolutionary technologies never spring forth from a vacuum. New devices always owe their existence to older ideas, and the computer is no exception. In particular, the computer and its programs are a natural step in an evolutionary process that began more than five thousand years ago with what are the most important of all technological innovations to date — writing and (much later in history) mechanical printing. Both of these technologies can be viewed as the representation of ideas in physical form: "petrified truth," as Mark Twain said. In the case of this book, for instance, we wrote down our ideas about Chapter 10 and could put the pages away and come back to them years later. For better or worse, they would still be there, unchanged, for us to read again. We could give the pages to others, for them to read at their leisure, even if we were no longer around to communicate the ideas contained therein. The book is not constrained by time.

What you now hold in your hands or your lap, though, is a comfortable old technology. The subject matter might be new, but the idea of a physical embodiment of ideas on paper would be familiar to a scribe of the time of the Pharaohs. The computer, however, represents a new way of thinking about information in physical form. Except for the comments you add in the margin, the information in this text, like all written and printed matter, is essentially static. A program on a disk, however, contains not only representations of information but also instructions to the computer on how to manipulate this information. The computer can perform arithmetic calculations, sort lists of numbers, solve algebraic equations, or, if the programmer's intent is to treat the data in the computer as characters rather than numbers, handle mailing lists of names and addresses. Furthermore, if the data are considered graphical rather than textual, the computer can use these data to display pictures on the screen.

In all of these examples, the computer and its program together take on the nature of an active metaphor—a microworld, if you will, having its own natural laws to govern its behavior. These microworlds are frequently models of a portion of the real world, from an attempt to imitate either the physical world or the environment of a job to be done. As we will see shortly, computer microworlds may begin by modeling familiar tasks but often evolve to include behavior far beyond the ranges of the tasks they originally imitated.

The Word Processor

At first, people thought of the computer solely as the apotheosis of the adding machine—a glorified calculator. It didn't take long to realize, though, that any information that could be expressed in numeric code could be grist for the computer's mill. By assigning a code number to each letter, digit, and punctuation mark, for instance, a text document could be stored in a computer's memory and then manipulated by a program. This, in simplest form, is all that a word processor really does.

Word processors began as models of typewriters. Indeed, one of the first word processors, the IBM magnetic tape Selectric of 1964, was actually a typewriter, with a way of electrically storing a coded version of what had been typed. In these early, paper-based word processors, the typist used special code sequences or keys to type a chosen range of lines and to enter or modify text in those lines, very much like we do in PasWord. To produce a perfectly typed document, then, one made a draft copy that was stored electrically, edited the paper copy, returned to the tape to make the corrections, and then typed the finished version. A master copy of a commonly used letter, for example, could be made and slightly modified (with the correct name and address) each time it was sent rather than having to be entirely retyped to make just a few changes.

As useful as early word processors were, they were of limited commercial impact until they were combined with display screens in the 1970s, and they didn't really take off until personal computers became popular in the late 1970s and early 1980s. With these *WYSIWYG* (for "What You See Is What You Get," pronounced "wizzy-wig") word processors, the user didn't have to insert special *control characters* while typing to produce special printed effects. Instead of having a document that looked like this:

```
{\bf 1.} Some of the {\it invisible benefits} of this plan
include: \cr
\tab \bullet Reduced {\ul downtime} for the \Sigma -7
units \cr
```

the user could see on the screen exactly what the finished document would look like:

1. Some of the *invisible benefits* of this plan include:
   - Reduced <u>downtime</u> for the Σ-7 units

On today's computers, for example, control of the typefaces, styles, and special characters is achieved by the typist pressing special characters or making selections from a menu. These are translated in turn into invisible control characters that are translated by the word processing program into instructions to the screen display. The internal representation of the document in the computer's memory still looks very much like the first example—the difference is that screen displays are sophisticated enough to show the letters in many forms.

Notice that the microworld that began as a model of the typewriter has evolved to include features that were either difficult or impossible to achieve with the typewriter, such as the mixing of fonts and typefaces in the example. This evolution beyond the original model also included such features as those you could program into PasWord, like the ability to cut a section of text and paste it elsewhere in the text (something that would have to be done with scissors and tape in the typewriter world, hence the terms *cut* and *paste*). The ability of a program to perform simple "reading" of a textfile also led to features that were undreamed of in the typewriter model, such as automatic spelling checkers and global search and replace commands.

While we are discussing enhancements of the typewriter model, we should make note of a new idea, still in its infancy at present. The computer allows us to link actions with data, producing what might be called "smart documents." One example of this is known as *hypertext*. In a hypertext document, the use of invisible control characters is extended to allow you to link parts of a document together. In such a document, you might read text on a screen as in a conventional word processor; in addition, you might select a word and be presented with a definition, a picture, or a more detailed background. In effect, a hypertext document can have "active footnotes" that can be called up and explored by the user. This mirrors the way we might browse through a book, looking first in the index, then in the text, then following a reference to a later section, then turning to the illustrations.

Though paper and ink provide a physical embodiment of the world of ideas, you can still pick up a paper and smudge the ink with greasy fingers. In this sense, the word processor is even closer to the world of ideas than the typewriter or pen, since the words cannot be touched. They are fleeting internal electrical currents, expressed by external patterns of light and dark dots on a screen. This "light writing," to use the words of Jack Harris, provides a flexibility impossible with paper and ink by dispensing (at least from the user's point of view) with the need to produce and manipulate physical objects.

	1	2	3	4	5	6
1		Spring	Summer	Fall	Winter	YTD
2	Sales	2275.91	1120.65			3396.56
3	Costs	1480.03	1289.98			2770.01
4	Profit	795.88	(169.33)			626.55

Figure 10.8. A sample spreadsheet

The Spreadsheet

A spreadsheet combines the attributes of a calculator and a word processor. Represented as a rectangular array of *cells*, the spreadsheet is modeled after an accountant's ledger sheet. In Figure 10.8, we illustrate a typical use for a spreadsheet with six columns, one for the row title, one for each quarter of the year, and one for the year to date, and four rows representing the column titles, and the sales, costs, and profits for each quarter.

Each cell of the spreadsheet contains not only visible information but also codes representing how the information is to be displayed. In Figure 10.8, for example, the numeric information is displayed with two decimal places of accuracy, right justified, with negative values enclosed in parentheses, whereas the textual information is centered in its cell. In this sense, the spreadsheet is very much like a modern word processor. The information can be edited by typing, cutting, copying, and pasting, while each piece of information carries with it a hidden collection of formatting information, as specified by the user. In a modern spreadsheet, this format information can be spread to each row or column. For example, to change the format of a column from integers to decimal numbers with two-place accuracy requires only changing the format of a single cell and issuing a command to expand the characteristics of that cell to its entire column, in much the same way that the margins of a paragraph could be made to apply to an entire document in a word processor. Knowing what we do now, we can even make a guess about how this is accomplished. We could envision the spreadsheet as a two-dimensional array of records, for example, where each record contained fields for display format, the cell's information, and other information, like references to other cells.

This by itself would be useful to accountants, saving the trouble of having to redo a ledger sheet to adapt to a client's stylistic wishes, but the true power of the spreadsheet goes much farther than mere "prettyprinting." When Daniel Bricklin

	1	2	3	4	5	6
1		Spring	Summer	Fall	Winter	YTD
2	Sales	2275.91	1120.65			3396.56
3	Costs	1480.03	1289.98			2770.01
4	Profit	795.88	(169.33)			626.55

row 2 – row 3 of this column   sum of (column 2 to column 5 of this row)

Figure 10.9. Spreadsheet formulas

and Robert Frankston designed VisiCalc, the first commercial spreadsheet, they began with a microworld that was dynamic rather than static. Along with numeric or textual data and format information, each cell of a spreadsheet can communicate with every other cell via a user-defined rule that describes the information to be stored in the cell.

Look at the YTD column in Figure 10.9, for example. We know that the total cost to date is the sum of the costs that have been entered so far, and the spreadsheet allows us to specify that the value in row 3 of column 6 will be the sum of the values in columns 2 through 5 of that row. When setting up the spreadsheet, then, the user enters a rule in row 2, column 6 and then enters the command to make that rule apply to all the cells in column 6. After all the formulas have been properly entered (including the "profit = sales − cost" rule for the cells in row 4), the user need only enter the numbers to be operated upon. As each number is entered in a cell, any other cell that uses that number is immediately recalculated. Of course, some cells, like the title cells in the first row and column, may have "empty rules" that say, in effect, "Just display the information in this cell."

Just as the word processor quickly evolved beyond its original typewriter model, the spreadsheet was soon recognized as not only a powerful and efficient tool for managing existing data but also a simulator—a "what-if" tool. Every faculty member, for instance, has had a student who comes to him or her with the plaintive cry, "What grade do I need on the final exam to pass this course?" If the course records have been kept in a spreadsheet, the instructor can use the spreadsheet, saying "Well, let's see . . . suppose you got a 65 on the final [types in "65" in the column for final exam, and the spreadsheet recalculates the course grade]. That'll give you a 59 average in the course, so maybe we'll try a 75 on the final . . . ," and so on, until the student is satisfied.

10.7 Reference

- The *record* type brings the number of Pascal types we know up to ten. Records are structured types, like arrays, but unlike arrays, the information in a record need not all be of a single type.
- Records are declared by listing their field names and types:

```
TypeName = record
              fieldName : Type;     {any type whatsoever}
              anotherFieldName : AnotherTypeName;
              ⋮
           end;
```

- Access to record fields is by *recordVariableName.fieldName*, using as the selector a period and a field name after the name of the record.
- Records can have any type of fields, including other record types and arrays. Also, records can be used as part of any other variables so that it is perfectly legal to have an array in which each element is a record.
- A common use of records is to collect logically related information that should be treated together.
- We can use records to define dynamic lists by using one field for the current length of the list and another for the array of data elements.

```
type
   CharArray = array [1 .. 256] of char;
   TextLine = record
                 length : integer;
                 chars : CharArray     Note: We have to declare CharArray before we
                                       can use it here.
              end;
```

- In a variant record, the fixed fields are followed by the variant fields. These fields are available or not, depending on the value of the tag field. A record with variant part is specified as follows:

```
TypeName = record
              fixed fields;
              case tag field name : ordinal type specification of
                 case constant : (field specifications);
                 another case constant : (field specifications)
                 ⋮
           end;
```

- The **with** statement (our eleventh statement) allows one to dispense with the name of a record variable. It looks like this:

  with *record variable name* **do**
     begin
       statements using field names without variable names in front
     end

10.8
Building Blocks

To declare and initialize a dynamic list, we would write the following:

```
Document = record
                totalLines: integer;
                theLine: array [1 .. MAXLINES] of Line
            end;

var
    doc: Document;    {current working document}
    ⋮
    doc.totalLines : = 0
```

The *ShiftArray* building block is, as we've seen, particularly useful for inserting and deleting elements from a dynamic list.

```
procedure ShiftArray (direction, start: integer; var d: Document);
    var
        i: integer;
begin
    if direction > 0 then
        for i : = d.totalLines + 1 downto start + 1 do
            d.theLine[i] : = d.theLine[i − 1]
    else if direction < 0 then
        for i : = start to d.totalLines − 1 do
            d.theLine[i] : = d.theLine[i + 1]
end;
```

Here's how we insert a new element into a dynamic list. There are a number of modifications we might make, like including the element to be inserted among the formal parameters.

```
procedure DoInsertion (var d: Document; lineNum: integer);
    var
        newLine: Line;
```

```
begin
    write('...');
    GetALine(newLine);                          {Get line to be inserted.}
    writeln;
    if d.totalLines = MAXLINES then
        writeln('***Sorry, no more room in this document.***')
    else
        begin
            if lineNum < 1 then                 {Fix lineNum if too low.}
                lineNum := 1;
            if lineNum > d.totalLines then      {Fix lineNum if too high, and insert.}
                d.theLine[d.totalLines + 1] := newLine
            else
                begin                           {Inserting into interior—shift to make room.}
                    ShiftArray(+1, lineNum, d);  {Shift up, starting at line number of insertion,}
                    d.theLine[lineNum] := newLine {and put the new line into 'hole'.}
                end;
            d.totalLines := d.totalLines + 1    {Update document line count.}
        end
end;
```

10.9 EXERCISES

1. Consider the following declaration section. For each of the identifiers in parts a–g, either list its type or explain why the identifier does not make sense.

```
type
    Word = array [1 .. 50] of char;
    Line = array [1 .. 125] of char;
    Numbers = array [1 .. 30] of integer;
    IndexEntry = record
                    key : Word;
                    occs : integer;
                    pags : Numbers
                 end;
    IndexRep = array [1 .. 100] of IndexEntry;
    BookRep = record
                    title : Line;
                    index : IndexRep
              end;
    ClassRep = array [1 .. 400] of BookRep;
    LibRep = array [1 .. 10000] of ClassRep;
```

```
var
    heading : Line;
    entry1, entry 2 : IndexEntry;
    Index : IndexRep;
    redBook, blueBook : BookRep;
    catalog : ClassRep;
    bigLib, smallLib : LibRep;
```

a. Index[4]
b. Index.title
c. Index[45].occs
d. bigLib[500]
e. bigLib[500].title
f. smallLib[500][200]
g. smallLib[500, 200].title[50]

2. Represent *bigLib* from Exercise 1 pictorially as we did for *thisClass* in Figure 10.4.

In Exercises 3 and 4, using the declarations of Exercise 1, tell whether the following statements or declarations are correct or not. For those that are incorrect, explain why. For variables that are not declared in Exercise 1, feel free to make any reasonable assumptions about their types.

3. **a.** catalog[3].title : = heading
   b. i : = IndexEntry.occs + 1
   c. read(index[3].key)
   d. **function** Retrieve(theKey : Word ; rep : IndexRep) : IndexEntry;

4. **a.** redBook.index : = index
   b. **if** redBook <> blueBook **then**
        writeln('Not the same')
   c. heading[index[4].pags] : = redBook.title[22]
   d. **if** bigLib[371, 1].index[2].key[1] = '$' **then**
        t : = t + 1

5. If a character requires 1 byte and an integer requires 2 bytes, how big are variables of the eight types in Exercise 1?

6. Can we declare a record anonymously within a record? For example, is this declaration legal?

```
License = record
            number : array [1 .. 20] of 0 .. 9;
            personal : record
                         name : array [1 .. 35] of char;
                         needsGlasses : boolean
                       end
          end;
```

In Exercises 7 and 8, write the **type** *declarations that would be appropriate to store the indicated data.*

7. **a.** A card in a deck of cards
   b. A deck of cards
   c. The current state of a game of checkers
   d. Entries in a phone book
   e. A phone book

8. a. Weather information for a city, consisting of high and low temperatures, sky condition (cloudy, partly cloudy, sunny, raining, snowing, fog), and barometric pressure at 2:00 P.M.

b. A year's worth of weather information for a city

c. A year's worth of weather information for 20 cities, to include the name of each city

d. Inventory information about a pair of pants. Inseam and waist size will be necessary but not sufficient. What other data are needed to determine a pair of pants?

e. Inventory information for a store that sells only pants

9. Does a record have to have at least one field, or is it possible to have an empty record with no fields?

10. Pascal doesn't have a predefined type to represent rational numbers, like 2/3 or $-355/113$. We can remedy this situation by defining a *package* of our own, which is to say a collection of **type** declarations and subprograms. We could define a rational number by

```
Rational = record
              numerator, denominator : integer
           end;
```

so that the number $-355/113$ would be represented by a record with *.numerator* field -355 and *.denominator* field 113.

a. Write subprograms to read a rational, represented as two integers with a slash (also known as *solidus* or *vergule*) between them, and to write a rational in this form.

b. Write **procedure** *Add(a, b : Rational ;* **var** *sum : Rational)*, which adds two rational numbers. The result should be in lowest terms by dividing the numerator and denominator by their greatest common divisor. *Hint:* See Chapter 7, Exercise 13.

c. Write **procedure** *Subtract(a, b : Rational ;* **var** *diff : Rational)*, which subtracts *b* from *a*.

d. Write **procedure** *Multiply(a, b : Rational ;* **var** *prod : Rational)*, which multiplies two rational numbers.

e. Give a collection of rational numbers for *a* and *b* that you would use to test *Add*.

f. What's interesting about the rational number 355/113?

11. a. Give a **type** declaration that we might use to represent time in hours, minutes, and seconds. We might have fractional seconds, but we'll never have fractional minutes and hours. We also won't allow seconds or minutes to be larger than 60 (so 132 seconds would be represented as 2 minutes, 12 seconds).

b. Using the declaration you gave in part a, write subprograms that read and write values of type *Time*. In each case, let time be represented as *hours:minutes:seconds*, so 7 hours, 43 minutes, and 89.6 seconds would be read and written as 7:43:89.6.

c. Write a subprogram that adds two values of type *Time*, producing an answer of this type.

d. Write a subprogram that converts time to dog time, where one unit of time is seven units of dog time. Dog time is expressed as *Time* is, using hours, minutes, and seconds.

12. A point in the plane can be described by its coordinates in the X and Y directions. A line in the plane can be described by the values a, b, and c in the equation $ax + by + c = 0$. A point (x_0, y_0) lies in the line $ax + by + c = 0$ if and only if $ax_0 + by_0 + c = 0$.

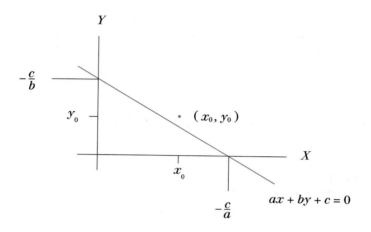

a. Write the declarations for *Point* and *Line*.

b. Using your declarations, write **function** *IsOn*$(p : Point ; l : Line) : boolean$, which returns *true* if and only if the point lies on the line.

c. Using your declarations, write **function** *Distance*$(p1, p2 : Point) : real$, which returns the distance between two points, where the distance between (x_0, y_0) and (x_1, y_1) is:

$$\sqrt{(x_0 - x_1)^2 + (y_0 - y_1)^2}$$

d. (You need to remember your high-school geometry here.) Using your declarations, write **procedure** *Intersection*$(l1, l2 : Line ; \textbf{var } p : Point)$, which returns the intersection of lines $l1$ and $l2$. *Hint:* Even if you know how to solve simultaneous linear equations, your job's not done.

13. Let's consider what would be necessary to write a grade-keeping program. Suppose that a course has twenty students and that each student will have scores for ten tests. Each student has a name consisting of not more than thirty characters, and each test score has a positive weight, which is some real number.

a. Write **type** declarations for this problem. You might want to look at part b before you do this part.

b. For the following tasks, describe how you would get the needed information.

    i. The name of the n-th student
    ii. The average of the test scores for the n-th student
    iii. The average of the test scores for a student with a given name
    iv. The class average on all tests
    v. The names of the students with average less than the class average

14. Do Exercise 13 assuming that a course may have from zero to twenty students and that each student will have scores for zero to ten tests.

15. We know that strings are an extension to Pascal and that they are not available in all Pascal environments.

  a. How could we change the declaration of *Line* in PasWord so that it makes no reference to strings?

  b. What changes would we have to make to the *DocHandler* unit if we used your definition of *Line* from part a?

16. Describe how the **with** statement is fundamentally different from the other Pascal statements you know.

17. The following data structure is intended to store the names and test scores of thirty students.

```
NameList = array [1 .. 30] of string [25];
Scores = array [1 .. 30, 1 .. 10] of 0 .. 100;
```

  a. Rewrite it so that it uses one, rather than two, arrays. Is there an advantage to this approach?

  b. Using your declarations from part a, write a procedure that displays a complete class roster, with names and scores for each student. Do the same thing for the structures as given originally.

18. Consider the following two data structures:

```
Struct1 = array [1 .. 7] of record
              x, y : real
          end;

Struct2 = record
              x, y : array [1 .. 7] of real
          end;
```

  a. Draw diagrams like Figure 10.4 to illustrate the two structures.

  b. How many real numbers does each structure represent?

  c. Which would be a better conceptual choice to represent the coordinates of seven points in the plane? Which would be better to represent a week's worth of high temperatures for Xenia, Ohio and Ypsilanti, Michigan?

  d. Give declarations for a single structure that could replace either of the two structures, without using records.

19. What would be an appropriate data structure to store information about a grid structure? In such a structure, we have a collection of *nodes*, each of which may be connected by *edges* to as many as four other nodes, as in the following diagram. In the diagram, there are six nodes (labeled for convenience and, perhaps, as a hint) and seven edges. Such structures are frequently used for designing the circuitry that makes up the processor chip in a computer, for instance.

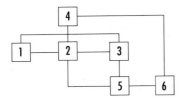

20. With the declaration of Exercise 19, write the following subprograms.

    a. **function** *Adjacent(n, m : Range) : boolean*, which returns *true* if and only if nodes *n* and *m* are joined by an edge.

    b. **procedure** *Delete(n : Range ; var g : Grid)*, which deletes node *n* from the grid along with all edges that are associated with that node. *Hint*: You have to do more than just change *n*.

21. In *ShiftArray*, what would happen if we replaced **downto** by **to**?

22. What other operations would be appropriate to add to PasWord? What operations would you like to include, but can't, because you haven't seen how to do them? What's the single biggest omission in PasWord at this stage in its development?

10.10 Answers

1. a. *IndexEntry*

    b. Meaningless. *Index* is an array, so requires an array selector rather than a field name (not to mention that *title* doesn't have anything to do with such a variable).

    c. *integer*

    d. *ClassRep*

    e. Meaningless. *Index*[500] is of type *ClassRep*, so the only selector that could follow is an array selector.

    f. *BookRep*

    g. *char*

3. a. Correct. Both sides of the assignment operator are of type *Line*.

    b. Incorrect. *IndexEntry* is a type name and has no business in an assignment statement. This would be correct if we had *entry1* in place of *IndexEntry*.

    c. Incorrect. *index*[3].*key* is a legal identifier, but it's of type *Word*, which is an array of characters. We can't read or write arrays as entire objects — we have to break them down until we're reading or writing a Pascal predefined type.

    d. Incorrect. Pascal functions can return only simple types, like *integer*, *real*, *char*, *boolean*, enumerated types, and subrange types (and pointers, as we'll see).

5. *Word* : 50 × 1 = 50 bytes
    Line : 125 bytes
    Numbers : 30 × 2 = 60 bytes
    IndexEntry : 50 + 2 + 60 = 112 bytes
    IndexRep : 100 × 112 = 11,200 bytes
    BookRep : 125 + 11,200 = 11,325 bytes (getting pretty big here)
    ClassRep : 400 × 11,325 = 4,530,000 bytes (too large for some systems)
    LibRep : 10,000 × 4,530,000 = 45,300,000,000 bytes (wow!)

7. a. Suit = (clubs, diamonds, hearts, spades);
    ValType = (two, three, four, five, six, seven, eight, nine, ten, jack, queen, king, ace);
    Card = **record**
            suit : SuitType;
            value : ValType
       end;

b. Deck = **array** [1 .. 52] **of** Card;   {Uses part a.}

c. PieceType = (single, king);
ColorType = (red, black);
SquareContents = **record**
                          case isEmpty : boolean **of**
                              true : ( );   {It's okay to have empty variant fields.}
                              false : (piece : PieceType ; color : ColorType)
                  end;
BoardContents = **array** [1 .. 8, 1 .. 8] **of** SquareContents;

d. TextLine = **array** [1 .. 30] **of** char;   {We could use strings here, too.}
NumberType = **array** [1 .. 7] **of** 0 .. 9;
Entry = **record**
            name, address : TextLine;
            number : NumberType
        end;

e. Directory = **array** [1 .. 100000] **of** Entry;   {Uses part d — may be too big.}

9. Refer to Figure 10.1. A record must have at least one field.

11. a. Time = **record**
                 hours : integer;
                 minutes : 0 .. 60;
                 seconds : real
             end;

b. We'll do reading. Writing is easier.

```
procedure ReadTime(var t : Time);
{No error-checking here. We assume that the }
{input is formatted as it should be.          }
   var
      dummy : char;   {This is the ':' that we read and discard.}
begin
   read(t.hours);
   read(dummy);
   read(t.minutes);
   read(dummy);
   read(t.seconds)
end;
```

c.
```
procedure AddTime(u, v : Time ; var t : Time);
   var
      sec : real;
      min : integer;
begin
   sec : = u.seconds + v.seconds;
   if sec > = 60.0 then
      begin
         t.seconds : = sec − 60.0;
         t.minutes : = 1
      end
```

```
      else
         begin
            t.seconds : = sec;
            t.minutes : = 0
         end;

   min : = u.minutes + v.minutes + t.minutes;
   if min > = 60 then
      begin
         t.minutes : = min − 60;
         t.hours : = 1
      end
   else
      begin
         t.minutes : = min;
         t.hours : = 0
      end;
   t.hours : = u.hours + v.hours + t.hours
end;
```

d. You're on your own here. It's somewhat similar to part c.

13. a. Here's one way:

```
StudentType = record
                 name : string [30];
                 test : array [1 .. 10] of 0 .. 100
              end;
Course = record
            weight : array [1 .. 10] of real;
            student : array [1 .. 30] of StudentType
         end;
```

b. We'll assume that we have a variable, c : *Course*.

i. c.student[n].name

ii.
```
sum : = 0.0;
weightSum : = 0.0;
for t : = 1 to 10 do
   begin
      sum : = sum + c.student[n].tests[t] * c.weight[t];
      weightSum : = weightSum + c.weight[t]
   end;
average : = sum / weightSum;
```

iii. We first do a linear search to find the index, n, corresponding to a name, and then we use part ii.

iv.
```
weightSum : = 0.0;
for t : = 1 to 10 do
   weightSum : = weightSum + c.weight[t];

sum : = 0.0;
for s : = 1 to 30 do
   for t : = 1 to 10 do
      sum : = sum + c.student[s].tests[t] * c.weight[t];
average : = sum / (weightSum * 30);
```

v. First, find the class average. Then loop through the students, computing each average. While still in the loop, if the average is less than the course average, then write the student's name. That's the most obvious way, but it's not the most efficient. How can this algorithm be improved?

15. a. We could use a dynamic array, as we did for the document. Change the type specification to:

```
Line = record
          length : 0 .. 80;
          ch : array [1 .. 80] of char
       end;
```

b. *GetALine* and *PrintALine* would have to be changed to read and write individual characters. You should be able to fill in the details. Refer to Chapter 6 for help.

17. a.
```
Student = record
             name : string [25];
             scores : array [1 .. 10] of 0 .. 100
          end;
Course = array [1 .. 30] of Student;
```

The main advantage is that this structure arranges the information in a logically coherent fashion. We don't have to keep track of two arrays for what is really a single conceptual object, the course.

b.
```
procedure WriteCourse(c : Course);
{This is for the version of part a.}
   var
      person, test : integer;
begin
   for person : = 1 to 30 do
      begin
         write(c[person].name, '   ');
         for test : = 1 to 10 do
            write(c[person].scores[test] : 3, '   ');
         writeln
      end
end;

procedure WriteCourse(n : NameList ; s : scores);
{This is for the original version.}
   var
      person, tests : integer;
begin
   for person : = 1 to 30 do
      begin
         write(n[person], '   ');
         for test : = 1 to 10 do
            write(s[person, test] : 3, '   ');
         writeln
      end
end;
```

19. const
     NUMNODES = 300;   {Or however large the grid will be.}
  type
     Range = 1 .. NUMNODES;
     Node = **record**
                  data :   {Anything that has to be stored in a node.};
                  up, right, down, left : 0 .. NUMNODES;
                  {This records the links to other nodes. A zero in }
                  {a field means that the node is not connected to}
                  {any other through that connection.   }
            end;
     Grid = **array** [Range] **of** Nodes;
  {We refer to a node by its index in the array.}

For the grid example in the exercise, we have the following representation:

	up	right	down	left
1	3	2	0	0
2	4	3	5	1
3	1	0	5	2
4	0	6	2	0
5	3	6	0	2
6	4	0	0	5
.				
.				
.				
300	0	0	0	0

21. In the example of Figure 10.6, after the shift, the lines would be 1, 2, 3, 3, 3, 3.

C H A P T E R

11

External Data Structures: Files

Y ou've learned a lot about programming so far. You have seen how to manipulate information and how to control the sequence of operations the computer will perform. You've also seen how to store information in Pascal's data structures in a way that permits efficient description and access. You have learned how to program efficiently, using a top-down approach with simple modules that encapsulate pieces of code in tidy conceptual units. In short, you are well on the way to being a competent programmer, able to write programs that do whatever you want them to. With one exception.

Until now, none of the programs you have written have any long-term memory. When your programs complete their intended tasks and quit, all the information they have saved is lost forever, gone to that great bit bucket in the sky. Clearly, if computers are to have any real practical use, there must be some way to store their results in a more or less permanent form. Consider the Pascal compiler that you have been using, for instance. In this case, there are two things that need to be stored permanently: your source code and the resulting object code. We could dispense with the object code and recompile the source code every time it's needed, but it would be an incredible bother to enter your source code, test and run it, quit for the day, and have to reenter the same source code the next day.

Almost all modern programming languages have the ability to save the output of a program in an external *file* that may reside on a floppy disk, for instance. Once the file is written to the disk (or tape, or compact disk, or any of a number of other media), it may be read at a later date and used as input for a program — either the same program that generated the file in the first place or an entirely different

445

program. In this chapter, we will discuss Pascal's **file** types. There are a few details we'll have to cover, but the essential ideas behind the care and feeding of files should already be familiar. In Pascal terms, writing to a file and reading from a file are very similar to writing to the screen and reading from the keyboard.

O B J E C T I V E S

In this chapter, we will:

- Introduce you to basic file concepts.
- Define and illustrate Pascal file types and their relationship to the standard *input* and *output* files.
- Describe how textfiles are created, written to, and read from by Pascal programs.
- Discuss standard file processing techniques, as illustrated by this chapter's PIP, an extended version of our PasWord program.
- Present additional examples that illustrate more advanced file processing techniques.

11.1   Files, Memory, and Permanent Storage

Files don't have to be external — they can reside solely in memory, just like any other Pascal data. We'll talk about such internal files in Section 11.5.

The most important fact about files is that they are generally stored on external devices. There are several nontrivial implications of this almost trivial observation. First, because there may be a large amount of room on a disk or tape, Pascal does not require that the size of a file be specified at compile time.

Unlike all other Pascal data types, there is no predefined limit to the size of a Pascal file. A file is dynamic, in that its size may grow and shrink during the time of its access.

The one-mode-only nature of file access may be circumvented in some compiler environments.

Another feature of files is dictated by the need to invent a type whose semantics do not depend on the nature of the external device on which files reside. In particular, at the time of Pascal's invention, it was inconvenient for a magnetic tape drive, for example, to switch between reading from the tape and writing to a tape. As a result, a file can be in one and only one of these two modes at any time.

A Pascal file may be in write-only mode or read-only mode. It cannot be in both modes simultaneously. Think of an ordinary cassette tape recorder: There's a button to record (our equivalent of writing to a file) and another button to play (to read), but there's no button to play *and* record simultaneously.

The magnetic tape drive is a good metaphor to keep in mind when thinking of Pascal files because it illustrates another important implication of storing files on an external device. To get to a particular location on a tape, the tape must be physically transported through the tape drive to position the piece to be read under the tape head that does the reading or writing. For example, in order to read the fifth piece of information from a tape, the first through fourth pieces must pass under the tape head. This holds true for all Pascal files, no matter how they are stored or accessed.

Files are *sequential access* entities. Unlike other compound structures where one has *random access* to any element by using the structure name and a selector, the only way to access file element n is to access elements 1 through $n - 1$ in sequence, whether or not they are needed by the program.

11.2 Textfiles

We'll begin our discussion of files by discussing a subtype, the *text* file type. The *text* type is really all we need for files, but it has disadvantages in size and speed that, in some cases, make us glad that there are file types other than *text*. We'll discuss other file types later, after you've had a chance to get comfortable with this simpler type. In this section, we will let you know when any part of our discussion doesn't apply to general **file** types, but most of what we say will be applicable to all files.

A file-type variable is declared just as all other Pascal variables are—the only difference is that we use the type name *text*. According to the language standard, the name of the file (that is, the variable name) must appear in the program header, so a typical program using files might begin

```
program FileUser(input, output, myFile);
    var
        myFile : text;
```

Such a declaration means that there is (or will be) an external file on your disk (or wherever it happens to be) referred to from within the program as *myFile*. Notice that the name *myFile* appears twice: as a variable in the program and as an identifier in the program parameter list, along with the standard files *input* and *output*. These last two we have seen before; they serve as indicators that the program will accept input from whatever device the compiler defines to be the usual one (the keyboard, in most cases) and that it will write to the standard output device (which, for our purposes, is almost always the screen). Both *input* and *output* are textfiles, at least as far as the computer is concerned, and in the preceding example, *myFile* is also a textfile. This means that life is very simple for us when we have to deal with reading from and writing to *myFile*.

You can read from and write to a textfile in almost exactly the same way as you read from the keyboard and write to the screen, using *read*, *readln*, *write*, *writeln*, and *eoln*. When we are using non-textfiles, we cannot use the procedures *readln*, *writeln*, or the function *eoln*.

Before we access a file, though, we must first *open* it. To open a file is to ready it for reading or writing and to establish a logical link between the file and our program. Recall that we mentioned that a file may be in one and only one mode at any time: read-only or write-only. To open a file in write-only mode, we use the command *rewrite(filename)*. This predefined procedure does several things: (1) It looks on the disk for a file with the name *filename*; (2) if no such file exists, an empty one with that name will be created on the disk; (3) if there is a file with the given name, that file will be emptied of its contents; and (4) in either case, the file will be readied for writing.[1]

Don't forget, *rewrite* destroys the contents of the file it opens.

To write to an open textfile, we can use *write* or *writeln*, almost exactly as we would write to the standard *output* file. The *writeln* command appends an end-of-line mark to the end of whatever was written on the file, and *write* doesn't. The only difference between writing to files and writing to *output* is that we must include the file name as the first parameter to *write* and *writeln*. When we leave a file name out (as we have up to now), output is directed by default to the standard output device. Finally, if we want the file to be saved and to exist after our program is finished (as is normally the case for files other than the standard *output* file), we

---

[1]The standard file *output* automatically has a *rewrite* call performed on it when the program begins execution. You don't have to rewrite it explicitly.

must formally close it, using a *close* statement.[2] This tells the machine to sever the connection between your program and the external file and to save the external file according to normal conventions for the computer and operating system under which your program is running.

Finally, note that textfiles can have any type of value stored in them. The term *text* merely describes how information will be represented in the file — that is, as characters. Any kind of data — integers, reals, characters, and strings — can be read from the keyboard and written to the screen, and the same is true with textfiles. For example, the following program reads two integers and an arbitrary string of characters from the user and writes them to a file *savedFile*.

```
program EchoToFile(input, savedFile);
    var
        num1, num2 : integer;
        c : char;
        savedFile : text;
begin
    rewrite(savedFile);              {Ready savedFile for writing.}
    readln(num1, num2);             {Read the two integers.}
    writeln(savedFile, num1, num2);  {Write the two numbers to savedFile.}
    while not eoln do               {Get characters until return is seen.}
        begin
            read(c);                {Read a character,}
            write(savedFile, c)     {and write it on the file.}
        end;
    close(savedFile)
end.
```

Figure 11.1 shows the contents of the file *savedFile* after the execution of the example program. There are two things to note here. First, the file consists of characters and is illustrated exactly as it would appear on disk. Just as with writing to the screen, the values of the integers *num1* and *num2* are converted from their internal binary representation to characters and written just as integers would be written on the screen. (We used a default integer width of six characters here, although that could be changed by the usual format-forcing, using colons after the integers.) Secondly, note that there are more markers than are explicitly generated by the program. There is an end-of-line mark after the last line, even though we didn't put one there (we could have by simply adding a *writeln* statement). There is also an *end-of-file* mark at the very end. The last end-of-line mark is inserted automatically in every textfile, and an end-of-file mark is likewise inserted at the end of every file.

Non-textfiles do not *have an end-of-line mark inserted.*

To open a file for reading, we use the command *reset(filename)*. This command looks on the disk for a file named *filename* and if it finds such a file, prepares

---

[2]The *close* procedure is not part of standard Pascal, but it is used in the compilers for which this text is written.

The user types:

102 –9001<RET>
Bob loves Mary <RET>

The file looks like:

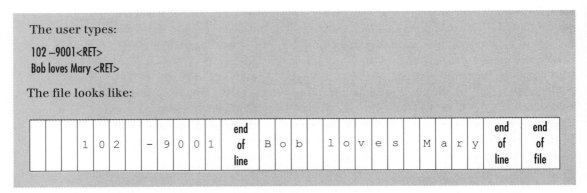

Figure 11.1.   The textfile created by the program *EchoToFile*

to read from the file, starting at the beginning.[3] It is an error to reset an external file that doesn't exist. Most compilers will let you know when your program tries to open a nonexistent file. Reading from an open file follows the same rules as reading from the keyboard: *read* reads what is requested and *readln* reads what is requested and then discards everything up to and including the first end-of-line mark encountered. When reading from a textfile other than the standard one (usually the keyboard), the file variable must appear as the first parameter, just as was the case with *write* and *writeln*. We could write a companion program to *EchoToFile* that reads *savedFile* and displays its contents on the screen. It would look like this:

```
program EchoToScreen(output, savedFile);
    var
        num1, num2 : integer;
        c : char;
        savedFile : text;
begin
    reset(savedFile);                   {Ready savedFile for reading.}
    readln(savedFile, num1, num2);      {Read the two integers from the file.}
    writeln(num1, num2);                {Write the two numbers to the screen.}
    while not eoln(savedFile) do        {Get characters until end mark is seen.}
        begin
            read(savedFile, c);         {Read a character from the file,}
            write(c)                    {and write it on the screen.}
        end;
    close(savedFile)
end.
```

[3]Just as *output* is automatically rewritten, the standard file *input* is automatically reset when a program begins execution.

Compare this program with *EchoToFile*, and you'll notice that they are structurally almost exactly the same. This makes perfect sense when you realize that they are indeed the same program — the only difference is the textfiles they use for input and output. *EchoToFile* gets information from *input* and sends it to *savedFile*, whereas *EchoToScreen* gets the same information from *savedFile* and sends it to the standard textfile *output*. This points out an important fact to keep in mind when using files: The external file *savedFile* was built by writing two integers with an end-of-line marker followed by a string of characters, so when we read from that file we must read two integers, discard the end-of-line marker, and then read a string of characters.

> **Y**ou should always read from a file in the same order and with the same types as were used when the file was originally created. In short, read 'em like you (or someone else) wrote 'em.

Speaking of strings, the **string** data type is particularly useful when dealing with textfiles. We have seen how conveniently a line of text can be read from the keyboard and written to the screen using strings, and this holds true generally for all textfiles. Indeed, the version of *EchoToScreen* can be considerably simplified as follows:

```
program EchoToScreen(output, savedFile);
   var
      num1, num2 : integer;
      s : string;
      savedFile : text;
begin
   reset(savedFile);
   readln(savedFile, num1, num2);
   writeln(num1, num2);
   readln(savedFile, s);    {Read an entire line at once,}
   writeln(s);              {and write it to the screen.}
   close(savedFile)
end.
```

From this point forward, we will use strings in our examples, as we have in our Program in Progress.

autions About Files

Files are different from any other Pascal data types. They may reside outside of memory and have a life that is independent of any program. So, it should come as no surprise that some of the things we are accustomed to doing with other types cannot be done with files. We have already mentioned, for example, that files can't be inspected or modified at will. A file can be in only one mode at a time, and to switch between reading and writing requires that we open it in the other mode by using *rewrite* or *reset*.

Another aspect in which files are different from other types is the way they are used as parameters in procedures or functions. You will recall that when we use a value parameter, the actual parameter is copied, and that copy is sent to the subprogram. Because files may reside on an external device, and because there is no predefined size for a file, this could cause problems in implementing files as value parameters, so Pascal avoids this problem by disallowing it.

> **F**ile-type variables may not be used as value parameters in a procedure or function call. Files may be sent to subprograms only as **var** parameters, whether or not they will be changed within the subprogram.

One last difference between files and other types is their use in assignment statements. We know that if *variable1* and *variable2* are arrays, for example, we can make the assignment *variable1* := *variable2*. Unfortunately, Pascal doesn't allow wholesale assignment of files.

> **I**f *file1* and *file2* are file-type variables, it is an error to assign one to the other by using *file1* := *file2*.

If we want the equivalent of the assignment statement for textfiles, we must write our own, as follows:

```
procedure Copy(var fromFile, toFile : text);
{Copies the contents of fromFile to the end of toFile. First, note the use }
{of the var parameter here, even though only toFile is being changed.      }
{Second, note that we don't rewrite toFile within the procedure; this      }
{procedure assumes that toFile has already been opened for writing.        }
    var
        s : string;
begin
    reset(fromFile);
    while not eof(fromFile) do      {as long as there's anything in the file . . .}
        begin
            readln(fromFile,s);        {Skip past the end-of-line mark.}
            writeln(toFile,s)          {Insert an end-of-line mark.}
        end
end;
```

Notice, first, the use of the predefined function *eof* to control the **while** loop in our example. The function *eof* accepts a file variable as its parameter and returns *true* or *false* to indicate whether or not the file in question has reached its end-of-file marker. Notice, too, as we mentioned in the header comments, we don't rewrite *toFile* within the procedure. We do this because we may want to keep *toFile* open for further copying. In this way, we could, for example, *concatenate* two files, putting one at the end of the other. If *file1*, *file2*, and *cat* were three textfiles, we could make *cat* contain the contents of *file1* followed by the contents of *file2* by doing the following:

```
rewrite(cat);
Copy(file1, cat);
Copy(file2, cat)
```

If *file1* contained the characters 'dog' and *file2* contained the characters 'food', then after the segment above, *cat* would contain the text 'dog food', where the space between 'dog' and 'food' denotes the end-of-line mark inserted by the *writeln* in *Copy*. You should convince yourself that it would in fact be impossible to use *Copy* for concatenation if we used *rewrite* on *toFile* within the procedure.

11.3   Problem Solving V: Modifying PasWord

We'll begin by calling your attention to the fact that what you see in the text isn't exactly like the version that is on the lab disk. This is the standard Pascal version, and your lab disk contains the version for your particular compiler. With the possible exception of the **string** type, there are more compiler-specific extensions to the **file** type than anywhere else in Pascal, and for good reason. The standard set of **file** features must apply over all machines, so there are lots of useful things that had to be left out of the standard and included in Pascal for specific compilers. This will require special care, then, if you ever have to port your file-using programs to another environment. Consider yourself warned.

Although most of PasWord 2.0 is the same as our original PasWord (version 1.0), it represents a significant improvement in that it saves documents and allows the user to modify previously saved documents. What we are posing, in essence, is a problem of program modification or maintenance. The nature of the proposed modifications localizes the required changes, most of which have to do with input and output. Notice how good programming practice helps us—the modular nature of PasWord 1.0 makes it easy for us to locate and change the code to produce version 2.0.

When reading the listing, notice that we have indicated explicitly the changes in the new version. The program header comments mention that this is version 2.0, and the procedure list indicates the subprograms that have been added by the notation **NEW**. In addition, any changes to the body of the program are also noted. This practice of annotating changes is so helpful that it is all but mandatory in the real world, where a team of several people would be working on a program, and would need to know what changes have been made by others. In such a development environment, we would have much more detailed annotations, including the dates of all changes and the names of the people who made them.

```
unit DocHandler2;
{————————————————————————————————————————————}
{                                                                            }
{              Support routines for managing a PasWord2 document.             }
{                                                                            }
{              This unit contains subprograms that handle insertion,         }
{              deletion, modification, and printing of lines in a document.  }
{              It also allows saving and retrieving a document from a        }
{              textfile.                                                      }
{                                                                            }
{————————————————————————————————————————————}
{              SUBPROGRAM LIST:                                              }
{              Initialize (var d: Document)                                   }
{              DoInsertion (var d: Document; lineNum: integer)                }
{              DoDeletion (var d: Document; lineNum: integer)                 }
{              DoChange (var d: Document; lineNum: integer)                   }
{              ShowDoc (d: Document; start, finish: integer)                  }
{              SaveDoc (d: Document ; var f : text)                **NEW**}
{              ReadDoc (var d: Document; var f : text)             **NEW**}
{————                                                                        }
{              ShiftArray (direction, start: integer; var d: Document)        }
{              GetALine (var newLine: Line)                                   }
{              PrintALine (d: Document; lineNum: integer)                     }
{              Swap (var thingOne, thingTwo: integer)                         }
{                                                                            }
{————————————————————————————————————————————}
interface
    const
        MAXLINES  = 64;      {max lines per document}
        MAXLENGTH = 80;      {max characters per line}
    type
        Line = string[MAXLENGTH];
        Document = record
                        totalLines: integer;
                        theLine: array [1 .. MAXLINES] of Line
                    end;
    procedure Initialize (var d: Document);
    procedure DoInsertion (var d: Document; lineNum: integer);
```

procedure DoDeletion (**var** d: Document; lineNum: integer);
procedure DoChange (**var** d: Document; lineNum: integer);
procedure ShowDoc (d: Document; start, finish: integer);
procedure SaveDoc (d: Document ; **var** f : text);
procedure ReadDoc (**var** d: Document ; **var** f : text);

implementation

{———————————————— PRIVATE ROUTINES ————————————————}

procedure ShiftArray (direction, start: integer; **var** d: Document);
begin
   {See Chapter 10.}
end;

procedure GetALine (**var** newLine: Line);
begin
   {See Chapter 10.}
end;

procedure PrintALine (d: Document; lineNum: integer);
begin
   {See Chapter 10.}
end;

procedure Swap (**var** thingOne, thingTwo: integer);
begin
   {See Chapter 10.}
end;

{———————————————— PUBLIC ROUTINES ————————————————}

procedure Initialize; {(var d: Document)}
{initializes document to zero lines}
begin
   {See Chapter 10.}
end;

procedure DoInsertion; {(var d: Document; lineNum: integer)}
begin
   {See Chapter 10.}
end;

procedure DoDeletion; {(var d: Document; lineNum: integer)}
begin
   {You've done this.}
end;

procedure DoChange; {(var d: Document; lineNum: integer)}
begin
   {You've done this.}
end;

```
       procedure ShowDoc; {(d: Document; start, finish: integer)}
       begin
          {See Chapter 10.}
       end;
```

{———————————————————— FILE ROUTINES ————————————————————}

```
       procedure SaveDoc; {(d: Document ; var f : text)}
       {Save the document d as file 'docFile'.}
          var
             thisLine : 1 .. MAXLINES;              {the line we are currently writing}
       begin
          writeln('Writing file . . .');
          rewrite(f);                               {Open and prepare the file to accept data.}
          for thisLine : = 1 to d.totalLines do
             writeln(f, d.theLine[thisLine]);
          close(f)
       end;

       procedure ReadDoc; {(var d: Document ; var f : text)}
       {Generates the document by reading it from file 'docFile'.}
          var
             currentLine : 0 .. MAXLINES;           {the line we are currently reading}
       begin
          writeln('Reading file . . .');
          reset(f);                                 {locates and opens the file for input}
          currentLine : = 0;                        {Initialize current line number.}
          while not eof(f) do                       {as long as there's anything left to read . . .}
             begin
                currentLine : = currentLine + 1; {Set the new line number.}
                readln(f, d.theLine[currentLine])   {Read a line from the file.}
             end;
          d.totalLines : = currentLine;             {Set the number of lines in the document.}
          close(f)
       end;

   end.
```

The *DocHandler2* unit is almost exactly the same as it was for PasWord 1.0, with the exception of the two file-management routines *SaveDoc* and *ReadDoc*. There are also very few changes in the main program. We added two routines, *Startup* and *DoQuit*, that handle reading a document from a file at the beginning of the session and saving the document to a file at the end of a session. Both of these subprograms require the user to respond to a question by typing a character, so we included a version of our building block subprogram that gets a legal character in response to the question (either "Enter n for new, or o for open" at the start or "Enter s to save document, or n for no saving") at the end.

The PIP

program PasWord2 (input, output, docFile);

```
{—————————————————————————————————————————————}
{                                                              }
{                    PROGRAM IN PROGRESS                       }
{                                                              }
{                        CHAPTER 11                            }
{                                                              }
{       Simple line-oriented word processor. Allows users to insert,  }
{       delete, change, display lines in a document. This program     }
{       also allows the user to read and write documents to           }
{       textfiles.                                                    }
{                                                              }
{—————————————————————————————————————————————}
{                                                              }
{       SUBPROGRAM LIST:                                       }
{       ShowMenu                                               }
{       GetAChar(prompt : string ; legal : ChrSet) : char            **NEW**}
{       GetCommand(var c : char; var param1, param2 : integer)       }
{       Startup(var d : Document ; var f : text)                     **NEW**}
{       DoQuit(d : Document ; var f : text)                          **NEW**}
{                                                              }
{—————————————————————————————————————————————}
```

uses
    DocHandler2;

type
    ChrSet = **set of** char;   {used in GetAChar   **NEW**}
var
    choice: char;   {command character}
    doc: Document;   {current working document}
    param1, param2: integer;   {line numbers for insert, delete, change, print commands}
    docFile : text;   {textfile for saving and retrieving a document   **NEW**}

procedure ShowMenu;
begin
    {See Chapter 10.}
end;

function GetAChar(prompt : **string** ; legal : ChrSet) : char;
{Returns a character entered by the keyboard.}
{If the character isn't in the set "legal," it   }
{writes the legal characters and keeps trying   }
{until the user enters a legal response.   }
{Called by : Startup, DoQuit   }

```
    var
        resp : char;
        i : integer;
begin
    writeln(prompt);
    readln(resp);
    while not (resp in legal) do
        begin
            writeln('** Sorry, that''s not a valid response **');
            writeln('Please type one of the following characters, followed by Return');
            writeln;
            for i : = 1 to 255 do
                if chr(i) in legal then
                    write(chr(i), ' ');
            writeln;
            writeln(prompt);
            readln(resp)
        end;
    GetAChar : = resp
end;

procedure GetCommand (var c: char; var param1, param2: integer);
begin
    {See Chapter 10.}
    {We could make use of GetAChar here, too.}
end;
```

```
{─────────────────────────── START, FINISH ───────────────────────────}

procedure Startup (var d: Document ; var f : text);
{Initializes document d to contain zero lines, or reads and }
{constructs a document from a file, and displays menu.       }
{Called by : Main                                            }
{Calls : GetAChar, Initialize, ReadDoc, ShowMenu            }
    var
        answer: char;
begin
    answer : = GetAChar('Enter n for new, or o for open:', ['n','N','o','O']);
    if (answer = 'n') or (answer = 'N') then
        Initialize(d)      {Create an empty document.}
    else
        ReadDoc(d, f);   {Read an existing document.}
    ShowMenu
end;

procedure DoQuit (d: Document ; var f : text);
{Save document if desired.                             }
{Called by : Main      Calls : GetAChar, SaveDoc}
```

```
   var
       answer: char;
   begin
       answer : = GetAChar('Enter s to save document, or n for no saving:', ['n','N','s','S']);
       if (answer = 's') or (answer = 'S') then
           SaveDoc(d, f)
   end;
{————————————————— MAIN PROGRAM —————————————————}
begin   {Main}
   Startup(doc, docFile);              (**NEW**)
   repeat
       GetCommand(choice, param1, param2);
       case choice of
           'i', 'I':
               DoInsertion(doc, param1);
           'd', 'D':
               DoDeletion(doc, param1);
           'c', 'C':
               DoChange(doc, param1);
           'p', 'P':
               ShowDoc(doc, param1, param2);
           '?':
               ShowMenu;
           'q', 'Q':
               DoQuit(doc, docFile)    (**NEW**)
       end   {case}
   until (choice = 'Q') or (choice = 'q')
end.
```

11.4 Using Files in PasWord 2.0

The primary difference between versions 1.0 and 2.0 of PasWord is the addition of two procedures, *ReadDoc* and *SaveDoc*. These routines build a document from an existing textfile and save the current document to a textfile, respectively. These two procedures, in turn, are called by two others, *Startup* and *DoQuit*, at the beginning and end of the session. Let's look first at *SaveDoc* and see how it saves the current document to a textfile.

```
procedure SaveDoc (d: Document ; var f : text);
   var
       thisLine : 1 .. MAXLINES;
```

```
begin
    writeln('writing file ...');
    rewrite(f);
    for thisLine := 1 to d.totalLines do
        writeln(f, d.theLine[thisLine]);
    close(f)
end;
```

This should look very familiar. It first creates an empty file, *docFile*, and readies the file for reading. The procedure then goes through every line in the document in order and writes each line to *docFile*, appending an end-of-line mark to the end of each line. After all lines have been written on *docFile*, the system automatically appends an end-of-file mark to the end of the file. The end-of-file mark serves as a second sentinel so that when we read from *docFile* we will know when to stop reading lines. Notice how similar *SaveDoc* is to the routine *ShowDoc* that we wrote in Chapter 10. They should be similar, after all, since they both do the same thing: write the contents of a document to a textfile. The only real difference between the two procedures is that *ShowDoc* writes to the standard file *output*, whereas *SaveDoc* writes to an external file, *docFile*. Figure 11.2 shows what *docFile* would look like for a typical document.

To reconstruct a document from the file and restore it to memory, we follow the principle we outlined earlier: *Read from a file in the same way as the file was originally generated*. In this case, that means that at the top conceptual level we will do the following:

```
currentLine := 0;
while we're not at the end of the file do
    begin
        currentLine := currentLine + 1;
        Read a line from the file, into d.theLine[currentLine]
    end;
d.totalLines := currentLine
```

That's simple enough—it mirrors *SaveDoc* almost exactly, except that we have to keep track of the number of the line we're currently reading so that we know in which line in the array *d.theLine* to place the characters we're reading. To read a line from the file into the array is just as simple; all we have to do is read a string from the file. We use a *readln* to accomplish this, since that's the way the file was built. Each logical line in the file is followed by an end-of-line sentinel. We can complete *ReadDoc* now.

```
procedure ReadDoc (var d: Document ; var f : text);
    var
        currentLine : 0 .. MAXLINES;
begin
    writeln('reading file ...');
    reset(f);
    currentLine := 0;
```

The document in memory:

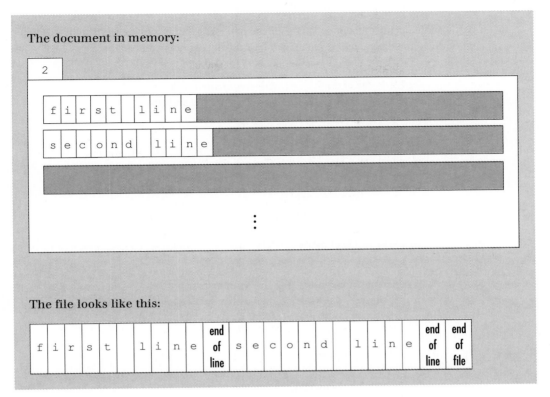

The file looks like this:

Figure 11.2.   Saving a document in PasWord 2.0

```
while not eof(f) do
   begin
      currentLine : = currentLine + 1;
      readln(f, d.theLine[currentLine])
   end;
   d.totalLines : = currentLine;
   close(f)
end;
```

11.5

Other **file** Types

A file, like an array, is a compound structure, which is to say that it is composed of *components* of simpler types. Also like an array, the components of a file may be of any type whatsoever, except that the components of a file may not be files, nor may they be structured types whose components include files. The most general declaration for files is **file of** *component type*. For example, the first two file declarations below are legal in Pascal, and the second two are not.

type

CharFile = **file of** char;		*OK — equivalent to* text.
TempData = **record**		*Standard record definition.*
	high, low : real	
end;		
TempFile = **file of** TempData;		*OK for components to be structured.*
WordFile = **file of** CharFile;		*NO. Can't have files of files.*
Weather = **record**		
	high, low : real;	
	report : CharFile	*Can use files as record fields.*
end;		
WeatherFile = **file of** Weather;		*NO. Can't have files whose components contain files.*

The components of a file are the smallest units that can be read or written. In the example above, for instance, if *f* were a variable of type *TempFile*, we could make the first two calls but not the second.

read(f, temps);	*If* temps *was of type* TempData *and* f *open to read.*
write(f, temps);	*If* temps *was of type* TempData *and* f *open to write.*
read(f, temps.high)	*NOPE.* temps.high *is real. Can only read things of type* TempData.

The nice feature of general files, especially if their components are structured types, is that a single *read* or *write* takes the place of potentially many calls that we would have to use with textfiles.

Remember that with general files we don't have *readln, writeln,* or *eoln* available.

In the *TempFile* example above, for instance, we could get one complete record with both high and low temperature from the file with a single *read*. We can then inspect the contents of the record we just read, as

read(f, temps);	*If* temps *was of type* TempData *and* f *open to read.*
spread : = temps.high − temps.low;	*Assuming* spread *was a real variable.*

Reading and writing general files are the *only* instances in the Pascal standard in which we can read or write a structured type in a single chunk. In general, arrays and records must be read piecewise, by reading their simple components one by one.

> **T**he only time we can break the rule of reading or writing structured types piecewise is when they are components of files.[4]

As with the other instances of the input/output procedures, the general file versions of *read* and *write* may take an arbitrary number of parameters, as long as the first parameter is a file variable. We could, for instance, read two components of *f* in a single *read* statement by saying

```
read(f, yesterdaysTemps, todaysTemps);   {read two components}
highChange : = todaysTemps.high − yesterdaysTemps.high
```

We could put general files to good use in PasWord if we wanted to introduce a new version, PasWord 2.1, with even simpler I/O (input/output) routines. We might, for example, decide that the basic unit of storage should be the document, and do the following:

```
type
   Document = record
                  totalLines : 0 .. MAXLINES;
                  theLine : array [1 .. MAXLINES] of Line
               end;
   ⋮
var
   ⋮
   doc: Document;
   docFile : file of Document;   NOTICE. A new file type.
   ⋮
procedure SaveDoc (d: Document);
{Version 2.1. Uses docFile : file of Document.}
begin
   writeln('writing file . . .');
   rewrite(docFile);
   write(docFile,d)   {Write a whole document component.}
end;
procedure ReadDoc (var d: Document);
{Version 2.1. Uses docFile : file of Document.}
begin
   writeln('reading file . . .');
   reset(docFile);
   read(docFile,d)   {Read a whole document component.}
end;
```

[4]Or when the Pascal implementation includes the nonstandard **string** extension, as you've seen.

This is considerably simpler than either of the textfile versions 2.0, since we can trust the system to handle the details of getting the line count and the string that makes up each line.

Again, we have to be careful, since PasWord 2.1 files are no longer compatible with any of the earlier versions. In fact, version 2.1 files are *very* much different from the earlier version, even though it may not appear so at first. Files created by versions 2.0 are textfiles: The information stored in them is in character form, as it would appear on the screen. In particular, each data item in textfiles is converted from its internal form to a form that people can read, so the integer 63 would appear in the file as the characters '   63' (six blank characters, followed by the characters '6' and '3', assuming a default width of eight characters for integers). Non-textfiles, however, store their information in almost exactly the same form as it is stored in memory, so the integer 63 would be stored in version 2.1 as its internal binary form 0000000000111111, using two 8-bit bytes rather than the eight bytes needed in a textfile.[5]

A File Example

One of the disadvantages of files, as we've already noted, is that they are sequential access entries. In order to read the nth component of a file, we must first read past the first, second, third, . . . $(n - 1)$th elements. It's sometimes handy to make a file appear to be a random access object, even though it really isn't. What we have in mind is a procedure, *ReadNthItem*, which takes a file variable f and a positive integer n as its argument and returns the nth component of the file if one exists. To implement *ReadNthItem*, we could reset f and then read and ignore the first $n - 1$ components to get us to the nth, which we'll return. The only thing we have to be careful about is the case when f has fewer than n components, in which case the procedure can't complete its task. So we'll include a boolean parameter, *success*, which will be true if and only if the procedure found an nth element in f.

We saw bounded linear searches in Section 9.4.

We've seen this kind of problem before—it's a bounded linear search, where the exit condition from the search loop will be $eof(f)$ **or** $(count = n)$, where *count* counts the number of components we've read so far. Notice that we have written our routine as a procedure, rather than as a function, even though it only returns a single value. We did that because the Pascal standard only allows functions to return simple types, such as reals, integers, characters, boolean values, subrange types, or user-defined ordinals. Since the returned value, *theData*, could be a structured type (depending on the type of *DataType*), we took the safe road and wrote our routine as a procedure.

---

[5]For this reason, non-textfiles are frequently referred to as *binary files*.

```
type
    DataType = any type you need (except file types);
    DataFile = file of DataType;
⋮
procedure ReadNthItem(var f : DataFile ; n : integer ; var theData : DataType ; var success :
                      boolean);
    var
        count : integer;
begin
    if n < = 0 then
        begin
            writeln('Improper file position in ReadNthItem. Must be positive.');
            success : = false
        end
    else
        begin
            reset(f);
            count : = 0;

            while (not eof(f)) and (count < n) do
            {We don't need a flagged loop here, since the two parts}
            {of the exit condition are logically independent. Either   }
            {one can be false without causing an error in the other. }
                begin
                    read(f, theData);    {Read past an element in the file.}
                    count : = count + 1
                end;

            if count = n then
                success : = true
            else
                begin
                    writeln('No position ', n : 1, ' in the file.');
                    success : = false
                end
        end
    end
end;
```

This is a good time to mention a quibble with *ReadNthItem* that may not be a problem in many cases but could turn out to be serious in a program that makes significant use of this procedure. Although *ReadNthItem* makes it appear that we have random access to a file, in that we can access any component with a single procedure call, in fact *ReadNthItem* simply hides the sequential access problem. If, for instance, we needed elements 4, 5, 8, 2, and 1 in a file, using five calls to *ReadNthItem* to get those elements would require 4 + 5 + 8 + 2 + 1 = 20 reads from the file. Since file access is very much slower than memory access, we would be better off in terms of time efficiency to declare an array to store data elements and first fill the array with file components 1 through 8, since that would require only eight reads rather than twenty.

Another File Example: Using Internal Files

To further illustrate the differences between a random access type and a sequential access one, let's consider the task of deleting the first element from a file. With arrays, this is straightforward, if cumbersome: All we have to do is shift each of the elements 2, 3, . . . one position to fill the hole in position 1, as we've seen in Chapter 10. How do we do this with a file, though?

The answer is that we can't do this shifting at all with files. We must, instead, resort to a *temporary file*—one that never resides on an external device—as a sort of internal scratch pad. If we call the temporary file *temp*, we can first read elements 2, 3, . . . from our main file, write them to file *temp*, empty the main file, and then write the contents of *temp* back onto our main file, as follows.

```
procedure DeleteFirst(var f : DataFile);
{Delete the first element of f. To simplify matters   }
{here, we assume that f has at least one element.      }
{Type declarations are the same as for ReadNthItem.}
    var
        temp : DataFile;
        theData : DataType;
begin
    reset(f);
    rewrite(temp);
    read(f, theData);            {Read past the first element of f.}
    while not eof(f) do
        begin
            read(f, theData);        {Read an element from f,}
            write(temp, theData)     {and copy it to temp.}
        end;
    reset(temp);                 {Change temp's mode from writing to reading.}
    rewrite(f);                  {Change f's mode to writing and empty it.}
    while not eof(temp) do
        begin
            read(temp, theData);     {Read an element from f,}
            write(f, theData)        {and copy it to temp.}
        end
end;
```

We're doing two things here that you haven't seen before. First, we're using an internal file *temp* that never gets saved to disk. (We don't include *temp* among the program parameters after the word **program**, so it doesn't get saved—it acts just like any other variable and expires when the program quits.) Second, we're changing the modes of both files while they're open. The call *reset(temp)* keeps *temp* open, changes its mode to read-only, and resets the active position back to the start. Similarly, the call *rewrite(f)* keeps *f* open, changes its mode to write-only, empties the file, and sets the active position to the first position in the file. A good exercise to test your understanding of this procedure would be to write *DeleteNth(f, n)*, which deletes the *n*th element from the file *f*.

Finally, we should stress that *DeleteFirst* deletes the first component of a file. For example, in PasWord 2.1 we are using a **file of** *Document*, which is to say that the individual components are entire documents. This means that if we were to use *DeleteFirst* on such a file we would delete an entire document from the file. On the other hand, if we had decided to write PasWord 2.1.1 to save documents as a **file of** *Line*, then *DeleteFirst* would delete just the first line from the file.

Primitive File Access

Although *read* and *write* are sufficient for most file access tasks, they are not the most basic Pascal file operations. If, for instance, we have a file *f* of reals and *r* is a real number, a call *read(f, r)* actually accomplishes two things: It retrieves the real number in the current position in the file and copies it into *r*, and it advances the current position by one. In a similar way, the call *write(f, r)* copies *r* into the current position of *f* (which is always the end of *f* when we are writing), advances the current position by one, and marks that the current position is the new end of *f*.

The operations *read* and *write* are each actually shorthand for even more primitive operations that make use of a variable associated with each file. The variable is called a *buffer variable* and is the actual "window" into the file (in fact, some sources refer to the file buffer as the *file window*). If *f* is a file variable of type **file of** *DataType*, then the buffer variable would be written $f^\wedge$ (with a caret, ^, or up-arrow, ↑, following the file variable[6]) and would be of type *DataType*. You do not declare the buffer variable with your other program variables—its declaration is implicit in the declaration of the file *f*.

If *f* is being generated (that is, has been opened by *rewrite*), the contents of the buffer variable $f^\wedge$ are what will next be written to the file. You can cause the contents of $f^\wedge$ to be appended to *f* by using the procedure *put(f)*. You may only *put* the file buffer into a file when the file is in write-only mode. In simple terms, the pair of statements

```
f^ := r;
put(f);
```

is equivalent to *write(f, r)*. The assignment $f^\wedge := r$ copies the value of *r* into the file buffer, and *put(f)* copies the contents of the buffer $f^\wedge$ to the end of the file and moves the reference location of $f^\wedge$ up one position, as illustrated in Figure 11.3, for a file *f* : **file of** *real*.

---

[6]We'll use the caret, since it avoids confusion with the arrow keys on many keyboards. On the keyboards of the computers for which this text is written, the arrow keys control the cursor and do not write arrows on the screen.

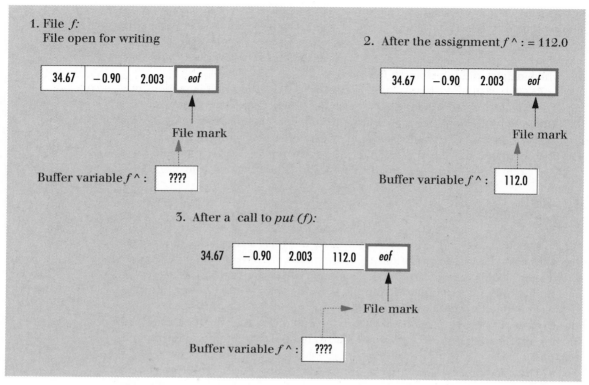

1. File *f:*
   File open for writing

34.67	−0.90	2.003	*eof*

   File mark

   Buffer variable *f* ^ : | ???? |

2. **After the assignment** *f* ^ : = 112.0

34.67	−0.90	2.003	*eof*

   File mark

   Buffer variable *f* ^ : | 112.0 |

3. **After a call to** *put (f):*

34.67	− 0.90	2.003	112.0	*eof*

   File mark

   Buffer variable *f* ^ : | ???? |

Figure 11.3.   Writing to a file using the file buffer and *put*

Notice that in write-only mode, the file mark for the active position is always at the end of the file (it's an error otherwise). Notice, too, that the value of the file buffer is undefined until you assign something to it and that after the value of the file buffer has been placed in the file by *put*, its value is again undefined. In other words, *put* acts differently from normal Pascal assignments in that it actually transfers the value in the file buffer to the file rather than just sending a copy.

The companion operation to *put* is *get*. This operation copies the value from the current position of the file into the file buffer and advances the current position by one. The low-level equivalent to *read(f, r)* is the pair of statements

```
get(f);
r := f^;
```

The procedure *get* may only be called when a file is in read-only mode, and it produces an error if the current position in the file is the end-of-file mark. Figure 11.4 illustrates the action of *get* and the file buffer on another **file of** *real*.

Why bother with the file buffer, *get*, and *put* when you have *read* and *write*? Good question. There can sometimes be a slight speed advantage to deferring

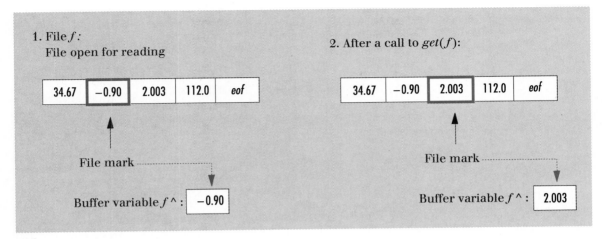

1. File *f*:
File open for reading

| 34.67 | −0.90 | 2.003 | 112.0 | *eof* |

File mark

Buffer variable *f* ^ :   −0.90

2. After a call to *get(f)*:

| 34.67 | −0.90 | 2.003 | 112.0 | *eof* |

File mark

Buffer variable *f* ^ :   2.003

Figure 11.4.   Reading from a file using the file buffer and *get*

actual file access (that is, making a call to *get* or *put*) until you need to do so, and there are times when you might want to use the file buffer to "peek" at the next component of a file, without actually transferring its value to your program via *read*. We don't use these low-level operations very much, and we'd guess that you won't either.

General Files and Textfiles Compared

We mentioned at the outset that the only kinds of files we really need are textfiles, and we hope that your experience in this chapter has convinced you that this is the case. In essence, if we can write it on the screen, we can store it in a textfile, and it's hard to imagine any information we would want to save from a Pascal program that we couldn't represent on a screen. Except for a desire for completeness, then, why did we include mention of binary, non-textfiles at all? As we've seen, at the heart of the majority of problems in computer science is an attention to the ecology of using a physical machine to manipulate information. This ecology is devoted to the efficient use of two scarce resources—storage space and time, and it's in these terms that we can compare textfiles and binary files.

The question of efficient use of time is the simpler, albeit less precise, of the two. Simply put, it takes longer to read and write textfiles than it does to read and write binary forms because the character representation of information must be converted to the computer's internal representations. The problem, however, is that though these conversions might take a few thousandths of a second, these milliseconds mount up when the system has to do them for what may be several thousand, or even tens of thousands of, reads or writes on a textfile.

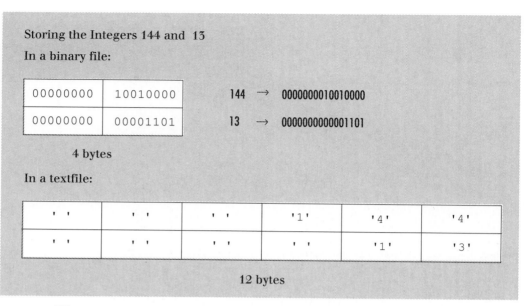

Storing the Integers 144 and 13

In a binary file:

00000000	10010000
00000000	00001101

144 → 0000000010010000

13 → 0000000000001101

4 bytes

In a textfile:

' '	' '	' '	'1'	'4'	'4'
' '	' '	' '	' '	'1'	'3'

12 bytes

Figure 11.5.   Storing integers in binary files and textfiles

Conversion between textfile character format and internal memory format takes time.

To investigate the difference between textfiles and binary files in terms of space, consider the following example. In many computers, the largest possible integer is 32767, which it obviously takes five characters to represent in human-readable textfile form. We'll allow an extra character at the front for either a blank or a minus sign so that the system can tell where one integer ends and the next begins. A character is typically stored in a byte of eight binary digits, so we need at least six bytes to store an integer in our hypothetical textfile. A binary file, on the other hand, represents integers in the same way that they are represented internally—by sixteen binary digits. Sixteen bits fit exactly in two 8-bit bytes, so the binary **file of** *integer* takes one-third as much space on disk to store the same amount of information as does a textfile of integers, assuming a default integer width of six characters. This is illustrated in Figure 11.5.

Binary files generally take up less space than the equivalent textfiles.

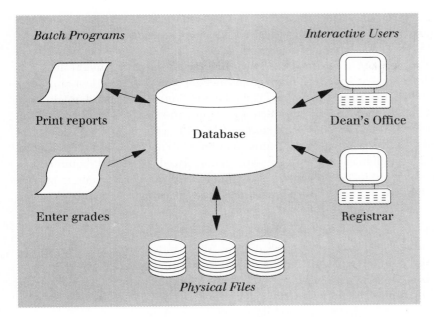

Batch Programs   *Interactive Users*

Print reports   Database   Dean's Office

Enter grades   Registrar

Physical Files

Figure 11.6. An overview of a database management system (DBMS)

11.6
Computer Science Interlude: Database Management

Once we can store information permanently and access it by a program, a wealth of applications become available that can be enhanced by computers. Today, we take for granted that airline reservations, factory inventory and personnel information, college and university record-keeping, banking, and the like are handled by computers. With a little work, we can all imagine what it must have been like to manage all these records without the computer. In this section, we'll look briefly at an example of a system that performs this kind of data management: a *database management system (DBMS)* for a college or university.

We can look at a DBMS as a large collection of logically related information that can be accessed and modified in controlled ways by any number of programs and users. Some of these programs will be *batch programs* that handle large amounts of information and that may take considerable amounts of time to accomplish their processing. Others will be *interactive programs*, requiring immediate action on a small subset of the available information. The DBMS will also access a number of files in which information is stored more or less permanently, as we illustrate in Figure 11.6.

In our example, typical batch programs would update grades for all students at the end of each term, produce student grade reports, print a summary of financial aid paid to all students in a given year, or generate the income tax information for all employees of the institution. Typical interactive programs might allow the Dean's Office to post a medical leave of absence for John Smith or look up John's performance in his courses last term. The registrar, on the other hand, might need to change John's grade in Computer Science 1 from "Incomplete" to "B" once John has recovered from mononucleosis and finished the coursework, or add a new section of a course to adjust for an increase in enrollments in CS1 in the fall term.

Database management systems are characterized by several requirements, many of which are just codifications of common sense. We don't intend to provide a comprehensive list here, but some features are easy enough to deduce. You can probably come up with a number of other criteria.

- First, such a system must permit the *handling of large amounts of information over extended periods of time*. Most students, for example, will be represented in the system for at least four years (much longer if the database is going to be used by the Alumni Office), and there could easily be thousands of students, enrolled in hundreds of courses, taught by hundreds of faculty members in dozens of departments.

- Second, the system must provide *efficient access to information*. The Dean of Students Office, for example, would not want to have to wait for two months after the end of the term to find out who is in academic trouble, nor would they want to write their own programs to determine this term's Dean's List candidates.

- Third, the system must be *internally consistent* so that a student who takes a leave of absence will not have his or her name remain active in the billing office. If a student record is updated, the new information should be available immediately in all contexts.

- Fourth, the system should permit *several modes of the information it stores*. The view of the database that the Registrar has will probably be very different from that of the Financial Aid Office.

- Fifth, the system should provide *security* by restricting the ability to inspect and modify information to only the information that a particular user has a need to know. For instance, the federal government requires the Registrar to record students' ethnic background, the Financial Aid Office needs to know the family income of scholarship recipients, and the Dean's Office needs access to any disciplinary information on a student. Your advisor might need to be able to look up your college address, the courses you've taken, and the grades you received in those courses but certainly should be denied access to information about your race or family income.

- Finally, the system should be *resilient* so that, for example, a power outage or flood will not destroy the records of all students who entered within the past fifteen years.

Part of most DBMSs is a *database language*, or *query language*, that allows users to communicate with the database in an efficient way. The Pascal language allows the programmer to manipulate the entities of a program, and query languages have a similar function in that they allow users to act on the database. A typical query, to find all the advisees of Rick Decker who are in serious academic difficulties, might look something like this:

```
SELECT NAME
FROM ADVISEES
WHERE FAC_NAME = 'Rick Decker'
    AND STUDENT.GPA < 2.0;
```

Designing a database as large as our example is a daunting task to contemplate. Just off the top of our heads, we can come up with a partial list of information that our example DBMS might use: Each student has a name, a student ID, a campus address, a home address, an expected year of graduation, a major (perhaps), and a list of courses in each term, along with the grades in each course. Each course has a list of students and their grades, one or more instructors, a name, and one or more departments responsible for the course. Each faculty member has a list of courses taught in a given term (if he or she isn't on leave), a collection of advisees, a name, an address, a rank and salary, and one or more departments with which he or she is associated. Just categorizing all the relevant information seems hideously difficult, and we haven't even begun to program yet.

As anxious as we might be to start writing code, the fact that we haven't done so yet is a good thing. Since a database is likely to be very complex, researchers in the field uniformly agree that we must have a logical model of the database before we can even begin to develop it. A considerable amount of work has gone into thinking about a good model for a database, and there is much research being done even as we write this. There are several logical models of databases; we'll present one of the most common, the *relational model*.

Starting at the bottom, we first identify the entities that will be represented in our database. An *entity* is any object that can be distinguished from others, so a person is an entity, as are a department and a course. An entity set is a set of similar entities, in whatever sense we define "similar," so {Classics, Mathematics, English} is an entity set of departments. An entity may have *attributes* associated with it, so a student as an entity has attributes such as a name, an ID number, an address, and so on. Some attributes characterize an entity uniquely: These are called *keys*, so though there may be two students named Jane Jones, only one has the key ID 277625090. An entity may have more than one key. For example, it may take a department name, course number, and section number to identify a course uniquely, since the Departments of Music, Physics, and Sociology all might offer a course numbered 100, and there may be more than one section of Sociology 100.

A *relation* is an ordered list of entity sets, generally expressed in tabular form. For example, we might have a relation TAKES that describes student enrollment in a course. The relation TAKES, shown in Figure 11.7, may be defined on the sets STUDENT, COURSE, and GRADE, which we would write

TAKES	STUDENT	COURSE	GRADE
	Jones, T.	CS 241	C+
	Wang, C-Y.	CS 241	B
	Kelly, R.	CS 241	C
	Wang, C-Y.	ART 101	B−
	Jain, N.	ART 101	A+
	Valence, M.	ECON 150	A−
	Smith, R.	ECON 150	B
	Wang, C-Y.	ECON 150	A

Figure 11.7.   A relation

TAKES(<u>STUDENT</u>, <u>COURSE</u>, GRADE), with the underlined sets being the keys, indicating that there will never be more than one row with the same student and course.

The relationship between students and courses is called *many-many*, since one student may take more than one course, just as one course will typically have many students. A relationship between faculty and department, on the other hand, might be *many-one* at institutions where each faculty member holds an appointment in a single department.

We can represent the overall structure of a database graphically in an *entity-relation diagram*, as in Figure 11.8. In such a diagram, entities are represented by rectangular boxes, their attributes by ovals, and the relations between entities by diamonds. These figures are connected by arcs, with an arrow indicating a many-one or one-one relationship. We can see, for example, that one faculty member may advise several students, each student has only one advisor, many students may take many courses, but for each (student, course) pair there is a unique grade.

After settling on a collection of entities, attributes, and relations, there are standard operations to convert these to one of several *normal forms*. The goal of reducing relations to normal form is to modify them so that the transition from logical model to physical model will be as painless as possible.

The *physical model* of a DBMS is where we implement the logical model on a computer, in terms of files and a programming language. We might, for instance, have a file of students in which each student is represented by a record that contains the key field *ID*, along with non–key fields for student name and a list (by course ID) of courses taken and grades for these courses. We might also have a course file, where each course is also represented by a record containing course

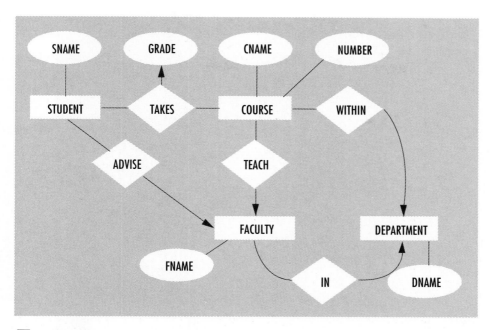

Figure 11.8.   An entity-relation diagram

name, ID, and a list of student IDs. These choices would have been dictated in part by the relations in our logical model. Notice that we resisted the temptation to include grades in the course file—when we normalized our logical model, we saw that it was redundant to put grades in two places.

To design the rest of our DBMS, we have to ask the same questions we ask whenever we begin to write a program. What data structures and algorithms shall we use to represent and manipulate information in our system? For instance, we could load the student records into an array, load the course records into another array, and have in the student records a list of indices to the courses, as in Figure 11.9. With this arrangement, it's easy to produce a course list, for example (for each course, run through the array of student pointers, find the indexed element in the array, and print the student name and grade).

We might also decide to keep the students sorted by name, since one of the requirements is fast response to queries. If the elements of the student array are sorted by name, it's much easier to select a student by name using a binary search. The point is, of course, that it is not enough to have done all the work of organizing the logical model—however much it helps us conceptualize the database—if the algorithms and data structures slow performance down to a crawl.

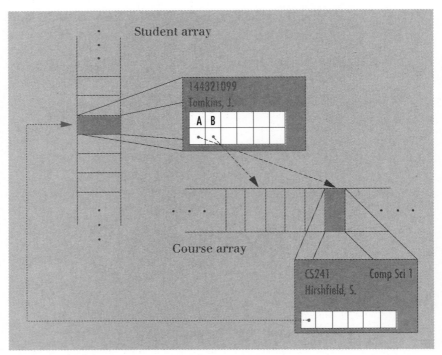

Figure 11.9.   Linking elements in two arrays

11.7 Reference

- The *text* type is a file of characters, usually stored on a disk. Textfiles are referred to in a program by a *file variable* of type *text*.
- Textfiles are opened by using the built-in procedures *reset* (for reading from a file) and *rewrite* (for writing information onto a file). Both procedures require a file variable and a file name as parameters. For example, to prepare a file named "My File" for reading, we might make the procedure call *reset(f, 'My File')*, which establishes a logical link in the program between the file variable *f* and the file named "My File." Thereafter, any reference to *f* would be understood to be a reference to "My File."
- With each textfile, there is a *file mark* that points to the location in the file where we are about to write or read. *Reset* sets the file mark to the beginning of the file so that the program will begin reading from the first character. *Rewrite* also sets the file mark to the first character, but it empties the file if the file name is that of an existing file, or it creates a new, empty file if there is no file on disk having the given file name.

- Textfiles are read and written just as the *standard files* for input from the keyboard and output to the screen. In other words, any input/output you can do to the standard files, you can also do to a file of your own. The procedures *read*, *readln*, *write*, *writeln*, and *eoln* can be used with textfiles by including the file variable as the first parameter. For example, the procedure call *read(f, ch)* will read a single character, *ch*, from the file associated with the file variable *f*. Similarly, the function call *eoln(f)* returns *true* if the character about to be read from the file *f* is the end-of-line character.

- An additional file function is *eof(fileVariable)*, which returns *true* if the file mark (the character about to be read) is the special end-of-file mark, indicating that there is nothing more in the file beyond the mark.

- File access in programs is generally performed in the following fashion:

```
reset(f);               {or rewrite, for writing}
while not eof(f) do     {as long as there is something left in the file}
  begin
    while not eoln(f) do   {Read a line.}
      begin
        Read information from the file and process it.
      end;
    readln(f)           {Discard eoln character.}
  end;
```

- Textfiles need not contain only characters — the information in a textfile can be integers or reals, as well. These are read and written just as characters are.

- The nonstandard procedure *close(fileVariable)* is used when you are finished reading or writing from a file. It severs the logical link between the file variable and a physical file on a disk. Any file that has been opened by *reset* or *rewrite* should be closed before the program ends.

- The predefined routines *get* and *put* explicitly manipulate the file buffer. If *f* is a file variable, *f^* refers to the contents of the file buffer. The procedure *get(f)* causes the value stored at the current file mark to be placed in the file buffer, and the procedure *put(f)* appends the contents of the file buffer to the end of the file *f*.

11.8
Building Blocks

To open a file for reading (input), we use the standard procedure *reset*:

var
   t : **text**;
   f : **file of** EmpRec;
⋮
reset(t);
reset(f);

To open a file for writing (output), we use the standard procedure *rewrite*:

var
   t : **text**;
   f : **file of** EmpRec;
⋮
rewrite(t);
rewrite(f);

Although we cannot use an assignment statement to copy the contents of one file to another, the following procedure accomplishes what we need.

```
procedure Copy(var fromFile, toFile : text);
    var
        s : string;
begin
    reset(fromFile);
    while not eof(fromFile) do
        begin
            readln(fromFile, s);
            writeln(toFile, s)
        end
end;
```

If we didn't have strings available, we could copy one textfile to another by reading and writing character by character, as follows. Note particularly what we had to do to duplicate the end-of-line marks, since they read as blanks.

```
procedure Copy(var fromFile, toFile : text);
    var
        c : char;
begin
    reset(fromFile);
    {We could rewrite toFile here, but we want to be}
    {able to use this routine for concatenation.      }
```

```
        while not eof(fromFile) do
            begin
                while not eoln(fromFile) do
                    begin
                        read(fromFile,c);
                        writeln(toFile,c)
                    end;
                readln(fromFile);   {Read past end-of-line mark.}
                writeln(toFile)     {Write an end-of-line mark.}
            end
    end;
```

Files are sequential access devices, as we've seen. We can simulate random access with the following procedure, which returns the n-th component of a file, if there is one.

```
    procedure ReadNthItem(var f : DataFile ; n : integer ; var theData : DataType ; var success :
                            boolean);
        var
            count : integer;
    begin
        if n < = 0 then
            begin
                writeln('Improper file position in ReadNthItem. Must be positive.');
                success : = false
            end
        else
            begin
                reset(f);
                count : = 0;
                while (not eof(f)) and (count < n) do
                    begin
                        read(f, theData);
                        count : = count + 1
                    end;
                if count = n then
                    success : = true
                else
                    begin
                        writeln('No position ', n : 1, ' in the file.');
                        success : = false
                    end
            end
    end;
```

The program *EchoToFile* acts like *Copy* (and, in fact, we could use *Copy* here, with only minor modification). *EchoToFile* writes to a text file exactly what was entered on the standard input device. Notice that the *reads* and *writes* are paired, in keeping with our "write in the same way you read" rule.

```
program EchoToFile(input, savedFile);
    var
        num1, num2 : integer;
        c : char;
        savedFile : text;
begin
    rewrite(savedFile);
    readln(num1, num2);
    writeln(savedFile, num1, num2);
    while not eoln do
        begin
            read(c);    {Read a character.}
            write(savedFile, c)
        end;
    close(savedFile)
end.
```

EchoToScreen is the reverse of *EchoToFile*, in that it displays the contents of a textfile on the standard output device.

```
program EchoToScreen(output, savedFile);
    var
        num1, num2 : integer;
        c : char;
        savedFile : text;
begin
    reset(savedFile);
    readln(savedFile, num1, num2);
    writeln(num1, num2);
    while not eoln(savedFile) do
        begin
            read(savedFile, c);
            write(c)
        end;
    close(savedFile)
end.
```

11.9

EXERCISES

xercises 1–5 refer to the following declarations.

```
type
    DataRec = record
                    name : string[25];
                    ID : integer;
                    hours : array[1 .. 366] of real
                end;
    Employees = array[1 .. 150] of DataRec;
    DataFile = file of DataRec;
    EmpFile = file of Employees;
var
    emp : Employees;
    thisPerson, thatPerson : DataRec;
    d : DataFile;
    e : EmpFile;
    f : text;
```

1. Identify which of the following statements are syntactically legal. For those that are not legal, explain why.

   a. reset(d, e, f)
   b. writeln(f, emp.name[3])
   c. writeln(emp[72].ID)
   d. read(d, thisPerson)
   e. read(f, thisPerson)
   f. for i := 1 to eof(d) do
          read(d, emp[i])

2. Identify which of the following statements are syntactically legal. For those that are not legal, explain why.

   a. read(e, thisPerson)
   b. writeln(d, emp[50])
   c. writeln(emp[72])
   d. read(e, emp)
   e. read(d, thisPerson, thatPerson)
   f. i := 0;
        while not eof(d) do
          begin
             i := i + 1;
             read(d, emp[i])
          end

3. The following procedure constructs the array *emp* from the file *d*. There's nothing syntactically wrong with it, but it may not run correctly. Explain the problem and fix it.

```
procedure ReadFile(var emp : Employees ; var d : DataFile);
    var
        i : integer;
begin
    reset(d);
    i := 0;
    while not eof(d) do
        begin
            i := i + 1;
            read(d, emp[i])
        end
end;
```

4. The following procedure stores the array *emp* in the textfile *f*. There are syntactic as well as run-time errors in the procedure. Rewrite it correctly.

```
procedure BuildFile(var emp : Employees ; f : text);
    var
        i, j : integer;
begin
    reset(f);
    for i := 1 to 150 do
        begin
            read(f, name, ID);
            for j := 1 to 366 do
                write(emp.hours[j]);
            writeln(f)
        end;
    close(f)
end;
```

5. Write the companion routine for Exercise 4 that will construct the array *emp* from the file *f*.

6. Why is a textfile allowed to contain end-of-line markers, whereas a binary file is not? Specifically, aren't there times when an end-of-line mark would be useful in a binary file?

Exercises 7 and 8 deal with a computerized inventory. The inventory for the Midnight Auto Parts Company is stored as a textfile. Each item in the inventory is stored in the file as follows:

> *Part number : integer*
> *Part name : a string of no more than 25 characters*
> *Number on hand : integer*
> *Price : real*

In the file, each element is separated from the next by an end-of-line mark. Write routines to perform the tasks specified in the next two exercises.

7. a. Create the initial file by asking the user for the data for the four fields for each part record and writing the values to a file. Close the file when the user enters -1 for the part number.

   b. Print a summary, suitably formatted, of the inventory represented by a file.

8. a. Create a new file of orders from a given inventory file, where an order is made for new items as follows:

   i. For each item with a price over $100.00, order enough items so that there is one item left in inventory.

   ii. For each item with a price less than or equal to $100.00, order enough items so that there will be five items on hand.

   For each item that needs to be ordered, the order file should contain the part number and the number to be ordered.

   b. Print the remaining inventory total in a file. In other words, print the total dollar value of all items on hand.

   c. Combine parts a and b to produce a complete inventory. In other words, given an inventory file and an order file, compute and display the retail price of items on hand less the cost of orders. Assume that the cost of ordering an item is half the price of the item.

   d. Update the inventory file, given a file of sales in a given day (part number and number sold) and the inventory file at the start of the day. The sales file might have several sales for a single item, so it might look like the following, where we've included explanatory comments that wouldn't be part of the file. Each record is separated from the next by an end-of-line mark, and the two numbers in each record are separated by blanks.

1013 3	*3 items of part number 1013*
239 1	*1 item of part number 239*
1013 1	*1 more item of part number 1013*
4774 12	*12 items of part number 4774*

9. Write **type** declarations that would be appropriate to store the following data objects in memory, and indicate briefly how you would save the objects as textfiles.

   a. A class list of students, including their names and scores (0 .. 20) on five quizzes, two exams (0 .. 100), and a final (0 .. 300).

   b. The current state of a game of chess (those of you who aren't chessplayers will have to do a little more research than those who are).

   c. A black and white picture, as on a computer screen. You may assume that a picture is made of black or white pixels (jargon for dots), 640 pixels across and 480 pixels down.

10. Do Exercise 9 for binary files, and describe the space saving in each case, if any. You may assume that in textfiles an integer or integer subrange will require six bytes, that boolean values require one byte, that characters require one byte, and that strings require as many bytes as their current length. In binary files, you may assume that an integer, integer subrange, or user-defined ordinal requires two bytes, boolean values and characters require one byte, and strings require 256 bytes.

11. How would you sort a file of integers, assuming that there was enough room in memory to store the entire file as an array of integers? You may assume that the file is of type *text*. Just give a high-level description—you needn't write detailed code.

12. How would you sort a file of integers, assuming that there was only enough room in memory to store half of the entire file as an array of integers? (This is a hard problem, and there are many acceptable answers.)

13. Suppose you had two textfiles of integers, each of which was sorted from smallest to largest. Write a subprogram to *merge* the two files, producing a single file consisting of the contents of the two input files arranged in sorted order. For example, the merge of files containing 3, 15, 18, 25, 39 and 4, 7, 22, 41, 44 would be 3, 4, 7, 15, 18, 22, 25, 39, 41, 44.

14. Write a subprogram that would take a file that had been opened for reading, and count and display the number of words, the average word length, the number of lines, and the average number of words per line. You may assume that the input file was a PasWord 2.0 file. You may want to look over Exercise 26 of Chapter 6.

15. Write a program that would take two PasWord 2.0 files and produce a file that reports how they differ. The resulting file should be of the same format as the input files and should consist of only the lines that were different in the two files. In other words, if the two files differed only in line six, both copies of line six would be included in the output file, one after the other.

16. Write a program that will:

a. Convert a PasWord 2.0 file to a PasWord 2.1 file.
b. Convert a PasWord 2.1 file to a PasWord 2.0 file.

17. Write a procedure that will completely reverse the contents of a PasWord 2.0 document, producing the lines in reverse order, and reversing the contents of each line. The input and output should be PasWord 2.0 files. For example, for the file consisting of the first part of this exercise, the output would be ".selif 0.2 droWsaP eb dluohs tuptuo dna tupni ehT .enil hcae . . ." and so on.

18. Revise PasWord 2.0 so that it performs automatic backup. In other words, after every five commands, the current document will be written to a file named *backup*. Include a new command, R, that will allow the user to revert to the backup copy, replacing the current document by the one saved in the backup file.

19. In Chapter 6, we counted the relative frequency of letters in the textfiles that we produced in writing Chapters 5 and 6. To do this, we wrote a program that opened and read the textfiles for Chapters 5 and 6, counted the number of instances of each letter ('a' .. 'z', 'A' .. 'Z'), and printed the number of letters of each kind (ignoring any differences between upper- and lowercase) divided by the total number of letters in each file. Show how we did that.

20. Do Exercise 19 using a textfile of your own. Most word processors allow you to convert their outputs to textfiles that you can use as input to your program. How do your results compare with the frequency table in Chapter 6?

21. Write a program that will read a textfile and count the number of times a character appeared adjacent to the same character. For example, given a file containing 'boob-bookkeeper', the program would display 2 2 2 2 2, corresponding to the two o's, b's, o's, k's, and e's.

22. Modify *EncryptCaesar* from Chapter 6 so that it accepts a textfile as input and produces a textfile as output.

23. Write a procedure that will interleave two textfiles, producing a file for the shuffled result. The result should consist of the first character of file 1, the first character of file 2, the second character of file 1, the second character of file 2, and so on. For example, if file 1 consisted of 'ABCDEF' and file 2 consisted of 'WXYZ', the result would be 'AWBXCYDZEF'. Your procedure should open and close all files as needed; don't assume that the files are open when the procedure is called.

In Exercises 24 and 25, suppose that f is of type IntFile, *which is a* **file of** *integer. Write the following routines, assuming throughout that the file has not been opened at the time of the subprogram call and is to be closed at the conclusion of the subprogram.*

24. a. function *Count*(**var** f : *IntFile*) : *integer*, which returns the number of integers in the file.
   b. procedure *Insert*(n, p : *integer* ; **var** f : *IntFile*), which inserts n into the file f at position p. If there are fewer than p elements in the file, or if p is less than or equal to zero, the procedure should do nothing.
   c. procedure *Prune*(**var** f : *IntFile*), which deletes the first, third, fifth, . . . elements from f.

25. a. function *Sum*(**var** f : *IntFile*) : *integer*, which returns the sum of the elements in f or returns zero if f is empty.
   b. procedure *Delete*(p : *integer* ; **var** f : *IntFile*), which deletes the element in position p from the file f. If there are fewer than p elements in the file, or if p is less than or equal to zero, the procedure should do nothing.
   c. procedure *Reverse*(**var** f : *IntFile*), which reverses the contents of f. *Hint:* There is a fairly simple recursive way to do this.

26. Which of the operations of Exercise 24 are substantially different from the way they would be if f were replaced by an array of integers?

27. Which of the operations of Exercise 25 are substantially different from the way they would be if f were replaced by an array of integers?

28. There's another reason why files must be passed as **var** parameters. When we perform any file operation, something is being changed, whether or not the contents of the file change. What is the "something" that is changed every time we do anything to a file?

29. What does the following routine do? Assume that *DataFile* = **file of** *DataType*.

```
procedure Whatsis(var f : DataFile ; n : integer ; var d : DataType);
   var
      i : integer;
   begin
      for i := 1 to n do
         get(f);
      d := f^
   end;
```

11.10 Answers

1. **a.** Illegal; the procedure *reset* may have only one parameter.
   b. Legal.
   c. Legal; we're writing an integer to the standard output device.
   d. Legal; we're writing a value of type *DataRec* to a **file of** *DataRec*.
   e. Illegal; we cannot write a compound variable to a textfile; we'd have to write each of the fields piecewise, including each element of the array.
   f. Yuck; very illegal. As we said, *eof* is a boolean function, so it would be completely inappropriate where an integer is expected.

3. There's no guarantee that the file contains less than or equal to 150 elements, so we might find ourselves in the position of running over the range of the array *emp*. The fix is to put another guard in the **while** loop, like this:

   ```
   while (not eof(d)) and (i < 150) do
   ```

5. ```
   procedure ReadFromFile(var emp : Employees ; var f : text);
       var
           i, j : integer;
   begin
       reset(f);
       for i : = 1 to 150 do
           begin
               write(f, emp[i].name, emp[i].ID);
               for j : = 1 to 366 do
                   write(emp[i].hours[j]);
               readln(f)
           end;
       close(f)
   end;
   ```

7. **a.** ```
   procedure BuildFile(var f : text);
       var
           partNum, onHand : integer;
           partName : string[25];
           price : real;
   begin
       rewrite(f);
       writeln('To stop building the file, enter −1 when asked for ');
       writeln('the part number. ');
       writeln;

       write('Part number? ');   {Prime the pump—get first number.}
       readln(partNum);
       while partNum <> −1 do   {Are we done yet?}
           begin
               writeln(f, partNum);   {If it's good, write it to the file,}
   ```

```
            write('Part name? ');      {and get the rest of the data.}
            readln(partName);
            writeln(f, partName);

            write('Number on hand? ');
            readln(onHand);
            writeln(f, onHand);

            write('Price? ');
            readln(price);
            writeln(f, price : 6 : 2);

            writeln;
            write('Part number? ');      {Get the next part number.}
            readln(partNum)
        end;
      close(f)
  end;
```

b. **procedure** PrintSummary(**var** f : text);
```
        var
            num, onHand : integer;
            name : string[25];
            price : real;
    begin
        reset(f);
            writeln(' Number      Name      OnHand Price');
            writeln('_____');
            while not eof(f) do
              begin
                readln(f, num);
                write(num : 8, ' ');
                readln(f, name);
                write(name : 25, ' ');
                readln(f, onHand);
                write(onHand : 8, ' ');
                readln(f, price);
                writeln(price : 6 : 2)
              end;
            close(f)
    end;
```

9. a. **type**
```
        StuRec = record
                    name : string [25];
                    quiz : array [1 .. 5] of 0 .. 20;
                    exam1, exam2 : 0 .. 100;
                    final : 0 .. 300
                  end;
        Class = array [1 .. 45] of StuRec;
```

We could write this to a file in much the same way as we did in Exercise 5.

b. type
```
    Piece = (pawn, knight, bishop, rook, king, queen);
    Color = (black, white, none);
    Square = record
                occupiedBy : Color;
                kind : Piece
             end;
    Board = array [1 .. 8, 1 .. 8] of Square;
```

Since we can't write ordinal types to a textfile, we'd have to send the *ord* of variables to type *Piece* and *Color*, and then translate the text values when we read the board from the file into memory.

c. type
```
    Picture = array [1 .. 640, 1 .. 480] of boolean;
```

As in part b, we can't write the boolean values to a textfile, so we could write to the file by writing ones and zeros, suitably formatted (using one character for each pixel, separated by blanks or end-of-line marks).

11. The most direct way would be to read the file into an array, use a sorting algorithm like *Quicksort* on the array, and then write the array back onto the file.

13. This is a somewhat complicated algorithm, but we provided a solution because it embodies a technique that can sometimes be useful. The basic idea of merging is to read a value from each of the two input files, compare them, and write the smaller value to the output file, after which we read a new value to replace the one we just transferred to output. The trick is to signal that there is no more to read from a file by sending *maxint*, since that will never be the smaller of the two values. To see the value of this technique, try writing this algorithm without it.

```
procedure Merge(var in1, in2, out : text);
    var
        n1,            {The most recent number read from file in1.}
        n2 : integer;  {The most recent number read from file in2.}

    function GetAValue(var f: text) : integer;
    {Reads a number from the file f, if possible. If there's}
    {nothing more to read, returns maxint as a signal.    }
        var
            n : integer;
    begin
        if not eof(in1) then
            read(f, n)
        else
            n := maxint;
        GetAValue := n
    end;

begin
    reset(in1);
    reset(in2);
    rewrite(out);

    n1 := GetAValue(in1);
    n2 := GetAValue(in2);
```

```
        while (n1 < maxint) or (n2 < maxint) do
            if n1 < n2 then
                begin
                    write(out, n1);
                    n1 := GetAValue(in1)
                end
            else
                begin
                    write(out, n2);
                    n2 := GetAValue(in2)
                end;
        close(in1);
        close(in2);
        close(out)
    end;
```

15. Use *ReadDoc* to read both files into memory. Then, for each line, use string comparisons to see if the corresponding lines in each document are the same. If they're not, write each to a change file. The only difficulty comes from the case where the two documents are not of the same length. In that case, run through all remaining lines of the larger document, writing them to the change file.

17. Use *ReadDoc* to read the file into memory. Then, for each line, use the procedure *Reverse* from Chapter 6 to reverse each line. Finally, modify *SaveDoc* so that it writes the lines from *doc.totalLines* **downto** 1 to the file. This, by the way, is a very common file-handling strategy: Place the file in memory, manipulate it, and extract the resulting memory image to the file. We did much the same thing in Exercise 15.

19.
```
program LetterCount(output, ch5, ch6);
    type
        CountArray : array ['A' .. 'Z'] of integer;
    var
        count : CountArray;
        ch5, ch6 : text;
        c : char;
        total : integer;

    procedure DoCount(var f : text ; var count : CountArray);
        var
            ch : char;
    begin
        reset(f);
        while not eof(f) do
            begin
                while not eoln(f) do
                    begin
                        read(f, ch);
                        if ('a' <= ch) and (ch <= 'z') then
                            ch := chr(ord(ch) - ord('a') + ord('A'));
                        if ('A' <= ch) and (ch <= 'Z') then
                            count [ch] := count [ch] + 1
                    end;
```

```
                readln(f)    {Discard end-of-line mark.}
            end;
        close(f)
    end;

begin
    for c : = 'A' to 'Z' do
        count[c] : = 0;

    DoCount(ch5, count);
    DoCount(ch6, count);

    total : = 0;
    for c : = 'A' to 'Z' do
        total : = total + count[c];
    for c : = 'A' to 'Z' do
        writeln(c, ' ', count[c]/total : 6 : 4)
end.
```

21.
```
program Duplicates(output, inFile);
    var
        inFile : text;
        oldChar, currentChar : char;
        dups : integer;           {Counts the number of adjacent duplicates seen so far.}
begin
    reset(inFile);
    oldChar : = chr(0);           {A dummy character, to get things started.}
    count : = 1;                  {Haven't seen any dups yet.}
    while not eof(inFile) do
        begin
            while not eoln(f) do
                begin
                    read(f, currentChar);
                    if currentChar = oldChar then
                        count : = count + 1
                    else           {We've reached the end of a run.}
                        begin
                            if count > 1 then
                                write(count, ' ');
                            count : = 1;
                            oldChar : = currentChar
                        end
                end;
            readln(f);            {Read past end-of-line mark.}
            if count > 1 then     {The end of a line is always the end of a run.}
                write(count, ' ');
            oldChar : = chr(0);
            count : = 1
        end;
    close(inFile)
end.
```

23. This is somewhat like *Merge* in Exercise 13 but much easier.

25. a. **function** Sum(**var** f : IntFile) : integer;
{Assumes f has been reset immediately before the call.}
    var
       n : integer;
  begin
    if eof(f) **then**
      Sum : = 0
    else
      begin
        read(f, n);
        Sum : = n + Sum(f)
      end;
    close(f)
  end;

b. **procedure** Delete(p : integer ; **var** f : IntFile);
    var
      i, n : integer;
      temp : text;
  begin
    reset(f);
    rewrite(temp);
    i : = 0;
    while $(i < p - 1)$ **and** (**not** eof(f)) **do**
    {Copy the first $p - 1$ elements from f to temp, if possible.}
      begin
        read(f, n);
        write(temp, n);
        i : = i + 1
      end;
    if (**not** eof(f)) **and** $(p >= 1)$ **then**   {We're okay—there is a p-th element to delete.}
      begin
        read(f, n);   {Read and discard the p-th element.}
        while not eof(f) **do**   {Put the rest of f, if any, into temp.}
          begin
            read(f, n);
            write(temp, n)
          end;
        rewrite(f);
        reset(temp);
        while not eof(temp) **do**   {Copy temp into f.}
          begin
            read(temp, n);
            write(f, n)
          end
      end;
    close(f);
    close(temp)
  end;

c. The key here is to stack the values from the file in pending procedure calls. Once all the values have been read, backing out of the pending calls while writing will reconstruct the file in reverse order. To understand what goes on, try drawing nested boxes as we did in Chapter 7.

```
procedure Reverse(var f : IntFile);
    var
        n : integer;
begin
    if eof(f) then
        rewrite(f)
    else
        begin
            read(f, n);
            Reverse(f);
            write(f, n)
        end
end;
```

27. *Delete* could be done much more efficiently with arrays. We could simply shift everything from position n to the end of the array by one position, as we did in Chapter 9. Although *Sum* and *Reverse* could be done recursively as in the answers to Exercise 25, it would be tidier (and simpler) to use **for** loops and avoid recursion entirely.

29. It's a simplified (and faster) version of *ReadNthItem*, with no error-checking.

Variables on the Fly: Pointers

There is just one more Pascal data type we have to cover, the *pointer* type. Pointers are very powerful and very useful in that they allow us to do things in Pascal that we simply couldn't do with the data types we know so far. They are also different in fundamental ways from any other Pascal data type, and this means that they may be difficult to understand at first. The first difference is that pointers are *dynamic*, in the sense that they may be created and destroyed explicitly by a program while it is running. The second difference between pointers and other types is that pointers require *indirect access* to information. This is a consequence of the dynamic nature of pointers, and it is where the major conceptual hurdle of pointers resides. We hope that when you finish this chapter you will agree with us that the time taken to learn to use pointers was time well spent.

OBJECTIVES

In this chapter, we will:

- Describe the process whereby storage for variables is allocated and deallocated (made available).
- Define the notion of a dynamic variable.
- Describe how information can be accessed "indirectly."
- Define and illustrate Pascal's **pointer** data type.

- Describe the predefined values and operations that help us work with pointers.
- Work with this chapter's PIP, a final, pointer-based implementation of PasWord.
- Describe and implement some established techniques for manipulating pointer-based structures.

12.1 Dynamic Variables

See Section 12.6 for a further discussion of operating systems and what they do.

Consider an integer variable *sum*. When your Pascal compiler sees the tokens *sum : integer*; in the variable declaration part of a program or subprogram, it generates code that, in effect, tells the system, "Find an integer-sized location in memory that's not currently being used, and assign that location now, and for as long as the program or subprogram runs, to the variable *sum*." The compiler generates this code in the form of instructions to the *operating system*, a program that is permanently in operation while the computer is running. The job of the operating system is to manage the *resources* of the machine—its memory, the central processing unit, and any other devices that are part of the system, like disk drives, the keyboard, and the screen. For example, the operating system allocates chunks of memory for our program and handles all the tedious details of opening files and writing to the screen and the disk.

For all the data types you've seen so far, once they are allocated in memory, they stay in memory for the duration of the program. They cannot be shrunk, enlarged, or destroyed—they are *static*.[1] This generally doesn't cause too much difficulty, and indeed you probably haven't given it much thought. One problem with static variables, though, is that we generally don't know ahead of time exactly how much room in memory we'll need to store all the information a program must manipulate. For instance, we may have to declare an array to be large enough to hold all the information we think we'll need, whether we actually use all of it or not.

PasWord is a good example. Because the central data structure of PasWord is an array of lines, we had to decide at the beginning that a document could contain no more than *MAXLINES* lines of text (64 in the Program in Progress of Chapter 10). This means that the documents we can process are smaller than the PasWord source code itself, which contains much more than 64 lines of code. We could make the upper limit larger by changing the constant declaration to *MAX-LINES* = 10000, but this creates two new problems. First, there is the distinct possibility that the system on which the program is to be run does not have enough memory to allocate storage for such a large array. Even if it does, the static nature

---

[1] Files aren't static, but they are also treated differently from other types, so our discussion really doesn't apply to them. You will notice some notational similarities between files and pointers shortly, which point out (pun intended) some functional similarities between the two.

of the array means that it will occupy a considerable chunk of memory that may never be used during the execution of the program. Although we *may* need a thousand (or more) lines in a document, there are many times when a PasWord document will be only five or ten lines long. In such cases, all the rest of the document is taking up space in memory (and, in PasWord 2.1, in the file) for no useful purpose.

The primary advantage of dynamic data types is that we can create and destroy variables at any time during the execution of a program, giving us much greater control over the amount of memory a program uses. If we could make our document dynamic, we could create a new line every time we needed one (for an insertion, for instance), and destroy a line whenever it was no longer needed (after a deletion, say). This way, the document would never be any larger in memory than it needed to be, thereby conserving the limited resource of memory in the most efficient way possible.

A secondary advantage of dynamic structures derives from the way they are allocated. When we declare an array of lines to hold PasWord's document, we assume that the lines are contiguous in memory—that is, right next to one another. That's why we had to write the *ShiftArray* procedure to move lines around in the static array. With dynamic lines, a document consists of a collection of separate objects in memory and is not part of a single monolithic variable. In a program like PasWord, this is a big win for two reasons. First, it means that we don't have to write the equivalent of a *ShiftArray* routine, since storage of the document is spread around in memory. Second, it means that we can avoid the problems that occur in some systems because single variables have a limited size. In other words, our document of logically linked but distinct objects could grow as large as the total amount of available memory if need be.

What we really need is to be able to construct a large object from small pieces so that instead of a large array-like entity, for instance, we have a logically equivalent linked collection of small objects. We can do this if we put a pointer in each element of the list that does not *contain* the next element in the list but rather *refers* to the next cell in the list. In the example of Figure 12.1, we would then have the equivalent of a large static structure, but it would be made of distinct dynamic parts, none of which had to be anywhere near the others in memory, and which could be rearranged at will. Bear this desideratum in mind—it vitally influences the way pointers are defined and used.

See the discussion of the ecological nature of computer science at the end of Section 11.5.

12.2 Pointer Data Types

A pointer to a given type is nothing but an address in memory where an object of that type may be stored. In other words, a pointer variable does not contain an object but instead contains a reference to that object.

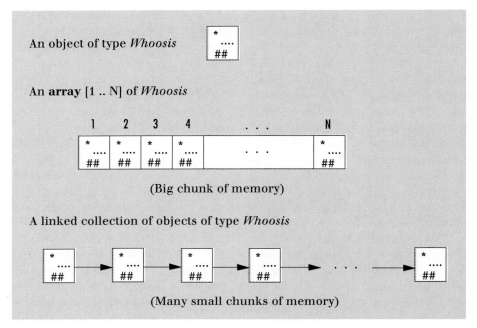

An object of type *Whoosis*

An **array** [1 .. N] of *Whoosis*

(Big chunk of memory)

A linked collection of objects of type *Whoosis*

(Many small chunks of memory)

Figure 12.1.   Two very different ways to represent a list

We declare a pointer to an object of a given type by using a **type** declaration that looks like ^*Type Name* or, if your keyboard contains the up-arrow character, ↑*Type Name*. As we did with the file window, we'll use carets in the body of the text and in the listing of the Program in Progress. All of the following are legal **type** declarations.

```
type
   IntPtr = ^integer;        Pointer to an integer.
   Temps = record
                high, low : real
            end;
   TempPtr = ^Temps;         Temps has been declared, so we can make a pointer to a
                             Temps-type object.

var
   p, q : IntPtr;
   t : TempPtr;
   realRef : ^real;          As usual, we can define anonymous types.
```

In the example, *p* may eventually contain an address in memory of the start of the location where an integer may be stored, and *t* may eventually contain an address of the start of a larger location in memory where the pair of real numbers of a *Temps*-type record may be stored.

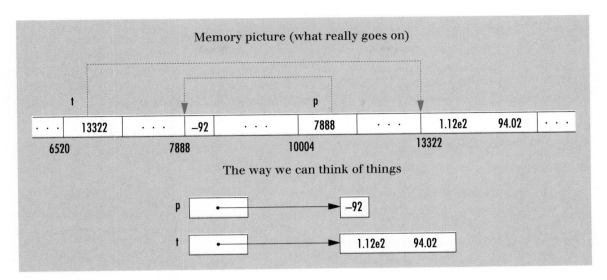

Figure 12.2. Two ways of thinking about pointers

As with other types, you cannot count on the fact that pointers will be initialized to anything useful. At the time of their declaration, all you know about p, q, t, and *realRef* is that the compiler has seen to it that these variables are large enough to hold memory addresses (usually 16, 24, or 32 bits). What they contain at this time, though, may not have anything to do with a real address in memory.

Eventually, the program will give these variables something to point to; we'll see how this is accomplished in a moment. For the time being, let's suppose that these pointers have been given something to point to. Then there are two levels of abstraction we may consider. We can think in terms of addresses in memory, or better still, we can think of a pointer as physically pointing to something.

In Figure 12.2, the pointer variable p is located in memory at address 10004 and contains as its value the address 7888. Memory location 7888 is, then, where p points. Similarly, the pointer variable t happens to be located at memory location 6520 and contains as its value the address 13322, which is where we consider t pointing to. All of this address manipulation is handled invisibly by the operating system, and we are free to think of variable p as pointing to some integer-sized location in memory and variable t as pointing to some location that is large enough to hold two real numbers. If this seems confusing, consider a real-world analogy: Rick Decker's office address is 219 Christian Johnson Hall, but to send mail to him, all you have to do is make sure it gets to Hamilton College. Mort, who delivers the mail, acts like the operating system: He knows the building and room address, so you don't need to be concerned with the details.[2]

---

[2]Unlike an operating system under the direction of a Pascal program, Mort will tell you the room and building, if asked.

Once we have declared a pointer variable, we can refer to the thing it points to by following the variable name with a caret or an up-arrow. In the example we have been using, then, $p\hat{}$ is the target of p and hence is of type integer.[3] In a similar way, $t\hat{}$ is a record of type *Temps*, and we can refer to it by itself, or we could use the field selectors to refer to its two fields, $t\hat{}.high$ or $t\hat{}.low$. These targets, followed by carets or up-arrows, may be used in any way that variables of the corresponding types may be used, as in the following examples.

N*otice how similar this is to the use of the caret that defines the file window: If* f *is a* **file of** *integer, then* f$\hat{}$ *is an integer variable, and if* p *is of type* $\hat{}$*integer, then* p$\hat{}$ *is an integer variable.*

```
p^ := q^ + 6;
readln(p^);
if p^ > 0 then
    spread := t^.high − t^.low;
```

Notice that the caret is used in two different ways: to declare a pointer type and to refer to the target of a pointer variable. This is a common enough cause of syntax errors that it is worth emphasizing.

> **T**o declare a pointer type, use the caret or up-arrow *before* a type name; to refer to the target of a pointer variable, use the caret or up-arrow *after* the variable name.

Pointer Operations

Since pointers are so different from other types, we should expect that the rules for their use are different, and indeed that's the case. There are only five things we can do with pointers. In the explanations that follow, assume that we have issued the following declarations:

```
type
    IntPtr = ^integer;
var
    p, q : IntPtr;      {pointers to integers}
    n, m : integer;     {ordinary integer variables}
```

OPERATION 1. *We can give a pointer something new to point to.* To do this, we make use of the predefined procedure *new(p)*. You can think of this as (1) an instruction to the operating system to find an available location in memory for p to point to (the size of which is dictated by the type of p), followed by (2) an instruction to store the address of the new location in p, thereby making p point to the new location.

---

[3]In technical terms, to refer to the target of a pointer is to *dereference* the pointer.

For example, after the compiler has read the preceding declarations, but before any statement has been executed, we have a memory snapshot that looks like this:

Remember these from Chapters 3 and 5?

```
p  |  ?? |
q  |  ?? |
n  | ?? |
m  | ?? |
```

The variables p, q, n, and m have been allotted places in memory, but they have not yet been initialized. We can initialize the pointer variables by using *new* on the pointers and by simple assignments to the static integer variables:

```
new(p);
new(q);
n := 13;
m := −8
```

After executing these statements, our memory snapshot would appear as:

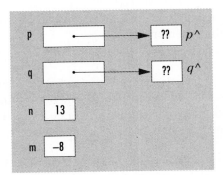

Notice now that all four variables contain information—two contain addresses and two contain integers. Notice also that we can now refer to $p\hat{}$ and $q\hat{}$, where we couldn't before, since p and q didn't have anything to point to until we called *new*.

Problem-solving technique

It is an error to refer to the target of a pointer if that pointer does not point to anything. If you have a program that uses pointers and you get a cryptic error message like "nil dereference," "address error," or "bus error," it is almost certainly because the program refers to the target of a pointer that doesn't point anywhere.

Notice also that $p\hat{}$ and $q\hat{}$ don't contain any useful information, since they have not yet been initialized. We can, of course, easily remedy this by making two more assignments,

```
p^ := n + m;
q^ := n - m
```

which would yield the following picture:

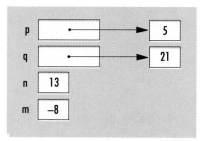

O P E R A T I O N **2.** *We can make assignments between pointers of the same type.* In our example, since p and q are both pointers to integers, we can assign one to the other. If, for instance, we made the statement

```
q := p
```

what would happen? Thinking of the address model, this assignment statement would cause the value in p (an address) to be copied into the variable q. In our conceptual model, the effect would be to cause q to point to the same location that p points to, yielding the following picture:

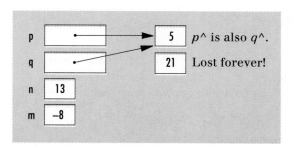

Notice two potential sources of error. First, by redirecting q we have destroyed the reference to the old location $q\hat{}$. Since q was the only pointer to—and the only way to reference—that location, the value in the old cell is irretrievably lost. The cell is still taking up room in memory, but there's no way of getting to its value, since its address is a closely kept secret, known only to the operating system. The same problem would have arisen if instead of $q := p$, we had called $new(q)$. This would have allocated a new cell and made q point to it, thereby leaving the old target of q lost in memory.

When redirecting pointers, be careful not to leave any "orphans" in memory—that is, cells with no pointers to them.

Another potential source of confusion in this example is that since p and q point to the same location, the targets $p\hat{}$ and $q\hat{}$ are two names for exactly the same variable. In other words, $p\hat{}$ and $q\hat{}$ are now aliases. That by itself is no problem, but you have to be aware that if you now performed the statement $p\hat{} := p\hat{} + 1$, you would also be changing the value of the (same) object known as $q\hat{}$. This could cause problems if you had made a logic error in your understanding of the program and expected $p\hat{}$ and $q\hat{}$ to be different objects.

*W*e saw aliasing before in Section 7.1.

OPERATION **3.** *We can compare pointers of the same type for equality and inequality.* This means that the boolean operators $=$ and $<>$ may take pointers (of the same type) as operands. We could use this to test whether we are in an aliasing situation, for example, by writing

```
if p = q then     {Test whether p and q point to the same location,}
   p^ := p^ + 1   {and if they are, we only need to change p^.}
else
   begin
      p^ := p^ + 1;
      q^ := q^ + 1
   end
```

By the way, beware that $=$ and $<>$ are the *only* relational operators that may act on pointers. In spite of the fact that pointers are addresses, and one can imagine testing whether one address is before another in memory, we can't do it in standard Pascal.

OPERATION **4.** *We can refer to a special pointer constant called* **nil.** The **nil** pointer has two peculiar properties: First, it is compatible with pointers of any type, and, second, it never has a target. We frequently use **nil** as a sentinel—an end marker—in a linked structure (as we pictured in Figure 12.2) to indicate that there are no further cells. We cannot dereference a **nil** pointer, which is to say we cannot refer to its target (since it has none), but we can assign **nil** to any pointer, and we can test whether any pointer is or is not equal to **nil**.

In our continuing example, we could make the assignment

q := **nil**

which would again redirect q, this time to the **nil** value, as follows.

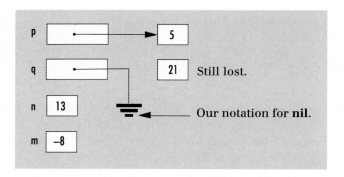

Having done so, it would be an error to refer to $q\hat{}$.

O P E R A T I O N **5.** *We can cancel the current reference of a pointer.* By calling the predefined procedure *dispose*(p), we do two things: (1) We return the target $p\hat{}$ to available (unused) memory, and (2) we leave p itself uninitialized, rendering any further reference to $p\hat{}$ invalid until we again give p something to point to (either by assigning p to another pointer or by using *new*(p)).

The purpose of *dispose* is to avoid cluttering memory with cells that are no longer being used.[4] In a sense, *dispose* is the inverse operation to *new*: Where *new* gives a pointer something to point to and forms a link between the pointer and its target, *dispose* cuts the link between a pointer and its target, thereby leaving the pointer with nothing to point at.

In our example, if we called

dispose(p)

we would not only free the old cell $p\hat{}$, but we would leave p as an uninitialized variable, containing nothing of any particular use. In particular, we could not then refer to $p\hat{}$, since p no longer has anything to point to. It's worth mentioning that we could not call *dispose*(q) in this example, since q already has no target.

---

[4]That's the intention, anyway. Since it's tricky to tell the operating system to change the status of a memory location from "used" to "available," some compilers allow calls to *dispose*, but don't generate any code when they translate the procedure call.

Problem-solving technique

Attempting to dispose of a **nil** pointer, or one that has already been disposed of, is a very common source of error.

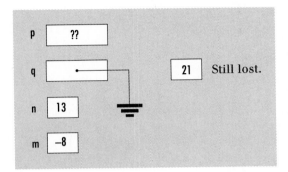

Finally, notice that in all the pictures we have drawn, the boxes for p and q haven't moved at all. The values in the boxes have changed, but p and q, like n and m, are static variables. This leads us to the following subtle, but more precise, characterization of pointers.

Pointers are static. What they point to is dynamic.

That's it — those are the only things one is allowed to do with pointers. We'll conclude with some examples of things we cannot do. You should try to figure out why each statement is illegal. Of course, the simplest reason in each case is, "It's not one of the five things we're allowed to do with pointers." By the way, all of these statements are perfectly legal if we replace the pointers p and q with their targets $p\hat{\ }$ and $q\hat{\ }$.

```
{A COLLECTION OF ERRONEOUS STATEMENTS,}
{assuming that p and q are pointers.}
p := q + 1;
readln(p);
write(p, q);
if p < q then
    writeln('Early in memory')
```

A Strange Example, with a Deferred Moral

Consider the following completely correct program segment. Look it over and see if you can figure out what it does. It will help to use a hand trace, drawing boxes and arrows, as we've done in the examples.

```
new(p);
new(q);
write('Enter two integers');
readln(p^, q^);
new(s);
s^ := p^ + q^;
writeln(s^);
dispose(p);
dispose(q);
dispose(s)
```

Got it? This segment gets two integers and writes their sum. Of course, it does so in a particularly inefficient fashion. We don't need the pointers at all in this example, since we could equally well have written the far simpler segment,

```
write('Enter two integers');
readln(n, m);
writeln(n + m)
```

We gave this example solely to force the question, "Why use pointers at all?" We'll readily admit that nothing we've covered in this section gives us the slightest indication that pointers have any use whatsoever, beyond complicating things that we can do perfectly well without them. Think of this section as practicing scales before you can become competent at the piano — it's apparently pointless but absolutely necessary. However, if you read the introduction of this chapter over, look at the Program in Progress, and pay careful attention to the explanation that follows, you'll be richly rewarded, as promised, with a powerful and indispensable tool for your programmer's kit.

12.3 Problem Solving III: Analyzing Pointers

Since our new design reflects a different choice for the program's central data structure, let's begin our dissection of PasWord 3.0 by looking at the **type** declaration part of the main program.

```
type
   ⋮
   LinePtr = ^LineCell;          {**NEW**}
   LineCell = record
                  theLine: Line;   {Line is defined as before.}
                  next: LinePtr
              end;
   Document = LinePtr;          {**NEW**}
```

In these declarations, the fundamental unit is the *LineCell* record. An object of this type consists of a line, defined as before as a string. Along with the line, the cell contains another field, *.next*, which is a pointer to another object of type *LineCell*, and that's where the promised power of pointers comes in.

> **T**he most common (and valuable) use of pointers is with pointers to a record, one or more fields of which are pointers to other records.

Take a look at Figure 12.3, in which we illustrate the use of records with pointers in PasWord 3.0. As with any compound data structure, simple parts are combined to create more complicated ones, which are then combined to make even more complex combinations. To create a document, we build a line cell for the first line, then create another line cell and link the first cell to that, then create a new third cell and link the second to that, and so on, for as many cells as we have lines. Notice in Figure 12.3 that we use a **nil** pointer in the last cell to indicate that no further cells follow.

Declarations

Conceptually, structures linked by pointers are quite simple. The complexity comes in the details, but we'll try to unravel the confusion as gently as possible. In the **type** declaration of our PIP, we have defined what is known as a *linked list*. The first detail to notice about the **type** declarations for the *Document* linked list is that there is an apparent error. If you've gotten into the habit of muttering "Declare before use, declare before use" while you write **type** declarations, you've probably noticed that we declared *LinePtr* = ^*LineCell* before we had declared *LineCell*. Unfortunately, there is simply no way to avoid violating the declare-before-use rule here: If we had declared *LineCell* before *LinePtr*, we'd still have a problem since the definition of *LineCell* uses *LinePtr*. Pascal allows us to break the rule in pointer-to-record declarations because there's no other way, but the standard does stipulate the order in which these declarations must occur.

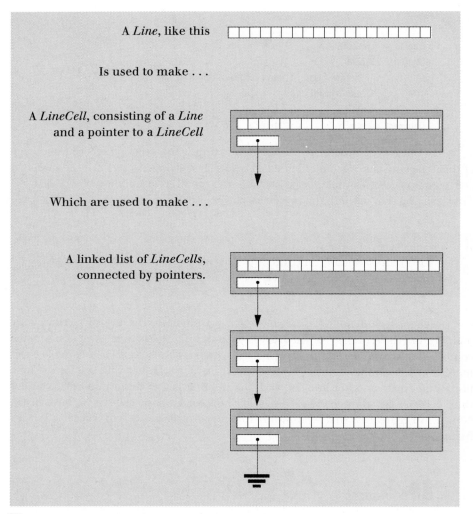

A *Line*, like this

Is used to make . . .

A *LineCell*, consisting of a *Line*
and a pointer to a *LineCell*

Which are used to make . . .

A linked list of *LineCells*,
connected by pointers.

Figure 12.3.   Representing a linked list

If you declare a pointer to a record, and the record uses a pointer of that type in its definition, the pointer type declaration must precede the record type declaration.

If we may anthropomorphize a bit, here's what the compiler may be regarded as saying to itself when it sees a pointer definition. "I haven't seen the type this pointer points to. Okay, I'll go back and fill in the definition as soon as I come to

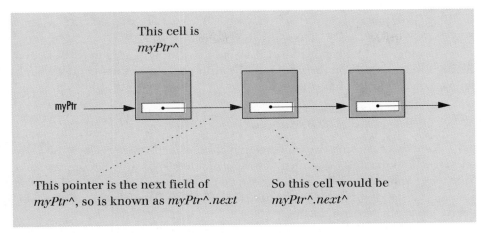

This cell is
*myPtr^*

myPtr

This pointer is the next field of
*myPtr^*, so is known as *myPtr^.next*

So this cell would be
*myPtr^.next^*

Figure 12.4.   Names of entities in a linked list

the **type** declaration for what the pointer points to, and if I don't get a declaration sooner or later, I'll give up and report an error." In a sense, declaring a pointer to a record acts like an implicit **forward** directive, similar to the one we saw in Chapter 7. Programming this is more work for the compiler designer, which is one reason for the declare-before-use rule in all other instances. We are allowed to violate the declare-before-use rule because a pointer is an address, and addresses are all the same size, regardless of the size of whatever they refer to.

Names

We've seen that the target of a pointer p may be referred to as $p\char"5E$. Names for targets get more complicated when we deal with linked structures. Suppose that *myPtr* was of type *LinePtr*, and pointed to a cell, as in Figure 12.4. The object *myPtr* points to is denoted *myPtr^* — that's simple enough. Now, *myPtr^* is a record, so we select its fields using the usual field name selector, and thus the pointer in the cell *myPtr^* would be called *myPtr^.next*. So far so good, but what about the rest of the linked list?

The second cell in the list is pointed to by the pointer *myPtr^.next*, so we would refer to it as *myPtr^.next^*. In a similar way, the third cell would be called *myPtr^.next^.next^*, the fourth cell would be called *myPtr^.next^.next^.next^*, and so on. In PasWord 3.0, each of these cells is a record, so we would refer to the line field of the second cell in the list as *myPtr^.next^.theLine*. We could further select within that line, since it's a string, so we could refer to the third character of the second line in the list by using *myPtr^.next^.theLine*[3]. Most people find this proliferation of carets and selectors somewhat confusing at first, but fortunately we rarely have to go to such lengths, as you'll see.

List Traversal

Issuing the "P" command in PasWord causes the procedure *ShowDoc* to display a range of lines on the screen. In the array version, this was controlled by a simple loop that looked something like:

> **for** lineNum : = start **to** finish **do**
>   *Write the* (lineNum)-*th line of the document*

That was easy, since we could refer to *doc.theLine*[*lineNum*] using the array selector to find the line we wanted to write. For a linked list, though, things are a trifle more complicated. For one thing, we don't have direct access to a particular line. As you saw, if *p* pointed to the first line cell in the list, the *i*-th cell would be referred to by the rather forbidding

> p^.next^.next^.next^. . . . .next^   {with *i* − 1 copies of *.next^*}

Clearly, there must be a better way. What we want is the pointer equivalent of $i := i + 1$, in effect moving a pointer one cell farther down the list, so that repeated invocations would cause a pointer to inspect every cell in the list in order. If you look back at Figure 12.4, you'll see how to do just that. If *p* points to a cell in a linked list with a pointer field *.next*, then the assignment

> p := p^.next

will have the effect of making *p* point to the same cell that *p^.next* currently points to. This is one of the fortunate side effects of having *p* and the *.next* field of each record be the same type. Figure 12.5 illustrates this effect.

> **T**o traverse a linked list, start with *p* pointing to the first cell in the list, and then repeatedly do *p* := *p^.next* (using the appropriate name for the pointer fields in the cells) until *p* has value **nil**, indicating that the end of the list has been reached.

Don't forget, the **nil** sentinel isn't put at the end of a list automatically. You have to put it there while you're building the list and make sure it stays there as you add and delete cells from the list.

Notice that the PasWord 3.0 *Document* type is defined by a pointer to the first line cell in the list. That means that to write the contents of the entire document, we must traverse the list, writing a line, *next*-ing our way down the list, and stopping when we find a *next* pointer that is the sentinel value **nil**.

> **procedure** WriteAll(d : Document);
> {This is NOT part of PasWord 3.0. It's a simplified}
> {version of the procedure ShowDoc.   }

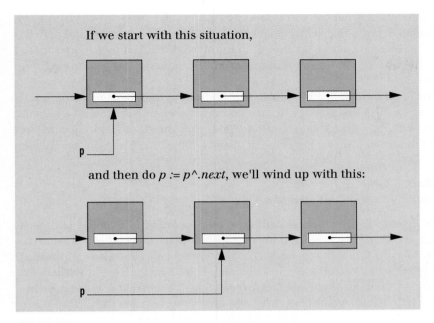

If we start with this situation,

p

and then do $p := p\hat{}.next$, we'll wind up with this:

p

Figure 12.5. Traversing a linked list

```
    var
        currentPtr : LinePtr;
begin
    currentPtr : = d;                    {Start at the first cell.⁵}
    while currentPtr <> nil do           {We're not at the end of the list, so}
        begin
            PrintALine(currentPtr^.theLine);   {write the current line,}
            currentPtr : = currentPtr^.next    {and advance to the next cell.}
        end
end;
```

More Traversal: Locating the *n*-th Cell

When called to show a document, PasWord doesn't always print the entire document but rather prints a range of lines. That's not hard, as long as we have two pointers, *startPtr* and *finishPtr*, that point to the first and last cells we want to display. How, though, do we find *startPtr* and *finishPtr*? The *ShowDoc* routine gets

---

⁵We don't really need *currentPtr* here. We could use *d* in its place, and upon completion of the procedure, *d* would still point to the first cell in the list. Do you see why?

two line numbers and not the corresponding pointers. We need a way, given n, to make a pointer to the n-th cell in a linked list. What we need is a function, *FindNth*, that takes an integer n and a pointer, d, to the start of a linked list, and returns a pointer to the n-th cell in the list if there is such a cell, and signals failure if there is no n-th cell.

This is very much like the problem of finding the n-th person standing in a line, and we can use this analogy to write the function *FindNth*. To find a person, we simply walk down the line, counting "One, two, three," and so on, until we either find the person we want or come to the end of the line. The loop statements, then, will be:

```
cellNum := cellNum + 1;      {Count,}
currentPtr := currentPtr^.next   {and advance.}
```

We should start the process with *currentPtr* pointing to the head of the list and initialize *cellNum* to 1, since if *currentPtr* points to the head of the list, that cell is the first. In other words, we want *currentPtr* and *cellNum* to advance in lockstep, referring at any time to the same cell. If we decide to use a **while** loop, what should the exit condition be? Well, we have two things that should cause the traversal to halt: Either we run out of cells in the list or we reach the one we want. The second condition is easily expressed—we've reached the cell we want when $cellNum = n$. The first exit condition is also simple if we adopt the convention that our list will have a **nil** sentinel. In that case, we see that we should get out of the loop when $currentPtr = $ **nil**. Putting these together, we exit the loop when $(currentPtr = $ **nil**$)$ **or** $(cellNum = n)$, and so the loop condition is just the negation of this statement, $(currentPtr <> $ **nil**$)$ **and** $(cellNum <> n)$. We can now write the entire function:

```
function FindNth (n: integer; d: Document): LinePtr;
{Returns a pointer to the n-th cell in the linked list d, }
{if such a cell exists, otherwise returns nil.          }
    var
        currentPtr: LinePtr;   {the current position in the list}⁶
        cellNum: integer;      {the number of the current cell}
begin
    currentPtr := d;
    cellNum := 1;
    while (currentPtr <> nil) and (cellNum <> n) do
        begin
            cellNum := cellNum + 1;
            currentPtr := currentPtr^.next
        end;
    FindNth := currentPtr
end;
```

[6]See if you can think of a way of writing *FindNth* without using either of the two local variables.

This function returns a pointer as its result, you'll notice. That's perfectly acceptable, since pointers are simple types (that is, without the compound structure of arrays, records, sets, and files) and the standard allows functions to return any simple type.[7] One other thing to notice is that the function returns *currentPtr* whether it succeeds or fails. The nice thing about this is that if *FindNth* fails to find an *n*-th cell (either by having fewer than *n* cells or by being given a meaningless value for *n*, like −4), it will return—after having traversed the entire list—with *currentCell* equal to **nil**. This can serve as a clear signal to the calling routine that there was no *n*-th cell in the list starting at *d*.

We are finally ready to write *ShowDoc* so that it displays a range of lines. Given integers representing the start and finish line numbers, we can use *FindNth* to convert the integer line numbers to their corresponding pointer values in our list. *ShowDoc* can then use the pointers to control its traversal. The segment of *ShowDoc* that does that looks like this:

```
PrintALine(startPtr^.theLine)      {Write the first line.}
printPtr := startPtr;              {Initialize our moving pointer.}
while printPtr <> finishPtr do     {If we haven't written the last line,}
  begin
    printPtr := printPtr^.next;    {then advance to the next one,}
      ...
    PrintALine(printPtr^.theLine); {and write it.}
  end;
```

In this segment, we "primed the pump" by writing the first line and then entered the loop to advance the cell pointer before printing again. We could have reversed the loop statements to print first and then advance to the next cell within the loop, but then the loop condition *printPtr <> finishPtr* would have stopped the loop before we printed the last line. To do things in this order would have required us to stop at the cell *after* the last cell, and that would have required the uglier condition *printPtr <> finishPtr^.next*. Things don't improve significantly if we use a **repeat** loop, since then we'd still have to check for the cell after the last cell.

Cautions About Pointers

There are two final details we need to cover about pointers. The first is very minor and is highly unlikely to occur. The second is a consequence of the nature of pointers that makes perfect sense once you've thought about it but is something that you might not consider unless it's been pointed out.

We talked about the **with** statement at the end of Chapter 10. Using the **with** statement with a record identifier eliminates the need to refer to the identifier when referring to its fields. Suppose that *currentLinePtr* was of type *LinePtr*. The

[7]We do have to be careful, though, since we're not allowed to dereference function calls that return pointers. In other words, it's wrong to write *thisLine := FindNth(3, d)^.theLine*, although it would be legal to do this with two statements: *q := FindNth(3, d) ; thisLine := q^.theLine*.

record name of the line cell, *currentLinePtr^*, is somewhat cumbersome, so we could use a **with** statement to simplify things. In this example, the intent is to dispose of a line that has no characters.

```
{ILLEGAL EXAMPLE}
with currentLinePtr^ do
   begin
      ⋮
      if Length(theLine) = 0 then
         dispose(currentLinePtr);
      ⋮
   end
```

That's perfectly reasonable, but we can't do it this way. The reason is that Pascal doesn't permit a pointer to be disposed of while it is still in use (by the **with** statement). That makes sense, since there might be field references after the *dispose* call. If there were, they would refer to fields of a line cell that no longer existed. In this case, we'd just have to bite the bullet, not use the **with** statement, and type in long identifier names.

The final caution concerns the use of pointers as parameters. Remember that a pointer is an address in memory where something else is stored. We might have a PasWord 3.0 routine, for example, that would be given a line pointer and a string and would replace the current line at that location with the string, like this:

```
procedure Update(p : LinePtr ; newLine : Line);
begin
   p^.theLine : = newLine
end;
```

If you think about it, you'll see that there's something going on here that's different from what happens with other types. We're not changing p at all in this procedure. The address it has is the same before and after the call, so there's no reason to make p a **var** parameter. We are, however, changing the contents of $p^$, the target of p. There's no way in the parameter list to indicate whether we're changing the target of a pointer, so Pascal was designed so that changes to the target of a pointer are always made globally, just as if the target was a global variable of a **var** parameter.

> **I**f a pointer is passed as a parameter to a subprogram, changes made to the target of the pointer are always available to the calling routine, whether the pointer was passed as a value or variable parameter. However, changes to the pointer itself are local to the subprogram if the pointer was passed as a value parameter. In short, pointers passed as parameters follow the usual value/variable rules of modification, whereas the targets of pointers always act as if they were **var** parameters.

12.4 Problem Solving V: Modifying PasWord

ur PIP for this chapter is an exercise in program reimplementation— we've taken a working program and rewritten it to reflect a new design. Functionally, PasWord 3.0 is identical to PasWord 2.0. It performs exactly the same operations as did the earlier versions. In the latest version of PasWord, the major change is in the structure of a document. As promised earlier, we no longer have a single large data structure for the document, but rather we have a linked collection of dynamic lines. Thus, a PasWord 3.0 document is limited in size only by the amount of available memory and has the added virtue of using memory much more efficiently.

The first difference you will see in reading the listing of *DocHandler3* is that there are several new subprograms, *FindNth*, *Tail*, *InsertAtHead*, *Insert*, *Delete-Head*, and *Delete*. These form a "package" of routines to maintain the linked structure that is used to represent a document. You'll also notice that the **type** declarations for a document and its supporting structures have been changed. About the only thing that hasn't changed is the definition of the *Line* type and— note carefully—the main program! One of the big advantages of using units is that if we design the unit as we should, hiding all of the implementation details from the program, we can make radical changes to the unit (as we do here) and never have to change the program that uses it.

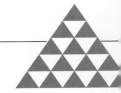

The PIP

unit DocHandler3;

```
{————————————————————————————————————————}
{                                                          }
{                    PROGRAM IN PROGRESS                    }
{                                                          }
{                        CHAPTER 12                         }
{                                                          }
{   This unit contains subprograms that handle insertion,  }
{   deletion, modification, and printing of lines in a document. }
{   It also allows saving and retrieving a document from a }
{   textfile.                                              }
{   NOTE: This version manages a document as a linked list, }
{   using pointers.                                        }
{                                                          }
```

```
{----------------------------------------------------------------}
{            SUBPROGRAM LIST:                                    }
{            Initialize (var d: Document)                         **CHANGED**}
{            DoInsertion (var d: Document; lineNum: integer)      **CHANGED**}
{            DoDeletion (var d: Document; lineNum: integer)       **CHANGED**}
{            DoChange (var d: Document; lineNum: integer)         **CHANGED**}
{            ShowDoc (d: Document; start, finish: integer)        **CHANGED**}
{            SaveDoc (d: Document ; var f: text)                  **CHANGED**}
{            ReadDoc (var d: Document; var f: text)               **CHANGED**}
{--------                                                        }
{            GetALine (var newLine: Line)                        }
{            PrintALine (d: Document; lineNum: integer)           **CHANGED**}
{            Swap (var thingOne, thingTwo: integer)             }
{--------                                                        }
{            FindNth (n: integer; d: Document): LinePtr           **NEW**}
{            Tail (d: Document): LinePtr                          **NEW**}
{            InsertAtHead (l: Line; var d: Document)             **NEW**}
{            Inert (l: Line; p: LinePtr; var d: Document)         **NEW**}
{            DeleteHead (var d: Document)                         **NEW**}
{            Delete (p: LinePtr; var d: Document)                **NEW**}
{                                                                }
{----------------------------------------------------------------}
```

interface

  const
    MAXLENGTH = 80;   {max characters per line}

  type
    Line = **string**[MAXLENGTH];

    LinePtr = ^LineCell;   {**NEW** definitions for a linked list of lines}
    LineCell = **record**
            theLine: Line;
            next: LinePtr;
        end;

    Document = LinePtr;   {**NEW** We refer to a document by a pointer to its first line.}

procedure Initialize (**var** d: Document);
procedure DoInsertion (**var** d: Document; lineNum: integer);
procedure DoDeletion (**var** d: Document; lineNum: integer);
procedure DoChange (**var** d: Document; lineNum: integer);
procedure ShowDoc (d: Document; start, finish: integer);
procedure SaveDoc (d: Document ; **var** f: text);
procedure ReadDoc (**var** d: Document ; **var** f: text);

implementation

{──────────────── PRIVATE UTILITY ROUTINES ────────────────}

```
procedure GetALine (var newLine: Line);
begin
   {See Chapter 10.}
end;

procedure PrintALine (theLine : Line);
begin
   writeln(theLine)
end;

procedure Swap (var thingOne, thingTwo: integer);
begin
   {See Chapter 10.}
end;
```

{──────────────── LINKED LIST ROUTINES ────────────────}

```
procedure Initialize;    {(var d: Document)}
{Initializes document to be an empty list of lines.}
begin
   d : = nil
end;

function FindNth (n: integer; d: Document): LinePtr;
{Returns a pointer to the n-th cell in the linked list d,}
{if such a cell exists, otherwise returns nil.           }
{Called by : DoInsertion, ShowDoc                        }
   var
      currentPtr: LinePtr;    {the current position in the list}
      cellNum: integer;       {the number of the current cell}
begin
   currentPtr : = d;
   cellNum : = 1;
   while (currentPtr <> nil) and (cellNum <> n) do
      begin
         cellNum : = cellNum + 1;
         currentPtr : = currentPtr^.next
      end;
   FindNth : = currentPtr
end;

function Tail (d: Document): LinePtr;
{Returns a pointer to the last cell of the linked list d,}
{if d is not empty, otherwise returns nil.               }
{Called by : DoInsertion, ShowDoc                        }
   var
      currentPtr: LinePtr;
```

```
begin
    currentPtr : = d;
    if currentPtr = nil then
        Tail : = nil
    else
        begin
            while currentPtr^.next <> nil do
                currentPtr : = currentPtr^.next;
            Tail : = currentPtr
        end
end;
procedure InsertAtHead (l: Line; var d: Document);
{Inserts line l at the head of the list d.}
{Called by : DoInsertion              }
    var
        temp: LinePtr;
begin
    new(temp);
    temp^.theLine : = l;
    temp^.next : = d;
    d : = temp
end;

procedure Insert (l: Line; p: LinePtr; var d: Document);
{Inserts line l after the cell pointed to by p in the list d.}
{Called by : DoInsertion                      }
    var
        temp: LinePtr;
begin
    new(temp);
    temp^.theLine : = l;
    temp^.next : = p^.next;
    p^.next : = temp
end;

procedure DeleteHead (var d: Document);
{Deletes the first cell in the list d.}
    var
        temp: LinePtr;
begin
    if d <> nil then    {Do nothing if the list d is empty.}
        begin
            temp : = d;
            d : = d^.next;
            dispose(temp)
        end
end;
```

```
procedure Delete (var p: LinePtr);
{Deletes the cell immediately after the cell pointed to }
{by p in list d. If there is no such cell, does nothing.  }
    var
        temp: LinePtr;
begin
    if p <> nil then     {shouldn't ever need this, but it protects the next statement}
        if p^.next <> nil then
            begin
                temp : = p^.next;
                p^.next : = p^.next^.next;
                dispose(temp)
            end
end;
```

{──────────────────────── COMMAND HANDLERS ────────────────────────}

```
procedure DoInsertion;    {(var d: Document; lineNum: integer)}
{Given a line number in the document, gets a new line and }
{inserts that line into the document, in position lineNum.    }
{If line number was out of range, automatically defaults      }
{to insertion at beginning or end of document.                }
{Calls : GetALine, FindNth, Tail, InsertAtHead, Insert        }
    var
        newLine: Line;
        insertionPtr: LinePtr;
begin
    write('...');
    GetALine(newLine);                         {Get line to be inserted.}
    writeln;
    if (lineNum <= 1) or (d = nil) then   {line num too low or empty document}
        InsertAtHead(newLine, d)
    else
        begin
            insertionPtr : = FindNth(lineNum — 1, d);
            if insertionPtr = nil then          {line num too high—insert at tail}
                Insert(newLine, Tail(d), d)
            else
                Insert(newLine, insertionPtr, d)    {line in interior—do ordinary insertion}
        end
end;

procedure DoDeletion;    {(var d: Document; lineNum: integer)}
{Deletes the line in position lineNum from the document }
{Calls :                                                }
```

```
begin
   {You'll fill this in.}
   writeln('Here"s where we"ll delete line ', lineNum : 1, '   NOT IMPLEMENTED')
end;

procedure DoChange;    {(var d: Document; lineNum: integer)}
{Change a specified line. Prints the original line, allows    }
{user to type in new line to replace one to be changed.      }
{Error if line number is out of range of lines in document.}
{Calls :                                                    }
begin
   {You'll fill this in later.}
   writeln('Changing line ', lineNum : 1, '   NOT IMPLEMENTED')
end;

procedure ShowDoc;    {(d: Document; start, finish: integer)}
{Prints lines of document from position 'start' to }
{position 'finish'. If these limits are invalid,    }
{defaults to printing entire document.              }
{Calls : PrintALine, FindNth                        }
   var
      lineNum: integer;
      startPtr, finishPtr, printPtr: linePtr;
begin
   if d = nil then
      writeln('Document is empty')
   else
      begin
      {Verify and fix parameters, if necessary.}
         if start > finish then              {limits out of order—swap them}
            Swap(start, finish);
         startPtr := FindNth(start, d);
         if startPtr = nil then              {lower limit out of range—set to list start}
            begin
               startPtr := d;
               start := 1
            end;
         finishPtr := FindNth(finish, d);
         if finishPtr = nil then             {upper limit out of range—set to list end}
            finishPtr := Tail(d);
         {Now that parameters are OK, do the printing.}
         printPtr := startPtr;
         lineNum := start;
```

```
        write(lineNum : 3, ' ');            {Write the first line number,}
        PrintALine(startPtr^.theLine);      {and print the first line}
        while printPtr <> finishPtr do      {for each subsequent line.}
           begin
              printPtr := printPtr^.next;    {Advance the pointer to the next cell,}
              lineNum := lineNum + 1;        {increase the line number,}
              write(lineNum : 3, ' ');       {write line number,}
              PrintALine(printPtr^.theLine)  {and print the line.}
           end
     end
end;
{————————————————— FILE ROUTINES —————————————————}
procedure SaveDoc;   {(d: Document ; var f : text)}
{Save current document as file f.}
   var
      currentLinePtr: LinePtr;
begin
   writeln('writing file . . .');
   rewrite(f);
   currentLinePtr := d;
   while currentLinePtr <> nil do                    {For every line . . .}
      begin
         writeln(f, currentLinePtr^.theLine);         {write the line to the file,}
         currentLinePtr := currentLinePtr^.next       {and advance the pointer to the next line.}
      end;
   close(f)
end;
procedure ReadDoc;   {(var d: Document ; var f : text)}
{Generates the document by reading it from file f.}
   var
      currentLinePtr: LinePtr;
begin
   writeln('reading file . . .');
   reset(f);
   if eof(f) then                                     {If the file is empty, create an empty document.}
      d := nil
   else                                               {If the file is nonempty, first create the first cell.}
      begin
         new(d);                                       {Save a pointer to the start of the document.}
         currentLinePtr := d;
         readln(f, currentLinePtr^.theLine);           {Read the first line into its cell.}
```

```
            while not eof(f) do                              {Now read the rest of the lines.}
              begin
                new(currentLinePtr^.next);                   {Build a new cell for the new line.}
                currentLinePtr := currentLinePtr^.next;      {Advance the line pointer.}
                readln(f, currentLinePtr^.theLine)           {Read a line into the cell.}
              end;
              currentLinePtr^.next := nil                    {Put a sentinel at the end of the list.}
          end;
        close(f)
      end;
    end.
```

12.5 Manipulating a Linked List

It's often necessary to be able to traverse a linked list, but if that were all we could do, there wouldn't be much point to going to all the trouble to learn pointers. Of course, PasWord does much more than that. The user can insert and delete lines, for example. Inserting and deleting entries from an array is a matter of shifting the contents of the array, either to make room for the new line or to fill the (conceptual) hole left by the deleted line. In this section, you'll discover that, although insertion and deletion in a linked list is not as simple to understand at first as it is in an array, the routines are considerably more efficient for linked lists than they are for arrays.

Insertion

Inserting a cell into a linked list is somewhat like inserting a new bead in a necklace of pop beads: We cut the link where we want the new cell to go and then connect the new cell to its neighbors on the left and right, thus restoring the integrity of the chain. For linked lists, this is an example of the kind of "pointer pushing" that is very common in such linked structures.

Figure 12.6 illustrates the steps we can use to insert a new cell. In this situation, the order of the steps is critical. If we reverse the steps and first link the list to *NewCell*, you can see that we would have destroyed any connection to the remaining part of the list, effectively losing it forever. We must first make sure that we have some connection to the list as a whole before we consider moving the pointer from the cell $p\hat{}$ to the cell $p\hat{}.next\hat{}$.

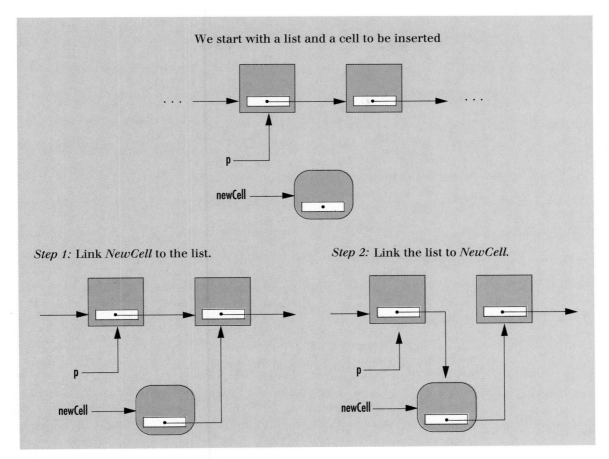

We start with a list and a cell to be inserted

Step 1: Link *NewCell* to the list. *Step 2:* Link the list to *NewCell.*

Figure 12.6. Inserting a cell into a linked list

How shall we write the code to do this? Step 1 tells us to "Make the *.next* pointer of *newCell^* point to the same location that the *.next* pointer of *p^* does." That's a direct assignment:

newCell^.next := p^.next

Step 2 tells us "Make the *.next* pointer of *p^* point to the same location as the pointer *newCell*," and that's another assignment:

p^.next := newCell

We're done—all we have to do now is fill in the other fields of the new cell, using

newCell^.*other fields* := *whatever belongs in those fields*

The generic procedure to insert a cell into a linked list now looks like this, written with its supporting **type** declarations:

```
type
    CellPtr = ^Cell;
    Cell = record
                data : Some data type;
                next : CellPtr
           end;
procedure Insert(d : Some data type ; var p : CellPtr);
{Inserts a cell with data d immediately}
{after the cell pointed to by p.           }
    var
        newCell : CellPtr;
begin
    new(newCell);                      {Build a new cell.}
    newCell^.next : = p^.next;         {Link the new cell to the cell after p's.}
    p^.next : = newCell;               {Change p's link to point to newCell.}
    newCell^.data : = d                {Put the rest of the data into newCell.}
end;
```

This insertion algorithm requires that we have a pointer p to the cell before the eventual location of *newCell*, for two reasons. First, we need p so that we can link *newCell^.next* to *p^.next*—otherwise we can't connect *newCell*'s cell to the rest of the list. Secondly, we need p so that we can link *p^.next* to *newCell*. This means that to insert a cell into position n in the list, we must call *FindNth*($n - 1$, d) to get the pointer to the cell before the n-th cell. You can see this is the listing of *DoInsertion* in the Program in Progress.

It also means that we cannot use this same routine to insert a new cell at the head of the list, since (1) there's no cell prior to the first cell in the list, and (2) we must change the pointer to the head of the list to refer to the new first cell. To do this, we can follow the steps of Figure 12.7.

Before you go on, see if you can translate the pictures in Figure 12.7 into code.

●   ●   ●

Got it? Here's how we did it. Take a look at PasWord 3.0 to see a functionally similar version, with the names changed.

```
procedure InsertAtHead(d : Some data type; var head : CellPtr);
{Inserts a cell with data d at the head}
{of the list pointed to by head.        }
    var
        newCell : CellPtr;
```

We start with a list and a cell to be inserted at the head.

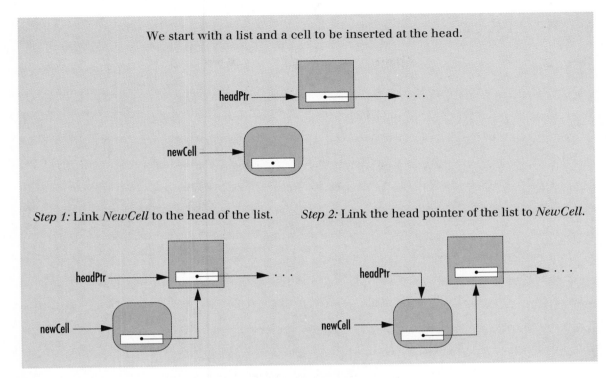

Step 1: Link *NewCell* to the head of the list.   *Step 2:* Link the head pointer of the list to *NewCell*.

Figure 12.7. Inserting a new cell at the head of a linked list

```
begin
   new(newCell);             {Build a new cell.}
   newCell^.next : = head;   {Link the new cell to the head of the list.}
   head : = newCell;         {Change the head pointer to point to newCell.}
   newCell^.data : = d       {Put the rest of the data into newCell.}
end;
```

This points out another significant difference between an array implementation of a list and a pointer implementation. In a sense, every position of an array is the same as any other. In a linked list, though, there may be significant programming differences between processing records in starting, ending, and interior positions.

Problem-solving technique

Linked lists may come in several logically distinct forms. In general, when using a pointer-based structure, be very careful to distinguish the "ordinary" cases from the exceptional ones. A routine that works flawlessly on the interior of a structure may fail on a structure that is empty or has only one cell.

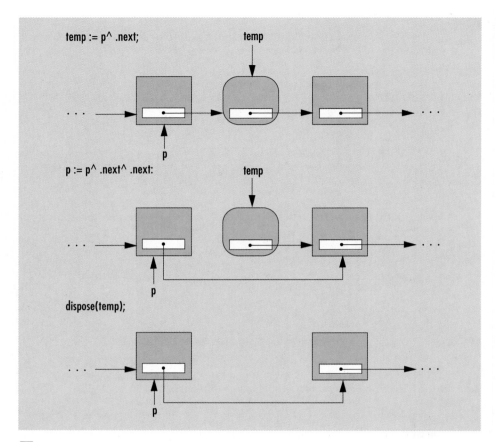

Figure 12.8.   Deleting a cell from a linked list

Deletion

Deletion from a linked list, like insertion, requires that we have a pointer to the cell before the one where all the real work is to take place.[8] Once we have a pointer, p, to a cell, we can delete the cell following p by "pointing around" it. This requires some minor housekeeping: We dispose of the deleted cell so that it doesn't clutter memory with what are known as *dangling references* — cells with nothing pointing to them. Figure 12.8 shows what to do to delete a cell from a linked list.

Deleting a cell from a linked list illustrates a commonly used technique. We knew that we were going to move the pointer to the deleted cell, so we generated a temporary pointer variable, *temp*, so that we would have a reference to that cell

---

[8]That's not strictly true. In the exercises, we explore a clever way to do insertion and deletion *at* the cell pointed to rather than after.

when the time came to dispose of it. If we hadn't done that, we would not have been able to refer to the cell to dispose of it later. Notice we did this by *temp* := *p^.next*. We didn't have to use *new(temp)*, since we already had a cell for *temp* to point to.

> ### Problem-solving technique
>
> A very common source of error is to use *new* when it's unnecessary. You need to call *new* only when you want to construct a new object for a pointer to point to.

Following our own advice to be particularly careful about the boundary cases, we should ask whether our deletion algorithm works correctly when we have to delete the first cell of a list. No, it doesn't, for the same reasons that insertion didn't—there is no cell prior to the one to be deleted. In our PIP, the definition of our data structure requires that there be a pointer to the first cell in the list and that the last cell in the list has a **nil** pointer in its *.next* field. The last condition is preserved no matter what cell we delete, but we can't use the deletion routine of Figure 12.8 to delete the head cell of a list. If we did, the reference to the first cell would be altered, and the Figure 12.8 code would never reflect the fact. The *DeleteHead* routine is to *Delete* as *InsertAtHead* is to *Insert*. We'll leave the details to you.

Linked Lists and Files

One final, and subtle, difference between PasWord 3.0 and PasWord 2.0 is how files are declared and manipulated. In a certain sense, PasWord 3.0 represents a regression from the file of the document we used in PasWord 2.1 back to the textfiles we used in version 2.0. This regression is dictated by the relationship (or lack thereof) between linked structures, like documents in PasWord 3.0, and external files.

As we have seen, PasWord 3.0 represents a document in memory simply by a pointer to where the first line of the document is stored. Similarly, subsequent lines of a document are accessed by pointers from within *LineCell* records. These pointers are allocated dynamically—while the PasWord program is running—based upon whatever memory is available in the machine at the moment storage is reserved for the pointer.

Although this allocation scheme is advantageous to the program in terms of making efficient use of memory, it interferes with its ability to use general files. That is, although we could easily do so, it does us no good to store a document in linked form. Such a document would be stored on disk with its pointer values intact, but when it was read back into memory, the machine's memory would be in a different condition from when the document had been saved. Thus, the pointer values saved as part of the document would be meaningless. They would still represent valid addresses in the computer's memory, but those addresses would more than likely not contain anything related to the current document. That's why we went back to using textfiles to store documents.

> **I**n general, although pointers help us to use and manage memory efficiently, they are of little use in saving and retrieving information from files.

12.6
Computer Science Interlude: Memory Management

We said before that the operating system of a computer is a program that is always running in the background, and that it is responsible for managing the resources of the computer. These resources include the screen, the keyboard, any peripheral devices such as printers and tape and disk drives, and memory. Most of the time you are unaware of the operating system. In a very real sense, though, it controls most of what you see when you use a computer—referred to as the *user interface*—as well as much of what you don't see. For example, both the MS/DOS operating system on IBM-compatible microcomputers and the Macintosh operating system use a menu bar to display commands that the user may select, but the two operating systems handle the menu bar in very different ways. To open the Edit menu (which resides in both systems) on an IBM-class machine, you typically press the F10 key to activate the menu bar, use the arrow keys to select an item, and press the Enter key to select an item. On the Macintosh, you use the mouse to move the pointer to the Edit menu, press and hold the mouse button to display the menu, drag the pointer to the menu item desired, and release the mouse button to select the desired menu item. However much these sequences of operations may differ,[9] they have in common the fact that they are controlled by the operating systems of the two computers.

In addition to the user interface, one of the things that the operating system must manage is allocation and deallocation of memory. One of the primitive operations of an operating system (OS) is *Allocate(a block in memory)*. We may think of *Allocate* as a function that, when given an integer representing the size of a needed block, returns the address of a location in memory that can serve as the beginning of a block of that size. For example, when a compiler sees a variable declaration for an integer *sum*, it generates code somewhat like *location1302* := *Allocate(2)*, setting aside memory locations starting at *location1302* for the two

---

[9]And the "best" operating system is a subject of much controversy among those people who attach a religious fervor to the differences between computers.

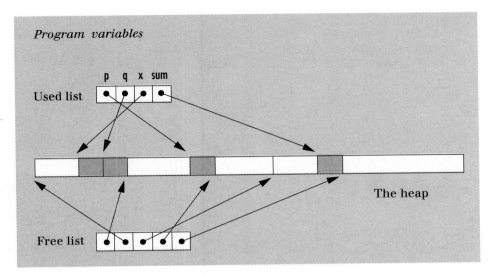

Figure 12.9.   Keeping track of memory with free and used lists

bytes necessary to store an integer, and uses the returned address in all subsequent code that refers to variable *sum*. Then, when translating *sum* := *sum* + 1, it might generate the code

```
LOD 1        ; Put 1 in the accumulator.
ADD loc1302  ; Add sum to 1,
STO loc1302  ; and store the result in sum.
```

In order to accomplish allocation and deallocation, the OS must keep track of which locations in memory are free and which are being used. For programs containing only static variables, that wouldn't be too much of a problem, since the allocation can be done all at once, just after compilation. Life gets more complicated when a source program deals with pointers, since *new*(*p*) and *dispose*(*p*) require that locations in memory be allocated and freed at run-time.

Most operating systems manage memory by keeping a *free list* of locations that are not presently being used in the *heap* (as the memory allotted for program variables and similar things, like code, is called), as well as a *used list* of locations that are presently occupied, as in Figure 12.9. When the OS receives a request for a block of memory of a given size, it clearly must decide to fill that request from a free block that is at least large enough to accommodate the request. This leads to all sorts of interesting problems.

Suppose that the request was for a block of 100 bytes and the free list contained, in order, blocks of size 250, 80, 16, 110, and 400. We could use a *first fit* scheme, in which we traverse the list from front to rear, stopping at the first block that was large enough to satisfy the request (the 250-byte block, in this case). Then, after allocation, the free list would look like 150, 80, 16, 110, and 400.

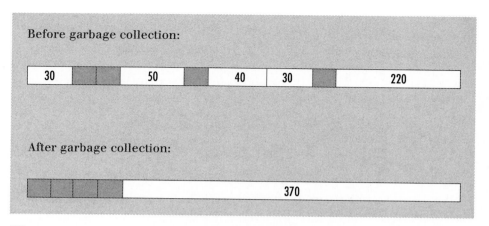

Figure 12.10. Garbage collection to build large free blocks

Another scheme would be to use a *best fit* algorithm, traversing the entire list and using the smallest block that was large enough — the 110-byte block in this case. After a best fit allocation, then, the free list would look like 250, 80, 16, 10, 400.

Which one is better? You can see that first fit will generally be faster, since it doesn't have to traverse the entire free list for each request, but it will also tend to leave the free list cluttered with small blocks at the start. On the other hand, best fit will generally leave the heap broken up into a collection of very small blocks (the 10-byte block in the example is one) that might never be used. Interestingly enough, you can show that there are some sequences of requests and free lists that can be satisfied by one scheme and not by the other. There's no final answer to which allocation scheme is better, although the consensus is that in most circumstances best fit simply isn't worth the extra effort.

If *p* is a pointer and we call *dispose(p)*, the easiest way to deal with the call is to remove the block from the used list, which is what some lazy compilers do. A much better way is to also add the deallocated block back to the free list, so it can be reused later. There are interesting problems involved with deallocation, as well. If the largest block in the free list is 100 and there are two adjacent free blocks of size 90, the largest request that could be filled would be 100, in spite of the fact that there was a block of 180 that could be made from the two adjacent blocks. Some operating systems handle this problem by *coalescing* — when a block is freed and it is adjacent to another free block, it and its free neighbor are merged into one large block.

Some operating systems go even further than that, employing a *garbage collection* algorithm. Every so often, the OS takes over and moves blocks in memory, collecting all the free blocks together, as we illustrate in Figure 12.10. There are a number of tricky points here, not the least of which is that the OS must inform all running applications that memory is being reorganized, so they can update their references to memory. Worst of all, though, is that the applications may not be aware of all references to memory.

We've highlighted only some of the most obvious OS topics — the rest belong in an operating systems course. It's a fascinating subject and of course vitally interesting to anyone designing system software, since without an operating system, there is no computer, at least in the sense that we understand the term.

12.7 Reference

- An object of *pointer* type is an address in memory where a value of another type is stored.
- Pointers are declared and referenced by a caret or an up-arrow, as follows:

```
type
    PointerType = ^PointedToType;    {caret before type name}
var
    ptr : PointerType;
    a : PointedToType;
begin
    ⋮
    a := ptr^                        {caret after variable name}
```

- There are only five things you can do with pointers:
  1. Give a pointer a new location in memory to point to using *New*.
  2. Refer to what a pointer points to, using the caret after the pointer.
  3. Compare two pointers for equality or inequality to determine whether they point to the same location in memory.
  4. Refer to the pointer constant **nil** (which can never point to anything).
  5. Destroy what a pointer points to using *Dispose*.
- The main use for pointers is as fields of records to make a logical link between records that may not be adjacent in memory. We can set up records this way by declarations like:

```
type
    CellPtr = ^Cell;              {must be declared before the record}
    Cell = record
               data : integer;    {or whatever you wish}
               next : CellPtr
           end;
```

- With declarations like the preceding ones, a typical data structure would take the form:

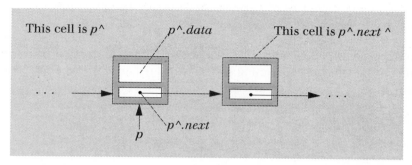

- In such *linked lists*, it is very common to use the **nil** pointer in the *next* field of the last record, as a sentinel to indicate the end of the list.
- One advantage to using pointers to manage lists is that the length of the list is limited only by the amount of available memory.
- The most common errors you will encounter when using pointers are the result of referring to a pointer's destination when there is nothing for a pointer to point to. These errors are generally reported to you by a compiler error message like "Nil dereference" (you're referring to $p\hat{}$ when p is **nil**); or "Bus error" or "Odd address exception" (you're referring to $p\hat{}$ when p hasn't been initialized, so it contains random garbage; that is, you neglected to use *New(p)*). Drawing box pictures can help.
- In arrays, every element behaves like every other, and you don't have to worry too much about the difference between empty arrays and nonempty ones. With linked structures, this difference may be very important.
- Pointers are perhaps the most confusing concept in Pascal programming. Take heart—if you persist in trying to understand them, the time will come when everything clicks into place, and you'll wonder why you ever thought they were obscure.

12.8 Building Blocks

Pointers are most frequently used as fields in records. In such a situation, the pointers point to other records and are declared as follows, with the pointer type declared before the record type:

```
type
    CellPtr = ^Cell;
    Cell = record
            data : whatever data fields you need;
            next : CellPtr    There's nothing wrong with having several pointer fields
        end;                  in the record.
```

We can use a declaration like this to implement a linked list. In such a structure, we might refer to a list by a pointer to its first cell and use a **nil** pointer in the last *next* field. Continuing the preceding declaration, we would declare:

List = CellPtr;

To traverse a linked list, we begin at the head and *next* our way down the list. Note that since *head* is a value parameter, we can use it as the pointer that tracks through the list without having to worry that we've lost our reference to the start of the list.

```
procedure Traverse(head : List);
{Assumes that the last cell in the list has a nil next field.}
begin
   while head <> nil do
      begin
         Process the cell headˆ ;
         head : = headˆ.next
      end
end;
```

We could do the same traversal recursively, if we wished, as follows. The advantage here is that by reversing the order of the two statements that process a cell and do a recursive call, we then have a routine that traverses the list in reverse order.

```
procedure Traverse(head : List);
begin
   if head <> nil then
      begin
         Traverse(headˆ.next);
         Process the cell headˆ
      end
end;
```

Another use of traversal is to find the *n*-th cell in a linked list using a pointer version of a bounded linear search.

```
function FindNth (n: integer; head : List): CellPtr;
{Returns a pointer to the n-th cell in the linked list starting}
{at head, if such a cell exists, otherwise returns nil.        }
   var
      currentPtr: CellPtr;        {the current position in the list}
      cellNum: integer;           {the number of the current cell}
begin
   currentPtr : = head;
   cellNum : = 1;
```

```
      while (currentPtr <> nil) and (cellNum <> n) do
         begin
            cellNum := cellNum + 1;       {Increase the position counter,}
            currentPtr := currentPtr^.next   {and move to the next cell.}
         end;
      FindNth := currentPtr
   end;
```

In order to ensure that the linked list will have a **nil** sentinel, we first
initialize the list by referring to an empty list by a **nil** head pointer.

```
procedure Initialize(var head : CellPtr);
{Creates an empty list}
begin
   head := nil
end;
```

Inserting a new element at the head of a linked list requires altering the
head pointer:

```
procedure InsertAtHead(d : Some data type; var head : CellPtr);
{Inserts a cell with data d at the head of}
{the list pointed to by head.            }
   var
      newCell : CellPtr;
begin
   new(newCell);               {Build a new cell,}
   newCell^.next := head;      {link the new cell to the head of the list,}
   head := newCell;            {change the head pointer to point to newCell,}
   newCell^.data := d          {and put the rest of the data into newCell.}
end;
```

To insert a new cell in the interior of a linked list, we need a pointer to the
cell immediately before the location where the new cell will go.

```
procedure Insert(d : Some data type ; var p : CellPtr);
{Inserts a cell with data d immediately after}
{the cell pointed to by p.                 }
   var
      newCell : CellPtr;
begin
   new(newCell);               {Build a new cell,}
   newCell^.next := p^.next;   {link the new cell to the cell after p's,}
   p^.next := newCell;         {change p's link to point to newCell,}
   newCell^.data := d          {put the rest of the data into newCell.}
end;
```

Deletion, like insertion, takes two forms, depending on whether or not we are deleting the first cell. To delete the first cell, we must remember to repoint the head pointer.

```
procedure DeleteHead (var head : List);
{Deletes the first cell in the list pointed to by head}
    var
        temp: CellPtr;
begin
    if head <> nil then          {Do nothing if the list is empty.}
        begin
            temp := head;        {Save a reference to the first cell,}
            head := head^.next;  {move the head pointer to the next cell,}
            dispose(temp)        {and dispose of the old first cell.}
        end
end;
```

As with insertion, deletion from the interior of a list requires that we have a pointer to the cell immediately before the one to be deleted.

```
procedure Delete (var p: CellPtr);
{Deletes the cell immediately after the cell pointed}
{to by p. If there is no such cell, does nothing.    }
    var
        temp: CellPtr;
begin
    if p <> nil then
        if p^.next <> nil then
            begin
                temp := p^.next;          {Save a reference to the cell to be deleted,}
                p^.next := p^.next^.next;  {bypass the cell to be deleted,}
                dispose(temp)             {and dispose of the cell.}
            end
end;
```

12.9 EXERCISES

Here are some declarations we'll use throughout these exercises.

```
type
    CellPtr = ^Cell;
    Cell = record
                data : integer;
                next : CellPtr
            end;
    IntFile = file of integer;
    IntArray = array [1 .. 200] of integer;
```

```
var
    p, q, r : CellPtr;
    s, t : ^integer;
    f : IntFile;
    a : IntArray;
    n, m : integer;
```

1. Given the preceding declarations, identify which of the following statements are incorrect. Explain.

   a. writeln(p)
   b. **if** p^ <> **nil then**
        p := p^.next
   c. dispose(p^.next^.next)
   d. p := s
   e. **while** p < q **do**
        p := p^.next

2. Given the preceding declarations, identify which of the following statements are incorrect. Explain.

   a. read(p^)
   b. write(f, s)
   c. p^.next^.data := a[9]
   d. **begin**
        s := **nil**;
        writeln(s^)
      end
   e. s^ := p^.data

3. What does the following procedure do to this linked list?

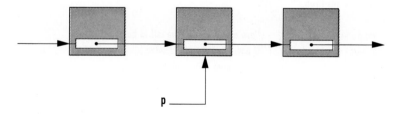

p

   What does it do in general? Will it do what you said it will do on all possible linked lists?

```
procedure Unknown(n : integer ; var p : CellPtr);
    var
        temp : CellPtr;
begin
    new(temp);
    temp^.data := p^.data;
    p^.data := n;
    temp^.next := p^.next;
    p^.next := temp
end;
```

4. In the version of *Delete* used in the text, we required a pointer to the cell before the one to be deleted. Not only is this requirement conceptually inelegant, but it means that we need a different routine to delete the first cell in a linked list. Write a **procedure** *Delete*(**var** *p* : *CellPtr*) that deletes the cell pointed to by *p* rather than the cell after the one pointed to by *p*. *Hint*: Exercise 3 might be helpful here.

5. Write **function** *Mid*(*p* : *CellPtr*) : *CellPtr*, which returns a pointer to the cell in the middle of the linked list that starts at the cell pointed to by *p*. You may assume that the linked list will have an odd number of cells.

6. Why does Pascal not allow the values of pointers to be inspected or directly manipulated?

7. Each of the following functions is supposed to return *true* if and only if the value *n* is in one of the cells in a linked list (starting at the cell pointed to by *p* and terminated with a **nil** sentinel). Why don't they work?

a. **function** Find(n : integer ; p : CellPtr) : boolean;
```
begin
    Find : = false;
    while p <> nil do
        if p^.data = n then
            Find : = true
        else
            p : = p^.next
end;
```

b. **function** Find(n : integer ; p : CellPtr) : boolean;
```
    var
        done : boolean;
begin
    done : = false;
    repeat
        if p^.data = n then
            done : = true
        else
            p : = p^.next
    until done or (p = nil);
    Find : = done
end;
```

c. **function** Find(n : integer ; p : CellPtr) : boolean;
```
begin
    Find : = false;
    if p^.data = n then
        Find : = true
    else
        Find : = Find(n, p^.next)
end;
```

8. The following routine is supposed to find the sum of the entries in a linked list pointed to by p.

```
q := p;
sum := 0;
while q <> nil do
    begin
        sum := sum + q^.data;
        q^.next := q
    end
```

a. Why doesn't it work?

b. Under what circumstances, if any, will it work as intended?

9. Suppose that a linked list contained its elements in sorted order, from smallest to largest.

a. We know that when we're implementing a sorted list using arrays, we can find an element very quickly, using binary search. Can we use the equivalent of binary search with a sorted linked list?

b. Write **procedure** *Insert*(n : *integer* ; **var** p : *CellPtr*), which inserts the value n in the sorted linked list pointed to by p. As usual, you may assume that the list ends with a **nil** sentinel.

10. The following statements interchange the two cells immediately following the one pointed to by p, as in the following diagram. The auxiliary pointer q is uninitialized at the start.

```
[1]   p^.next := q
[2]   p^.next^.next := p^.next^.next^.next
[3]   q := p^.next^.next
[4]   q^.next := p^.next
```

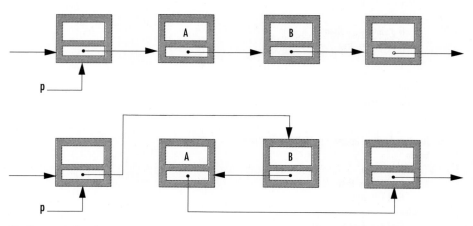

Unfortunately, the statements aren't in the correct order. Which of these orders is correct?

   $1, 3, 2, 4$ $2, 4, 1, 3$ $3, 2, 1, 4$ $3, 2, 4, 1$ $4, 1, 2, 3$

Bonus: There are 24 ways to arrange these statements. Are any of them correct, aside from the one correct one in the preceding list?

11. Suppose that a free list contained, in order, blocks of size 200, 50, and 100 bytes. Suppose also that requests came in for blocks of size 100, 80, 50, and 70, starting with a request for the 100-byte block. Describe the contents of the free list at each stage, using the following allocation strategies:

   a. First-fit
   b. Best-fit
   c. *Worst-fit*, in which the current largest block is the one from which allocation is made.

12. For the free list of Exercise 11, give a sequence of requests:

   a. That can be satisfied by first-fit but not by best-fit.
   b. That can be satisfied by best-fit but not by first-fit.

13. Write **procedure** *ConvertToLinkedList*(**var** p : *CellPtr* ; a : *IntArray*), which will set p to point to the first cell in a linked list that contains the elements of the array a.

14. Reverse Exercise 13 by writing a procedure that will take a pointer, p, to the first cell in a linked list and will set the contents of array a to the contents of the linked list.

   a. Do this problem assuming that the linked list contains exactly 200 cells.
   b. Do this problem assuming you know nothing about the size of the linked list. If the list is longer than 200 cells, just put the first 200 cells in the array.

   We could give a recursive definition of lists by saying that a list is either (1) empty or (2) consists of a head element followed by a list. This is a common way to regard lists and lends itself naturally to recursive algorithms. In Exercises 15–20, we'll explore some recursive list algorithms.

15. What does the following procedure do?

```
procedure DoSomething(var head : CellPtr);
begin
    if head <> nil then
        begin
            DoSomething(head^.next);
            dispose(head)
        end
end;
```

16. Write **function** *Sum*(*head* : *CellPtr*) : *integer*, which returns the sum of all the elements in the list pointed to by *head*. It's helpful in this kind of problem to think in terms like this: "If a list is empty, the sum is zero. Otherwise, the sum of a list is the value in the head cell plus the sum of the rest of the list."

17. Write **function** *Size*(*head* : *CellPtr*) : *integer*, which returns the number of cells in the list pointed to by *head*.

18. a. Write **function** *Max*(*head* : *CellPtr*) : *integer*, which returns the largest value in the list pointed to by *head*. You may assume that the list contains only positive integers and that the function should return zero if given an empty list.
   b. Write **function** *MaxLoc*(*head* : *CellPtr*) : *CellPtr*, which returns a pointer to the largest value in the list pointed to by *head*. You may assume that the list contains only positive integers and that the function should return **nil** if given an empty list.

19. Write **function** $Copy(head : CellPtr) : CellPtr$, which returns a pointer to the head of a new list that is a duplicate of the one pointed to by $head$.

20. Write **function** $Tail(head : CellPtr) : CellPtr$, which returns a pointer to the last cell in the list pointed to by $head$.

There's no reason why we have to restrict ourselves to cells with just one pointer field. In Exercises 21–24, we'll explore some things we can do with extra pointers in our cells.

21. In a *doubly linked list*, each cell contains a pointer to the prior cell, as well as one to the next cell. The declarations and the list look like this:

```
type
    DoubleCellPtr = ^DoubleCell;
    DoubleCell = record
                    data : some type;
                    prior, next : DoubleCellPtr
                 end;
```

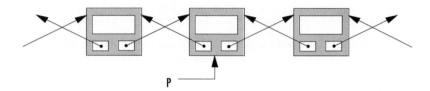

P

a. Write a routine to delete the cell pointed to by p in a doubly linked list. To make life easier, assume that the cell to be deleted is neither at the head nor at the tail of the list.

b. Why would we want to use doubly linked lists? Are they just devices to bedevil students?

22. If we have a long linked list that doesn't require insertions or deletions, we could put an extra pointer in each cell that points to the cell twice as far along in the list so that the cell in position 6 would have a pointer to the cell in position 7 and one to the cell in position 12 (if the list is long enough to have a twelfth cell, that is).

a. Draw such a structure with sixteen cells, and for each cell, indicate how many moves it would take from the first cell to get there.

b. Find a way to describe how to get to cell n. In other words, given n, what should be the sequence of "steps" (going to the next cell) and "hops" (going to the twice-as-far cell) to get to cell n in the least amount of time?

c. Let $M(n)$ be a function that counts the least number of moves to get to the n-th cell. What can you say about M? A suitable answer might be "$M(n)$ never gets any larger than [some function involving n]." Even better would be something exact, like "$M(n)$ is equal to the number of digits in the binary expression of n, plus the number of 1s in the binary expression of n, minus 2."

d. Does this data structure make *FindNth* significantly faster than was the case with a simple linked list?

e. *Bonus*: The "hop" pointers in the upper half of the list are never used. Can you think of a good use for them that would speed up access even further?

23. A *binary tree* is a data structure in which each cell (called a *node* in this context) has references to zero, one, or two other nodes (usually called the *children* of the original node). If we implemented such a structure with pointers, we might have declarations and pictures like this:

```
type
    NodePtr = ^Node;
    Node = record
                data : some type;
                left, right : NodePtr   {pointers to the left and right children}
            end;
var
    root : NodePtr;              {Access to the tree is through a pointer to the top node.}
```

a. Given these declarations, what does this procedure do when called with *root* as its parameter? Try it with the following tree illustrated in simplified form.

```
procedure Inorder(p : NodePtr);
begin
    if root <> nil then
        begin
            Inorder(p^.left);
            writeln(p^.data);
            Inorder(p^.right)
        end
end;
```

b. This tree is an example of a *binary search tree*. Such trees have the property that for every node, the value in the node is greater than that in its left child or any of its left child's descendants and less than that in its right child or any of its right child's descendants. Write a routine to find the node containing a given value in a binary search tree. In other words, $Find(n : DataType ; root : NodePtr) : NodePtr$ should return a pointer to the node containing n, if any, or should return **nil** if n isn't in the tree. In the preceding example, for instance, $Find(10, root)$ would be the left child pointer of the node containing 13, since placing 10 to the left of the 13 node would still result in a binary search tree.

c. How is $Find$ in binary search trees like the array binary search version of $Find$ in sorted lists?

24. In a *braid* or *multilist*, there are two or more key data fields, and as many pointer fields, in each node. In the example that follows, we have a small telephone directory with a name and a number field. There are two sets of pointers, arranged so that one set (the upper set in the picture) links the cells in sorted order by name, and the other set (the lower ones) links the cells in increasing order of numbers.

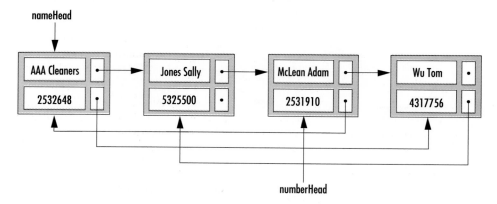

a. What would be the advantage of such a data structure?
b. Write a deletion routine for the two-braid shown.
c. Write a routine to insert a new cell in a two-braid.

25. A *stack* is a list for which all insertions, deletions, and inspections are made at the head (called the *top* of the stack). This mirrors a stack of plates at a cafeteria, where you would select a plate from the top of the stack and where new plates would always be added to the top.

a. Write the **type** declarations for a pointer-based implementation of a stack of real numbers.
b. Write a routine to *Create* a new, empty stack.
c. Write a routine, *Push*, that would put a new value on the top of the stack, pushing all other values down by one position.
d–f. Redo parts a through c for an array-based implementation.
g. Compare the array and pointer implementations.

26. A *queue* is another linear data structure for which insertions are made at one end of the list and deletions and inspections are made at the other end. Queues are commonly used to model real-world situations like people waiting in line at a bank or supermarket.

a. Write the **type** declarations for a pointer-based implementation of a queue of real numbers.

b. Write a routine to *Create* a new, empty queue.
c. Write a routine, *Enqueue*, that would put a new value on the tail of a queue.
d. Write a routine, *Dequeue*, that would remove the value at the head of a queue.
e–h. Redo parts a through d for an array-based implementation.
i. Compare the array and pointer implementations.

12.10 Answers

1. a. Incorrect; we cannot inspect the value of a pointer.
 b. Incorrect; the boolean expression compares $p\hat{\ }$ with **nil**, but $p\hat{\ }$ is a record (of type *Cell*, here), so it can't be compared with a pointer. This would be legal if we used p rather than $p\hat{\ }$.
 c. No problem here. We're just disposing of a pointer.
 d. Incorrect; we are making an assignment between two pointers, but what they point to are of incompatible types, so the assignment isn't allowed.
 e. Incorrect; the only comparisons we can make between pointers are equality and inequality.

3. This is a very clever algorithm. Draw the memory snapshots, and you'll see that the effect of this routine is to insert a new cell containing the data n at the position pointed to by p. This means that if we're willing to pay the price of moving the data (which could be considerable if the *.data* field was very large), we don't really need a pointer to the cell before the one where we want to do an insert. This routine will work equally well at any position in the list: first, interior, or last. It will not, however, work correctly to insert a new cell into an empty list, nor will it allow us to insert a new element after the last cell in a list.

5. We use an auxiliary pointer, q, that makes one step for every two that p makes. Notice that we're not losing the anchor to the head of the list by advancing p, since p is a value parameter, so it reverts to its original value upon termination of the function. This technique of having an auxiliary pointer that tracks behind another is fairly common.

```
function Mid(p : CellPtr) : CellPtr;
    var
        q : CellPtr;
begin
    q := p;
    if p^.next = nil then          {No need to do anything for a one-cell list.}
        Mid := p
    else
        begin
            while p <> nil do      {The list is longer than one cell.}
                begin
                    q := q^.next;       {Advance q one step,}
                    p := p^.next^.next  {for every two steps of p.}
                end;
            Mid := q               {When p's at the end, return q.}
        end
end;
```

7. a. This will work just fine if n isn't in the list. On a successful search, though, it gets hung up in the loop, never advancing p.

b. A good try, but it fails on empty lists.

c. This almost works, but it will eventually crash trying to dereference a **nil** pointer. The exit case of the recursion should test whether p is **nil**, as follows:

```
function Find(n : integer ; p : CellPtr) : boolean;
begin
    if p = nil then    {This guards the subsequent reference to p^.data.}
        Find : = false
    else if p^.data = n then
        Find : = true
    else
        Find : = Find(n, p^.next)
end;
```

9. a. No. Binary search requires the ability to find the middle cell of a sublist. We can do this with arrays, since we can do arithmetic on indices, but we can't do any better than a linear search with linked lists (but see Exercise 22).

b. This is easiest to do recursively. We argue as follows: If the list is empty, then make the list consist of a new cell containing n. In case the list is nonempty, if n is less than the head of the list, insert n at the head of the list; otherwise, insert n where it belongs in the rest of the list.

```
procedure Insert(n : integer ; var p : CellPtr);
    var
        temp : CellPtr;
begin
    if p = nil then
        begin
            new(temp);
            temp^.data : = n;
            temp^.next : = nil;
            p : = temp
        end
    else if n < p^.data then
        begin
            new(temp);
            temp^.data : = n;
            temp^.next : = p;
            p : = temp
        end
    else
        Insert(n, p^.next)
end;
```

Note, by the way, that although the two code segments are almost identical (and could be made so), we can't fold them together under the single condition **if** ($p =$ **nil**) **or** ($n < p^.data$) **then** . . . , since p could be **nil**, and Pascal might still try to refer to $p^$.

11. a. (200, 50, 100)
    Request 100
    (100, 50, 100)
    Request 80
    (20, 50, 100)
    Request 50
    (20, 100)
    Request 70
    (20, 30)
b. (200, 50, 100)
    Request 100
    (200, 50)
    Request 80
    (120, 50)
    Request 50
    (120)
    Request 70
    (50)
c. (200, 50, 100)
    Request 100
    (100, 50, 100)
    Request 80
    (20, 50, 100)
    Request 50
    (20, 50, 50)
    Request 70; can't be fulfilled.

13. procedure ConvertToLinkedList(**var** p : CellPtr ; a : IntArray);
    var
        i : integer;
        q : CellPtr;
    begin
    new(p);
    p^.data : = a[1];
    q : = p;
    for i : = 2 **to** 200 **do**
        begin
            new(q^.next);
            q^.next^.data : = a[i];
            q : = q^.next
        end;
    q^.next : = **nil**
    end;

15. It destroys a linked list, disposing of every cell. This is a good recursive example. It says, "To destroy a list, (1) do nothing to an empty list, and (2) if the list is nonempty, destroy all but the head of the list, then dispose of the head element." Note that this algorithm would not work if we reversed the order of the statements *DoSomething(head^.next)* and *dispose(head)*.

17. function Size(head : CellPtr) : integer;
    begin
        if p = **nil then**
            Size : = 0
        else
            Size : = 1 + Size(p^.next)
    end;

19. function Copy(head : CellPtr) : CellPtr;
        var
            newHead : CellPtr;
    begin
    if head = **nil then**
        Copy : = **nil**
    else
        begin
            new(newHead);
            newHead^.data : = head^.data;
            newHead^.next : = Copy(head^.next);
            Copy : = newHead
        end
    end;

21. a. There's a pleasing symmetry here. If you understand this, pointers should hold no further terrors for you.

    p^.prior^.next : = p^.next;
    p^.next^.prior : = p^.prior;
    dispose(p)

    b. Singly linked lists permit traversal in one direction only; with doubly linked lists, we can move forward or backward. They do also serve to bedevil students, if the truth be known.

23. a. This routine traverses the tree, inspecting and writing the contents of each node. In English, the routine says, "To inspect the nodes of a binary tree, inspect everything to the left of the root, then inspect the root, then inspect everything to the right of the root." When applied to the sample tree, this routine writes 5, 8, 13, 21, 34. Other tree traversals can be made by moving the *writeln* call before or after the two recursive calls.

    b. function Find(n : DataType ; root : NodePtr) : NodePtr;
        begin
        if root = **nil then**   {Didn't find n, and there's nothing left to search.}
            Find : = **nil**
        else if n = root^.data **then**   {Found it!}
            Find : = root
        else if n < root^.data **then**   {If it's anywhere, it's to the left of the root.}
            Find : = Find(n, root^.left)
        else   {If it's anywhere, it's to the right of the root.}
            Find : = Find(n, root^.right)
        end;

c. It's structurally identical if we flatten the tree into a list (by sitting on it, for instance). The root is conceptually the middle of the list, the left child is conceptually the middle of the left half of the list, and so on.

25. a. We use the usual linked list implementation, using the head of the list as the top of the stack.

```
type
    StackPtr = ^Cell;
    Cell = record
                data : real;
                next : StackPtr
           end;
    Stack = StackPtr;
```

Here's a picture of a stack in this implementation:

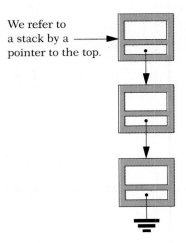

We refer to
a stack by a ———→
pointer to the top.

b.
```
procedure Create(var s : Stack);
begin
    s := nil
end;
```

c. Note that *Push* is nothing more than our old friend *InsertAtHead*.

```
procedure Push(r : real ; var s : Stack);
    var
        newCell : StackPtr;
begin
    new(newCell);
    newCell^.data := r;
    newCell^.next := s;
    s := newCell
end;
```

d. We use the usual dynamic array implementation from Chapter 10, with an array for the data and an integer *.size* field. To eliminate array shifting, we'll put the bottom at the low end of the array.

```
const
   STACKMAX = 200;
type
   Stack = record
              size : 0 .. STACKMAX;
              data : array [1 .. STACKMAX]
           end;
```

Here's a picture of a stack in this implementation:

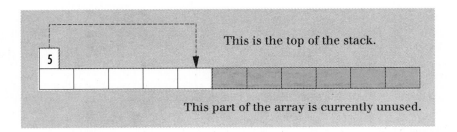

e.
```
procedure Create(var s : Stack);
begin
   s.size : = 0
end;
```

f. Note that in this implementation we have to test whether we're trying to *Push* something onto a full stack.

```
procedure Push(r : real ; var s : Stack);
begin
   if s.size = MAXSIZE then
      writeln('There"s no room to Push an element on the stack.')
   else
      begin
         s.size : = s.size + 1;
         s.data[s.size] : = r
      end
end;
```

g. There's no real saving of time between the routines we've seen in either version. The array version cannot grow arbitrarily large and may have wasted space in the array that's not currently used for the stack. Overall, there's no clear reason for preferring one over the other.

Introduction to Abstract Data Types: Linked Lists

A lthough you may not consider yourself a master programmer, you have now seen (with the exception of a few minor details we chose to omit) all there is to Pascal. You've completed your apprenticeship and are ready to move on to more challenging projects. As apprentices have done for centuries in other crafts, you've learned the basic tools of this trade and have made some tools of your own to take with you when you leave us. Traditionally, the last task of an apprentice is to complete a major work: PasWord was your apprentice project, and now you're prepared to begin your journey. In keeping with the tradition, we will bid you farewell in this chapter and leave you with some words about what is ahead if you continue your progress to becoming a master yourself. In the standard computer science curriculum, the next two courses will constitute the journeyman portion of your training, in which you see that the subject matter of computer science is devoted in one way or another to the question, "What are the general principles that serve to organize our thinking about computers and their programs?"

Nicklaus Wirth can be credited with more than inventing the Pascal language; among his other accomplishments, he also wrote a delightful book with perhaps the most felicitous title of any text on computer science, *Algorithms + Data Structures = Programs*. If you continue beyond this course, you can expect very shortly to take a course on data structures and one on algorithms. The data structures of a program are the major structural forms for the efficient representation of information, and the algorithms act on instances of these structures to process their information. Together, they should constitute an introduction to a more sophisticated view of programs and the programming process. The point of view that distinguishes an apprentice from a master is that the apprentice approaches each problem as completely unrelated to any others, whereas the master can see that different structures or algorithms are really not as unrelated as they seem but are rather just different ways of viewing the same problem. This ability to "abstract"—to recognize and exploit common structural and procedural themes—is one (if not *the*) organizing principle of computer science.

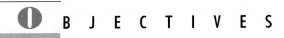

OBJECTIVES

In this chapter, we will:

- Describe the notion of an abstract data type (ADT).
- Provide examples of two implementations of a list ADT.
- Discuss the memory and processing tradeoffs between the two list implementations.
- Describe object-oriented programming as a design technique that exploits ADTs.

13.1 Levels of Abstraction, Again

We will spend most of our time in this chapter on another modification of PasWord. Unlike the prior modifications, this time we won't introduce any new functionality to our word processor. Instead, we'll look at PasWord in a different light and redesign part of it so that it's written the way an expert programmer would have done from the start.

PasWord 2.0 in Chapter 11 and Chapter 12's PasWord 3.0 both perform the same tasks, but they represent and manipulate a document in ways that are as different as bagels and doughnuts. In both versions, the logical structure of a document is the same—a collection of elements (lines in this case) arranged conceptually so that there is a first element, followed immediately by a second, which is followed immediately by a third, and so on, up to a last element that has no successor. This organization is common enough that it is worth studying as an abstract entity in its own right, and that's just what we'll do. Biologists classify living things into categories like the *ursidae*, including black bears, brown bears, and polar bears; similarly, computer scientists group data structures into classes like the *list*, instances of which include lines in a document, airplanes waiting to land at an airport, entries in a telephone book, customers in line at a bank, and, as in our PIP for this chapter, simple integers to be processed. In a critical sense, as far as writing a program to store and manipulate a list is concerned, it is unimportant what type of information resides in the list as long as the linear structure of first element, second element, . . . , last element is there.

Once we have conceived the structure of a list *abstract data type*, the next thing to decide is what operations are appropriate on structures of this type. The choice of what operations to include in the *list* abstract data type is to some degree a judgment call, but we would probably agree that the *list* operations should at least include the following:

1. *Create* a new, empty list.
2. *Destroy* a list, setting it to be empty again and freeing as much of its memory as we can.
3. *Insert* an element at a given position in a list.
4. *Delete* the element in a given position in a list.
5. Given a potential element in the list, *Search* for the position of that element in the list.
6. Tell whether a list is *Empty* or not.
7. Given a potential position in the list, tell whether it is a *BadPosition* or whether it represents a legitimate position in the list.
8. Determine the *Length* of a list.
9. Identify the first position (or *Head*) of a list.
10. Identify the last position (or *Tail*) of a list.
11. Given an integer, *n*, *Find* the *n*-th position in the list, if one exists.
12. Given a position in a list, find the position *Prior* to the one given.
13. Given a position in a list, find the *Next* position after the one given.

Look familiar? It should, since many of these are generalizations of the operations that PasWord performs on its list of lines that we call a *Document*. After all, at one level of abstraction PasWord is really nothing more than a specialized list processor. It should not be surprising, then, that the operations it performs are specializations of the operations on the *list* abstract data type.

An *abstract data type* is characterized by

1. A structure of *positions*.
2. The *data* that is stored in each position.
3. A collection of structure-preserving *operations* that act on the positions or the data associated with positions.

Indeed, the notion of an ADT should not seem so new to you if you think back only a couple of months ago to your first exposure to Pascal. We mentioned back then that the Pascal language had a number of built-in, predefined data types. Admittedly these types (integer, real, boolean, char) are atomic in nature, so their "structure" is rather uninteresting. Still, in using these data types in your early programs, you didn't concern yourself with how they were actually going to be implemented (such as how much storage they required or how that storage was organized) on your computer. You simply used them.

Notice, too, that each predefined atomic type came with a predefined set of operations that could be applied to elements of that type. It makes sense, for example, to apply arithmetic operations to integers and logical operations to booleans, but not vice versa. Though not presented this way, you can imagine an integer ADT that encapsulates the detailed structure and operations that describe Pascal integers. Just as Pascal allows us to extend its base of primitive types to define more complex, composite types of our own, we are free to build and package our own ADTs.

In a very real sense, the *list* ADT is the starting point for the study of all other ADTs. We can make other structures from lists either by changing the set of operations while keeping the structure fixed or by modifying the structure itself. If, for example, we limit the operations so that all modifications — like insertion and deletion — are done only at the head, the resulting ADT is called a *stack*. If we relax the restriction that each position has at most one successor, we have a hierarchical ADT called a *tree*. Both of these ADTs have numerous real-world applications and are worthy of study in their own right.

When considering ADTs, we don't concern ourselves so much with the eventual use of the data; instead, we look at the abstract structure and operations and consider how we can represent them efficiently. In other words, we want the representation of the positions and associated data to use as little room in memory as possible, and we want the implementations of the operations to take as little time as possible. In this chapter, we will look closely at two different implementations of the *list* ADT, and we will see that there is often a tradeoff between time and space. If we choose a space-efficient representation of positions and data, we frequently find that the algorithms that manipulate the structures may not be as time-efficient or as easy to understand as they would be if we began with a somewhat less compact representation of the data.

13.2   Problem Solving II: Developing Two LIST Packages

The first thing you will notice about the Program in Progress for this chapter is that it is not a program at all but rather two program units. In the listings that follow, the two units are written in parallel, on facing pages, so that you can compare them. As you do so, notice that all of the public routines have an "L" (for *List*) as the first character of their names. We did this for two reasons. First, we wanted you to be able to read the main program and quickly spot the list routines.

We also wanted to reduce the likelihood that the author of the program that uses either unit might have to change the names of the program's subprograms to avoid name conflicts, since it is highly unlikely that an author would independently name a subprogram *LPrior*, for instance.

As you read the listings, bear in mind that the array implementation is on the left, even-numbered pages and that the linked list implementation is on the right. Look carefully at the subprograms, noting that some operations are nearly trivial in one implementation and are quite complicated in the other. This, of course, reflects the engineering emphasis of software design that we've talked about before — we almost never can say with certainty that one solution is *the* best, only that one solution is better in some respects than the other. We'll have much more to say about this after you've had a chance to analyze the PIP.

$\mathbf{T}$he PIP

unit ArrayList;

```
{——————————————————————————————————————————}
{                                                                              }
{                          PROGRAM IN PROGRESS                                 }
{                                                                              }
{                               CHAPTER 13                                     }
{                                                                              }
{        This unit is a list-manipulation package, using an array              }
{        implementation for lists.                                             }
{                                                                              }
{        In this implementation, a list is a record consisting of an           }
{        integer length field, indicating the number of elements in            }
{        the list, along with an array that contains the list elements.        }
{                                                                              }
{        Positions in the list are integers in the range                       }
{        1 .. MAXLENGTH, and we use the value 0 as a "pseudo-                   }
{        position" to indicate an illegal position in a list.                   }
{                                                                              }
{——————————————————————————————————————————}
```

interface

const
    MAXLENGTH = 1000;   {This should be private, but we need it for the type declarations.}

type
    DataType = integer;   {or any type needed}

    Position = 0 .. MAXLENGTH;

    List = **record**
            length: Position;
            data: **array**[1 .. MAXLENGTH] **of** DataType
        end;

unit LinkedList;

```
{———————————————————————————————————}
{                                                                      }
{                     PROGRAM IN PROGRESS                              }
{                                                                      }
{                          CHAPTER 13                                  }
{                                                                      }
{    This unit is a list-manipulation package, using a pointer         }
{    implementation for lists.                                         }
{                                                                      }
{    In this implementation, a list is composed of a linked            }
{    collection of cells, each of which has a data field and a         }
{    pointer field that points to the next cell in the list. We use    }
{    a nil pointer as a sentinel in the last cell in the list.         }
{                                                                      }
{    A list is referred to by a header record, containing an          }
{    integer length field, indicating the number of elements in       }
{    the list, along with a pointer to the head of the linked         }
{    collection of cells that contain the list elements.              }
{                                                                      }
{    Positions in the list are pointers, and we use the nil pointer    }
{    as a "pseudo-position" to indicate an illegal position in a       }
{    list.                                                             }
{                                                                      }
{———————————————————————————————————}
```

interface

```
type
    DataType  =  integer;                    {or any type needed}

    Position  =  ^Cell;
    Cell  =  record
                data: DataType;
                next: Position
            end;
    List  =  record
                length: integer;
                head: Position
            end;
```

```
procedure LInit (var l: List);
procedure LDestroyList (var l: List);

function LEmpty (l: List): boolean;
function LBadPosition (p: Position; l: List): boolean;
function LLength (l: List): integer;

function LHead (l: List): Position;
function LTail (l: List): Position;
function LPrior (p: Position; l: List): Position;
function LNext (p: Position; l: List): Position;

function LFindNth (n: integer; l: List): Position;
function LSearch (d: DataType; l: List): Position;

procedure LInsert (d: DataType; var p: Position; var l: List);
procedure LDelete (var p: Position; var l: List);
```
implementation
```
procedure LInit    {var l: List};
{Initializes a list with no elements.}
begin
    l.length : = 0
end;


procedure LDestroyList    {var l: List};
{Resets a list to be empty.}
begin
    l.length : = 0
end;
```

```
function LEmpty    {(l: List): boolean};
{Returns true if and only if the list is empty.}
begin
    LEmpty : = (l.length = 0)
end;
```

```
procedure LInit (var l: List);
procedure LDestroyList (var l: List);

function LEmpty (l: List): boolean;
function LBadPosition   {(p: Position; l: List): boolean};
function LLength (l: List): integer;

function LHead (l: List): Position;
function LTail (l: List): Position;
function LPrior (p: Position; l: List): Position;
function LNext (p: Position; l: List): Position;

function LFindNth (n: integer; l: List): Position;
function LSearch (d: DataType; l: List): Position;

procedure LInsert (d: DataType; var p: Position; var l: List);
procedure LDelete (var p: Position; var l: List);
```

implementation

```
procedure LInit   {var l: List};
{Initializes a list with no elements.}
begin
   l.length : = 0;
   l.head : = nil
end;

procedure LDestroyList   {var l: List};
{Resets a list to be empty.}
   var
      current, temp: Position;
begin
   current : = l.head;
   while current <> nil do
      begin
         temp : = current;
         current : = current^.next;
         dispose(temp)
      end;
   l.length : = 0
end;

function LEmpty   {(l: List): boolean};
{Returns true if and only if the list is empty.}
begin
   LEmpty : = (l.length = 0)
end;
```

```
function LBadPosition (p: Position; l: List): boolean;
{Returns true if and only if p not in the list l.}
begin
    LBadPosition : = (p = 0) or (p > l.length)
end;
```

```
function LLength    {(l: List): integer};
{Returns the number of elements in the list.}
begin
    LLength : = l.length
end;
```

```
function LHead    {(l: List): Position};
{Returns the position of the head of the list.}
begin
    LHead : = 1     This is a "one," not an "el."
end;
```

```
function LTail    {(l: List): Position};
{Returns the position of the tail of the list.}
begin
    LTail : = l.length
end;
```

```
function LPrior    {(p: Position; l: List): Position};
{Returns the position immediately before p,}
{if such a position exists, otherwise returns }
{the null pseudo-position.                    }
```

function LBadPosition   {(p: Position; l: List): boolean};
{Returns true if and only if p is not in the list l.}
   var
      current: Position;
begin
  current : = l.head;
  while (current $<>$ **nil**) **and** (current $<>$ p) **do**
    current : = current^.next;
  LBadPosition : = (current = **nil**)
end;

function LLength   {(l: List): integer};
{Returns the number of elements in the list.}
begin
  LLength : = l.length
end;

function LHead   {(l: List): Position};
{Returns the position of the head of the list.}
begin
  LHead : = l.head
end;

function LTail   {(l: List): Position};
{Returns the position of the tail of the list.}
   var
      p: Position;
begin
  if l.head = **nil then**
    LTail : = **nil**   {There is no tail in an empty list.}
  else
    begin
      p : = l.head;
      while p^.next $<>$ **nil do**
        p : = p^.next;
      LTail : = p
    end
end;

function LPrior   {(p: Position; l: List): Position};
{Returns the position immediately before p,}
{if such a position exists, otherwise returns }
{the null pseudo-position.   }
   var
      current: Position;
      done: boolean;

```
begin
  if (p < = 1) or (p > l.length) then
    LPrior := 0              {no prior position or bad position error}
  else
    LPrior := p − 1
end;


function LNext    {(p: Position; l: List): Position};
{Returns the position immediately after p, }
{if such a position exists, otherwise returns}
{the null pseudo-position.                  }
begin
  if (p > = l.length) or (p = 0) then
    LNext := 0              {no next position or bad position error}
  else
    LNext := p + 1
end;

function LFindNth    {(n: integer; l: List): Position};
{Returns the n-th position in the list,      }
{if such a position exists, otherwise returns}
{the null pseudo-position.                   }
begin
  if (n < 1) or (n > l.length) then
    LFindNth := 0              {bad position error}
  else
    LFindNth := n
end;


function LSearch    {(d: DataType; l: List): Position};
{Returns the first position in the list with data }
{equal to d, if such a position exists, otherwise }
{returns the null pseudo-position.                }
```

```
begin
   current : = l.head;
   done : = false;

   while not done do
      if current = nil then              {Failed—ran out of positions to inspect.}
         done : = true

      else if current^.next = p then     {Succeeded—found the position.}
         done : = true

      else
         current : = current^.next;      {Keep looking.}

   LPrior : = current
end;

function LNext   {(p: Position; l: List): Position};
{Returns the position immediately after p, }
{if such a position exists, otherwise returns}
{the null pseudo-position.              }
begin
   if p = nil then
      LNext : = nil
   else
      LNext : = p^.next
end;

function LFindNth   {(n: integer; l: List): Position};
{Returns the n-th position in the list,      }
{if such a position exists, otherwise returns}
{the null pseudo-position.              }
   var
      count: integer;
      p: Position;
begin
   count : = 1;
   p : = l.head;

   while (count <> n) and (p <> nil) do
      begin
         count : = count + 1;
         p : = p^.next
      end;

   LFindNth : = p
end;

function LSearch   {(d: DataType; l: List): Position};
{Returns the first position in the list with data }
{equal to d, if such a position exists, otherwise}
{returns the null pseudo-position.        }
```

```
        var
            i: Position;
            done: boolean;
    begin
        i := 1;
        done := false;
        while not done do
            if i > l.length then              {Failed—ran out of elements to inspect.}
                begin
                    done := true;
                    LSearch := 0
                end
            else if l.data[i] = d then    {Succeeded—found the element.}
                begin
                    done := true;
                    LSearch := i
                end
            else                          {Keep looking.}
                i := i + 1
    end;

procedure ShiftArray (offset: integer; start: Position; var l: List);
{PRIVATE: Shifts the contents of an array from start}
{to the end of the array by the amount offset.      }
{NOTE: It is the responsibility of the calling routine }
{to make sure that the shifted part is within the     }
{range of the array indices.                          }
{Called by : LInsert, LDelete                         }
        var
            i: Position;
    begin
        if offset > 0 then
            for i := l.length + offset downto start + offset do
                l.data[i] := l.data[i − offset]
        else if offset < 0 then
            for i := start to l.length − offset do
                l.data[i] := l.data[i + offset]
    end;

procedure LInsert   {d: DataType; var p: Position; var l: List};
{Insert d into the list l, at position p.}
{NOTE: It is the responsibility of the }
{calling routine to guarantee that p  }
{is a valid position in l.            }
```

```
    var
        p: Position;
        done: boolean;
begin
    p := l.head;
    done := false;

    while not done do
        if p = nil then          {Failed—ran out of elements to inspect.}
            done := true

        else if p^.data = d then  {Succeeded—found the element.}
            done := true

        else                     {Keep looking.}
            p := p^.next;

    LSearch := p
end;
```

```
procedure LInsert   {d: DataType; var p: Position; var l: List};
{Insert d into the list l, at position p. If p is nil, we }
{insert the new element after the last cell in the list.}
{NOTE: It is the responsibility of the calling routine }
{to guarantee that p is a valid position in l.           }
    var
        newCell: Position;
```

```
begin
  if l.length = MAXLENGTH then
    writeln('No room in the list to insert a new element.')
  else
    begin
      if p < l.length + 1 then
      {We only need to shift elements if we're not appending onto the tail.}
        ShiftArray( + 1, p, l);

      l.data[p] := d;              {Insert new element.}
      l.length := l.length + 1   {Update length field.}
    end
end;
```

```
begin
    if l.length = 0 then                              {We're inserting into an empty list.}
      begin
        new(l.head);
        l.head^.data : = d;
        l.head^.next : = nil
      end
    else if p = nil then                              {We're inserting after the tail.}
      begin
        newCell : = l.head;
        while newCell^.next <> nil do                 {Find the last cell in the list,}
          newCell : = newCell^.next;
        new(newCell^.next);                           {and place the new cell after the end.}
        newCell^.next^.data : = d;
        newCell^.next^.next : = nil
      end
    else                                              {We're inserting into the interior of the list.}
      begin
        new(newCell);
        newCell^.data : = p^.data;
        newCell^.next : = p^.next;
        p^.data : = d;
        p^.next : = newCell
      end;
    l.length : = l.length + 1                         {In any case, update the length field.}
end;

procedure DeleteTail (var l: List);
{PRIVATE: Deletes the tail of the list.}
{NOTE: Assumes l is not empty.    }
{Called by : LDelete             }
    var
      p: Position;
begin
    p : = l.head;
    if p^.next = nil then                             {We're disposing of the only cell in the list.}
      begin
        l.head : = nil;
        dispose(p)
      end
```

```
procedure LDelete    {var p: Position; var l: List};
{Deletes the element at position p from the list l.    }
{NOTE: It is the responsibility of the calling         }
{routine to guarantee that p is a valid position in l.}
begin
    if p < l.length then              {We only need to shift elements if we're not deleting the tail.}
        ShiftArray( −1, p, l);

    l.length := l.length − 1
end;

end.                              {of unit ArrayList}
```

```
      else
        begin
          while p^.next^.next <> nil do    {Find a pointer to the cell before the tail,}
            p := p^.next;
          dispose(p^.next);                {and delete the tail.}
          p^.next := nil
        end;
      l.length := l.length - 1             {In either case, decrease the length field.}
  end;

procedure LDelete   {var p: Position; var l: List};
{Deletes the element at position p from the list l.   }
{NOTE: It is the responsibility of the calling routine}
{to guarantee that p is a valid position in l.        }
  var
    temp: Position;
  begin
    if p^.next = nil then                  {We have to treat the tail differently.}
      DeleteTail(p, l)
    else
      begin
        p^.data := p^.next^.data;
        temp := p^.next;
        p^.next := p^.next^.next;
        dispose(temp);
        l.length := l.length - 1
      end
  end;
end.                                       {of unit LinkedList}
```

13.3 Comparing Data Structures

The two implementations of *List* that we will investigate here are not the only possible ones, but they are the most common and probably look familiar to you. We represent a list first as an array of data elements, along with a length field, describing how many elements of the array contain useable information. Second, we describe a list as a linked list of records with a header record, containing a length field and a pointer to the first element of the list. Here are the **type** declarations for the two implementations:

Array implementation
const
   MAX = 1000;

type
   DataType = integer;

   Position = 0 .. MAX;
   List = **record**
       length: Position;
       data: **array**[1 .. MAX] **of** DataType
   end;

Pointer implementation
type
   DataType = integer;
   Position = ^Cell;
   Cell = **record**
       data: DataType;
       next: Position
      end;
   List = **record**
       length: integer;
       head: Position
     end;

Figure 13.1 illustrates these two implementations. Both, of course, are simply generalizations of data structures we have used in PasWord's various versions. How shall we compare these two? There's not much difference in the complexity of the **type** declarations, as you can see, so there's no reason on those grounds to prefer one over the other. You might prefer the array implementation simply because you've had more time to get accustomed to arrays, but with practice you'd probably be equally at home with the pointer version.

We find a significant difference between the two, however, when we look at their memory requirements. Suppose that pointers require four bytes of memory, integers use two bytes, and an object of type *DataType* takes d bytes. We want to see how much space will be required to store a list of L elements. The array version requires *MAX* (which we'll abbreviate as M in the formulas below) cells in the array, no matter how long the list is and so will require $2 + Md$ bytes to store a list, regardless of its length: 2 bytes for the length field and M array cells, each of size d.

The linked list version, on the other hand, will use only as many cells as the list has elements (L, in our notation). Each cell is larger than an array cell, since each cell in a linked list requires a pointer. The header record consists of an integer and a pointer, for a total of 6 bytes in this example, so to represent a list we will need $6 + L(d + 4)$ bytes. Thus, the array version will require less space than the

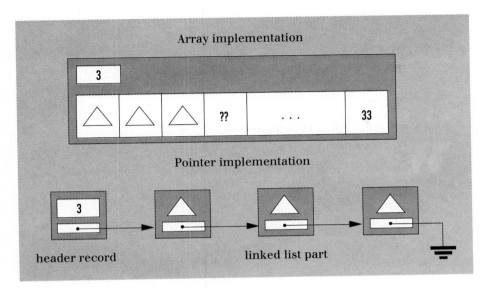

Array implementation

Pointer implementation

header record   linked list part

Figure **13.1.** Two implementations of the *List* ADT

pointer version whenever

$$2 + Md < 6 + L(d + 4)$$

With a little elementary algebra, we can solve for d, and so determine that the array version uses less memory whenever

$$d < \frac{4(L + 1)}{M - L}$$

As an example, suppose we consider lists that are half of the maximum size, with $L = 500$ and $M = 1000$. For these lists, the array version will require less space whenever the data size, d, is less than 4.008, so arrays are more efficient only for quite small data sizes. You can verify that for very small lists, with $L = 10$, arrays are more efficient only when $d < 0.044 \ldots$ Since no data types can be represented in .044 ... bytes, it is safe to say that small linked lists will use less space no matter what size *DataType* is.

Before we leave this comparison, let's see just how much more memory-efficient the linked list version is. We'll take the more extreme of the two preceding examples and look at how much space is required to store a small list of size 10. Suppose that we had a list of integers, so $d = 2$ in this case. The array will require $2 + 1000 \times 2 = 2002$ bytes, whereas the linked version will take only $6 + 10(2 + 4) = 66$ bytes, which is just a bit more than one thirtieth of the array version! If an application using lists needed to store 100 lists, for instance, and we knew that most were very small but one or two might be very large, we might be able to stop right here, since that many lists in array form could take more memory than the system had available. In that case, it would make no difference whether the array version ran faster,[1] since the only choice would be between a program that ran and one that wouldn't run at all.

13.4 Comparing Algorithms

When we descend from the ADT level and look at implementations in a real programming language, the abstract structures of the positions become *data structures*, described by constant and type declarations. Analogously, operations become *algorithms*, described by procedure and function declarations. Just as we can compare the space used by different implementations of an abstract structure, we can also compare the time required by the subprograms that implement the abstract operations.

Computing Timing Functions

Since we've decided that the time an algorithm takes to run will be expressed as a function of how long the input to the algorithm is, we need to decide how to measure time. One thing we could do is code the algorithm, run it for various input sizes, and count the number of seconds the algorithm takes to complete. The problem, of course, is that the values we get will apply only to one machine/ compiler combination and so will be useless for other systems. What we'll do instead is analyze the algorithm to count the maximal number of statements that are executed over all inputs of a given size.

Often our job is very simple, since many algorithms take a constant amount of time, regardless of the input. Take, for instance, the initialization routine, *LInit*, which initializes the list to the empty list (a list with no elements).

procedure LInit (var l: List);

Array implementation	*Pointer implementation*
begin	**begin**
l.length : = 0	l.length : = 0;
end;	l.head : = **nil**
	end;

Clearly, each of these routines will run in an amount of time that is independent of the size of the list it is initializing. In a similar way, we see that *LEmpty*, *LLength*, *LHead*, and *LNext* run in "constant time" for both implementations. In terms we introduced in Chapter 9, we would say that the running times of these algorithms were all $O(1)$.

-----

[1] It doesn't, by the way—at least not for all of the operations on *list*.

LSearch, however, is an $O(n)$ algorithm in either implementation, since it requires a traversal of the list and so could take as many as n steps through the traversal loop (where n is the size of the list) to discover that the desired element is or is not in the list. That both these implementations may take time proportional to the size of the list should come as no surprise, since they are almost line-for-line identical. The steps these implementations use are the same, since they are really the same algorithm in two different guises: "Starting from the head, inspect each element in turn until you find d or run out of elements in the list."

function LSearch (d: DataType; l: List): Position;

Array implementation	*Pointer implementation*
var	**var**
i: Position;	p: Position;
done: boolean;	done: boolean;
begin	**begin**
i := 1;	p := l.head;
done := false;	done := false;
while not done **do**	**while not** done **do**
if i > l.length **then**	**if** p = **nil then**
begin	
done := true;	done := true
LSearch := 0	
end	
else if l.data[i] = d **then**	**else if** p^.data = d **then**
begin	
done := true;	done := true
LSearch := i	
end	
else	**else**
i := i + 1	p := p^.next;
end;	LSearch := p
	end;

There are cases, though, in which the choice of implementation makes a great deal of difference in processing time. Consider the function *LPrior*, for instance. Given a position, p, in the array implementation (an array index), we check whether p is in the list, and if it is, we return $p - 1$. We simply use the value of the length field and have no need even to traverse the list. That clearly takes $O(1)$ time. However, to find the position prior to the pointer p in a linked list, we must do a linear search, starting at the head of the list and inspecting each cell until we find one whose next cell is the one pointed to by p, or we find that there is no such cell. We have to do this since pointers are one-way devices, so there is no pointer equivalent to the integer statement $p := p - 1$. This linear search could take time proportional to the length of the list, if the position p happens not to be in the list or is at the end of the list, for example. This means, of course, that the pointer implementation of *Prior* is a linear, $O(n)$, algorithm on lists of size n.

function LPrior (p: Position; l: List): Position;

Array implementation	*Pointer implementation*
Runs in constant time	*Could take time proportional to* n

Array implementation

Runs in constant time

```
begin
  if (p <= 1) or (p > l.length) then
    LPrior := 0
  else
    LPrior := p − 1
end;
```

Pointer implementation

Could take time proportional to n

```
var
  current: Position;
  done: boolean;
begin
  current := l.head;
  done := false;
  while not done do
    if current = nil then
      done := true
    else if current^.next = p then
      done := true
    else
      current := current^.next;
  LPrior := current
end;
```

You should be able to verify the timing estimates for the two implementations of the *List* operations given in Table 13.1.

Table 13.1.   Timing estimates for array and pointer implementations of the *List* operations

Operation	Array Implementation	Pointer Implementation
LInit	1	1
LDestroyList	1	*n*
LEmpty	1	1
LBadPosition	1	*n*
LLength	1	1
LHead	1	1
LTail	1	*n*
LPrior	1	*n*
LNext	1	1
LFindNth	1	*n*
LSearch	*n*	*n*
(ShiftArray)	*n*	—
LInsert	*n*	1 (unless inserting after tail)
(DeleteTail)	—	*n*
LDelete	*n*	1 (unless deleting from tail)

Note: 1 = constant time, *n* = time proportional to the length of the list

Tradeoffs

We've compared two implementations of the *List* ADT. Which is better? If we intend that question to mean which is better for all list-manipulating programs, we can't answer it, since there is no answer. On one hand, we've seen that the array implementation of the *list* operations runs at least as fast as the pointer versions in most cases and runs significantly faster for operations like *Destroy*, *Tail*, *Prior*, and *FindNth*. On the other hand, we shouldn't rush to choose the array implementation, since we've also demonstrated that it uses more space, as a rule, than the pointer version.

As is often the case, programmers are faced with the kinds of decisions engineers have to make all the time. An engineer would never say with certainty what the best design for a bridge is without knowing what other factors are involved: How long will the bridge be, what loads will it have to bear, how much money is available for the project? Although in the abstract it would make sense to plate the bridge with gold, for instance, since gold is very resistant to corrosion and would never need to be repainted, that suggestion for an implementation would invariably be rejected because of cost. In a similar way, a programmer needs to know the relative memory and speed costs of the available implementations and the nature of the program and then base the decision of implementation on all these considerations.

To take a simple example, imagine that space was at a premium (if, for instance, the program would have to maintain a large number of lists of varying sizes) and that insertions and deletions were to be made only at the heads of lists. The pointer version would be a winner in terms of both memory use and speed, since the pointer versions of insertion and deletion at the head of linked lists runs in constant time, whereas the array version requires that we shift the entire contents of the array. Of course, not all decisions about implementation are this easy, but this example points out the importance of knowing the properties of several implementations of a single abstract data type.

Finally, we should never take the implementation of an ADT as graven in stone. These routines provide ways to do the list operations, but there will invariably be options that experience will suggest. Insertion in a list, for example, will take time proportional to the length of the list with arrays because of the need to shift elements to make room for the new one. We can modify insertion in a linked list to run in constant time, though, if the data is not too large, or if we are fortunate enough to know the position pointer to the cell prior to where the new data will go. The exercises explore ways to do this and illustrate that we should always be open to the possibility of modifying the package of routines in our toolkit.

13.5   Computer Science Interlude: Object-Oriented Programming

Over the past few years, a number of researchers have observed that programming is very similar to preindustrial technology. An eighteenth-century gunsmith, for example, would have constructed the gunstock from a piece of wood, forged and bored the barrel from a piece of iron, and constructed the firing mechanism from scratch for each weapon. Such a gun could take several months to produce, and would cost more than most people could afford, since it required the complete attention of a skilled craftsperson for a considerable length of time. Even worse, if the gun later broke, it would be repaired only by another highly skilled gunsmith.

Many programs today are constructed in the same way—they are built from scratch by highly skilled individuals and can be repaired and modified only by equally skilled workers. Parts of different programs are not interchangeable and must be custom-fitted for each new job. As a result, building large programs is time consuming, expertise intensive, and prone to error. This explains, in part, why software is expensive and comes with disclaimers that translate from legalese to something like "If our software fails and you lose a bundle because of the failure, you can't sue us." No automobile or toaster comes with a legal document like that. The reason has very much to do with the way cars and household appliances are built and how programs are not.

Building libraries of useful routines like the two units in this chapter is one way to simplify the technology of crafting programs. Having a library of procedures and functions is like having a stock of screws, trigger guards, and barrels on hand that can be used to make guns quickly and reliably, not to mention that the same stock parts can be used to make shotguns and pistols, as well as rifles.

Object-oriented programming (which we abbreviate to *OOP*) begins with the notion of encapsulation of structure and operations that we saw in the units of the Program in Progress and takes this notion several steps further. The first object-oriented language, Smalltalk, was developed at the Xerox Palo Alto Research Center at about the same time Nicklaus Wirth was working on Pascal, in the early 1970s. Since then, as computer scientists have seen the potential of the object-oriented approach, a number of other object-oriented languages have been developed. Some, like Object Pascal, C++, and Objective-C, are extensions of traditional languages. Others, like Smalltalk, Trellis, and Eiffel, are more nearly attempts to develop a language from the ground up.

Classes and Objects

The basic concepts of the object-oriented approach are the *class* and the *object*. Classes in object-oriented programming are very much like abstract data types, in that they describe a structure, the data that are associated with positions in the structure, and the operations that act on the structure and data. An *object* is similar to a variable, in that it is a particular instance of a class. Since it is an instance of a class, an object carries with it the ability to perform operations on its data. This is the major difference between object-oriented languages and *procedural languages* like Pascal. In Pascal, the programmer thinks of performing operations on variables; in object-oriented languages, the programmer thinks of sending messages to objects, telling them to perform actions on themselves.

For example, in an object-oriented version of PasWord, we might have a class, *Line*, that contained a list of characters and an integer representing the length of the list. Along with this data structure, the template *Line* would also contain declarations of procedures and functions that act on the line, such as a printing routine that would display the characters in the line. Then when it was necessary to print the contents of the object *thisLine*, the programmer would send a message to a particular *Line* object, telling it, in effect, "Print your contents." In Pascal, the equivalent would be to call a procedure that would take a line as one of its parameters and print it. The difference is that in the object-oriented paradigm, the details of printing are private to the line itself and do not appear in the calling routine.

The goal of object-oriented programming is to make the programming process easier. It does so in two basic ways. First, generally useful classes and objects, like lists, can be defined and used by any program intended to operate on them. This allows one to produce a program by plugging together a collection of predefined routines rather than designing these routines from scratch. The obvious advantages of this approach are that (1) much of the programming work is already done for you, (2) the predefined routines are reuseable across many applications, and (3) it significantly reduces the amount of sensitive code that is dependent purely on the application and must be carefully treated at any modification. In the gunsmithing example, it is as if the smith can rely on the facts that (1) there is no need to make gun barrels from scratch, (2) a 37-inch, 55-calibre barrel from one gun is guaranteed to fit another, and (3) the entire gun doesn't have to be rebuilt if the smith decided to change from a 55-calibre barrel to a 45-calibre one.

Using classes and objects also offers a distinct, nonprocedural means of program decomposition and design. Throughout this text, we have used decomposition as a means for describing large problems in terms of smaller ones and thus making them more tractable. Our basis for performing this "breaking down" has been primarily algorithmic — when a step in our algorithm is conceptually complex, we break it into two or more processing steps and encapsulate it as a subprogram. Many programs, on the other hand, lend themselves to data decomposition. That is, the program can be described as a model of *things*, as opposed to *actions*. In such cases, programs can be broken down into subprograms by describing the thing being modeled in terms of its constituent parts (a knob on the device, a functional unit of a business, a person with specific responsibilities, and so on) rather than the specifics of its processing.

This model is important because recent studies have confirmed that people naturally classify information in an object-oriented way and because, as you can now see, the functions of a program during its lifetime tend to change much more rapidly than the objects. Thus, we have evidence that an OOP approach not only makes programs easier to write but easier to maintain as well.

Keeping with our attempt to bring gunsmithing into the industrial era, we might observe that the basic production steps are much the same for barrels of rifles, pistols, shotguns, and cannons. In all four, one makes a straight cylinder of the appropriate material and dimension with a circular hole through the length of the cylinder. In our terms, we have a *barrel* class (which could be used as is for instances such as shotguns and cannons) and a subclass of barrels with grooves in the bore (for rifles and pistols). Almost all of the manufacturing directions are the same for rifles and shotguns—the *rifleBarrel* class just has some extra steps and inherits the rest from its parent class.

Inheritance

Typically, an object-oriented language has a large number of classes built in already. The class *CList*, for example, might have the thirteen list operations we defined in Section 13.1. If we want to write a program that manipulates sorted lists, in which the data elements are arranged in order of their values, we might consider defining a class *CSortedList* to encapsulate the details of storing and manipulating such lists. Many of the operations on sorted lists, such as creating empty instances, finding the length, and finding the head element, depend only on the list-like structure, not on the fact that the elements are in sorted order, and so don't need to be specific to the subclass *CSortedList*. Others, like searching for an element, can be tailored to the subclass (since it's much easier to find an element in a sorted list than in an unsorted list, as we've seen).

In Object Pascal, we define our own classes by extending (overloading) the **type** declaration to include the **class**, so we could define our *CSortedList* class as follows:

```
type
    CSortedList = object(CList);
    {The class CSortedList is a subclass of CList.}
        function Search(theObject : CObject) : CObject; override;
        {Search is defined for objects in CList. We are indicating}
        {here that within the subclass we're using a different    }
        {definition that overrides the definition in CList.        }
        function Min : CObject;
        {Min, on the other hand, is not an operation defined for CList,}
        {so to use it in CSortedList, we have to define it here.       }
    end;
```

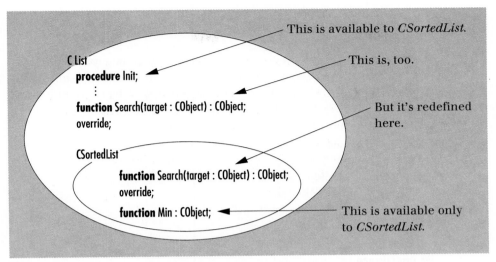

The following text appears within the figure:

C List
  procedure Init;   This is available to *CSortedList*.
    ⋮   This is, too.
  function Search(target : CObject) : CObject;
  override;   But it's redefined
                                 here.
  CSortedList
      function Search(target : CObject) : CObject;
      override;
      function Min : CObject;   This is available only
                                    to *CSortedList*.

Figure 13.2.   Inheritance from a class to a subclass

The subprogram declarations for the functions *Search* and *Min* are distinguished from the corresponding functions in *CList* by placing their class names in front, like this:

```
function CSortedList.Search(target : CObject) : CObject;
begin
    Statements here
end;
function CSortedList.Min : CObject;
begin
    Statements here
end;
```

Don't worry about syntactic details — this is not a tutorial on object-oriented programming in Object Pascal but rather just a taste. The important thing to notice is that the class *CSortedList* inherits the operations of its superclass *CList*, as shown in Figure 13.2. For programming purposes, this means that many of the routines we'd have to include among the sorted list routines are already written for us simply because they are part of the parent class that deals with general lists. If the predefined library of classes is large enough, then the programmer's job is considerably simplified.

The class inheritance structure in an object-oriented programming system guarantees that subclasses can use all the procedures and functions defined for their parent classes. All the programmer has to do is rewrite the ones that need to be made particular to the subclass and add ones that the parent class doesn't provide.

Polymorphism

We mentioned variant records in Section 10.5

Suppose we had to write a geometry program that, among its other actions, computed the areas of plane geometric figures like squares, triangles, and circles. In Pascal, we might use variant records to represent these figures and a single procedure to find their areas, as follows.

```
type
    Shape = (square, triangle, circle);
    Figure = record
                    case theShape : Shape of
                        square : (side : real);
                        triangle : (base, height : real);
                        circle : (radius : real)
                end;
function ComputeArea(f : Figure) : real;
    const
        PI = 3.14159;
begin
    if f.theShape = square then
        ComputeArea : = sqr(f.side)
    else if f.theShape = triangle then
        ComputeArea : = 0.5 * f.base * f.height
    else if f.theShape = circle then
        ComputeArea : = PI * sqr(f.radius)
end;
```

It would be generous to say that this is somewhat confusing. Not only is it hard to read, but adding another shape would require that we change the record definition, the function *ComputeArea*, and any other routines that rely on the shape of a geometric figure. In an object-oriented language, we might instead have a class *CFigure* with subclasses *CSquare*, *CTriangle*, and *CCircle*, each of which might have its own *ComputeArea* routine. If *theFigure* was an object of one of these classes and we wanted it to report its area, all we would have to do is send it a message invoking its *ComputeArea* function message, as

```
area : = theFigure.ComputeArea
```

The system would look at the class of the object *theFigure* and decide which of the several functions called *ComputeArea* would be the appropriate one to apply to *theFigure*. When writing the program, we wouldn't have to have any idea which class *theFigure* belonged to—we could use the same function name for all of them and let the system sort it out. The ability to use the same name for an operation on different classes of objects is called *polymorphism*. The advantage in this case is that we keep the notion of computing area separated from the details of how we perform the computations. In the spirit of object-orientation, we leave the details entirely in the hands of the objects themselves.

The only equivalents of polymorphism in standard Pascal are some of the numeric operators like +, which may perform integer addition, real addition, or set union (which are implemented in three very different ways), and the I/O procedures like *write* (which act in very different ways, depending on whether they are called to operate on integers, reals, or characters). Object-oriented languages allow us to define polymorphic operations of our own.

If the object-oriented paradigm is such a good way of enhancing programmer productivity, why didn't we teach you Object Pascal right from the start? To be honest, we considered it seriously but eventually decided in favor of standard Pascal for two main reasons. The practical reason was that Pascal is big enough all by itself so that it's a tight fit to get all of Pascal and program design techniques into one term. Simply speaking, it would be impossible to do all that and object-oriented programming in one course. The pedagogical reason is that, as they exist now, object-oriented languages are bulky and not easy to learn. With their dozens of classes and hundreds of operations, they impose a significant burden on both the programmer and the system. Your authors regularly use object-oriented languages for large projects; we believe this paradigm does lead to more effective programming. But there's a big difference between using a language and advocating it as a first experience for novices. We hope that there will come a time when someone will invent an object-oriented language that's as easy to learn as Pascal — and when that time comes, you'll hear from us again.

13.6 Reference

- Computer science is devoted to discovering, analyzing, and utilizing the general principles that describe computers and their programs. One of these general principles is the abstract data type (ADT).
- An abstract data type is defined by (1) a structure of positions, (2) the data associated with the positions, and (3) the operations that act on the positions and their data. The *list* ADT, for example, has its positions in a linear order with any data type we choose associated with the positions and has a collection of operations that perform actions such as creating an empty list, telling the length of a list, inserting an element in a list, and so on.
- When we implement an ADT, we represent its structure and data as a data structure defined in a particular language, and we represent its operations as procedures and functions in the language.
- We can compare implementations of an ADT by looking at the space required by the data structures and the time taken by the algorithms, generally expressing each as functions of the size of the objects being stored or acted upon.

- When comparing implementations of an ADT, there is generally not a clear winner. Often we gain speed at the expense of space, and *vice versa*.
- Object-oriented programming (OOP) extends the notions of encapsulation and information-hiding by providing:
  - *Classes* that contain data structures and operations on these structures.
  - *Objects* that are instances of classes and that communicate to other objects by passing messages to perform some actions on themselves.
  - *Inheritance*, in which a class and its objects may inherit the definitions of its parent classes.
  - *Polymorphism*, in which a collection of related actions across several classes may be given the same name.

13.7 Building Blocks

We won't list the building blocks in this chapter, since the Program in Progress consists almost entirely of building blocks. The two units are examples of what one should strive for when building a library of useful routines—an entire package of building blocks, all tailored for a particular structure. In doing this, a program that uses a linear structure can consist of nothing but the description of what should be done with these lists. All of the programming details of list manipulation are hidden in the units, where they don't stand in the way of understanding what the program itself does.

Finally, notice that if we design a program this way, we can completely change the implementation by changing just the **uses** clause—apart from that we don't have to touch the program at all. We did just that when we upgraded PasWord from version 2.0 to version 3.0. We could think of the program as a person given the task of getting from San Francisco to Detroit and having available the means of getting the job done by driving, flying, or taking a train. These choices are analogous to units, and all the person has to do is choose which one he or she will use. Some choices are fast but expensive, and some are cheap but tedious—the traveler, like the programmer, needs only to choose wisely. The knowledge on which to base your choices is what awaits you in the computer science courses that lie ahead.

13.8

EXERCISES

1. Sometimes we can improve the efficiency of operations on a data structure if we modify it slightly.

   a. For example, would any of the operations on the pointer version of *List* be faster if we included in the header record a pointer to the list tail?

   b. Would this change require modification of any of the other operations besides the ones you mentioned in part a? If so, give an example by rewriting one operation for this modified implementation.

2. Let's look at whether it would be worth our time to modify the pointer implementation of *List* by using doubly linked lists, as we did in Chapter 12, Exercise 21.

   a. Which operations would be faster in this implementation?

   b. Considering the changes that would have to be made to other operations, would you say the change of implementation was worth it? Justify your answer, explaining your reasons in detail.

3. We've left some operations out of our *List* ADT. Think of at least one that would be appropriate to include.

4. For your choice of operation in Exercise 3, write implementations for arrays and linked lists.

   For Exercises 5–10, describe as clearly as possible the structure of the abstract data types (remember that pictures are worth 2^{10} words), and provide descriptions of what would be a reasonable collection of operations on instances of each structure.

5. *Stacks*, mentioned in Exercise 25 of Chapter 12.

6. *Queues*, mentioned in Exercise 26 of Chapter 12.

7. *Rings*, consisting of a circular arrangement of positions, along with a reference to a current position. The current position is where all insertions, deletions, and inspections are made. Such a data structure is sometimes used for time-sharing the resources of a computer. Each job has a record describing it, and when the current position advances to a job's description, that job is given a small slice of time to run, after which the current position advances to the next job, which is then given a small slice of time, and so on.

8. *Binary trees*, mentioned in Exercise 23 of Chapter 12.

9. *Sorted lists*, which have the linear structure of *List* but have the elements arranged in sorted order.

10. *Graphs*, where a graph consists of a collection of positions, some of which are linked to others. We might use a graph to model cities and airline connections between them.

6 + *n*. For Exercises $n = 5$ to 10, provide an implementation by (a) giving **type** declarations and descriptions of whatever operations that (b) create a new empty instance of the type, (c) do the equivalent of insertion, and (d) do the equivalent of deletion.

17. It is quite often the case that a list (or almost any other ADT, for that matter) has elements that are more complicated than integers. Frequently, the elements of a list are records like employee records, and one record field, called a *key field*, is singled out for special consideration. In the case of employee records, for instance, the key field might be an integer ID number that uniquely distinguishes each employee. If that was the case, what modifications might you make to the *List* ADT?

18. If you were to design an object-oriented language, what classes would you include? What would your hierarchy look like? This is not a trivial question—a good answer might require only three pages but might be the result of considerable thought. Think of this as an essay question.

19. Write a class hierarchy for polygons (like triangles, squares, rectangles, and so on), including the operations for each class.

20. Of the four distinguishing features of object-oriented languages—classes, objects, inheritance, and polymorphism, which one would you jettison if you were told you could keep only three in an object-oriented language you were designing?

21. We could represent polynomials in one variable—like 4, or $2 + x$, or $8.3 - 2x + 3.4x^2$—as lists, consisting of the coefficients of each term. For instance, the polynomial $3.9 + 45.7x^2 - 0.901x^3$ could be represented by the list (3.9, 0, 45.7, −0.901). Suppose we wanted to write a package to manipulate polynomials.

a. Which of the *List* operations would be appropriate for this application?
b. What operations would you have to include that were not provided by the *List* ADT?

22. Rewrite PasWord using either of the two *List* units. Which unit you use, of course, will make no difference at all to the code of PasWord, although you'll have to modify the unit you choose so that it refers to a list of lines rather than a list of integers. You might want to include another unit that uses the list unit and is used by the main program. Such a unit would handle all the details that are specific to the word-processing functionality of the program, as opposed to the list-handling aspect.

13.9
Answers

1. a. *LTail*, of course, would be faster. It would change the running time from $O(n)$ to $O(1)$.
  b. We'll give two examples of the changes we'd have to make, one simple and one not quite so simple. When we create a new list, we must now make the *l.tail* pointer **nil**, and when we insert a new element and the new element happens to go at the tail of the list, we must update the *l.tail* pointer. *LInsert* now runs in $O(1)$ time, no matter where the insertion occurs.

```
procedure LCreate(var l : List);
begin
    l.length : = 0;
    l.head : = nil;
    l.tail : = nil                    (**CHANGE**)
end;
```

```
procedure LInsert    {d: DataType; var p: Position; var l: List};
    var
        newCell: Position;
begin
    if l.length = 0 then                    {We're inserting into an empty list.}
        begin
            new(l.head);
            l.head^.data := d;
            l.head^.next := nil;
            l.tail := l.head                (**CHANGE**)
        end

    else if p = nil then                    {We're inserting after the tail.}
        begin
            new(newCell);                   (**CHANGE**)
            newCell^.data := d;             (**CHANGE**)
            newCell^.next := nil;           (**CHANGE**)
            l.tail^.next := newCell         (**CHANGE**)
        end

    else                                    {We're inserting into the interior of the list.}
        begin
            new(newCell);
            newCell^.data := p^.data;
            newCell^.next := p^.next;
            p^.data := d;
            p^.next := newCell;
            if newCell^.next = nil then     (**CHANGE**)
                l.tail := newCell           (**CHANGE**)
        end;
    l.length := l.length + 1                {In any case, update the length field.}
end;
```

3. One would be to *Retrieve* the element in position p in a list so that it can be inspected.

5. We discussed the structure in Chapter 12. It's a linear structure, like *List*. The customary operations on stacks are *Create* a new, empty, stack, *Push* a new element on a stack, *Pop* an element from the stack, removing it and its position, *Top*, which returns the top element on a stack without removing it, and an operation that would tell whether a stack was *Empty*.

7. The structure is a circular arrangement of positions, that is, one for which each position has exactly one immediate successor and one immediate predecessor, and every position is eventually reachable from every other.

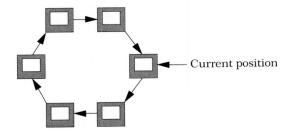
Current position

Operations might include *Create* an empty ring, *Advance* the current position to its successor, *Insert* a new element in the ring at the current position, *Delete* the element in the current position, *Retrieve* the element in the current position, *Update* the element in the current position, replacing it by another, and tell whether the ring is *Empty*.

9. The structure is exactly that of a list. The operations would be those of the *List* ADT, but we wouldn't need the position parameter in *Insert*, since there would be only one place to insert a new element (assuming that there were no duplicate elements).

11. a–c. See Exercise 25 of Chapter 12 for the **type** declarations and for the definitions of *Create* and *Push*.

d. If we used the pointer implementation, the delete procedure *Pop* would look like this:

```
procedure Pop(var s : Stack);
    var
        temp : StackPtr;
begin
    if s = nil then
        writeln('Can''t Pop from an empty stack.')
    else
        begin
            temp := s;
            s := s^.next;
            dispose(temp)
        end
end;
```

It's worth mentioning here that quite a few authors fold *Pop* and *Top* into one subprogram that returns the top element from the stack and then deletes it from the stack. It's good to know that, not only because it will prepare you for other definitions of *Stack*, but also to illustrate that the definitions for even the most common ADTs are open to different interpretations.

13. We'll use a pointer-based implementation, referring to a ring by a pointer to the current cell in the ring.

a. type
```
JobRec = some appropriate type;
JobPtr = ^JobCell;
JobCell = record
              data : JobRec;
              next : JobPtr
          end;
Ring = JobPtr;
```

b. procedure RCreate(**var** r : Ring);
```
begin
    r := nil
end;
```

c. **procedure** RInsert(j : JobRec ; **var** r : Ring);
    var
        newCell : JobPtr;
  begin
    new(newCell);
    if r = **nil then**   {The ring is empty.}
      begin
        newCell^.data : = j;
        newCell^.next : = newCell;
        r : = newCell
      end
    else   {The ring has at least one cell.}
      begin
        newCell^.data : = r^.data;
        r^.data : = j;
        newCell^.next : = r^.next;
        r^.next : = newCell
      end
  end;

d. **procedure** RDelete(**var** r : Ring);
    var
        temp : JobPtr;
  begin
    if r = **nil then**   {The ring is empty.}
      writeln('Can''t delete an element from an empty ring.')
    else if r^.next = r **then**   {The ring has only one cell.}
      begin
        dispose(r);
        r : = **nil**
      end
    else   {The ring has more than one cell.}
      begin
        temp : = r^.next;
        r^.data : = temp^.data;
        r^.next : = temp^.next;
        dispose(temp)
      end
  end;

15. a, b. The array implementation of *List* would be appropriate here, since it permits us to find an element in $O(\log n)$ time. We'd rewrite *LSearch* to use the binary search routine we discussed in Chapter 9. See **unit** *ArrayList* for the **type** declarations and the definition of *LInit*. Note that although we can find where to place the new element in $\log n$ time, insertion is still $O(n)$, since we have to shift the array to make room for the new element.

c. **function** LSearch (d: DataType ; start, finish : Position ; l: SortedList): Position;
{Returns the position in the list l where the element d should be inserted.}
    var
        mid: Position;

```
    begin
      if start = finish then
      {The sublist is of length 1, so figure where d belongs, at or after the one element.}
          if d < = l.data[start] then
            LSearch : = start
          else
            LSearch : = start + 1
      else
      {The sublist we're searching is longer than one, so find the sublist where d belongs.}
          begin
            mid : = (start + finish) div 2;
            if d = l.data[mid] then
              LSearch : = mid
            else if d < l.data[mid] then
              LSearch : = Lsearch(d, start, mid, l)
            else
              LSearch : = Lsearch(d, mid + 1, finish, l)
          end
    end;
    procedure LInsert(d : DataType ; var l : SortedList);
      var
        where : Position;
    begin
      if l.length = MAXLENGTH then
        writeln('No room in the list to insert a new element.')
      else
        begin
          where : = LSearch(d, 1, l.length, l);
          if where < l.length + 1 then
            ShiftArray( +1, where, l);
          l.data[where] : = d;
          l.length : = l.length + 1
        end
    end;
```

d. Deletion was done in *ArrayList*.

17. We would modify *LSearch* so that it searched for an employee's position in the list by key field. It would also be appropriate to include operations to *Update* the other fields of a record in a given position, to account for name changes, changes in pay rate, and so on. This modification moves our *List* ADT toward becoming a database, which we discussed in Chapter 11.

19. The class hierarchy might be arranged like this, in part:

    Polygon
        Triangle (Three-sided figures)
            Right (Contains a right angle)
            Isosceles (Contains two equal angles and two equal sides)
            Equilateral (All sides and angles are the same length)

Quadrilateral (Four-sided figures)
Trapezoid (Two sides are parallel)
Parallelogram (All opposite sides are parallel)
Rectangle (All angles are right angles)
Rhombus (All sides are of the same length)
Square (Could be a subclass of *Rectangle* or *Rhombus*)

Typical operations might be to have an object return its area, to create a new instance of an object when given suitable information, to destroy an object, to have an object determine whether it intersects another object, to have an object return the object formed by the intersection of itself with another object, to have an object draw itself on a display screen, and so on.

21. a. *LInit, LDestroyList, LInsert, LDelete.*
  b. We would probably want to include routines to add, subtract, multiply, and divide polynomials and to evaluate a polynomial for a given x value.

Reserved Words

and	end	mod	repeat
array	file	nil	set
begin	for	not	then
case	forward	of	to
const	function	or	type
div	goto	packed	until
do	if	procedure	var
downto	in	program	while
else	label	record	with

Standard Identifiers

abs	false	pack	sin
arctan	get	page	sqr
boolean	input	pred	sqrt
char	integer	put	succ
chr	ln	read	text
cos	maxint	readln	true
dispose	new	real	trunc
eof	odd	reset	unpack
eoln	ord	rewrite	write
exp	output	round	writeln

In these definitions, terms that are defined elsewhere are italicized.

Abstract data type (ADT) A formal description of a class of information consisting of a structure of positions, the data associated with the positions, and the structure-preserving operations that may be applied to instances of the *data type*.

Accumulator variable A *variable* to which the same operation may be performed repeatedly. For example, a variable that keeps a running sum of input values.

Activation record The information that must be saved upon invocation of a *function* or *procedure* in order to guarantee an orderly return.

Actual parameters The *parameters* that are used when a *function* or *procedure* is *called* in a *program*. See also *Formal parameters*.

Algorithm A clearly defined and unambiguous sequence of operations needed to perform an information-processing task. When *implemented* in a particular programming language, an algorithm takes the form of a *program* or *subprogram*.

Aliases Two or more seemingly distinct *identifiers* that refer to the same object. To be avoided whenever possible.

Allocation The action an *operating system* takes to set aside a location in *memory* for use by a *program*. See also *Used list*.

Anonymous type A *type* definition that is made directly, rather than using the name of a previously defined type. In Pascal, *formal parameters* cannot be defined anonymously.

Array In programming languages, a *structured data type*, consisting of a collection of elements of one type, indexed by one or more *ordinal* values.

Artificial Intelligence The branch of computer science devoted to the study of the computer solution of problems that require what we would call intelligent behavior if performed by humans. Distinguished from the much more common field of Artificial Stupidity, which produces programs that generate $10-million phone bills.

ASCII American Standard Code for Information Interchange; a code used to represent *character* information as a sequence of *bits*.

Assembly language A programming language that closely parallels *machine language* but uses descriptive references that people can read and understand more readily.

Assignment statement A statement that sets a *variable* equal to the value of an *expression*. In Pascal, an assignment statement takes the form *variable := expression*.

Back-to-front reading A *top-down* approach to *program* reading, starting with the *subprogram* calls in the main statement body and proceeding through the subprograms. The reverse of *front-to-back reading*.

Best-fit An *algorithm* for *allocation* that chooses the smallest available block that will fill an allocation request.

Big-O notation An upper estimate for a function. A function *f* is *O(g)* if *f* eventually is always less than some fixed multiple of a function *g*.

Binary file A *file* whose *components* are data values represented as they are stored in *memory*. Distinguished from a *textfile*.

Binary notation Base-2 *positional notation*; a way of expressing numeric information as sums of powers of two, using the digits 0 and 1.

Binary search A search *algorithm*, commonly used with *arrays*, that repeatedly divides the search domain into two nearly equal parts. A *logarithmic-time algorithm*.

Bit A binary digit, either 0 or 1.

Bit bucket The mythical location where data go when they are lost or destroyed. Commonly encountered when using *pointers*.

Block A portion of a Pascal program that begins with the *parameters* of a *program* or *subprogram* and ends with the last **end** in the statement part of the program or subprogram. Every object in a Pascal program

has a *scope* consisting of the block within which the object is defined.

Boolean A *data type* that consists of two values, true and false.

Bottom-up design The process of design that works toward a solution by repeatedly combining small units to form larger ones. The reverse process is known as *top-down design*.

Bounded linear search A *linear search* algorithm characterized by an *exit condition* that may terminate the search before all data have been inspected.

Braid See *Multilist*.

Buffer *Memory* used for temporary storage, generally used to store input or output until needed by a *program* or output device.

Byte A sequence of eight *bits*. Half a byte is a nybble or nibble.

Call In Pascal, a location in a *program* where a *function* or *procedure* is invoked and caused to be executed.

Capitalization of identifiers A consistent scheme to indicate the nature of an identifier by the way it is capitalized. In this text, we indicate variables with initial lowercase letters, like *totalAmount*; we write constants using all uppercase, like *ARRAYSIZE*; and we use initial caps for subprogram names, like *SphereVol*.

Case-sensitive The property whereby upper- and lowercase letters are considered to be different, as, for example, in Pascal *strings*. Distinguished from *case-insensitive*, where there is no logical difference between upper- and lowercase letters, as in Pascal *identifiers*.

Central processing unit (CPU) That part of a computer that performs the information-processing operations. A computer may be regarded as consisting of a CPU, a *memory*, and *input/output (I/O) units*.

Character An instance of the *char* data type; a single character, such as 'A' or '#'. In Pascal, a character *literal* is represented between single quotes.

Class In *object-oriented programming*, an implementation of an *abstract data type* consisting of data and routines for manipulating the data.

Comment Explanatory text in a *source code* program that is not translated into executable code. Useless to computers, comments are indispensable to humans.

Compiler A program that takes *source code* in a language like Pascal and translates it into *object code* that may be executed by a computer. Unlike an *interpreter*, a compiler translates all of the source code before any of the translated statements are executed.

Compiler directive An instruction to a *compiler*; compiler directives appear in *source code* programs, but they are not translated into *object code* as statements are. In Pascal, **forward** is a compiler directive.

Component A constituent part of a *structured data type*, such as an element of an *array* or a *field* of a *record*.

Compound statement A *statement* that is comprised of more than one simpler statements grouped by a **begin..end** pair.

Constant An *identifier* that represents a value that may not be changed during the execution of any *statement* within its *scope*.

Contiguous Adjacent, with no intervening gaps. For example, the *integer subrange* 2 .. 9 consists of eight contiguous integers.

Control The order of execution of *statement*s in a *program*. In Pascal, control passes from one statement to the one following unless control is transferred to another location in a program by a **goto** statement, an **if** or **case** statement, a *loop*, or a *subprogram* call.

Control variable A variable that controls a **for** *loop*; also known as an index variable. More generally, any variable that may change its value at every iteration of a loop and that is used to determine the exit from a loop.

Counted loop A loop controlled by a *counter variable*.

Counter variable A special case of an *accumulator variable*; a variable that is increased by one at various times, to count the number of times a condition has occurred.

Crash In programming, a catastrophic error from which recovery is impossible. A situation to be avoided whenever possible.

Dangling reference When using *pointers*, a memory location for which there is no longer any pointer reference. See also *Bit bucket*.

Data type An organization of information supported by the features of a programming language. In Pascal, there are eleven basic data types: *integer, real, character, boolean, enumerated, subrange, set, array, record, file,* and *pointer*.

Deallocation The action an *operating system* takes to set free a location in *memory* that was formerly used by a *program*. See also *Free list*.

Debugging The process of finding and repairing errors in a program. The term "bug," meaning an error, was popularized by Grace Murray Hopper when a moth flew into a computer, causing a short circuit.

Declaration Those parts of a Pascal program where *labels, constants, types, variables,* and *subprograms* are defined.

Delimiter A *character* that separates functional units in a *program*. For example, a blank character may serve to delimit the end of a number, separating it from what follows.

Divide and conquer An *algorithm* design process in which a problem is divided into smaller problems, the smaller problems are solved, and then they are suitably combined to produce a solution to the larger problem.

Documentation The comments in a *program* and the supporting explanations, such as technical manuals, that describe the action and design of the program. See also *Comment*.

Doubly-linked list A collection of data values arranged in a list by being linked in each direction with *pointers*. See also *Linked list*.

Dynamic data structure A data structure whose actual or conceptual size may vary during the execution of a *program*.

Empty statement In Pascal, a *statement* that is translated into a no-operation instruction to the computer. For example, an empty statement is understood to lie between apparently adjacent semicolons.

Encapsulation The process of collecting logically related data declarations and operations in one place, to hide internal details and make the resulting code easier to understand.

End-of-file mark In Pascal, an indicator of the end of a data file. Unlike the *end-of-line mark*, the end-of-file mark cannot be read, but rather must be inspected by the *eof* function.

End-of-line mark In Pascal, a special *character* that represents the end of a line of *input* or *output*. Generally, one uses the function *eoln* to test for the presence of the end-of-line mark.

Enumerated type An *ordinal* type for which the *literal* names of its values are defined within a program. Also called a user-defined ordinal type.

Execute In computer science, to perform one or more instructions on a computer.

Exit condition A condition that is true upon exit from a *loop* or *recursive subprogram*. Also, a condition that causes a *program* to exit from a loop or recursive subprogram.

Expert system A *program* that performs humanlike diagnostic and analytical functions in a specific field, such as medical diagnosis.

Exponential-time algorithm An *algorithm* whose *timing function* is exponential. An exponential algorithm is computationally infeasible for all but the smallest inputs.

Expression A part of a *statement* that consists of a formula for computing a single value.

Extension Features of a language that are not included in the *standard*, so cannot be relied on to exist in all *compilers*.

Fetch-execute cycle In a *stored-program computer*, this describes the process of fetching an *object code* statement from *memory* and then performing the statement.

Field In Pascal, a *component* of a *record*.

File Generally, a collection of information stored on an external device, such as a magnetic disk. In Pascal, an instance of the file *data type*. See also *Input* and *Output*.

File mark The current location in a *file* where reading or writing will take place.

File window In Pascal, a *buffer* that contains the most recent value that will be read from or written to a *file*.

First-fit An *algorithm* for *allocation* that chooses the first available block in the *free list* that will fill an allocation request.

Fixed part In Pascal, the *fields* of a *record* that are guaranteed to be available throughout the existence of the record. Distinguished from the *variant part* of a record.

Flagged loop A *loop* that is controlled by a single *boolean* variable, called a flag.

Formal parameters The *parameters* that are used in a *function* or *procedure declaration*.

Free-format language Like Pascal, a language that places few restrictions on the use of spaces, tabs, and returns in the *source code* program.

Free list In an *operating system*, a list of references to *memory* that are not currently being used.

Front-to-back reading A *bottom-up* approach to reading a *program*, starting from the declarations and reading toward the main statement body. The reverse of *back-to-front reading*.

Function A *subprogram* that is called within an *expression* and returns a single value. Differs from a *procedure* in that its call is not a *statement*.

Garbage collection An *algorithm*, used by an *operating system*, that periodically searches for and frees memory blocks that are no longer used. See also *Deallocation*.

Global object A Pascal entity, such as a *variable* or *type*, whose *scope* is all of a *program*.

Graph An *abstract data type* in which each position (called a node) may have several predecessors and several successors; a network structure. In mathematics, a collection of nodes connected by edges.

Guard A *statement* that prevents a subsequent statement from being executed in situations of potential error. The computer equivalent of an ounce of prevention.

Handle A *pointer* to a pointer.

Header The part of a *program* or *subprogram* that contains the program or subprogram name and the *parameters* to the program or subprogram. A Pascal program or subprogram consists of a header, a declaration part, and a *statement* part.

Heap That portion of *memory* where *allocation* and *deallocation* of *dynamic variables* takes place; where the targets of *pointers* live.

Hexadecimal notation Base-16 *positional notation*, using 0 through 9, along with the symbols A through F, for the "digits" 10 through 15.

High-level language Like Pascal, a language that is designed for ease of use and comprehension by programmers. The form of a high-level language generally bears very little resemblance to the *machine language* of a computer and must be translated by a *compiler* or *interpreter* before execution.

Hydra A mythological beast of unpleasant disposition in each of its several heads. Difficult to defeat since cutting off a head causes two to grow in its place.

Hypertext A computer application consisting of a collection of textual, graphical, and audio material with complex cross-references that can be accessed (and often modified) by the user.

Identifier A name for a *program*, *subprogram*, *variable*, *constant*, *type*, or other element of a program.

Implementation The process of coding an *abstract data type* or *algorithm* in a programming language. Also, the private part of a *unit*.

Index variable See *Control variable*.

Infinite loop A *loop* whose *exit condition* is never met, so that once entered, *control* will never be transferred out of the loop. The program equivalent of a black hole; usually (but not always) something one doesn't want to do.

Infinite recursion A *recursive subprogram* whose *exit condition* is never satisfied. Almost always an error.

Information hiding The process of concealing details of an *algorithm* or data structure to improve the readability of a *program*. For example, *encapsulating* the actions of an algorithm and its *local objects* within a *subprogram*.

Inheritance In *object-oriented programming*, the use within a *class* of a feature of its parent class (that is, the class containing the given class).

Input Information used by a program that comes from an external source, such as the keyboard, disk, or magnetic tape. See also *Output*.

Input/output (I/O) units The devices, such as the keyboard or screen, that enable a *program* to communicate to the outside world.

Integer An instance of the *data type* that consists of whole numbers, like -5 and 32767.

Interface In computer science, the conceptual region where communication takes place between entities. For example, the "user interface" between a *program* and its user. Also, the public part of a *unit*. Loosely used in slang as well, as in "the interface between our staff and the public."

Interpolation search A search *algorithm* that estimates the location where a data element will lie in an ordered list and that uses that estimate to reduce the size of the search domain. Similar to *binary search*, but much faster in many cases.

Interpreter A program that translates *source code* into *object code*. Unlike a *compiler*, an interpreter translates a *statement* of source code and causes it to be executed before going on to the next source code statement.

Key A data value, usually part of a *record*, that is used for sorting, searching, or retrieval.

Label A *string* that represents the destination of a **goto** statement. In Pascal, a label consists of one to four digits.

Levels of abstraction The conceptualization of a complex problem or system at any of several levels of detail. For example, one may consider a *program* from the point of view of the organization of its *subprograms* or at the (lower) level of its individual *statements*.

Lexical analysis See *scanning*.

Lexicographic order A *linear order*, defined on *strings*, that is an extension of the underlying order on *characters*. Similar, but not exactly identical, to the rules used to order words in a dictionary or names in a bibliography.

Linear order An ordering on a set of values that has the same properties as $\leq$ on the real numbers. Loosely speaking, under a linear order all elements of the set may be arranged in a line according to their ordering.

Linear search A search algorithm that inspects every value in a list in sequential in order. See also *Bounded linear search*.

Linked list A collection of data values arranged in a list by linking each element to its successor with *pointers*.

Literal A data value written explicitly in a *program*, rather than being computed during execution.

Local object A Pascal entity, such as a *variable* or *type*, whose *scope* is a *block* within a *program*.

Logarithmic-time algorithm An *algorithm* whose *timing function* is a logarithmic function of the size of the input. Logarithmic algorithms are fast, all other things being equal.

Logic error An error in the design of an *algorithm*, as opposed to *syntax* or *semantic* errors.

Loop A section of code that is executed repeatedly, generally under the control of a **for**, **while**, or **repeat** *statement*.

Loop invariant A condition that, if it is true at the start of one iteration of a *loop*, will be true at the end of that iteration.

Machine language The language used to control the hardware of a computer. Machine language is dictated by the design of the computer.

Memory That part or parts of a computer where information is stored for later reference.

Memory snapshot A description of the values, at a particular time, of the *variables* and *expressions* used in a segment of code. Used to *trace* the action of a segment of code.

Message In *object-oriented programming*, an instruction to an *object* to perform an action on itself.

Method of relaxation The technique of repeatedly performing a calculation until successive results differ by a predetermined small amount.

Multilist A list, generally implemented with *pointers*, that has two or more *key* fields with as many pointers as keys, such that the pointers associated with each key link the list in an order determined by the associated keys.

Mutual recursion The situation in which a *subprogram* calls itself indirectly, through calls to other subprograms. For example, when procedure *A* calls procedure *B*, which then calls procedure *A*.

Nested loop A *loop* that appears within the body of another loop. In most programming languages, an inner loop performs all of its iterations for each iteration of the enclosing loop.

Nil pointer In Pascal, the only *literal* value for a *pointer*; a pointer constant that is compatible with all types and never has a target.

Null string A *string* of length zero; a string with no characters.

Numerical analysis A field within the intersection of mathematics and computer science devoted to the design and analysis of *algorithms* for numerical computations.

Object In *object-oriented programming*, an instance of a *class*. Object is to class (object-oriented) as *variable* is to *data type* (Pascal), roughly speaking.

Object code The output from a *compiler* or *interpreter*; the result of translating *source code* into instructions that a computer can execute.

Object-oriented programming (OOP) A programming methodology characterized by *classes* of *objects*, with *inheritance* of class properties. In object-oriented programming, the fundamental action is sending *messages* to *objects*.

Off-by-one error A *logic error* that causes a *loop* to be performed one more or one less time than it should be. Also known as fencepost error, from the analogy of assuming that a fence has as many rails as it does posts.

Operating system A *program* that is responsible for managing the resources of a computer, such as *memory*, the screen, the keyboard, and the disk drive.

Ordinal Any *data type* characterized by a *linear order* wherein each value except the largest has a unique successor and each value except the smallest has a unique predecessor. In Pascal, *integers* are an ordinal type, while *reals* are not.

Out-of-range error A *run-time* error, caused by an *ordinal* expression taking a value out of the range of values allowed for its type.

Output Information, generated by a *program*, that is sent to an external destination, such as the screen, disk, or magnetic tape. See also *File* and *Input*.

Overloading Using a *variable* for more than one purpose.

Parameter An *identifier* that serves to indicate information that is sent to or from a *subprogram*. See also *Formal* and *Actual parameters*.

Parsing The process of determining the *syntax* of a string of *tokens*, according to the specifications of a (programming) language.

Pascal, Blaise (1623–1662) French mathematician of prodigious accomplishments, among the lesser of which was the invention of a mechanical calculator. After stunning successes in mathematics, he abandoned his career at age twenty-five and devoted the remainder of his life to the study of philosophy and religion.

Pointer An instance of a *data type* that contains a reference to information, rather than the information itself.

Polymorphism In *object-oriented programming*, the use of the same *message* name over several *classes*. In Pascal, the nearest equivalents are operators like +, which has different meanings depending on whether it is applied to *reals*, *integers*, or *sets*.

Polynomial-time algorithm An *algorithm* whose *timing function* is a polynomial function of the size of the input. Generally speaking, polynomial algorithms are midway in efficiency between *logarithmic* and *exponential algorithms*.

Positional notation The scheme for representing numbers as multiples of powers of an integer, called the base. For example, base-10 positional notation is the customary way of expressing numbers in decimal form. See also *Binary notation* and *Hexadecimal notation*.

Postcondition An assertion that is intended to be true after execution of a section of program code.

Precedence The rules that govern the order of operations in an *expression*. In Pascal, for example, multiplication has a higher precedence

than addition; so in the absence of parentheses, all multiplications would be performed before any additions.

Precondition An assertion that is assumed to be true prior to execution of a section of program code.

Procedure A collection of *statements* that are defined in one location and *called* into execution in one or more different locations in a program. Differs from a *function* in that a procedure call is a statement, while a function call is used within an *expression*. Procedures and functions are collectively known as *subprograms*.

Program A list of instructions to a computer. An *algorithm* that has been *implemented* in a particular programming language. Similar to a *subprogram*, but a program can be executed on its own.

Prompt An instruction to the operator of a *program*, telling the operator what input is needed and what form it must take.

Pseudocode An informal description of a *program*, in which some *statements* are expressed in human, rather than programming, language.

Queue An *abstract data type* that has a *linear* structure, in which insertion is done at one end of the list and inspection and deletion are done at the other.

Random access That property of a *data type* characterized by the ability to access any element within an instance of the type with equal efficiency. In Pascal, *arrays* and *records* are random-access structures. Distinguished from *sequential access*.

Real In Pascal, an instance of a *data type* that is capable of representing numeric information with fractional parts. Distinguished from, but containing, *integers*.

Record An instance of a *structured data type* that may contain data of several different types. In Pascal, a data type containing one or more *fields*.

Recursive definition A definition that uses the term defined as part of its definition. A recursive *function* or *procedure* includes one or more calls to itself, either directly or indirectly. See this definition, for example.

Recursive descent A *parsing algorithm* that uses *mutually recursive* routines to analyze the *syntax* of a language (usually a programming language).

Reserved word In Pascal, any of the 36 *tokens* that have meanings that cannot be redefined within a *program*. For example, **and**, **begin**, **if**, and **procedure** are reserved words. Distinguished from *standard identifiers*, which may be redefined. See the Appendix.

Robustness The features of a *program* that contribute to immunity from errors. A robust program will anticipate errors and handle them without *crashing*.

Run-time That time during which a *program* is executing.

Scanning That part of program translation that identifies the *tokens* in the *source code*.

Scope That portion of a *program* in which an *identifier* has meaning. See also *Block*.

Selector The *syntactic* feature that allows selection of a *component* of a *structured type*. In Pascal, for example, an element of an *array* is selected by following the array name by an *ordinal expression* within square brackets, and an element of a *record* is selected by following the record name by a period and a *field* name.

Self-documentation Generally, writing a *program* so that its form suggests its function, using descriptive *identifiers* and *encapsulation*. In an ideal world and an ideal language, a self-documenting program would have no need for *comments*. In the real world, we *document*, and document again.

Semantics In computer science, the meaning of the *statements* and *declarations* of a *program*. See also *Syntax*.

Sentinel A value used to signal the end of a list of data. See also *Overloading*.

Sequential access That property of a *data type* characterized by the need to access the first $n - 1$ elements before the n-th may be accessed. In Pascal, *files* are sequential-access structures. Distinguished from *random access*.

Set In Pascal, an unordered collection of data elements of the same type. Distinguished from an *array*, which is an ordered collection of elements of one type.

Side effect A modification of a relatively *global variable* within a *subprogram*, circumventing the transfer of information by *parameters*. Generally, not a good idea.

Simple type A *data type* with a simple structure; not a *structured type*. The simple types in Pascal are the *ordinal types* (*integer*, *character*, and *boolean*), *enumerated types*, *subrange types*, *reals*, and *pointers*.

Software life cycle One description of the design process used to build and maintain *programs*, consisting of design, development, analysis, testing, and maintenance. An idealized description of a much less precise process.

Sorted list A list in which the positional order of each element corresponds to the underlying *linear order* of the element type. For example, a row of people arranged by height.

Source code The input to a *compiler* or *interpreter*; a *program* that is translated into *object code* that a computer can *execute*.

Stack An *abstract data type* that has a *linear* structure and in which insertion, deletion, and inspection are done at the head of the list.

Standard identifiers In Pascal, any of the 40 *tokens* that have predefined meaning but that can be redefined within a *program*. For example, *dispose*, *eof*, *false*, *maxint*, and *readln* are standard identifiers. Distinguished from *reserved words*, which may not be redefined. See the Appendix.

Standard language An agreed-upon description of the *syntax* and *semantics* of a programming language, generally published by an organization devoted to maintaining common standards. The Pascal described in this text is ISO (International Standards Organization) Pascal, unless otherwise noted.

Standard textfiles In Pascal, the *textfiles input* and *output*, used to transfer information from the standard input device (usually the keyboard) to a program, and from a program to the standard output device (usually the screen).

State A complete description of all the data values of a *program* at a specific time.

Statement The basic active unit of a *program*; an instruction to perform some action on information. In Pascal, there are eleven kinds of statements: assignment, **case**, *compound*, *empty*, **for**, **goto**, **if**, *procedure calls*, **repeat**, **while**, and **with**.

Stepwise refinement *Top-down design* applied to coding; the process of coding the highest-level tasks before writing code for subordinate tasks.

Stored-program computer A computer in which a *program* is stored in *memory*.

String An instance of a *data type* consisting of sequences of *characters*. This is a nonstandard but common *extension* to Pascal.

Structured data type A *data type* that is composed of several simpler types. In Pascal, the structured types are *arrays*, *files*, *records*, *sets*, and *strings*.

Structured statement A statement that monitors and controls the execution of other statements. In Pascal, the structured statements are **case**, **for**, **if**, **if..else**, **repeat**, **while**, and **with**.

Stub A *subprogram* that consists of a complete *header* but that may not have its statement part fully implemented. Stubs are used during program design, to defer code writing until the logical organization of the *program* has been satisfactorily developed.

Subprogram In Pascal, a *function* or *procedure*; generally, an action, defined within a *program* or subprogram, that may be invoked elsewhere.

Subrange A *data type* consisting of a *contiguous* range of values of some *ordinal type*.

Subscript In Pascal, the expression whose value refers to a particular *component* of an *array*.

Syntax In computer science, the grammatical form that the elements of a *program* must take. See also *Semantics*.

Tag field In Pascal, a *field* of a *record* that is used to determine which of several *variant fields* may be referenced.

Temporary file A file that exists only within memory and is never saved to an external device.

Terminating condition See *Exit condition*.

Textfile A *file* whose *components* are data values represented as *characters*. Distinguished from a *binary file*.

Timing function A function that describes the running time of an *algorithm* in terms of the size of the input to the algorithm.

Token Any of the smallest meaningful elements of a *program*. In Pascal, for instance, the characters '+' and ':', any *identifiers*, and all *reserved words* are tokens.

Top-down design The process of design that works toward a solution by repeatedly dividing large units into smaller ones. The reverse process is known as *bottom-up design*.

Trace The process of executing by hand what a section of code will do when executed by a computer. See also *Memory snapshot*.

Transfer function A *function* that takes a value of one type and returns the equivalent value of another type. In Pascal, *trunc* and *round* are transfer functions.

Tree An *abstract data type* in which each position may have more than one successor, but may have at most one predecessor; a hierarchical data structure.

Truth table A tabular description of the values taken by an expression composed of *boolean* variables. Each row contains a set of values for the *variables*, along with the resultant value of the expression.

Type See *Data type*.

Type coercion Assigning an *expression* of one type to a *variable* of another type. In Pascal, for example, it is possible to assign an *integer* expression to a *real* variable.

Unit A common, but nonstandard, *extension* to Pascal; a separately compileable collection of *statements* and *declarations*. A unit cannot be executed on its own, but must be referenced by a program

via a **uses** directive. Units are useful in that they support *encapsulation* and *information hiding*.

Used list In an *operating system*, a list of references to *memory* that are currently being used by some *program*.

Value parameter In Pascal, a *parameter* of a *subprogram* that passes a copy of its *actual parameter* to the subprogram. Changes to value parameters within a subprogram have no effects on the values of the *actual parameters* that were used in the *call* to the subprogram. Distinguished from *variable parameters*.

Variable In Pascal, a named data object, used to store information.

Variable (var) parameter In Pascal, a *parameter* of a *subprogram* that passes a reference to its *actual parameter* to the subprogram. Changes to variable parameters within a subprogram immediately change the values of the corresponding actual parameters that were used in the *call* to the subprogram. Distinguished from *value parameter*s.

Variant part In Pascal, the *fields* of a *record* that are available only when a *tag field* contains a suitable value. Distinguished from the *fixed part* of a record.

Verification The process of proving that a section of code does what it is intended to do; constructing a proof of correctness using logical elements such as *preconditions*, *postconditions*, and *loop invariants*.

Virtual computer The computer as it appears to a user at a given level of abstraction. For example, a Pascal user would see a virtual computer that appeared to execute Pascal statements directly.

The symbols appear in ASCII order.

INDEX